P9-AGT-310

UNCOMMON WEALTH

An Anthology of Poetry in English

EDITED BY

Neil Besner, Deborah Schnitzer, and Alden Turner

WITHDRAWN

DAVID JUN 2 8 2024 BRARY
RICKS COLLEGE
REXBURG, IDAHO 83460-0405

Toronto New York Oxford
OXFORD UNIVERSITY PRESS
1997

Oxford University Press
70 Wynford Drive, Don Mills, Ontario M3C 1J9

Oxford   New York
Athens   Auckland   Bangkok   Bombay
Calcutta   Cape Town   Dar es Salaam   Delhi
Florence   Hong Kong   Istanbul   Karachi
Kuala Lumpur   Madras   Madrid   Melbourne
Mexico City   Nairobi   Paris   Singapore
Taipei   Tokyo   Toronto

and associated companies in
Berlin   Ibadan

Oxford is a trademark of Oxford University Press

Canadian Cataloguing in Publication Data

Main entry under title:

Uncommon wealth : an anthology of poetry in English

Includes index.
ISBN 0–19–541076–9

1. English poetry.   I. Besner, Neil Kalman, 1949–   .
II. Schnitzer, Deborah, 1950–   .   III. Turner, Alden R.

PN6101.U52   1997   821.008   C96–932005–1

Text & Cover Design: Brett Miller
Composition: IBEX Graphic Communications Inc.

Since this page cannot accommodate all the copyright notices,
pages XXXIX–LVI constitute an extension of the copyright page.

Copyright © Oxford University Press Canada 1997

1 2 3 4 — 00 99 98 97

This book is printed on permanent (acid-free) paper ∞.

Printed in Canada

TABLE OF CONTENTS

XXXIII   INTRODUCTION

XXXIX   ACKNOWLEDGEMENTS

MARY QUEEN OF SCOTS   1   *from* The Kings and Queens of Scotland
Scotland. 1542–1587

EDMUND SPENSER   *from* Amoretti
England/Ireland. 1552–1599   2   Sonnet 1
  2   Sonnet 15

MICHAEL DRAYTON   3   To the Virginian Voyage
England. 1563–1631

WILLIAM SHAKESPEARE   5   Sonnet 18
England. 1564–1616   5   Sonnet 107

SIR JOHN DAVIES   6   Epigram 36: Of Tobacco
England. 1569–1626

EMILIA LANIER   7   from *Salve Deus Rex Judæorum*
England. 1569–1645   Eves Apologie

MAIRI NIGHEAN   9   Luinneag Mhic Leoid/MacLeod's Lilt
ALASDAIR RUAIDH/
MARY MACLEOD
Scotland. *c.* 1569–*c.* 1674

JOHN DONNE   14   The Canonization
England. 1572–1631   15   Song ('Go and catch a falling star')

THOMAS MORTON   16   The Song
England/America. 1575–1646

ROBERT HAYMAN   from *Quodlibets*
England/N. America.   17   To the first planters of Newfoundland
c. 1579–*c.* 1631   18   A Skeltonical continued rhyme in praise
of my Newfoundland

ROBERT HERRICK   18   To the Virgins, to Make Much of Time
England. 1591–1674

ROGER WILLIAMS   19   Of Their Government
England/America. 1603–1683   19   Of Their Persons and Parts of Body

EDMUND WALLER   20   Of English Verse
England. 1606–1687

JOHN MILTON   21   from *Paradise Lost*
England. 1608–1674   Book 1: The Argument

ANNE BRADSTREET   26   The Author to Her Book
England/America.   27   Before the Birth of One of Her Children
c. 1612–1672

ANDREW MARVELL   28   To His Coy Mistress
England. 1621–1678

MICHAEL WIGGLESWORTH   29   from *The Day of Doom: or, a Description of*
England/America. 1631–1705   *the Great and Last Judgement*

KATHERINE FOWLER   31   Friendship's Mystery, To my dearest Lucasia
PHILIPS
England. 1632–1664

ANONYMOUS   32   from *The Bay Psalm Book*
America. 1640   Psalm 23: A Psalm of David

APHRA BEHN   33   To the Most Illustrious Prince Christopher
England. 1640–1689   Duke of Albemarle on His Voyage to His
          Government of Jamaica. A Pindarick.
    36   A Song in Dialogue

Edward Taylor   37   from *Preparatory Meditations*
America. c. 1644–1729   Prologue
    38   from *Sacramental Meditations*
          Meditation 38

ANONYMOUS   39   Dónall Óg/Donal Óg
Ireland. after 1650; c. 1902   43   Donal Óg

MRS ANNE KILLIGREW   44   Penelope to Ulysses
England. 1660–1685   45   To the Queen

ANONYMOUS   47   London Mourning in Ashes
England. 1661

ANNE FINCH,   51   The Unequal Fetters
COUNTESS OF WINCHILSEA   51   To the Nightingale
England. 1661–1720

JONATHAN SWIFT   53   Verses Said to be Written on the Union
Ireland. 1667–1745   53   Verses Made for the Women Who Cry
                              Apples, etc.

SARAH EGERTON   55   The Emulation
(NÉE FYGE, LATER FIELD)
England. c. 1669–c. 1722

HENRY KELSEY   57   from *Henry Kelsey His Book*
England/N. America.   Prologue
c. 1670–1724

ELIZABETH THOMAS   60   The Triumvirate
England. 1675–1731

ANONYMOUS   61   from *The New England Primer*
America. 1683   Alphabet

GEORGE BERKELEY   62   Verses on the Prospect of Planting Arts and
Ireland. 1685–1753   Learning in America

ALEXANDER POPE   from the Seventh Book of Homer's *Odysses*
England. 1688–1744   63   The Gardens of Alcinous
                          from An Essay on Man
                     64   Epistle I
                     70   Epistle II, verse 1

LADY MARY WORTLEY   71   from *Six Town Eclogues: With Some*
MONTAGU   *Other Poems*
England. 1689–1762   Saturday: The Small Pox: Flavia

MARY COLLIER   74   The Woman's Labour: An Epistle to
England. c. 1690–c. 1762   Mr Stephen Duck; In Answer to his Late
                              Poem, Called 'The Thresher's Labour'

MARY COOPER   80   A was an Archer, and shot at a Frog
England. c. 1700–1761

JAMES THOMSON   81   A Hymn [On the Seasons]
Scotland/England. 1700–1748   84   Ode: Rule, Britannia

THOMAS GRAY   85   Elegy Written in a Country Churchyard
England. 1716–1771

MARY LEAPOR   89   An Essay on Woman
England. 1722–1746

MERCY OTIS WARREN   91   To a Young Lady
USA. 1728–1814   92   A Thought on the Inestimable Blessing of
                           Reason, Occasioned by its Privation to a
                           Friend of Very Superior Talents and
                           Virtues, 1770

OLIVER GOLDSMITH   93   *from* The Deserted Village
Ireland/England. *c.* 1730–1774

JOHN DICKINSON   97   The Liberty Song
America. 1732–1808

ANNA SEWARD   99   The Lake; or, Modern Improvement in
Scotland. 1742–1809   Landscape

ANNA LAETITIA (AIKEN)   102 Epistle to William Wilberforce, Esq. on the
BARBAULD   Rejection of the Bill for Abolishing the
England. 1743–1825   Slave Trade, 1791
                        105 The Rights of Woman

SUSANNA BLAMIRE   106   I've Gotten a Rock, I've Gotten a Reel
Scotland. 1747–1794

CHARLOTTE SMITH   107   'The Dead Beggar, an Elegy addressed to a
England. 1749–1806   Lady, who was affected at seeing the
                           Funeral of a nameless Pauper, buried
                           at the Expence of the Parish, in the
                           Church-Yard at Brighthelmstone, in
                           November 1792'

LADY ANNE LINDSAY   108   Auld Robin Gray
Scotland. 1750–1825

PHILIP FRENEAU   109   The Indian Burying Ground
USA. 1752–1832   110   On Mr Paine's Rights of Man

PHILLIS WHEATLEY   112   On Being Brought from Africa to America
America. *c.* 1754–1784 112   On Imagination

WILLIAM BLAKE   114   The Little Black Boy
England. 1757–1827   115   The Garden of Love

ROBERT BURNS   115   A Poet's Welcome to his love-begotten
Scotland. 1759–1796   Daughter; the first instance that entitled
                           him to the venerable appellation of
                           Father—
                        117 Auld lange syne

SARAH WENTWORTH   118   Memento, for My Infant Who Lived But
MORTON   Eighteen Hours
USA. 1759–1846   118   The African Chief

CAROLINA OLIPHANT,   120   The Regalia
BARONESS NAIRNE
Scotland. 1766–1845

WILLIAM WORDSWORTH   122   Lucy Gray; or, Solitude
England. 1770–1850   124   My Heart Leaps Up When I Behold

SIR WALTER SCOTT   124   Proud Maisie
Scotland. 1771–1832

SAMUEL TAYLOR   125   Kubla Khan; or, A Vision in a Dream.
COLERIDGE   A Fragment.
England. 1772–1834

ANONYMOUS   127   Alphabet
America. 1775

ANONYMOUS   128   Burrowing Yankees
America/Canada. 1776; 1780   129   An Appeal

GEORGE GORDON,   130   *from* Childe Harold's Pilgrimage
LORD BYRON   Canto 3, verses 1–8
Scotland/England. 1788–1824

PERCY BYSSHE SHELLEY   132   The Indian Girl's Song
England. 1792–1822   133   England in 1819

JANET HAMILTON   134   A Phase of the War in America, 1864
Scotland. 1795–1873   135   Comparative Slavery

JOHN KEATS   137   La Belle Dame sans Merci
England. 1795–1821   138   Ode on a Grecian Urn

SOJOURNER TRUTH   140   Ain't I a Woman?
USA. c. 1797–1883

JOHN DUNMORE LANG   141   Colonial Nomenclature
Australia. 1799–1878

BAMEWAWASGEZHIKAQUAY/   142   To My Ever Beloved and Lamented Son
JANE SCHOOLCRAFT   William Henry
Chippewa. 1800–1841

RALPH WALDO EMERSON   144   Concord Hymn
USA. 1803–1882   144   The Problem

JAMES CLARENCE   146   The Nameless One
MANGAN
Ireland. 1803–1849

JOSEPH HOWE   148   The Micmac
Canada. 1804–1873

ELIZABETH BARRETT   149   The Runaway Slave at Pilgrim's Point
BROWNING
England. 1806–1861

HENRY WADSWORTH   157   *from* The Song of Hiawatha
LONGFELLOW   XXII: Hiawatha's Departure
USA. 1807–1882

HENRY L. DEROZIO   163   To the Pupils of the Hindu College
India. 1809–1831

EDGAR ALLAN POE   163   Annabel Lee
USA. 1809–1849

ALFRED, LORD TENNYSON   165   Ulysses
England. 1809–1892

ROBERT BROWNING   167   My Last Duchess
England. 1812–1889   168   The Bishop Orders His Tomb at Saint
Praxed's Church

EMILY BRONTË   171   The Prisoner: A Fragment
England. 1818–1848

FREDERICK DOUGLASS   173   A Parody
USA. *c.* 1818–*c.* 1895

HERMAN MELVILLE   175   A Utilitarian View of the Monitor's Fight
USA. 1819–1891   176   Monody

WALT WHITMAN   177   *from* Song of Myself
USA. 1819–1892

WILLIAM WILSON   192   England and British America
Ojibway. *c.* 1820–1839

MATTHEW ARNOLD   197   To Marguerite—Continued
England. 1822–1888

WILLIAM ALLINGHAM   198   from *Laurence Bloomfield in Ireland:*
Ireland. 1824–1889   *A Modern Poem in Twelve Chapters*
                                        Chapter I, Laurence, lines 1–111

CHEESQUATALAWNY/   201   The Atlantic Cable
YELLOW BIRD/
JOHN ROLLIN RIDGE
Cherokee. 1827–1867

EMILY DICKINSON   203   #632: The Brain—is wider than the Sky—
USA. 1830–1886   204   #1082: Revolution is the Pod

CHRISTINA ROSSETTI   204   'That where I am, there ye may be also'
England. 1830–1894

WILLIAM MORRIS   from *The Earthly Paradise*
England. 1834–1896   205   An Apology
                      206   November

HENRY KENDALL   207   The Last of His Tribe
Australia. 1839–1882

THOMAS HARDY   208   The Darkling Thrush
England. 1840–1928

GERARD MANLEY   209   Pied Beauty
HOPKINS
England. 1844–1889

EMILY LAWLESS   210   Clare Coast: *Circa* 1720
Ireland. 1845–1913

ALICE MEYNELL   213   Renouncement
England. 1847–1922   214   A Father of Women

ISABELLA VALANCY   215   The Dark Stag
CRAWFORD   216   Said the Canoe
Canada. 1850–1887

ROBERT LOUIS STEVENSON   219   Foreign Children
Scotland/England/Samoa.
1850–1894

TORU DUTT   220   Our Casuarina Tree
India. 1856–1877

CHARLES G. D. ROBERTS   221   The Skater
Canada. 1860–1943

BLISS CARMAN   223   Low Tide on Grand Pré
Canada. 1861–1929

MARY COLERIDGE   224   The Other Side of a Mirror
England. 1861–1907

ARCHIBALD LAMPMAN   225   Heat
Canada. 1861–1899   227   In November

RABINDRANATH TAGORE   228   from The Child
India. 1861–1941

TEKAHIONWAKE/   230   As Red Men Die
EMILY PAULINE JOHNSON   231   A Cry from an Indian Wife
Mohawk. 1861–1913

DUNCAN CAMPBELL SCOTT   233   The Forsaken
Canada. 1862–1947

SWAMI VIVEKANANDA   236   The Cup
India. 1863–1902

ANDREW BARTON   237   The Man from Snowy River
('THE BANJO') PATERSON
Australia. 1864–1941

MARY GILMORE   240   Eve-song
Australia. 1865–1962   241   Never Admit the Pain

WILLIAM BUTLER YEATS   241   The Magi
Ireland. 1865–1939   242   Easter 1916

HENRY LAWSON   244   The Bastard from the Bush
Australia. 1867–1922

W.E.B. DU BOIS   246   The Song of the Smoke
USA. 1868–1963

MARY FULLERTON ('E')   247   Flesh
Australia. 1868–1946   248   Cubes

MANMOHAN GHOSE   249   London
India. 1869–1924

CHARLOTTE MEW   250   The Farmer's Bride
England. 1869–1928   251   Monsieur Qui Passe (Quai Voltaire)

JAMES WELDON JOHNSON 252   O Black and Unknown Bards
USA. 1871–1938

J.M. SYNGE   254   The Curse
Ireland. 1871–1909   254   A Question

PAUL LAURENCE DUNBAR 255   We Wear the Mask
USA. 1872–1906

JOHN SHAW NEILSON   256   The Orange Tree
Australia. 1872–1942

NGUNAITPONI/   257   The Song of Hungarrda
DAVID UNAIPON
Australia. 1873–1967

ALEXANDER POSEY   258   Ode to Sequoyah
Creek. 1873–1908

ROBERT FROST   259   In White
USA. 1874–1963   260   Design
                      260   Desert Places

AMY LOWELL   261   The Sisters
USA. 1874–1925   265   New Heavens for Old

GERTRUDE STEIN   266   from Tender Buttons
USA/France. 1874–1946

EDWARD THOMAS   270   The Gypsy
England. 1878–1917

JOSEPH CAMPBELL   271   The Newspaper-Seller
Ireland. 1879–1944

FREDERICK PHILIP GROVE 273 Arctic Woods
Prussia/Canada. 1879–1948

SAROJINI NAIDU   274   Awake!
India. 1879–1949   275   Bangle-Sellers

PATRICK (PADRAIC)   276   The Mother
HENRY PEARSE
Ireland. 1879–1916

WALLACE STEVENS   277   Of Mere Being
USA. 1879–1955   277   The Planet on the Table

E.J. PRATT   278   from *Brébeuf and His Brethren*
Canada. 1882–1964   [The Martyrdom of Brébeuf and
                Lalemant, 16 March 1649] XII
        282   from *Towards the Last Spike*
                The Pre-Cambrian Shield (i) and
                (ii) Dynamite on the North Shore

T.E. HULME   284   The Blanket-makers
England. 1883–1917   285   Autumn

EDITH ANNE ROBERTSON   285   Pyatie Beauty/Pied Beauty
Scotland. 1883–c. 1978   286   Country boy on a motor cycle

WILLIAM CARLOS   286   Danse Russe
WILLIAMS   287   This Is Just to Say
USA. 1883–1963

ANNA WICKHAM   288   The Fired Pot
England. 1884–1947   288   The Sick Assailant

D.H. LAWRENCE   289   Figs
England. 1885–1930

DOROTHEA MACKELLAR   292   In a Southern Garden
Australia. 1885–1968

EZRA POUND   293   A Pact
USA/England. 1885–1972   293   L'art, 1910

HELEN B. CRUICKSHANK   294   On Being Eighty
Scotland. 1886–1975

H.D. (HILDA DOOLITTLE)   295   At Baia
USA/England. 1886–1961   296   *from* Sigil

RUPERT BROOKE   300   Dining-Room Tea
England. 1887–1915

MARIANNE MOORE   302   Poetry (1921 version)
USA. 1887–1972   303   Poetry (1924 version)
                      303   Poetry (1967 version)

EDWIN MUIR   304   For Ann Scott-Moncrieff
Scotland. 1887–1959

EDITH SITWELL   305   Lullaby
England. 1887–1964

T.S. ELIOT   307   The Hollow Men
USA/England. 1888–1965

KATHERINE MANSFIELD   310   To Stanislaw Wyspianski
New Zealand. 1888–1923

CLAUDE McKAY   311   If We Must Die
Jamaica/USA. 1889–1948   312   America

IVOR GURNEY   312   The Silent One
England. 1890–1937

ISAAC ROSENBERG   313   Break of Day in the Trenches
England. 1890–1918

FRANCIS LEDWIDGE   314   To One Dead
Ireland. 1891–1917

HUGH MACDIARMID/   315   from *A Drunk Man Looks at the Thistle*
CHRISTOPHER MURRAY
GRIEVE
Scotland. 1892–1978

VERA BRITTAIN   319   To My Brother
England. 1893–1970

SYLVIA TOWNSEND   320   Honey for Tea
WARNER
England. 1893–1978

e.e. cummings   322   [the Cambridge ladies who live in
USA. 1894–1962   furnished souls]
                      322   [somewhere i have never travelled,gladly
                             beyond]

LOUISE BOGAN   323   Women
USA. 1897–1970

HART CRANE   324   Black Tambourine
USA. 1899–1932   324   *from* Voyages

ROLLA LYNN RIGGS   325   Shadow on Snow
Cherokee. 1899–1954

F.R. SCOTT   326   Laurentian Shield
Canada. 1899–1985

ERNEST G. MOLL   327   A Gnarled Riverina Gum-tree
Australia. 1900–1979

SIX NATIONS COUNCIL, 328   Condolence Ceremony
IROQUOIS CONFEDERACY 330   *from* The Ceremony Called 'At the Wood's
Canada/America. 1900   Edge'

KENNETH SLESSOR   333   Five Bells
Australia. 1901–1971

GWENDOLYN B. BENNETT 336   Heritage
USA. 1902–1981

KENNETH FEARING   337   Cultural Notes
USA. 1902–1961

LANGSTON HUGHES   338   The Weary Blues
USA. 1902–1967

A.J.M. SMITH   339   The Lonely Land
Canada. 1902–1980

STEVIE SMITH   340   Not Waving But Drowning
England. 1902–1971   341   Emily Writes Such a Good Letter

LORINE NIEDECKER   342   [I married]
USA. 1903–1970

EARLE BIRNEY   343   Can. Lit.
Canada. 1904–1995   343   The Bear on the Delhi Road

GLADYS MAY   345   Junior Geography Lesson
CASELY-HAYFORD
('AQUAH LALUAH')
Ghana/Sierra Leone.1904–1950

PATRICK KAVANAGH   346   *from* The Great Hunger
Ireland. 1904–1967

LOUIS ZUKOFSKY   349   from 'A'—11
USA. 1904–1978

KENNETH REXROTH   350   from *The Love Poems of Marichiko*
USA. 1905–1982

SAMUEL BECKETT   352   Something There
Ireland. 1906–1989

W.H. AUDEN   353   Letter to a Wound
England/USA. 1907–1973   355   Lullaby

A.D. HOPE   356   The End of a Journey
Australia. b. 1907

LOUIS MACNEICE   357   Reflections
Ireland. 1907–1963

DENIS DEVLIN   358   Liffey Bridge
Scotland/Ireland. 1908–1959

KATHLEEN RAINE   360   Spell to Bring Lost Creatures Home
England/Scotland. b. 1908

THEODORE ROETHKE   361   My Papa's Waltz
USA. 1908–1963

CHARLES BRASCH   362   Ambulando
New Zealand. 1909–1973

JEAN EARLE   363   Young Girls Running
England/Wales. b. 1909

OLIVE FRASER   364   Lines Written after a Nervous
Scotland. 1909–1977   Breakdown (II)

ROBERT GARIOCH   365   The Wire
(SUTHERLAND)
Scotland. 1909–1987

VINAYAK KRISHNA GOKAK   370   The Song of India
India. b. 1909

RALPH GUSTAFSON   371   In the Yukon
Canada. 1909–1995

A. M. KLEIN   372   Montreal
Canada. 1909–1972   374   Political Meeting

DOROTHY LIVESAY   375   Day and Night
Canada. b. 1909   380   Bartok and the Geranium

MARIE MAKINO   381   'Ilda
England. [b. date unknown]

CHARLES OLSON   382   from *The Maximus Poems*, Book III
USA. 1910–1970   The Festival Aspect

P.S. REGE   385   Dream
India. 1910–1978

ELIZABETH BISHOP   386   The Moose
USA. 1911–1979   390   In the Waiting Room

ALLEN CURNOW   393   Landfall in Unknown Seas
New Zealand. b. 1911   395   An Incorrigible Music

SOMHAIRLE   396   Ban-Ghàidheal/A Highland Woman
MACGILL-EAIN/
SORLEY MACLEAN
Scotland. b. 1911

JOHN CAGE   399   *from* Diary: How to Improve the World
USA. 1912–1992   (You Will Only Make Matters Worse)
                1965–1967

IRVING LAYTON   406   From Colony to Nation
Canada. b. 1912   407   Keine Lazarovitch 1870–1959

BHARATI SARABHAI   408   from *The Well of the People*
India. b. 1912   Chorus of Workers

MURIEL RUKEYSER   411   from *The Lynchings of Jesus*
USA. 1913–1980   Passage to Godhead

R.S. THOMAS   412   Welsh History
Wales. b. 1913   413   Expatriates

DOUGLAS LEPAN   414   A Country Without a Mythology
Canada. b. 1914

DYLAN THOMAS   415   Fern Hill
Wales. 1914–1953

DOROTHY AUCHTERLONIE   417   Apopemptic Hymn
(GREEN)
England/Australia. 1915–1991

G. S. FRASER   418   An Elegy for Keith Bullen
Scotland. 1915–1980

ALUN LEWIS   419   Goodbye
Wales. 1915–1944

ROLAND MATHIAS   420   Laus Deo
Wales. b. 1915

SYDNEY GOODSIR SMITH   421   The Grace of God and the Meth-Drinker
New Zealand/Scotland.
1915–1975

JUDITH WRIGHT   423   The Hawthorn Hedge
Australia. b. 1915   424   At Cooloola

P.K. PAGE   425   The Permanent Tourists
Canada. b. 1916

GWENDOLYN BROOKS   426   The Mother
USA. b. 1917

ROBERT LOWELL   427   For the Union Dead
USA. 1917–1977

JAMES MCAULEY   429   Because
Australia. 1917–1976

MIRIAM WADDINGTON   430   Déjà Vu
Canada. b. 1917

MARGARET AVISON   432   The Swimmer's Moment
Canada. b. 1918

W.S. GRAHAM   433   Johann Joachim Quantz's Five Lessons
Scotland. 1918–1986

AL PURDY   436   Lament for the Dorsets
Canada. b. 1918   438   The Runners

MURIEL SPARK   440   Bluebell Among the Sables
Scotland. b. 1918   441   Created and Abandoned

LAWRENCE FERLINGHETTI   441   I Am Waiting
USA. b. 1919

ELMA MITCHELL   446   Thoughts After Ruskin
Scotland/England. b. 1919

MAY SWENSON   447   Under the Baby Blanket
USA. 1919–1989

GWEN HARWOOD   448   New Music
Australia. b. 1920 449   Suburban Sonnet

EDWIN MORGAN   450   Canedolia: an off-concrete scotch fantasia
Scotland. b. 1920

OODGEROO (FORMERLY 451   We Are Going
KATH WALKER)
Australia. 1920–1993

ANONYMOUS   452   Salute to the Elephant
Nigeria. c. 1921

GEORGE MACKAY BROWN 454   King of Kings
Scotland. b. 1921

RUARAIDH MACTHÒMAIS/ 457   Clann-Nighean an Sgadain/The Herring
DERICK THOMSON   Girls
Scotland. b. 1921

GABRIEL OKARA   459   One Night at Victoria Beach
Nigeria. b. 1921   460   Suddenly the air cracks

RICHARD WILBUR   462   Pangloss's Song: A Comic-Opera Lyric
USA. b. 1921

PHILIP LARKIN   463   Faith Healing
England. 1922–1985

ELI MANDEL   464   Houdini
Canada. 1922–1992

KENDRICK SMITHYMAN 465   The Last Moriori
New Zealand. b. 1922

HONE TUWHARE 466 Snowfall
New Zealand. b. 1922

DANNIE ABSE 467 Epithalamion
Wales. b. 1923 468 X-Ray

MARI EVANS 469 I Am a Black Woman
USA.

DENISE LEVERTOV 470 A Tree Telling of Orpheus
England/USA. b. 1923

JOHN ORMOND 474 Certain Questions for Monsieur Renoir
Wales. 1923–1990

NISSIM EZEKIEL 476 Very Indian Poem in Indian English
India. b. 1924 477 Enterprise

JANET FRAME 478 The Clown
New Zealand. b. 1924

EFUA SUTHERLAND 479 A Professional Beggar's Lullaby
Ghana. b. 1924

IAN HAMILTON FINLAY 479 Ballad
Scotland. b. 1925 480 Little Calendar

CAROLYN KIZER 480 Exodus
USA. b. 1925

ANNE RANASINGHE 482 Auschwitz From Colombo
Sri Lanka. b. 1925

JAMES K. BAXTER 483 The Ikons
New Zealand. 1926–1972

RAYMOND GARLICK 484 Map Reading
Wales. b. 1926

ALLEN GINSBERG 485 A Supermarket in California
USA. b. 1926

FRANK O'HARA 486 Why I Am Not a Painter
USA. 1926–1966

JOHN ASHBERY 487 The Painter
USA. b. 1927

ROBERT KROETSCH   488   Stone Hammer Poem
Canada. b. 1927

PHYLLIS WEBB   493   Poetics Against the Angel of Death
Canada. b. 1927

MAYA ANGELOU   494   A Good Woman Feeling Bad
USA. b. 1928

KWESI BREW   495   The Search
Ghana. b. 1928

IAIN MACA'GHOBHAINN/   496   Shall Gaelic Die?
IAIN CRICHTON SMITH
Scotland. b. 1928

JAYANTA MAHAPATRA   500   Hunger
India. b. 1928   500   The Abandoned British Cemetery
at Balasore

ANNE SEXTON   502   The Death Baby
USA. 1928–1974

U. A. FANTHORPE   506   Not My Best Side
England. b. 1929   508   Knowing about Sonnets

THOM GUNN   509   On the Move
England/USA. b. 1929   510   Lament

PETER PORTER   513   Phar Lap in the Melbourne Museum
Australia. b. 1929

A.K. RAMANUJAN   514   Still Another View of Grace
India/USA. 1929–1993

ADRIENNE RICH   515   Diving into the Wreck
USA. b. 1929   517   (The Floating Poem, Unnumbered)

CHINUA ACHEBE   518   Mango Seedling
Nigeria. b. 1930

E.K. BRATHWAITE   519   Calypso
Barbados. b. 1930

TED HUGHES   521   Dust As We Are
England. b. 1930

MAZISI KUNENE   522   Elegy
South Africa. b. 1930

ALDA LARA   523   Testament
Angola. 1930–1962

GARY SNYDER   524   Riprap
USA. b. 1930   525   What You Should Know to Be a Poet

DEREK WALCOTT   526   from *Omeros*, Chapter LXIV
St Lucia b. 1930

JAY MACPHERSON   527   The Fisherman
Canada. b. 1931

ARUN BALKRISHNA   528   An Old Woman
KOLATKAR
India. b. 1932

CHRISTOPHER OKIGBO   529   Elegy for Slit-Drum
Nigeria. 1932–1967

LENRIE PETERS   532   Isatou Died
The Gambia. b. 1932

SYLVIA PLATH   533   Daddy
USA. 1932–1963

SIPHO SEPAMLA   535   'Measure for Measure'
South Africa. b. 1932

ANNE STEVENSON   536   A Letter from an English novelist: Paul
England. b. 1933   Maxwell, author of 'A Second Eve',
                           writes to Ruth Arbeiter in Vermont

FLEUR ADCOCK   538   Wife to Husband
New Zealand/England. b. 1934   538   For a Five-Year-Old

AMIRI BARAKA   539   An Agony. As Now
USA. b. 1934   540   Numbers, Letters

LEONARD COHEN   541   I Have Not Lingered in European
Canada. b. 1934   Monasteries
                542   French and English

KAMALA DAS   544   The Old Playhouse
India. b. 1934   545   An Introduction

AUDRE LORDE   546   Power
USA. 1934–1992

DAVID MALOUF   548   Off the Map
Australia. b. 1934

N. SCOTT MOMADAY   549   Rainy Mountain Cemetery
Kiowa. b. 1934

R. PARTHASARATHY   550   *from* Ghosts
Tamil/USA. b. 1934   I: Luiz Vaz de Camoëns, 1524?–1580

SONIA SANCHEZ   551   under a soprano sky
USA. b. 1934   552   haiku (for the police on osage ave)

WOLE SOYINKA   552   Telephone Conversation
Nigeria. b. 1934   553   'No!' He Said

CHRIS WALLACE-CRABBE   555   Love Poem
Australia. b. 1934   556   A Wintry Manifesto

ARONIAWENRATE/   557   Rattle
PETER BLUE CLOUD
Mohawk. b. 1935

KOFI AWOONOR   560   Afro-American Beats
Ghana. b. 1935

JOHN PEPPER CLARK   563   A Child Asleep
BEKEDEREMO
Nigeria. b. 1935

GEORGE BOWERING   564   Grandfather
Canada. b. 1935

YASMINE GOONERATNE   565   Menika
Sri Lanka/Australia. b. 1935

SALLY ROBERTS JONES   567   Lletherneuadd Uchaf, 1868
Wales. b. 1935

TITUS CHUKWENEKA   568   Combat
NWOSU
Nigeria. b. 1935

STEWART CONN   570   'Kitchen-Maid'
Scotland. b. 1936

K. D. KATRAK   571   Malabar Hill
India. b. 1936   574   The Kitchen Door

MARGE PIERCY   575   The woman in the ordinary
USA. b. 1936   576   Unlearning to not speak

PRAKASH BANDEKAR   577   Afternoon Massacre
India. b. 1937

GILLIAN CLARKE   579   On Air
Wales. b. 1937

K.N. DARUWALLA   580   The Epileptic
India. b. 1937

CLAIRE HARRIS   581   In the Dark, Father
Trinidad and Tobago/
Canada. b. 1937

G.S. SHARAT CHANDRA   582   Bangla (water pipe) Desh
India. b. 1938

DILIP CHITRE   584   Poem in Self-Exile
India. b. 1938   584   Mumbai: A Song

JONATHAN KARIARA   587   A Leopard Lives in a Muu Tree
Kenya. b. 1938

LES A. MURRAY   588   An Absolutely Ordinary Rainbow
Australia. b. 1938

JOHN NEWLOVE   589   Samuel Hearne in Wintertime
Canada. b. 1938

PAULA GUNN ALLEN   591   Kopis'taya (A Gathering of Spirits)
Laguna/Sioux. b. 1939

MARGARET ATWOOD   593   Progressive Insanities of a Pioneer
Canada. b. 1939   595   Notes Towards a Poem That Can Never
                            Be Written

bill bissett   598   th wundrfulness uv th mountees our secret
Canada. b. 1939   police

SEAMUS HEANEY   599   Digging
Ireland. b. 1939   600   from Whatever You Say Say Nothing

PATRICK LANE   602   Passing into Storm
Canada. b. 1939

DENNIS LEE   603   *from* Civil Elegies
Canada. b. 1939

MUDROOROO/   606   Crow
COLIN JOHNSON
Nyoongah/Australia. b. 1939

FRED WAH   607   Waiting for Saskatchewan
Canada. b. 1939

EUNICE DE SOUZA   608   Encounter at a London Party
India. b. 1940

ADIL JUSSAWALLA   608   A Bomb-site
India. b. 1940

JUDITH KAZANTZIS   609   For my sister pregnant
England. b. 1940

GEOFFREY LEHMANN   611   Night Flower
Australia. b. 1940

RACHEL MCALPINE   611   Here it is
New Zealand. b. 1940

MOLARA   612   song at the african middle class
OGUNDIPE-LESLIE
Nigeria. b. 1940

GIEVE PATEL   613   Nargol
India. b. 1940

JAMES WELCH   615   In My Lifetime
Blackfoot. b. 1940

MICHAEL HARTNETT   616   *from* A Farewell to English
Ireland. b. 1941

GWENDOLYN MACEWEN   618   Dark Pines Under Water
Canada. 1941–1987

ATUKWEI OKAI/   619   Elavanyo Concerto
JOHN OKAI
Ghana. b. 1941

SIMON J. ORTIZ   622   Waiting for You to Come By
Acoma Pueblo. b. 1941

PAULINE STAINER   623   Sighting the Slave Ship
England. b. 1941

LAKDASA   624   Don't Talk To Me About Matisse
WIKKRAMASINHA
Sri Lanka. 1941–1978

ANNHARTE   625   Raced Out to Write This Up
Anishinabe. b. 1942

EILÉAN NÍ CHUILLEANÁIN   626   The Second Voyage
Ireland. b. 1942   627   Amelia

GAURI DESHPANDE   628   The Female of The Species
India. b. 1942

DOUGLAS DUNN   629   Empires
Scotland. b. 1942

DAPHNE MARLATT   630   Imperial Cannery, 1913
Australia/Canada. b. 1942

MICERE GITHAE MUGO   631   Where Are Those Songs?
Kenya. b. 1942

MUKHTARR MUSTAPHA   633   Gbassay—blades in regiment
Sierra Leone. b. 1942

ANDREW SUKNASKI   634   Overland to the Southern Plain
Canada. b. 1942

HUGO WILLIAMS   636   The Couple Upstairs
England. b. 1942

GRACE AKELLO   636   Encounter
Uganda. b. 1940s

AMELIA BLOSSOM HOUSE   638   We Still Dance
South Africa. b. 1940s

LOUISE GLÜCK   639   Aubade
USA. b. 1943   639   Dedication to Hunger

PAULETTE JILES   642   Windigo
USA/Canada. b. 1943

THOMAS KING   643   The City on the Hill
Cherokee. b. 1943

MICHAEL ONDAATJE   644   Bearhug
Sri Lanka/Canada. b. 1943   644   The Cinnamon Peeler

OLIVE SENIOR   646   Colonial Girls School
Jamaica. b. 1943

EAVAN BOLAND   647   Mise Eire
Ireland. b. 1944   649   Listen. This is the Noise of Myth

DENNIS COOLEY   651   a curse on a critic
Canada. b. 1944

PAUL DURCAN   652   Crinkle, near Birr
Ireland. b. 1944   655   The Jewish Bride

TOM LEONARD   656   Jist ti Let Yi No
Scotland. b. 1944   657   A Priest Came on at Merkland Street

bpNichol   663   Two Words: A Wedding
Canada. 1944–1988

SALEEM PEERADINA   664   There Is No God
India/USA. b. 1944

CRAIG RAINE   665   In the Kalahari Desert
England. b. 1944

CAROL RUMENS   667   Rules for Beginners
England. b. 1944

MONGANE (WALLY)   668   The Growing
SEROTE
South Africa. b. 1944

KIT WRIGHT   669   I Found South African Breweries Most
England. b. 1944   Hospitable

SYL CHENEY-COKER   670   Letter to a Tormented Playwright
Sierra Leone. b. 1945

GILLIAN HANSCOMBE   671   An Apostrophe to Her Majesty Queen
Australia/England. b. 1945   Elizabeth II

SELIMA HILL   672   The Significance of Significance
England. b. 1945   673   Eating Chocolates in the Dark

JACK MAPANJE   674   At the Metro: Old Irrelevant Images
Malawi. b. 1945

BRONWEN WALLACE   675   The Woman in This Poem
Canada. 1945–1989

TOM WAYMAN   677   Saving the World
Canada. b. 1945

ROBERT BRINGHURST   679   These Poems, She Said
USA/Canada. b. 1946

CHRYSTOS   680   Ceremony for Completing a Poetry Reading
Menominee/USA/Canada.
b. 1946

TONY CURTIS   681   Thoughts from the Holiday Inn
Wales. b. 1946

PATRICK FRIESEN   686   talking new york: waiting on love
Canada. b. 1946

LEONA GOM   687   University
Canada. b. 1946

WAYNE KEON   688   I'm Not in Charge of This Ritual
Algonkin-Iroquois. b. 1946

KOJO LAING   690   Senior lady sells garden eggs
Ghana. b. 1946

BILL MANHIRE   691   Wellington
New Zealand. b. 1946   692   Party Going

MIGUEL PIÑERO   692   The Book of Genesis According to
Puerto Rico/USA. b. 1946   Saint Miguelito

PETER READING   from *Evagatory*
England. b. 1946   695   [Province of hyperborean bleakness]
696   [East End of London . . .]
696   [Forest, Sarawak, limestone outcrop]

SHARON THESEN   696   Loose Woman Poem
Canada. b. 1946   697   Po-It-Tree

PENNY WINDSOR   698   Advice on Pregnancy
Wales. b. 1946

KOFI ANYIDOHO   700   *from* Soul in Birthwaters (Suite for the
Ghana. b. 1947   Revolution)
                        II. Radio Revolution

PETER FINCH   702   Visual Text Makes It As Super Hero
Wales. b. 1947

VERONICA FORREST- 703   Identi-kit
THOMSON
Scotland. 1947–1975

KERI HULME   703   Mushrooms and Other Bounty
New Zealand. b. 1947

LIZ LOCHHEAD   704   Six Men Monologues
Scotland. b. 1947

ARVIND KRISHNA   708   The Sale
MEHROTRA
India. b. 1947

M. NOURBESE PHILIP 710 Somewhere in the Dark Continent
Trinidad and Tobago/Canada.
b. 1947

ROBERTA HILL WHITEMAN 712   Scraps Worthy of Wind
Oneida. b. 1947

CIARAN CARSON   714   Belfast Confetti
Ireland b. 1948   714   Narrative in Black and White

LORNA CROZIER   716   On the Seventh Day
Canada. b. 1948

KRISTJANA GUNNARS 718   Stefán Eyjólfsson XIV
Iceland/Canada. b. 1948

WENDY ROSE   719   Story Keeper
Hopi. b. 1948

LESLIE MARMON SILKO   722   Lullaby
Laguna Pueblo. b. 1948

MURRAY EDMOND   722   My Return to Czechoslovakia
New Zealand. b. 1949   724   House

CILLA McQUEEN   725   Matinal
New Zealand. b. 1949   726   Weekend Sonnets

CAROLYN FORCHÉ   727   Kalaloch
USA. b. 1950

LENORE KEESHIG-TOBIAS   730   Resistance
Ojibway. b. 1950

MEDBH McGUCKIAN   731   Venus and the Rain
Ireland. b. 1950

GRACE NICHOLS   732   Tropical Death
Guyana/England. b. 1950

ODIA OFEIMUN   733   A Handle for the Flutist
Nigeria. b. 1950

SHEENAGH PUGH   734   Going back to Hlidarendi
England/Wales. b. 1950

PHILIP SALOM   735   The World of Dreams
Australia. b. 1950

RAY A. YOUNG BEAR   737   Our Bird Aegis
Meskwaki. b. 1950

CATHERINE OBIANUJU   738   Nigeria in the year 1999
ACHOLONU
Nigeria. b. 1951

MEENA ALEXANDER   739   Boating
India/USA. b. 1951

CHRISTOPHER DEWDNEY   741   The Dialectic Criminal: Hand in Glove with
Canada. b. 1951   an Old Hat

JOY HARJO   743   Anchorage
Creek. b. 1951   744   I Am a Dangerous Woman

FRANK KUPPNER   745   from *A Bad Day for the Sung Dynasty*
Scotland. b. 1951

PAUL MULDOON   749   Why Brownlee Left
Ireland. b. 1951

SUSAN MUSGRAVE   750   Burial of the Dog
USA/Canada. b. 1951

ROO BORSON   751   City Lights
Canada. b. 1952

DI BRANDT   752   questions i asked my mother
Canada. b. 1952

HELEN DUNMORE   754   Sisters leaving before the dance
England. b. 1952   755   Poem for December 28

LINTON KWESI JOHNSON   756   Mekkin Histri
Jamaica/England. b. 1952

DANIEL DAVID MOSES   757   The Line
Delaware. b. 1952

CHRISTINE QUNTA   759   The know
South Africa. b. 1952

VIKRAM SETH   760   Work and Freedom
India. b. 1952

DIONNE BRAND   761   *from* No Language Is Neutral
Trinidad and Tobago/Canada.
b. 1953

ABENA P.A. BUSIA   763   Exiles
Ghana. b. 1953   763   Liberation

MONIZA ALVI   764   The Sari
Pakistan/England. b. 1954

IMITIAZ DHARKER   765   Another Woman
India. b. 1954

IAN DUHIG   767   I'r Hen Iaith A'i Chaneuon/To the Old
Ireland/England. b. 1954   Tongue and Its Songs

LOUISE ERDRICH   768   Dear John Wayne
Chippewa. b. 1954

NUALA ARCHER   770   Whale on the Line
USA/Ireland. b. 1955

DAVID DABYDEEN   771   The Canecutters' Song
British Guyana/England b. 1955   772   The New Poetry

CAROL ANN DUFFY   773   Standing Female Nude
Scotland. b. 1955   774   The Captain of the 1964 Top of the
Form Team

RITA ANN HIGGINS   775   Woman's Inhumanity to Woman
Ireland. b. 1955   (Galway Labour Exchange)

ERIN MOURÉ   776   Cherish
Canada. b. 1955

VÉRONIQUE TADJO   777   Five Poems
Ivory Coast. b. 1955

SUJATA BHATT   780   White Asparagus
India. b. 1956   781   A Different Way to Dance

JEAN BINTA BREEZE   784   Ordinary Mawning
Jamaica/England. b. 1956

ANNE FRENCH   786   Collisions
New Zealand. b. 1956   786   In absentia

IYAMIDÉ HAZELEY   787   When You Have Emptied Our Calabashes
Sierra Leone. b. 1957

LI-YOUNG LEE   788   This Room and Everything in It
Indonesia/USA. b. 1957

IAN MCMILLAN   790   Just the Facts, Just the
England. b. 1957

ARCHIE WELLER   791   The Legend of Jimmy's Axe
Australia. b. 1957   792   Untitled

MOYA CANNON   793   'Taom'
Ireland. b. 1958

DERMOT BOLGER   794   Snuff Movies
Ireland. b. 1959

JOANNE ARNOTT   795   Abortion (Like Motherhood) Changes
Canada. b. 1960   Nothing

CHERRY SMYTH   796   Black Leather Jacket
Ireland/England. b. 1960

MAUD SULTER   798   Azania
Scotland. b. 1960

KATHLEEN JAMIE   799   The Queen of Sheba
Scotland. b. 1962

JACKIE KAY   802   from The Adoption Papers
Scotland. b. 1962   Chapter 4: Baby Lazarus

KRISTINA RUNGANO   804   The Woman
Zimbabwe. b. 1963

MÉIRA COOK   805   a fine grammar of bones
South Africa/Canada. b. 1964

807   AUTHOR INDEX

INTRODUCTION

The poems in *Uncommon Wealth* were written over a period of four hundred years by four hundred and twenty-six authors from territories and countries on almost every continent. We have selected poets from Canada, the United States, India, Australia, New Zealand, the Caribbean, parts of Africa, and the United Kingdom. In these sites of colonization and citadels of empire, the writing of poetry in English may appear to be a marginal activity relative to the grand designs of competing histories and cultures. But in fact, the poets in *Uncommon Wealth* explore the deepest implications of these historical and cultural assumptions by revealing the essential, diverse, and changing character of language itself.

When widely different texts are collected in anthologies, 'maps' of people, places, and time take shape—maps that are subject to altered conditions and provisional boundaries. Too often, though, we are reticent about marking new boundaries or recognizing emerging states where literary (as well as economic, social, and political) transformations occur. The organization of the poems in *Uncommon Wealth* releases poetry from traditional categories, and may inspire readers to consider anew three commanding questions: What poetry do we read? Why do we read poetry? How do we read it?

The tables of contents in poetry anthologies have usually reflected the positions attained by individual poets and their works. The more frequently authors' names and texts appeared, the more authority they acquired. With time, it became unthinkable to exclude from any representative collection T.S. Eliot's 'The Love Song of J. Alfred Prufrock', John Keats's 'Ode to a Nightingale', Robert Frost's 'Mending Wall', John Betjeman's 'In Westminster Abbey', or Elizabeth Barrett Browning's 'How Do I Love Thee?' As readers of poetry in the Canadian prairie, colonized by English and French literary history and activity and the canonizing of British and American texts, we have been schooled in these traditions—but we have also become aware of the consequences of this schooling, especially on readers whose heritages, languages, and vision lie elsewhere. Why should poetry come to us as if we were stranded orphans or adoptees whose identities are defined primarily by what has been lost: colonial status with Britain, some prospect of unification with the United States, the political viability of the British Commonwealth? The symptoms of this condition are described in Dennis Lee's essay, 'Cadence, Country, Silence: Writing in Colonial Space', in which he discusses the conditions of language in a colony: 'My sense when I began writing . . . was that I had access to a great many words: those of the British, the American, and (so far as anyone took it seriously) the Canadian traditions. Yet at the same time those words seemed to lie in a great random heap, which glittered with promise so long as I considered it in the mass but within which each individual word somehow clogged with sludge, the moment I tried to move it into place in a poem. I could stir words, prod at them, cram them into position; but there was no way I could speak them directly.

They were completely external to me, though since I had never known the words of poetry in any other way I assumed that was natural.'

Contemporary readers are not simply pseudo-British or anti-American. John Donne, W.B. Yeats, Walt Whitman, Adrienne Rich, Chinua Achebe, Archibald Lampman, Rabindranath Tagore, Margaret Atwood, Mudrooroo, and Imitiaz Dharker look, sound, and signify differently from various regional, national, and international perspectives. Reading along the sweep of poetic history recorded in this anthology makes new connections among these poets and allows us to recognize that our postcolonial vulnerability, self-consciousness, and alienation are not simply weaknesses. These patterns evolve as strengths we develop in landing those cumbersome beasts known as the anthologized Eliot or Yeats.

No anthology can or should represent all interests and possibilities, but each collection has the capacity to make both magic and mischief. In *Uncommon Wealth* we have tried to balance pros and cons: what can be put aside and what has been passed over? What needs to be protected and what needs exposure? To what extent do our selections necessarily imply that we have reproduced the fixity of a canon? On the one hand, our criteria are associated with reputation, nationality, class, gender, culture, and ideology. On the other, these criteria are also linked to what each of us believes (amidst all of these contexts) are good poems, poems worth reading, remembering, and arguing over— regardless of their positions in or out of a canon or their indebtedness to local or foreign traditions.

Part of our answer to these questions about selection came through the poems themselves and their refusal to be neatly categorized into any system: we have simply arranged the poems in *Uncommon Wealth* in chronological order according to their authors' dates of birth, and alphabetically within that chronological system. The history of North America's evolution, including the naming of aboriginal authors' communities, has been made as clear as possible, recognizing that for other regions this history may be less easy to trace, but is nonetheless equally important. The notes that precede each poet's work provide brief biographical and bibliographical introductions to individual poets.

We took Irish poet Michael Hartnett's 'Advice' seriously: 'Never believe/the poem's caged/once written down/or captured like a wall's with bricks/or heat beneath a roof/trapped by slates./Each poem is a bunch of grapes/that thin skins restlessly press—/about to explode in a living juice,/about to explode in drunkenness.' The relationships Hartnett describes bristle with the energy of alternate crossings and unexpected continuities. It is one thing to read Emily Brontë among other mid-nineteenth century British women poets; it is quite another to read her in *Uncommon Wealth*, where her poem 'The Prisoner. A Fragment' sits beside 'A Parody' by the American poet Frederick Douglass and in the company of 'England and British America' by the Ojibway poet William Wilson. In this anthology, those poets who had been driven into hiding are 'discovered', manuscripts surface, poems scribbled on the backs of shopping lists are found in hope chests, and some local unknown becomes known in relation to an Old World giant of letters. With time, we hope, it may become just as unthinkable not to hear Keats's 'Ode to a Nightingale' in relation to more contemporary invocations to the muse, or Alexander Pope's 'Essay on Man' in relation to New World meditations on a related theme, or to read Robert Browning's 'My Last Duchess' without Vikram Seth's 'Work and Freedom', Thomas Hardy's 'The Darkling Thrush' without Catherine Obianuju Acholonu's 'Nigeria in the year 1999', or Australian poet Andrew Barton Paterson's 'The Man from Snowy River' without his aboriginal compatriot Archie Weller's 'The Legend of Jimmy's Axe'.

When we recognize that the boundaries constructed by anthologies are provisional, we discover what persists—what 'alters when it alteration finds'—what remains of the colonial condition, and how the patterns which advance liberation and imprisonment, ownership and freedom are recursive. This dialectical perspective informs Anne Stevenson's assessment of her own bicultural roots. Born in England of American parents, raised in America, and a practising poet in Scotland and Wales, Stevenson re-evaluates the shaping forces which she has carried back and forth across the Atlantic. In the introduction to her *Selected Poems 1956–1986* (1986), she writes: 'I was brought up in a tradition of self-improvement, self-pity, self-advertising [in America]. First in Scotland and later in Wales, it began to sink in on me that "I" is not the best foundation upon which to build an art. Any art needs a tradition, a history, a mythology, a faith. The religious work-ethic in America . . . has led to the rule of technocrats and capitalists . . . but there is another way of going about things, what one might call a "work-aesthetic" in which an artist commits himself (herself) to craft almost at the expense of self. . . . I have tried . . . to lay, as it were, on the altar of making.'

Whatever traditions influence individual writers, many poets focus on how the facts of empire have affected their imaginative work. In the introduction to his anthology, *Poems Of Black Africa* (1975), Wole Soyinka advises that the 'ghostly influence' exercised by European models is cause for neither 'self-flagellation' nor isolationism among African poets: 'The excesses committed in a small part of the poetic output achieve an importance only for those who fail to see the poet's preoccupations as springing from the same source of creativity which activates the major technological developments: town planning, sewage-disposal, hydro-electric power. None of these and others—including the making of war— has taken place or will ever again take place without the awareness of foreign thought and culture patterns, and their exploitation. To recommend, on the one hand, that the embattled general or the liberation fighter seek the more sophisticated weaponry of Europe, America, or China, while, on the other, that the poet totally expunge from his consciousness all knowledge of foreign tradition in his own craft, is an absurdity.' Soyinka's insights apply to poems as diverse as Manmohan Ghose's 'London', W.H. Auden's 'Lullaby', Nissim Ezekiel's 'Very Indian Poem in Indian English', Sonia Sanchez's 'haiku (for the police on osage ave)', Atukwei Okai's 'Elavanyo Concerto', Tom Leonard's 'Jist ti Let Yi No', and Gillian Hanscombe's 'An Apostrophe to Her Majesty Queen Elizabeth II'.

In European classical and national traditions, the question of why we read poetry inevitably sets a living theorist against the inherited influences of particularly active, 'ghostly' presences. Responding to the notorious critique of poets and poetry by his own mentor, Plato, 'that all poetical imitations are ruinous to the understanding of hearers', Aristotle advised that the desire to imitate—to use language to re-present external reality, for example—was a fundamental component of our human nature, instrumental to our learning, essential to our delight. Although Aristotle's defense of poetry has been a theme upon which others have composed variations—Sir Philip Sidney's 'Apology for Poetry' (1595), William Wordsworth's 'Preface' to *Lyrical Ballads* (1802), and Percy Bysshe Shelley's *A Defence of Poetry* (1821)—such theoretical evidence of our belief that poetry matters does not appear to meet the ongoing challenge to readers' sensibilities expressed in Thomas Love Peacock's satirical comments in 'The Four Ages of Poetry' (1820): 'While the historian and the philosopher are advancing in, and accelerating, the progress of knowledge, the poet is wallowing in the rubbish of departed ignorance, and raking up the ashes of dead savages to find gewgaws and rattles for the grown babies of the age . . . for the maturity of mind to make a serious business of the play-things of its childhood, is as absurd as for a full-grown man to rub his gums with coral and cry to be charmed to sleep by the jingle of silver bells.'

Attacks like Peacock's persist, but we may no longer respond to them in the tradition of Wordsworth, who confidently proclaimed: 'What we have loved,/Others will love, and we will teach them how.' Contemporary readers might be guided by Wallace Stevens's suggestion in *The Necessary Angel* (1951): 'One function of the poet at any time is to discover by his own thought and feeling what seems to him to be poetry at that time.' In her introduction to *Façade*, for example, Edith Sitwell attempts to understand what critics referred to as the 'strangeness' of her sound experiments. She describes the processes through which she was 'finding [her] way' as a poet, recalling how particular poems come into being. Sitwell acknowledges the poet's frustration when an intended meaning is 'misread'—critics who did not see that her piece 'The Shadow of Cain' was about the dropping of the bomb on Hiroshima, for example—even as she acknowledges that 'a line can mean several things—all equally true.' Readers of poetry experience similar paradoxes and apparent contradictions. They become aware that a poet may have one intention, that a particular reading has enjoyed a privileged reputation, that original contexts may not be recovered, and that words acquire different meanings over time.

The act of reading poetry is a process of finding one's way. And one of the many pleasures in this process is asking questions and looking for answers by engaging in always interesting, sometimes fascinating, and occasionally even intimate dialogues and conversations—rather than simply absorbing information. Reading a poem is seldom a matter of taking a writer's meaning out of her words as if one were removing a button from a box or a sweater from a closet. We can resist assumptions that would dictate meaning—assumptions that insist on strict consensus about what a poem ultimately means; that one is reading rightly or wrongly; that connections between standard readings and standards of reading must be preserved; that poets have to be protected from their own insights.

While there may be 'right readings' dangled as carrots to ensure that some interpretations remain more powerful than others, there are moments of release when meanings coded by the medium of language itself cunningly emerge. Gertrude Stein, for example, opens linguistic surfaces closed by prevailing heterosexist convention and so expresses the love of one woman for another by using the very rules of grammar and lexical meaning to dislodge customary associations and patterns of agreement. In this way, the reader's experience of a same-sex relationship appears in *Tender Buttons* as an error in agreement between subject and verb: 'A sight a whole sight and a little groan grinding makes a trimming such a sweet singing trimming and a red thing not a round thing but a white thing, a red thing and a white thing.'

Of course, we work with different and, at times, idiosyncratic strategies and assumptions, and struggle to understand their impact on poems, which are themselves determined internally by poets' choices in language and voice, form, rhythm, and metrical pattern. In some cases, the dialogue between context and text, language and emerging action is the substance of the poem itself, as in Leonard Cohen's 'French and English' or Cilla McQueen's 'Weekend Sonnets'. These poems take poetry—the process of its creation—as their theme and/or technical focus. In so doing, they may celebrate (or lament) the poet's awareness of self as maker or artisan.

Poetry restores a sense of vitality to language and the capacity of the medium to construct experiences, to cultivate, as Marianne Moore observes in 'Poetry', 'imaginary gardens with real toads in them' or to take the most ancient of journeys through the language of the street and the jostling of the subway coach as in Tom Leonard's 'A Priest Came on at Merkland Street'. And the figurative language in poetry—similes, metaphors, images, conceits—often engage in dialogue with other art forms—music, painting, sculpture, dance—enhancing our appreciation of the way in which any art form both refers to and departs from the familiar dimensions of our everyday condition. Examples of this inter-art tradition in *Uncommon Wealth* include Keats's 'Ode on a Grecian Urn', Frank O'Hara's 'Why I Am Not a Painter', and Elma Mitchell's 'Thoughts after Ruskin'. In Lakdasa Wikkramasinha's 'Don't Talk To Me About Matisse', the art of European painters—'the aboriginal shot by the great white hunter Matisse', or 'crucified by Gauguin'—is seen as a violent act of appropriation, with 'the murderers sustained/by the beauty robbed of savages.'

Some of the poetry in *Uncommon Wealth* protests against presumptuous answers to questions of identity, form, and meaning. The 'Black Madonna on the Cross' which soars 'above Soweto' in Maud Sulter's 'Azania', restricted by her position beneath the 'Christ of St John on the Cross', is 'Ready to write in her womens tongue a/message. In blood. To her sisterhood. A society closed to/the taint of men. Ready to leave her mark of the past.' In response to changing meanings and ideologies, poetry may enact rebellion, articulating rights and freedoms on behalf of gender, ethnicity, race, class, and national identities and communities: Kofi Anyidoho's 'Radio Revolution', Sujata Bhatt's 'A Different Way to Dance', and Paula Gunn Allen's 'Kopis'taya (A Gathering of Spirits)'. In Gunn Allen's poem, protest affirms indigenous community values and traditions rather than overtly confronting established figures of authority. Many poems, as we might expect, take up issues of language rights—Marge Piercy's 'Unlearning

to Not Speak', Seamus Heaney's 'Whatever You Say Say Nothing'. And some-
times poems purportedly redress a wrong, but in reality perpetuate oppressive
conventions representative of the time and place in which the poet lives and
works. Anna Seward's presentation of the destruction of Mother Nature wrought
by landscape architects in 'The Lake; or, Modern Improvement in Landscape',
for example, depends on misogynist conventions: the 'gaudy despot' Fashion, a
'Resistless goddess' whose 'idiot hour' drives the outraged, 'injured' 'Genius of
the scene' from his 'Fall'n' 'woods'.

Other poems invite our appreciation of poetry as performance, both in oral
traditions and in technological media, where the value of language is derived
from the sound of the accompanied or unaccompanied human voice more than
from the visual appearances of the word: Afro-American spirituals, rock lyrics,
folk ballads, chants, dirges, and hymns. In addition to individual and group
harmonies and dissonances, performances in poetry may employ gestures,
rituals, and formulae as dramatizing strategies to express a community's integral
activities. In 'The Canecutters' Song', David Dabydeen foregrounds the work of
the drum in the poem's accelerating rhythms and the closing 'chorus of lust' to
establish how the 'ritualistic' elements of the song approximate 'a perverse
replica' of the Hindu fertility ceremony. And other versions of poetry as perfor-
mance occur in written form—the dramatic monologues of Anne Bradstreet,
Li-Young Li, and Allen Ginsberg—where scenes of writing and/or speaking
declare the speakers' awareness of an audience (or the lack thereof).

What cannot be fully anthologized in *Uncommon Wealth* is our affection for
language and its possibilities. We hope readers hear and see how these poems
mark and transcend every border.

NEIL BESNER
DEBORAH SCHNITZER
ALDEN TURNER

ACKNOWLEDGEMENTS ❧

We began discussing our ideas for *Uncommon Wealth* in 1992, and we are thankful for the insights and encouragement of Brian Henderson at that early stage. At Oxford University Press, Ric Kitowski, Director of the College Division, Phyllis Wilson, Managing Editor, and Jane McNulty, Editor, are largely responsible for bringing the book to completion, and we value their uncommon creativity and professionalism.

We are grateful to all of our friends and colleagues at the University of Winnipeg who offered us their generous advice and shared their expertise on this project, including Valerie Baseley, Carlene Besner, Per Brask, Keith Louise Fulton, Patty Hawkins, Beryle Jones, Debbie Keahey, Lena McCourtie, Rakesh Mittoo, Mark Morton, Perry Nodelman, Uma Parameswaran, Lloyd Siemens, and Clement Wyke.

Hours of research would have become infinite if not for the dedicated assistance of the University of Winnipeg's reference librarians, particularly Linwood DeLong; the staff of the Interlibrary Loan Department, co-ordinated by Allison Dixon; and Jan Horner in the Dafoe Library, University of Manitoba. The help of our research assistants—Karen Green, Carolyn Smallwood, and Chris Wiebe—was invaluable. The University of Winnipeg offered generous, ongoing research funding, and Erin Booth kindly expedited our requests for financial support.

We have also appreciated the help and advice of Nathalie Cooke (McGill University), Dennis Cooley and Gaby Divay (University of Manitoba), Susan Rudy Dorscht (University of Calgary), Terry Goldie (York University), Norman S. Grabo (University of Tulsa), Charlene Diehl Jones (University of Waterloo), David Kent (Centennial College), Alan Lawson (University of Queensland, Australia), Carol Morrell (University of Saskatchewan), David Staines (University of Ottawa), Leighton Steele (University of Manitoba), and Mark Williams (University of Canterbury, New Zealand).

The most vital contributors to *Uncommon Wealth* have been the students of our colloquia, seminars, and classes.

Those closest to us in our readings and re-readings of these poems are our families, especially Barbara and Daniel Besner, Ben, Zachary, and Mendel Schnitzer, Kelsey and Caitlin Turner, and Connie Turner.

DANNIE ABSE. 'Epithalamion' from *Walking Under Water* by Dannie Abse (Hutchinson Publishing Group, 1952). Copyright © 1952. 'X-Ray' from *Way Out in the Centre* by Dannie Abse (Hutchinson Publishing Group, 1981). Copyright © 1981. Both reprinted by permission of Sheil Land Associates.

CHINUA ACHEBE. 'Mango Seedling' from *Christmas in Biafra and Other Poems* by Chinua Achebe. Copyright © 1973 by Chinua Achebe. Reprinted by permission of Doubleday, a division of Bantam Doubleday Dell Publishing Group, Inc. and by permission of Harold Ober Associates Incorporated.

CATHERINE OBIANUJU ACHOLONU. 'Nigeria in the year 1999' from *The Heinemann Book of African Poetry in English*, selected by Adewale Maja-Pearce, William Heinemann, 1990 (Catherine Obianuju Acholonu).

FLEUR ADCOCK. 'For a Five-Year-Old' from *Selected Poems* by Fleur Adcock (Oxford University Press, 1983). Reprinted by permission of Oxford University Press. 'Wife to Husband'. Reprinted by permission of the author.

GRACE AKELLO. 'Encounter' from *My Barren Song*, Dangaroo Press, 1979.

MEENA ALEXANDER. 'Boating' from *Night-Scene, The Garden* (New York: Red Dust, 1992) © Meena Alexander, 1992.

PAULA GUNN ALLEN. 'Kopis'taya (A Gathering of Spirits)' from *The Greenfield Review*, 1984. Reprinted by permission of Greenfield Review Press.

MONIZA ALVI. 'The Sari' from *The Country at My Shoulder* by Moniza Alvi (Oxford University Press, 1993). Reprinted by permission of Oxford University Press.

MAYA ANGELOU. 'A Good Woman Feeling Bad' from *Shaker, Why Don't You Sing?* by Maya Angelou. Copyright © 1983 by Maya Angelou. Reprinted by permission of Random House, Inc. And from *And Still I Rise* by Maya Angelou (Virago Press, 1986). Reprinted by permission of Virago Press, a division of Little, Brown and Company (UK).

ANNHARTE. 'Raced Out to Write This Up'.

ANONYMOUS. Translated by Adeboye Babalowa. 'Salute to the Elephant' from *A Selection of African Poetry*, edited by Senanu and Vincent, London: Longmans, 1976 (Professor Adeboye Babalowa).

KOFI ANYIDOHO. 'Radio Revolution' from *Soul in Birthwaters (Suite for the Revolution)* from *Aftermath*, Greenfield Review Press, 1977. Reprinted by permission of Greenfield Review Press.

NUALA ARCHER. 'Whale on the Line' is reprinted by kind permission of the author and The Gallery Press from *Whale on the Line* (1981).

JOANNE ARNOTT. 'Abortion (Like Motherhood) Changes Nothing' is reprinted with permission of the author and the publisher from *Wiles of Girlhood* (Vancouver: Press Gang Publishers, 1991).

ARONIAWENRATE/PETER BLUE CLOUD. 'Rattle' from *The Other Side of Nowhere* by Peter Blue Cloud, White Pine Press, 1990. Reprinted by permission of the author.

JOHN ASHBERY. 'The Painter', from *Some Trees* by John Ashbery. Copyright © 1956 by John Ashbery. First published by The Ecco Press in 1978. Reprinted by permission.

MARGARET ATWOOD. 'Progressive Insanities of a Pioneer' from *The Animals in That Country* by Margaret Atwood. Copyright © Oxford University Press Canada 1968. Reprinted by permission of Oxford University Press Canada. 'Notes Towards a Poem That Can Never Be Written' from *Selected Poems II: Poems Selected and New*. Copyright © 1987 by Margaret Atwood. Reprinted by permission of Houghton Mifflin Company. All rights reserved. And from *True Stories* © Margaret Atwood 1981. Reproduced with permission of Oxford University Press Canada and Curtis Brown Ltd., London on behalf of Margaret Atwood. Copyright © O.W. Toad 1981.

DOROTHY AUCHTERLONIE (GREEN). 'Apopemptic Hymn' is reprinted from *The Dolphin* (Australian National University Press, 1967) by permission of the Literary Estate of Dorothy Green.

W.H. AUDEN. 'Letter to a Wound' and 'Lullaby' from *The English Auden: Poems, Essays and Dramatic Writings 1927–1939* by W.H. Auden. Reprinted by permission of Faber and Faber Ltd. And from *Collected Poems* by W.H. Auden. Copyright © 1934 and renewed 1962 by W.H. Auden. Copyright © 1973 by The Estate of W.H. Auden. Reprinted by permission of Random House, Inc.

MARGARET AVISON. 'The Swimmer's Moment' from *Selected Poems* by Margaret Avison. Copyright © Margaret Avison 1991. Reprinted by permission of Oxford University Press Canada.

KOFI AWOONOR. 'Afro-American Beats' from *Ride Me, Memory*. Reprinted by permission of Greenfield Review Press.

PRAKASH BANDEKAR. 'Afternoon Massacre' from *An Anthology of Marathi Poetry (1945–65)*, ed. Dilip Chitre.

AMIRI BARAKA. 'Numbers, Letters' from *Black Magic Poetry* and 'An Agony. As Now' from *The Dead Lecturer*. Reprinted by permission of Sterling Lord Literistic, Inc. Copyright © 1969 by Amiri Baraka.

JAMES K. BAXTER. 'The Ikons' from *Collected Poems* by James K. Baxter (Oxford University Press, 1979). Reprinted by permission of Oxford University Press and Mrs. J. Baxter.

SAMUEL BECKETT. 'Something There' from *Collected Poems 1930–1978* by Samuel Beckett, Calder Publications Limited, London. Reproduced by permission of the Samuel Beckett Estate and The Calder Educational Trust, London. Copyright © Samuel Beckett 1974, 1984. And from *Collected Poems in English and French* by Samuel Beckett. Copyright © 1977 by Samuel Beckett. Used by permission of Grove/Atlantic, Inc.

JOHN PEPPER CLARK BEKEDEREMO. 'A Child Asleep' from *Black Orpheus* (Lagos University Press).

GWENDOLYN B. BENNETT. 'Heritage' from *Opportunity*, Volume 1, December 1923.

SUJATA BHATT. 'White Asparagus' and 'A Different Way to Dance' from *Monkey Shadows* by Sujata Bhatt (Carcanet Press, 1991). Reprinted by permission of Carcanet Press Limited.

EARLE BIRNEY. 'Can. Lit.' and 'The Bear on the Delhi Road' from *Selected Poems of Earle Birney* by Earle Birney. Used by permission of the Canadian Publishers, McClelland & Stewart, Toronto.

ELIZABETH BISHOP. 'The Moose' and 'In the Waiting Room' from *The Complete Poems 1927–1979* by Elizabeth Bishop. Copyright © 1979, 1983 by Alice Helen Methfessel. Reprinted by permission of Farrar, Straus & Giroux, Inc.

BILL BISSETT. 'th wundrfulness uv th mountees our secret police' from *sailor* by bill bissett (Talonbooks, 1980). Reprinted by permission of the author.

LOUISE BOGAN. 'Women' from *The Blue Estuaries: Poems 1923–1968* by Louise Bogan. Copyright © 1968 by Louise Bogan. Reprinted by permission of Farrar, Straus & Giroux, Inc.

EAVAN BOLAND. 'Mise Eire' and 'Listen. This is the Noise of Myth' from *Selected Poems* by Eavan Boland (Carcanet Press, 1989). Reprinted by permission of Carcanet Press Limited. And from *An Origin Like Water: Collected Poems 1967–1987* by Eavan Boland. Copyright © 1996 by Eavan Boland. Reprinted by permission of W.W. Norton & Company, Inc.

DERMOT BOLGER. 'Snuff Movies' from *Internal Exiles: Poems* by Dermot Bolger is reprinted by permission of A.P. Watt Ltd on behalf of Dermot Bolger.

ROO BORSON. 'City Lights' reprinted from *Night Walk: Selected Poems* (Oxford University Press Canada, 1994), by permission of the author.

GEORGE BOWERING. 'Grandfather' from *Selected Poems* by George Bowering. Used by permission of the Canadian Publishers, McClelland & Stewart, Toronto.

DIONNE BRAND. Excerpt from 'No Language Is Neutral' © Dionne Brand, 1990. Reprinted from *No Language Is Neutral* with the permission of Coach House Press.

DI BRANDT. 'questions i asked my mother' from *questions i asked my mother*. Copyright © Di Brandt 1987. Reprinted by permission of Turnstone Press Limited.

CHARLES BRASCH. 'Ambulando' from *Ambulando* by Charles Brasch (Caxton Press, 1964). Reprinted by permission of Alan Roddick, for the Estate of Charles Brasch.

E.K. BRATHWAITE. 'Calypso' from *The Arrivants* by Edward Kamau Brathwaite (Oxford University Press, 1973). Reprinted by permission of Oxford University Press.

JEAN BINTA BREEZE. 'Ordinary Mawning' from *Riddym Ravings and Other Poems*, ed. Mervyn Morris, Race Today Publications, 1988.

KWESI BREW. 'The Search' from *Okyeame*.

ROBERT BRINGHURST. 'These Poems, She Said' from *The Beauty of the Weapons* by Robert Bringhurst. Used by permission of the Canadian Publishers, McClelland & Stewart, Toronto.

VERA BRITTAIN. 'To My Brother' from *Verses of a V.A.D.*, Erskine Macdonald Ltd, 1918.

GWENDOLYN BROOKS. 'The Mother' from *The World of Gwendolyn Brooks*.

GEORGE MACKAY BROWN. 'King of Kings' from *Poems: New and Selected* by George Mackay Brown is reprinted by permission of John Murray (Publishers) Ltd.

ABENA P.A. BUSIA. 'Liberation' and 'Exiles' from *Testimonies of Exile*. Reprinted by permission of Africa World Press Inc.

JOHN CAGE. Excerpt from *A Year from Monday*, © 1967 by John Cage, Wesleyan University. Reprinted by permission of University Press of New England.

MOYA CANNON. '"Taom"' from *Oar* by Moya Cannon published by Salmon Publishing Ltd., 1990. Reprinted by permission of Salmon Publishing Ltd., Knockeven, Cliffs of Moher, Co. Clare, Ireland.

CIARAN CARSON. 'Belfast Confetti' and 'Narrative in Black and White' from *Belfast Confetti*, Bloodaxe Books, 1989.

GLADYS MAY CASELY-HAYFORD ('AQUAH LALUAH'). 'Junior Geography Lesson'.

G.S. SHARAT CHANDRA. 'Bangla (water pipe) Desh' from *Aftermath*, Greenfield Review Press, 1977. Reprinted by permission of Greenfield Review Press.

SYL CHENEY-COKER. 'Letter to a Tormented Playwright' from *The Graveyard Also Has Teeth*, © 1980. Reprinted by permission of the author.

DILIP CHITRE. 'Poem in Self-Exile' and 'Mumbai: A Song' from *Travelling in a Cage*, Clearing House Press, 1980.

CHRYSTOS. 'Ceremony for Completing a Poetry Reading' is reprinted with permission of the publisher from *Not Vanishing* (Vancouver: Press Gang Publishers, 1988).

EILÉAN NÍ CHUILLEANÁIN. 'Amelia' is reprinted by kind permission of the author and The Gallery Press from *The Rose-Geranium* (1981). 'The Second Voyage' is reprinted by kind permission of the author and The Gallery Press from *The Second Voyage*. Lines from 'The Second Voyage' from *The Second Voyage* by Eiléan Ní Chuilleanáin are reprinted with the permission of Wake Forest University Press.

GILLIAN CLARKE. 'On Air' from *The King of Britain's Daughter* by Gillian Clarke (Carcanet Press, 1993). Reprinted by permission of Carcanet Press Limited.

LEONARD COHEN. 'I Have Not Lingered in European Monasteries' and 'French and English' from *Stranger Music* by Leonard Cohen. Used by permission of the Canadian Publishers, McClelland & Stewart, Toronto, and Stranger Music Inc.

STEWART CONN. 'Kitchen-Maid' is reprinted by permission of Bloodaxe Books Ltd from: *In the Kibble Palace: New and Selected Poems* by Stewart Conn (Bloodaxe Books, 1987).

MÉIRA COOK. 'a fine grammar of bones' from *A Fine Grammar of Bones*. Copyright © Méira Cook 1993. Reprinted by permission of Turnstone Press Limited.

DENNIS COOLEY. 'a curse on a critic' from *Dedications* by Dennis Cooley (Thistledown Press, 1988). Reprinted by permission of the author.

LORNA CROZIER. 'On the Seventh Day' from *Inventing the Hawk* by Lorna Crozier. Used by permission of the Canadian Publishers, McClelland & Stewart, Toronto.

HELEN B. CRUICKSHANK. 'On Being Eighty' from *Collected Poems* (Reprographia, 1971). Reprinted by permission of A.C. Hunter.

E.E. CUMMINGS. '[the Cambridge ladies who live in furnished souls]', copyright 1923, 1951, © 1991 by the Trustees for the e.e. cummings Trust. '[somewhere i have never travelled,gladly beyond]', copyright 1931, © 1959, 1991 by the Trustees for the e.e. cummings Trust. Copyright © 1979 by George James Firmage, from *Complete Poems: 1904–1962* by e.e. cummings, edited by George J. Firmage. Reprinted by permission of Liveright Publishing Corporation.

ALLEN CURNOW. 'Landfall in Unknown Seas' from *Island and Time* is reprinted by permission of the author. 'An Incorrigible Music' from *An Incorrigible Music* is reprinted by permission of Auckland University Press and Allen Curnow.

TONY CURTIS. 'Thoughts from the Holiday Inn' from *The Last Candles* (Seren, 1989). Reprinted by permission.

DAVID DABYDEEN. 'The Canecutters' Song' from *Slave Song*, Dangaroo Press, 1984. 'The New Poetry' from *Coolie Odyssey*, Dangaroo Press, 1988.

K.N. DARUWALLA. 'The Epileptic' is reprinted from *Under Orion* by permission of the author.

KAMALA DAS. 'The Old Playhouse' from *The Descendants*, Writers Workshop, 1967. 'An Introduction' from *Summer in Calcutta* by Kamala Das. Reprinted by permission of the author.

GAURI DESHPANDE. 'The Female of The Species' from *Between Births*, Calcutta: Writer's Workshop, 1968.

EUNICE DE SOUZA. 'Encounter at a London Party' from *Ranters, Ravers & Rhymers*, William Collins, 1990.

DENIS DEVLIN. 'Liffey Bridge' from *Collected Poems of Denis Devlin*, The Dedalus Press, Dublin, 1989. Reprinted by permission of The Dedalus Press.

CHRISTOPHER DEWDNEY. 'The Dialectic Criminal: Hand in Glove with an Old Hat' from *Predators of the Adoration* by Christopher Dewdney. Used by permission of the Canadian Publishers, McClelland & Stewart, Toronto.

IMITIAZ DHARKER. 'Another Woman' from *Pardah and Other Poems* by Imitiaz Dharker (New Delhi: Oxford University Press, 1989). Reprinted by permission of Oxford University Press.

H.D. (HILDA DOOLITTLE). 'Sigil XIV–XIX' and 'At Baia' by H.D., from *Collected Poems, 1912–1944*. Copyright © 1982 by The Estate of Hilda Doolittle. Reprinted by permission of New Directions Publishing Corp. and Carcanet Press Limited.

W.E.B. DU BOIS. 'The Song of the Smoke'.

CAROL ANN DUFFY. 'The Captain of the 1964 Top of the Form Team' is taken from *Mean Time* published by Anvil Press Poetry in 1993. 'Standing Female Nude' is taken from *Standing Female Nude* published by Anvil Press Poetry in 1985.

IAN DUHIG. 'I'r Hen Iaith A'i Chaneuon/To the Old Tongue and Its Songs' is reprinted by permission of Bloodaxe Books Ltd from *The Bradford Count* by Ian Duhig (Bloodaxe Books, 1991).

HELEN DUNMORE. 'Sisters leaving before the dance' and 'Poem for December 28' are reprinted by permission of Bloodaxe Books Ltd from *Short Days Long Nights* by Helen Dunmore (Bloodaxe Books, 1991).

DOUGLAS DUNN. 'Empires' from *Douglas Dunn: New and Selected Poems 1966–1988* by Douglas Dunn. Copyright © 1989 by Douglas Dunn. First published by The Ecco Press in 1989. Reprinted by permission.

PAUL DURCAN. 'The Jewish Bride', from the collection *A Snail In My Prime*. First published in Great Britain in 1993 by Harvill. © Paul Durcan. Reproduced by permission of the Harvill Press. 'Crinkle, near Birr' from *Daddy, Daddy* (Thistledown Press Ltd, 1990). Reprinted by permission of Thistledown Press Ltd.

JEAN EARLE. 'Young Girls Running' from *Selected Poems* (Seren, 1990). Reprinted by permission.

MURRAY EDMOND. 'My Return to Czechoslovakia' and 'House' from *End Wall*, Melbourne: Oxford University Press, 1981. Reprinted by permission of the author.

T.S. ELIOT. 'The Hollow Men' from *Collected Poems 1909–1962* by T.S. Eliot. Reprinted by permission of Faber and Faber Ltd. And from *Collected Poems 1909–1962* by T.S. Eliot, copyright 1936 by Harcourt Brace & Company, copyright © 1964, 1963 by T.S. Eliot, reprinted by permission of the publisher.

LOUISE ERDRICH. 'Dear John Wayne' from *Jacklight* by Louise Erdrich. Copyright © 1984 by Louise Erdrich. Reprinted by permission of Henry Holt and Co., Inc.

MARI EVANS. 'I Am a Black Woman' from *I Am a Black Woman*, published by Wm. Morrow & Co., 1970, by permission of the author.

NISSIM EZEKIEL. 'Very Indian Poem in Indian English' and 'Enterprise' from *Collected Poems 1952–1988* by Nissim Ezekiel. Reprinted by permission of the author and Oxford University Press, New Delhi.

U.A. FANTHORPE. 'Not My Best Side' copyright U.A. Fanthorpe, from *Side Effects* (1978), and 'Knowing about Sonnets' copyright U.A. Fanthorpe, from *Selected Poems* (1986), reproduced by permission of Peterloo Poets.

KENNETH FEARING. 'Cultural Notes' from *New and Selected Poems* by Kenneth Fearing. Reprinted by permission of Indiana University Press.

LAWRENCE FERLINGHETTI. 'I Am Waiting' by Lawrence Ferlinghetti, from *A Coney Island of the Mind*. Copyright © 1958 by Lawrence Ferlinghetti. Reprinted by permission of New Directions Publishing Corp.

PETER FINCH. 'Visual Text Makes It As Super Hero' from *Selected Poems* (Poetry Wales Press, 1987). Reprinted by permission.

IAN HAMILTON FINLAY. 'Ballad' and 'Little Calendar' are reprinted by permission of the author.

CAROLYN FORCHÉ. 'Kalaloch' from *Gathering the Tribes* by Carolyn Forché. Copyright © 1976 by Carolyn Forché. Reprinted by permission of Yale University Press.

VERONICA FORREST-THOMSON. 'Identi-kit' from *Collected Poems and Translations* (London, Lewes, Berkeley: Allardyce, Barnett, Publishers, 1990). Copyright © Jonathan Culler and the Estate of Veronica Forrest-Thomson, 1990 and Copyright © Allardyce, Barnett, Publishers, 1990. First printed in *Identi-kit*. Copyright Veronica Forrest-Thomson, 1967. Printed by permission of Allardyce, Barnett, Publishers.

JANET FRAME. 'The Clown' from *The Pocket Mirror*. Reprinted by permission of Curtis Brown, Australia.

G.S. FRASER. 'An Elegy for Keith Bullen' reproduced from *Poems of G.S. Fraser* (Leicester University Press, 1981) by permission of Leicester University Press (a Cassell imprint) London. All rights reserved.

OLIVE FRASER. 'Lines Written after a Nervous Breakdown (II)' from *The Wrong Music: The Poems of Oliver Fraser 1909–77* edited by Helena M. Shire, published by Canongate Books, Edinburgh. Reprinted by permission of Canongate Books.

ANNE FRENCH. 'Collisions' from *All Cretans Are Liars* (Auckland University Press, 1987) and 'In absentia' from *The Male as Evader* (Auckland University Press, 1988) are reprinted by permission of the author.

PATRICK FRIESEN. 'talking new york: waiting on love' from *Blasphemer's Wheel: Selected and New Poems*. Copyright © Patrick Friesen 1994. Reprinted by permission of Turnstone Press.

ROBERT FROST. 'Design' ('In White') and 'Desert Places' from *The Poetry of Robert Frost* edited by Edward Connery Lathem. Copyright 1936 by Robert Frost. Copyright © 1964 by Lesley Frost Ballantine. Copyright © 1967 by Henry Holt and Co., Inc. Reprinted by permission of Henry Holt and Co., Inc., and Jonathan Cape.

MARY FULLERTON ('E'). 'Flesh' and 'Cubes' from *Moles Do So Little With Their Privacy*. Reprinted by permission of HarperCollins Publishers Pty. Limited.

ROBERT GARIOCH (SUTHERLAND). We are grateful for permission to include 'The Wire' from *Complete Poetical Works* by Robert Garioch (ed. R. Fulton), Macdonald Publishers, Edinburgh 1983. Reprinted by permission of The Saltire Society.

RAYMOND GARLICK. 'Map Reading' from *A Sense of Time* by Raymond Garlick. Reprinted by permission of Gomer Press.

MARY GILMORE. 'Eve-song' and 'Never Admit the Pain' from *Selected Poems* by Mary Gilmore. (ETT Imprint, Sydney, 1997). Reprinted by permission of ETT Imprint.

ALLEN GINSBERG. All lines from 'A Supermarket in California' from *Collected Poems 1947–1980* by Allen Ginsberg. Copyright © 1955 by Allen Ginsberg. Copyright renewed. Reprinted by permission of HarperCollins Publishers, Inc. and Penguin Books Ltd.

LOUISE GLÜCK. 'Dedication to Hunger' and 'Aubade' from *Descending Figure* by Louise Glück. Copyright © 1976, 1977, 1978, 1979, 1980 by Louise Glück. First published by The Ecco Press in 1980. Reprinted by permission.

VINAYAK KRISHNA GOKAK. 'The Song of India' from *In Life's Temple*, Madras: Blackie & Son, 1965.

LEONA GOM. 'University' from *The Collected Poems* by Leona Gom (Sono Nis Press, 1991). Reprinted with permission from Sono Nis Press.

YASMINE GOONERATNE. 'Menika' is reprinted by permission of the author.

W.S. GRAHAM. 'Johann Joachim Quantz's Five Lessons' from *Collected Poems 1942–1977* by W.S. Graham (Faber and Faber, 1979). Copyright © The Estate of W.S. Graham. Reprinted by permission.

FREDERICK P. GROVE. 'Arctic Woods' is reprinted by permission of A. Leonard Grove, Toronto, Canada.

THOM GUNN. 'On the Move' and 'Lament' from *Collected Poems* by Thom Gunn. Copyright © 1994 by Thom Gunn. Reprinted by permission of Farrar, Straus & Giroux, Inc and Faber and Faber Ltd.

KRISTJANA GUNNARS. 'Stefán Eyjólfsson XIV' from *Settlement Poems I*. Copyright © Kristjana Gunnars 1992. Reprinted by permission of Turnstone Press Limited.

RALPH GUSTAFSON. 'In the Yukon' from *The Moment is All* by Ralph Gustafson. Used by permission of the Canadian Publishers, McClelland & Stewart, Toronto.

GILLIAN HANSCOMBE. 'An Apostrophe to Her Majesty Queen Elizabeth II' from *Beautiful Barbarians: Lesbian Feminist Poetry*, ed. Mohin, Lilian, Onlywomen Press Ltd., London, 1986.

JOY HARJO. 'Anchorage' and 'I Am a Dangerous Woman' from *She Had Some Horses*, Thunder's Mouth Press, 1983.

CLAIRE HARRIS. 'In the Dark, Father' is reprinted from *Fables from Women's Quarters* © Claire Harris, 1984. Reprinted with the permission of Goose Lane Editions.

MICHAEL HARTNETT. 'A Farewell to English' from *Selected and New Poems* (The Gallery Press and Wake Forest University Press, 1994). Reprinted by kind permission of the author and The Gallery Press.

GWEN HARWOOD. 'New Music' and 'Suburban Sonnet' from *Selected Poems* by Gwen Harwood (ETT Imprint, Sydney, 1996). Reprinted by permission of ETT Imprint.

IYAMIDÉ HAZELEY. 'When You Have Emptied Our Calabashes' from *Daughters of Africa*.

SEAMUS HEANEY. Excerpt from 'Whatever You Say Say Nothing' and 'Digging' from *New Selected Poems 1966–1987* by Seamus Heaney. Reprinted by permission of Faber and Faber Ltd. And from *Selected Poems 1966–1987* by Seamus Heaney. Copyright © 1990 by Seamus Heaney. Reprinted by permission of Farrar, Straus & Giroux, Inc.

RITA ANN HIGGINS. 'Woman's Inhumanity to Woman (Galway Labour Exchange)' originally published in *Witch in the Bushes*, 1988, Salmon Publishing, reprinted in *Goddess and Witch*, 1990, Salmon Publishing Ltd.

SELIMA HILL. 'Eating Chocolates in the Dark' and 'The Significance of Significance' from *Trembling Hearts in the Bodies of Dogs: New and Selected Poems* published by Bloodaxe Books, 1995. Copyright © Selima Hill. Reprinted by permission of the author.

A.D. HOPE. 'The End of a Journey' from *Selected Poems* by A.D. Hope. Reprinted by permission of HarperCollins Publishers Pty Limited.

AMELIA BLOSSOM HOUSE. 'We Still Dance' from *Our Sun Will Rise* (Three Continents Press, 1989). Reprinted by permission of Three Continents Press.

LANGSTON HUGHES. 'The Weary Blues' from *Collected Poems* by Langston Hughes. Copyright © 1994 by the Estate of Langston Hughes. Reprinted by permission of Alfred A. Knopf Inc. and Harold Ober Associates Incorporated.

TED HUGHES. 'Dust As We Are' from *Wolfwatching* by Ted Hughes. Copyright © 1991 by Ted Hughes. Reprinted by permission of Farrar, Straus & Giroux, Inc. and Faber and Faber Ltd.

KERI HULME. 'Mushrooms and Other Bounty' from *Moeraki Conversations*, Auckland University Press, 1983.

KATHLEEN JAMIE. 'The Queen of Sheba' is reprinted by permission of Bloodaxe Books Ltd from *The Queen of Sheba* by Kathleen Jamie (Bloodaxe Books, 1994).

PAULETTE JILES. 'Windigo' from *Celestial Navigation* by Paulette Jiles. Used by permission of McClelland & Stewart, Inc., Toronto, *The Canadian Publishers*.

LINTON KWESI JOHNSON. 'Mekkin Histri' is reprinted by permission of Bloodaxe Books Ltd from *Tings an Times* by Linton Kwesi Johnson (Bloodaxe Books, 1991).

SALLY ROBERTS JONES. 'Lletherneuadd Uchaf, 1868' from *The Forgotten Country* by Sally Roberts Jones. Reprinted by permission of Gomer Press.

ADIL JUSSAWALLA. 'A Bomb-site'.

JONATHAN KARIARA. 'A Leopard Lives in a Muu Tree' from *Penguin Book of Modern African Poetry* (Penguin Books Ltd).

K.D. KATRAK. 'Malabar Hill' and 'The Kitchen Door' from *Contemporary Indian Poetry in English*, Macmillan, 1972. Reprinted by permission of the author.

PATRICK KAVANAGH. Section I, 'The Great Hunger' from *Collected Poems* by Patrick Kavanagh. Reprinted by kind permission of the Trustees of the Estate of Patrick Kavanagh, c/o Peter Fallon, Literary Agent, Loughcrew, Oldcastle, Co. Meath, Ireland.

JACKIE KAY. 'Baby Lazarus' is reprinted by permission of Bloodaxe Books Ltd from *The Adoption Papers* by Jackie Kay (Bloodaxe Books, 1991).

JUDITH KAZANTZIS. 'For my sister pregnant' from *The Wicked Queen*, Sidgwick & Jackson, 1980.

LENORE KEESHIG-TOBIAS. 'Resistance' from *Fireweed*, Winter 1986. Reprinted by permission of the author.

WAYNE KEON. 'I'm Not In Charge Of This Ritual' is reprinted by permission of the author.

THOMAS KING. 'The City on the Hill' is reprinted by permission of the author.

CAROLYN KIZER. 'Exodus', copyright © 1984 by Carolyn Kizer. Reprinted from *Yin*, by Carolyn Kizer, with the permission of BOA Editions, Ltd., 92 Park Ave., Brockport, NY 14420.

A.M. KLEIN. 'Political Meeting' and 'Montreal' from *A.M. Klein: Complete Poems*, ed. Zailig Pollock (University of Toronto Press, 1990). Reprinted by permission of University of Toronto Press Incorporated.

ARUN BALKRISHNA KOLATKAR. 'An Old Woman' from *Jejuri*, Clearing House Press, 1976.

ROBERT KROETSCH. 'Stone Hammer Poem' © 1989 Robert Kroetsch. From *Completed Field Notes: The Long Poems of Robert Kroetsch* (McClelland & Stewart). Reprinted by permission of Westwood Creative Artists Ltd.

MAZISI KUNENE. 'Elegy' (Heinemann Publishers Pty Ltd).

FRANK KUPPNER. Excerpts from *A Bad Day for the Sung Dynasty* by Frank Kuppner (Carcanet Press, 1984). Reprinted by permission of Carcanet Press Limited.

KOJO LAING. 'Senior lady sells garden eggs' © Kojo Laing. Reprinted by permission of the author.

PATRICK LANE. 'Passing into Storm' from *Selected Poems* (Oxford University Press Canada, 1987) is reprinted by permission of the author.

ALDA LARA. 'Testament' from *A Horse of White Clouds: Poems from Lusophone Africa*, translated by Don Burness (The Ohio University Monographs in International Studies, 1989). Reprinted by permission.

PHILIP LARKIN. 'Faith Healing' from *The Whitsun Weddings* by Philip Larkin. Reprinted by permission of Faber and Faber Ltd.

IRVING LAYTON. 'Keine Lazarovitch 1870–1959' and 'From Colony to Nation' from *Collected Poems* by Irving Layton. Used by permission of the Canadian Publishers, McClelland & Stewart, Toronto.

DENNIS LEE. 'Elegy #1' from *Civil Elegies* by Dennis Lee (House of Anansi, 1972). Reprinted by permission of Stoddart Publishing Co. Limited, Don Mills, Ontario.

LI-YOUNG LEE. 'This Room and Everything in It', copyright © 1990 by Li-Young Lee. Reprinted from *City in Which I Love You*, by Li-Young Lee, with the permission of BOA Editions, Ltd., 92 Park Avenue, Brockport, NY 14420.

GEOFFREY LEHMANN. 'Night Flower' from *A Voyage of Lions*, Angus & Robertson. Reprinted by permission of Curtis Brown (Australia) Pty. Ltd.

TOM LEONARD. 'Jist ti Let Yi No' and 'A Priest Came on at Merkland Street' from *Intimate Voices: Selected Poetry 1965–83*, Vintage Press, © Tom Leonard.

DOUGLAS LEPAN. 'A Country Without a Mythology' from *Weathering It* by Douglas LePan. Used by permission of McClelland & Stewart, Inc., Toronto, *The Canadian Publishers*.

DENISE LEVERTOV. 'A Tree Telling of Orpheus' by Denise Levertov, from *Poems 1968–1972*. Copyright © 1970 by Denise Levertov. Reprinted by permission of New Directions Publishing Corp. and Laurence Pollinger Limited.

ALUN LEWIS. 'Goodbye' from *Ha! Ha! Among the Trumpets*, George Allen & Unwin (HarperCollins Publishers Ltd).

DOROTHY LIVESAY. 'Day and Night' and 'Bartok and the Geranium' from *Collected Poems*. Copyright © Dorothy Livesay. Reprinted by permission of the author.

LIZ LOCHHEAD. 'Six Men Monologues' from *True Confessions & New Cliches* © Liz Lochhead 1985. Reprinted by permission of Polygon.

AUDRE LORDE. 'Power' from *The Black Unicorn* by Audre Lorde. Copyright © 1978 by Audre Lorde. Reprinted by permission of W.W. Norton & Company, Inc.

ROBERT LOWELL. 'For the Union Dead' from *Selected Poems* by Robert Lowell. Copyright © 1977 by Robert Lowell. Reprinted by permission of Farrar, Straus & Giroux, Inc. and Faber and Faber Ltd.

IAIN MACA'GHOBHAINN/IAIN CRICHTON SMITH. 'Shall Gaelic Die?' from *Selected Poems* by Iain Crichton Smith (Carcanet Press, 1985). Reprinted by permission of Carcanet Press Limited.

RACHEL McALPINE. 'Here it is' from *Selected Poems* by Rachel McAlpine (Mallinson Rendel, 1988). Reprinted by permission of the author.

JAMES McAULEY. 'Because' from *Collected Poems* by James McAuley. Reprinted by permission of HarperCollins Publishers Pty. Limited.

HUGH MacDIARMID/CHRISTOPHER MURRAY GRIEVE. From 'A Drunk Man Looks at the Thistle'. Reprinted with the permission of Simon & Schuster from *The Collected Poems* of Hugh MacDiarmid. Copyright © 1948, 1962 by Christopher Murray Grieve.

GWENDOLYN MacEWEN. 'Dark Pines Under Water' from *Magic Animals* (Stoddart, 1984). Reprinted by permission of Stoddart Publishing Co. Limited, Don Mills, Ontario.

SOMHAIRLE MacGILL-EAIN/SORLEY MacLEAN. 'Ban-Ghàidheal/A Highland Woman' from *From Wood to Ridge: Collected Poems in Gaelic and English* by Sorley MacLean (Carcanet Press, 1989). Reprinted by permission of Carcanet Press Limited.

MEDBH McGUCKIAN. 'Venus and the Rain' is reprinted by kind permission of the author and The Gallery Press from *Venus and the Rain* (1994).

CLAUDE McKAY. 'If We Must Die' and 'America' from *Selected Poems of Claude McKay*, Twayne Publishers, 1981. Used by permission of The Archives of Claude McKay, Carl Cowl, Administrator.

DOROTHEA MACKELLAR. 'In a Southern Garden' is reprinted courtesy of Curtis Brown (Australia) Pty. Ltd.

IAN McMILLAN. 'Just the Facts, Just the' from *Selected Poems* by Ian McMillan (Carcanet Press, 1987). Reprinted by permission of Carcanet Press Limited.

LOUIS MacNEICE. 'Reflections' from *Collected Poems* by Louis MacNeice (Faber and Faber, 1966). Reprinted by permission of David Higham Associates.

JAY MACPHERSON. 'The Fisherman' from *Poems Twice Told* by Jay Macpherson. Copyright © Oxford University Press Canada 1981. Reprinted by permission of Oxford University Press Canada.

CILLA McQUEEN. 'Matinal' and 'Weekend Sonnets' from *The Oxford Book of Contemporary New Zealand Poetry*, Melbourne: Oxford University Press, 1982.

RUARAIDH MacTHÒMAIS/DERICK THOMSON. 'Clann-Nighean an Sgadain/The Herring Girls' from *Collected Poems, Creachadh Na Clàrsaich*, available from Gairm Publications, Glasgow G26 B2. Reprinted by permission of the author.

JAYANTA MAHAPATRA. 'Hunger' and 'The Abandoned British Cemetery at Balasore' from *Selected Poems* by Jayanta Mahapatra (New Delhi: Oxford University Press, 1987). Reprinted by permission of Oxford University Press.

MARIE MAKINO. ''Ilda' from *Best Music Hall and Vanity Songs*, EMI Music Publishing Ltd.

DAVID MALOUF. 'Off the Map' copyright © David Malouf 1994. Reproduced by permission of the author c/o Rogers, Coleridge & White Ltd., 20 Powis Mews, London W11 1JN.

ELI MANDEL. 'Houdini' is reprinted by permission of the Estate of Eli Mandel.

BILL MANHIRE. 'Wellington' and 'Party Going' from *Sheet Music: Poems 1967–1982* by Bill Manhire (Victoria University Press, 1996). Reprinted by permission of the author.

JACK MAPANJE. 'At the Metro: Old Irrelevant Images' from *Of Chameleons and Gods* by Jack Mapanje. Copyright © Jack Mapanje 1981. Reprinted by permission of Heinemann Publishers Oxford.

DAPHNE MARLATT. 'Imperial Cannery, 1913' from *Steveston* (first edition: Talonbooks, 1974; second edition: Longspoon Press, 1984) © Daphne Marlatt and Robert Minden (photographs). Reprinted by permission of the author.

ROLAND MATHIAS. 'Laus Deo' from *Burning Brambles: Selected Poems 1944–1979* by Roland Mathias. Reprinted by permission of Gomer Press.

ARVIND KRISHNA MEHROTRA. 'The Sale' from *Ten Twentieth-Century Indian Poets*, edited by R. Parthasarathy (Oxford University Press Delhi, 1989). Reprinted by permission.

ELMA MITCHELL. 'Thoughts After Ruskin' copyright Elma Mitchell, from *The Poor Man in the Flesh* (1976), reproduced by permission of Peterloo Poets.

ERNEST G. MOLL. 'A Gnarled Riverina Gum-tree' from *Poems 1940–1955* by Ernest G. Moll. Reprinted by permission of HarperCollins Publishers Pty. Limited.

N. SCOTT MOMADAY. 'Rainy Mountain Cemetery' from *The Way to Rainy Mountain* by N. Scott Momaday, © 1969, The University of New Mexico Press. Reprinted by permission.

MARIANNE MOORE. 'Poetry' is reprinted with the permission of Simon & Schuster from *The Collected Poems of Marianne Moore*. Copyright © 1935 by Marianne Moore, renewed 1963 by Marianne Moore and T.S. Eliot. And from *The Complete Poems* by Marianne Moore. Reprinted by permission of Faber and Faber Ltd.

EDWIN MORGAN. 'Canedolia: an off-concrete scotch fantasia' from *The Second Life* by Edwin Morgan (Carcanet Press, 1968). Reprinted by permission of Carcanet Press Limited.

DANIEL DAVID MOSES. 'The Line' is reprinted by permission of the author.

ERIN MOURÉ. 'Cherish' from *Domestic Fuel* by Erin Mouré is reprinted with the permission of Stoddart Publishing Co. Limited, Don Mills, Ontario.

MUDROOROO. 'Crow' from *Dalwurra: The Black Bittern*. Reprinted by permission.

MICERE GITHAE MUGO. 'Where Are Those Songs?' from *Daughter of My People, Sing!*, pp. 2–4, East African Literature Bureau, 1976. Reprinted by permission.

EDWIN MUIR. 'For Ann Scott-Moncrieff' from *Collected Poems* by Edwin Muir. Copyright © 1960 by Willa Muir. Reprinted by permission of Faber and Faber Ltd and Oxford University Press, Inc.

PAUL MULDOON. 'Why Brownlee Left' from *Why Brownlee Left* by Paul Muldoon. Reprinted by permission of Faber and Faber Ltd and Wake Forest University Press.

LES A. MURRAY. 'An Absolutely Ordinary Rainbow' from *The Vernacular Republic Poems 1961–1983*, Collins/Angus & Robertson, 1988 (HarperCollins Publishers, Melbourne).

SUSAN MUSGRAVE. 'Burial of the Dog' from *Selected Strawberries and Other Poems* (Sono Nis Press, 1977). Reprinted by permission of Susan Musgrave.

MUKHTARR MUSTAPHA. 'Gbassay—blades in regiment' from *A Selection of African Poetry*, Longman, 1976.

SAROJINI NAIDU. 'Awake!' and 'Bangle-Sellers' from *The Sceptred Flute*, Allahabad: Kitabistan Publishing, 1958.

JOHN NEWLOVE. 'Samuel Hearne in Wintertime' from *The Fat Man* by John Newlove. Used by permission of the Canadian Publishers, McClelland & Stewart, Toronto.

BPNICHOL. 'Two Words: A Wedding' from *As Elected: Selected Writing* (Talonbooks, 1980). Reprinted by permission of the Estate of bpNichol.

GRACE NICHOLS. 'Tropical Death' from *Fat Black Woman's Poems* by Grace Nichols (Virago Press, 1984). Reprinted by permission of Little, Brown and Company (UK) Ltd.

LORINE NIEDECKER. '[I married]' from *From This Condensery: The Complete Poems of Lorine Niedecker*, edited by Robert Bertholf, Jargon Society, 1985.

TITUS CHUKWENEKA NWOSU. 'Combat' from *A Selection of African Poetry*, Longman, 1988 (Editorial Consultancy & Agency Services).

ODIA OFEIMUN. 'A Handle for the Flutist' from *The Poet Lied*, Lagos: Update Communications, 1988.

MOLARA OGUNDIPE-LESLIE. 'song at the african middle class' from *Penguin Book of Modern African Poetry* (Penguin Books Ltd).

FRANK O'HARA. 'Why I Am Not a Painter' from *Collected Poems* by Frank O'Hara. Copyright © 1958 by Maureen Granville-Smith, Administratrix of the Estate of Langston Hughes. Reprinted by permission of Alfred A. Knopf Inc.

ATUKWEI OKAI/JOHN OKAI. 'Elavanyo Concerto' is reprinted from *Lorgorligi Logarithms* with the kind permission of Ghana Publishing Corporation, Publishing Division.

GABRIEL OKARA. 'One Night at Victoria Beach' from *Black Orpheus*, African Universities Press (Lagos University Press). 'Suddenly the air cracks'.

CHRISTOPHER OKIGBO. 'Elegy for Slit-Drum' from *Labyrinths with Path of Thunder* by Christopher Okigbo (New York: Africana Publishing Corporation, 1971). Copyright © 1971 by Legal Personal Representatives of Christopher Okigbo. Reproduced by the permission of the publisher.

CHARLES OLSON. 'The Festival Aspect' from *The Maximus Poems* by Charles Olson, translated/edited by George Butterick. Copyright © 1983 The Regents of the University of California. Reprinted by permission of University of California Press.

MICHAEL ONDAATJE. 'Bear Hug' and 'The Cinnamon Peeler' from *The Cinnamon Peeler* (McClelland & Stewart, 1992). Reprinted by permission of the author.

OODGEROO. 'We Are Going' by Oodgeroo of the tribe Noonuccal (formerly known as Kath Walker) in *My People*, Third Edition, 1990, published by Jacaranda Press, Australia.

JOHN ORMOND. 'Certain Questions for Monsieur Renoir' from *Definition of the Waterfall: Poems* by John Ormond (Oxford University Press, 1973). Reprinted by permission of the Estate of John Ormond.

SIMON J. ORTIZ. 'Waiting for You to Come By' is reprinted by permission of the author.

P.K. PAGE. 'The Permanent Tourists' © P.K. Page. Reprinted by permission of the author.

R. PARTHASARATHY. 'Luiz Vaz de Camoëns, 1524?–1580' from *Contemporary Indian Poetry in English*. Copyright © 1972 by R. Parthasarathy. Reprinted by permission of the author.

GIEVE PATEL. 'Nargol'.

SALEEM PEERADINA. 'There Is No God'.

LENRIE PETERS. 'Isatou Died' from *Black Orpheus* (Lagos University Press).

M. NOURBESE PHILIP. 'Somewhere in the Dark Continent' from *Looking for Livingstone*. First published by The Mercury Press. Reprinted by permission of the author.

MARGE PIERCY. 'The woman in the ordinary' and 'Unlearning to not speak' from *Circles on the Water* by Marge Piercy. Copyright © 1982 by Marge Piercy. Reprinted by permission of Alfred A. Knopf Inc. 'The woman in the ordinary' copyright © 1971, 1973 by Marge Piercy. 'Unlearning to not speak' copyright © 1971, 1973 by Marge Piercy. Published in *Circles on the Water: Selected Poems of Marge Piercy*, Alfred A. Knopf, Inc., 1982. Used by permission of the Wallace Literary Agency, Inc.

MIGUEL PIÑERO. 'The Book of Genesis According to Saint Miguelito' by Miguel Piñero is reprinted with permission from the publisher of *La Bodega Sold Dreams* (Houston: Arte Público Press–University of Houston, 1985).

SYLVIA PLATH. All lines from 'Daddy' from *Ariel* by Sylvia Plath. Copyright © 1963 by Ted Hughes. Copyright renewed. Reprinted by permission of HarperCollins Publishers, Inc and Faber and Faber Ltd.

PETER PORTER. 'Phar Lap in the Melbourne Museum' from *Collected Poems*, Oxford University Press, 1983. Reprinted by permission of Oxford University Press.

EZRA POUND. 'A Pact' and 'L'art, 1910' by Ezra Pound, from *Personae*. Copyright © 1926 by Ezra Pound. Reprinted by permission of New Directions Publishing Corp. And from *Collected Shorter Poems* by Ezra Pound. Reprinted by permission of Faber and Faber Ltd.

E.J. PRATT. From 'Brébeuf and His Brethren': '[The Martyrdom of Brébeuf and Lalemant, 16 March 1649]' XII and from 'Towards the Last Spike': 'The Pre-Cambrian Shield' (i) and (ii) from *E.J. Pratt: Complete Poems*, ed. Sandra Djwa (University of Toronto Press, 1988). Reprinted by permission of University of Toronto Press Incorporated.

SHEENAGH PUGH. 'Going Back to Hlidarendi' from *What a Place to Grow Flowers* (Christopher Davies Publishers, 1979) is reprinted by permission of Christopher Davies Publishers Ltd.

AL PURDY. 'Lament for the Dorsets' and 'The Runners' from *Rooms for Rent in the Outer Planets*, Harbour Publishing, 1996. Reprinted courtesy of Harbour Publishing.

CHRISTINE QUNTA. 'The know' from *Hoyi Na! Axania: Poems of an African Struggle*, Sydney: Marimba Press, 1979.

CRAIG RAINE. 'In the Kalahari Desert' from *A Martian Sends a Postcard Home* by Craig Raine (Oxford University Press, 1979). Reprinted by permission of Oxford University Press.

KATHLEEN RAINE. 'Spell to Bring Lost Creatures Home' from *Collected Poems* by Kathleen Raine. Reprinted by permission of HarperCollins Publishers Ltd.

A.K. RAMANUJAN. 'Still Another View of Grace' from *The Striders* by A.K. Ramanujan (New Delhi: Oxford University Press, 1966). Reprinted by permission of Oxford University Press.

ANNE RANASINGHE. 'Auschwitz From Colombo' is reprinted by permission of the author from *Poems* (1971).

PETER READING. Excerpts from *Evagatory* by Peter Reading are reprinted by permission from Bloodaxe Books (1996) Ltd.

P.S. REGE. 'Dream'.

KENNETH REXROTH. From 'The Love Poems of Marichiko' by Kenneth Rexroth, from *Flower Wreath Hill*. Copyright © 1979 by Kenneth Rexroth. Reprinted by permission of New Directions Publishing Corp.

ADRIENNE RICH. 'Diving into the Wreck', '(The Floating Poem, Unnumbered)' from *Twenty-One Love Poems* from *The Fact of a Doorframe: Poems Selected and New 1950–1984* by Adrienne Rich. Copyright © 1984 by Adrienne Rich. Copyright © 1975, 1978 by W.W. Norton & Company, Inc. Copyright © 1981 by Adrienne Rich. Reprinted by permission of the author and W.W. Norton & Company, Inc.

ROLLA LYNN RIGGS. 'Shadow on Snow'.

EDITH ANNE ROBERTSON. 'Pyatie Beauty/Pied Beauty' from *Translations into the Scots Tongue of Poems by Gerard Manley Hopkins*, Aberdeen University Press, 1968. 'Country boy on a motor cycle' from *Forest Voices and Other Poems*, Aberdeen University Press, 1969 (The Estate of Edith Anne Robertson).

THEODORE ROETHKE. 'My Papa's Waltz', copyright 1942 by Hearst Magazines, Inc. from *The Collected Poems of Theodore Roethke* by Theodore Roethke. Used by permission of Doubleday, a division of Bantam Doubleday Dell Publishing Group, Inc and Faber and Faber Ltd.

WENDY ROSE. 'Story Keeper' from *The Greenfield Review*. Reprinted by permission of Greenfield Review Press.

MURIEL RUKEYSER. 'Passage to Godhead' from 'The Lynchings of Jesus' from *Theory of Flight*, from *Collected Poems of Muriel Rukeyser*, © 1978, McGraw-Hill, New York, by permission of William L. Rukeyser.

CAROL RUMENS. 'Rules for Beginners' is reprinted by permission of Bloodaxe Books Ltd from *Thinking of Skins* by Carol Rumens (Bloodaxe Books, 1993).

KRISTINA RUNGANO. 'The Woman' from *A Storm is Brewing* is reprinted by permission of the author.

PHILIP SALOM. 'The World of Dreams' from *The New Oxford Book of Australian Verse*, Melbourne: Oxford University Press, 1986. Reprinted by permission of the author.

SONIA SANCHEZ. 'under a soprano sky' and 'haiku (for the police on osage ave)' from *Under a Soprano Sky* by Sonia Sanchez. Copyright © 1987. Reprinted by permission of Africa World Press Inc.

BHARATI SARABHAI. From *The Well of the People*, 'Chorus of Workers' from *The Well of the People*, Vish-Bharati, 1943.

DUNCAN CAMPBELL SCOTT. 'The Forsaken' is reprinted with the permission of John G. Aylen, Ottawa, Canada.

F.R. SCOTT. 'Laurentian Shield' from *Collected Poems* by F.R. Scott. Used by permission of the Canadian Publishers, McClelland & Stewart, Toronto.

OLIVE SENIOR. 'Colonial Girls School' from *Creation Fire: An Anthology of Caribbean Women Poets*, edited by Ramabai Espinet, Sister Vision Press, 1990.

SIPHO SEPAMLA. '"Measure for Measure"' from *The Soweto I Love* (Rex Collings Ltd).

MONGANE (WALLY) SEROTE. 'The Growing', Allen & Unwin (HarperCollins Publishers Ltd).

VIKRAM SETH. 'Work and Freedom' from *All You Who Sleep Tonight* by Vikram Seth. Copyright © 1987, 1990 by Vikram Seth. Reprinted by permission of Alfred A. Knopf Inc.

ANNE SEXTON. 'The Death Baby', from *The Death Notebooks*. Copyright © 1974 by Anne Sexton. Reprinted by permission of Houghton Mifflin Co. All rights reserved and reprinted by permission of Sterling Lord Literistic, Inc. Copyright © 1974 by Anne Sexton.

LESLIE MARMON SILKO. 'Lullaby' from *Heath Anthology of American Literature*, Volume II.

EDITH SITWELL. 'Lullaby' from *The Collected Poems* (Sinclair Stevenson, 1993). Reprinted by permission of David Higham Associates.

KENNETH SLESSOR. 'Five Bells' from *Selected Poems* by Kenneth Slessor. Reprinted by permission of HarperCollins Publishers Pty. Limited.

A.J.M. SMITH. 'The Lonely Land' from *The Classic Shade* by A.J.M. Smith. Used by permission of the Canadian Publishers, McClelland & Stewart, Toronto.

STEVIE SMITH. 'Not Waving But Drowning' and 'Emily Writes Such a Good Letter' from *The Collected Poems of Stevie Smith* (Penguin 20th Century Classics). Reprinted by permission. Copyright © 1972 by Stevie Smith. Reprinted by permission of New Directions Publishing Corp.

SYDNEY GOODSIR SMITH. 'The Grace of God and the Meth-Drinker' from *Collected Poems 1941–1975* by Sydney Goodsir Smith, John Calder (Publishers) Ltd., London. Reprinted by permission of The Sydney Goodsir Smith Estate and The Calder Educational Trust, London.

KENDRICK SMITHYMAN. Acknowledgement is made to Margaret Edgcumbe and Auckland University Press for permission to use 'The Last Moriori' by Kendrick Smithyman from *Stories About Wooden Keyboards* (AUP, 1985).

CHERRY SMYTH. 'Black Leather Jacket', copyright © Cherry Smyth, from *Of Eros and of Dust: Poems from the City* edited by Steve Anthony, The Oscars Press, 1992. Reprinted by permission of the author.

GARY SNYDER. 'Riprap' from *Riprap and Cold Mountain Poems* by Gary Snyder. Copyright © 1965 by Gary Snyder. Reprinted by permission of North Point Press, a division of Farrar, Straus & Giroux, Inc and Gary Snyder. 'What You Should Know to Be a Poet' by Gary Snyder, from *Regarding Wave*. Copyright © 1970 by Gary Snyder. Reprinted by permission of New Directions Publishing Corp.

WOLE SOYINKA. 'Telephone Conversation' from *Black Orpheus* (Lagos University Press).

WOLE SOYINKA. '"No!" He Said' from *The Heinemann Book of African Poetry in English*, selected by Adewale Maja-Pearce, William Heinemann, 1990 (Wole Soyinka).

MURIEL SPARK. 'Bluebell Among the Sables' and 'Created and Abandoned' from *Going up to Sotheby's and Other Poems* by Muriel Spark (Granada, 1984). Reprinted by permission of David Higham Associates.

PAULINE STAINER. 'Sighting the Slave Ship' is reprinted by permission of Bloodaxe Books Ltd from *Sighting the Slave Ship* by Pauline Stainer (Bloodaxe Books, 1992).

WALLACE STEVENS. 'Of Mere Being' and 'The Planet on the Table' from *The Collected Poems of Wallace Stevens*. Reprinted by permission of Faber and Faber Ltd and Alfred A. Knopf, Inc.

ANNE STEVENSON. 'A Letter from an English novelist: Paul Maxwell, author of "A Second Eve", writes to Ruth Arbeiter in Vermont' from *Correspondences* from *The Collected Poems 1955–1995* by Anne Stevenson (Oxford University Press, 1996). Reprinted by permission of Oxford University Press.

ANDREW SUKNASKI. 'Overland to the Southern Plain' is reprinted by permission of the author.

MAUD SULTER. 'Azania' from *As a Black Woman*, London: Akira Press, 1985.

EFUA SUTHERLAND. 'A Professional Beggar's Lullaby'.

MAY SWENSON. 'Under the Baby Blanket' from *New and Selected Things Taking Place*. Used with permission of The Literary Estate of May Swenson.

VÉRONIQUE TADJO. 'Five Poems' from *Laterite*, Hatier, 1984.

SHARON THESEN. 'Po-It-Tree' and 'Loose Woman Poem' are reprinted from *Artemis Hates Romance* (Coach House Press, 1980) by permission of the author.

DYLAN THOMAS. 'Fern Hill' from *The Poems* (J.M. Dent, 1974). Reprinted by permission of David Higham Associates. And from *The Poems of Dylan Thomas*. Copyright © 1945 by The Trustees for the copyrights of Dylan Thomas. Reprinted by permission of New Directions Publishing Corp.

R.S. THOMAS. 'Welsh History' from *Song at the Year's Turning* and 'Expatriates' from *Poetry for Supper*, Rupert Hart-David.

HONE TUWHARE. 'Snowfall' from *Deep River Talk: Collected Poems* by Hone Tuwhare (University of Hawaii Press, 1994). Reprinted by permission of University of Hawaii Press.

NGUNAITPONI/DAVID UNAIPON. 'The Song of Hungarrda'.

MIRIAM WADDINGTON. 'Déjà Vu' from *Collected Poems* by Miriam Waddington. Copyright © Miriam Waddington 1986. Reprinted by permission of Oxford University Press Canada.

FRED WAH. 'Waiting for Saskatchewan' from *Waiting for Saskatchewan,* Turnstone Press, 1985. Reprinted by permission of the author.

DEREK WALCOTT. Chapter LXIV, section III from *Omeros* by Derek Walcott. Copyright © 1990 by Derek Walcott. Reprinted by permission of Farrar, Straus & Giroux, Inc and Faber and Faber Ltd.

BRONWEN WALLACE. 'The Woman in This Poem' by Bronwen Wallace is reprinted from *Signs of the Former Tenant* by permission of Oberon Press.

CHRIS WALLACE-CRABBE. 'Love Poem' from *The Music of Division* by Chris Wallace-Crabbe. © Chris Wallace-Crabbe. Reprinted by permission of the author. 'A Wintry Manifesto' from *Selected Poems, 1956–1994* (Oxford University Press, 1995). Reprinted by permission of Oxford University Press.

SYLVIA TOWNSEND WARNER. 'Honey for Tea' from *Collected Poems* by Sylvia Townsend Warner, edited by Claire Harman (Carcanet Press, 1982). Reprinted by permission of Carcanet Press Limited.

TOM WAYMAN. 'Saving the World' from *The Face of Jack Munro* (Harbour Publishing, Madeira Park, BC, 1986). Reprinted by permission.

PHYLLIS WEBB. 'Poetics Against the Angel of Death' is reprinted with permission of the author.

JAMES WELCH. 'In My Lifetime' is reprinted from *Riding the Earthboy 40* by James Welch, Copyright © 1990 by James Welch. Reprinted by permission of Confluence Press, Inc. at Lewis-Clark State College, Lewiston, Idaho.

ARCHIE WELLER. 'The Legend of Jimmy's Axe' and 'Untitled' are reprinted by permission of the author.

ROBERTA HILL WHITEMAN. 'Scraps Worthy of Wind' from *Star Quilt* © 1984. Reprinted by permission of Holy Cow! Press.

ANNA WICKHAM. 'The Fired Pot' and 'The Sick Assailant' from *The Writings of Anna Wickham*, edited by R.D. Smith (Virago Press, 1984). Reprinted by permission of George and Margaret Hepburn.

LAKDASA WIKKRAMASINHA. 'Don't Talk To Me About Matisse' from *An Anthology of Modern Writing*, University of Arizona Press, 1981.

RICHARD WILBUR. 'Pangloss's Song: A Comic-Opera Lyric' from *Advice to a Prophet and Other Poems*, copyright © 1957 and renewed 1985 by Richard Wilbur, reprinted by permission of Harcourt Brace & Company. And from *New and Collected Poems* by Richard Wilbur. Reprinted by permission of Faber and Faber Ltd.

HUGO WILLIAMS. 'The Couple Upstairs' from *Selected Poems* by Hugo Williams (Oxford University Press, 1989). Reprinted by permission of Oxford University Press.

WILLIAM CARLOS WILLIAMS. 'Danse Russe' and 'This is Just to Say' by William Carlos Williams, from *Collected Poems: 1909–1939*, Volume I. Copyright © 1938 by New Directions Publishing Corp. Reprinted by permission of New Directions Publishing Corp. and Carcanet Press Limited.

PENNY WINDSOR. 'Advice on Pregnancy' was published in 1990 by Honno, The Welsh Women's Press, in *Exchanges: Poems by Women from Wales* edited by Jude Brigley.

JUDITH WRIGHT. 'The Hawthorn Hedge' and 'At Cooloola' from *A Human Pattern* by Judith Wright (ETT Imprint, Sydney, 1996). Reprinted by permission of ETT Imprint.

KIT WRIGHT. 'I Found South African Breweries Most Hospitable' from *Poems 1974–1983* by Kit Wright (Hutchinson, 1988). Reprinted by permission of Random House UK Ltd.

RAY A. YOUNG BEAR. 'Our Bird Aegis', first published in *Callaloo*, Volume 17, Number 1, 1994. Reprinted by permission of the author.

LOUIS ZUKOFSKY. '11' from 'A'. Copyright © 1978. Reprinted by permission of the Johns Hopkins University Press.

Every effort has been made to determine and contact copyright owners. In the case of any omissions, the publisher will be pleased to make suitable acknowledgement in future editions.

MARY QUEEN OF SCOTS

Scotland 1542-1587

Mary was a patron of poetry and poets; witness Ronsard's 'o belle et plus que belle et agréable Aurore' and Joachim du Bellay's 'Astrae'. For some, she is a romantic heroine martyred by Elizabeth, Henry VIII's bastard daughter, and for others, a harlot, murderess of her second husband, Henry, Lord Darnley. Her 'The Kings and Queens of Scotland' forms part of Antonia Fraser's *Mary Queen of Scots*, a 1981 anthology which presents an intriguing collection of responses to Mary's charismatic historical circumstance.

from THE KINGS AND QUEENS OF SCOTLAND

What am I, alas, what purpose has my life?
I nothing am, a corpse without a heart,
A useless shade, a victim of sad strife,
One who lives yet, and wishes to depart.
My enemies, no envy hold for me;
My spirit has no taste for greatness now.
Sorrow consumes me in extreme degree,
Your hatred shall be satisfied, I vow.
And you, my friends, you who have held me dear,
Reflect that I, lacking both health and fortune,
Cannot aspire to any great deed here.
Welcome, therefore, my ultimate misfortune.
And pray that when affliction ends my story,
Then I may have some share in Heaven's glory.   [1873]

Translated by Caroline Bingham

EDMUND SPENSER

England/Ireland 1552–1599

The son of a tradesman, Spenser graduated from Cambridge and then served as a secretary to several prominent noblemen in England. He subsequently held colonial government posts in Ireland. His literary circle included Sir Philip Sidney, Sir Edward Dyer, and Sir Walter Raleigh. Spenser's staunch Protestant and patriot commitments are reflected in his major contributions to the English Renaissance: the pastoral eclogues of *The Shepheardes Calender* (1579) and an epic allegory, *The Faerie Queene* (1590; 1596). His *Epithalamion* and the *Amoretti* sequence of 89 Petrarchan sonnets were written for his second wife, Elizabeth Boyle, and published in 1595. Spenser's uses of archaic diction, figurative language, and verse forms show the influences of medieval, Latin, and Greek writers, most notably Chaucer and Virgil.

from AMORETTI

SONNET 1

Happy ye leaves when as those lilly hands,
Which hold my life in their dead doing might,
Shall handle you and hold in loves soft bands,
Lyke captives trembling at the victors sight.
And happy lines, on which with starry light,
Those lamping eyes will deigne sometimes to look
And reade the sorrowes of my dying spright,
Written with teares in harts close bleeding book.
And happy rymes bathed in the sacred brooke,
Of Helicon whence she derivéd is,
When ye behold that Angels blessed looke,
My soules long lackéd foode, my heavens blis.
Leaves, lines, and rymes, seeke her to please alone,
Whom if ye please, I care for other none.   [1595]

SONNET 15

Ye tradefull merchants, that with weary toyle
Do seeke most pretious things to make your gain,
And both the Indias of their treasures spoile,
What needeth you to seeke so farre in vaine?
For loe my love doth in her selfe containe
All this world's riches that may farre be found.
If saphyres, loe her eyes be saphyres plaine;
If rubies, loe her lips be rubies sound;
If pearls, her teeth be pearls both pure and round;
If yvorie, her forhead yvory weene;
If gold, her locks are finest gold on ground;
If silver, her faire hands are silver sheene.
But that which fairest is, but few behold:
Her mind, adornd with vertues manifold.   [1595]

MICHAEL DRAYTON

England 1563-1631

'To the Virginian Voyage' celebrates the heroic adventure of Britain's quest to take possession of the New World. Written in honour of an expedition which was ordered in April, 1606 and sailed in December after Drayton's poem was published, the ode concludes with an invitation to Richard Hakluyt (1553–1616), author of *The Principal Navigations, Traffics, Voyages and Discoveries of the English Nation* (1589). Hakluyt is asked to immortalize this event and so 'inflame/Men to see fame' such that in 'after-times', his 'wit' will be 'much commend[ed]'.

TO THE VIRGINIAN VOYAGE

You brave heroic minds
Worthy your country's name,
That honour still pursue,
Go, and subdue,
Whilst loit'ring hinds
Lurk here at home with shame.

Britons, you stay too long;
Quickly aboard bestow you,
And with a merry gale
Swell your stretched sail,
With vows as strong
As the winds that blow you.

Your course securely steer,
West and by south forth keep;
Rocks, lee shores, nor shoals,
When Aeolus scowls,
You need not fear,
So absolute the deep.

And cheerfully at sea
Success you still entice
To get the pearl and gold,
And ours to hold
Virginia,
Earth's only paradise.

Where nature hath in store
Fowl, venison, and fish,
And the fruitfullest soil,
Without your toil,
Three harvests more,
All greater than your wish.

And the ambitious vine
Crowns with his purple mass
The cedar reaching high
To kiss the sky,
The cypress, pine,
And useful sassafras.

To whom the golden age
Still nature's laws doth give;
No other cares attend,
But them to defend
From winter's rage,
That long there doth not live.

When as the luscious smell
Of that delicious land
Above the seas that flows
The clear wind throws,
Your hearts to swell
Approaching the dear strand,

In kenning of the shore
(Thanks to God first given)
O you the happiest men,
Be frolic then;
Let cannons roar,
Frighting the wide heaven.

And in regions far,
Such heroes bring ye forth
As those from whom we came,
And plant our name
Under that star
Not known unto our North.

And as there plenty grows
Of laurel everywhere,
Apollo's sacred tree,
You it may see
A poet's brows
To crown, that may sing there.

Thy *Voyages* attend,
Industrious Hakluyt,
Whose reading shall inflame
Men to see fame,
And much commend
To after-times thy wit.

[1606]

William Shakespeare

England 1564-1616

Shakespeare was born of middle-class parents in Stratford-on-Avon in 1564. There is almost no record of his education or life before 1592 when he was working as an actor and playwright in London with a company called Lord Chamberlain's Men. Shakespeare's tragedies, comedies, and romances contain many remarkable verse soliloquies and dialogue as well as songs, ballads, and dirges; although some printed versions circulated, no collected edition of his plays was published until after his death (*The First Folio*, 1623). Unlike the plays he wrote for stage performance, his sonnets were private meditations circulated among friends and associates; the majority of his 154 sonnets were written between 1593 and 1596, and were published without his permission in 1609.

SONNET 18

Shall I compare thee to a summer's day?
Thou art more lovely and more temperate.
Rough winds do shake the darling buds of May,
And summer's lease hath all too short a date.
Sometime too hot the eye of heaven shines,
And often is his gold complexion dimmed;
And every fair from fair sometime declines,
By chance, or nature's changing course, untrimmed:
But thy eternal summer shall not fade
Nor lose possession of that fair thou ow'st,
Nor shall Death brag thou wand'rest in his shade
When in eternal lines to time thou grow'st.
    So long as men can breathe or eyes can see,
    So long lives this, and this gives life to thee.   [1609]

SONNET 107

Not mine own fears, nor the prophetic soul
Of the wide world, dreaming on things to come,
Can yet the lease of my true love control,
Supposed as forfeit to a confined doom.
The mortal moon hath her eclipse endured,
And the sad augurs mock their own presage;
Incertainties now crown themselves assured,
And peace proclaims olives of endless age.
Now with the drops of this most balmy time
My love looks fresh, and Death to me subscribes,
Since, spite of him, I'll live in this poor rime,
While he insults o'er dull and speechless tribes:
    And thou in this shalt find thy monument
    When tyrants' crests and tombs of brass are spent.   [1609]

SIR JOHN DAVIES

England 1569-1626

Davies enjoyed a distinguished and sometimes colourful legal career: solicitor-general and attorney-general for Ireland, an appointment as Lord Chief Justice of the King's Bench (though he died before taking up office), disbarment from the bench from 1598–1601 for fighting. His epigram on tobacco forms one of a sequence he published as *Epigrammes* (c. 1590), shrewd observations on local custom and prevailing points of view. Davies's advertisement lauds the medicinal benefit of tobacco, which had found its way to London markets around 1565. To Davies's mind, tobacco becomes a legitimate descendant of the royal family of herbal cures and charms celebrated in Homer's *Odyssey*.

EPIGRAM 36: OF TOBACCO

Homer of Moly and Nepenthe sings:
Moly, the gods' most sovereign herb divine;
Nepenthe, Helen's drink, which gladness brings,
Heart's grief expels, and doth the wits refine.
But this our age another world hath found,
From whence an herb of heavenly power is brought;
Moly is not so sovereign for a wound,
Nor hath Nepenthe so great wonders wrought:
It is Tobacco, whose sweet substantial fume
The hellish torment of the teeth doth ease
By drawing down and drying up the rheum,
The mother and the nurse of each disease:
It is Tobacco, which doth cold expel,
And clears the obstructions of the arteries,
And surfeits, threat'ning death, digesteth well,
Decocting all the stomach's crudities:
It is Tobacco, which hath power to clarify
The cloudy mists before dim eyes appearing:
It is Tobacco, which hath power to rarefy
The thick gross humour which doth stop the hearing;
The wasting hectic, and the quartaine fever,
Which doth of physic make a mockery;
The gout it cures, and helps ill breaths for ever,
Whether the cause in teeth or stomach be;
And though ill breaths were by it but confounded,
Yet that vile medicine it doth far excel,
Which by Sir Thomas Moore hath been propounded,
For this is thought a gentleman-like smell.
O, that I were one of those Mountebanks
Which praise their oils and powders which they sell!
My customers would give me coin with thanks;

I for this ware, for sooth a tale would tell,
Yet would I use none of these terms before;
I would but say, that it the pox will cure.
This were enough, without discoursing more,
All our brave gallants in the town t'allure.   [c. 1590]

EMILIA LANIER

England 1569-1645

Tentatively identified as the 'dark lady' of Shakespeare's sonnets by scholar A.L. Rowse who edited
Lanier's religious poems in *Salve Deus* under the title *The Poems of Shakespeare's Dark Lady* (1978),
Lanier significantly alters the traditional reading of the events of the 'fall', by arguing that Eve's
'betrayal' was in fact motivated by her simple goodness. Eve gave to 'Adam what shee held most
deare' in 'undiscerning Ignorance', and is thus more blameless than her mate who consciously and
'in malice Gods deare Sonne betray[ed].' Lanier's challenge to the established readings finds kin-
ship among the continuing reconceptualization of legend and myth conducted by women writers.

from SALVE DEUS REX JUDÆORUM

EVES APOLOGIE

Till now your indiscretion sets us free
And makes our former fault much less appeare;
Our Mother *Eve*, who tasted of the Tree,
Giving to *Adam* what shee held most deare,
Was simply good, and had no powre to see,
The after-comming harme did not appeare:
        The subtile Serpent that our Sex betraide,
        Before our fall so sure a plot had laide.

That undiscerning Ignorance perceav'd
No guile, or craft that was by him intended;
For had she knowne, of what we were bereav'd,
To his request she had not condiscended.
But she (poor soule) by cunning was deceav'd,
No hurt therein her harmelesse Heart intended:
        For she alleadg'd Gods word, which he denies,
        That they should die, but even as Gods, be wise.

But surely *Adam* can not be excusde,
Her fault though great, yet hee was most too blame;
What Weaknesse offered, Strength might have refusde,
Being Lord of all, the greater was his shame:
Although the Serpents craft had her abusde,
Gods holy word ought all his actions frame,
        For he was Lord and King of all the earth,
        Before poore *Eve* had either life or breath.

Who being fram'd by Gods eternall hand,
The perfect'st man that ever breath'd on earth;
And from Gods mouth receiv'd that strait command,
The breach whereof he knew was present death:
Yea having powre to rule both Sea and Land,
Yet with one Apple wonne to loose that breath
    Which God had breathed in his beauteous face,
    Bringing us all in danger and disgrace.

And then to lay the fault on Patience backe,
That we (poore women) must endure it all;
We know right well he did discretion lacke,
Beeing not perswaded thereunto at all;
If Eve did erre, it was for knowledge sake,
The fruit being faire perswaded him to fall:
    No subtill Serpents falshood did betray him,
    If he would eate it, who had powre to stay him?

Not *Eve*, whose fault was onely too much love,
Which made her give this present to her Deare,
That what shee tasted, he likewise might prove,
Whereby his knowledge might become more cleare;
He never sought her weakenesse to reprove,
With those sharpe words, which he of God did heare;
    Yet Men will boast of Knowledge, which he tooke
    From *Eves* faire hand, as from a learned Booke.

If any Evill did in her remaine,
Beeing made of him, he was the ground of all;
If one of many Worlds could lay a staine
Upon our Sexe, and worke so great a fall
To wretched Man, by Satans subtill traine;
What will so fowle a fault amongst you all?
    Her weakenesse did the Serpents words obay,
    But you in malice Gods deare Sonne betray.

Whom, if unjustly you condemne to die,
Her sinne was small, to what you doe commit;
All mortal sinnes that doe for vengeance crie,
Are not to be compared unto it:
If many worlds would altogether trie,
By all their sinnes the wrath of God to get;
    This sinne of yours, surmounts them all as farre
    As doth the Sunne, another little starre.

Then let us have our Libertie againe,
And challendge to your selves no Sov'raigntie;
You came not in the world without our paine,
Make that a barre against your crueltie;
Your fault being greater, why should you disdaine
Our beeing your equals, free from tyranny?
    If one weake woman simply did offend,
      This sinne of yours, hath no excuse, nor end.

To which (poore soules) we never gave consent,
Witnesse thy wife (O *Pilate*) speakes for all;
Who did but dreame, and yet a message sent,
That thou should'st have nothing to doe at all
With that just man; which, if thy heart relent,
Why wilt thou be a reprobate with *Saul*?
    To seeke the death of him that is so good,
      For thy soules health to shed his dearest blood.   [1611]

MAIRI NIGHEAN ALASDAIR RUAIDH/ MARY MACLEOD

Scotland c. 1569 - c. 1674

'Poetess of Harris and Skye', MacLeod was a member of a company of remarkable women, song-makers in Gaelic, who flourished between 1645 and 1725. MacLeod's songs were composed during the transition from classical (syllabic versification) to modern (stressed metre) poetry and begin the tradition of court poetry in popular diction and versification; most of her surviving pieces are laments (panegyrics) praising distinguished members of hereditary houses. While written in the vernacular, they retain the spirit and character of the classic bard. The first complete collection of her work is the *Gaelic Songs Of Mary MacLeod* (ed. Watson, 1965).

LUINNEAG MHIC LEOID

Is mi am shuidhe air an tulaich
    Fo mhulad 's fo imcheist,
Is mi ag coimhead air Ile,
    Is ann de m' iongnadh 's an ám so;
Bha mi uair nach do shaoil mi,
    Gus an do chaochail air m'aimsir,
Gun tiginn an taobh so
    Dh'amharc Dhiùraidh á Sgarbaidh.

      I hurabh o i hoiriunn o,
        i hurabh o i hoiriunn o,
      I hurabh o i hogaidh ho ro,
        hi ri ri rithibh ho i ag o.

Gun tiginn an taobh so
   Dh'amharc Dhiùraidh á Sgarbaidh;
Beir mo shoraidh do'n dùthaich
   Tha fo dhubhar nan garbhbheann,
Gu Sir Tormod ùr allail
   Fhuair ceannas air armailt,
Is gun cainte anns gach fearann
   Gum b'airidh fear t'ainm air.

Gun cainte anns gach fearann
   Gum b'airidh fear t'ainm air,
Fear do chéille is do ghliocais,
   Do mhisnich 's do mheanmain,
Do chruadail 's do ghaisge,
   Do dhreach is do dhealbha,
Agus t'fholachd is t'uaisle
   Cha bu shuarach ri leanmhainn.

Agus t'fholachd is t'uaisle
   Cha bu shuarach ri leanmhainn;
D'fhuil dìrich rìgh Lochlainn
   B'e sud toiseach do sheanchais.
Tha do chàirdeas so-iarraidh
   Ris gach Iarla tha an Albainn,
Is ri h-uaislean na h-Eireann:
   Cha bhreug ach sgeul dearbhta e.

Is ri h-uaislean na h-Eireann:
   Cha bhreug ach sgeul dearbhta e.
A Mhic an fhir chliuitich,
   Bha gu fiùghantach ainmeil;
Thug barrachd an gliocas
   Air gach Ridir bha an Albainn
Ann an cogadh 's an sìothshaimh,
   Is ann an dìoladh an airgid.

Ann an cogadh 's an sìothshaimh,
   Is ann an dìoladh an airgid.
Is beag an t-iongnadh do mhac-sa
   Bhith gu beachdail mór meanmnach,
Bhith gu fiùghant' fial farsaing,
   O'n a ghlac sibh mar shealbh e:
Clann Ruairidh nam bratach,
   Is e mo chreach-sa na dh'fhalbh dhiubh.

Clann Ruairidh nam bratach,
 Is e mo chreach-sa na dh'fhalbh dhiubh;
Ach an aon fhear a dh'fhuirich
 Nìor chluinneam sgeul marbh ort;
Ach, eudail de fhearaibh,
 Ge do ghabh mi uat tearbadh
Fhir a' chuirp as glan cumadh,
 Gun uireasbhuidh dealbha.

Fhir a' chuirp as glan cumadh,
 Gun uireasbhuidh dealbha;
Cridhe farsaing fial fearail
 Is maith thig geal agus dearg ort.
Sùil ghorm as glan sealladh
 Mar dhearcaig na talmhainn,
Làmh ri gruaidh ruitich
 Mar mhucaig na fearradhris.

Làmh ri gruaidh ruitich
 Mar mhucaig na fearradhris.
Fo thagha na gruaige
 Cùl dualach nan camlùb.
Gheibhte sud ann ad fhàrdaich
 An càradh air ealchainn,
Miosair is adharc
 Is rogha gach armachd.

Miosair is adharc
 Is rogha gach armachd,
Agus lanntainean tana
 O'n ceannaibh gu'm barrdhéis.
Gheibhte sud air gach slios dhiubh
 Isneach is cairbinn,
Agus iubhair chruaidh fhallain
 Le an taifeidean cainbe.

Agus iubhair chruaidh fhallain
 Le an taifeidean cainbe,
Is cuilbheirean caola
 Air an daoiread gun ceannaichte iad;
Glac nan ceann lìomhta
 Air chur sìos ann am balgaibh
O iteach an fhìreoin
 Is o shìoda na Gailbhinn.

O iteach an fhìreoin
   Is o shìoda na Gailbhinn;
Tha mo chion air a' churaidh,
   Mac Mhuire chur sealbh air.
Is e bu mhiannach le m' leanabh
   Bhith am beannaibh na sealga,
Gabhail aighir na frìthe
   Is a' dìreadh nan garbhghlac.

Gabhail aighir na frìthe
   Is a' dìreadh nan garbhghlac,
A' leigeil nan cuilean
   Is a' furan nan seanchon;
Is e bu deireadh do'n fhuran ud
   Fuil thoirt air chalgaibh
O luchd nan céir geala
   Is nam falluingean dearga.

O luchd nan céir geala
   Is nam falluingean dearga,
Le do chomhlan dhaoine naisle
   Rachadh cruaidh air an armaibh;
Luchd aithneachadh latha
   Is a chaitheadh an fhairge
Is a b'urrainn g'a seòladh
   Gu seòlaid an tarruinte i.

MacLeod's Lilt

Sitting here on the knoll, forlorn and unquiet, I gaze upon Islay
   and marvel the while; there was a time I never thought, till
   my times took a change, that hither I should come to view
   Jura from Scarba.

I hurabh o.

Hither to come and view Jura from Scarba! Bear my greetings to
   the land that lieth shadowed by the rugged peaks, to the
   young renowned Sir Norman that hath won headship over an
   armed host, for it is said in every land that one of his
   name were worthy thereof.

In every land they say one of thy name were worthy thereof, one
   of thy prudence and thy wisdom, thy courage and thy spirit,
   one of thy hardihood and valour, of thy mien and of thy
   mould; and thy lineage and thy nobility were no trifle to
   trace.

Thy lineage and nobility were no trifle to trace; from the blood
   of Lochlann's kings thine ancestry unbroken takes its rise;
   thy kinship is not far to seek with every earl that is in
   Scotland, and with the nobles of Ireland; no lie is this but
   a proven tale.

No lie but a tale well proven, thou son of the renowned sire that
   was open-handed and far-famed, that in wisdom excelled every
   one of Scotland's knights, in war and in peace and in the
   bestowal of silver.

In war and in peace and in the bestowal of silver; no marvel that
   his son should be prudent, great and spirited, should be
   liberal and free-handed, since ye have received that
   character as an inheritance, ye sons of Roderick of
   war-banners! My sorrow, that so many of you are dead and
   gone!

So many of you are dead and gone, ye sons of Roderick! but thou
   one that remainest, news of thy death may I never hear; thou
   treasure among men, though I am sundered from thee, thou
   whose form is so fair, without flaw of fashioning.

Thou of form so fair, without flaw of fashioning, thou heart
   manly and generous, well do red and white become thee; thy
   clear-seeing eye blue as the blaeberry, set by thy cheek
   ruddy as the berry of the dog-rose.

Thy cheek is ruddy as the berry of the dog-rose, and under the
   choicest head of hair thy curling locks entwine. In thy
   dwelling would be found, ranged upon the weapon-rack,
   powder-horn and shot-horn and the pick of every armoury.

Powder-horn and shot-horn and the pick of every armoury, and
   sword-blades slender-tapering from hilt to tip; would be
   found on each side of them rifle and carabine, and bows
   tough and sound with their bowstrings of hemp.

Bows tough and sound with their bowstrings of hemp, and narrow
   culverins would be bought though they be dear; a handful of
   polished arrows thrust down into quivers, fledged from the
   plumage of the eagle and the silk of Galway.

Fledged from the eagle's plumage and the silk of Galway; the hero
   hath my love, may Mary's Son prosper him! It would be my
   dear one's pleasure to be a-hunting in the peaks, taking joy
   of the forest and ascending the rough dells.

Taking joy of the forest and ascending the rough dells, letting
   slip the young hounds and inciting the old ones; of that
   incitement it would come that blood would flow on the
   bristles of the folk of white flanks and russet mantles.

Blood on the deer white-flanked and russet-mantled, at the hands
   of thy company of nobles that bear hardly on their weapons;
   men that well would read the day, and speed over the ocean,
   and fit to sail the vessel to the haven wherein she would be
   beached.   [1934]

JOHN DONNE
England 1572–1631

Donne became Dean of St Paul's Cathedral in 1621; his public sermons and private devotions
(published in 1624) established his reputation as one of the greatest preachers of his day. In his
hands, Elizabethan decorative conceits (elaborate metaphors) acquired a new kind of intellectual
intensity and emotional complexity, producing a poetry which has come to be known as Meta-
physical. While this approach influenced subsequent writers like Andrew Marvell, Donne's 'con-
ceited' style was for the most part neglected until revived among twentieth-century modernists like
T.S. Eliot, whose essay 'The Metaphysical Poets' (1921) contributed to a re-evaluation of Donne's
stylistic energy and innovation. While few of Donne's poems were published during his lifetime,
collected editions of his work began appearing in 1633 and 1635.

THE CANONIZATION

For God's sake hold your tongue, and let me love,
   Or chide my palsy, or my gout,
My five gray hairs, or ruined fortune, flout,
     With wealth your state, your mind with arts improve,
        Take you a course, get you a place,
        Observe His Honor, or His Grace,
Or the King's real, or his stampèd face
     Contemplate; what you will, approve,
     So you will let me love.

Alas, alas, who's injured by my love?
   What merchant's ships have my sighs drowned?
Who says my tears have overflowed his ground?
     When did my colds a forward spring remove?
        When did the heats which my veins fill
        Add one man to the plaguy bill?
Soldiers find wars, and lawyers find out still
     Litigious men, which quarrels move,
     Though she and I do love.

Call us what you will, we are made such by love;
    Call her one, me another fly,
We're tapers too, and at our own cost die,
    And we in us find the eagle and the dove.
        The phoenix riddle hath more wit
        By us: we two being one, are it.
So, to one neutral thing both sexes fit.
    We die and rise the same, and prove
    Mysterious by this love.

We can die by it, if not live by love,
    And if unfit for tombs and hearse
Our legend be, it will be fit for verse;
    And if no piece of chronicle we prove,
        We'll build in sonnets pretty rooms;
        As well a well-wrought urn becomes
The greatest ashes, as half-acre tombs,
    And by these hymns, all shall approve
    Us canonized for love:

And thus invoke us: You whom reverend love
    Made one another's hermitage;
You, to whom love was peace, that now is rage;
Who did the whole world's soul contract, and
    drove
        Into the glasses of your eyes
        (So made such mirrors, and such spies,
That they did all to you epitomize)
        Countries, towns, courts: Beg from above
    A pattern of your love!   [1633]

Song

Go and catch a falling star,
    Get with child a mandrake root,
Tell me where all past years are,
    Or who cleft the Devil's foot,
Teach me to hear mermaids singing,
Or to keep off envy's stinging,
        And find
        What wind
Serves to advance an honest mind.

If thou beest born to strange sights,
    Things invisible to see,
Ride ten thousand days and nights,
    Till age snow white hairs on thee,

Thou, when thou return'st, wilt tell me
All strange wonders that befell thee,
    And swear
    No where
Lives a woman true, and fair.

If thou findst one, let me know,
    Such a pilgrimage were sweet;
Yet do not, I would not go,
    Though at next door we might meet;
Though she were true when you met her,
And last till you write your letter,
    Yet she
    Will be
False, ere I come, to two, or three.   [1635]

THOMAS MORTON

England/America 1575-1646

Morton's *New English Canaan* (1637) is a promotional prose tract, based on his trading-post experiences at Passanagessit, New England, between 1622 and 1630. Morton encourages colonization among indigenous peoples and satirizes the Puritan settlers as fanatic religious extremists. His account of conflict with the Puritan military leader, Myles Standish, over a traditional English May Day celebration at Ma-re Mount (Passanagessit) epitomizes religious and cultural differences among English colonists. Morton's argument in favour of the earthly bounties and natural pleasures of life in New England, as exemplified by this rousing song, provides evidence of the influence of English popular culture in the early colonies.

THE SONG

Chorus.
Drink and be merry, merry, merry boys;
Let all your delight be in the Hymen's joys;
Io to Hymen, now the day is come,
About the merry Maypole take a room.
    Make green garlands, bring bottles out
    And fill sweet nectar freely about.
    Uncover thy head and fear no harm,
    For here's good liquor to keep it warm.
Then drink and be merry, &c.
Io to Hymen, &c.
    Nectar is a thing assigned
    By the Deity's own mind
    To cure the heart oppressed with grief,
    And of good liquors is the chief.

Then drink, &c.
Io to Hymen, &c.
> Give to the melancholy man
> A cup or two of't now and then;
> This physic will soon revive his blood,
> And make him be of a merrier mood.

Then drink, &c.
Io to Hymen, &c.
> Give to the nymph that's free from scorn
> No Irish stuff nor Scotch over worn.
> Lasses in beaver coats come away,
> Ye shall be welcome to us night and day.

To drink and be merry, &c.
Io to Hymen, &c. [1637]

ROBERT HAYMAN

England/N. America c. 1579-c. 1631

The first permanent English settlement in North America was founded at Cupar's Cove, New-foundland, in 1610 by Governor John Guy. During the next twenty years the Cupar's Cove colonists produced many literary works, including the first book of verse written in English in a North American colony, *Quodlibets, Lately Come Over from New Britaniola, Old Newfound-land* (1628). Composed by Hayman, Governor of Cupar's Cove from 1622 to 1628, *Quodlibets's* 350 epigrams moralize on the excesses of Europe and advertise the bounty of North America.

from QUODLIBETS

TO THE FIRST PLANTERS OF NEWFOUNDLAND

What aim you at in your plantation?
Sought you the honour of our nation?
Or did you hope to raise your own renown?
Or else to add a kingdom to a crown?
Or Christ's true doctrine for to propagate?
Or draw savages to a blessed state?
Or our o'er-peopled kingdom to relieve?
Or show poor men where they may richly live?
Or poor men's children goodly to maintain?
Or aim'd you at your own sweet private gain?
All these you had achiev'd before this day,
And all these you have balk'd by your delay.

A SKELTONICAL CONTINUED RHYME IN PRAISE OF MY NEWFOUNDLAND

Although in clothes, company, buildings fair,
With England, Newfoundland cannot compare,
Did some know what contentment I found there,
Always enough, most times somewhat to spare,
With little pains, less toil and lesser care,
Exempt from taxings, ill news, lawing, fear,
If clean, and warm, no matter what you wear,
Healthy, and wealthy, if men careful are,
With much much more, then I will now declare,
I say if some wise men knew what this were
I do believe they'd live no other where.   [1628]

ROBERT HERRICK

England 1591–1674

A Londoner who somewhat reluctantly assumed a parish in Devon's West Country, lost it during the civil wars, and reclaimed it when Charles was restored to the throne in 1660, Herrick published a single volume of his work (1,400 sacred and secular lyrics) in 1648. 'To the Virgins' relies on the poet's playful and ironic temperament, and a sense of timing that has its philosophical root in the popular *Carpe diem* ('Seize the day') ideology of many sixteenth- and seventeenth-century love poems.

TO THE VIRGINS, TO MAKE MUCH OF TIME

Gather ye rosebuds while ye may,
    Old time is still a-flying;
And this same flower that smiles today,
    Tomorrow will be dying.

The glorious lamp of heaven, the sun,
    The higher he's a-getting,
The sooner will his race be run,
    And nearer he's to setting.

That age is best which is the first,
    When youth and blood are warmer;
But being spent, the worse, and worst
    Times still succeed the former.

Then be not coy, but use your time,
    And while ye may, go marry;
For having lost but once your prime,
    You may forever tarry.   [1648]

ROGER WILLIAMS

England/America 1603-1683

Williams sailed to New England with the Massachusetts Bay Company led by Governor John Winthrop in 1630. As minister of the First Church in Boston, Williams promoted separation from the Church of England, but his increasingly radical views alienated him from Winthrop's theocratic orthodoxy. Banished in 1635, Williams founded a colony in Narragansett territory at Providence, Rhode Island, for members of dissenting religious groups, including antinomians, Quakers, and Jews. Williams's writings on liberty of conscience, separation of church and state, and indigenous peoples' traditional entitlements are regarded as classic documents of cultural pluralism and religious toleration. Selections of verse from *A Key into the Language of America* satirize the barbarism of colonizing and 'civilizing' so-called 'Heathen' peoples without regard for their common humanity.

OF THEIR GOVERNMENT

The wildest of the sons of men have ever found a necessity (for preservation of themselves, their families, and properties) to cast themselves into some mold or form of government.

More particular:

> Adulteries, murders, robberies, thefts,
> Wild Indians punish these!
> And hold the scales of justice so,
> That no man farthing leese.
>
> When Indians hear the horrid filths
> Of Irish, English men,
> The horrid oaths and murders late,
> Thus say these Indians then,
>
> 'We wear no clothes, have many gods,
> And yet our sins are less.
> You are barbarians, pagans wild,
> Your land's the wilderness.'   [1643]

OF THEIR PERSONS AND PARTS OF BODY

Nature knows no difference between Europe and Americans in blood, birth, bodies, etc., God having of one blood made all mankind, Acts 17, and all by nature being children of wrath, Ephesians 2.

More particularly:

> Boast not proud English, of thy birth and blood,
>   Thy brother Indian is by birth as good.
> Of one blood God made him, and thee and all,
>   As wise, as fair, as strong, as personal.
>
> By nature wrath's his portion, thine no more,
>   Till grace his soul and thine in Christ restore.
> Make sure thy second birth, else thou shalt see,
>   Heaven ope to Indians wild, but shut to thee.   [1643]

EDMUND WALLER

England 1606–1687

In contrast to the secure position of Latin and Greek, established languages of composition in England, Waller presents the special conditions that define the fragile nature of the vernacular, 'a daily changing tongue' whose prospects are only as 'long-lived' perhaps 'as present love'. His verse enjoyed a keen audience in its day; his handling of counterpoint, metre (his piece on Prince Charles's escape from shipwreck at Santander in 1625, 'His Majesty's Escape at St Andere' is one of the first examples of heroic couplets in English verse, a form that enjoyed 200 years of prominence) and word choice commanded the attention of John Dryden who called Waller 'the father of our English numbers'. Waller's works include *Poems* (1645), *Divine Poems* (1685), and the two-volume *Poems* (ed. G. Thorn-Drury, 1893).

OF ENGLISH VERSE

Poets may boast, as safely vain,
Their work shall with the world remain;
Both bound together live or die,
The verses and the prophecy.

But who can hope his lines should long
Last in a daily changing tongue?
While they are new, envy prevails,
And as that dies, our language fails.

When architects have done their part,
The matter may betray their art;
Time, if we use ill-chosen stone,
Soon brings a well-built palace down.

Poets that lasting marble seek
Must carve in Latin or in Greek;
We write in sand, our language grows,
And like the tide our work o'erflows.

Chaucer his sense can only boast,
The glory of his numbers lost!
Years have defaced his matchless strain;
And yet he did not sing in vain.

The beauties which adorned that age,
The shining subjects of his rage,
Hoping they should immortal prove,
Rewarded with success his love.

This was the generous poet's scope,
And all an English pen can hope,
To make the fair approve his flame
That can so far extend their name.

Verse thus designed has no ill fate
If it arrive but at the date
Of fading beauty, if it prove
But as long-lived as present love.   [1668]

JOHN MILTON

England 1608–1674

Milton's self-directed education after his Cambridge degrees was so intense that biographers spec-
ulate he read almost every significant work written in English. A reformer, his political activities
included the writing of a series of pamphlets that advocated the restraint of the power enjoyed by
bishops (*The Reason of Church Government Urged Against Prelaty*, 1642); the freeing of the press
from government control (*Aeropagitica*, 1644); less restrictive divorce laws (the first stage of his
first marriage lasted three weeks, though his bride returned three years later in 1645 and died in
1652); and continuing opposition to the restoration of Charles II. With the help of his friend
Andrew Marvell, Milton survived Charles's return, and though blind and somewhat impoverished,
composed *Paradise Lost* (1667), *Paradise Regained* (1671), and *Samson Agonistes* (1671)—works
commandingly textured by classical reference that explore humanity's response to the enigmatic
series of paradoxes defining Milton's understanding of the story of the Christ and the nature of
heroic action.

from PARADISE LOST

BOOK 1

The Argument
   This first book proposes, first in brief, the whole subject, man's disobedience,
and the loss thereupon of Paradise, wherein he was placed: then touches
the prime cause of his fall, the serpent, or rather Satan in the serpent; who,
revolting from God, and drawing to his side many legions of angels, was, by the
command of God, driven out of Heaven with all his crew, into the great deep.

Which action passed over, the poem hastes into the midst of things; presenting Satan, with his angels, now fallen into Hell—described here not in the center (for heaven and earth may be supposed as yet not made, certainly not yet accursed), but in a place of utter darkness, fitliest called Chaos. Here Satan with his angels lying on the burning lake, thunderstruck and astonished, after a certain space recovers, as from confusion; calls up him who, next in order and dignity, lay by him; they confer of their miserable fall. Satan awakens all his legions, who lay till then in the same manner confounded. They rise: their numbers; array of battle; their chief leaders named, according to the idols known afterwards in Canaan and the countries adjoining. To these Satan directs his speech; comforts them with hope yet of regaining Heaven; but tells them, lastly, of a new world and new kind of creature to be created, according to an ancient prophecy or report in Heaven; for that angels were long before this visible creation was the opinion of many ancient fathers. To find out the truth of this prophecy, and what to determine thereon, he refers to a full council. What his associates thence attempt. Pandemonium, the palace of Satan, rises, suddenly built out of the deep: the infernal peers there sit in council.

   Of man's first disobedience, and the fruit
Of that forbidden tree whose mortal taste
Brought death into the world, and all our woe,
With loss of Eden, till one greater Man
Restore us, and regain the blissful seat,
Sing, Heavenly Muse, that on the secret top
Of Oreb, or of Sinai, didst inspire
That shepherd who first taught the chosen seed
In the beginning how the heavens and earth
Rose out of Chaos: or, if Sion hill
Delight thee more, and Siloa's brook that flowed
Fast by the oracle of God, I thence
Invoke thy aid to my adventurous song,
That with no middle flight intends to soar
Above th' Aonian mount, while it pursues
Things unattempted yet in prose or rhyme.
And chiefly thou, O Spirit, that dost prefer
Before all temples th' upright heart and pure,
Instruct me, for thou know'st; thou from the first
Wast present, and, with mighty wings outspread,
Dovelike sat'st brooding on the vast abyss,
And mad'st it pregnant: what in me is dark
Illumine; what is low, raise and support;
That to the height of this great argument
I may assert Eternal Providence,
And justify the ways of God to men.
  Say first (for Heaven hides nothing from thy view,
Nor the deep tract of Hell), say first what cause

Moved our grand parents, in that happy state,
Favored of Heaven so highly, to fall off
From their Creator, and transgress his will
For one restraint, lords of the world besides?
Who first seduced them to that foul revolt?
   Th' infernal serpent; he it was, whose guile,
Stirred up with envy and revenge, deceived
The mother of mankind, what time his pride
Had cast him out from Heaven, with all his host
Of rebel angels, by whose aid aspiring
To set himself in glory above his peers,
He trusted to have equaled the Most High,
If he opposed; and with ambitious aim
Against the throne and monarchy of God
Raised impious war in Heaven and battle proud,
With vain attempt. Him the Almighty Power
Hurled headlong flaming from th' ethereal sky
With hideous ruin and combustion down
To bottomless perdition, there to dwell
In adamantine chains and penal fire,
Who durst defy th' Omnipotent to arms.
   Nine times the space that measures day and night
To mortal men, he with his horrid crew
Lay vanquished, rolling in the fiery gulf
Confounded though immortal. But his doom
Reserved him to more wrath; for now the thought
Both of lost happiness and lasting pain
Torments him; round he throws his baleful eyes,
That witnessed huge affliction and dismay,
Mixed with obdùrate pride and steadfast hate.
At once, as far as angels ken, he views
The dismal situation waste and wild:
A dungeon horrible, on all sides round
As one great furnace flamed; yet from those flames
No light, but rather darkness visible
Served only to discover sights of woe,
Regions of sorrow, doleful shades, where peace
And rest can never dwell, hope never comes
That comes to all, but torture without end
Still urges, and a fiery deluge, fed
With ever-burning sulphur unconsumed:
Such place Eternal Justice had prepared
For those rebellious; here their prison ordained
In utter darkness and their portion set
As far removed from God and light of Heaven
As from the center thrice to th' utmost pole.

O how unlike the place from whence they fell!
There the companions of his fall, o'erwhelmed
With floods and whirlwinds of tempestuous fire,
He soon discerns; and, weltering by his side,
One next himself in power, and next in crime,
Long after known in Palestine, and named
Beëlzebub. To whom th' arch-enemy,
And thence in Heaven called Satan, with bold words
Breaking the horrid silence thus began:
    'If thou beëst he—but O how fallen! how changed
From him who in the happy realms of light
Clothed with transcendent brightness didst outshine
Myriads, though bright! if he whom mutual league,
United thoughts and counsels, equal hope
And hazard in the glorious enterprise,
Joined with me once, now misery hath joined
In equal ruin; into what pit thou seest
From what height fallen, so much the stronger proved
He with his thunder: and till then who knew
The force of those dire arms? Yet not for those,
Nor what the potent Victor in his rage
Can else inflict, do I repent or change,
Though changed in outward luster, that fixed mind
And high disdain, from sense of injured merit,
That with the Mightiest raised me to contend,
And to the fierce contention brought along
Innumerable force of spirits armed,
That durst dislike his reign, and me preferring,
His utmost power with adverse power opposed
In dubious battle on the plains of Heaven,
And shook his throne. What though the field be lost?
All is not lost: the unconquerable will,
And study of revenge, immortal hate,
And courage never to submit or yield:
And what is else not to be overcome?
That glory never shall his wrath or might
Extort from me. To bow and sue for grace
With suppliant knee, and deify his power
Who from the terror of this arm so late
Doubted his empire—that were low indeed;
That were an ignominy and shame beneath
This downfall; since, by fate, the strength of gods
And this empyreal substance cannot fail;
Since, through experience of this great event,
In arms not worse, in foresight much advanced,
We may with more successful hope resolve

To wage by force or guile eternal war,
Irreconcilable to our grand Foe,
Who now triùmphs, and in th' excess of joy
Sole reigning holds the tyranny of Heaven.'
  So spake th' apostate angel, though in pain,
Vaunting aloud, but racked with deep despair;
And him thus answered soon his bold compeer:
  'O prince, O chief of many thronèd powers,
That led th' embattled seraphim to war
Under thy conduct, and in dreadful deeds
Fearless, endangered Heaven's perpetual King,
And put to proof his high supremacy,
Whether upheld by strength, or chance, or fate!
Too well I see and rue the dire event
That with sad overthrow and foul defeat
Hath lost us Heaven, and all this mighty host
In horrible destruction laid thus low,
As far as gods and heavenly essences
Can perish: for the mind and spirit remains
Invincible, and vigor soon returns,
Though all our glory extinct, and happy state
Here swallowed up in endless misery.
But what if he our Conqueror (whom I now
Of force believe almighty, since no less
Than such could have o'erpowered such force as ours)
Have left us this our spirit and strength entire,
Strongly to suffer and support our pains,
That we may so suffice his vengeful ire,
Or do him mightier service as his thralls
By right of war, whate'er his business be,
Here in the heart of Hell to work in fire,
Or do his errands in the gloomy deep?
What can it then avail though yet we feel
Strength undiminished, or eternal being
To undergo eternal punishment?'
  Whereto with speedy words th' arch-fiend replied:
'Fallen cherub, to be weak is miserable,
Doing or suffering: but of this be sure,
To do aught good never will be our task,
But ever to do ill our sole delight,
As being the contrary to his high will
Whom we resist. If then his providence
Out of our evil seek to bring forth good,
Our labor must be to pervert that end,
And out of good still to find means of evil;
Which ofttimes may succeed, so as perhaps

Shall grieve him, if I fail not, and disturb
His inmost counsels from their destined aim.
But see! the angry Victor hath recalled
His ministers of vengeance and pursuit
Back to the gates of Heaven; the sulphurous hail,
Shot after us in storm, o'erblown hath laid
The fiery surge that from the precipice
Of Heaven received us falling; and the thunder,
Winged with red lightning and impetuous rage,
Perhaps hath spent his shafts, and ceases now
To bellow through the vast and boundless deep.
Let us not slip th' occasion, whether scorn
Or satiate fury yield it from our Foe.
Seest thou yon dreary plain, forlorn and wild,
The seat of desolation, void of light,
Save what the glimmering of these livid flames
Casts pale and dreadful? Thither let us tend
From off the tossing of these fiery waves;
There rest, if any rest can harbor there;
And reassembling our afflicted powers,
Consult how we may henceforth most offend
Our enemy, our own loss how repair,
How overcome this dire calamity,
What reinforcement we may gain from hope,
If not, what resolution from despair.'   [1674]

ANNE BRADSTREET

England/America c. 1612-1672

Bradstreet received a private education in England before she emigrated to the Massachusetts Bay
colony with her husband, Simon. The daughter of well-educated parents, Dorothy Yorke and
Thomas Dudley (Governor of Massachusetts Bay after John Winthrop), she read widely in Eliza-
bethan and Metaphysical verse. Her poetry derived from English and European literary influences
as well as orthodox Puritan doctrine emphasizing resignation to God's will and an acceptance of
the insignificance of earthly life. Bradstreet's *The Tenth Muse Lately Sprung Up in America*, published
in London in 1650 without her knowledge, was the first book of poetry published by a colonist in
North America. Her creative self-assertion and self-deprecation resulted in an ironic, often satiric
voice attentive to the complexities of woman's experiences of love, death, faith, and resignation.

THE AUTHOR TO HER BOOK

Thou ill-form'd offspring of my feeble brain,
Who after birth did'st by my side remain,
Till snatcht from thence by friends, less wise than true,
Who thee abroad expos'd to public view,

Made thee in rags halting to th' press to trudge,
Where errors were not lessened (all may judge).
At thy return my blushing was not small,
My rambling brat (in print) should mother call;
I cast thee by as one unfit for light,
Thy visage was so irksome in my sight;
Yet being mine own, at length affection would
Thy blemishes amend, if so I could:
I wash'd thy face, but more defects I saw,
And rubbing off a spot, still made a flaw.
I stretcht thy joints to make thee even feet,
Yet still thou run'st more hobbling than is meet;
In better dress to trim thee was my mind,
But nought save homespun cloth i' th' house I find;
In this array, 'mongst vulgars may'st thou roam,
In critic's hands, beware thou dost not come;
And take thy way where yet thou art not known,
If for thy father asked, say thou had'st none:
And for thy mother, she alas is poor,
Which caus'd her thus to send thee out of door.   [1678]

BEFORE THE BIRTH OF ONE OF HER CHILDREN

All things within this fading world hath end,
Adversity doth still our joys attend;
No ties so strong, no friends so dear and sweet,
But with death's parting blow is sure to meet.
The sentence past is most irrevocable,
A common thing, yet oh inevitable;
How soon, my dear, death may my steps attend,
How soon't may be thy lot to lose thy friend,
We both are ignorant, yet love bids me
These farewell lines to recommend to thee,
That when that knot's untied that made us one,
I may seem thine, who in effect am none.
And if I see not half my days that's due,
What nature would, God grant to yours and you;
The many faults that well you know I have,
Let be interr'd in my oblivion's grave;
If any worth or virtue were in me,
Let that live freshly in thy memory,
And when thou feel'st no grief, as I no harms,
Yet love thy dead, who long lay in thine arms:
And when thy loss shall be repaid with gains,
Look to my little babes, my dear remains.
And if thou love thy self, or loved'st me,

These O protect from step-dame's injury.
And if chance to thine eyes shall bring this verse,
With some sad sighs honor my absent hearse;
And kiss the paper for thy love's dear sake,
Who with salt tears this last farewell did take.   [1678]

ANDREW MARVELL

England 1621–1678

Marvell became aide to Milton during the latter's tenure as Assistant Latin Secretary to Cromwell's
Council of State. When the monarchy was restored, he translated his own continuing disenchant-
ment into political satire. While his poetry was generally unknown during his lifetime and pub-
lished only after his death in 1681, his exploration of the psychology of the fall, particularly in its
secular and spiritual formulations, intrigues twentieth-century readers. The argument in 'To His
Coy Mistress' is wrought with appealing, albeit superficial logic, that establishes a new low for an
already fallen art which has as its antecedents Petrarchan love merchants, avid Virgilian suitors,
and the robust though unscrupulous pick-up artists of classical mythologies.

TO HIS COY MISTRESS

Had we but world enough, and time,
This coyness, lady, were no crime.
We would sit down, and think which way
To walk, and pass our long love's day.
Thou by the Indian Ganges' side
Shouldst rubies find; I by the tide
Of Humber would complain. I would
Love you ten years before the Flood,
And you should, if you please, refuse
Till the conversion of the Jews.
My vegetable love should grow
Vaster than empires, and more slow.
An hundred years should go to praise
Thine eyes, and on thy forehead gaze.
Two hundred to adore each breast:
But thirty thousand to the rest;
An age at least to every part,
And the last age should show your heart.
For, lady, you deserve this state;
Nor would I love at lower rate.
But at my back I always hear
Time's wingèd chariot hurrying near:
And yonder all before us lie
Deserts of vast eternity.
Thy beauty shall no more be found;

Nor, in thy marble vault, shall sound
My echoing song; then worms shall try
That long-preserved virginity,
And your quaint honor turn to dust;
And into ashes all my lust:
The grave's a fine and private place,
But none, I think, do there embrace.
　　Now therefore, while the youthful hue
Sits on thy skin like morning dew,
And while thy willing soul transpires
At every pore with instant fires,
Now let us sport us while we may;
And now, like amorous birds of prey,
Rather at once our time devour,
Than languish in his slow-chapped power.
Let us roll all our strength and all
Our sweetness up into one ball:
And tear our pleasures with rough strife,
Thorough the iron gates of life.
Thus, though we cannot make our sun
Stand still, yet we will make him run.   [1681]

MICHAEL WIGGLESWORTH

England/America 1631–1705

A 1651 graduate of Harvard and ordained as a Puritan minister in 1656, Wigglesworth wrote colonial America's first bestseller, a 'fire-and-brimstone' 224-stanza epic on the Christian Judgement Day, *The Day of Doom*. Written in traditional ballad form, *The Day of Doom* is a memorable adaptation of standard tenets of Puritan doctrine: God's omnipotence and grace, human depravity, Christ's atonement, and predestination. Wigglesworth's 1662 long poem entitled 'God's Controversy with New England' was unpublished until 1873. A second collection of his verse, *Meat Out of the Eater*, appeared in 1670.

from THE DAY OF DOOM: OR, A DESCRIPTION OF THE GREAT AND LAST JUDGEMENT

217
But woe, woe, woe our souls unto!
　　we would not happy be;
And therefore bear God's vengeance here
　　to all eternity.
Experience and woeful sense
　　must be our painful teachers
Who n'ould believe, nor credit give,
　　unto our faithful preachers.

218
Thus shall they lie, and wail, and cry,
    tormented, and tormenting
Their galléd hearts with poisoned darts
    but now too late repenting.
There let them dwell i' th' flames of hell;
    there leave we them to burn,
And back again unto the men
    whom Christ acquits, return.

219
The saints behold with courage bold,
    and thankful wonderment,
To see all those that were their foes
    thus sent to punishment:
Then do they sing unto their King
    a song of endless praise:
They praise His name, and do proclaim
    that just are all His ways.

220
Thus with great joy and melody
    to heav'n they all ascend,
Him there to praise with sweetest lays,
    and hymns that never end,
Where with long rest they shall be blessed,
    and nought shall them annoy:
Where they shall see as seen they be,
    and whom they love enjoy.

221
O glorious place! where face to face
    Jehovah may be seen,
By such as were sinners whilere
    and no dark veil between.
Where the sun shine, and light divine,
    of God's bright countenance,
Doth rest upon them every one,
    with sweetest influence.

222
O blessed state of the renate!
    O wondrous happiness,
To which they're brought, beyond what thought
    can reach, or words express!
Grief's water-course, and sorrow's source,
    are turned to joyful streams.
Their old distress and heaviness
    are vanishéd like dreams.

223
For God above in arms of love
   doth dearly them embrace,
And fills their sprites with such delights,
   and pleasures in His grace;
As shall not fail, nor yet grow stale
   through frequency of use:
Nor do they fear God's favor there,
   to forfeit by abuse.

224
For there the saints are perfect saints,
   and holy ones indeed,
From all the sin that dwelt within
   their mortal bodies freed:
Made kings and priests to God through Christ's
   dear love's transcendency,
There to remain, and there to reign
   with Him eternally.   [1662]

KATHERINE FOWLER PHILIPS

England 1632-1664

Philips's neoclassical nickname 'the Matchless Orinda' operated as a pseudonym within her circle of intellectuals and artists who formed the Society of Friendship. Many of her poems are dedicated to women like Anne Owen, Viscountess Dungannon (Philips's 'dearest Lucasia')—women who perceived themselves as soulmates dedicated to one another's spiritual, emotional, and artistic development. These friendships for Philips were 'Nobler than kindred or than marriage-band, Because more free' ('A Friend'). When Philips died of smallpox in London while trying to recover a pirated edition of her work (an authorized version was published in 1667), her contemporaries acknowledged their admiration. Later, Anne Killigrew would observe that 'every laurel to her laurel bowed'.

FRIENDSHIP'S MYSTERY, TO MY DEAREST LUCASIA

Come my Lucasia, since we see
That miracles men's faith do move,
By wonder and by prodigy
To the dull angry world let's prove
There's a religion in our love.

For though we were design'd t'agree,
That Fate no liberty destroys,
But our election is as free
As angels', who with greedy choice
Are yet determin'd to their joys.

Our hearts are doubled by the loss,
Here mixture is addition grown;
We both diffuse, and both ingross:
And we whose minds are so much one,
Never, yet ever are alone.

We court our own captivity
Than thrones more great and innocent:
'Twere banishment to be set free,
Since we wear fetters whose intent
Not bondage is but ornament.

Divided joys are tedious found,
And griefs united easier grow:
We are ourselves but by rebound,
And all our titles shuffled so,
Both princes, and both subjects too.

Our hearts are mutual victims laid,
While they (such power in friendship lies)
Are altars, priests, and off'rings made:
And each heart which thus kindly dies,
Grows deathless by the sacrifice.   [1667]

ANONYMOUS

America

The Bay Psalm Book, the result of the collaborative effort of Puritan ministers, is a utilitarian, 'plain and familiar translation' of the Hebrew psalms of David which would fit metrically with tunes familiar to their congregations. The 1640 edition of 1700 copies was the first publication on the printing press established in 1638 at Massachusetts Bay in the town of Cambridge. Over fifty revised editions were subsequently published in the colonies, England, and Scotland. As a result, personal faith and communal morality were instilled among the seventeenth- and eighteenth-century Puritans and Calvinists as they sang the psalms at church and at home.

from THE BAY PSALM BOOK

PSALM 23

A Psalm of David

The Lord to me a shepherd is,
    want therefore shall not I.
He in the folds of tender grass,
    doth cause me down to lie.
To waters calm me gently leads;
    restore my soul doth He;

He doth in paths of righteousness
　for His name's sake lead me.
Yea though in valley of death's shade
　I walk, none ill I'll fear,
Because Thou art with me; Thy rod
　and staff my comfort are.
For me a table Thou hast spread,
　in presence of my foes.
Thou dost anoint my head with oil;
　my cup it overflows.
Goodness and mercy surely shall
　all my days follow me;
And in the Lord's house I shall dwell
　so long as days shall be.　　　　　　　　　　[1640]

APHRA BEHN

England 1640–1689

Behn's career included a stint as a spy in Antwerp, for which she received such little recompense that in 1668 she ended up in debtor's prison for a time. She was the first woman to write for money, a decision motivated by poverty, widowhood, and prodigious energy and ability. As a professional playwright, she wrote 20 plays and chafed at the common charge of plagiarism routinely launched against women writers. As political intrigue intensified and theatrical markets became less reliable, she turned to the writing of prose fiction and developed both the genre and its capacity to respond to issues of moral and social justice. Her last novel, *Oroonoko* (1688), based on her own experience in the West Indies, protests against slavery. Behn's poetry is most recently available in volume 1 (1992) of Janet Todd's proposed multi-volume, complete edition of Behn's often pioneering literary practice.

TO THE MOST ILLUSTRIOUS PRINCE CHRISTOPHER DUKE OF ALBEMARLE ON HIS VOYAGE TO HIS GOVERNMENT OF JAMAICA. A PINDARICK.

It is resolv'd! His Word and Honour's past!
We must submit, and let the *Heroe* go:
This Scanty Isle He long has Serv'd and Grac't,
And distant Worlds expect Him now.
　　No Grateful Laurels this allows,
　　To Crown the Noble Victor's Brows:
Supinely here His Generous Youth was lost,
Which shou'd more memorable Glories boast,
　　Such as shou'd more Renown His Name,
And still maintain aloft His spreading Fame.
His Soul by Nature Bravely Rough and Great,
Scorns the Confinement of a Home-Retreat;
　　But soft Repose, that Court-Disease,

Infectious to the Great and Young,
Subdu'd His Martial Mind to Ease,
And Charm'd Him with her Pleasures long.
Born for Great Action, but compell'd to Sloth,
He yields to all the Splendid Baits for Youth.

II

So the Young Victor did at *Capua* lie,
      Tamely unnerv'd in Luxury;
While all his gilded Arms hung Useless by:
In daz'ling Riots wanton'd with his Fair,
Despising Conquests, and renouncing War,
Till Glory wak'd him from th' Inchanting Dream,
And pointing out his Youth a Nobler Theam.
He rowses now, and puts his Armour on,
      Gives Order for his Warlike Steeds;
In vain the Lovely Charmer Weeps and Pleads,
He'll be no more by Idle Love undone;
In vain the shining Goblets take their Round,
      And with Obliging Healths are Crown'd,
The Ivory Tables bending with the Weight
      Of Costly Fare, in O'er-charg'd Plate:
He now for Fame Ignoble Ease disdains;
Bravely Resolv'd, he breaks the Lazy Chains.

III

      Well did Great *Cæsar* know,
      His Grandeur and Magnificence
      To New-found Worlds He cou'd not shew
      So greatly to His Fame, as now,
         In so Renown'd a Prince:
Already to the utmost Bounds of Shore
      His Mighty Name is gone before.
Great *Albemarle* the Sea-born *Nereids* sung,
      Upon that Memorable Day,
When all the Floods let loose their joyful Throng,
And bore the *Martyr's Sons* in Triumph o'er the Sea:
      And still between the Monarchs Praise
      The Fame of *Albemarle* they raise;
Crowns to the Royal Youths they brought, and to the Victor Bays.

IV

How must that Wond'ring World rejoyce to see
Their Land so Honour'd, and themselves so Blest,
When on their Shores (*Great Prince*) they Welcom Thee,
Whose Brave Hereditary Loyalty
Has been so many generous ways exprest?

What Homage must Your Ravisht Subjects pay
For the vast Condescention You have shewn?
What Treasures offer, how enough Obey,
   Their Humble Gratitude to own,
   When they behold a Prince so Great
   From an Illustrious Court retreat,
To render all their Happiness compleat?
A Prince whom no Ignoble Interest sways
To trust his Fortune with the Fickle Seas,
Altho' its Tributary Waves before
   Allow'd Him so immense a Store,
As if the Wonders of the Deep till now,
   Of which we have so oft been told,
   Did never yet its meaning shew,
Till yielding up the Miracle in Gold:
   And 'tis Great *Albemarle* alone
Has found the Secret of the Philosophic Stone.

V

   With Him, his Princess, whose High Birth
     Must Adoration claim
   O'er all the Habitable Earth
That ever heard the Great *Newcastle*'s Name.
How justly is our Verse a Tribute due,
   Illustrious Patroness, to You!
Descended from a Prince and Poet too!
That Honour which no Mortal Pow'r can give,
And is alone the Gods Prerogative;
Like that bright Vertue which do's in You shine,
And, more than Mortal, renders You Divine.
Prepare, ye Sun-scorch'd Natives of the Shore,
Prepare another Rising Sun t'adore,
Such as has never blest your Horizon before.
   And you the Brave Inhabitants of the Place,
   Who have by Conquest made it all your own,
     Whose Generous and Industrious Race
Has paid such Useful Tribute to the Crown;
See what your Grateful King for you has done!
Behold a Prince high in His Favor plac'd,
By Fortune Blest, and lavish Honour Grac'd,
Lov'd by the Great, and Worshipp'd by the Crowd,
Of whom the Nation has so long been proud,
The Souldiers Honour, and the Brave Mans Friend,
   The Muses best-lov'd Theme,
To whom their Noblest Verse they Recommend,
And to whose Vertues pay their Noblest Flame.

VI

This Prince, thus Lov'd, we do resign to you,
   Yet must but lend Him for a space:
Fond Parents lose their Darling so,
To Dangers thus they let him go,
With tender Tears, and many a soft Embrace;
Loth to forego the Treasure of their Heart,
   And yet wou'd have him Honour share,
With trembling Doubts and Fears at last they part,
With Vows and Pray'rs commit Him to Heav'ns Care.
We lend Him to eternize you a Fame,
That to the Coming Age your Land may boast,
Of all that e'er Obey'd Great *Cæsar's* Name,
   He Honour'd yours the Most.
Prepare your Triumphs, and your Songs of Joy,
   Let *Albemarle's* Great Name resound
To all your Happy Shores, and let the Sea
To the glad Echo's and the Nymphs convey
   The grateful Tidings all around,
   While the soft Breezes prune their Wings,
   And gather all their Gentlest Air,
(In the Rich Groves, drest with Perpetual Springs)
To Fan and Entertain the *Hero* there.
   Let all your World be Glad and Gay,
     To make His Joys Compleat,
   Eternal *Zephires* round Him play,
     And Flowers beneath His Feet.
Thus for Our Honour, and for your Repose,
We are content Our Happiness to lose:
But, like the Souls to Bodies newly Born,
He is but Lent, more Glorious to Return.   [1687]

A SONG IN DIALOGUE

She[pherd]. *Silvi*[a], when will you be kind,
   Ah, *Silvi*[a], when will you be kind.
Sil. When Constancy in Swains I find,
   Ah, when Constancy in Swains I find.
She. Ah my *Silvia*, you're too Fair,
   E'er to give me cause to change,
   Ah! do not let me then despair,
   For my Heart's not given to range.
Sil. Men will Sigh, Protest, and Weep,
   Ah! what a coyle with love you'll keep,
     Till our Blushes you o'er-come:
   Ah! till the blessing you have won,

Which, having once obtain'd, you fly:
Or if, by chance, you linger on,
    Can see us Sigh, can see us Dye,
And Triumph when we are undone.
She. Oh! may my Flocks forget to feed,
    And Wolves into my Sheepfold break:
May Heaven forget me in my need,
    And thou disdain me when I speak,
If ever I thy Love betray,
    Or with false Vows thy faith repay.
Sil. Then take my hand, which ne'er to Swain
    Was render'd, on the score of Love:
But, oh! I give it you with pain,
    For fear you shou'd Inconstant prove.   [1691]

EDWARD TAYLOR

America c. 1644-1729

Taylor was born in Leicestershire, England, studied at Cambridge, emigrated to the Massachusetts Bay colony in 1668, and graduated from Harvard in 1671. For the rest of his life, he ministered to a Puritan congregation in the frontier village of Westfield, Massachusetts. Although Taylor wrote poetry in concert with his religious duties, his two major works, *Preparatory Meditations before my Approach to the Lord's Supper* (c. 1682) and *God's Determinations touching his Elect* (c. 1680), remained unpublished until 1937. Taylor's Metaphysical imagery may be compared with that of Richard Crashaw, George Herbert, and John Donne. His Meditations were his form of secret prayer and self-examination derived from the biblical texts for his communion sermons. All 217 poems use the same iambic pentameter lines (rhyming ababcc). Against this formal dialectical diction are striking analogies invoking Christ's aid in human salvation.

from PREPARATORY MEDITATIONS

PROLOGUE

Lord, Can a Crumb of Earth the Earth outweigh:
    Outmatch all mountains, nay the Chrystall Sky?
Imbosom in't designs that shall Display
    And trace into the Boundless Deity?
    Yea, hand a Pen whose moysture doth guild ore
    Eternall Glory with a glorious glore.

If it its Pen had of an Angels Quill,
    And sharpened on a Pretious Stone ground tite,
And dipt in Liquid Gold, and mov'de by skill
    In Chrystall leaves should golden Letters write,
    It would but blot and blur: yea, jag and jar,
    Unless thou mak'st the Pen and Scribener.

I am this Crumb of Dust which is design'd
  To make my Pen unto thy Praise alone,
And my dull Phancy I would gladly grinde
  Unto an Edge on Zions Pretious Stone:
  And Write in Liquid Gold upon thy Name
  My Letters till thy glory forth doth flame.

Let not th' attempts breake down my Dust I pray,
  Nor laugh thou them to scorn, but pardon give.
Inspire this Crumb of Dust till it display
  Thy Glory through 't: and then thy dust shall live.
  Its failings then thou'lt overlook I trust,
  They being Slips slipt from thy Crumb of Dust.

Thy Crumb of Dust breaths two words from its breast;
  That thou wilt guide its pen to write aright
To Prove thou art, and that thou art the best,
  And shew thy Properties to shine most bright.
  And then thy Works will shine as flowers on Stems,
  Or as in Jewellary Shops, do jems.   [c. 1682]

from SACRAMENTAL MEDITATIONS

MEDITATION 38

1 JOHN II: 1: And if any man sin, we have an advocate with the Father.

Oh! What a thing is Man? Lord, Who am I?
  That thou shouldst give him Law (Oh! golden Line)
To regulate his Thoughts, Words, Life thereby:
  And judge him wilt thereby too in thy time.
  A Court of Justice thou in heaven holdst,
  To try his Case while he's here housd on mould.

How do thy Angells lay before thine eye
  My Deeds both White and Black I dayly doe?
How doth thy Court thou Pannellst there them try?
  But flesh complains. What right for this? let's know!
  For right or wrong, I can't appeare unto't.
  And shall a sentence Pass on such a suite?

Soft; blemish not this golden Bench, or place.
  Here is no Bribe, nor Colourings to hide,
Nor Pettifogger to befog the Case;
  But Justice hath her Glory here well tri'de:
  Her spotless Law all spotted Cases tends;
  Without Respect or Disrespect them ends.

God's Judge himselfe, and Christ Atturny is;
   The Holy Ghost Regesterer is founde.
Angells the sergeants are, all Creatures kiss
   The booke, and doe as Evidence abounde.
All Cases pass according to pure Law,
And in the sentence is no Fret nor flaw.

What saith, my soule? Here all thy Deeds are tri'de.
   Is Christ thy Advocate to pleade thy Cause?
Art thou his Client? Such shall never slide.
   He never lost his Case: he pleads such Laws
   As Carry do the same, nor doth refuse
   The Vilest sinners Case that doth him Choose.

This is his Honour, not Dishonour: nay,
   No Habeas-Corpus 'gainst his Clients came;
For all their Fines his Purse doth make down pay.
   He Non-Suites Satan's suite or Casts the same.
   He'l plead thy Case, and not accept a Fee.
   He'l plead Sub Forma Pauperis for thee.

My Case is bad. Lord, be my Advocate.
   My sin is red: I'me under Gods Arrest.
Thou hast the Hit of Pleading; plead my state.
   Although it's bad, thy Plea will make it best.
   If thou wilt plead my Case before the King,
   I'le Waggon Loads of Love and Glory bring.   [1690]

ANONYMOUS

Ireland

A classic example of Modern Irish verse since 1650, 'Dónall Óg/Donal Óg' belongs to a category of folksong called the *chanson de jeune fille*, the lament of the love-lorn maiden whose faithless lover has robbed her of identity, place, and spiritual passion. The poem exists in any number of translations from Munster to Scotland, as P.L. Henry observes in his headnote to the Gaelic original and the translation he provides in *Dánta Ban: Poems of Irish Women Early And Modern*. The second translation is by Lady Augusta Gregory, an Irish poet and playwright who with William Butler Yeats established Ireland's first national theatre.

DÓNALL ÓG

A Dhónaill Óig, má théir thar farraige,
Beir mé féin leat, as ná déan mo dhearmad;
As beidh agat féirín lá aonaigh is margaidh,
Is iníon rí Gréige mar chéile leapa agat.

Má théir-se anonn, tá comhartha agam ort:
Tá cúl fionn agus dhá shúil ghlasa agat,
Dhá chocán déag i do chúl buí bachallach,
Mar bheadh béal na bó nó rós i ngarraithe.

Is déanach aréir do labhair an gadhar ort,
Do labhair an naoscach sa churraichín doimhin ort,
Is tú id chaonaí aonair ar fud na gcoillte,
Is go rabhair gan chéile go héag go bhfaghair me!

Do gheallais domh-sa, agus d'innsis bréag dom,
Go mbeitheá romham-sa ag cró na gcaorach;
Do leigeas fead agus trí chéad ghlaoch chút,
Is ní bhfuaras ann ach uan ag méiligh.

Do gheallais domh-sa ní ba dheacair duit:
Loingeas óir fá chrann seoil airgid,
Dhá bhaile dhéag de bhailtibh margaidh,
Is cúirt bhreágh aolga cois taobh na farraige.

Do gheallais domh-sa ní nár bhféidir,
Go dtabharfá lámhainne de chroiceann éisc dom,
Go dtabharfá bróga de chroiceann éan dom,
Is culaith den tsíoda ba dhaoire in Éirinn.

A Dhónaill Óig, b'fhearr duit mise agat
Ná bean uasal uaibhreach iomarcach;
Do chrúfainn bó is do dhéanfainn cuigeann duit,
Is dá mba chruaidh é bhuailfinn buille leat.

Och, ochón! agus ní le hocras,
Uireasa bí, dí ná codlata
Fá ndear domh-sa bheith tanaí triuchalga,
Ach grá fir óig is é bhreoigh go follas mé.

Is moch ar maidin do chonnac-sa an t-óigfhear
Ar muin chapaill ag gabháil an bhóthair,
Níor dhruid sé liom is níor chuir ná streo orm,
Is ar mo chasadh abhaile dhom sea ghoileas mo dhóthain.

Nuair théim-se féin go Tobar an Uaignis
Suím síos ag déanamh buartha,
Nuair chím an saol is ná feicim mo bhuachaill,
Go raibh scáil an ómair i mbarr a ghruanna.

Siúd é an Domhnach do thugas grá duit,
An Domhnach díreach roimh Domhnach Cásca,
Is mise ar mo ghlúinibh ag léamh na Páise,
Sea bhí mo dhá shúil ag síor-thabhairt an ghrá dhuit.

Dúirt mo mháithrín liom gan labhairt leat
Inniu ná amárach ná Dia Domhnaigh.
Is olc an tráth do thug sí rabhadh dom
's é dúnadh an dorais é i ndiaidh na foghla.

Ó a dhe, a mháithrín, tabhair mé féin dó.
Is tabhair a bhfuil agat den tsaol go léir dó;
Éirigh féin ag iarraidh déirce,
Agus ná gabh siar ná aniar ar m'éileamh.

Do bhainis soir dhíom, is do bhainis siar dhíom,
Do bhainis romham is do bhainis im'dhiadh dhíom,
Do bhainis gealach is do bhainis grian díom,
's is ró-mhór m'eagla gur bhainis Dia dhíom.

DONAL ÓG

O Donal Óg, if you go oversea,
Take myself with you—and do not forget me!
And you'll have a keepsake on fair and market day,
And the Greek king's daughter as your bedmate.

If you go over, I have your mark:
You have a head of fair hair and two grey eyes,
Twelve curls in your yellow ringlets behind,
The cowslip or the garden rose—that would be their like.

The dog cried out to you late last night,
From the depths of the quagmire cried the snipe,
You were moving all alone through the woodlands wild,
And I pray that you will never wed until you are mine.

You promised me—'twas the lie you told—
That you'd be before me at the sheepfold,
I whistled and called out to you three hundred times,
But the bleating of the lone lamb was all I got in reply.

You promised me a thing right hard:
A ship of gold with a silver mast,
Twelve towns where markets are wont to be,
And a fair limed court beside the sea.

You promised what could never be,
That you'd give me gloves of the skin of fish,
That you'd give me boots of the skin of birds,
And a suit of the dearest Irish silk.

O Donal Óg, you'd be better with me
Than with a noblewoman, proud and haughty,
I'd milk the cow for you and do the churning,
And strike a blow with you if your need was urgent.

Woe, alas! Not from hunger,
Lack of food or drink or sleep
That I am pining, pinched and peaked,
But a young man's love has wasted me.

In the early morning I saw the young man
Riding on horseback along the road;
He didn't come near me and he gave no greeting,
And I cried my fill as I turned back home.

Whenever I go to the Well of Loneliness,
I sit me down and take to mourning,
When I see all the world except only my dear,
With the shade of amber high on his cheeks.

That was the Sunday I gave my love to your keeping,
At the Mass of the Palms before Sunday of Easter,
Christ's Passion of branches on my knees I was reading,
But my two eyes were on you and my heart was bleeding.

My mother has told me not to speak to you,
Today nor tomorrow nor on Sunday:
'Twas an ill time she gave me her caution—
Closing the door after the robbing.

O darling mother, give me away to him,
And give all you have in the whole wide world to him,
Go out yourself with the beggar's bowl,
And grant what I ask without toing and froing.

You've taken east from me, you've taken west from me,
The road behind me, and the road before,
You've taken moon, you've taken sun from me,
And I'm in dread you've taken the God I adore.   [after 1650]

Translated by P.L. Henry

DONAL ÓG

It is late last night the dog was speaking of you;
the snipe was speaking of you in her deep marsh.
It is you are the lonely bird through the woods;
and that you may be without a mate until you find me.

You promised me, and you said a lie to me,
that you would be before me where the sheep are flocked;
I gave a whistle and three hundred cries to you,
and I found nothing there but a bleating lamb.

You promised me a thing that was hard for you,
a ship of gold under a silver mast;
twelve towns with a market in all of them,
and a fine white court by the side of the sea.

You promised me a thing that is not possible,
that you would give me gloves of the skin of a fish;
that you would give me shoes of the skin of a bird;
and a suit of the dearest silk in Ireland.

When I go by myself to the Well of Loneliness,
I sit down and I go through my trouble;
when I see the world and do not see my boy,
he that has an amber shade in his hair.

It was on that Sunday I gave my love to you;
the Sunday that is last before Easter Sunday.
And myself on my knees reading the Passion;
and my two eyes giving love to you for ever.

My mother said to me not to be talking with you today,
or tomorrow, or on the Sunday;
it was a bad time she took for telling me that;
it was shutting the door after the house was robbed.

My heart is as black as the blackness of the sloe,
or as the black coal that is on the smith's forge;
or as the sole of a shoe left in white halls;
it was you put that darkness over my life.

You have taken the east from me; you have taken the west from me;
you have taken what is before me and what is behind me;
you have taken the moon, you have taken the sun from me;
and my fear is great that you have taken God from me!   [c. 1902]

Translated by Lady Augusta Gregory

MRS ANNE KILLIGREW

England 1660–1685

Killigrew's *Poems* (1686), published posthumously by her father, was accompanied by an encomium by the playwright, poet, and critic John Dryden entitled 'To the Pious Memory of the accomplished Young Lady Mrs Anne Killigrew'. Dryden addressed Killigrew as 'Excellent in the two Sister-Arts of Poesie, and Painting', and a self-portrait fronts the 1686 collection. Killigrew combines stock Court verse conventions (she was for a time companion of Anne Finch and Maid of Honour to Mary of Modena, Duchess of York) with her own distinctive interest in poetic theory, the individual voice, and mythological and biblical subjects.

PENELOPE TO ULYSSES

Return my dearest Lord, at length return,
Let me no longer your sad absence mourn,
Ilium in Dust, does no more Work afford,
No more Employment for your Wit or Sword.

　Why did not the fore-seeing Gods destroy,
Helin the Fire-brand both of *Greece* and *Troy*,
E're yet the Fatal Youth her Face had seen,
E're lov'd and born away the wanton Queen?
Then had been stopt the mighty Floud of Woe,
Which now both *Greece* and *Phrygia* over-flow:
Then I, these many Teares, should not have shed,
Nor thou, the source of them, to War been led:
I should not then have trembled at the Fame
Of *Hectors* warlike and victorious Name.

　Why did I wish the Noble *Hector* Slain?
Why *Ilium* ruin'd? Rise, O rise again!
Again great City flourish from thine Urne:
For though thou'rt burn'd, my Lord does not return.
Sometimes I think, (but O most Cruel Thought,)
That, for thy Absence, th'art thy self in fault:
That thou art captiv'd by some captive Dame,
Who, when thou fired'st *Troy*, did thee inflame
And now with her thou lead'st thy am'rous Life,
Forgetful, and despising of thy Wife.   [1686]

TO THE QUEEN

As those who pass the *Alps* do say,
The Rocks which first oppose their way,
And so amazing-High do show,
By fresh Ascents appear but low,
And when they come unto the last,
They scorn the dwarfish Hills th'ave past.

So though my *Muse* at her first flight,
Thought she had chose the greatest height,
And (imp'd with *Alexander's* Name)
Believ'd there was no further Fame:
Behold an Eye wholly Divine
Vouchsaf'd upon my Verse to Shine!
And from that time I'gan to treat
With Pitty him the World call'd *Great*;
To smile at his exalted Fate,
Unequal (though Gigantick) State.
I saw that Pitch was not sublime,
Compar'd with this which now I climb;
His Glories sunk, and were unseen,
When once appear'd the Heav'n-born Queen:
Victories, Laurels, Conquer'd Kings,
Took place among inferiour things.

Now surely I shall reach the Clouds,
For none besides such Vertue shrouds:
Having scal'd this with holy Strains,
Nought higher but the Heaven remains!
No more I'll Praise on them bestow,
Who to ill Deeds their Glories owe;
Who build their *Babels* of Renown,
Upon the poor oppressed Crown,
Whole Kingdoms do depopulate,
To raise a Proud and short-Liv'd State:
I prize no more such Frantick Might,
Than his that did with Wind-Mills Fight:
No, give me Prowess, that with Charms
Of Grace and Goodness, not with Harms,
Erects a Throne i'th' inward Parts,
And Rules mens Wills, but with their Hearts;
Who with Piety and Vertue thus
Propitiates God, and Conquers us.
O that now like *Araunah* here,
Altars of Praises I could rear,
Suiting her worth, which might be seen
Like a Queens Present, to a Queen!

'Alone she stands for Vertues Cause,
'When all decry, upholds her Laws:
'When to Banish her is the Strife,
'Keeps her unexil'd in her Life;
'Guarding her matchless Innocence
'From Storms of boldest Impudence;
'In spight of all the Scoffs and Rage,
'And Persecutions of the Age,
'Owns Vertues Altar, feeds the Flame,
'Adores her much-derided Name;
'While impiously her hands they tie,
'Loves her in her Captivity;
'Like *Perseus* saves her, when she stands
'Expos'd to the *Leviathans*.
'So did bright Lamps once live in Urns,
'So Camphire in the water burns,
'So *Ætna's* Flames do ne'er go out,
'Though Snows do freeze her head without.

How dares bold Vice unmasked walk,
And like a Giant proudly stalk?
When Vertue's so exalted seen,
Arm'd and Triumphant in the Queen?
How dares its Ulcerous Face appear,
When Heavenly Beauty is so near?
But so when God was close at hand,
And the bright Cloud did threatning stand
(In sight of *Israel*) on the Tent,
They on in their Rebellion went.

O that I once so happy were,
To find a nearer Shelter there!
Till then poor Dove, I wandering fly
Between the Deluge and the Skie:
Till then I Mourn, but do not sing,
And oft shall plunge my wearied wing:
If her bless'd hand vouchsafe the Grace,
I'th' Ark with her to give a place,
I safe from danger shall be found,
When Vice and Folly others drown'd.   [1686]

ANONYMOUS

England

This poem was printed as a broadside ballad and sold in September, 1666, shortly after the Great Fire of London. It was one of the ballads later collected and published by Samuel Pepys.

LONDON MOURNING IN ASHES

Of Fire, Fire, Fire I sing,
   that have more cause to cry,
In the Great Chamber of the King
   (a City mounted high);
Old London that
Hath stood in state
   above six hundred years,
In six days' space,
Woe and alas!
   is burned and drowned in tears.

The second of September in
   the middle time of night,
In Pudding Lane it did begin
   to burn and blaze outright;
Where all that gazed
Were so amazed
   at such a furious flame,
They knew not how
Or what to do
   that might expel the same.

It swallowed Fish Street Hill, and straight
   it licked up Lombard Street;
Down Canon Street in blazing state
   it flew with flaming feet;
Down to the Thames
Whose shrinking streams
   began to ebb away,
As thinking that
The power of Fate
   had brought the latter day.

Eurus the God of eastern gales
   was Vulcan's bellows now,
And did so fill the flagrant sails
   that high-built churches bow;

The leads they bear
Dropped many a tear
  to see their fabrics burn;
The sins of men
Made churches then
  in dust and ashes mourn.

With hand and feet, in every street,
  they pack up goods and fly;
Pitch, tar, and oil increase the spoil
  old Fish Street 'gins to fry;
The fire doth range
Up to the Change,
  and every King commands,
But in despite
Of all its might,
  the stout old Founder stands.

Out of the shops the goods are ta'en,
  and haled from every shelf,
As in a shipwrack every man
  doth seek to save himself;
The Fire so hot,
A strength hath got
  no water can prevail;
An hundred ton
Were it poured on,
  would prove but like a pail.

The crackling flames do fume and roar,
  as billows do retire;
The City, though upon the shore,
  doth seem a sea of fire,
Where steeple spires
Show in the Fires
  like vessels sinking down.
The open fields
More safety yields,
  and thither fly the Town.

Up to the head of aged Paul's
  the flame doth fluttering fly;
Above a hundred thousand souls
  upon the ground do lie;
Sick souls and lame
All fly the flame;
  women with child we know

Are forced to run,
The Fire to shun,
   have not a day to go.

Cradles were rocked in every field,
   and food was all their cry,
Till the King's bowels bread did yield,
   and sent them a supply;
A Father he
Of his country,
   himself did sweetly show,
Both day and night,
With all his might,
   he sought to ease our woe.

The King himself in person there
   was, and the Duke of York,
And likewise many a Noble Peer
   assisted in the work;
To quell the ire
Of this wild Fire,
   whose army was so high,
And did invade,
So that it made
   ten hundred thousand fly.

From Sunday morn till Thursday at night
   it roared about the Town;
There was no way to quell its might
   but to pull houses down;
And so they did,
As they were bid
   By Charles, his great command;
The Duke of York
Some say did work
   with bucket in his hand.

At Temple Church, and Holborn Bridge,
   and Pie corner 'tis stenched;
The water did the Fire besiege,
   at Aldersgate it quenched;
At Cripplegate
(Though very late)
   and eke at Coleman Street,
At Basinghall
The Fire did fall;
   we all were joyed to see't.

Bishopsgate Street to Cornhill end,
   And Leadenhall's secure;
It to the postern did extend;
   Fenchurch doth still endure;
Clothworker's Hall
Did ruined fall,
   yet stopped the Fire's haste;
Mark Lane, Tower Dock,
Did stand the shock,
   And all is quenched at last.

Many of French and Dutch were stopped,
   and also are confined;
'Tis said that they their fire-balls dropped,
   and this plot was designed
By them and those
That are our foes;
   yet some think nothing so,
But that our God
With his flaming rod
   for sin sends all this woe.

Although the Fire be fully quenched,
   yet if our sins remain,
And that in them we still are drenched,
   the Fire will rage again;
Or what is worse,
A heavier curse,
   in Famine will appear;
Where shall we tread
When want of bread
   and hunger draweth near?

If this do not reform our lives,
   a worse thing will succeed;
Our kindred, children, and our wives
   will die for want of bread;
When Famine comes,
'Tis not our drums,
   our ships, our horse or foot
That can defend;
But if we mend,
   we never shall come to't.   [1661]

ANNE FINCH, COUNTESS OF WINCHILSEA

England 1661–1720

The unique combination of privileged status, financial security, childlessness, colleagues, and a congenial husband encouraged Winchilsea to pursue an interest in nature and female friendship, and to find poetic expression for her sensitivity to the passion, commitment, and understanding women bring to the 'unequal fetters' of marriage itself. While there is no complete edition of her work, the *Selected Poems of Anne Finch* was published in 1978.

THE UNEQUAL FETTERS

Could we stop the time that's flying
   Or recall it when 'tis past
Put far off the day of dying
   Or make youth for ever last
To love would then be worth our cost.

But since we must lose those graces
   Which at first your hearts have won
And you seek for in new faces
   When our spring of life is done
It would but urge our ruin on.

Free as Nature's first intention
   Was to make us, I'll be found
Nor by subtle Man's invention
   Yield to be in fetters bound
By one that walks a freer round.

Marriage does but slightly tie men
   Whilst close prisoners we remain
They the larger slaves of Hymen
   Still are begging love again
At the full length of all their chain.   [1713]

TO THE NIGHTINGALE

Exert thy voice, sweet harbinger of spring!
   This moment is thy time to sing,
   This moment I attend to praise,
And set my numbers to thy lays.
   Free as thine shall be my song;
   As thy music, short, or long.

Poets, wild as thee, were born,
  Pleasing best when unconfined,
  When to please is least designed,
Soothing but their cares to rest;
  Cares do still their thoughts molest,
  And still th'unhappy poet's breast,
Like thine, when best he sings, is placed against a thorn.
She begins, Let all be still!
  Muse, thy promise now fulfill!
Sweet, oh! sweet, still sweeter yet
Can thy words such accents fit,
Canst thou syllables refine,
Melt a sense that shall retain
Still some spirit of the brain,
Till with sounds like these it join.
  'Twill not be! then change thy note;
  Let division shake thy throat.
Hark! Division now she tries;
Yet as far the Muse outflies.
  Cease then, prithee, cease thy tune;
  Trifler, wilt thou sing till June?
Till thy business all lies waste,
And the time of building's past!
  Thus we poets that have speech,
Unlike what thy forests teach,
  If a fluent vein be shown
  That's transcendent to our own,
Criticize, reform, or preach,
Or censure what we cannot reach.   [1713]

JONATHAN SWIFT

Ireland 1667–1745

Swift left Ireland for England following the abdication of James II in 1688, but returned as chaplain to the Lord Justice, the Earl of Berkeley in 1699. Spirited, controversial, and the most prominent political satirist of his time, Swift, unswervingly loyal to the Anglican Church and the Tory party, was rewarded by the deanship of St Patrick's Cathedral in Dublin in 1713 though he had hoped for an appointment in England. Swift's genius was valued by a distinguished circle which included Alexander Pope, John Gay, author of the famous *Beggar's Opera* (1728), and Irish poet Thomas Parnell. While criticized for misanthropy, Swift maintained that it was mankind's failure to take advantage of its capacity for reasoned behaviour that roused his cutting edge in works like *Gulliver's Travels* (1726). The standard edition of Swift's poems is Sir Harold Williams's three-volume collection, published in 1937 and revised in 1958.

VERSES SAID TO BE WRITTEN ON THE UNION

The Queen has lately lost a part
Of her entirely English heart,
For want of which by way of botch,
She pieced it up again with Scotch.
Blessed revolution, which creates
Divided hearts, united states.
See how the double nation lies;
Like a rich coat with skirts of frieze:
As if a man in making posies
Should bundle thistles up with roses.
Whoever yet a union saw
Of kingdoms, without faith or law.
Henceforward let no statesman dare,
A kingdom to a ship compare;
Lest he should call our commonweal,
A vessel with a double keel:
Which just like ours, new rigged and manned,
And got about a league from land,
By change of wind to leeward side
The pilot knew not how to guide.
So tossing faction will o'erwhelm
Our crazy double-bottomed realm.   [1746]

VERSES MADE FOR THE WOMEN WHO CRY APPLES, ETC.

APPLES

Come buy my fine wares,
Plums, apples, and pears,
A hundred a penny,
In conscience too many,

Come, will you have any;
My children are seven,
I wish them in heaven,
My husband's a sot,
With his pipe and his pot,
Not a farthing will gain 'em,
And I must maintain 'em.

ASPARAGUS

Ripe 'sparagrass,
Fit for lad or lass,
To make their water pass:
   O, 'tis a pretty picking
   With a tender chicken.

ONIONS

Come, follow me by the smell,
Here's delicate onions to sell,
I promise to use you well.
They make the blood warmer,
You'll feed like a farmer:
For this is every cook's opinion,
No savoury dish without an onion;
But lest your kissing should be spoiled,
Your onions must be thoroughly boiled;
   Or else you may spare
   Your mistress a share,
The secret will never be known;
   She cannot discover
   The breath of her lover
But think it as sweet as her own.

OYSTERS

   Charming oysters I cry,
   My masters come buy,
   So plump and so fresh,
   So sweet is their flesh,
   No Colchester oyster,
   Is sweeter and moister,
   Your stomach they settle,
   And rouse up your mettle,
   They'll make you a dad
   Of a lass or a lad;
   And Madam your wife
   They'll please to the life;

Be she barren, be she old,
Be she slut, or be she scold,
Eat my oysters, and lie near her,
She'll be fruitful, never fear her.

HERRINGS

Be not sparing,
Leave off swearing,
Buy my herring
Fresh from Malahide,
Better ne'er was tried.
Come eat 'em with pure fresh butter and mustard,
Their bellies are soft, and as white as a custard.
Come, sixpence a dozen to get me some bread,
Or, like my own herrings, I soon shall be dead.

ORANGES

Come, buy my fine oranges, sauce for your veal,
And charming when squeezed in a pot of brown ale.
Well roasted, with sugar and wine in a cup,
They'll make a sweet bishop when gentlefolks sup.   [1746]

SARAH EGERTON (NÉE FYGE, LATER FIELD)

England c. 1669– c. 1722

Egerton began her career at fourteen with the composition in 1683 of *The Female Advocate*, a response to contemporary Robert Gould's attack on women which he titled 'Love given O'er, or a Satyr against the Pride, Lust, and Inconstancy, Etc. of Woman' (1683). Egerton's piece, published in 1686, so enraged her father that she was exiled to country relatives. Nevertheless, Egerton's inquiry into the enslavement of women by 'Tyrant Custom' continued, deepened by her collaboration with a group of women writers who together produced *The Nine Muses*, a collection of elegiac poems honouring John Dryden. A photo-reproduction of her *Poems On Several Occasions* (1703) was made available in 1987.

THE EMULATION

Say Tyrant Custom, why must we obey,
The impositions of thy haughty Sway;
From the first dawn of Life, unto the Grave,
Poor Womankind's in every State, a Slave.
The Nurse, the Mistress, Parent and the Swain,
For Love she must, there's none escape that Pain;
Then comes the last, the fatal Slavery,

The Husband with insulting Tyranny
Can have ill Manners justify'd by Law;
For Men all join to keep the Wife in awe.
Moses who first our Freedom did rebuke,
Was Marry'd when he writ the Pentateuch;
They're Wife to keep us Slaves, for well they know,
If we were loose, we soon should make them, so.
We yeild like vanquish'd Kings whom Fetters bind,
When chance of War is to Usurpers kind;
Submit in Form; but they'd our Thoughts controul,
And lay restraints on the impassive Soul:
They fear we should excel their sluggish Parts,
Should we attempt the Sciences and Arts.
Pretend they were design'd for them alone,
So keep us Fools to raise their own Renown;
Thus Priests of old their Grandeur to maintain,
Cry'd vulgar Eyes would sacred Laws Prophane.
So kept the Mysteries behind a Screen,
There Homage and the Name were lost had they been seen:
But in this blessed Age, such Freedom's given,
That every Man explains the Will of Heaven;
And shall we Women now sit tamely by,
Make no excursions in Philosophy,
Or grace our Thoughts in tuneful Poetry?
We will our Rights in Learning's World maintain,
Wits Empire, now, shall know a Female Reign;
Come all ye Fair, the great Attempt improve,
Divinely imitate the Realms above:
There's ten celestial Females govern Wit,
And but two Gods that dare pretend to it;
And shall these finite Males reverse their Rules,
No, we'll be Wits, and then Men must be Fools.   [1703]

HENRY KELSEY

England/N. America c. 1670–1724

As the first writer of English poetry in the region of central Canada, Kelsey expresses fear and isolation amid the 'Emynent Dangers' of an unfamiliar landscape where he brought the inhabitants 'to a Commerce' in 'my masters interest'. Elsewhere in his writings, however, Kelsey suggests how he learned from the language and art of Cree 'poets' (his term) that 'Every man maketh his own songs by vertu of what he dreams.' Kelsey's manuscript journal of his experiences as a young Hudson Bay Company apprentice clerk at York Fort was discovered in 1926. It consists of this little-known prologue written in verse as well as a narrative daily logbook of his travels during 1690 and 1691 with Cree peoples in Rupertsland, now northern Manitoba.

from HENRY KELSEY HIS BOOK

PROLOGUE

Henry Kelsey his Book being ye Gift of James Hubbud
in the year of our Lord 1693

Now Reader Read for I am well assur'd
Thou dost not know the hardships I endur'd
In this same desert where Ever y^t I have been
Nor wilt thou me believe without y^t thou had seen
The Emynent Dangers that did often me attend
But still I lived in hopes y^t once it would amend
And makes me free from hunger & from Cold
Likewise many other things wch I cannot here unfold
For many times I have often been oppresst
With fears & Cares y^t I could not take my rest
Because I was alone & no friend could find
And once y^t in my travels I was left behind
Which struck fear & terror into me
But still I was resolved this same Country for to see
Although through many dangers I did pass
Hoped still to undergo y^m, at the Last
Now Considering y^t it was my dismal fate
for to repent I thought it now to late
Trusting still unto my masters Consideration
Hoping they will Except of this my small Relation
Which here I have pend & still will Justifie
Concerning of those Indians & their Country
If this wont do farewell to all as I may say

[2]
And for my living i'll seek some other way
In sixteen hundred & ninety'th year
I set forth as plainly may appear
Through Gods assistance for to understand
The natives language & to see their land
And for my masters interest I did soon
Sett from ye house ye twealth of June
Then up ye River I with heavy heart
Did take my way & from all English part
To live amongst y^e ₐNatives of this place
If god permits me for one two years space
The Inland Country of Good report hath been
By Indians but by English yet not seen
Therefore I on my Journey did not stay
But making all ye hast I could upon our way
Gott on ye borders of ye stone Indian Country
I took possession on ye tenth Instant July
And for my masters I speaking for y^m, all
This neck of land I deerings point did call
Distance from hence by Judgement at ye lest
From ye house six hundred miles southwest
Through Rivers wch run strong with falls
thirty three Carriages five lakes in all
The ground begins for to be dry with wood
Poplo & birch with ash thats very good
For the Natives of that place w^ch, knows
No use of Better than their wooden Bows
According to ye use & custom of this place
In September I brought those Natives to a peace
But I had no sooner from those Natives turnd my back
Some of the home Indians came upon their track
And for old grudges & their minds to fill

[3]
Came up with them Six tents of w^ch, they kill'd
This ill news kept secrett was from me
Nor none of those home Indians did I see
Untill that they their murder all had done
And the Chief acter was he y^ts called ye Sun
So far I have spoken concerning of the spoil
And now will give acco^t. of that same Country soile
Which hither part is very thick of wood
Affords small nutts wth little cherryes very good
Thus it continues till you leave ye woods behind
And then you have beast of severall kind
The one is a black a Buffillo great

Another is an outgrown Bear wch is good meat
His skin to gett I have used all y^e, m_∧eans I can
He is mans food & he makes food of man
His hide they would not me it preserve
But said it was a god & they should Starve
This plain affords nothing but Beast & grass
And over it in three days time we past
getting unto ye woods on the other side
It being about forty sixe miles wide
This wood is poplo ridges with small ponds of water
there is beavour in abundance but no Otter
with plains & ridges in the Country throughout
Their Enemies many whom they cannot rout
But now of late they hunt their Enemies
And with our English guns do make y^m, flie
At deerings point after the frost
I set up their a Certain Cross
In token of my being their there
Cut out on it ye date of year
And Likewise for to veryfie the same
added to it my master sir Edward deerings name
So having not more to trouble you wth all I am
Sir your most obedient & faithfull Servt. at Command

HENRY KELSEY
[c. 1690–1692]

ELIZABETH THOMAS

England 1675–1731

When Thomas showed her early poetry to an aging John Dryden, he thought her verses 'too good to be a Woman's'. A 'widowed' fiancée (a 16-year courtship with lawyer Richard Gwinnet ended with his death before the proposed marriage was concluded), she was probably mistress to Oliver Cromwell. Reduced circumstances led to isolation and debtor's prison. Thomas attempted to secure funds by selling private correspondences from Dryden and early letters written by Pope given to her by Cromwell. But poverty and a damaged reputation (in retaliation for the sale of his letters, Pope sullied her further in a vitriolic portrait in his *Dunciad*) were never overcome. Thomas's poems were published in 1722; 'The Triumvirate' demonstrates her bold and concentrated realization of the chilling consequence of infidelity.

THE TRIUMVIRATE

Oh! wondrous force of sympathy,
Where three unite in harmony;
Where master with the maid combines,
And mistress with them issue joins;
Where all unanimous agree
To club for future progeny.

Ah! may the household gods adorn
This happy infant, yet unborn,
With mother's cleanliness and air
(A stately, silly, tattered fair);
The mistress' form may it partake,
Her awkward mien and clumsy make,
Her broken mouth, her Judas grin,
And all the fiend which reigns within.

　 But Daddy's lines! oh, let the face
Reflect, with such expressive grace!
That all who shall this infant see
May cry at sight, ''Tis very he!'

[1722]

ANONYMOUS

America

First published on the Massachusetts Bay printing press in 1683, editions of *The New England Primer* were used in American schools until the 1830s. This collection of verses, aphorisms, hymns, prayers, and catechism employ rhyme and metre as mnemonic devices for (initially Puritan) doctrine. Its enforcement of religious and social conformity through literacy and education reflected significant shifts in American cultural values. This historical text suggests how the iconic verbal and visual representations used to teach alphabets in literacy instruction to this day have a profound effect on readers' strategies and repertoires.

from THE NEW ENGLAND PRIMER

ALPHABET

A — In *Adam's* Fall / We Sinned all.

B — Thy Life to Mend / This *Book* Attend.

C — The *Cat* doth play / And after flay.

D — A *Dog* will bite / A Thief at night.

E — An *Eagles* flight / Is out of fight.

F — The Idle *Fool* / Is whipt at School.

G — As runs the *Glafs* / Mans life doth pafs.

H — My *Book* and *Heart* / Shall never part.

J — *Job* feels the Rod / Yet blefses GOD.

K — Our *KING* the good / No man of blood.

L — The *Lion* bold / The *Lamb* doth hold.

M — The *Moon* gives light / In time of night.

N — *Nightingales* fing / In Time of Spring.

O — The *Royal Oak* / it was the Tree / That fav'd His / Royal Majeftie.

P — *Peter* denies / His Lord and cries

Q — Queen *Efther* comes / in Royal State / To Save the JEWS / from difmal Fate

R — *Rachel* doth mour, / For her firft born

S — *Samuel* anoints / Whom God appoint:

T — *Time* cuts down all / Both great and fmall.

U — *Uriah*'s beauteous Wife / Made *David* feek his / Life.

W — *Whales* in the Sea / God's Voice obey.

X — *Xerxes* the great did / die, / And fo muft you & I,

Y — *Youth* forward flips / Death fooneft nips.

Z — *Zacheus* he / Did climb the Tree / His Lord to fee,

[1683]

GEORGE BERKELEY

Ireland 1685–1753

Berkeley's philosophical study, *The Treatise Concerning the Principles of Human Knowledge* (1716) argued from the premise 'esse est percepi' ('to be is to be perceived'), an assertion of the provisional nature of material reality and the mind-dependence of ideas. He wrote 'Verses on the Prospect of Planting Arts and Learning in America' before his own voyage to America in 1728, made as part of an unsuccessful plan to establish a missionary college in the Bermudas. Berkeley's poem expresses the popular enthusiasm for a second chance at a golden age in the New World, an opportune reprieve from a pox'd cultural and spiritual Old World.

VERSES ON THE PROSPECT OF PLANTING ARTS AND LEARNING IN AMERICA

The Muse, disgusted at an age and clime
   Barren of every glorious theme,
In distant lands now waits a better time,
   Producing subjects worthy fame.

In happy climes, where from the genial sun
   And virgin earth such scenes ensue,
The force of art by nature seems outdone,
   And fancied beauties by the true.

In happy climes, the seat of innocence,
   Where nature guides and virtue rules,
Where men shall not impose for truth and sense
   The pedantry of courts and schools:

There shall be sung another golden age,
   The rise of empire and of arts,
The good and great inspiring epic rage,
   The wisest heads and noblest hearts.

Not such as Europe breeds in her decay;
   Such as she bred when fresh and young,
When heav'nly flame did animate her clay,
   By future poets shall be sung.

Westward the course of empire takes its way;
   The four first acts already past,
A fifth shall close the drama with the day;
   Time's noblest offspring is the last.

[1752]

ALEXANDER POPE

England 1688–1744

Because of his Roman Catholicism, Pope was denied the right to vote, pursue public office, or attend university. His profitable and much admired English translations of Homer's *Iliad* and *Odyssey* and his editions of Shakespeare, however, provided financial independence. Pope was, in fact, the first English writer to make his living by the pen with works that include commentaries on aesthetic theory (*An Essay on Criticism*, 1711), mock epic accounts of social customs (*The Rape of the Lock*, 1712), pastorals (*Windsor Forrest*, 1713), satires on popular literatures and taste (*The Dunciad*, 1728), and epistles which express the poet's allegiance to classical ideals and principles. Pope felt himself to be a legitimate descendant of the 'Patriarch wits' of the 'golden age' where order survived amidst diversity, a philosophical position expressed in technique as well: his stylistic genius found in the metrical uniformity of the heroic couplet unprecedented rhythmic variety. The multi-volume *Twickendon Edition* of Pope's work (1939–67) remains the standard edition.

from THE SEVENTH BOOK OF HOMER'S ODYSSES

THE GARDENS OF ALCINOUS

Close to the gates a spacious garden lies,
From storms defended, and inclement skies:
Four acres was th' allotted space of ground,
Fenc'd with a green enclosure all around.
Tall thriving trees confess'd the fruitful mold;
The red'ning apple ripens here to gold,
Here the blue fig with luscious juice o'erflows,
With deeper red the full pomegranate glows,
The branch here bends beneath the weighty pear,
And verdant olives flourish round the year.
The balmy spirit of the western gale
Eternal breathes on fruits untaught to fail:
Each dropping pear a following pear supplies,
On apples apples, figs on figs arise:
The same mild season gives the blooms to blow,
The buds to harden, and the fruits to grow.
  Here order'd vines in equal ranks appear
With all th' united labours of the year,
Some to unload the fertile branches run,
Some dry the black'ning clusters in the sun,
Others to tread the liquid harvest join,
The groaning presses foam with floods of wine.
Here are the vines in early flow'r descry'd,
Here grapes discolour'd on the sunny side,
And there in autumn's richest purple dy'd.
  Beds of all various herbs, for ever green,

In beauteous order terminate the scene.
  Two plenteous fountains the whole prospect
      crown'd;
This thro' the gardens leads its streams around,
Visits each plant, and waters all the ground:
While that in pipes beneath the palace flows,
And thence its current on the town bestows;
To various use their various streams they bring,
The People one, and one supplies the King.   [1713]

from AN ESSAY ON MAN

To Henry St John, Lord Bolingbroke

EPISTLE I. OF THE NATURE AND STATE OF MAN, WITH RESPECT TO THE UNIVERSE

  Awake, my St John! leave all meaner things
To low ambition, and the pride of kings.
Let us (since life can little more supply
Than just to look about us and to die)
Expatiate free o'er all this scene of man;
A mighty maze! but not without a plan;
A wild, where weeds and flowers promiscuous shoot,
Or garden, tempting with forbidden fruit.
Together let us beat this ample field,
Try what the open, what the covert yield;
The latent tracts, the giddy heights, explore
Of all who blindly creep, or sightless soar;
Eye Nature's walks, shoot folly as it flies,
And catch the manners living as they rise;
Laugh where we must, be candid where we can;
But vindicate the ways of God to man.
  1. Say first, of God above, or man below,
What can we reason, but from what we know?
Of man, what see we but his station here,
From which to reason, or to which refer?
Through worlds unnumbered though the God be known,
'Tis ours to trace him only in our own.
He, who through vast immensity can pierce,
See worlds on worlds compose one universe,
Observe how system into system runs,
What other planets circle other suns,
What varied Being peoples every star,
May tell why Heaven has made us as we are.
But of this frame the bearings, and the ties,
The strong connections, nice dependencies,

Gradations just, has thy pervading soul
Looked through? or can a part contain the whole?
   Is the great chain, that draws all to agree,
And drawn supports, upheld by God, or thee?
   2. Presumptuous man! the reason wouldst thou find,
Why formed so weak, so little, and so blind?
First, if thou canst, the harder reason guess,
Why formed no weaker, blinder, and no less!
Ask of thy mother earth, why oaks are made
Taller or stronger than the weeds they shade?
Or ask of yonder argent fields above,
Why Jove's satellites are less than Jove?
   Of systems possible, if 'tis confessed
That Wisdom Infinite must form the best,
Where all must full or not coherent be,
And all that rises, rise in due degree;
Then, in the scale of reasoning life, 'tis plain,
There must be, somewhere, such a rank as man:
And all the question (wrangle e'er so long)
Is only this, if God has placed him wrong?
   Respecting man, whatever wrong we call,
May, must be right, as relative to all.
In human works, though labored on with pain,
A thousand movements scarce one purpose gain;
In God's, one single can its end produce;
Yet serves to second too some other use.
So man, who here seems principal alone,
Perhaps acts second to some sphere unknown,
Touches some wheel, or verges to some goal;
'Tis but a part we see, and not a whole.
   When the proud steed shall know why man restrains
His fiery course, or drives him o'er the plains;
When the dull ox, why now he breaks the clod,
Is now a victim, and now Egypt's god:
Then shall man's pride and dullness comprehend
His actions', passions', being's use and end;
Why doing, suffering, checked, impelled; and why
This hour a slave, the next a deity.
   Then say not man's imperfect, Heaven in fault;
Say rather, man's as perfect as he ought:
His knowledge measured to his state and place,
His time a moment, and a point his space.
If to be perfect in a certain sphere,
What matter, soon or late, or here or there?
The blest today is as completely so,
As who began a thousand years ago.

  3. Heaven from all creatures hides the book of Fate,
All but the page prescribed, their present state:
From brutes what men, from men what spirits know:
Or who could suffer Being here below?
The lamb thy riot dooms to bleed today,
Had he thy reason, would he skip and play?
Pleased to the last, he crops the flowery food,
And licks the hand just raised to shed his blood.
O blindness to the future! kindly given,
That each may fill the circle marked by Heaven:
Who sees with equal eye, as God of all,
A hero perish, or a sparrow fall,
Atoms or systems into ruin hurled,
And now a bubble burst, and now a world.
  Hope humbly then; with trembling pinions soar;
Wait the great teacher Death, and God adore!
What future bliss, he gives not thee to know,
But gives that hope to be thy blessing now.
Hope springs eternal in the human breast:
Man never is, but always to be blest:
The soul, uneasy and confined from home,
Rests and expatiates in a life to come.
  Lo! the poor Indian, whose untutored mind
Sees God in clouds, or hears him in the wind;
His soul proud Science never taught to stray
Far as the solar walk, or milky way;
Yet simple Nature to his hope has given,
Behind the cloud-topped hill, an humbler heaven;
Some safer world in depth of woods embraced,
Some happier island in the watery waste,
Where slaves once more their native land behold,
No fiends torment, no Christians thirst for gold!
To Be, contents his natural desire,
He asks no angel's wing, no seraph's fire;
But thinks, admitted to that equal sky,
His faithful dog shall bear him company.
  4. Go, wiser thou! and, in thy scale of sense,
Weigh thy opinion against Providence;
Call imperfection what thou fancy'st such,
Say, here he gives too little, there too much;
Destroy all creatures for thy sport or gust,
Yet cry, if man's unhappy, God's unjust;
If man alone engross not Heaven's high care,
Alone made perfect here, immortal there:
Snatch from his hand the balance and the rod,
Rejudge his justice, be the God of God!

In pride, in reasoning pride, our error lies;
All quit their sphere, and rush into the skies.
Pride still is aiming at the blest abodes,
Men would be angels, angels would be gods.
Aspiring to be gods, if angels fell,
Aspiring to be angels, men rebel:
And who but wishes to invert the laws
Of order, sins against the Eternal Cause.
    5. Ask for what end the heavenly bodies shine,
Earth for whose use? Pride answers, ''Tis for mine:
For me kind Nature wakes her genial power,
Suckles each herb, and spreads out every flower;
Annual for me, the grape, the rose renew
The juice nectareous, and the balmy dew;
For me, the mine a thousand treasures brings;
For me, health gushes from a thousand springs;
Seas roll to waft me, suns to light me rise;
My footstool earth, my canopy the skies.'
    But errs not Nature from this gracious end,
From burning suns when livid deaths descend,
When earthquakes swallow, or when tempests sweep
Towns to one grave, while nations to the deep?
'No,' 'tis replied, 'the first Almighty Cause
Acts not by partial, but by general laws;
The exceptions few; some change since all began,
And what created perfect?'—Why then man?
If the great end be human happiness,
Then Nature deviates; and can man do less?
As much that end a constant course requires
Of showers and sunshine, as of man's desires;
As much eternal springs and cloudless skies,
As men forever temperate, calm, and wise.
If plagues or earthquakes break not Heaven's design,
Why then a Borgia, or a Catiline?
Who knows but he whose hand the lightning forms,
Who heaves old ocean, and who wings the storms,
Pours fierce ambition in a Caesar's mind,
Or turns young Ammon loose to scourge mankind?
From pride, from pride, our very reasoning springs;
Account for moral, as for natural things:
Why charge we Heaven in those, in these acquit?
In both, to reason right is to submit.
    Better for us, perhaps, it might appear,
Were there all harmony, all virtue here;
That never air or ocean felt the wind;
That never passion discomposed the mind:

But ALL subsists by elemental strife;
And passions are the elements of life.
The general ORDER, since the whole began,
Is kept in Nature, and is kept in man.
    6. What would this man? Now upward will he soar,
And little less than angel, would be more,
Now looking downwards, just as grieved appears
To want the strength of bulls, the fur of bears.
Made for his use all creatures if he call,
Say what their use, had he the powers of all?
Nature to these, without profusion, kind,
The proper organs, proper powers assigned;
Each seeming want compensated of course,
Here with degrees of swiftness, there of force;
All in exact proportion to the state;
Nothing to add, and nothing to abate.
Each beast, each insect, happy in its own;
Is Heaven unkind to man, and man alone?
Shall he alone, whom rational we call,
Be pleased with nothing, if not blessed with all?
    The bliss of man (could pride that blessing find)
Is not to act or think beyond mankind;
No powers of body or of soul to share,
Bur what his nature and his state can bear.
Why has not man a microscopic eye?
For this plain reason, man is not a fly.
Say what the use, were finer optics given,
To inspect a mite, not comprehend the heaven?
Or touch, if tremblingly alive all o'er,
To smart and agonize at every pore?
Or quick effluvia darting through the brain,
Die of a rose in aromatic pain?
If nature thundered in his opening ears,
And stunned him with the music of the spheres,
How would he wish that Heaven had left him still
The whispering zephyr, and the purling rill?
Who finds not Providence all good and wise,
Alike in what it gives, and what denies?
    7. Far as creation's ample range extends,
The scale of sensual, mental powers ascends:
Mark how it mounts, to man's imperial race,
From the green myriads in the peopled grass:
What modes of sight betwixt each wide extreme,
The mole's dim curtains, and the lynx's beam.
Of smell, the headlong lioness between,
And hound sagacious on the tainted green:

Of hearing, from the life that fills the flood,
To that which warbles through the vernal wood:
The spider's touch, how exquisitely fine!
Feels at each thread, and lives along the line:
In the nice bee, what sense to subtly true
From poisonous herbs extracts the healing dew:
How instinct varies in the groveling swine,
Compared, half-reasoning elephant, with thine!
'Twixt that, and reason, what a nice barrier;
Forever separate, yet forever near!
Remembrance and reflection how allied;
What think partitions sense from thought divide:
And middle natures, how they long to join,
Yet never pass the insuperable line!
Without this just gradation, could they be
Subjected, these to those, or all to thee?
The powers of all subdued by thee alone,
Is not thy reason all these powers in one?
   8. See, through this air, this ocean, and this earth,
All matter quick, and bursting into birth.
Above, how high progressive life may go!
Around, how wide! how deep extend below!
Vast Chain of Being! which from God began,
Natures ethereal, human, angel, man,
Beast, bird, fish, insect, what no eye can see,
No glass can reach! from Infinite to thee,
From thee to nothing.—On superior powers
Were we to press, inferior might on ours:
Or in the full creation leave a void,
Where, one step broken, the great scale's destroyed:
From Nature's chain whatever link you strike,
Tenth or ten thousandth, breaks the chain alike.
   And, if each system in gradation roll
Alike essential to the amazing Whole,
The least confusion but in one, not all
That system only, but the Whole must fall.
Let earth unbalanced from her orbit fly,
Planets and suns run lawless through the sky,
Let ruling angels from their spheres be hurled,
Being on being wrecked, and world on world,
Heaven's whole foundations to their center nod,
And Nature tremble to the throne of God:
All this dread ORDER break—for whom? for thee?
Vile worm!—oh, madness, pride, impiety!
   9. What if the foot, ordained the dust to tread,
Or hand, to toil, aspired to be the head?

What if the head, the eye, or ear repined
To serve mere engines to the ruling Mind?
Just as absurd for any part to claim
To be another, in this general frame:
Just as absurd, to mourn the tasks or pains,
The great directing MIND of ALL ordains.

    All are but parts of one stupendous whole,
Whose body Nature is, and God the soul;
That, changed through all, and yet in all the same,
Great in the earth, as in the ethereal frame,
Warms in the sun, refreshes in the breeze,
Glows in the stars, and blossoms in the trees,
Lives through all life, extends through all extent,
Spreads undivided, operates unspent,
Breathes in our soul, informs our mortal part,
As full, as perfect, in a hair as heart;
As full, as perfect, in vile man that mourns,
As the rapt seraph that adores and burns;
To him no high, no low, no great, no small;
He fills, he bounds, connects, and equals all.

    10. Cease then, nor ORDER imperfection name:
Our proper bliss depends on what we blame.
Know thy own point: this kind, this due degree
Of blindness, weakness, Heaven bestows on thee.
Submit—In this, or any other sphere,
Secure to be as blest as thou canst bear:
Safe in the hand of one disposing Power,
Or in the natal, or the mortal hour.
All Nature is but art, unknown to thee;
All chance, direction, which thou canst not see;
All discord, harmony not understood;
All partial evil, universal good:
And, spite of pride, in erring reason's spite,
One truth is clear: Whatever IS, is RIGHT.

from EPISTLE II. OF THE NATURE AND STATE OF MAN
WITH RESPECT TO HIMSELF, AS AN INDIVIDUAL

    1. Know then thyself, presume not God to scan;
The proper study of mankind is Man.
Placed on this isthmus of a middle state,
A being darkly wise, and rudely great:
With too much knowledge for the skeptic side,
With too much weakness for the Stoic's pride,
He hangs between; in doubt to act, or rest,
In doubt to deem himself a god, or beast;

In doubt his mind or body to prefer,
Born but to die, and reasoning but to err;
Alike in ignorance, his reason such,
Whether he thinks too little, or too much:
Chaos of thought and passion, all confused;
Still by himself abused, or disabused;
Created half to rise, and half to fall;
Great lord of all things, yet a prey to all;
Sole judge of truth, in endless error hurled:
The glory, jest, and riddle of the world!   [1733–34]

LADY MARY WORTLEY MONTAGU

England 1689–1762

A woman of independent means and mind, Montagu taught herself Latin, avoided an arranged marriage and eloped with a man she loved, helped introduce smallpox inoculation to England, and published nine numbers of a periodical titled *The Nonsense of Common-Sense* (1737–38) whose last number explicitly attacked male stereotypes. She enjoyed the friendship of the more lively members of London's literary circles, including Pope (though later Montagu became the 'furious Sappho' in his imitation of Horace's Second Satire, a portrait he composed in retaliation for her attack on his moral and artistic character in 'Verses Addressed to the Imitator of Horace'). Her published letters, written during her residence in Constantinople in 1716 where her husband was ambassador, express learning and sensitivity. Robert Halsband presented his three-volume edition of Montagu's letters in 1965–67, and, with Isobel Gundy, the *Essays and Poems and Simplicity, a Comedy,* in 1977.

from SIX TOWN ECLOGUES: WITH SOME OTHER POEMS

SATTURDAY: THE SMALL POX: FLAVIA

The wretched Flavia, on her Couch reclin'd,
Thus breath'd the Anguish of a wounded mind.
A Glass revers'd in her right hand she bore;
For now she shunn'd the Face she sought before.
     How am I chang'd! Alas, how am I grown
A frightfull Spectre to my selfe unknown!
Where's my Complexion, where the radiant bloom
That promis'd Happyness for Years to come?
Then, with what Pleasure I this Face survey'd!
To look once more, my Visits oft delay'd!
Charm'd with the veiw,* a fresher red would rise,
And a new Life shot sparkling from my Eyes.
Ah Faithless Glass, my wonted bloom restore!
Alas, I rave! that bloom is now no more!

Montagu's spelling is reproduced exactly from the original.

The Greatest Good the Gods on Men bestow,
Even Youth it selfe to me is useless now.
There was a Time, (Oh that I could forget!)
When Opera Tickets pour'd before my Feet,
And at the Ring where brightest Beauties shine,
The earliest Cherrys of the Park were mine.
Wittness oh Lilly! and thou Motteux tell!
How much Japan these Eyes have made you sell,
With what contempt you saw me oft despise
The humble Offer of the raffled Prize:
For at each raffle still the Prize I bore,
With Scorn rejected, or with Triumph wore:
Now Beautie's Fled, and Presents are no more.

  For me, the Patriot has the House forsook,
And left debates to catch a passing look,
For me, the Soldier has soft verses writ,
For me, the Beau has aim'd to be a Wit,
For me, the Wit to Nonsense was betraid,
The Gamester has for me his Dun delaid,
And overseen the Card, I would have paid.
The bold and Haughty, by Success made vain,
Aw'd by my Eyes has trembled to complain,
The bashful 'Squire touch'd with a wish unknown
Has dar'd to speak with Spirit not his own,
Fir'd by one Wish, all did alike Adore,
Now Beauty's fled, and Lovers are no more.

  As round the Room I turn my weeping Eyes,
New unaffected Scenes of Sorrow rise;
Far from my Sight that killing Picture bear,
The Face disfigure, or the Canvas tear!
That Picture, which with Pride I us'd to show,
The lost ressemblance but upbraids me now.
And thou my Toilette! where I oft have sate,
While Hours unheeded pass'd in deep Debate,
How Curls should fall, or where a Patch to place,
If Blue or Scarlet best became my Face;
Now on some happier Nymph thy Aid bestow,
On Fairer Heads, ye useless Jewells, glow!
No borrow'd Lustre can my Charms restore,
Beauty is fled, and Dress is now no more.

  Ye meaner Beauties, I permit you, shine,
Go triumph in the Hearts, that once were mine,
But midst your Triumphs, with Confusion know,
'Tis to my Ruin all your Charms ye owe.
Would pitying Heaven restore my wonted mein,
You still might move, unthought of, and unseen—

But oh, how vain, how wretched is the boast,
Of Beauty faded, and of Empire lost!
What now is left, but weeping to Deplore
My Beauty fled, and Empire now no more!
   Ye cruel Chymists, what with held your Aid?
Could no Pomatums save a trembling Maid?
How false and triffling is that Art you boast;
No Art can give me back my Beauty lost!
In tears surrounded by my Freinds I lay,
Mask'd o're, and trembling at the light of Day,
Mirmillo came my Fortune to deplore
(A golden headed Cane, well carv'd he bore),
Cordials, he cry'd, my Spirits must restore,—
Beauty is fled, and Spirit is no more!
Galen the Grave, Officious Squirt was there,
With fruitless Greife and unavailing Care;
Machaon too, the Great Machaon, known
By his red Cloak, and his Superior frown,
And why (he cry'd) this Greife, and this Dispair?
You shall again be well, again be fair,
Beleive my Oath (with that an Oath he swore),
False was his Oath! my Beauty is no more.
   Cease hapless Maid, no more thy Tale persue,
Forsake Mankind, and bid the World Adieu.
Monarchs, and Beauties rule with equal sway,
All strive to serve, and Glory to obey,
Alike unpity'd when depos'd they grow,
Men mock the Idol of their Former vow.
   'Adieu, ye Parks—in some obscure recess,
Where Gentle streams will weep at my distress,
Where no false Freind will in my Greife take part.
And mourn my Ruin with a Joyful Heart,
There let me live, in some deserted Place,
There hide in shades this lost Inglorious Face.
Operas, Circles, I no more must view!
My Toilette, Patches, all the World, Adieu!'   [1747]

MARY COLLIER

England c. 1690 – c. 1762

While Mr Duck's depiction of the Herculean response of the day labourer to field work in contrast
to the 'throng of prattling' idle females may have appealed to Queen Caroline, Collier's response,
published again by public subscription in 1762, argues that he so under-represents the true nature
of women's work that she must speak to right the 'wrong'. Born into poverty, Collier worked
throughout her life as a field hand, washer-woman, and farmhouse manager. Self-taught, she wrote
when she could. Collier had hoped to see some profit from the sale of 'The Woman's Labour' or
perhaps enjoy some patronage, but neither prospect materialized. Rather, she was often to defend
the authenticity of her verse against sceptics little disposed to accept even the novelty of an uned-
ucated woman poet. Her *Poems on Several Occasions* appeared in 1762.

THE WOMAN'S LABOUR: AN EPISTLE TO MR STEPHEN DUCK; IN ANSWER TO HIS LATE POEM, CALLED 'THE THRESHER'S LABOUR'

Immortal bard! thou fav'rite of the Nine!
Enrich'd by Peers, advanc'd by Caroline!
Deign to look down on one that's poor and low,
Rememb'ring you yourself was lately so;
Accept these lines: Alas! what can you have
From her, who ever was, and's still, a slave!
No learning ever was bestow'd on me;
My life was always spent in drudgery:
And not alone; alas! with grief I find,
It is the portion of poor woman-kind.
Oft have I thought as on my bed I lay,
Eas'd from the tiresome labours of the day,
Our first extraction from a mass refin'd,
Could never be for slavery design'd;
Till time and custom by degrees destroy'd
That happy state our sex at first enjoyed.
When men had us'd their utmost care and toil,
Their recompense was but a female smile;
When they by arts or arms were render'd great,
They laid their trophies at a woman's feet;
They, in those days, unto our sex did bring
Their hearts, their all, a free-will offering;
And as from us their being they derive,
They back again should all due homage give.

Jove once descending from the clouds, did drop
In show'rs of gold on lovely Danae's lap;
The sweet-tongu'd poets, in those generous days,
Unto our shrine still offer'd up their lays;

But now, alas! that Golden Age is past;
We are the objects of your scorn at last.
And you, great Duck, upon whose happy brow
The Muses seem to fix the garland now,
In your late *Poem* boldly did declare
Alcides' labours can't with your's compare;
And of your annual task have much to say,
Of threshing, reaping, mowing corn and hay;
Boasting your daily toil, and nightly dream,
But can't conclude your never-dying theme,
And let our hapless sex in silence lie
Forgotten, and in dark oblivion die;
But on our abject state you throw your scorn,
And women wrong, your verses to adorn.
You of hay-making speak a word or two,
As if our sex but little work could do:
This makes the honest farmer smiling say,
He'll seek for women still to make his hay;
For if his back be turn'd, their work they mind
As well as men, as far as he can find.
For my own part, I many a summer's day
Have spent in throwing, turning, making hay;
But ne'er could see, what you have lately found,
Our wages paid for sitting on the ground.
'Tis true, that when our morning's work is done,
And all our grass expos'd unto the sun,
While that his scorching beams do on it shine,
As well as you, we have a time to dine:
I hope, that since we freely toil and sweat
To earn our bread, you'll give us time to eat.
That over, soon we must get up again,
And nimbly turn our hay upon the plain;
Nay, rake and prow it in, the case is clear;
Or how should cocks in equal rows appear?
But if you'd have what you have wrote believ'd,
I find that you to hear us talk are griev'd:
In this, I hope, you do not speak your mind,
For none but Turks, that ever I could find,
Have Mutes to serve them, or did e'er deny
Their slaves, at work, to chat it merrily.
Since you have liberty to speak your mind,
And are to talk, as well as we, inclin'd,
Why should you thus repine, because that we,
Like you, enjoy that pleasing liberty?
What! would you lord it quite, and take away
The only privilege our sex enjoy?

When ev'ning does approach, we homeward hie,
And our domestic toils incessant ply:
Against your coming home prepare to get
Our work all done, our house in order set;
Bacon and dumpling in the pot we boil,
Our beds we make, our swine we feed the while;
Then wait at door to see you coming home,
And set the table out against you come:
Early next morning we on you attend;
Our children dress and feed, their cloaths we mend;
And in the field our daily task renew,
Soon as the rising sun has dry'd the dew.

When harvest comes, into the field we go,
And help to reap the wheat as well as you;
Or else we go the ears of corn to glean;
No labour scorning, be it e'er so mean;
But in the work we freely bear a part,
And what we can, perform with all our heart.
To get a living we so willing are,
Our tender babes into the field we bear,
And wrap them in our cloaths to keep them warm,
While round about we gather up the corn;
And often unto them our course do bend,
To keep them safe, that nothing them offend:
Our children that are able, bear a share
In gleaning corn, such is our frugal care.
When night comes on, unto our home we go,
Our corn we carry, and our infant too;
Weary, alas! but 'tis not worth our while
Once to complain, or *rest at ev'ry stile*;
We must make haste, for when we home are come,
Alas! we find our work has just begun;
So many things for our attendance call,
Had we ten hands, we could employ them all.
Our children put to bed, with greatest care
We all things for your coming home prepare:
You sup, and go to bed without delay,
And rest yourselves till the ensuing day;
While, we, alas! but little sleep can have,
Because our froward children cry and rave;
Yet, without fail, soon as daylight doth spring,
We in the field again our work begin,
And there, with all our strength, our toil renew,
Till *Titan's* golden rays have dry'd the dew;
Then home we go unto our children dear,

Dress, feed, and bring them to the field with care.
Were this your case, you justly might complain
That day nor night you are secure from pain;
Those mighty troubles which perplex your mind
(*Thistles* before, and *females* come behind),
Would vanish soon, and quickly disappear,
Were you, like us, encumber'd thus with care.
What you would have of us we do not know:
We oft take up the corn that you do mow;
We cut the peas, and always ready are
In ev'ry work to take our proper share;
And from the time that harvest doth begin,
Until the corn be cut and carry'd in,
Our toil and labour's daily so extreme,
That we have hardly ever *Time to dream*.

The harvest ended, respite none we find;
The hardest of our toil is still behind:
Hard labour we most cheerfully pursue,
And out, abroad, a charing often go:
Of which I now will briefly tell in part,
What fully to declare is past my art;
So many hardships daily we go through,
I boldly say, the like *you* never knew.

When bright Orion glitters in the skies
In winter nights, then early we must rise;
The weather ne'er so bad, wind, rain, or snow,
Our work appointed, we must rise and go;
While you on easy beds may lie and sleep,
Till light does thro' your chamber-windows peep.
When to the house we come where we should go,
How to get in, alas! we do not know:
The maid quite tir'd with work the day before,
O'ercome with sleep; we standing at the door
Oppress'd with cold, and often call in vain,
E're to our work we can admittance gain:
But when from wind and weather we get in,
Briskly with courage we our work begin;
Heaps of fine linen we before us view,
Whereon to lay our strength and patience too;
Cambricks and muslins, which our ladies wear,
Laces and edgings, costly, fine, and rare,
Which must be wash'd with utmost skill and care;
With holland shirts, ruffles and fringes too,
Fashions which our fore-fathers never knew.

For several hours here we work and slave,
Before we can one glimpse of day-light have;
We labour hard before the morning's past,
Because we fear the time runs on too fast.

At length bright Sol illuminates the skies,
And summons drowsy mortals to arise;
Then comes our mistress to us without fail,
And in her hand, *perhaps*, a mug of ale
To cheer our hearts, and also to inform
Herself what work is done that very morn;
Lays her commands upon us, that we mind
Her linen well, nor *leave the dirt behind*:
Not this alone, but also to take care
We don't her cambrics nor her ruffles tear;
And *these* most strictly does of us require,
To save her soap, and sparing be of fire;
Tells us her charge is great, nay furthermore,
Her clothes are fewer than the time before.
Now we drive on, resolv'd our strength to try,
And what we can, we do most willingly;
Until with heat and work, 'tis often known,
Not only sweat, but blood runs trickling down
Our wrists and fingers; still our work demands
The constant action of our lab'ring hands.

Now night comes on, from whence you have relief,
But that, alas! does but increase our grief;
With heavy hearts we often view the sun,
Fearing he'll set before our work is done;
For either in the morning, or at night,
We piece the summer's day with candle-light.
Tho' we all day with care our work attend,
Such is our fate, we know not when 'twill end:
When ev'ning's come, you homeward take your way,
We, till our work is done, are forc'd to stay;
And after all our toil and labour past,
Six-pence or eight-pence pays us off at last;
For all our pains, no prospect can we see
Attend us, but old age and poverty.

The washing is not all we have to do:
We oft change work for work as well as you.
Our mistress of her pewter doth complain,
And 'tis our part to make it clean again.
This work, tho' very hard and tiresome too,

Is not the worst we hapless females do:
When night comes on, and we quite weary are,
We scarce can count what falls unto our share;
Pots, kettles, sauce-pans, skillets, we may see,
Skimmers and ladles, and such trumpery,
Brought in to make complete our slavery.
Tho' early in the morning 'tis begun,
'Tis often very late before we've done;
Alas! our labours never know an end;
On brass and iron we our strength must spend;
Our tender fingers scratch and tear:
All this, and more, with patience we must bear.
Colour'd with dirt and filth we now appear;
Your threshing *sooty peas* will not come near.
All the perfections woman once could boast,
Are quite obscur'd, and altogether lost.

   Once more our mistress sends to let us know
She wants our help, because the beer runs low:
Then in much haste for brewing we prepare,
The vessels clean, and scald with greatest care;
Often at midnight from our bed we rise;
At other times, ev'n *that* will not suffice;
Our work at ev'ning oft we do begin,
And ere we've done, the night comes on again.
Water we pump, the copper we must fill,
Or tend the fire; for if we e'er stand still,
Like you, when threshing, we a watch must keep,
Our wort boils over if we dare to sleep.

   But to rehearse all labour is in vain,
Of which we very justly might complain:
For us, you see, but litle rest is found;
Our toil increases as the year runs round.
While you to Sisyphus yourselves compare,
With Danaus' daughters we may claim a share;
Fow while *he* labours hard against the hill,
Bottomless tubs of water *they* must fill.

   So the industrious bees do hourly strive
To bring their loads of honey to the hive;
Their sordid owners always reap the gains,
And poorly recompense their toil and pains.   [1739]

MARY COOPER

England c. 1700–1761

The first printed version of this alphabet rhyme appeared in a twelve-page primer compiled by 'T.W.', *A little book for little children: wherein are set down in a plain and pleasant way, directions for spelling, and other remarkable matters* (c. 1710). However, the most popular and widely reprinted version was this one published by Mary Cooper in *A child's new play-thing being a spelling-book intended to make the learning to read a diversion instead of a task* (2nd edition, 1743). Following the death of her husband, Thomas, Mary Cooper took over his business as a printer, publisher, and bookseller in Paternoster Row, London, from about 1742 until 1761. She also published two well-known collections of nursery rhymes, *Tom Thumb's Song Book* and *Tom Thumb's Pretty Song Book*. Cooper's alphabet was reprinted in a first American edition of *A child's new play-thing* published in Boston (1750) and under the title 'Tom Thumb's Alphabet' in *Tom Thumb's play-book to teach children their letters as soon as they can speak. Being a new and pleasing method to allure little ones in the first principles of learning* (1758). Her version also served as the text for the earliest known Canadian picture-book, *The Illustrated Comic Alphabet* (1859), by Amelia Frances Howard-Gibbon (1826–1874).

A WAS AN ARCHER, AND SHOT AT A FROG

A was an Archer, and shot at a Frog.
B was a Butcher who kept a great Dog.
C was a Captain, covered with Lace.
D was a Drunkard, with a red Face.
E was an Esquire, with pride on his Brow.
F was a Farmer and followed the Plough.
G was a Gamester, and he had ill Luck.
H was a Hunter and hunted a Buck.
J was a Joiner and built up a House.
K was a King and governed a Mouse.
L was a Lady, with a white Hand.
M was a Merchant to a foreign Land.
N was a Nobleman, gallant and bold.
O was an Oyster Wench, one that could scold.
P was a Parson who wore a silk gown.
Q was a Quaker who would not bow down.
R was a Robber, who wanted the Whip.
S was a Sailor who sailed in a Ship.
T was a Tinker who mended a Pot.
V was a Vintner, a very great Sot.
W was a Watchman, who guarded the door.
X was Xpensive and so became poor.
Y was a Youth who did not love School.
Z was a Zany, and looked like a Fool.

[1743]

JAMES THOMSON

Scotland/England 1700-1748

'Rule, Britannia' was composed by Thomson for *Alfred*, a masque (a court drama involving dance, disguise, elaborate sets, and political elements) which he wrote in collaboration with fellow Scottish playwright David Mallet. Thomson is most completely known as a landscape poet; his *The Seasons* (begun with 'Winter' in 1726) went through fifty printings from 1730 to 1800. Thomson's work exhibits the representative features of the eighteenth-century genre, Topographical Poetry: an emphasis on the descriptive integrity of the observing eye, an attachment to a survey of the scene below—usually nature 'methodized' in distinguished estates, parks, and gardens—and a conviction that the multi-dimensional properties of the divine are present in all aspects of external reality. The most scholarly edition of *The Seasons* is Sambrook's (1981).

A HYMN [ON THE SEASONS]

These, as they change, Almighty Father! these
Are but the varied God. The rolling year
Is full of thee. Forth in the pleasing Spring
Thy beauty walks, thy tenderness and love.
Wide flush the fields; the softening air is balm;
Echo the mountains round; the forest smiles;
And every sense, and every heart, is joy.
Then comes thy glory in the Summer months,
With light and heat refulgent. Then thy sun
Shoots full perfection through the swelling year;
And oft thy voice in dreadful thunder speaks;
And oft at dawn, deep noon, or falling eve,
By brooks and groves, in hollow-whispering gales.
Thy bounty shines in Autumn unconfined,
And spreads a common feast for all that lives.
In Winter, awful thou! with clouds and storms
Around thee thrown, tempest o'er tempest rolled,
Majestic darkness! on the whirlwind's wing
Riding sublime, thou bidd'st the world adore,
And humblest nature with thy northern blast.
    Mysterious round! what skill, what force divine,
Deep-felt, in these appear! a simple train,
Yet so delightful mixed, with such kind art,
Such beauty and beneficence combined,
Shade, unperceived, so softening into shade,
And all so forming an harmonious whole
That, as they still succeed, they ravish still.
But wandering oft, with brute unconscious gaze,
Man marks not thee, marks not the mighty hand,
That, ever busy, wheels the silent spheres,

Works in the secret deep, shoots steaming thence
The fair profusion that o'erspreads the Spring,
Flings from the sun direct the flaming day,
Feeds every creature, hurls the tempest forth,
And, as on earth this grateful change revolves,
With transport touches all the springs of life.
    Nature, attend! join every living soul
Beneath the spacious temple of the sky,
In adoration join; and, ardent, raise
One general song! To him, ye vocal gales,
Breathe soft, whose spirit in your freshness breathes:
Oh! talk of him in solitary glooms,
Where, o'er the rock, the scarcely-waving pine
Fills the brown shade with a religious awe.
And ye, whose bolder note is heard afar,
Who shake th' astonished world, lift high to heaven
Th' impetuous song, and say from whom you rage.
His praise, ye brooks, attune, ye trembling rills;
And let me catch it as I muse along.
Ye headlong torrents, rapid and profound;
Ye softer floods, that lead the humid maze
Along the vale; and thou, majestic main,
A secret world of wonders in thyself,
Sound his stupendous praise, whose greater voice
Or bids you roar, or bids your roarings fall.
Soft roll your incense, herbs, and fruits, and flowers,
In mingled clouds to him, whose sun exalts,
Whose breath perfumes you, and whose pencil paints.
Ye forest bend; ye harvests wave, to him;
Breathe your still song into the reaper's heart,
As home he goes beneath the joyous moon.
Ye that keep watch in heaven, as earth asleep
Unconscious lies, effuse your mildest beams,
Ye constellations! while your angels strike,
Amid the spangled sky, the silver lyre.
Great source of day! best image here below
Of thy Creator, ever pouring wide
From world to world the vital ocean round!
On nature write with every beam his praise.
The thunder rolls: be hushed the prostrate world;
While cloud to cloud returns the solemn hymn.
Bleat out afresh, ye hills; ye mossy rocks,
Retain the sound; the broad responsive low,
Ye valleys, raise; for the Great Shepherd reigns,
And his unsuffering kingdom yet will come.
Ye woodlands all, awake: a boundless song

Burst from the groves; and when the restless day,
Expiring, lays the warbling world asleep,
Sweetest of birds! sweet Philomela, charm
The listening shades, and teach the night his praise.
Ye chief, for whom the whole creation smiles,
At once the head, the heart, the tongue of all,
Crown the great hymn! in swarming cities vast,
Assembled men, to the deep organ join
The long-resounding voice, oft breaking clear,
At solemn pauses, through the swelling bass;
And, as each mingling flame increases each,
In one united ardour rise to heaven.
Or if you rather choose the rural shade,
And find a fane in every sacred grove,
There let the shepherd's flute, the virgin's lay,
The prompting seraph, and the poet's lyre,
Still sing the God of Seasons as they roll.
For me, when I forget the darling theme,
Whether the blossom blows, the Summer ray
Russets the plain, inspiring Autumn gleams,
Or Winter rises in the blackening east,
Be my tongue mute, may fancy paint no more,
And, dead to joy, forget my heart to beat!
    Should fate command me to the farthest verge
Of the green earth, to distant barbarous climes,
Rivers unknown to song, where first the sun
Gilds Indian mountains, or his setting beam
Flames on the Altantic isles, 'tis nought to me;
Since God is ever present, ever felt,
In the void waste as in the city full;
And where he vital spreads there must be joy.
When even at last the solemn hour shall come,
And wing my mystic flight to future worlds,
I cheerful will obey; there, with new powers,
Will rising wonders sing: I cannot go
Where Universal Love not smiles around,
Sustaining all yon orbs, and all their sons;
From seeming evil still educing good,
And better thence again, and better still,
In infinite progression. But I lose
Myself in him, in Light ineffable!
Come then, expressive Silence, muse his praise.   [1730]

ODE: RULE, BRITANNIA

1

When *Britain* first, at heaven's command,
  Arose from out the azure main;
This was the charter of the land,
  And guardian angels sung *this* strain:
    'Rule, *Britannia*, rule the waves;
    Britons never will be slaves.'

2

The nations, not so blest as thee,
  Must, in their turns, to tyrants fall:
While thou shalt flourish great and free,
  The dread and envy of them all.
    'Rule,' etc.

3

Still more majestic shalt thou rise,
  More dreadful, from each foreign stroke:
As the loud blast that tears the skies,
  Serves but to root thy native oak.
    'Rule,' etc.

4

Thee haughty tyrants ne'er shall tame:
  All their attempts to bend thee down,
Will but arouse thy generous flame;
  But work their woe, and thy renown.
    'Rule,' etc.

5

To thee belongs the rural reign;
  Thy cities shall with commerce shine:
All thine shall be the subject main,
  And every shore it circles thine.
    'Rule,' etc.

6

The Muses, still with freedom found,
  Shall to thy happy coast repair:
Blest isle! with matchless beauty crowned,
  And manly hearts to guard the fair.
    'Rule, *Britannia*, rule the waves;
    Britons never will be slaves.'

[1745–46]

THOMAS GRAY

England 1716-1771

This elegy is among the best known and best loved in English, praised by even the most severe of critics, Samuel Johnson (1709–84). Part of Gray's originality lies in his substituting references to native traditions and national histories for the classical allusions that were initially part of the verse. By absorbing his wide reading in Anglo-Saxon, English, Welsh, and Norse literatures, he foregrounds the indigenous character of the hamlet, its more illustrious members, and the 'obscure' yet significant life of the region. Standard editions of Gray's poems are by Starr and Hendrickson (1966) and Lonsdale (with Collins, 1977).

ELEGY WRITTEN IN A COUNTRY CHURCHYARD

The curfew tolls the knell of parting day,
The lowing herd wind slowly o'er the lea,
The ploughman homeward plods his weary way,
And leaves the world to darkness and to me.

Now fades the glimmering landscape on the sight,
And all the air a solemn stillness holds,
Save where the beetle wheels his droning flight,
And drowsy tinklings lull the distant folds;

Save that from yonder ivy-mantled tow'r
The moping owl does to the moon complain
Of such as, wand'ring near her secret bow'r,
Molest her ancient solitary reign.

Beneath those rugged elms, that yew-tree's shade,
Where heaves the turf in many a mould'ring heap,
Each in his narrow cell for ever laid,
The rude forefathers of the hamlet sleep.

The breezy call of incense-breathing Morn,
The swallow twitt'ring from the straw-built shed,
The cock's shrill clarion, or the echoing horn,
No more shall rouse them from their lowly bed.

For them no more the blazing hearth shall burn,
Or busy housewife ply her evening care;
No children run to lisp their sire's return,
Or climb his knees the envied kiss to share.

Oft did the harvest to their sickle yield,
Their furrow oft the stubborn glebe has broke;
How jocund did they drive their team afield!
How bowed the woods beneath their sturdy stroke!

Let not Ambition mock their useful toil,
Their homely joys and destiny obscure;
Nor Grandeur hear, with a disdainful smile,
The short and simple annals of the poor.

The boast of heraldry, the pomp of pow'r,
And all that beauty, all that wealth e'er gave,
Awaits alike th' inevitable hour.
The paths of glory lead but to the grave.

Nor you, ye Proud, impute to these the fault,
If Mem'ry o'er their tomb no trophies raise,
Where through the long-drawn aisle and fretted vault
The pealing anthem swells the note of praise.

Can storied urn or animated bust
Back to its mansion call the fleeting breath?
Can Honour's voice provoke the silent dust,
Or Flatt'ry soothe the dull cold ear of Death?

Perhaps in this neglected spot is laid
Some heart once pregnant with celestial fire;
Hands that the rod of empire might have swayed,
Or waked to ecstasy the living lyre.

But Knowledge to their eyes her ample page
Rich with the spoils of time did ne'er unroll;
Chill Penury repressed their noble rage,
And froze the genial current of the soul.

Full many a gem of purest ray serene
The dark unfathomed caves of ocean bear:
Full many a flower is born to blush unseen,
And waste its sweetness on the desert air.

Some village-Hampden that with dauntless breast
The little tyrant of his fields withstood;
Some mute inglorious Milton here may rest,
Some Cromwell guiltless of his country's blood.

Th' applause of list'ning senates to command,
The threats of pain and ruin to despise,
To scatter plenty o'er a smiling land,
And read their hist'ry in a nation's eyes,

Their lot forbade: nor circumscribed alone
Their growing virtues, but their crimes confined;
Forbade to wade through slaughter to a throne,
And shut the gates of mercy on mankind,

The struggling pangs of conscious truth to hide,
To quench the blushes of ingenuous shame,
Or heap the shrine of Luxury and Pride
With incense kindled at the Muse's flame.

Far from the madding crowd's ignoble strife
Their sober wishes never learned to stray;
Along the cool sequestered vale of life
They kept the noiseless tenor of their way.

Yet ev'n these bones from insult to protect
Some frail memorial still erected nigh,
With uncouth rhymes and shapeless sculpture decked,
Implores the passing tribute of a sigh.

Their name, their years, spelt by th' unlettered muse,
The place of fame and elegy supply:
And many a holy text around she strews,
That teach the rustic moralist to die.

For who to dumb Forgetfulness a prey,
This pleasing anxious being e'er resigned,
Left the warm precincts of the cheerful day,
Nor cast one longing ling'ring look behind?

On some fond breast the parting soul relies,
Some pious drops the closing eye requires;
Ev'n from the tomb the voice of Nature cries,
Ev'n in our ashes live their wonted fires.

For thee who, mindful of th' unhonoured dead,
Dost in these lines their artless tale relate;
If chance, by lonely Contemplation led,
Some kindred spirit shall inquire thy fate,

Haply some hoary-headed swain may say,
'Oft have we seen him at the peep of dawn
Brushing with hasty steps the dews away
To meet the sun upon the upland lawn.

'There at the foot of yonder nodding beech
That wreathes its old fantastic roots so high,
His listless length at noontide would he stretch,
And pore upon the brook that babbles by.

'Hard by yon wood, now smiling as in scorn,
Mutt'ring his wayward fancies he would rove,
Now drooping, woeful wan, like one forlorn,
Or crazed with care, or crossed in hopeless love.

'One morn I missed him on the customed hill,
Along the heath and near his fav'rite tree;
Another came; nor yet beside the rill,
Nor up the lawn, nor at the wood was he;

'The next with dirges due in sad array
Slow through the church-way path we saw him borne.
Approach and read (for thou canst read) the lay,
Graved on the stone beneath yon aged thorn.'

The Epitaph
Here rests his head upon the lap of Earth
A youth to Fortune and to Fame unknown.
Fair Science frowned not on his humble birth,
And Melancholy marked him for her own.

Large was his bounty, and his soul sincere,
Heav'n did a recompense as largely send:
He gave to Mis'ry all he had, a tear,
He gained from heav'n ('twas all he wished) a friend.

No farther seek his merits to disclose,
Or draw his frailties from their dread abode
(There they alike in trembling hope repose),
The bosom of his Father and his God.   [1751]

MARY LEAPOR

England 1722-1746

Leapor's working-class heritage, gender, and vocation make her one of the many eighteenth-century 'peasant poets', men and women with limited status and insufficient means whose learning was self-made and whose opportunities depended on the vagaries of patronage and public subscription. Under the pen name 'Mira' (also 'Myra'), Leapor wrote about disenfranchisement and privilege with her ear skilfully tuned to the heroic couplet, the mock epic, and the frailty of the species, especially the 'Stygian' effect of its hypocrisy and indifference. Leapor's *Poems upon Several Occasions* was published by subscription in 1748 (after she succumbed to measles), and a second volume of her work appeared in 1751.

AN ESSAY ON WOMAN

Woman, a pleasing but a short-lived flower,
Too soft for business and too weak for power:
A wife in bondage, or neglected maid;
Despised, if ugly; if she's fair, betrayed.
'Tis wealth alone inspires every grace,
And calls the raptures to her plenteous face.
What numbers for those charming features pine,
If blooming acres round her temples twine!
Her lip the strawberry, and her eyes more bright
Than sparkling Venus in a frosty night;
Pale lilies fade and, when the fair appears,
Snow turns a negro and dissolves in tears,
And, where the charmer treads her magic toe,
On English ground Arabian odours grow;
Till mighty Hymen lifts his sceptred rod,
And sinks her glories with a fatal nod,
Dissolves her triumphs, sweeps her charms away,
And turns the goddess to her native clay.

But, Artemisia, let your servant sing
What small advantage wealth and beauties bring.
Who would be wise, that knew Pamphilia's fate?
Or who be fair, and joined to Sylvia's mate?
Sylvia, whose cheeks are fresh as early day,
As evening mild, and sweet as spicy May:
And yet that face her partial husband tires,
And those bright eyes, that all the world admires.
Pamphilia's wit who does not strive to shun,
Like death's infection or a dog-day's sun?
The damsels view her with malignant eyes,
The men are vexed to find a nymph so wise:

And wisdom only serves to make her know
The keen sensation of superior woe.
The secret whisper and the listening ear,
The scornful eyebrow and the hated sneer,
The giddy censures of her babbling kind,
With thousand ills that grate a gentle mind,
By her are tasted in the first degree,
Though overlooked by Simplicus and me.
Does thirst of gold a virgin's heart inspire,
Instilled by nature or a careful sire?
Then let her quit extravagance and play,
The brisk companion and expensive tea,
To feast with Cordia in her filthy sty
On stewed potatoes or on mouldy pie;
Whose eager eyes stare ghastly at the poor,
And fright the beggars from her hated door;
In greasy clouts she wraps her smoky chin,
And holds that pride's a never-pardoned sin.

If this be wealth, no matter where it falls;
But save, ye Muses, save your Mira's walls:
Still give me pleasing indolence and ease,
A fire to warm me and a friend to please.

Since, whether sunk in avarice or pride,
A wanton virgin or a starving bride,
Or wondering crowds attend her charming tongue,
Or, deemed an idiot, ever speaks the wrong;
Though nature armed us for the growing ill
With fraudful cunning and a headstrong will;
Yet, with ten thousand follies to her charge,
Unhappy woman's but a slave at large.   [1751]

MERCY OTIS WARREN

USA 1728–1814

Warren lived with her husband James near Plymouth, Massachusetts. She was best known as an outspoken proponent of independence for the American colonies, a cause she furthered through her writing of patriotic histories and plays. Warren's philosophical, political, and religious poetry was collected and published under her name in 1890 as *Poems, Dramatic and Miscellaneous*, but for many years these poems had been published anonymously.

TO A YOUNG LADY

On shewing an excellent Piece of PAINTING, much faded

Come, and attend, my charming maid;
See how the gayest colours fade;
As beauteous paintings lose their dye,
Age sinks the lustre of your eye.

Then seize the minutes as they pass;
Behold! how swift runs down the glass;
The hasty sands that measure time,
Point you to pleasures more sublime;
And bid you shun the flow'ry path,
That cheats the millions into death.

Snatch every moment time shall give,
And uniformly virtuous live;
Let no vain cares retard thy soul,
But strive to reach the happy goal;
When pale, when unrelenting Death,
Shall say, resign life's vital breath!
May you, swift as the morning lark
That stems her course to heav'n's high arch,
Leave every earthly care, and soar,
Where numerous seraphims adore;
Thy pinions spread and wafted high,
Beyond the blue etherial sky,
May you there chant the glorious lays,
The carols of eternal praise,
To that exhaustless source of light,
Who rules the shadows of the night,
Who lends each orb its splendid ray,
And points the glorious beams of day.

Time and eternity he holds;
Nor all eternity unfolds,
The glories of Jehovah's name;
Nor highest angels can proclaim,
The wonders of his boundless grace,
They bow, and veil before his face.

What then shall mortals of an hour,
But bend submissive to his power;
And learn at wisdom's happy lore,
Nature's great author to adore.   [1790]

A THOUGHT ON THE INESTIMABLE BLESSING OF REASON, OCCASIONED BY ITS PRIVATION TO A FRIEND OF VERY SUPERIOR TALENTS AND VIRTUES, 1770

What is it moves within my soul,
And as the needle to the pole,
Directs me to the final cause,
The central point of nature's laws?
'Tis reason, Lord, which thou hast given,
A ray divine, let down from Heaven,
A spark struck from effulgent light,
Transcendent, clear, divinely bright,
Thou hast bestow'd lest man should grope
In endless darkness, void of hope.
    Creative being! who reason gave,
And by whose aid the powers we have
To think, to judge, to will, to know,
From whom these reasoning powers flow,
Thy name be ever magnified
That thus to angels we're allied,
Distinguish'd thus in the great chain,
Nor left the least in thy domain.
    Yet should'st thou but a moment frown,
Or wink this boasted reason down,
'Twould level proud imperious man
With the least worm in nature's plan.
Then humbly will I Thee implore,
Whom worlds of rationals adore,
That thou this taper should preserve,
From reason's laws let me ne'er swerve,
But calmly, mistress of my mind,
A friend to virtue and mankind,
Oh! gently lead me on to peace,
May years the heavenly gleam increase,

Nor waste beneath the frown of age
As I tread down time's narrow stage,
But brighter burn as life decays,
More fit to join the heavenly lays.
And when the tenement shall fall,
When broken down this feeble wall,
Then may the glad enlighten'd soul
Freed from these clogs, this dull control,
Expand her wings, shake off her load,
And rise to glorify her God.   [1790]

OLIVER GOLDSMITH

Ireland/England c. 1730-1774

Goldsmith believed that rural depopulation was a consequence of an eighteenth-century scorched-earth policy embraced by an emerging commercial class determined to transform common property into private enclosure. Combining elements of pastoral elegy, Topographical Poetry, and a pre-Romantic emphasis on the subjective experience of the poet, Goldsmith's evocation of rural innocence and a lost order appeared to detractors as a beautifully constructed but idiosyncratic fantasy barely accountable to existing conditions. Others found Goldsmith's lament prophetic, his nostalgia significant, and his politics sensitive to a real tension that existed between material and spiritual conceptions of well-being. Goldsmith's body of work, including his two comedies *The Good-Natured Man* (1768) and *She Stoops to Conquer* (1773), was edited by Arthur Friedman in 1966.

from THE DESERTED VILLAGE

TO SIR JOSHUA REYNOLDS
DEAR SIR,
I can have no expectations in an address of this kind, either to add to your reputation, or to establish my own. You can gain nothing from my admiration, as I am ignorant of that art in which you are said to excel; and I may lose much by the severity of your judgment, as few have a juster taste in poetry than you. Setting interest therefore aside, to which I never paid much attention, I must be indulged at present in following my affections. The only dedication I ever made was to my brother, because I loved him better than most other men. He is since dead. Permit me to inscribe this Poem to you.

How far you may be pleased with the versification and mere mechanical parts of this attempt, I do not pretend to enquire; but I know you will object (and indeed several of our best and wisest friends concur in the opinion) that the depopulation it deplores is no where to be seen, and the disorders it laments are only to be found in the poet's own imagination. To this I can scarcely make any other answer than that I sincerely believe what I have written; that I have taken all possible pains, in my country's excursions, for these four or five years past, to be certain of what I allege; and that all my views and enquiries have led me to believe those miseries real, which I here attempt to display. But this is not the place to enter into an enquiry, whether the country be depopulating, or not; the discussion would take up much room, and I should prove myself, at best, an indifferent politician, to tire the reader with a long preface, when I want his unfatigued attention to a long poem.

In regretting the depopulation of the country, I inveigh against the increase of our luxuries; and here also I expect the shout of modern politicians against me. For twenty or thirty years past, it has been the fashion to consider luxury as one of the greatest national advantages; and all the wisdom of antiquity in that particular, as erroneous. Still, however, I must remain a professed ancient on that head, and continue to think those luxuries prejudicial to states, by which so many vices are introduced, and so many kingdoms have been undone. Indeed so much has been poured out of late on the other side of the question, that, merely for the sake of novelty and variety, one would sometimes wish to be in the right.

> I am, Dear Sir,
> Your sincere friend, and ardent admirer,
> OLIVER GOLDSMITH.

Sweet Auburn, loveliest village of the plain,
Where health and plenty cheered the labouring swain,
Where smiling spring its earliest visit paid,
And parting summer's lingering blooms delayed:
Dear lovely bowers of innocence and ease,
Seats of my youth, when every sport could please,
How often have I loitered o'er thy green,
Where humble happiness endeared each scene;
How often have I paused on every charm,
The sheltered cot, the cultivated farm,
The never-failing brook, the busy mill,
The decent church that topped the neighbouring hill,
The hawthorn bush, with seats beneath the shade,
For talking age and whispering lovers made.
How often have I blessed the coming day,
When toil remitting lent its turn to play,
And all the village train, from labour free,
Led up their sports beneath the spreading tree,
While many a pastime circled in the shade,
The young contending as the old surveyed;
And many a gambol frolicked o'er the ground,
And sleights of art and feats of strength went round.
And still as each repeated pleasure tired,
Succeeding sports the mirthful band inspired;
The dancing pair that simply sought renown,
By holding out to tire each other down;

The swain mistrustless of his smutted face,
While secret laughter tittered round the place;
The bashful virgin's sidelong looks of love,
The matron's glance that would those looks reprove.
These were thy charms, sweet village; sports like these,
With sweet succession, taught even toil to please;
These round thy bowers their cheerful influence shed,
These were thy charms—but all these charms are fled.
    Sweet smiling village, loveliest of the lawn,
Thy sports are fled and all thy charms withdrawn;
Amidst thy bowers the tyrant's hand is seen,
And desolation saddens all thy green:
One only master grasps the whole domain,
And half a tillage stints thy smiling plain.
No more thy glassy brook reflects the day,
But, choked with sedges, works its weedy way.
Along thy glades, a solitary guest,
The hollow-sounding bittern guards its nest;
Amidst thy desert walks the lapwing flies,
And tires their echoes with unvaried cries.
Sunk are thy bowers in shapeless ruin all,
And the long grass o'ertops the mouldering wall;
And trembling, shrinking from the spoiler's hand,
Far, far away, thy children leave the land.
    Ill fares the land, to hastening ills a prey,
Where wealth accumulates and men decay:
Princes and lords may flourish or may fade;
A breath can make them, as a breath has made;
But a bold peasantry, their country's pride,
When once destroyed, can never be supplied.
    A time there was, ere England's griefs began,
When every rood of ground maintained its man;
For him light labour spread her wholesome store,
Just gave what life required, but gave no more:
His best companions, innocence and health;
And his best riches, ignorance of wealth.
    But times are altered; trade's unfeeling train
Usurp the land and dispossess the swain;
Along the lawn, where scattered hamlets rose,
Unwieldy wealth and cumbrous pomp repose;
And every want to opulence allied,
And every pang that folly pays to pride.
These gentle hours that plenty bade to bloom,
Those calm desires that asked but little room,
Those healthful sports that graced the peaceful scene,
Lived in each look and brightened all the green;

These, far departing, seek a kinder shore,
And rural mirth and manners are no more.
   Sweet Auburn! parent of the blissful hour,
Thy glades forlorn confess the tyrant's power.
Here as I take my solitary rounds,
Amidst thy tangling walks and ruined grounds,
And, many a year elapsed, return to view
Where once the cottage stood, the hawthorn grew,
Remembrance wakes with all her busy train,
Swells at my breast and turns the past to pain.
   In all my wanderings round this world of care,
In all my griefs—and God has given my share—
I still had hopes my latest hours to crown,
Amidst these humble bowers to lay me down;
To husband out life's taper at the close
And keep the flame from wasting by repose.
I still had hopes, for pride attends us still,
Amidst the swains to show my book-learned skill,
Around my fire an evening group to draw,
And tell of all I felt and all I saw;
And, as an hare whom hounds and horns pursue,
Pants to the place from whence at first she flew,
I still had hopes, my long vexations past,
Here to return—and die at home at last.
   O blest retirement, friend to life's decline,
Retreats from care that never must be mine,
How happy he who crowns in shades like these
A youth of labour with an age of ease;
Who quits a world where strong temptations try,
And, since 'tis hard to combat, learns to fly.
For him no wretches, born to work and weep,
Explore the mine or tempt the dangerous deep;
No surly porter stands in guilty state
To spurn imploring famine from the gate;
But on he moves to meet his latter end,
Angels around befriending virtue's friend;
Bends to the brave with unperceived decay,
While resignation gently slopes the way;
And, all his prospects brightening to the last,
His heaven commences ere the world be past!
   Sweet was the sound, when oft at evening's close
Up yonder hill the village murmur rose;
There, as I passed with careless steps and slow,
The mingling notes came softened from below;
The swain responsive as the milkmaid sung,
The sober herd that lowed to meet their young;

The noisy geese that gabbled o'er the pool,
The playful children just let loose from school;
The watchdog's voice that bayed the whispering wind,
And the loud laugh that spoke the vacant mind;
These all in sweet confusion sought the shade,
And filled each pause the nightingale had made.
But now the sounds of population fail,
No cheerful murmurs fluctuate in the gale,
No busy steps the grassgrown foot-way tread,
For all the bloomy flush of life is fled.
All but yon widowed, solitary thing
That feebly bends beside the plashy spring;
She, wretched matron, forced, in age, for bread,
To strip the brook with mantling cresses spread,
To pick her wintry faggot from the thorn,
To seek her nightly shed and weep till morn;
She only left of all the harmless train,
The sad historian of the pensive plain.   [1770]

JOHN DICKINSON

America 1732–1808

Dickinson, the author of this popular American Patriot ballad, was a lawyer, politician, and writer
who lived in Philadelphia; he published *Letters from a Farmer in Pennsylvania* in 1768.

THE LIBERTY SONG

Come join hand in hand, brave Americans all,
And rouse your bold hearts at fair Liberty's call;
No tyrannous acts, shall suppress your just claim,
Or stain with dishonor America's name.
    In freedom we're born, and in freedom we'll live;
        Our purses are ready
        Steady, Friends, steady,
    Not as *slaves*, but as *freemen* our money we'll give.

Our worthy forefathers—let's give them a cheer—
To climates unknown did courageously steer;
Thro' oceans to deserts, for freedom they came,
And, dying, bequeath'd us their freedom and fame.

Their generous bosoms all dangers despis'd,
So highly, so wisely, their birthrights they priz'd;
We'll keep what they gave, we will piously keep,
Nor frustrate their toils on the land or the deep.

The Tree, their own hands had to Liberty rear'd,
They lived to behold growing strong and rever'd;
With transport then cried,—'Now our wishes we gain,
For our children shall gather the fruits of our pain.'

How sweet are the labors that freemen endure,
That they shall enjoy all the profit, secure,—
No more such sweet labors Americans know,
If Britons shall reap what Americans sow.

Swarms of placemen and pensioners soon will appear,
Like locusts deforming the charms of the year:
Suns vainly will rise, showers vainly descend,
If we are to drudge for what others shall spend.

Then join hand in hand brave Americans all,
By uniting we stand, by dividing we fall;
In so righteous a cause let us hope to succeed,
For Heaven approves of each generous deed.

All ages shall speak with amaze and applause,
Of the courage we'll show in support of our laws;
To die we can bear,—but to serve we disdain,
For shame is to freemen more dreadful than pain.

This bumper I crown for our sovereign's health,
And this for Britannia's glory and wealth:
That wealth, and that glory immortal may be,
If she is but just, and we are but free.
     In freedom we're born, &c.   [1768]

ANNA SEWARD

Scotland 1742–1809

Known as the 'Swan of Lichfield' and much admired by Sir Walter Scott who edited a three-volume presentation of her work in 1810, Seward was inspired by the classical tradition of English literature her father favoured even though his fear of producing 'that dreaded phenomenon, a learned lady' (Scott, Biographical Preface to *The Poetical Works*, ix), prompted him to deny her access to the study of poetry for a period of ten years. It was not until the tragic loss of her younger sister Sarah, just before Sarah's marriage and Anna's own coming of age, that he allowed her poetic interests freer rein.

THE LAKE; OR, MODERN IMPROVEMENT IN LANDSCAPE

Grand, ancient, gothic, mark this ample dome,
Of fashion's slave, the uncongenial home!
Long have its turrets braved the varying clime,
And mock'd the ravage of relentless time.

  The owner shrugs his shoulders, and deplores
One vile effect of his self-squander'd stores,
That the triste edifice must still remain
To shock his lordship's gaze, and blot the plain;
That no gay villa may supply its place,
Rise in Italian, or in Gallic grace.

  'But, yet,' he cries, 'by Fashion's aid divine,
'Rescued from sylvan shrouds, my scenes may shine;
'Resistless goddess, to thy votary come,
'And chace the horrors of this leafy gloom!'

  She comes!—the gaudy despot stands confest,
Known by her mien assur'd, and motley vest;
The vest, mistaken by her servile train
For beauty's robe of sky-enwoven grain,
Deck'd with each varying form, each living hue,
That Nature hallow'd, and her REPTON drew.

  Scorning their power, and reckless of expense,
The foe of beauty, and the bane of sense;
Close by my lord, and with strange projects warm,
Stalks o'er the scenes her edicts shall deform.

  'Yon broad, brown wood, now darkening to the sky,
'Shall prostrate soon with perish'd branches lie;
'Yield golden treasures for our great design,
'Till all the scene one glassy surface shine.'

Mid shrubs, and tangled grass, with sparkling waves,
A little vagrant brook the valley laves;
Now hid, now seen, the wanton waters speed,
Hurrying loquacious o'er their pebbly bed.

'A Lake! she cries, this source can never fail,
'A lake shall fill our undulating dale!
'No more the dingles shall sink dark and deep,
'No waving hedgerows round the meadows sweep;
'All must be Lake this level lawn between,
'And those bare hills, and rocks, that form the screen,
'Peer o'er the yet proud woods, and close the scene.'

What recks it her that, many a tedious year,
Barren and bleak its naked banks appear!
Since, tho' the pliant Naiad swiftly pours
Her urn exhaustless to receding shores,
Sullen and tardy found, the Dryad train
Are still, thro' circling seasons, woo'd in vain,
Ere the dusk umbrage shall luxuriant flow,
And shadowy tremble o'er the lake below;
Which curtain'd thus, changes its leaden hue,
Rising a silver mirror to the view.

See, at the pert behest, subservient toil
Plough with the victim woods the echoing soil!
See, the forced flood th' o'erwhelmed valley laves,
O'er fields, lanes, thickets, spread the silent waves!—
No lively hue of spring they know to wear,
No gorgeous glow of the consummate year;
No tinge that gold-empurpled autumn spreads
O'er the rich woodland, sloping from the meads,
But stagnant, mute, unvarying, cold, and pale,
They meet the winter-wind, and summer-gale.

Between the base of yonder gothic pile,
Whose towers frown sullen o'er the wat'ry spoil,
And the chill lake's uncomfortable breast,
Lo! on the lawn, with venerable crest,
A few old oaks defend the tired survey,
In part, from that dull pool's eternal grey;
While, gleaming, underneath their darksome boughs,
With better grace the torpid water shows.
Again the dame her swarthy agents calls,
Raised is the ready axe—and—ah! it falls!
They who had seen whole centuries roll away,
No more half-veil the lake, and mitigate the day.

Too late the slumbering Genius of the scene
Starts from his mossy couch, with wilder'd mien;
Dismay'd beholds, and all too late to save,
His graces destined to a watery grave;
His winding brook, green wood, and mead and dell,
His grassy lanes, and moss-encircled well;
And for the guardian oaks, now prostrate laid,
His winter screen, his sultry summer's shade,
Sees the weak saplings, dotted on the lawn,
With dark and clumsy fence around them drawn,
Warp in the noon-tide ray, with shrivell'd rind,
And shrink, and tremble in the rising wind.

In vain he curses the fantastic power,
And the pale ravage of her idiot-hour;
But no vindictive ire the spell revokes,
Fall'n are the woods, and lawn-adorning oaks!
Fled every varied charm boon Nature gave,
No green field blossoms, and no hedge-rows wave!
On the dim waters nods the useless sail,
And Eurus howls along the deluged vale.

His reign usurp'd, since Time can ne'er restore,
Indignant rising to return no more,
His eyes concealing with one lifted hand,
Shadowing the waters, as his wings expand,
The injured Genius seeks the distant coast,
Like Abdiel, flying from the rebel host.   [1810]

ANNA LAETITIA (AIKEN) BARBAULD

England 1743-1825

Barbauld felt that her early publications in poetry and prose placed her 'out of the bounds of female reserve', a position she did not at first encourage among her sex. Her later pamphlets and occasional pieces which critiqued discriminatory policies in matters of religion, sex, and race were met with insult. Thus reviled, she retreated from public life and according to the Memoir prepared by Lucy Aiken as part of the two-volume *Works of Anna Laetitia Barbauld* (1825), Barbauld 'even laid aside the intention which she had entertained of preparing a new edition of her Poems.'

EPISTLE TO WILLIAM WILBERFORCE, ESQ. ON THE REJECTION OF THE BILL FOR ABOLISHING THE SLAVE TRADE, 1791

Cease, Wilberforce, to urge thy generous aim!
Thy Country knows the sin, and stands the shame!
The Preacher, Poet, Senator in vain
Has rattled in her sight the Negro's chain;
With his deep groans assailed her startled ear,
And rent the veil that hid his constant tear;
Forced her averted eyes his stripes to scan,
Beneath the bloody scourge laid bare the man,
Claimed Pity's tear, urged Conscience' strong controul,
And flashed conviction on her shrinking soul.
The Muse too, soon awaked, with ready tongue
At Mercy's shrine applausive pæans rung;
And Freedom's eager sons in vain foretold
A new Astrean reign, an age of gold:
She knows and she persists—Still Afric bleeds,
Unchecked, the human traffic still proceeds;
She stamps her infamy to future time,
And on her hardened forehead seals the crime.

In vain, to thy white standard gathering round,
Wit, Worth, and Parts and Eloquence are found:
In vain, to push to birth thy great design,
Contending chiefs, and hostile virtues join;
All, from conflicting ranks, of power possesst
To rouse, to melt, or to inform the breast.
Where seasoned tools of Avarice prevail,
A Nation's eloquence, combined, must fail:
Each flimsy sophistry by turns they try;
The plausive argument, the daring lie,
The artful gloss, that moral sense confounds,
Th' acknowledged thirst of gain that honour wounds:
Bane of ingenuous minds!—th' unfeeling sneer,

Which sudden turns to stone the falling tear:
They search assiduous, with inverted skill,
For forms of wrong, and precedents of ill;
With impious mockery wrest the sacred page,
And glean up crimes from each remoter age:
Wrung Nature's tortures, shuddering, while you tell,
From scoffing fiends bursts forth the laugh of hell;
In Britain's senate, Misery's pangs give birth
To jests unseemly, and to horrid mirth—
Forbear!—thy virtues but provoke our doom,
And swell th' account of vengeance yet to come;
For, not unmarked in Heaven's impartial plan,
Shall man, proud worm, contemn his fellow-man!
And injured Afric, by herself redresst,
Darts her own serpents at her tyrant's breast.
Each vice, to minds depraved by bondage known,
With sure contagion fastens on his own;
In sickly languors melts his nerveless frame,
And blows to rage impetuous Passion's flame:
Fermenting swift, the fiery venom gains
The milky innocence of infant veins;
There swells the stubborn will, damps learning's fire,
The whirlwind wakes of uncontrouled desire,
Scars the young heart to images of woe,
And blasts the buds of Virtue as they blow.

Lo! where reclined, pale Beauty courts the breeze,
Diffused on sofas of voluptuous ease;
With anxious awe her menial train around
Catch her faint whispers of half-uttered sound;
See her, in monstrous fellowship, unite
At once the Scythian and the Sybarite!
Blending repugnant vices, misallied,
Which frugal nature purposed to divide;
See her, with indolence to fierceness joined,
Of body delicate, infirm of mind,
With languid tones imperious mandates urge;
With arm recumbent wield the household scourge;
And with unruffled mien, and placid sounds,
Contriving torture, and inflicting wounds.

Nor, in their palmy walks and spicy groves,
The form benign of rural Pleasure roves;
No milk-maid's song, or hum of village talk,
Soothes the lone poet in his evening walk:
No willing arm the flail unwearied plies,

Where the mixed sounds of cheerful labour rise;
No blooming maids and frolic swains are seen
To pay gay homage to their harvest queen:
No heart-expanding scenes their eyes must prove
Of thriving industry and faithful love:
But shrieks and yells disturb the balmy air,
Dumb sullen looks of woe announce despair,
And angry eyes through dusky features glare.
Far from the sounding lash the Muses fly,
And sensual riot drowns each finer joy.

Nor less from the gay East, on essenced wings,
Breathing unnamed perfumes, Contagion springs;
The soft luxurious plague alike pervades
The marble palaces and rural shades;
Hence thronged Augusta builds her rosy bowers,
And decks in summer wreaths her smoky towers;
And hence, in summer bowers, Art's costly hand
Pours courtly splendours o'er the dazzled land:
The manners melt;—one undistinguished blaze
O'erwhelms the sober pomp of elder days;
Corruption follows with gigantic stride,
And scarce vouchsafes his shameless front to hide:
The spreading leprosy taints every part,
Infects each limb, and sickens at the heart.
Simplicity, most dear of rural maids,
Weeping reigns her violated shades:
Stern Independence from his glebe retires,
And anxious Freedom eyes her drooping fires;
By foreign wealth are British morals changed,
And Afric's sons, and India's, smile avenged.

For you, whose tempered ardour long has borne
Untired the labour, and unmoved the scorn;
In Virtue's fasti be inscribed your fame,
And uttered yours with Howard's honoured name;
Friends of the friendless—Hail, ye generous band!
Whose efforts yet arrest Heaven's lifted hand,
Around whose steady brows, in union bright,
The civic wreath and Christian's palm unite:
Your merit stands, no greater and no less,
Without, or with the varnish of success:
But seek no more to break a nation's fall,
For ye have saved yourselves—and that is all.
Succeeding times your struggles, and their fate,
With mingled shame and triumph shall relate;

While faithful History, in her various page,
Marking the features of this motley age,
To shed a glory, and to fix a stain,
Tells how you strove, and that you strove in vain.   [1825]

THE RIGHTS OF WOMAN

Yes, injured Woman! rise, assert thy right!
Woman! too long degraded, scorned, opprest;
O born to rule in partial Law's despite,
Resume thy native empire o'er the breast!

Go forth arrayed in panoply divine;
That angel pureness which admits no stain;
Go, bid proud Man his boasted rule resign,
And kiss the golden sceptre of thy reign.

Go, gird thyself with grace; collect thy store
Of bright artillery glancing from afar;
Soft melting tones thy thundering cannon's roar,
Blushes and fears thy magazine of war.

Thy rights are empire: urge no meaner claim,—
Felt, not defined, and if debated, lost;
Like sacred mysteries, which withheld from fame,
Shunning discussion, are revered the most.

Try all that wit and art suggest to bend
Of thy imperial foe the stubborn knee;
Make treacherous Man thy subject, not thy friend;
Thou mayst command, but never canst be free.

Awe the licentious, and restrain the rude;
Soften the sullen, clear the cloudy brow:
Be, more than princes' gifts, thy favours sued;—
She hazards all, who will the least allow.

But hope not, courted idol of mankind,
On this proud eminence secure to stay;
Subduing and subdued, thou soon shalt find
Thy coldness soften, and thy pride give way.

Then, then, abandon each ambitious thought,
Conquest or rule thy heart shall feebly move,
In Nature's school, by her soft maxims taught,
That separate rights are lost in mutual love.   [1825]

SUSANNA BLAMIRE

Scotland 1747-1794

Blamire's work came to public attention through the combined efforts of Patrick Maxwell and Dr Henry Carlisle. Their persistence led to the 1842 edition of *The Poetical Works of Miss Susanna Blamire*, 'The Muse of Cumberland'—material that had been circulated anonymously by Blamire in musical miscellanies or found in the safekeeping of family members. 'I've Gotten a Rock, I've Gotten a Reel' offers a deft counterpoint to the male seducer Marvell sets up in 'To His Coy Mistress'. Both Marvell and Blamire preferred the 'shorten'd measure' of an octosyllabic line rather than the established ten-syllable heroic couplet as the medium within which to show their appreciation for the devious character of the 'make haste while the sun shines' advance.

I'VE GOTTEN A ROCK, I'VE GOTTEN A REEL

I've gotten a rock, I've gotten a reel,
I've gotten a wee bit spinning-wheel;
An' by the whirling rim I've found
How the weary, weary warl goes round.
'Tis roun' an' roun' the spokes they go,
Now ane is up, an' ane is low;
'Tis by ups and downs in Fortune's wheel,
That mony ane gets a rock to reel.

I've seen a lassie barefoot gae,
Look dashed an' blate, wi' nought to say;
But as the wheel turned round again,
She chirped an' talked, nor seemed the same:
Sae fine she goes, sae far aglee,
That folks she kenned she canna see;
An' fleeching chiels around her thrang,
Till she miskens her a' day lang.

There's Jock, when the bit lass was poor,
Ne'er trudged o'er the lang mossy moor,
Though now to the knees he wades, I trow,
Through winter's weet an' winter's snow:
An' Pate declared the ither morn
She was like a lily amang the corn;
Though ance he swore her dazzling een
Were bits o' glass that blacked had been.

Now, lassies, I hae found it out,
What men make a' this phrase about;
For when they praise your blinking ee,
'Tis certain that your gowd they see:

An' when they talk o' roses bland,
They think o' the roses o' your land;
But should dame Fortune turn her wheel,
They'd aff in a dance of a threesome reel.   [1842]

CHARLOTTE SMITH

England 1749-1806

Driven to write professionally by an extravagant, bankrupt husband, Smith supported herself and
her ten children (she ultimately had twelve) initially while resident in debtor's prison, publishing
a book almost yearly. Her works include Gothic novels, English translations of French children's
stories, a series of legal cases presented as *The Romance of Real Life*, and verse. The immensely
popular *Elegiac Sonnets and Other Essays* (1784) went through 11 editions by 1851. Influenced by
the ideals of Jean-Jacques Rousseau, Smith's work anticipates the Romantics; her compassion for
the poor and the disenfranchised is haunted by her own 30-year struggle to recover something of
the large estate left to her children by their paternal grandfather. *The Poems Of Charlotte Smith* (ed.
Curran) was published in 1993.

'THE DEAD BEGGAR, AN ELEGY ADDRESSED TO A LADY, WHO WAS AFFECTED AT SEEING THE FUNERAL OF A NAMELESS PAUPER, BURIED AT THE EXPENCE OF THE PARISH, IN THE CHURCH-YARD AT BRIGHTHELMSTONE, IN NOVEMBER 1792'

Swells then thy feeling heart, and streams thine eye
    O'er the deserted being, poor and old,
Whom cold, reluctant, Parish Charity
    Consigns to mingle with his kindred mould?

Mourn'st thou, that *here* the time-worn sufferer ends
    Those evil days still threatening woes to come;
Here, where the friendless feel no want of friends,
    Where even the housless wanderer finds an home?

What tho' no kindred crowd in sable forth,
    And sigh, or seem to sigh, around his bier;
Tho' o'er his coffin with the humid earth
    No children drop the unavailing tear?
Rather rejoice that *here* his sorrows cease,
    Whom sickness, age, and poverty oppress'd;
Where Death, the Leveller, restores to peace
    The wretch who living knew not where to rest.

Rejoice, that tho' an outcast spurn'd by fate,
   Thro' penury's rugged path his race he ran;
In earth's cold bosom, equall'd with the great,
   Death vindicates the insulted rights of Man.

Rejoice, that tho' severe his earthly doom,
   And rude, and sown with thorns the way he trod,
Now, (where unfeeling Fortune cannot come)
   He rests upon the mercies of his God.   [1792]

LADY ANNE LINDSAY

Scotland 1750–1825

Family members had known of Lindsay's version of this old Scottish air ('The Bridegroom greets when the Sun gangs down'), but she felt her ability as a writer would discomfort those 'who could write nothing'. Lindsay's 'secret' offered little recompense; while the ballad was welcomed with enthusiasm, Lindsay was left to hug herself in 'obscurity'. This is the only poem for which Lindsay is known, though she was well established in literary and political salons in Edinburgh and London.

AULD ROBIN GRAY

When the sheep are in the fauld, when the cows come hame,
When a' the weary world to quiet rest are gane,
The woes of my heart fa' in showers frae my ee,
Unken'd by my gudeman, who soundly sleeps by me.

Young Jamie loo'd me weel, and sought me for his bride;
But saving ae crown-piece, he'd naething else beside.
To make the crown a pound, my Jamie gaed to sea;
And the crown and the pound, oh! they were baith for me!

Before he had been gane a twelvemonth and a day,
My father brak his arm, our cow was stown away;
My mither she fell sick—my Jamie was at sea—
And auld Robin Gray, oh! he came a-courting me.

My father cou'dna work, my mother cou'dna spin;
I toil'd day and night, but their bread I cou'dna win;
And Rob maintain'd them baith, and, wi' tears in his ee,
Said, 'Jenny, oh! for their sakes, will you marry me?'

My heart it said na, and I look'd for Jamie back;
But hard blew the winds, and his ship was a wrack:
His ship it was a wrack! Why didna Jenny dee?
Or, wherefore am I spared to cry out, Woe is me!

My father argued sair—my mother didna speak,
But she look'd in my face till my heart was like to break:
They gied him my hand, but my heart was in the sea;
And so auld Robin Gray, he was gudeman to me.

I hadna been his wife, a week but only four,
When mournfu' as I sat on the stane at my door,
I saw my Jamie's ghaist—I cou'dna think it he,
Till he said, 'I'm come hame, my love, to marry thee!'

O sair, sair did we greet, and mickle say of a';
Ae kiss we took, nae mair—I bade him gang awa.
I wish that I were dead, but I'm no like to dee;
For O, I am but young to cry out, Woe is me!

I gang like a ghaist, and I carena much to spin;
I darena think o' Jamie, for that wad be a sin.
But I will do my best a gude wife aye to be,
For auld Robin Gray, oh! he is sae kind to me.   [1776]

PHILIP FRENEAU

USA 1752–1832

Freneau, born in New York and educated at Princeton, was the most prolific and political poet of the American revolutionary and early nationalist period. He is appreciated today for his meditative, lyric poems on the frailty of human and physical nature. In these, he draws on his interests in speculative theology and philosophy. His works include *A Poem on the Rising Glory of America* (1771) (co-written with Hugh Henry Brackenridge), 'The Power of Fancy' (1770), 'The House of Night' (1779), and 'To Sir Toby' (1792).

THE INDIAN BURYING GROUND

In spite of all the learned have said,
I still my old opinion keep;
The *posture*, that *we* give the dead,
Points out the soul's eternal sleep.

Not so the ancients of these lands—
The Indian, when from life released,
Again is seated with his friends,
And shares again the joyous feast.*

The North American Indians bury their dead in a sitting posture; decorating the corpse with wampum, the images of birds, quadrupeds, &c: And (if that of a warrior) with bows, arrows, tomhawks and other military weapons.

His imaged birds, and painted bowl,
And venison, for a journey dressed,
Bespeak the nature of the soul,
ACTIVITY, that knows no rest.

His bow, for action ready bent,
And arrows, with a head of stone,
Can only mean that life is spent,
And not the old ideas gone.

Thou, stranger, that shalt come this way,
No fraud upon the dead commit—
Observe the swelling turf, and say
They do not *lie*, but here they *sit*.

Here still a lofty rock remains,
On which the curious eye may trace
(Now wasted, half, by wearing rains)
The fancies of a ruder race.

Here still an aged elm aspires,
Beneath whose far-projecting shade
(And which the shepherd still admires)
The children of the forest played!

There oft a restless Indian queen
(Pale *Shebah*, with her braided hair)
And many a barbarous form is seen
To chide the man that lingers there.

By midnight moons, o'er moistening dews,
In habit for the chase arrayed,
The hunter still the deer pursues,
The hunter and the deer, a shade!

And long shall timorous fancy see
The painted chief, and pointed spear,
And Reason's self shall bow the knee
To shadows and delusions here.   [1788]

ON MR PAINE'S RIGHTS OF MAN

Thus briefly sketched the sacred rights of man,
How inconsistent with the royal plan!
Which for itself exclusive honor craves,
Where some are masters born, and millions slaves.

With what contempt must every eye look down
On that base, childish bauble called a crown,
The gilded bait, that lures the crowd, to come,
Bow down their necks, and meet a slavish doom;
The source of half the miseries men endure,
The quack that kills them, while it seems to cure,
   Roused by the reason of his manly page,
Once more shall Paine a listening world engage:
From Reason's source, a bold reform he brings,
In raising up mankind, he pulls down kings,
Who, source of discord, patrons of all wrong,
On blood and murder have been fed too long:
Hid from the world, and tutored to be base,
The curse, the scourge, the ruin of our race,
Theirs was the task, a dull designing few,
To shackle beings that they scarcely knew,
Who made this globe the residence of slaves,
And built their thrones on systems formed by knaves
—Advance, bright years, to work their final fall,
And haste the period that shall crush them all.
   Who, that has read and scanned the historic page
But glows, at every line, with kindling rage,
To see by them the rights of men aspersed,
Freedom restrained, and Nature's law reversed,
Men, ranked with beasts, by monarchs willed away,
And bound young fools, or madmen to obey:
Nor driven to wars, and now oppressed at home,
Compelled in crowds o'er distant seas to roam,
From India's climes the plundered prize to bring
To glad the strumpet, or to glut the king.
   Columbia, hail! immortal be thy reign:
Without a king, we till the smiling plain;
Without a king, we trace the unbounded sea,
And traffic round the globe, through each degree;
Each foreign clime our honored flag reveres,
Which asks no monarch, to support the stars:
Without a king, the laws maintain their sway,
While honor bids each generous heart obey.
Be ours the task the ambitious to restrain,
And this great lesson teach—that kings are vain;
That warring realms to certain ruin haste,
That kings subsist by war, and wars are waste:
So shall our nation, formed on Virtue's plan,
Remain the guardian of the Rights of Man,
A vast republic, famed through every clime,
Without a king, to see the end of time.   [1795]

PHILLIS WHEATLEY

America c. 1754-1784

'On Being Brought from Africa to America' bespeaks the pious Christian and classical education Wheatley received in the Boston household to which she was sold as a slave at the age of seven. The racial prejudices of American readers undermined Wheatley's attempts in 1772 and 1779 to publish her own work. However, her owner, Susanna Wheatley, facilitated the 1773 publication of Wheatley's *Poems* in London; a posthumous American reprint of this volume was not made until 1786. Although she wrote rather conventional Christian elegies and occasional patriotic poems, Wheatley was acutely sensitive to the vagaries of democracy.

ON BEING BROUGHT FROM AFRICA TO AMERICA

'Twas mercy brought me from my *Pagan* land,
Taught my benighted soul to understand
That there's a God, that there's a *Saviour* too:
Once I redemption neither sought nor knew.
Some view our sable race with scornful eye,
'Their colour is a diabolic dye.'
Remember, *Christians*, *Negroes*, black as *Cain*,
May be refined, and join th' angelic train.   [1773]

ON IMAGINATION

Thy various works, imperial queen, we see,
How bright their forms! how decked with pomp by thee!
Thy wond'rous acts in beauteous order stand,
And all attest how potent is thine hand.

    From *Helicon's* refulgent heights attend,
Ye sacred choir, and my attempts befriend:
To tell her glories with a faithful tongue.
Ye blooming graces, triumph in my song.

    Now here, now there, the roving *Fancy* flies,
Till some loved object strikes her wand'ring eyes,
Whose silken fetters all the senses bind,
And soft captivity involves the mind.

    Imagination! who can sing thy force?
Or who describe the swiftness of thy course?
Soaring through air to find the bright abode,
Th' empyreal palace of the thund'ring God,
We on thy pinions can surpass the wind,
And leave the rolling universe behind:
From star to star the mental optics rove,

Measure the skies, and range the realms above.
There in one view we grasp the mighty whole,
Or with new worlds amaze th' unbounded soul.

Though *Winter* frowns to *Fancy's* raptured eyes
The fields may flourish, and gay scenes arise;
The frozen deeps may break their iron bands,
And bid their waters murmur o'er the sands.
Fair *Flora* may resume her fragrant reign,
And with her flow'ry riches deck the plain;
Sylvanus may diffuse his honours round,
And all the forest may with leaves be crowned:
Show'rs may descend, and dews their gems disclose,
And nectar sparkle on the blooming rose.

Such in thy pow'r, nor are thine orders vain,
O thou the leader of the mental train:
In full perfection all thy works are wrought,
And thine the sceptre o'er the realms of thought.
Before thy throne the subject-passions bow,
Of subject-passions sov'reign ruler Thou,
At thy command joy rushes on the heart,
And through the glowing veins the spirits dart.

Fancy might now her silken pinions try
To rise from earth, and sweep th' expanse on high;
From *Tithon's* bed now might *Aurora* rise,
Her cheeks all glowing with celestial dyes,
While a pure stream of light o'er flows the skies.
The monarch of the day I might behold,
And all the mountains tipt with radiant gold,
But I reluctant leave the pleasing views,
Which *Fancy* dresses to delight the *Muse*;
Winter austere forbids me to aspire,

And northern tempests damp the rising fire;
They chill the tides of *Fancy's* flowing sea,
Cease then, my song, cease the unequal lay.   [1773]

WILLIAM BLAKE

England 1757-1827

Deeply disturbed by what he saw as the brute materialism of his age and its tendency toward the sacrifice of spiritual values, Blake used his enormous gifts as a visual and verbal artist to champion human rights. He composed a group of 'prophetic' works, visionary narratives the reader was to experience in the company of the engraved designs and illustrations, a method of 'illuminated printing' the poet had created. Blake believed in the hieratic function of the imagination, the 'Great Code of Art' embodied in the Old and New Testaments. He lived all his life in the presence of a fourth dimension—he had visions and conversed with the spirit world—and while some consigned him to a lunatic fringe, the mythology he constructed inspired a younger generation of artists. *Songs Of Experience* (1794) and *Songs Of Innocence* (1789) are lyric sequences that articulate what Blake called the 'two contrary states of the human soul'. The most recent edition of Blake's collected works is *The Poetry and Prose of William Blake* (eds Erdman and Bloom, 1982).

THE LITTLE BLACK BOY

My mother bore me in the southern wild,
And I am black, but O! my soul is white;
White as an angel is the English child,
But I am black, as if bereav'd of light.

My mother taught me underneath a tree,
And sitting down before the heat of day,
She took me on her lap and kissed me,
And pointing to the east, began to say:

'Look on the rising sun: there God does live
And gives his light, and gives his heat away;
And flowers and trees and beasts and men receive
Comfort in morning, joy in the noonday.

'And we are put on earth a little space,
That we may learn to bear the beams of love;
And these black bodies and this sun-burnt face
Is but a cloud, and like a shady grove.

'For when our souls have learn'd that heat to bear,
The cloud will vanish: we shall hear his voice,
Saying: "Come out from the grove, my love & care,
And round my golden tent like lambs rejoice."'

Thus did my mother say, and kissed me;
And thus I say to little English boy:
When I from black and he from white cloud free,
And round the tent of God like lambs we joy,

I'll shade him from the heat till he can bear
To lean in joy upon our father's knee;
And then I'll stand and stroke his silver hair,
And be like him, and he will then love me.   [1789]

THE GARDEN OF LOVE

I went to the Garden of Love,
And saw what I never had seen:
A Chapel was built in the midst,
Where I used to play on the green.

And the gates of this Chapel were shut,
And 'Thou shalt not' writ over the door;
So I turn'd to the Garden of Love,
That so many sweet flowers bore,

And I saw it was filled with graves,
And tomb-stones where flowers should be:
And Priests in black gowns were walking their rounds,
And binding with briars my joys & desires.   [1794]

ROBERT BURNS

Scotland 1759-1796

The publication in 1786 of *Poems, chiefly in the Scottish Dialect* immediately established Burns's
name among the élite as a homegrown and 'Heaven-taught ploughman'. A lifelong commitment to
the preservation of traditional tunes and words combined with his own considerable song-writing
abilities to produce immensely popular pieces like 'Auld lang syne', collections like *Select Scottish
Airs* (1792), and the four volumes of *The Scots Musical Museum*. The vigour of the native lyric
tradition is also present in his satirical commentary on the everyday and the common folk
available in the three-volume *Poems and Songs* (1968) which preserves the eighteenth-century form
of the song and direct transcripts from the music books themselves.

A POET'S WELCOME TO HIS LOVE-BEGOTTEN DAUGHTER;
THE FIRST INSTANCE THAT ENTITLED HIM TO THE VENERABLE
APPELLATION OF FATHER—

Thou's welcome, Wean! Mischanter fa' me,
If thoughts o' thee, or yet thy Mamie,
Shall ever daunton me or awe me,
          My bonie lady;
Or if I blush when thou shalt ca' me
          Tyta, or Daddie.—

Tho' now they ca' me, Fornicator,
And tease my name in kintra clatter,
The mair they talk, I'm kend the better;
        E'en let them clash!
An auld wife's tongue's a feckless matter
        To gie ane fash.—

Welcome! My bonie, sweet, wee Dochter!
Tho' ye come here a wee unsought for;
And tho' your comin I hae fought for,
        Baith Kirk and Queir;
Yet by my faith, ye're no unwrought for,
        That I shall swear!

Wee image o' my bonie Betty,
As fatherly I kiss and daut thee,
As dear and near my heart I set thee,
        Wi' as gude will,
As a' the Priests had seen me get thee
        That's out o' h ——. —

Sweet fruit o' monie a merry dint,
My funny toil is no a' tint;
Tho' ye come to the warld asklent,
        Which fools may scoff at,
In my last plack your part's be in't,
        The better half o't.—

Tho' I should be the waur bestead,
Thou's be as braw and bienly clad,
And thy young years as nicely bred
        Wi' education,
As ony brat o' Wedlock's bed,
        In a' thy station.—

[Lord grant that thou may ay inherit
Thy Mither's looks an' gracefu' merit;
An' thy poor, worthless Daddie's spirit,
        Without his failins!
'Twad please me mair to see thee heir it
        Than stocked mailins!]

For if thou be, what I wad hae thee,
And tak the counsel I shall gie thee,
I'll never rue my trouble wi' thee,
        The cost nor shame o't,
But be a loving Father to thee,
        And brag the name o't. —

                                        [c. 1801]

AULD LANG SYNE

Should auld acquaintance be forgot
  And never brought to mind?
Should auld acquaintance be forgot,
  And auld lang syne!

Chorus
For auld lang syne, my jo,
  For auld lang syne,
We'll tak a cup o' kindness yet
  For auld lang syne.

And surely ye'll be your pint stowp!
  And surely I'll be mine!
And we'll tak a cup o' kindness yet,
  For auld lang syne.
    For auld, &c.

We twa hae run about the braes,
  And pou'd the gowans fine;
But we've wander'd mony a weary fitt,
  Sin auld lang syne.
    For auld, &c.

We twa hae paidl'd in the burn,
  Frae morning sun till dine;
But seas between us braid hae roar'd,
  Sin auld lang syne.
    For auld, &c.

And there's a hand, my trusty fiere!
  And gie's a hand o' thine!
And we'll tak a right gude-willie-waught,
  For auld lang syne.
    For auld, &c.

[1796]

SARAH WENTWORTH MORTON

USA 1759–1846

Morton was well-known in early nineteenth-century Boston literary circles for her progressive anti-slavery and women's suffrage writings, but she also wrote with equal sensitivity and conviction about her personal affections and losses. She often published collections of her poetry and essays under the pen-name 'Philenia Constantia'; her best-known volume is *My Mind and Its Thoughts* (1823).

MEMENTO, FOR MY INFANT WHO LIVED BUT EIGHTEEN HOURS

As the pure snow-drop, child of April tears,
　Shook by the rough wind's desolating breath—
Scarce o'er the chilly sod its low head rears,
　And trembling dies upon the parent heath,

So my lost boy, arrayed in fancy's charms,
　Just born to mourn—with premature decay
To the cold tyrant stretched his feeble arms,
　And struggling sighed his little life away.

As not in vain the early snow-drop rose,
　Though short its date, and hard the withering gale;
Since its pale bloom ethereal balm bestows,
　And cheers with vernal hope the wasted vale.

My perished child, dear pledge of many a pain!
　Torn from this ruffian world, in yon bright sphere,
Joins with awakened voice the cherub train,
　And pours his sweet breath on a mother's ear.

Kind dreams of morn his fairy phantom bring,
　And floating tones of ecstacy impart,
Soft as when seraphs strike the heavenly string
　To charm the settled sorrow of the heart.   [1823]

THE AFRICAN CHIEF

See how the black ship cleaves the main,
　High bounding o'er the dark blue wave,
Remurmuring with the groans of pain,
　Deep freighted with the princely slave!

Did all the Gods of Afric sleep,
   Forgetful of their guardian love,
When the white tyrants of the deep
   Betrayed him in the palmy grove?

A chief of Gambia's golden shore,
   Whose arm the band of warriors led,
Or more—the lord of generous power,
   By whom the foodless poor were fed.

Does not the voice of reason cry,
   Claim the first right that nature gave,
From the red scourge of bondage fly,
   Nor deign to live a burdened slave?

Has not his suffering offspring clung,
   Desponding round his fettered knee;
On his worn shoulder, weeping hung,
   And urged one effort to be free?

His wife by nameless wrongs subdued,
   His bosom's friend to death resigned;
The flinty path-way drenched in blood,
   He saw with cold and frenzied mind.

Strong in despair, then sought the plain,
   To heaven was raised his steadfast eye,
Resolved to burst the crushing chain,
   Or mid the battle's blast to die.

First of his race, he led the band,
   Guardless of danger, hurling round,
Till by his red avenging hand,
   Full many a despot stained the ground.

When erst Messenia's sons oppressed
   Flew desperate to the sanguine field,
With iron clothed each injured breast,
   And saw the cruel Spartan yield,

Did not the soul to heaven allied,
   With the proud heart as greatly swell,
As when the Roman Decius died,
   Or when the Grecian victim fell?

Do later deeds quick rapture raise,
   The boon Batavia's William won,
Paoli's time-enduring praise,
   Or the yet greater Washington?

If these exalt thy sacred zeal,
   To hate oppression's mad control,
For bleeding Afric learn to feel,
   Whose Chieftain claimed a kindred soul.

Ah, mourn the last disastrous hour,
   Lift the full eye of bootless grief,
While victory treads the sultry shore,
   And tears from hope the captive chief.

While the hard race of pallid hue,
   Unpracticed in the power to feel,
Resign him to the murderous crew,
   The horrors of the quivering wheel,

Let sorrow bathe each blushing cheek,
   Bend piteous o'er the tortured slave,
Whose wrongs compassion cannot speak,
   Whose only refuge was the grave.   [1823]

CAROLINA OLIPHANT, BARONESS NAIRNE

Scotland 1766–1845

Inspired by the 'auld warld tales' of her kinsfolk, Oliphant collected Scots songs, sometimes adapting them, and presenting them under the pseudonym 'B.B.' or 'Mrs Bogan of Bogan'. When she married and moved to Edinburgh, she and Mr Purdie, a local music dealer, published the six-volume collection *The Scottish Minstrel* in 1842. Oliphant's Jacobite heritage is felt equally in 'The Regalia', for Scotland's union with England deprived the Highlanders of their cultural identity, undermining indigenous customs like the one which had provided that the Scottish Regalia should be forever kept in Scotland.

THE REGALIA

We hae the crown without a head,
   The sceptre's but a hand, O;
The ancient warlike royal blade,
   Might be a willow wand, O!
Gin they had tongues to tell the wrangs

That laid them useless by, a',
Fu' weel I wot, there's ne'er a Scot
   Could boast his cheek was dry, a'.

   Then flourish, thistle, flourish fair,
      Tho' ye've the crown nae langer,
   They'll hae the skaith that cross ye yet,
      Your jags grow aye the stranger.

O for a touch o' warlock's wand,
   The byegane back to bring a',
And gi'e us ae lang simmer's day
   O' a true-born Scottish king a'!
We'd put the crown upon his head,
   The sceptre in his hand a',
We'd rend the welkin wi' the shout,
   Bruce and his native land, a'.

   Then flourish, thistle, &c.

The thistle ance it flourish'd fair,
   An' grew maist like a tree a',
They've stunted down its stately tap,
   That roses might luik hie a'.
But though its head lies in the dust,
   The root is stout and steady;
The thistle is the warrior yet,
   The rose its tocher'd leddy.

   Then flourish, thistle, &c.

The rose it blooms in safter soil,
   And strangers up could root it;
Aboon the grund he ne'er was fand
   That pu'd the thistle oot yet.

   Then flourish, thistle, flourish fair,
      Tho' ye've the crown nae langer,
   They'll hae the skaith that cross ye yet,
      Your jags grow aye the stranger.   [n. d.]

WILLIAM WORDSWORTH

England 1770–1850

With Samuel Coleridge, whom he met in 1795, Wordsworth published *Lyrical Ballads* (1798). Its *Preface to the Second Edition* (1800), written by Wordsworth (and inspired by conversations with Coleridge) became a manifesto for the Romantic Movement. Wordsworth defines the purpose of poetry as the poetic re-creation of a common language and the common events of a rural life: a 'selection of the real language of men in a state of vivid sensation'. The poet's 'impassioned expression' integrates meditative and descriptive elements to achieve the illusion of a 'spontaneous overflow of powerful feelings' whose 'origin' derives 'from emotions recollected in tranquillity'. Wordsworth became Poet Laureate in 1843, and many argue that his position and the growing conservatism of his religious and political points of view diminished his poetic power.

LUCY GRAY; OR, SOLITUDE

Oft I had heard of Lucy Gray:
And, when I crossed the wild,
I chanced to see at break of day
The solitary child.

No mate, no comrade Lucy knew;
She dwelt on a wide moor,
—The sweetest thing that ever grew
Beside a human door!

You yet may spy the fawn at play,
The hare upon the green;
But the sweet face of Lucy Gray
Will never more be seen.

'To-night will be a stormy night—
You to the town must go;
And take a lantern, Child, to light
Your mother through the snow.'

'That, Father! will I gladly do:
'Tis scarcely afternoon—
The minster-clock has just struck two,
And yonder is the moon!'

At this the Father raised his hook,
And snapped a faggot-band;
He plied his work;—and Lucy took
The lantern in her hand.

Not blither is the mountain roe:
With many a wanton stroke
Her feet disperse the powdery snow,
That rises up like smoke.

The storm came on before its time:
She wandered up and down;
And many a hill did Lucy climb:
But never reached the town.

The wretched parents all that night
Went shouting far and wide;
But there was neither sound nor sight
To serve them for a guide.

At day-break on a hill they stood
That overlooked the moor;
And thence they saw the bridge of wood,
A furlong from their door.

They wept—and, turning homeward, cried,
'In heaven we all shall meet;'
—When in the snow the mother spied
The print of Lucy's feet.

Then downwards from the steep hill's edge
They tracked the footmarks small;
And through the broken hawthorn hedge,
And by the long stone-wall;

And then an open field they crossed:
The marks were still the same;
They tracked them on, nor ever lost;
And to the bridge they came.

They followed from the snowy bank
Those footmarks, one by one,
Into the middle of the plank;
And further there were none!

—Yet some maintain that to this day
She is a living child;
That you may see sweet Lucy Gray
Upon the lonesome wild.

O'er rough and smooth she trips along,
And never looks behind;
And sings a solitary song
That whistles in the wind.

[1800]

MY HEART LEAPS UP WHEN I BEHOLD

My heart leaps up when I behold
  A rainbow in the sky:
So was it when my life began;
So is it now I am a man;
So be it when I shall grow old,
  Or let me die!
The Child is father of the Man;
And I could wish my days to be
Bound each to each by natural piety.

                                                                [1807]

SIR WALTER SCOTT

Scotland 1771–1832

In his poems and his historical novels, Scott drew on his encyclopedic knowledge of Scottish history, myth, and legend; 'Proud Maisie', sung by crazy Madge Wildfire on her deathbed in Scott's novel *The Heart of Midlothian*, is one among many examples of Scott's uses of local speech, dialogue, and setting. His three-volume collection of popular ballads, *Minstrelsy of the Scottish Border* (1802–3) shows how widely read Scott was in his own tradition, while the metrical romances that he wrote between 1805 and 1813—including classics like *The Lay of the Last Minstrel* (1805) and *The Lady of the Lake* (1810)—established Scott as the best-known poet of his day.

PROUD MAISIE

Proud Maisie is in the wood
  Walking so early;
Sweet Robin sits on the bush,
  Singing so rarely.

'Tell me, thou bonny bird,
  When shall I marry me?'—
'When six braw gentlemen
  Kirkward shall carry ye.'

'Who makes the bridal bed,
  Birdie, say truly?'—
'The gray-headed sexton
  That delves the grave duly.

'The glowworm o'er grave and stone
  Shall light thee steady,
The owl from the steeple sing,
  "Welcome, proud lady."'

                                                                [1818]

SAMUEL TAYLOR COLERIDGE

England 1772–1834

Coleridge's intellectual and imaginative power developed despite a debilitating addiction to laudanum, a liquid form of opium (routinely prescribed for ailments such as rheumatism, from which Coleridge suffered), a failed marriage, and chronic bouts of depression and anxiety. His gifts are felt in the incantatory, archetypal power of works like 'The Rime of the Ancient Mariner', and in the meditative and conversational values of descriptive poems like 'Frost at Midnight' and 'Dejection: An Ode'. His influence as a theorist of the religious and poetic imagination is palpable among nineteenth- and twentieth-century thinkers. The collected edition of Coleridge's poems and literary, religious, and political writing under the general editorship of Kathleen Coburn was begun in 1969.

KUBLA KHAN: OR, A VISION IN A DREAM. A FRAGMENT.

The following fragment is here published at the request of a poet of great and deserved celebrity, and, as far as the Author's own opinions are concerned, rather as a psychological curiosity, than on the ground of any supposed poetic merits.

In the summer of the year 1797, the Author, then in ill health, had retired to a lonely farmhouse between Porlock and Linton, on the Exmoor confines of Somerset and Devonshire. In consequence of a slight indisposition, an anodyne had been prescribed, from the effects of which he fell asleep in his chair at the moment that he was reading the following sentence, or words of the same substance, in Purchas's Pilgrimage: 'Here the Khan Kubla commanded a palace to be built, and a stately garden thereunto. And thus ten miles of fertile ground were inclosed with a wall.' The Author continued for about three hours in a profound sleep, at least of the external senses, during which time he has the most vivid confidence, that he could not have composed less than from two to three hundred lines; if that indeed can be called composition in which all the images rose up before him as things, with a parallel production of the correspondent expressions, without any sensation or consciousness of effort. On awaking he appeared to himself to have a distinct recollection of the whole, and taking his pen, ink, and paper, instantly and eagerly wrote down the lines that are here preserved. At this moment he was unfortunately called out by a person on business from Porlock, and detained by him above an hour, and on his return to his room, found, to his no small surprise and mortification, that though he still retained some vague and dim recollection of the general purport of the vision, yet, with the exception of some eight or ten scattered lines and images, all the rest had passed away like the images on the surface of a stream into which a stone has been cast, but, alas! without the after restoration of the latter!

Then all the charm

Is broken—all that phantom-world so fair
Vanishes, and a thousand circlets spread,
And each mis-shape the other. Stay awhile,
Poor youth! who scarcely dar'st lift up thine eyes—
The stream will soon renew its smoothness, soon
The visions will return! And lo, he stays,
And soon the fragments dim of lovely forms
Come trembling back, unite, and now once more
The pool becomes a mirror.

Yet from the still surviving recollections in his mind, the Author has frequently purposed to finish for himself what had been originally, as it were, given to him. Σαμερον αδιον ασω: *but the to-morrow is yet to come.*

As a contrast to this vision, I have annexed a fragment of a very different character, describing with equal fidelity the dream of pain and disease.

In Xanadu did Kubla Khan
A stately pleasure-dome decree:
Where Alph, the sacred river, ran
Through caverns measureless to man
   Down to a sunless sea,
So twice five miles of fertile ground
With walls and towers were girdled round:
And there were gardens bright with sinuous rills,
Where blossomed many an incense-bearing tree;
And here were forests ancient as the hills,
Enfolding sunny spots of greenery.

But oh! that deep romantic chasm which slanted
Down the green hill athwart a cedarn cover!
A savage place! as holy and enchanted
As e'er beneath a waning moon was haunted
By woman wailing for her demon-lover!
And from this chasm, with ceaseless turmoil seething,
As if this earth in fast thick pants were breathing,
A mighty fountain momently was forced:
Amid whose swift half-intermitted burst
Huge fragments vaulted like rebounding hail,
Or chaffy grain beneath the thresher's flail:
And 'mid these dancing rocks at once and ever
It flung up momently the sacred river.
Five miles meandering with a mazy motion
Through wood and dale the sacred river ran,
Then reached the caverns measureless to man,
And sank in tumult to a lifeless ocean:
And 'mid this tumult Kubla heard from far
Ancestral voices prophesying war!
   The shadow of the dome of pleasure
   Floated midway on the waves;
   Where was heard the mingled measure
   From the fountain and the caves.
It was a miracle of rare device,
A sunny pleasure-dome with caves of ice!

A damsel with a dulcimer
In a vision once I saw:
It was an Abyssinian maid,
And on her dulcimer she played,
Singing of Mount Abora.
Could I revive within me
Her symphony and song,
To such a deep delight 'twould win me,
That with music loud and long,
I would build that dome in air,
That sunny dome! those caves of ice!
And all who heard should see them there,
And all should cry, Beware! Beware!
His flashing eyes, his floating hair!
Weave a circle round him thrice,
And close your eyes with holy dread,
For he on honey-dew hath fed,
And drunk the milk of Paradise.   [1816]

ANONYMOUS

America

'Alphabet' was a patriotic ballad composed for children during the American Revolution. Its overt political message may contrast with *The New England Primer*'s theocratic version of the alphabet, but both impress upon their readers the uses of language as ideological instruments.

ALPHABET

A, stands for Americans, who scorn to be slaves;
B, for Boston, where fortitude their freedom saves;
C, stands for Congress, which, though loyal, will be free;
D, stands for defence, 'gainst force and tyranny.
    Stand firmly, A and Z,
    We swear for ever to be free!

E, stands for evils, which a civil war must bring;
F, stands for fate, dreadful to both people and king;
G, stands for George, may God give him wisdom and grace;
H, stands for hypocrite, who wears a double face.

J, stands for justice, which traitors in power defy,
K, stands for king, who should to such the axe apply;
L, stands for London, to its country ever true,
M, stands for Mansfield, who hath another view.

N, stands for North, who to the House the mandate brings,
O, stands for oaths, binding on subjects not on kings:
P, stands for people, who their freedom should defend,
Q, stands for *quere*, when will England's troubles end?

R, stands for rebels, not at Boston but at home,
S, stands for Stuart, sent by Whigs abroad to roam,
T, stands for Tories, who may try to bring them back,
V, stands for villains, who have well deserved the rack.

W, stands for Wilkes, who us from warrants saved,
Y, for York, the New, half corrupted, half enslaved,
Z, stands for Zero, but means the Tory minions,
Who threatens us with fire and sword, to bias our opinions.
    Stand firmly A and Z,
    We swear for ever to be free!
                                      [1775]

ANONYMOUS

America/Canada

These songs were popular among Loyalists during the American Revolution in so far as they pro-
moted loyalty, truth, and faith in the 'old English cause'. Their writers' poetic uses of invective and
chauvinistic appeals to readers' social and religious prejudices are blatant but effective illustrations
of popular rhetoric in America.

BURROWING YANKEES

Ye Yankees who, mole-like, still throw up the earth,
And like them, to your follies are blind from your birth;
Attempt not to hold British troops at defiance,
True Britons, with whom you pretend an alliance.

Mistake not; such blood ne'er run in your veins,
'Tis no more than the dregs, the lees, or the drains:
Ye affect to talk big of your hourly attacks;
Come on! and I'll warrant, we'll soon see your backs.

Such threats of bravadoes serve only to warm
The true British hearts, you ne'er can alarm;
The Lion once rous'd, will strike such a terror,
Shall show you, poor fools, your presumption and error.

And the time will soon come when your whole rebel race
Will be drove from the lands, nor dare show your face:
Here's a health to great *George*, may he fully determine,
To root from the earth all such insolent vermin.
                                      [1776]

AN APPEAL

The old English cause knocks at every man's door,
   And bids him stand up for religion and right;
It addresses the rich as well as the poor;
   And fair liberty, bids them, like Englishmen fight.
      And suffer no wrong,
      From a rebel throng,
Who, if they're not quelled, will enslave us ere long;
Most bravely then let us our liberty prize,
Nor suffer the Congress to blind all our eyes;
   Or each rebel cut-purse, will soon give us law,
   For they are as bad as a Tyler or Straw.

From France, D'Estaing to America has come.
   The French banditti will rob our estates;
These robbers are all protected by Rome,
   Consult but their annals, record but their dates,
      It's their politics
      To burn heretics,
Or poison by water that's fetch'd from the Styx.
Let Frenchified rebels, in vain then attempt
To bring our own church, or our king to contempt;
   For no rebel cut-purse shall e'er give us law,
   Should they prove as daring as Tyler or Straw.

The farces of Rome, with carrying her hosts,
   Are laugh'd at and jeer'd by the learned and wise,
And all her thin tinsels apparently lost,
   Her stories of relics, and sanctified lies.
      Each ignorant joke
      Believe, or you smoke,
And if we are conquer'd we receive the Pope's yoke;
But despising the counsels of Adams and Lee,
As loyal Americans, we'll die or be free.
   For no rebel cut-throat shall e'er give us law,
   Should they prove as daring as Tyler or Straw.

Let curses most vile, and anathemas roar,
   Let half-ruin'd France, to the Pope tribute pay;
Britain's thundering cannon, shall guard safe our shore;
   Great George shall defend us, none else we'll obey.
      Then France, join'd by Spain,
      May labor in vain,
For soon the Havana shall be ours again.
The French then will scamper and quit every state,
And find themselves bubbled, when *morbleu* it's too late.
   For no Frenchman, or rebel imp of the law,
   In our old constitution can point out a flaw.   [1780]

GEORGE GORDON, LORD BYRON

Scotland/England 1788–1824

The notorious aspects of Byron's life (his aristocracy, promiscuity, generosity, daring, and volatile nature) contributed to the immediate popularity of the Byronic hero whose first instalment in Byron's poetry came in the opening two cantos of *Childe Harold's Pilgrimage* (1812). Byron's superman—estranged, haunted, 'un homme unique', rebel of unspoken causes, and fatally attractive—was continually developed by the poet in *Manfred* (1817), for example, and in *Don Juan*. Byron began the latter in 1819 and continued writing until his death in 1824 in the town of Missolonghi where he had gone to support the Greek bid for independence from Turkey. Byron's reputation soared in Europe in the nineteenth century, to the extent that French critic Hyppolyte Taine singled him out as 'the greatest and most English' of the Romantics. Current estimates are less flattering, an observation indicative of the irony Byron appreciated with respect to the shifting sands of literary judgment and taste.

from CHILDE HAROLD'S PILGRIMAGE

CANTO 3

'Once More Upon the Waters'

1

Is thy face like thy mother's, my fair child!
Ada! sole daughter of my house and heart?
When last I saw thy young blue eyes they smiled,
And then we parted—not as now we part,
But with a hope.—
            Awaking with a start,
The waters heave around me; and on high
The winds lift up their voices; I depart,
Whither I know not; but the hour's gone by,
When Albion's lessening shores could grieve or glad mine eye.

2

Once more upon the waters! yet once more!
And the waves bound beneath me as a steed
That knows his rider. Welcome to their roar!
Swift be their guidance, wheresoe'er it lead!
Though the strained mast should quiver as a reed,
And the rent canvas fluttering strew the gale,
Still must I on; for I am as a weed,
Flung from the rock on Ocean's foam, to sail
Where'er the surge may sweep, the tempest's breath prevail.

3

In my youth's summer I did sing of One,
The wandering outlaw of his own dark mind;
Again I seize the theme, then but begun,
And bear it with me, as the rushing wind
Bears the cloud onwards: in that tale I find
The furrows of long thought, and dried-up tears,
Which, ebbing, leave a sterile track behind,
O'er which all heavily the journeying years
Plod the last sands of life—where not a flower appears.

4

Since my young days of passion—joy, or pain—
Perchance my heart and harp have lost a string,
And both may jar: it may be that in vain
I would essay as I have sung to sing.
Yet, though a dreary strain, to this I cling,
So that it wean me from the weary dream
Of selfish grief or gladness—so it fling
Forgetfulness around me—it shall seem
To me, though to none else, a not ungrateful theme.

5

He, who grown agèd in this world of woe,
In deeds, not years, piercing the depths of life,
So that no wonder waits him—nor below
Can love, or sorrow, fame, ambition, strife,
Cut to his heart again with the keen knife
Of silent, sharp endurance—he can tell
Why thought seeks refuge in lone caves, yet rife
With airy images, and shapes which dwell
Still unimpaired, though old, in the soul's haunted cell.

6

'Tis to create, and in creating live
A being more intense, that we endow
With form our fancy, gaining as we give
The life we image, even as I do now.
What am I? Nothing: but not so art thou,
Soul of my thought! with whom I traverse earth,
Invisible but gazing, as I glow
Mixed with thy spirit, blended with thy birth,
And feeling still with thee in my crushed feelings' dearth.

7

Yet must I think less wildly—I *have* thought
Too long and darkly, till my brain became,
In its own eddy boiling and o'erwrought,
A whirling gulf of phantasy and flame:
And thus, untaught in youth my heart to tame,
My springs of life were poisoned. 'Tis too late!
Yet am I changed; though still enough the same
In strength to bear what time can not abate,
And feed on bitter fruits without accusing Fate.

8

Something too much of this—but now 'tis past,
And the spell closes with its silent seal.
Long absent HAROLD reappears at last;
He of the breast which fain no more would feel,
Wrung with the wounds which kill not but ne'er heal;
Yet Time, who changes all, had altered him
In soul and aspect as in age: years steal
Fire from the mind as vigor from the limb,
And life's enchanted cup but sparkles near the brim.   [1816]

PERCY BYSSHE SHELLEY

England 1792-1822

In the Preface to the lyrical drama *Prometheus Unbound*, Shelley celebrates the possibility of heroic action and his own 'passion for reforming the world', a passion borne out in his nonconformist politics. His pamphlet *The Necessity of Atheism*, written with Thomas Jefferson Hogg, prompted Shelley's expulsion from Oxford in 1811. Equally renegade were his advocacy of Catholic emancipation in Ireland and his criticism of matrimony. His own experiment with an open-marriage practice led to permanent exile in Italy. Integral to Shelley's approach to heroic action is the concept of the redemptive function of the imagination: poets are 'the unacknowledged legislators of the world', for their art 'redeems from decay the visitations of divinity in man' (*A Defence of Poetry*, 1840). Shelley hoped that his emotional and visionary symbols would apprehend the immutable world of ultimate forms and so transform the human heart. The most accepted standard edition is *Shelley's Poetry and Prose* (eds Reiman and Powers, 1977).

THE INDIAN GIRL'S SONG

I arise from dreams of thee
In the first sleep of night—
The winds are breathing low
And the stars are burning bright.
I arise from dreams of thee—

And a spirit in my feet
Has borne me—Who knows how?
To thy chamber window, sweet!—

The wandering airs they faint
On the dark silent stream—
The champak odours fail
Like sweet thoughts in a dream;
The nightingale's complaint—
It dies upon her heart—
As I must die on thine
O beloved as thou art!

O lift me from the grass!
I die, I faint, I fail!
Let thy love in kisses rain
On my lips and eyelids pale.

My cheek is cold and white, alas!
My heart beats loud and fast.
Oh press it close to thine again
Where it will break at last.   [1822]

ENGLAND IN 1819

An old, mad, blind, despised, and dying king;
Princes, the dregs of their dull race, who flow
Through public scorn—mud from a muddy spring;
Rulers who neither see, nor feel, nor know,
But leech-like to their fainting country cling
Till they drop, blind in blood, without a blow;
A people starved and stabbed in the untilled field;
An army, which liberticide and prey
Makes as a two-edged sword to all who wield;
Golden and sanguine laws which tempt and slay;
Religion Christless, Godless—a book sealed;
A Senate—Time's worst statute unrepealed,—
Are graves, from which a glorious Phantom may
Burst to illumine our tempestuous day.   [1839]

JANET HAMILTON

Scotland 1795–1873

Spinner, weaver, mother of ten, Hamilton did not learn to write until she was 54. In the Preface to *Poems, Essays, And Sketches* (1870), Hamilton apologises for the 'egotistical sketch' which she prepared only because it had been so 'urgently requested' by enthusiasts who found her 'power of language and ability for composition' nothing short of remarkable given the conditions in which she wrote. Hamilton explains: 'I can only say, that they must have been acquired during a long course of reading the works of good authors, and thus, insensibly acquiring something of their manner and style.' The most complete edition of her work is *Poems and Prose Works of Janet Hamilton* (1885).

A PHASE OF THE WAR IN AMERICA, 1864

Give me angel wing and eye,
   Give me arm and strength Herculean;
With the speed of light I'd fly—
   Not to yonder bright cerulean.

Westward far my flight should be,
   O'er the wide and wild Atlantic;
I the fated land would see
   Drunk with blood whose sons are frantic.

Horror, fed on carnage, lowers
   O'er corruption rankly steaming;
O'er Virginia's Eden bowers
   Thousand vultures hover screaming.

In one gory mass they lie—
   Husband, father, son, and lover—
Festering 'neath a burning sky,
   Earth no more her slain can cover.

Crippled victims, weak and wan,
   Back a ghastly tide are flowing;
Angel eyes will weep to scan
   Bootless slaughter onward going.

See, recording angels stand
   On each side of death's dark portals,
Noting with unerring hand
   Entering hordes of ghastly mortals.

From a cloud-capp'd tower I gaze,
    From the battle field arising
Myriad souls, with dread amaze,
    I behold—my soul surprising.

Civil war, thou demon, fell,
    Shall thy bloody hand for ever
Ring the dreadful tocsin bell?
    Britain's heart-strings quail and quiver.

War, thou Lernæan hydra dire,
    I would strangle and uncoil thee;
Close thy tracks of blood and fire,
    Of thy venomed fangs despoil thee.

Through thy Augean stables vile,
    With long-horded rank pollution,
(Heaven my help) I'd pour the while
    One strong, sweeping, vast ablution.

Father of the waters flow,
    Flow each transatlantic river,
O'er your land of death and woe
    Cleanse her soil of blood for ever.

Time was when we lightly spoke,
    Smiled at each defeat and blunder,
Now, alas! the spell is broke—
    We can only weep and wonder.   [1870]

COMPARATIVE SLAVERY

Tell me not of negro slavery,
    Of its shackles, stripes, and woes—
Shackles stronger, stripes more cruel,
    Deeper woe the drunkard knows.

Ah! what fetters adamantine
    Bind and hold him in their thrall,
Oft the scorpion scourge of horror
    On his shrinking soul will fall.

Tell me not of buying, selling,
    Like the beasts in field or fold,
Human beings—lo! the drunkard—
    Body, soul, and heart hath sold.

Sold! is it to plant the cotton,
  Hoe the soil, and pick the pod?
No; to drink the demon tyrant,
  Foe to man, accursed of God.

Tell me not the negro mother
  Rears her children for the mart,
To be torn, when master wills it,
  From her clinging arms and heart.

We have thousand British mothers
  Who, in want, neglect, and cold,
See their infant victims pining
  To the fiend intemperance sold.

Do we loathe the beastly orgies
  Of the negro breeding pens?
Look within our thousand brothels,
  Viler far than negro dens.

Why do we descern so clearly
  Beams that dim our brother's eye,
While the motes, that mar our vision,
  We so seldom can descry?

Heritage of British freeman
  Never can a drunkard claim;
Slave of drink, and thrall of misery,
  His the heritage of shame.

Men of temperance, men of action,
  Ye who work, and think, and feel,
For the cause heaven smiles upon you,
  Labouring for your country's weal.

On the battle-field of temperance,
  Are no garments rolled in blood!
Nor the sound of shouting warrior
  Wading in the purple flood.

Patriotic zeal and pity,
  Effort born of brother love,
These your arms go on and conquer,
  Success waits you from above.   [1870]

JOHN KEATS

England 1795–1821

In a December 1816 letter Keats wrote of Negative Capability: 'that is when man is capable of being in uncertainties, Mysteries, doubts, without any irritable reaching after fact & reason.' Keats's valuing of ambiguity and his rapt attention to the dialectical process of apperception gave life and meaning to those 'untrodden region[s]' of the mind that he believed to be poetry's new frontier. Keats died of tuberculosis at the age of 25 having produced a wealth of poetic material: sonnets, narrative and epic poems ('Lamia', 1820, *Hyperion*, 1818), poetic romances (*Endymion*, 1817, 'The Eve of St Agnes', 1820), and odes which show the resources of a poet who could become 'characterless' and so evoke alternate states of mind. In a letter to Richard Woodhouse (27 October 1818) he observes: 'A Poet is the most unpoetical of any thing in existence; because he has no Identity— he is continually in for—and filling some other Body.' The standard edition of Keats's poetry is Jack Stillinger's *The Poems of John Keats* (1978).

LA BELLE DAME SANS MERCI

O what can ail thee, Knight at arms,
   Alone and palely loitering?
The sedge has withered from the Lake
   And no birds sing!

O what can ail thee, Knight at arms,
   So haggard, and so woebegone?
The squirrel's granary is full
   And the harvest's done.

I see a lily on thy brow
   With anguish moist and fever dew,
And on thy cheeks a fading rose
   Fast withereth too.

I met a Lady in the Meads,
   Full beautiful, a faery's child,
Her hair was long, her foot was light
   And her eyes were wild.

I made a Garland for her head,
   And bracelets too, and fragrant Zone,
She looked at me as she did love
   And made sweet moan.

I set her on my pacing steed
   And nothing else saw all day long,
For sidelong would she bend and sing
   A faery's song.

She found me roots of relish sweet,
  And honey wild, and manna dew,
And sure in language strange she said
  'I love thee true.'

She took me to her elfin grot
  And there she wept and sighed full sore,
And there I shut her wild wild eyes
  With kisses four.

And there she lulléd me asleep,
  And there I dreamed, Ah woe betide!
The latest dream I ever dreamt
  On the cold hill side.

I saw pale Kings, and Princes too,
  Pale warriors, death-pale were they all;
They cried, 'La belle dame sans merci
  Thee hath in thrall!'

I saw their starved lips in the gloam
  With horrid warning gapéd wide,
And I awoke, and found me here
  On the cold hill's side.

And this is why I sojourn here,
  Alone and palely loitering;
Though the sedge is withered from the Lake
  And no birds sing.   [1820]

ODE ON A GRECIAN URN

1
Thou still unravish'd bride of quietness,
  Thou foster-child of silence and slow time,
Sylvan historian, who canst thus express
  A flowery tale more sweetly than our rhyme:
What leaf-fring'd legend haunts about thy shape
  Of deities or mortals, or of both,
    In Tempe or the dales of Arcady?
  What men or gods are these? What maidens loth?
What mad pursuit? What struggle to escape?
    What pipes and timbrels? What wild ecstasy?

2

Heard melodies are sweet, but those unheard
   Are sweeter; therefore, ye soft pipes, play on;
Not to the sensual ear, but, more endear'd,
   Pipe to the spirit ditties of no tone:
Fair youth, beneath the trees, thou canst not leave
    Thy song, nor ever can those trees be bare;
      Bold lover, never, never canst thou kiss
Though winning near the goal—yet, do not grieve;
    She cannot fade, though thou hast not thy bliss,
    For ever wilt thou love, and she be fair!

3

Ah, happy, happy boughs! that cannot shed
   Your leaves, nor ever bid the spring adieu;
And, happy melodist, unwearied,
   Forever piping songs forever new;
More happy love! more happy, happy love!
    Forever warm and still to be enjoy'd,
      Forever panting, and forever young;
All breathing human passion far above,
    That leaves a heart high-sorrowful and cloy'd,
      A burning forehead, and a parching tongue.

4

Who are these coming to the sacrifice?
   To what green altar, O mysterious priest,
Lead'st thou that heifer lowing at the skies,
   And all her silken flanks with garlands drest?
What little town by river or sea shore,
    Or mountain-built with peaceful citadel,
      Is emptied of this folk, this pious morn?
And, little town, thy streets for evermore
    Will silent be; and not a soul to tell
      Why thou art desolate, can e'er return.

5

O Attic shape! Fair attitude! with brede
   Of marble men and maidens overwrought,
With forest branches and the trodden weed;
   Thou, silent form, dost tease us out of thought
As doth eternity: Cold Pastoral!
    When old age shall this generation waste,
      Thou shalt remain, in midst of other woe
Than ours, a friend to man, to whom thou say'st,
'Beauty is truth, truth beauty,'—that is all
    Ye know on earth, and all ye need to know.　　　　　　[1820]

Sojourner Truth

USA c. 1797–1883

Invited to read at US President Clinton's inauguration in 1993, Maya Angelou chose this poem by Sojourner Truth, read first at the 1852 National Women's Suffrage Convention. With its insistent rhetorical question, 'Ain't I a Woman?', the poem draws powerfully on oral tradition to make the speaker's case; when she turns her attention to woman's traditional place in the Bible, her gathering up of women's strengths has made her diagnosis of women's calling seem inevitable.

AIN'T I A WOMAN?

Ain't I a woman?
  Look at me
Look at my arm!
  I have plowed and planted
and gathered into barns
  and no man could head me. . . .
And ain't I a woman?
  I could work as much
And eat as much as a man—
  When I could get it—
And bear the lash as well
  and ain't I a woman?
I have born thirteen children
  and seen most all sold into slavery
and when I cried out a mother's grief
  none but Jesus heard me . . .
and ain't I a woman? . . .
  If the first woman God ever made
was strong enough to turn the world
  upside down, all alone
together women ought to be able to turn it
  rightside up again.   [1851]

JOHN DUNMORE LANG

Australia 1799–1878

Lang, a prominent clergyman, political reformer, and writer, was born in Greenock, Scotland. He emigrated to Australia in 1823 to become Sydney's first Presbyterian minister; dismissed by the synod for his controversial views, he established the Scots Church for his congregation. A member of the Legislative Council, Lang campaigned relentlessly for social causes including convicts' rights and a national education system, founded Australian College in Sydney, and wrote numerous historical, political, and religious books and pamphlets. Lang's religious and satirical verse is collected in his *Poems: Sacred and Secular* (1872).

COLONIAL NOMENCLATURE

'Twas said of Greece two thousand years ago,
　　That every stone i' the land had got a name.
Of New South Wales too, men will soon say so too;
　　But every stone there seems to get the same.
'Macquarie' for a name is all *the* go:
　　The old Scotch Governor was fond of fame.
Macquarie Street, Place, Port, Fort, Town, Lake, River:
'Lachlan Macquarie, Esquire, Governor,' for ever!

I like the native names, as Parramatta,
　　And Illawarra, and Woolloomoolloo;
Nandowra, Woogarora, Bulkomatta,
　　Tomah, Toongabbie, Mittagong, Meroo;
Buckobble, Cumleroy, and Coolingatta.
　　The Warragumby, Bargo, Burradoo;
Cookbundoon, Carrabaiga, Wingecarribbee,
The Wollondilly, Yurumbon, Bungarribbee.

I hate your Goulburn Downs and Goulburn Plains,
　　And Goulburn River and the Goulburn Range,
And Mount Goulburn and Goulburn Vale! One's brains
　　Are turned with Goulburns! Vile scorbutic mange
For immortality! Had I the reins
　　Of Government a fortnight, I would change
These Downing Street appellatives, and give
The country names that should deserve to live.

I'd have Mount Hampden and Mount Marvell, and
　　Mount Wallace and Mount Bruce at the old Bay.
I'd have them all the highest in the land,
　　That men might see them twenty leagues away.

I'd have the Plains of Marathon beyond
　Some mountain pass yclept Thermopylae.
Such are th' immortal names that should be written
On all thy new discoveries, Great Britain!

Yes! let some badge of liberty appear
　On every mountain and on every plain
Where Britain's power is known, or far or near,
　That freedom there may have an endless reign!
Then though she die, in some revolving year,
　A race may rise to make her live again!
The future slave may lisp the patriot's name
And his breast kindle with a kindred flame!   [1824]

BAMEWAWASGEZHIKAQUAY/ JANE SCHOOLCRAFT

Chippewa 1800–1841

Schoolcraft's grandfather was the Chippewa chief and renowned orator, Waubojeeg; her mother, Susan, was a well-known teller of traditional stories and her father was John Johnston, a British trader at the Sault Ste Marie frontier trading post. Educated in Ireland but fluent in the Ojibway language and oral literature as well as in English literature and history, Jane Johnston married prominent ethnologist and writer Henry Rowe Schoolcraft in 1823, a union not uncommon in the border area between the United States and Canada. Under the pen-name Rosa she wrote stories and poetry for her husband's ethnographic magazine, *The Literary Voyageur or Muzzeniegun* (1826–27).

TO MY EVER BELOVED AND LAMENTED SON WILLIAM HENRY

Who was it, nestled on my breast,
'And on my cheeks sweet kisses prest'
And in whose smile I felt so blest?
　　　Sweet Willy.

Who hail'd my form as home I stept,
And in my arms so eager leapt,
And to my bosom joyous crept?
　　　My Willy.

Who was it, wiped my tearful eye,
And kiss'd away the coming sigh,
And smiling bid me say 'good boy'?
　　　Sweet Willy.

Who was it, look'd divinely fair,
Whilst lisping sweet the evening pray'r
Guileless and free from earthly care?
    My Willy.

Where is that voice attuned to love,
That bid me say 'my darling dove'
But oh! that soul has flown above,
    Sweet Willy.

Whither has fled the rose's hue?
The lilly's whiteness blending grew,
Upon thy cheek—so fair to view,
    My Willy.

Oft have I gaz'd with wrapt delight,
Upon those eyes that sparkled bright,
Emitting beams of joy and light!
    Sweet Willy.

Oft have I kiss'd that forehead high,
Like polished marble to the eye,
And blessing, breathed an anxious sigh.
    For Willy.

My Son! thy coral lips are pale,
Can I believe the heart-sick tale,
That I, thy loss must ever wail?
    My Willy.

The clouds in darkness seemed to low'r,
The storm has past with awful pow'r,
And nipt my tender, beauteous flow'r!
    Sweet Willy.

But soon my spirit will be free,
And I my lovely Son shall see,
For God, I know, did this decree!
    My Willy.   [1827]

RALPH WALDO EMERSON

USA 1803–1882

Emerson was born in Boston, educated at Harvard, and ordained as a Unitarian minister but his religious scepticism ended this career in 1832. Under the influence of Wordsworth, Coleridge, and Carlyle he developed Puritan and Calvinist doctrinal beliefs into a transcendentalist philosophy. Emerson's rhetorically and intellectually sophisticated public addresses and essays profoundly influenced Whitman, Frost, Stevens, and cummings. His poetry reflects his thought in a more meditative, self-conscious, and conventionally Romantic form of expression.

CONCORD HYMN

SUNG AT THE COMPLETION OF THE BATTLE MONUMENT, JULY 4, 1837

By the rude bridge that arched the flood,
    Their flag to April's breeze unfurled,
Here once the embattled farmers stood
    And fired the shot heard round the world.

The foe long since in silence slept;
    Alike the conqueror silent sleeps;
And Time the ruined bridge has swept
    Down the dark stream which seaward creeps.

On this green bank, by this soft stream,
    We set to-day a votive stone;
That memory may their deed redeem,
    When, like our sires, our sons are gone.

Spirit, that made those heroes dare
    To die, and leave their children free,
Bid Time and Nature gently spare
    The shaft we raise to them and thee.   [1837]

THE PROBLEM

I like a church; I like a cowl;
I love a prophet of the soul;
And on my heart monastic aisles
Fall like sweet strains, or pensive smiles;
Yet not for all his faith can see
Would I that cowled churchman be.

Why should the vest on him allure,
Which I could not on me endure?

Not from a vain or shallow thought
His awful Jove young Phidias brought;
Never from lips of cunning fell
The thrilling Delphic oracle;
Out from the heart of nature rolled
The burdens of the Bible old;
The litanies of nations came,
Like the volcano's tongue of flame,
Up from the burning core below,—
The canticles of love and woe;
The hand that rounded Peter's dome,
And groined the aisles of Christian Rome,
Wrought in a sad sincerity;
Himself from God he could not free;
He builded better than he knew;—
The conscious stone to beauty grew.

Know'st thou what wove yon woodbird's nest
Of leaves, and feathers from her breast?
Or how the fish outbuilt her shell,
Painting with morn each annual cell?
Or how the sacred pine-tree adds
To her old leaves new myriads?
Such and so grew these holy piles,
Whilst love and terror laid the tiles.
Earth proudly wears the Parthenon,
As the best gem upon her zone;
And Morning opes with haste her lids,
To gaze upon the Pyramids;
O'er England's abbeys bends the sky,
As on its friends, with kindred eye;
For, out of Thought's interior sphere,
These wonders rose to upper air;
And Nature gladly gave them place,
Adopted them into her race,
And granted them an equal date
With Andes and with Ararat.

These temples grew as grows the grass;
Art might obey, but not surpass.
The passive Master lent his hand
To the vast soul that o'er him planned;
And the same power that reared the shrine,
Bestrode the tribes that knelt within.
Ever the fiery Pentecost
Girds with one flame the countless host,

Trances the heart through chanting choirs,
And through the priest the mind inspires.
The word unto the prophet spoken
Was writ on tables yet unbroken;
The word by seers or sibyls told,
In groves of oak, or fanes of gold,
Still floats upon the morning wind,
Still whispers to the willing mind.
One accent of the Holy Ghost
The heedless world hath never lost.
I know what say the fathers wise,—
The Book itself before me lies,
Old *Chrysostom*, best Augustine,
And he who blent both in his line,
The younger *Golden Lips* or mines,
Taylor, the Shakspeare of divines.
His words are music in my ear,
I see his cowled portrait dear;
And yet, for all his faith could see,
I would not the good bishop be.   [1847]

JAMES CLARENCE MANGAN

Ireland 1803–1849

Though supported by friends who helped secure him occasional employment, Mangan could never recover from a lifelong addiction to drugs and alcohol. He died malnourished and spent. In many ways he lived out the drama of the accursed, suffering artist conceived by Symbolist poets like Verlaine and visual artists like Gauguin: the artist who deliberately offers his or her life to atone for the hypocrisies of the age. In his Foreword to *The Selected Poems of James Clarence Mangan* (1974), the poet Anthony Cronin reminds the reader that the figure of the suffering artist in Mangan's work resists the stereotype of the inebriated, broken genius often sold as the 'anthologized Irish poet'. The anguish Mangan is forced to explore is the 'genuine article', Cronin affirms.

THE NAMELESS ONE

BALLAD

Roll forth, my song, like the rushing river,
    That sweeps along to the mighty sea;
God will inspire me while I deliver
        My soul of thee!

Tell thou the world, when my bones lie whitening
    Amid the last homes of youth and eld,
That there was once one whose veins ran lightning
        No eye beheld.

Tell how his boyhood was one drear night-hour,
   How shone for *him*, through his griefs and gloom,
No star of all heaven sends to light our
       Path to the tomb.

Roll on, my song, and to after ages
   Tell how, disdaining all earth can give,
He would have taught men, from wisdom's pages,
       The way to live.

And tell how trampled, derided, hated,
   And worn by weakness, disease, and wrong,
He fled for shelter to God, who mated
       His soul with song—

With song which always, sublime or vapid,
   Flowed like a rill in the morning beam,
Perchance not deep, but intense and rapid—
       A mountain stream.

Tell how this Nameless, condemned for years long
   To herd with demons from hell beneath,
Saw things that made him, with groans and tears, long
       For even death.

Go on to tell how, with genius wasted,
   Betrayed in friendship, befooled in love,
With spirit shipwrecked, and young hopes blasted,
       He still, still strove.

Till, spent with toil, dreeing death for others,
   And some whose hands should have wrought for *him*
(If children live not for sires and mothers,)
       His mind grew dim.

And he fell far through that pit abysmal
   The gulf and grave of Maginn and Burns,
And pawned his soul for the devil's dismal
       Stock of returns.

But yet redeemed it in days of darkness,
   And shapes and signs of the final wrath,
When death, in hideous and ghastly starkness,
       Stood on his path.

And tell how now, amid wreck and sorrow,
  And want, and sickness, and houseless nights,
He bides in calmness the silent morrow,
      That no ray lights.

And lives he still, then? Yes! Old and hoary
  At thirty-nine, from despair and woe,
He lives enduring what future story
      Will never know.

Him grant a grave to, ye pitying noble,
  Deep in your bosoms! There let him dwell!
He, too, had tears for all souls in trouble,
      Here and in hell.   [1903]

JOSEPH HOWE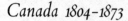

Canada 1804–1873

Howe, the leading journalist and politician of his time in Nova Scotia, founded the *Novascotian* in
1828 and edited it until 1840. He was premier of the province from 1860 to 1863. Howe used the
Novascotian as a vehicle to encourage the region's cultural and political life. His considerable prose
works are represented in *The Heart of Howe: Selections from the Letters and Speeches of Joseph Howe*
(ed. Harvey, 1939). His poetry, collected in *Poems and Essays* (1874, rev. ed. Parks, 1973), renders
a vision of hope and destiny for Nova Scotia.

THE MICMAC

Though o'er Acadia's hills and plains
  The wand'ring Micmac listless strays,
While scarce a single trace remains
  Of what he was in other days.

And though he now an outcast seems
  Upon the lands his Fathers trod,
And his dark eye no longer beams
  With pride which bent but to his God,—

Though the fire-water's deadly wave
  Which even pride could not control,
Has drown'd each feeling high that gave
  Such innate grandeur to his soul;—

There was a time when Nature's child
  With nobler port and manner bore him,
And ranged with joy his native wild,
  Or slept with Heaven's blue curtain o'er him.

Long ere the white man's axe was heard
  Resounding in the forest shade,
Long ere the rifle's voice had stirr'd
  The stillness of the Sylvan glade,—

Ere Science, with her plastic hand,
  And Labor, with his patient toil,
Had changed the features of the land,
  And dispossess'd him of the soil.

Then let fair Fancy change the scene,
  While gazing on the Micmac's brow,
And showing what he once has been,
  Make us forget what he is now.   [1874]

ELIZABETH BARRETT BROWNING

England 1806–1861

Browning secretly married Robert Browning and fled with him to Florence, escaping years of invalidism supervised by the tyrannical eye of a jealous father. The title of her *Sonnets from the Portuguese* (1850) was initially chosen to suggest that the verses were translated from Portuguese, to conceal their autobiographical elements. Browning's writing demonstrates the breadth of her political activism: a meditation in support of Italian unification, commentaries on the reality of child poverty, and fierce affirmations of the right to self-determination. The standard *Complete Works of Elizabeth Barrett Browning*, edited by Porter and Clarke in six volumes, was published in 1900.

THE RUNAWAY SLAVE AT PILGRIM'S POINT

I

I stand on the mark beside the shore
  Of the first white pilgrim's bended knee,
Where exile turned to ancestor,
  And God was thanked for liberty.
I have run through the night, my skin is as dark,
I bend my knee down on this mark:
  I look on the sky and the sea.

II

O pilgrim-souls, I speak to you!
  I see you come proud and slow
From the land of the spirits pale as dew
  And round me and round me ye go.
O pilgrims, I have gasped and run
All night long from the whips of one
  Who in your names works sin and woe!

III

And thus I thought that I would come
   And kneel here where ye knelt before,
And feel your souls around me hum
   In undertone to the ocean's roar;
And lift my black face, my black hand,
Here, in your names, to curse this land
   Ye blessed in freedom's, evermore.

IV

I am black, I am black,
   And yet God made me, they say:
But if He did so, smiling back
   He must have cast his work away
Under the feet of his white creatures,
With a look of scorn, that the dusky features
   Might be trodden again to clay.

V

And yet He has made dark things
   To be glad and merry as light:
There's a little dark bird sits and sings,
   There's a dark stream ripples out of sight,
And the dark frogs chant in the safe morass,
And the sweetest stars are made to pass
   O'er the face of the darkest night.

VI

But we who are dark, we are dark!
   Ah God, we have no stars!
About our souls in care and cark
   Our blackness shuts like prison-bars:
The poor souls crouch so far behind
That never a comfort can they find
   By reaching through the prison-bars.

VII

Indeed we live beneath the sky,
   That great smooth Hand of God stretched out
On all his children fatherly,
   To save them from the dread and doubt
Which would be if, from this low place,
All opened straight up to his face
   Into the grand eternity.

VIII

And still God's sunshine and his frost,
   They make us hot, they make us cold,
As if we were not black and lost;
   And the beasts and birds, in wood and fold,
Do fear and take us for very men:
Could the whippoorwill or the cat of the glen
   Look into my eyes and be bold?

IX

I am black, I am black!
   But, once, I laughed in girlish glee,
For one of my color stood in the track
   Where the drivers drove, and looked at me,
And tender and full was the look he gave—
Could a slave look *so* at another slave?—
   I look at the sky and the sea.

X

And from that hour our spirits grew
   As free as if unsold, unbought:
Oh, strong enough, since we were two,
   To conquer the world, we thought.
The drivers drove us day by day;
We did not mind, we went one way,
   And no better a freedom sought.

XI

In the sunny ground between the canes,
   He said 'I love you' as he passed;
When the shingle-roof rang sharp with the rains,
   I heard how he vowed it fast:
While others shook he smiled in the hut,
As he carved me a bowl of the cocoanut
   Through the roar of the hurricanes.

XII

I sang his name instead of a song,
   Over and over I sang his name,
Upward and downward I drew it along
   My various notes,—the same, the same!
I sang it low, that the slave-girls near
Might never guess, from aught they could hear,
   It was only a name—a name.

XIII
I look on the sky and the sea.
  We were two to love and two to pray:
Yes, two, O God, who cried to Thee,
  Though nothing didst Thou say!
Coldly Thou sat'st behind the sun:
And now I cry who am but one,
  Thou wilt not speak today.

XIV
We were black, we were black,
  We had no claim to love and bliss,
What marvel if each went to wrack?
  They wrung my cold hands out of his,
They dragged him—where? I crawled to touch
His blood's mark in the dust . . . not much,
  Ye pilgrim-souls, though plain as *this!*

XV
Wrong, followed by a deeper wrong!
  Mere grief's too good for such as I:
So the white men brought the shame ere long
  To strangle the sob of my agony.
They would not leave me for my dull
Wet eyes!—it was too merciful
  To let me weep pure tears and die.

XVI
I am black, I am black!
  I wore a child upon my breast,
An amulet that hung too slack,
  And, in my unrest, could not rest:
Thus we went moaning, child and mother,
One to another, one to another,
  Until all ended for the best.

XVII
For hark! I will tell you low, low,
  I am black, you see,—
And the babe who lay on my bosom so,
  Was far too white, too white for me;
As white as the ladies who scorned to pray
Beside me at church but yesterday,
  Though my tears had washed a place for my knee.

XVIII
My own, own child! I could not bear
    To look in his face, it was so white;
I covered him up with a kerchief there,
    I covered his face in close and tight:
And he moaned and struggled, as well might be,
For the white child wanted his liberty—
    Ha, ha! he wanted the master-right.

XIX
He moaned and beat with his head and feet,
    His little feet that never grew;
He struck them out, as it was meet,
    Against my heart to break it through:
I might have sung and made him mild,
But I dared not sing to the white-faced child
    The only song I knew.

XX
I pulled the kerchief very close:
    He could not see the sun, I swear,
More, then, alive, than now he does
    From between the roots of the mango . . . where?
I know where. Close! A child and mother
Do wrong to look at one another
    When one is black and one is fair.

XXI
Why, in that single glance I had
    Of my child's face, . . . I tell you all,
I saw a look that made me mad!
    The *master's* look, that used to fall
On my soul like his lash . . . or worse!
And so, to save it from my curse,
    I twisted it round in my shawl.

XXII
And he moaned and trembled from foot to head,
    He shivered from head to foot;
Till after a time, he lay instead
    Too suddenly still and mute.
I felt, beside, a stiffening cold:
I dared to lift up just a fold,
    As in lifting a leaf of the mango-fruit.

XXIII
But *my* fruit . . . ha, ha!—there, had been
    (I laugh to think on't at this hour!)
Your fine white angels (who have seen
    Nearest the secret of God's power)
And plucked my fruit to make them wine,
And sucked the soul of that child of mine
    As the hummingbird sucks the soul of the flower.

XXIV
Ha, ha, the trick of the angels white!
    They freed the white child's spirit so.
I said not a word, but day and night
    I carried the body to and fro,
And it lay on my heart like a stone, as chill.
—The sun may shine out as much as he will:
    I am cold, though it happened a month ago.

XXV
From the white man's house, and the black man's hut,
    I carried the little body on:
The forest's arms did round us shut,
    And silence through the trees did run:
They asked no question as I went,
They stood too high for astonishment,
    They could see God sit on his throne.

XXVI
My little body, kerchiefed fast,
    I bore it on through the forest, on;
And when I felt it was tired at last,
    I scooped a hole beneath the moon:
Through the forest-tops the angels far,
With a white sharp finger from every star,
    Did point and mock at what was done.

XXVII
Yet when it was all done aright,—
    Earth, 'twixt me and my baby, strewed,—
All, changed to black earth,—nothing white,—
    A dark child in the dark!—ensued
Some comfort, and my heart grew young;
I sate down smiling there and sung
    The song I learnt in my maidenhood.

XXVIII

And thus we two were reconciled,
  The white child and black mother, thus;
For as I sang it soft and wild,
  The same song, more melodious,
Rose from the grave whereon I sate:
It was the dead child singing that,
  To join the souls of both of us.

XXIX

I look on the sea and the sky.
  Where the pilgrims' ships first anchored lay
The free sun rideth gloriously,
  But the pilgrim ghosts have slid away
Through the earliest streaks of the morn:
My face is black, but it glares with a scorn
  Which they dare not meet by day.

XXX

Ha!—in their stead, their hunter sons!
  Ha, ha! they are on me—they hunt in a ring!
Keep off! I brave you all at once,
  I throw off your eyes like snakes that sting!
You have killed the black eagle at nest, I think:
Did you ever stand still in your triumph, and shrink
  From the stroke of her wounded wing?

XXXI

(Man, drop that stone you dared to lift!—)
  I wish you who stand there five abreast,
Each, for his own wife's joy and gift,
  A little corpse as safely at rest
As mine in the mangoes! Yes, but *she*
May keep live babies on her knee,
  And sing the song she likes the best.

XXXII

I am not mad: I am black.
  I see you staring in my face—
I know you staring, shrinking back,
  Ye are born of the Washington-race,
And this land is the free America,
And this mark on my wrist—(I prove what I say)
  Ropes tied me up here to the flogging-place.

XXXIII

You think I shrieked then? Not a sound
  I hung, as a gourd hangs in the sun;
I only cursed them all around
  As softly as I might have done
My very own child: from these sands
Up to the mountains, lift your hands,
  O slaves, and end what I begun!

XXXIV

Whips, curses; these must answer those!
  For in this union you have set
Two kinds of men in adverse rows,
  Each loathing each; and all forget
The seven wounds in Christ's body fair,
While He sees gaping everywhere
  Our countless wounds that pay no debt.

XXXV

Our wounds are different. Your white men
  Are, after all, not gods indeed,
Nor able to make Christs again
  Do good with bleeding. We who bleed
(Stand off!) we help not in our loss!
We are too heavy for our cross,
  And fall and crush you and your seed.

XXXVI

I fall, I swoon! I look at the sky.
  The clouds are breaking on my brain;
I am floated along, as if I should die
  Of liberty's exquisite pain.
In the name of the white child waiting for me
In the death-dark where we may kiss and agree,
White men, I leave you all curse-free
  In my broken heart's disdain!

[1850]

HENRY WADSWORTH LONGFELLOW
USA 1807–1882

Born in Portland, Massachusetts (later Maine), Longfellow was a student and professor of languages at Bowdoin College, and a professor of European literatures at Harvard. He was highly popular in his own time due to his works' sentimentality, accessible diction, and simplified metres. The romantic stereotypes in 'The Song of Hiawatha' of indigenous peoples and their relations with Europeans have become embedded and elaborated in the iconography of North American popular culture. The works published during Longfellow's lifetime include half a dozen books of poetry, a translation of Dante's *Divine Comedy* (1867–70), and an influential anthology, *The Poets and Poetry of Europe* (1845).

from THE SONG OF HIAWATHA

XXII

Hiawatha's Departure
By the shore of Gitche Gumee,
By the shining Big-Sea-Water,
At the doorway of his wigwam,
In the pleasant summer morning,
Hiawatha stood and waited.
All the air was full of freshness,
All the earth was bright and joyous,
And before him, through the sunshine,
Westward toward the neighboring forest
Passed in golden swarms the Ahmo,
Passed the bees, the honey-makers,
Burning, singing in the sunshine.

Bright above him shone the heavens,
Level spread the lake before him;
From its bosom leaped the sturgeon,
Sparkling, flashing in the sunshine;
On its margin the great forest
Stood reflected in the water,
Every tree-top had its shadow,
Motionless beneath the water.

From the brow of Hiawatha
Gone was every trace of sorrow,
As the fog from off the water,
As the mist from off the meadow.
With a smile of joy and triumph,
With a look of exultation,
As of one who in a vision
Sees what is to be, but is not,
Stood and waited Hiawatha.

Toward the sun his hands were lifted,
Both the palms spread out against it,
And between the parted fingers
Fell the sunshine on his features,
Flecked with light his naked shoulders,
As it falls and flecks an oak-tree
Through the rifted leaves and branches.
    O'er the water floating, flying,
Something in the hazy distance,
Something in the mists of morning,
Loomed and lifted from the water,
Now seemed floating, now seemed flying,
Coming nearer, nearer, nearer.
    Was it Shingebis the diver?
Was it the pelican, the Shada?
Or the heron, the Shuh-shuh-gah?
Or the white goose, Waw-be-wawa,
With the water dripping, flashing
From its glossy neck and feathers?
    It was neither goose nor diver,
Neither pelican nor heron,
O'er the water, floating, flying,
Through the shining mist of morning,
But a birch canoe with paddles,
Rising, sinking on the water,
Dripping, flashing in the sunshine;
And within it came a people
From the distant land of Wabun,
From the farthest realms of morning
Came the Black-Robe chief, the Prophet,
He the Priest of Prayer, the Pale-face,
With his guides and his companions.
    And the noble Hiawatha,
With his hands aloft extended,
Held aloft in sign of welcome,
Waited, full of exultation,
Till the birch canoe with paddles
Grated on the shining pebbles,
Stranded on the sandy margin,
Till the Black-Robe chief, the Pale-face,
With the cross upon his bosom,
Landed on the sandy margin.
    Then the joyous Hiawatha
Cried aloud and spake in this wise:
'Beautiful is the sun, O strangers,
When you come so far to see us!

All our town in peace awaits you;
All our doors stand open for you;
You shall enter all our wigwams,
For the heart's right hand we give you.
   'Never bloomed the earth so gayly,
Never shone the sun so brightly,
As to-day they shine and blossom
When you come so far to see us!
Never was our lake so tranquil,
Nor so free from rocks and sand-bars;
For your birch canoe in passing
Has removed both rock and sand-bar.
   'Never before had our tobacco
Such a sweet and pleasant flavor,
Never the broad leaves of our corn-fields
Were so beautiful to look on,
As they seem to us this morning,
When you come so far to see us!'
   And the Black-Robe chief made answer,
Stammered in his speech a little,
Speaking words yet unfamiliar:
'Peace be with you, Hiawatha,
Peace be with you and your people,
Peace of prayer, and peace of pardon,
Peace of Christ, and joy of Mary!'
   Then the generous Hiawatha
Led the strangers to his wigwam,
Seated them on skins of bison,
Seated them on skins of ermine,
And the careful old Nokomis
Brought them food in bowls of bass-wood,
Water brought in birchen dippers,
And the calumet, the peace-pipe,
Filled and lighted for their smoking.
   All the old men of the village,
All the warriors of the nation,
All the Jossakeeds, the prophets,
The magicians, the Wabenos,
And the medicine-men, the Medas,
Came to bid the strangers welcome;
'It is well,' they said, 'O brothers,
That you come so far to see us!'
   In a circle round the doorway,
With their pipes they sat in silence,
Waiting to behold the strangers,
Waiting to receive their message;

Till the Black-Robe chief, the Pale-face,
From the wigwam came to greet them,
Stammering in his speech a little,
Speaking words yet unfamiliar;
'It is well,' they said, 'O brother,
That you come so far to see us!'
　　Then the Black-Robe chief, the prophet,
Told his message to the people,
Told the purport of his mission,
Told them of the Virgin Mary,
And her blessed Son, the Saviour,
How in distant lands and ages
He had lived on earth as we do;
How he fasted, prayed, and labored;
How the Jews, the tribe accursed,
Mocked him, scourged him, crucified him;
How he rose from where they laid him,
Walked again with his disciples,
And ascended into heaven.
And the chiefs made answer, saying:
'We have listened to your message,
We have heard your words of wisdom,
We will think on what you tell us.
It is well for us, O brothers,
That you come so far to see us!'
　　Then they rose up and departed
Each one homeward to his wigwam,
To the young men and the women
Told the story of the strangers
Whom the Master of Life had sent them
From the shining land of Wabun.
　　Heavy with the heat and silence
Grew the afternoon of Summer,
With a drowsy sound the forest
Whispered round the sultry wigwam,
With a sound of sleep the water
Rippled on the beach below it;
From the corn-fields shrill and ceaseless
Sang the grasshopper, Pah-puk-keena;
And the guests of Hiawatha,
Weary with the heat of Summer,
Slumbered in the sultry wigwam.
　　Slowly o'er the simmering landscape
Fell the evening's dusk and coolness,
And the long and level sunbeams
Shot their spears into the forest,

Breaking through its shields of shadow,
Rushed into each secret ambush,
Searched each thicket, dingle, hollow;
Still the guests of Hiawatha
Slumbered in the silent wigwam.
    From his place rose Hiawatha,
Bade farewell to old Nokomis,
Spake in whispers, spake in this wise,
Did not wake the guests, that slumbered:
    'I am going, O Nokomis,
On a long and distant journey,
To the portals of the Sunset,
To the regions of the home-wind,
Of the Northwest wind, Keewaydin.
But these guests I leave behind me,
In your watch and ward I leave them;
See that never harm comes near them,
See that never fear molests them,
Never danger nor suspicion,
Never want of food or shelter,
In the lodge of Hiawatha!'
    Forth into the village went he,
Bade farewell to all the warriors,
Bade farewell to all the young men,
Spake persuading, spake in this wise:
    'I am going, O my people,
On a long and distant journey;
Many moons and many winters
Will have come, and will have vanished,
Ere I come again to see you.
But my guests I leave behind me;
Listen to their words of wisdom,
Listen to the truth they tell you,
For the Master of Life has sent them
From the land of light and morning!'
    On the shore stood Hiawatha,
Turned and waved his hand at parting;
On the clear and luminous water
Launched his birch canoe for sailing,
From the pebbles of the margin
Shoved it forth into the water;
Whispered to it, 'Westward! westward!'
And with speed it darted forward.
    And the evening sun descending
Set the clouds on fire with redness,
Burned the broad sky, like a prairie,

Left upon the level water
One long track and trail of splendor,
Down whose stream, as down a river,
Westward, westward Hiawatha
Sailed into the fiery sunset,
Sailed into the purple vapors,
Sailed into the dusk of evening.
    And the people from the margin
Watched him floating, rising, sinking,
Till the birch canoe seemed lifted
High into that sea of splendor,
Till it sank into the vapors
Like the new moon, slowly, slowly
Sinking in the purple distance.
    And they said, 'Farewell forever!'
Said, 'Farewell, O Hiawatha!'
And the forests, dark and lonely,
Moved through all their depths of darkness,
Sighed, 'Farewell, O Hiawatha!'
And the waves upon the margin
Rising, rippling on the pebbles,
Sobbed, 'Farewell, O Hiawatha!'
And the heron, the Shuh-shuh-gah,
From her haunts among the fen-lands,
Screamed, 'Farewell, O Hiawatha!'
    Thus departed Hiawatha,
Hiawatha the Beloved,
In the glory of the sunset,
In the purple mists of evening,
To the regions of the home-wind,
Of the Northwest wind, Keewaydin,
To the Islands of the Blessed,
To the kingdom of Ponemah,
To the land of the Hereafter!   [1855]

HENRY L. DEROZIO

India 1809-1831

Of Indian and Portuguese parentage, Derozio taught English Literature and Language at Hindu College, Calcutta, where his own interest in the Romanticism of Byron and Scott inspired parallel allegiances among his students and within the Indo-Anglian poetry movement itself. At the same time, Derozio seems fully aware of the cost British influence imposes on a first language and culture.

TO THE PUPILS OF THE HINDU COLLEGE

Expanding like the petals of young flowers
I watch the gentle opening of your minds,
And the sweet loosening of the spell that binds
Your intellectual energies and powers
That stretch (like young birds in soft summer hours)
Their wings to try their strength. O how the winds
Of circumstances and freshening April showers
Of early knowledge and unnumbered kinds
Of new perceptions shed their influence,
And how you worship truth's omnipotence!
What joyance rains upon me when I see
Fame in the mirror of futurity,
Weaving the chaplets you have yet to gain,
Ah then I feel I have not lived in vain.   [1923]

EDGAR ALLAN POE

USA 1809-1849

Poe's personality and circumstances—his drinking problems, his poor health and poverty, and his unhappy relationships with women—are legendary. Poe was born in Boston, orphaned at two, and then adopted by a foster father, John Allan of Richmond, Virginia; his stormy but highly pro- ductive life ended at forty. In poetry, Poe wished for brevity and beauty, noting in 'The Poetic Principle' (1850) that 'Beauty is the sole legitimate province of the poem'. Among his books of poems are *Tamerlane and Other Poems* (1827), *Poems by Edgar A. Poe* (1831), and *The Raven and Other Poems* (1849).

ANNABEL LEE

It was many and many a year ago,
    In a kingdom by the sea,
That a maiden there lived whom you may know
    By the name of Annabel Lee;—
And this maiden she lived with no other thought
    Than to love and be loved by me.

She was a child and *I* was a child,
   In this kingdom by the sea,
But we loved with a love that was more than love—
   I and my Annabel Lee—
With a love that the wingéd seraphs of Heaven
   Coveted her and me.

And this was the reason that, long ago,
   In this kingdom by the sea,
A wind blew out of a cloud by night
   Chilling my Annabel Lee;
So that her highborn kinsmen came
   And bore her away from me,
To shut her up, in a sepulchre
   In this kingdom by the sea.

The angels, not half so happy in Heaven,
   Went envying her and me:—
Yes! that was the reason (as all men know,
   In this kingdom by the sea)
That the wind came out of the cloud, chilling
   And killing my Annabel Lee.

But our love it was stronger by far than the love
   Of those who were older than we—
   Of many far wiser than we—
And neither the angels in Heaven above
   Nor the demons down under the sea
Can ever dissever my soul from the soul
   Of the beautiful Annabel Lee:—

For the moon never beams without bringing me dreams
   Of the beautiful Annabel Lee;
And the stars never rise but I see the bright eyes
   Of the beautiful Annabel Lee;
And so, all the night-tide, I lie down by the side
Of my darling, my darling, my life and my bride
   In her sepulchre there by the sea—
   In her tomb by the side of the sea.

[1849]

ALFRED, LORD TENNYSON

England 1809-1892

Tennyson succeeded Wordsworth as Poet Laureate in 1850. Post-Victorian poets may have admired Tennyson's lyrical strength, but felt his politics and mood were of a 'drawing room' variety. Currently, there is particular interest in the psychiatric and spiritual response to persons' moments of crisis, and the visionary and experimental qualities of that exploration. Tennyson's narrative, epic, and long poems include *In Memoriam* (1850), an extended meditation on the grieving process, *Enoch Arden* (1864), an account of co-dependency, and *Maud* (1854), a monodrama. The first collection of Tennyson's poetry in a single volume is *The Poems Of Tennyson* (ed. Ricks, 1969).

ULYSSES

It little profits that an idle king,
By this still hearth, among these barren crags,
Match'd with an aged wife, I mete and dole
Unequal laws unto a savage race,
That hoard, and sleep, and feed, and know not me.

   I cannot rest from travel: I will drink
Life to the lees: all times I have enjoy'd
Greatly, have suffer'd greatly, both with those
That loved me, and alone; on shore, and when
Thro' scudding drifts the rainy Hyades
Vext the dim sea: I am become a name;
For always roaming with a hungry heart
Much have I seen and known; cities of men
And manners, climates, councils, governments,
Myself not least, but honour'd of them all;
And drunk delight of battle with my peers,
Far on the ringing plains of windy Troy.
I am a part of all that I have met;
Yet all experience is an arch wherethro'
Gleams that untravell'd world, whose margin fades
For ever and for ever when I move.
How dull it is to pause, to make an end,
To rust unburnish'd, not to shine in use!
As tho' to breathe were life. Life piled on life
Were all too little, and of one to me
Little remains: but every hour is saved
From that eternal silence, something more,
A bringer of new things; and vile it were
For some three suns to store and hoard myself,
And this gray spirit yearning in desire
To follow knowledge like a sinking star,
Beyond the utmost bound of human thought.

This is my son, mine own Telemachus,
To whom I leave the sceptre and the isle—
Well-loved of me, discerning to fulfil
This labour, by slow prudence to make mild
A rugged people, and thro' soft degrees
Subdue them to the useful and the good.
Most blameless is he, centred in the sphere
Of common duties, decent not to fail
In offices of tenderness, and pay
Meet adoration to my household gods,
When I am gone. He works his work, I mine.

There lies the port; the vessel puffs her sail:
There gloom the dark broad seas. My mariners,
Souls that have toil'd, and wrought, and thought with me—
That ever with a frolic welcome took
The thunder and the sunshine, and opposed
Free hearts, free foreheads—you and I are old;
Old age hath yet his honour and his toil;
Death closes all: but something ere the end,
Some work of noble note, may yet be done,
Not unbecoming men that strove with Gods.
The lights begin to twinkle from the rocks:
The long day wanes: the slow moon climbs: the deep
Moans round with many voices. Come, my friends,
'Tis not too late to seek a newer world.
Push off, and sitting well in order smite
The sounding furrows; for my purpose holds
To sail beyond the sunset, and the baths
Of all the western stars, until I die.
It may be that the gulfs will wash us down:
It may be we shall touch the Happy Isles,
And see the great Achilles, whom we knew.
Tho' much is taken, much abides; and tho'
We are not now that strength which in old days
Moved earth and heaven; that which we are, we are;
One equal temper of heroic hearts,
Made weak by time and fate, but strong in will
To strive, to seek, to find, and not to yield.

[1842]

ROBERT BROWNING

England 1812-1889

Ezra Pound claimed Browning as his artistic father, finding in the earlier poet's verse key elements that seemed synchronized with twentieth-century North American and continental Modernism. Browning's dramatic monologues seemed particularly able to tolerate, indeed to revel in, ambiguity. Combining a desire to subvert inherited assumptions about class and gender, an appreciation for the vernacular, and techniques of compression particularly suited to the syntactic 'swing' of a speaker thinking aloud, Browning achieved an original psychological realism. A Cambridge edition of his work prepared by G. Robert Strange was published in 1974, and a projected seven-volume, annotated edition of *The Poetical Works of Robert Browning* by Ian Jack and Margaret Smith was begun in 1983.

MY LAST DUCHESS

FERRARA

That's my last Duchess painted on the wall,
Looking as if she were alive. I call
That piece a wonder, now: Frà Pandolf's hands
Worked busily a day, and there she stands.
Will 't please you sit and look at her? I said
'Frà Pandolf' by design, for never read
Strangers like you that pictured countenance,
The depth and passion of its earnest glance,
But to myself they turned (since none puts by
The curtain I have drawn for you, but I)
And seemed as they would ask me, if they durst,
How such a glance came there; so, not the first
Are you to turn and ask thus. Sir, 'twas not
Her husband's presence only, called that spot
Of joy into the Duchess' cheek: perhaps
Frà Pandolf chanced to say 'Her mantle laps
Over my lady's wrist too much,' or 'Paint
Must never hope to reproduce the faint
Half-flush that dies along her throat': such stuff
Was courtesy, she thought, and cause enough
For calling up that spot of joy. She had
A heart—how shall I say?—too soon made glad,
Too easily impressed; she liked whate'er
She looked on, and her looks went everywhere.
Sir, 'twas all one! My favor at her breast,
The dropping of the daylight in the West,
The bough of cherries some officious fool
Broke in the orchard for her, the white mule
She rode with round the terrace—all and each

Would draw from her alike the approving speech,
Or blush, at least. She thanked men—good! but thanked
Somehow—I know not how—as if she ranked
My gift of a nine-hundred-years-old name
With anybody's gift. Who'd stoop to blame
This sort of trifling? Even had you skill
In speech—(which I have not)—to make your will
Quite clear to such an one, and say, 'Just this
Or that in you disgusts me; here you miss,
Or there exceed the mark'—and if she let
Herself be lessoned so, nor plainly set
Her wits to yours, forsooth, and made excuse
—E'en then would be some stooping; and I choose
Never to stoop. Oh sir, she smiled, no doubt,
Whene'er I passed her; but who passed without
Much the same smile? This grew; I gave commands;
Then all smiles stopped together. There she stands
As if alive. Will 't please you rise? We'll meet
The company below, then. I repeat,
The Count your master's known munificence
Is ample warrant that no just pretense
Of mine for dowry will be disallowed;
Though his fair daughter's self, as I avowed
At starting, is my object. Nay, we'll go
Together down, sir. Notice Neptune, though,
Taming a sea horse, thought a rarity,
Which Claus of Innsbruck cast in bronze for me!   [1842]

THE BISHOP ORDERS HIS TOMB AT SAINT PRAXED'S CHURCH

ROME, 15—

Vanity, saith the preacher, vanity!
Draw round my bed: is Anselm keeping back?
Nephews—sons mine . . . ah God, I know not! Well—
She, men would have to be your mother once,
Old Gandolf envied me, so fair she was!
What's done is done, and she is dead beside,
Dead long ago, and I am Bishop since,
And as she died so must we die ourselves,
And thence ye may perceive the world's a dream.
Life, how and what is it? As here I lie
In this state-chamber, dying by degrees,
Hours and long hours in the dead night, I ask
'Do I live, am I dead?' Peace, peace seems all.
Saint Praxed's ever was the church for peace;
And so, about this tomb of mine. I fought

With tooth and nail to save my niche, ye know:
—Old Gandolf cozened me, despite my care;
Shrewd was that snatch from out the corner South
He graced his carrion with, God curse the same!
Yet still my niche is not so cramped but thence
One sees the pulpit o' the epistle-side,
And somewhat of the choir, those silent seats,
And up into the aery dome where live
The angels, and a sunbeam's sure to lurk:
And I shall fill my slab of basalt there,
And 'neath my tabernacle take my rest,
With those nine columns round me, two and two,
The odd one at my feet where Anselm stands:
Peach-blossom marble all, the rare, the ripe
As fresh-poured red wine of a mighty pulse.
—Old Gandolf with his paltry onion-stone,
Put me where I may look at him! True peach,
Rosy and flawless: how I earned the prize!
Draw close: that conflagration of my church
—What then? So much was saved if aught were missed!
My sons, ye would not be my death? Go dig
The white-grape vineyard where the oil-press stood,
Drop water gently till the surface sink,
And if ye find . . . Ah God, I know not, I! . . .
Bedded in store of rotten fig-leaves soft,
And corded up in a tight olive-frail,
Some lump, ah God, of *lapis lazuli*,
Big as a Jew's head cut off at the nape,
Blue as a vein o'er the Madonna's breast . . .
Sons, all have I bequeathed you, villas, all,
That brave Frascati villa with its bath,
So, let the blue lump poise between my knees,
Like God the Father's globe on both his hands
Ye worship in the Jesu Church so gay,
For Gandolf shall not choose but see and burst!
Swift as a weaver's shuttle fleet our years:
Man goeth to the grave, and where is he?
Did I say basalt for my slab, sons? Black—
'Twas ever antique-black I meant! How else
Shall ye contrast my frieze to come beneath?
The bas-relief in bronze ye promised me,
Those Pans and Nymphs ye wot of, and perchance
Some tripod, thyrsus, with a vase or so,
The Saviour at his sermon on the mount,
Saint Praxed in a glory, and one Pan
Ready to twitch the Nymph's last garment off,

And Moses with the tables . . . but I know
Ye mark me not! What do they whisper thee,
Child of my bowels, Anselm? Ah, ye hope
To revel down my villas while I gasp
Bricked o'er with beggar's mouldy travertine
Which Gandolf from his tomb-top chuckles at!
Nay, boys, ye love me—all of jasper, then!
'Tis jasper ye stand pledged to, lest I grieve
My bath must needs be left behind, alas!
One block, pure green as a pistachio-nut,
There's plenty jasper somewhere in the world—
And have I not Saint Praxed's ear to pray
Horses for ye, and brown Greek manuscripts,
And mistresses with great smooth marbly limbs?
—That's if ye carve my epitaph aright,
Choice Latin, picked phrase, Tully's every word,
No gaudy ware like Gandolf's second line—
Tully, my masters? Ulpian serves his need!
And then how I shall lie through centuries,
And hear the blessed mutter of the mass,
And see God made and eaten all day long,
And feel the steady candle-flame, and taste
Good strong thick stupefying incense-smoke!
For as I lie here, hours of the dead night,
Dying in state and by such slow degrees,
I fold my arms as if they clasped a crook,
And stretch my feet forth straight as stone can point,
And let the bedclothes, for a mortcloth, drop
Into great laps and folds of sculptor's-work:
And as yon tapers dwindle, and strange thoughts
Grow, with a certain humming in my ears,
About the life before I lived this life,
And this life too, popes, cardinals and priests,
Saint Praxed at his sermon on the mount,
Your tall pale mother with her talking eyes,
And new-found agate urns as fresh as day,
And marble's language, Latin pure, discreet,
—Aha, ELUCESCEBAT quoth our friend?
No Tully, said I, Ulpian at the best!
Evil and brief hath been my pilgrimage.
All *lapis*, all, sons! Else I give the Pope
My villas! Will ye ever eat my heart?
Ever your eyes were as a lizard's quick,
They glitter like your mother's for my soul,
Or ye would heighten my impoverished frieze,
Piece out its starved design, and fill my vase

With grapes, and add a visor and a Term,
And to the tripod ye would tie a lynx
That in his struggle throws the thyrsus down,
To comfort me on my entablature
Whereon I am to lie till I must ask
'Do I live, am I dead?' There, leave me, there!
For ye have stabbed me with ingratitude
To death—ye wish it—God, ye wish it! Stone—
Gritstone, a-crumble! Clammy squares which sweat
As if the corpse they keep were oozing through—
And no more *lapis* to delight the world!
Well, go! I bless ye. Fewer tapers there,
But in a row: and, going, turn your backs
—Ay, like departing altar-ministrants,
And leave me in my church, the church for peace,
That I may watch at leisure if he leers—
Old Gandolf—at me, from his onion-stone,
As still he envied me, so fair she was!   [1845]

EMILY BRONTË

England 1818-1848

In 1845, Charlotte Brontë, Emily's older sister, 'accidentally alighted' on a MS volume of Emily's poems, and added verses of her own and her sister Anne's. Together they published *Poems by Currer, Ellis, and Acton Bell* in 1846. The volume sold only two copies, yet it was followed by Emily's *Wuthering Heights*, as well as Charlotte's *Jane Eyre* and Anne's *Agnes Grey*. The last poem that Emily wrote before her death, 'No Coward Soul Is Mine', offers an ecstatic affirmation of the divine presence in every mortal shape, an inward liberty in circumstances as dire as those in 'The Prisoner'. The theme of the 'chainless soul' pervades Brontë's work, which is collected by C.W. Hatfield in *The Complete Poems of Emily J. Brontë* (1941).

THE PRISONER

A FRAGMENT

In the dungeon crypts idly did I stray,
Reckless of the lives wasting there away;
'Draw the ponderous bars! open, Warder stern!
He dared not say me nay—the hinges harshly turn.

'Our guests are darkly lodged,' I whispered, gazing through
The vault, whose grated eye showed heaven more gray than blue
(This was when glad Spring laughed in awaking pride);
'Aye, darkly lodged enough!' returned my sullen guide.

Then, God forgive my youth! forgive my careless tongue!
I scoffed, as the chill chains on the damp flagstones rung:
'Confined in triple walls, art thou so much to fear,
That we must bind thee down and clench thy fetters here?'

The captive raised her face; it was as soft and mild
As sculptured marble saint; or slumbering unweaned child;
It was so soft and mild, it was so sweet and fair,
Pain could not trace a line, or grief a shadow there!

The captive raised her hand and pressed it to her brow;
'I have been struck,' she said, 'and I am suffering now;
Yet these are little worth, your bolts and irons strong:
And, were they forged in steel, they could not hold me long.'

Hoarse laughed the jailor grim: 'Shall I be won to hear;
Dost think, fond, dreaming wretch, that *I* shall grant thy prayer?
Or, better still, wilt melt my master's heart with groans?
Ah! sooner might the sun thaw down these granite stones.

'My master's voice is low, his aspect bland and kind,
But hard as hardest flint the soul that lurks behind;
And I am rough and rude, yet not more rough to see
Than is the hidden ghost that has its home in me.'

About her lips there played a smile of almost scorn.
'My friend,' she gently said, 'you have not heard me mourn;
When you my kindred's lives, *my* lost life can restore,
Then may I weep and sue—but never, friend, before!

'Still, let my tyrants know, I am not doomed to wear
Year after year in gloom, and desolate despair;
A messenger of Hope comes every night to me,
And offers for short life, eternal liberty.

'He comes with western winds, with evening's wandering airs,
With that clear dusk of heaven that brings the thickest stars,
Winds take a pensive tone, and stars a tender fire,
And visions rise, and change, that kill me with desire.

'Desire for nothing known in my maturer years,
When Joy grew mad with awe, at counting future tears.
When, if my spirit's sky was full of flashes warm,
I knew not whence they came, from sun or thunderstorm.

But, first, a hush of peace—a soundless calm descends;
The struggle of distress and fierce impatience ends;
Mute music soothes my breast—unuttered harmony,
That I could never dream, till Earth was lost to me.

'Then dawns the Invisible; the Unseen its truth reveals;
My outward sense is gone, my inward essence feels:
Its wings are almost free—its home, its harbor found,
Measuring the gulf, it stoops—and dares the final bound.

'Oh! dreadful is the check—intense the agony—
When the ear begins to hear, and the eye begins to see;
When the pulse begins to throb, the brain to think again;
The soul to feel the flesh, and the flesh to feel the chain.

'Yet I would lose no sting, would wish no torture less;
The more that anguish racks, the earlier it will bless;
And robed in fires of hell, or bright with heavenly shine,
If it but herald death, the vision is divine!'

She ceased to speak, and we, unanswering, turned to go—
We had no further power to work the captive woe:
Her cheek, her gleaming eye, declared that man had given
A sentence, unapproved, and overruled by Heaven.   [1846]

FREDERICK DOUGLASS

USA c. 1818–c. 1895

'A Parody', which concludes Douglass's *Narrative of the Life of an American Slave*, mocks 'Heavenly Union', a popular hymn in the southern United States. Born Frederick Augustus Washington Bailey, a slave in Maryland, Douglass struggled to become literate and then in 1838 obtained his legal freedom, fled to New York City, and changed his name. Speaking from his experience of slavery, Douglass began to address audiences about abolition and Black liberation in 1841, and eventually became the most prominent Black spokesperson in nineteenth-century America; he also delivered speeches on emancipation in England, founded a newspaper (*The North Star*), participated in the Seneca Falls and Rochester women's rights conventions in 1848, and held several important political posts from 1865 to 1895.

A PARODY

'Come, saints and sinners, hear me tell
How pious priests whip Jack and Nell,
And women buy and children sell,
And preach all sinners down to hell,
    And sing of heavenly union.

'They'll bleat and baa, dona like goats,
Gorge down black sheep, and strain at motes,
Array their backs in fine black coats,
Then seize their negroes by their throats,
    And choke, for heavenly union.

'They'll church you if you sip a dram,
And damn you if you steal a lamb;
Yet rob old Tony, Doll, and Sam,
Of human rights, and bread and ham;
    Kidnapper's heavenly union.

'They'll loudly talk of Christ's reward,
And bind his image with a cord
And scold, and swing the lash abhorred,
And sell their brother in the Lord
    To handcuffed heavenly union.

'They'll read and sing a sacred song,
And make a prayer both loud and long,
And teach the right and do the wrong,
Hailing the brother, sister throng,
    With words of heavenly union.

'We wonder how such saints can sing,
Or praise the Lord upon the wing,
Who roar, and scold, and whip, and sting,
And to their slaves and mammon cling,
    In guilty conscience union.

'They'll raise tobacco, corn, and rye,
And drive, and thieve, and cheat, and lie,
And lay up treasures in the sky,
By making switch and cowskin fly,
    In hope of heavenly union.

'They'll crack old Tony on the skull,
And preach and roar like Bashan bull,
Or braying ass, of mischief full,
Then seize old Jacob by the wool,
    And pull for heavenly union.

'A roaring, ranting, sleek man-thief,
Who lived on mutton, veal, and beef,
Yet never would afford relief
To needy, sable sons of grief,
    Was big with heavenly union.

'"Love not the world," the preacher said,
And winked his eye, and shook his head;
He seized on Tom, and Dick, and Ned,
Cut short their meat, and clothes, and bread,
    Yet still loved heavenly union.

'Another preacher whining spoke
Of One whose heart for sinners broke:
He tied old Nanny to an oak,
And drew the blood at every stroke,
    And prayed for heavenly union.

'Two others oped their iron jaws,
And waved their children-stealing paws;
There sat their children in gewgaws;
By stinting negroes' backs and maws,
    They kept up heavenly union.

'All good from Jack another takes,
And entertains their flirts and rakes,
Who dress as sleek as glossy snakes,
And cram their mouths with sweetened cakes;
    And this goes down for union.'   [1845]

HERMAN MELVILLE

USA 1819–1891

Born in New York City, Melville once wrote that 'a whale-ship was my Yale College and my Harvard.' From 1839 to 1844, his exploits as a sailor who travelled to places such as the Marquesas, Tahiti, and Hawaii shaped his later adventures into his imagination, such that he became the first American writer to envision America as 'other': racist, capitalist, imperialist, and patriarchal. Melville's poetry was published in four collections—*Battle-Pieces* (1866); *Clarel: A Poem and Pilgrimage in the Holy Land* (1876); *John Marr and Other Sailors* (1888); and *Timoleon* (1891)—well after the precipitous decline of his intensive ten-year career as a writer of short stories and novels, including 'Bartleby, the Scrivener' (1853), *Typee: A Peep at Polynesian Life* (1846), *Moby-Dick* (1851), and *Billy Budd* (1891).

A UTILITARIAN VIEW OF THE MONITOR'S FIGHT

Plain be the phrase, yet apt the verse,
    More ponderous than nimble;
For since grimed War here laid aside
His Orient pomp, 'twould ill befit
        Overmuch to ply
    The rhyme's barbaric cymbal.

Hail to victory without the gaud
   Of glory; zeal that needs no fans
Of banners; plain mechanic power
Plied cogently in War now placed—
    Where War belongs—
   Among the trades and artisans.

Yet this was battle, and intense—
   Beyond the strife of fleets heroic;
Deadlier, closer, calm 'mid storm;
No passion; all went on by crank,
    Pivot, and screw,
   And calculations of caloric.

Needless to dwell; the story's known.
   The ringing of those plates on plates
Still ringeth round the world—
The clangor of that blacksmiths' fray.
    The anvil-din
   Resounds this message from the Fates:

War shall yet be, and to the end;
   But war-paint shows the streaks of weather;
War yet shall be, but warriors
Are now but operatives; War's made
    Less grand than Peace,
   And a singe runs through lace and feather.   [1866]

MONODY

To have known him, to have loved him
   After loneless long;
And then to be estranged in life,
   And neither in the wrong;
And now for death to set his seal—
   Ease me, a little ease, my song!

By wintry hills his hermit-mound
   The sheeted snow-drifts drape,
And houseless there the snow-bird flits
   Beneath the fir-trees' crape:
Glazed now with ice the cloistral vine
   That hid the shyest grape.   [1891]

WALT WHITMAN

USA 1819–1892

Born in New York, Whitman transformed the earlier mystical as well as utilitarian urges of New England's poets into the self-conscious and self-revealing poetic drama of identity and democracy anticipated in the prophesying rhetoric of Emerson. Whitman professes his devotion to the language of experience and the divinity of men and women in the 1855 Preface to *Leaves of Grass*: 'They shall find their inspiration in real objects today, symptoms of the past and future. . . . They shall not deign to defend immortality or God or the perfection of things or liberty or the exquisite beauty and reality of the soul. They shall arise in America and be responded to from the remainder of the earth.' Erotic, confessional, visionary, compassionate, bombastic, and seemingly unfettered, 'Song of Myself' appeared in the six editions of *Leaves of Grass* Whitman revised, expanded, and altered from 1855 to 1881.

from SONG OF MYSELF

1

I celebrate myself, and sing myself,
And what I assume you shall assume,
For every atom belonging to me as good belongs to you.

I loafe and invite my soul,
I lean and loafe at my ease observing a spear of summer grass.

My tongue, every atom of my blood, form'd from this soil, this air,
Born here of parents born here from parents the same, and their parents the
     same,
I, now thirty-seven years old in perfect health begin,
Hoping to cease not till death.

Creeds and schools in abeyance,
Retiring back a while sufficed at what they are, but never forgotten,
I harbor for good or bad, I permit to speak at every hazard,
Nature without check with original energy.

2

Houses and rooms are full of perfumes, the shelves are crowded with
     perfumes,
I breathe the fragrance myself and know it and like it,
The distillation would intoxicate me also, but I shall not let it.

The atmosphere is not a perfume, it has no taste of the distillation, it is
     odorless,
It is for my mouth forever, I am in love with it,
I will go to the bank by the wood and become undisguised and naked,
I am mad for it to be in contact with me.

The smoke of my own breath,
Echoes, ripples, buzz'd whispers, love-root, silk-thread, crotch and vine,
My respiration and inspiration, the beating of my heart, the passing of blood
  and air through my lungs,
The sniff of green leaves and dry leaves, and of the shore and dark-color'd
  sea-rocks, and of hay in the barn,
The sound of the belch'd words of my voice loos'd to the eddies of the wind,
A few light kisses, a few embraces, a reaching around of arms,
The play of shine and shade on the trees as the supple boughs wag,
The delight alone or in the rush of the streets, or along the fields and hill-
  sides,
The feeling of health, the full-noon trill, the song of me rising from bed and
  meeting the sun.

Have you reckon'd a thousand acres much? have you reckon'd the earth
  much?
Have you practis'd so long to learn to read?
Have you felt so proud to get at the meaning of poems?

Stop this day and night with me and you shall possess the origin of all poems,
You shall possess the good of the earth and sun, (there are millions of suns
  left,)
You shall no longer take things at second or third hand, nor look through the
  eyes of the dead, nor feed on the spectres in books,
You shall not look through my eyes either, nor take things from me,
You shall listen to all sides and filter them from your self.

3
I have heard what the talkers were talking, the talk of the beginning and the
  end,
But I do not talk of the beginning or the end.

There was never any more inception than there is now,
Nor any more youth or age than there is now,
And will never be any more perfection than there is now,
Nor any more heaven or hell than there is now.

Urge and urge and urge,
Always the procreant urge of the world.
Out of the dimness opposite equals advance, always substance and increase,
  always sex,
Always a knit of identity, always distinction, always a breed of life.

To elaborate is no avail, learn'd and unlearn'd feel that it is so.
Sure as the most certain sure, plumb in the uprights, well entretied, braced in
  the beams,
Stout as a horse, affectionate, haughty, electrical,
I and this mystery here we stand.

Clear and sweet is my soul, and clear and sweet is all that is not my soul.

Lack one lacks both, and the unseen is proved by the seen,
Till that becomes unseen and receives proof in its turn.

Showing the best and dividing it from the worst age vexes age,
Knowing the perfect fitness and equanimity of things, while they discuss I am
  silent, and go bathe and admire myself.

Welcome is every organ and attribute of me, and of any man hearty and clean,
Not an inch nor a particle of an inch is vile, and none shall be less familiar
  than the rest.

I am satisfied—I see, dance, laugh, sing;
As the hugging and loving bed-fellow sleeps at my side through the night, and
  withdraws at the peep of the day with stealthy tread,
Leaving me baskets cover'd with white towels swelling the house with their
  plenty,
Shall I postpone my acceptation and realization and scream at my eyes,
That they turn from gazing after and down the road,
And forthwith cipher and show me to a cent,
Exactly the value of one and exactly the value of two, and which is ahead?

4
Trippers and askers surround me,
People I meet, the effect upon me of my early life or the ward and city I live
  in, or the nation,
The latest dates, discoveries, inventions, societies, authors old and new,
My dinner, dress, associates, looks, compliments, dues,
The real or fancied indifference of some man or woman I love,
The sickness of one of my folks or of myself, or ill-doing or loss or lack of
  money, or depressions or exaltations,
Battles, the horrors of fratricidal war, the fever of doubtful news, the fitful
  events;
These come to me days and nights and go from me again,
But they are not the Me myself.

Apart from the pulling and hauling stands what I am,
Stands amused, complacent, compassionating, idle, unitary,
Looks down, is erect, or bends an arm on an impalpable certain rest,
Looking with side-curved head curious what will come next,
Both in and out of the game and watching and wondering at it.

Backward I see in my own days where I sweated through fog with linguists
  and contenders,
I have no mockings or arguments, I witness and wait.

5

I believe in you my soul, the other I am must not abase itself to you,
And you must not be abased to the other.

Loafe with me on the grass, loose the stop from your throat,
Not words, not music or rhyme I want, not custom or lecture, not even the
    best,
Only the lull I like, the hum of your valvèd voice.

I mind how once we lay such a transparent summer morning,
How you settled your head athwart my hips and gently turn'd over upon me,
And parted the shirt from my bosom-bone, and plunged your tongue to my
    bare-stript heart,
And reach'd till you felt my beard, and reach'd till you held my feet.

Swiftly arose and spread around me the peace and knowledge that pass all the
    argument of the earth,
And I know that the hand of God is the promise of my own,
And I know that the spirit of God is the brother of my own,
And that all the men ever born are also my brothers, and the women my
    sisters and lovers,
And that a kelson of the creation is love,
And limitless are leaves stiff or drooping in the fields,
And brown ants in the little wells beneath them,
And mossy scabs of the worm fence, heap'd stones, elder, mullein and
    pokeweed.

6

A child said What is the grass? fetching it to me with full hands;
How could I answer the child? I do not know what it is any more than he.

I guess it must be the flag of my disposition, out of hopeful green stuff woven.

Or I guess it is the handkerchief of the Lord,
A scented gift and remembrancer designedly dropt,
Bearing the owner's name someway in the corners, that we may see and
    remark, and say Whose?

Or I guess the grass is itself a child, the produced babe of the vegetation.

Or I guess it is a uniform hieroglyphic,
And it means, Sprouting alike in broad zones and narrow zones,
Growing among black folks as among white,
Kanuck, Tuckahoe, Congressman, Cuff, I give them the same, I receive them
    the same.

And now it seems to me the beautiful uncut hair of graves.

Tenderly will I use you curling grass,
It may be you transpire from the breasts of young men,
It may be if I had known them I would have loved them,
It may be you are from old people, or from offspring taken soon out of their
     mothers' laps,
And here you are the mothers' laps.

This grass is very dark to be from the white heads of old mothers,
Darker than the colorless beards of old men,
Dark to come from under the faint red roofs of mouths.

O I perceive after all so many uttering tongues,
And I perceive they do not come from the roofs of mouths for nothing.

I wish I could translate the hints about the dead young men and women,
And the hints about old men and mothers, and the offspring taken soon out
     of their laps.

What do you think has become of the young and old men?
And what do you think has become of the women and children?

They are alive and well somewhere,
The smallest sprout shows there is really no death,
And if ever there was it led forward life, and does not wait at the end to
     arrest it,
And ceas'd the moment life appear'd.

All goes onward and outward, nothing collapses,
And to die is different from what any one supposed, and luckier.

. . .

20
Who goes there? hankering, gross, mystical, nude;
How is it I extract strength from the beef I eat?

What is a man anyhow? what am I? what are you?

All I mark as my own you shall offset it with your own,
Else it were time lost listening to me.

I do not snivel that snivel the world over,
That months are vacuums and the ground but wallow and filth.

Whimpering and truckling fold with powders for invalids, conformity goes to
     the fourth-remov'd,
I wear my hat as I please indoors or out.

Why should I pray? why should I venerate and be ceremonious?

Having pried through the strata, analyzed to a hair, counsel'd with doctors
     and calculated close,
I find no sweeter fat than sticks to my bones.

In all people I see myself, none more and not one a barley-corn less,
And the good or bad I say of myself I say of them.

I know I am solid and sound,
To me the converging objects of the universe perpetually flow,
All are written to me, and I must get what the writing means.

I know I am deathless,
I know this orbit of mine cannot be swept by a carpenter's compass,
I know I shall not pass like a child's carlacue cut with a burnt stick at night.

I know I am august,
I do not trouble my spirit to vindicate itself or be understood,
I see that the elementary laws never apologize,
(I reckon I behave no prouder than the level I plant my house by, after all.)

I exist as I am, that is enough,
If no other in the world be aware I sit content,
And if each and all be aware I sit content.

One world is aware and by far the largest to me, and that is myself,
And whether I come to my own to-day or in ten thousand or ten million
     years,
I can cheerfully take it now, or with equal cheerfulness I can wait.

My foothold is tenon'd and mortis'd in granite,
I laugh at what you call dissolution,
And I know the amplitude of time.

21
I am the poet of the Body and I am the poet of the Soul,
The pleasures of heaven are with me and the pains of hell are with me,
The first I graft and increase upon myself, the latter I translate into a new
     tongue.

I am the poet of the woman the same as the man,
And I say it is as great to be a woman as to be a man,
And I say there is nothing greater than the mother of men.

I chant the chant of dilation or pride,
We have had ducking and deprecating about enough,
I show that size is only development.

Have you outstript the rest? are you the President?
It is a trifle, they will more than arrive there every one, and still pass on.

I am he that walks with the tender and growing night,
I call to the earth and sea half-held by the night.

Press close bare-bosom'd night—press close magnetic nourishing night!
Night of south winds—night of the large few stars!
Still nodding night—mad naked summer night.

Smile O voluptuous cool-breath'd earth!
Earth of the slumbering and liquid trees!
Earth of departed sunset—earth of the mountains misty-topt!
Earth of the vitreous pour of the full moon just tinged with blue!
Earth of shine and dark mottling the tide of the river!
Earth of the limpid gray of clouds brighter and clearer for my sake!
Far-swooping elbow'd earth—rich apple-blossom'd earth!
Smile, for your lover comes.

Prodigal, you have given me love—therefore I to you give love!
O unspeakable passionate love.

22
You sea! I resign myself to you also—I guess what you mean,
I behold from the beach your crooked inviting fingers,
I believe you refuse to go back without feeling of me,
We must have a turn together, I undress, hurry me out of sight of the land,
Cushion me soft, rock me in billowy drowse,
Dash me with amorous wet, I can repay you.

Sea of stretch'd ground-swells,
Sea breathing broad and convulsive breaths,
Sea of the brine of life and of unshovell'd yet always-ready graves,
Howler and scooper of storms, capricious and dainty sea,
I am integral with you, I too am of one phase and of all phases.

Partaker of influx and efflux I, extoller of hate and conciliation,
Extoller of amies and those that sleep in each others' arms.

I am he attesting sympathy,
(Shall I make my list of things in the house and skip the house that supports
    them?)

I am not the poet of goodness only, I do not decline to be the poet of
    wickedness also.

What blurt is this about virtue and about vice?
Evil propels me and reform of evil propels me, I stand indifferent,
My gait is no fault-finder's or rejecter's gait,
I moisten the roots of all that has grown.

Did you fear some scrofula out of the unflagging pregnancy?
Did you guess the celestial laws are yet to be work'd over and rectified?

I find one side a balance and the antipodal side a balance,
Soft doctrine as steady help as stable doctrine,
Thoughts and deeds of the present our rouse and early start.

This minute that comes to me over the past decillions,
There is no better than it and now.

What behaved well in the past or behaves well to-day is not such a wonder,
The wonder is always and always how there can be a mean man or an infidel.

23
Endless unfolding of words of ages!
And mine a word of the modern, the word En-Masse.

A word of the faith that never balks,
Here or henceforward it is all the same to me, I accept Time absolutely.

It alone is without flaw, it alone rounds and completes all,
That mystic baffling wonder alone completes all.

I accept Reality and dare not question it.
Materialism first and last imbuing.

Hurrah for positive science! long live exact demonstration!
Fetch stonecrop mixt with cedar and branches of lilac,
This is the lexicographer, this the chemist, this made a grammar of the old
     cartouches,
These mariners put the ship through dangerous unknown seas,
This is the geologist, this works with the scalpel, and this is a mathematician.

Gentlemen, to you the first honors always!
Your facts are useful, and yet they are not my dwelling,
I but enter by them to an area of my dwelling.

Less the reminders of properties told my words,
And more the reminders they of life untold, and of freedom and extrication,
And make short account of neuters and geldings, and favor men and women
     fully equipt,
And beat the gong of revolt, and stop with fugitives and them that plot and
     conspire.

24
Walt Whitman, a kosmos, of Manhattan the son,
Turbulent, fleshy, sensual, eating, drinking and breeding,
No sentimentalist, no stander above men and women or apart from them,
No more modest than immodest.

Unscrews the locks from the doors!
Unscrews the doors themselves from their jambs!

Whoever degrades another degrades me,
And whatever is done or said returns at last to me.

Through me the afflatus surging and surging, through me the current and
    index.

I speak the pass-word primeval, I give the sign of democracy,
By God! I will accept nothing which all cannot have their counterpart of on
    the same terms.

Through me many long dumb voices,
Voices of the interminable generations of prisoners and slaves,
Voices of the diseas'd and despairing and of thieves and dwarfs,

Voices of cycles of preparation and accretion,
And of the threads that connect the stars, and of wombs and of the
    father-stuff,
And of the rights of them the others are down upon,
Of the deform'd, trivial, flat, foolish, despised,
Fog in the air, beetles rolling balls of dung.

Through me forbidden voices,
Voices of sexes and lusts, voices veil'd and I remove the veil,
Voices indecent by me clarified and transfigur'd.

I do not press my fingers across my mouth,
I keep as delicate around the bowels as around the head and heart,
Copulation is no more rank to me than death is.

I believe in the flesh and the appetites,
Seeing, hearing, feeling, are miracles, and each part and tag of me is a miracle.

Divine am I inside and out, and I make holy whatever I touch or am touch'd
    from,
The scent of these arm-pits aroma finer than prayer,
This head more than churches, bibles, and all the creeds.

If I worship one thing more than another it shall be the spread of my own
    body, or any part of it,
Translucent mould of me it shall be you!
Shaded ledges and rests it shall be you!
Firm masculine colter it shall be you!
Whatever goes to the tilth of me it shall be you!
You my rich blood! your milky stream pale strippings of my life!
Breast that presses against other breasts it shall be you!
My brain it shall be your occult convolutions!
Root of wash'd sweet-flag! timorous pond-snipe! nest of guarded duplicate
    eggs! it shall be you!
Mix'd tussled hay of head, beard, brawn, it shall be you!
Trickling sap of maple, fibre of manly wheat, it shall be you!
Sun so generous it shall be you!
Vapors lighting and shading my face it shall be you!
You sweaty brooks and dews it shall be you!
Winds whose soft-tickling genitals rub against me it shall be you!
Broad muscular fields, branches of live oak, loving lounger in my winding
    paths, it shall be you!
Hands I have taken, face I have kiss'd, mortal I have ever touch'd, it shall
    be you.

I dote on myself, there is that lot of me and all so luscious,
Each moment and whatever happens thrills me with joy,
I cannot tell how my ankles bend, nor whence the cause of my faintest wish,
Nor the cause of the friendship I emit, nor the cause of the friendship I take
    again.

That I walk up my stoop, I pause to consider if it really be,
A morning-glory at my window satisfies me more than the metaphysics of
    books.

To behold the day-break!
The little light fades the immense and diaphanous shadows,
The air tastes good to my palate.

Hefts of the moving world at innocent gambols silently rising freshly exuding,
Scooting obliquely high and low.

Something I cannot see puts upward libidinous prongs,
Seas of bright juice suffuse heaven.

The earth by the sky staid with, the daily close of their junction,
The heav'd challenge from the east that moment over my head,
The mocking taunt, See then whether you shall be master!

. . .

46
I know I have the best of time and space, and was never measured and never
   will be measured.

I tramp a perpetual journey, (come listen all!)
My signs are a rain-proof coat, good shoes, and a staff cut from the woods,
No friend of mine takes his ease in my chair,
I have no chair, no church, no philosophy,
I lead no man to a dinner-table, library, exchange,
But each man and each woman of you I lead upon a knoll,
My left hand hooking you round the waist,
My right hand pointing to landscapes of continents and the public road.

Not I, not any one else can travel that road for you,
You must travel it for yourself.

It is not far, it is within reach,
Perhaps you have been on it since you were born and did not know,
Perhaps it is everywhere on water and on land.

Shoulder your duds dear son, and I will mine, and let us hasten forth,
Wonderful cities and free nations we shall fetch as we go.

If you tire, give me both burdens, and rest the chuff of your hand on my hip,
And in due time you shall repay the same service to me,
For after we start we never lie by again.

This day before dawn I ascended a hill and look'd at the crowded heaven,
And I said to my spirit When we become the enfolders of those orbs, and the
   pleasure and knowledge of every thing in them, shall we be fill'd and satisfied
   then?
And my spirit said No, we but level that lift to pass and continue beyond.

You are also asking me questions and I hear you,
I answer that I cannot answer, you must find out for yourself.

Sit a while dear son,
Here are biscuits to eat and here is milk to drink,
But as soon as you sleep and renew yourself in sweet clothes, I kiss you
   with a good-by kiss and open the gate for your egress hence.

Long enough have you dream'd contemptible dreams,
Now I wash the gum from your eyes,
You must habit yourself to the dazzle of the light and of every moment of
   your life.

Long have you timidly waded holding a plank by the shore,
Now I will you to be a bold swimmer,
To jump off in the midst of the sea, rise again, nod to me, shout, and laugh-
    ingly dash with your hair.

47
I am the teacher of athletes,
He that by me spreads a wider breast than my own proves the width of my
    own,
He most honors my style who learns under it to destroy the teacher.

The boy I love, the same becomes a man not through derived power, but in
    his own right,
Wicked rather than virtuous out of conformity or fear,
Fond of his sweetheart, relishing well his steak,
Unrequited love or a slight cutting him worse than sharp steel cuts,
First-rate to ride, to fight, to hit the bull's eye, to sail a skiff, to sing a song or
    play on the banjo,
Preferring scars and the beard and faces pitted with small-pox over all
    latherers,
And those well-tann'd to those that keep out of the sun.

I teach straying from me, yet who can stray from me?
I follow you whoever you are from the present hour,
My words itch at your ears till you understand them.

I do not say these things for a dollar or to fill up the time while I wait for a
    boat,
(It is you talking just as much as myself, I act as the tongue of you,
Tied in your mouth, in mine it begins to be loosen'd.)

I swear I will never again mention love or death inside a house,
And I swear I will never translate myself at all, only to him or her who pri-
    vately stays with me in the open air.

If you would understand me go to the heights or water-shore,
The nearest gnat is an explanation, and a drop or motion of waves a key,
The maul, the oar, the hand-saw, second my words.

No shutter'd room or school can commune with me,
But roughs and little children better than they.

The young mechanic is closest to me, he knows me well,
The woodman that takes his axe and jug with him shall take me with him all
    day,
The farm-boy ploughing in the field feels good at the sound of my voice,
In vessels that sail my words sail, I go with fishermen and seamen and love
    them.

The soldier camp'd or upon the march is mine,
On the night ere the pending battle many seek me, and I do not fail them,
On that solemn night (it may be their last) those that know me seek me.

My face rubs to the hunter's face when he lies down alone in his blanket,
The driver thinking of me does not mind the jolt of his wagon,
The young mother and old mother comprehend me,
The girl and the wife rest the needle a moment and forget where they are,
They and all would resume what I have told them.

48
I have said that the soul is not more than the body,
And I have said that the body is not more than the soul,
And nothing, not God, is greater to one than one's self is,
And whoever walks a furlong without sympathy walks to his own funeral
    drest in his shroud,
And I or you pocketless of a dime may purchase the pick of the earth,
And to glance with an eye or show a bean in its pod confounds the learning
    of all times,
And there is no trade or employment but the young man following it may
    become a hero,
And there is no object so soft but it makes a hub for the wheel'd universe,
And I say to any man or woman, Let your soul stand cool and composed
    before a million universes.

And I say to mankind, Be not curious about God,
For I who am curious about each am not curious about God,
(No array of terms can say how much I am at peace about God and about
    death.)

I hear and behold God in every object, yet understand God not in the least,
Nor do I understand who there can be more wonderful than myself.

Why should I wish to see God better than this day?
I see something of God each hour of the twenty-four, and each moment then,
In the faces of men and women I see God, and in my own face in the glass,
I find letters from God dropt in the street, and every one is sign'd by God's
    name,
and I leave them where they are, for I know that wheresoe'er I go,
Others will punctually come for ever and ever.

49
And as to you Death, and you bitter hug of mortality, it is idle to try to alarm
    me.

To his work without flinching the accoucheur comes,
I see the elder-hand pressing receiving supporting,
I recline by the sills of the exquisite flexible doors,
And mark the outlet, and mark the relief and escape.

And as to you Corpse I think you are good manure, but that does not offend me,
I smell the white roses sweet-scented and growing,
I reach to the leafy lips, I reach to the polish'd breasts of melons.

And as to you Life I reckon you are the leavings of many deaths,
(No doubt I have died myself ten thousand times before.)

I hear you whispering there O stars of heaven,
O suns—O grass of graves—O perpetual transfers and promotions,
If you do not say any thing how can I say any thing?

Of the turbid pool that lies in the autumn forest,
Of the moon that descends the steeps of the soughing twilight,
Toss, sparkles of day and dusk—toss on the black stems that decay in the
     muck,
Toss to the moaning gibberish of the dry limbs.

I ascend from the moon, I ascend from the night,
I perceive that the ghastly glimmer is noonday sunbeams reflected,
And debouch to the steady and central from the offspring great or small.

50
There is that in me—I do not know what it is—but I know it is in me.

Wrench'd and sweaty—calm and cool then my body becomes, I sleep—
     I sleep long.

I do not know it—it is without name—it is a word unsaid,
It is not in any dictionary, utterance, symbol.

Something it swings on more than the earth I swing on,
To it the creation is the friend whose embracing awakes me.

Perhaps I might tell more. Outlines! I plead for my brothers and sisters.

Do you see O my brothers and sisters?
It is not chaos or death—it is form, union, plan—it is eternal life—it is
     Happiness.

51
The past and present wilt—I have fill'd them, emptied them,
And proceed to fill my next fold of the future.

Listener up there! what have you to confide to me?
Look in my face while I snuff the sidle of evening,
(Talk honestly, no one else hears you, and I stay only a minute longer.)

Do I contradict myself?
Very well then I contradict myself,
(I am large, I contain multitudes.)

I concentrate toward them that are nigh, I wait on the door-slab.

Who has done his day's work? who will soonest be through with his supper?

Who wishes to walk with me?

Will you speak before I am gone? will you prove already too late?

52
The spotted hawk swoops by and accuses me, he complains of my gab and
    my loitering.

I too am not a bit tamed, I too am untranslatable,
I sound my barbaric yawp over the roofs of the world.

The last scud of day holds back for me,
It flings my likeness after the rest and true as any on the shadow'd wilds,
It coaxes me to the vapor and the dusk.

I depart as air, I shake my white locks at the runaway sun,
I effuse my flesh in eddies, and drift it in lacy jags.

I bequeath myself to the dirt to grow from the grass I love,
If you want me again look for me under your boot-soles.

You will hardly know who I am or what I mean,
But I shall be good health to you nevertheless,
And filter and fibre your blood.

Failing to fetch me at first keep encouraged,
Missing me one place search another,
I stop somewhere waiting for you.   [1881]

WILLIAM WILSON

Ojibway c. 1820-1839

While studying at Upper Canada Academy, Wilson recited 'England and British America' at a public examination in April 1838. The poem, an ambiguously patriotic tribute to British colonialism and a polemical response to indigenous peoples' dispossession, was reprinted widely after it appeared in *The Christian Guardian* (May 1838). In 1839 Wilson died in New York City of smallpox.

ENGLAND AND BRITISH AMERICA

Babel! whose primal empire erst did rise
In peerless pomp 'neath fair and fervid skies,
Where now thy lofty tower, whose summit proud
Attempted heav'n, and pierc'd the ambient cloud?
Assyria where? against whose vices bold
The prophet's ire in dread denouncement told,—
Along whose streets betimes his warnings swept,
And o'er her doom in plaintive accents wept,—
Till, loudly echoing, flash'd the bolts of heav'n,
Launch'd by Jehovah's arm in thunder giv'n,
And dire revenge from giant slumber burst,
Hurling her smitten fabrics to the dust!
Where Carthage now? against whose rival coast
Triumphant Rome led forth her conquering host,
Ere warring Scipio bends her prostrate walls,
And Romans shout exulting as she falls!
Where do the myriad spires of Egypt gleam
Along the banks of Nile's extended stream,—
Rearing aloft her monumental pyre,
Whose cloudy top would fain to heaven aspire?
And where her halls by learned Magi grac'd,
Whose gifted minds the path of science trac'd?
Where too her sceptred kings that proudly shone
In pomp barbaric on th' empurpled throne,
Commanding nations far, by stern decree,
In adoration low to bend the knee?
And Greece! oh where that mighty empire now
That bade the Perse with trembling homage bow?
Bright clime of that immortal bard, whose name
With deathless hues shall live in brightest fame,
Who tun'd his hallow'd harp, all wild and free,
To rapturous strains of heav'nly harmony,—
Of him whose thunder did the forum shake,
And made the throne of haughty Philip quake,
While rude Oppression from his seat was hurl'd

And Freedom's banner o'er his corse unfurl'd!
Where now her classic field, her sylvan grove,
Made vocal with the muses' lays of love?
Arcadia where, where sacred Science dwelt,
At whose fair shrine exalted sages knelt?
Alas! the lamp that brightly shone of yore
On her its light effulgent sheds no more;
No more with her doth Genius rear his throne,
And fondly view a realm from zone to zone:
For lo! her sons by Moslem tyrants fall,
And slavish chains their captive minds enthrall.
Where is the mighty Alexander now,
Who fought the world to deck ambition's brow,
Who dar'd in arms to match all-conquering Jove,
And boldly spurn the laws of Heaven above?
Rolling his chariot fierce to realms afar,
And with rebellious arms wag'd dastard war;
While nations wild with consternation stare,
And groans of slaughter'd millions fill the air;
Until he made, by more than mortal skill,
A fated world obsequious to his will.
Th' Eternal City where, imperial Rome,
Whose standard proudly wav'd o'er realms unknown,
And through the earth her battling legions bore,
To glut their madden'd ranks with human gore?
Where now those rock-built tow'rs that darkly frown'd
In mystic awe o'er Tiber's stream profound,
And rear'd their impious heads in height sublime,
Scowling defiance 'gainst the blasts of time?

To this bless'd land I turn from Empires' fall,
O'er which stern fate has stretch'd oblivion's pall,—
Have fled like ocean's spray before his nod,
That dar'd the brunt of his relentless rod.
Here would the muse kneel at Apollo's shrine,
In votive strains t'invoke the tuneful Nine,
Perchance t'imbibe alike th' enlivening fire
Of him who did the early bards inspire.
But Britain first behold, that 'sea-girt isle',
With pow'r and wealth as boundless as the Nile,
With genius, learning, art, and science bless'd,
And reason's nobler ray at her behest;
Her sons, the first in glory's ballow'd field,
The last in battle's darker hour to yield,
Behold, in firm recluse from tyrants' shock,
Around the standard of their country flock,—

A formidable front to despots show,
While to the field they dare the angry foe:
Contentment, peace, and good their steps attend,
Their sacred hearths from ruthless vice defend;
To them each genial year its charms renews,
The fruitful earth their thousand wants pursues;
For them wing'd commerce wafts from distant climes
The treasures of their land and richest mines;
Harmonious laws their kindred hearts unite,
And wisdom's ways their nobler thoughts delight.
Behold her red-cross flag unfurling far,
Victorious Wellington directs her ear;
Triumphant too at Waterloo he rode,
Beneath its wheels the vain tricolor trode,—
Inglorious bade the proud usurper bow,
And own his conqu'ring arm in suppliance low.
Behold, 'midst yonder deep and princely hall,
Where godlike Justice sits in awful pall,
Where Freedom's matchless champions mutual join
To shield the laws, and for their rights combine,
Immortal Pitt with conscious boldness rise;
Destructive lightning flashes from his eyes;
Now threat'ning vengeance sits upon his brow,
His glowing cheeks bespeak his fervour now;
Through all his frame th' inspiring god is seen,
And all his pow'rs with mingled terror gleam.
Hark! through the long-drawn aisle his voice resounds,
And dreadly now re-echo back the sounds;
Like when th' Olympian sire in thunder pours
His vengful wrath, and arrowy tempests showers:
On schemes corrupt he wreaks his fell desire,
And fiercely vents his all-devouring ire,
While round the pompous heads of tyrant kings
Aloud his dread denunciation rings,—
In thunder loud his vengeance flings retort,
While heaven and earth revere the dread report.
Before his voice now brazen discord shrinks,
Now lordly quilt in meek submission sinks;
Insatiate ease now startles from his couch,
In frantic terror factious minions crouch:
The sable sons of Afric gladly hear
His welcome voice, and lend a list'ning ear;
He bids the captive slave from bondage flee—
He fondly sets the iron-bound pris'ner free.
Amid the crowd of patriots, heroes, view,
That grace proud Albion's clime with bright halo,

The train of star-eyed Science' devotees,
Who to her altar bow with suppliant knees.
On learning's pinions proud they take their way,
And through the maze of latent myst'ries stray;
Far as imagination's piercing ken
With philosophic eye their flight they wend;
Stay with firm hand the planets in their course,
Direct the pathless comet, trace its source,
Chief to her bards is due the meed of praise,
Though feebly giv'n in low discordant lays:
High on Parnassus' cliffs they glorious stand,
They strike the lyre with more than mortal hand;
Melodious sounds retreat on heav'nly wings,
As sweet the muse in pensive sorrow sings,
And o'er romantic vales and distant plains
In fitful echoes die the mystic strains.
But first enroll'd on list of genius' throng,
Who scal'd the proudest heights of lofty song,
With dazzling rays, as shines the morning star,
Her Milton stands on fame's dread mount afar,
And gently beckons the aspiring muse,
As o'er his soul his sacred beams diffuse.

   The clime of Canada in fondness gleams,
And western wilds awake more pleasing themes:
From where the eagle gluts his hungry beak
On Labrador's far coast of barren peak,
To where the Rocky Mountains sternly rise,
O'erlook the land, and half invade the skies,
Its fair and undulating soil extends,
And to the eye its bright enchantment lends.
Here Nature's God in matchless splendor rears
His living fane, and in wild pomp appears.
Here placid lakes like molten silver beam,
The full-orb'd sun reflects the glassy stream,—
Alluvial mountains lift their verdant heads,
And on the prairies prone their influence spreads.
Here fertile vales their rich luxuriance show,
Where nature's works in loveliest beauty glow;
From whose retreats, or sounds the woodman's hymn,
Far from the bustling throng of madd'ning din,
Or 'mid their haunts aerial spirits stray,
While to the breeze they chaunt they roundelay.
Here cataracts vast the echoing forests wake,
And all the ground with quick vibrations shake;
Where dread Niagara in thunder roars,

As o'er the rocky steep his deluge pours,—
Along whose banks the lonely Indian wound,
And in the scene his kindred spirit found.
Here boundless plains in fragrant verdure stretch,
Bright landscapes there invite the artist's sketch;
Here forests dark their stately branches wave,
And rivers there in solemn silence lave.
But though this land with ev'ry good is crown'd,
And choicest gifts on ev'ry hand surround,—
Though Nature here has wrought her grandest plan,
Yet does the mind deplore the fate of man.
Those lordly tribes that lin'd these mighty lakes
Have fled, and disappear'd like wintry flakes.
Lo! on the mountain-tops their fires are out,
In blithesome vales all silent is their shout;
A solemn voice is heard from ev'ry shore,
That now the Indian nations are no more,—
A remnant scarce remain to tell their wrongs,
But soon will fade to live in poets' songs.

   Hail to thee, Canada! the brightest gem
That decks Victoria's brilliant diadem;
Thine is the happy seat, the blissful clime
Where art and nature form one vast sublime;
Where temp'rate skies effuse their golden rays,
The fertile land the labourer's toil repays;
Plenty and peace at ev'ry footstep smile,
And sunny scenes to gentler thoughts beguile.
A voice is heard upon thy mighty floods,
A voice resounds throughout thy trackless woods,—
Heard in the plaintive rill and cataract's roar,
Heard in the whisp'ring breeze on ev'ry shore:
'Tis Freedom's voice; 'tis on thy rivers roll'd,
That in their course the sacred theme have told,
And bid the dwellers on the mountains swell
The choral strain, and wake the joyful knell,—
Till all mankind shall hear the gladd'ning sound,
Rouse from the trammel yoke of sleep profound,
And o'er the earth Britannia's banner wave,
Each foeman crush'd—unshackled ev'ry slave.

                                          [1838]

MATTHEW ARNOLD

England 1822-1888

Arnold was the most eloquent spokesperson among the Victorians for the virtues of literature as the means to educate and civilize a culture, to preserve the classical and religious values of Western civilization. Arnold's stance as a critic and educator remains a touchstone; his poetic vision reveals a yearning to reconcile the life of the body with the more spiritual life of the mind. This struggle towards serenity at times imbues Arnold's poetry with a resignation to the sorrows of seeking love in a clamorous world. Arnold's works are available in several multi-volume collections, including *The Poems of Matthew Arnold* (ed. Allott, 1965) and *Complete Prose Works* (11 vols, ed. Super, 1960–77).

TO MARGUERITE—CONTINUED

Yes! in the sea of life enisled,
With echoing straits between us thrown,
Dotting the shoreless watery wild,
We mortal millions live *alone*.
The islands feel the enclasping flow,
And then their endless bounds they know.

But when the moon their hollows lights,
And they are swept by balms of spring,
And in their glens, on starry nights,
The nightingales divinely sing;
And lovely notes, from shore to shore,
Across the sounds and channels pour—

Oh! then a longing like despair
Is to their farthest caverns sent;
For surely once, they feel, we were
Parts of a single continent!
Now round us spreads the watery plain—
Oh might our marges meet again!

Who ordered that their longing's fire
Should be, as soon as kindled, cooled?
Who renders vain their deep desire?—
A God, a God their severance ruled!
And bade betwixt their shores to be
The unplumbed, salt, estranging sea.   [1852]

WILLIAM ALLINGHAM

Ireland 1824–1889

Allingham left County Donegal for England in 1863 where he enjoyed the influence of the Pre-Raphaelite Brotherhood, formed in the late 1840s by poets like Dante Gabriel Rossetti, which developed a distinctive design and vision guided by fifteenth-century Italian art. Allingham wrote about Ireland for an English readership—a Victorian middle class largely unable and often unwilling to understand the forces that shaped Irish politics and culture. In *Laurence Bloomfield in Ireland* (1864), Allingham counters Paddyism—the trivialization of things Irish directed by English condescension—and offers a more realistic vision of the integrity of a peasantry disenfranchised by the corrupt policies and practices of absentee landlords and agents.

from LAURENCE BLOOMFIELD IN IRELAND

A MODERN POEM
IN TWELVE CHAPTERS

I.

Laurence
Autumnal sunshine spread on Irish hills
Imagination's bright'ning mirror fills,
Wherein a Horseman on a handsome grey
Along the high road takes his easy way,
Saluted low by every ragged hat,
Saluting kindly every Teague and Pat
Who plods the mud or jolts on lazy wheels,
Or loudly drives a patient ass with creels,
(Short pipe removed before obeisance made)
Or checks, regardant, his potato-spade;
'Fine day,' the young man says with friendly nod,
'Fine day, your honour,—glory be to God!'
Then, too polite to stare, they talk their fill
Of Minor Bloomfield (so they call him still,
Though six-and-twenty now) come back of late
From foreign countries to his own estate,
And who in turn has no incurious eye
For each, and all the world, in passing by;
The cornstacks seen through rusty sycamores,
Pigs, tatter'd children, pools at cabin doors,
Unshelter'd rocky hill-sides, browsed by sheep,
Summer's last flow'rs that nigh some brooklet creep,
Black flats of bog, stone-fences loose and rough,
A thorn-branch in a gap thought gate enough,
And all the wide and groveless landscape round,
Moor, stubble, aftermath, or new-plough'd ground,
Where with the crows white seagulls come to pick;

Or many a wasteful acre crowded thick
With docken, coltsfoot, and the hoary weed
Call'd fairy-horse, and tufted thistle-seed
Which *for* the farm, *against* the farmer tells;
Or wrinkled hawthorns shading homestead wells,
Or, saddest sight, some ruin'd cottage-wall,
The roof-tree cut, the rafters forced to fall
From gables with domestic smoke embrown'd,
Where Poverty at worst a shelter found,
The scene, perhaps, of all its little life,
Its humble joys, and unsuccessful strife.
Th' observant rider pass'd too many such;
Let them do more (he thought) who do so much,
Nor, where they've kill'd a human dwelling-place,
Unburied leave the skeleton's disgrace.
Though Irish, he was of the absentees,
And unaccustom'd yet to sights like these.

At twelve years old his birthplace he had left,
A child endow'd with much, of much bereft;
Return'd a boy—a lad—the third time now
Returns, a man, with broad and serious brow.
A younger son (the better lot at first),
And by a Celtic peasant fondly nurst,
Bloomfield is Irish born and English bred,
Surviving heir of both his parents dead;
One who has studied, travell'd, lived, and thought,
Is brave, and modest, as a young man ought;
Calm—sympathetic; hasty—full of tact;
Poetic, but insisting much on fact;
A complex character and various mind,
Where all, like some rich landscape, lies combined.

From school to Ireland, Laurence first return'd
A patriot vow'd; his soul for Ireland burn'd.
Oft did his schoolmates' taunts in combat end,
And high his plans with one Hibernian friend,
Who long'd like him for manhood, to set free
Their emerald Inisfail from sea to sea,
With army, senate, all a nation's life,
Copartner in the great world's glorious strife,
Peer in all arts, gay rival in each race,
Illustrious, firm, in her peculiar place.
The glories and the griefs of Erin fill'd
Heart and imagination. How he thrill'd
To every harp-note of her ancient fame,

How, to her storied wounds, his cheek would flame!
And hearing some great speaker, on a day,
Whose urgent grasp held thousands under sway
While thus he thunder'd,—'Tis for slaves alone
'To live without a country of their own!
'Alas for Ireland! she whose sons are born
'The wide earth's pity and proud England's scorn,
'England whose fraud and guilt have sunk us low.
'Speak, Irishmen, shall this be always so?'
Judge how young Laurence felt. 'Like a young fool,'
His guardian growl'd, and shipp'd him back to school.

Not such was he at Cambridge; for he found
Thought's new horizons daily opening round,
While History spread her pictures grave and vast;
And living Britain startled him at last
To recognise the large imperial tone,
And all the grandeur of a well-built throne.
O joy, a part in England's pride to claim,
To flush with triumph in her force and fame,
See distant powers confess with wondering awe
Her martial strength, her majesty of law,
And every child of hers throughout the world
Stand safe beneath her banner, broad unfurl'd!

A beardless Burke of college parliament
The loyal Laurence back to Ireland went,
On visit to a rich relation's house;
Where boldly to Sir Ulick he avows
An alter'd mind, and sees with alter'd sight
Reckless provincials, hating rule and right,
Busy for mischief without aim or sense,
Their politics mere factious turbulence,
Drawn this and that way by the word or nod
Of noisy rogues and stealthy men-of-God;
And checks them with a small ideal band
Who, brothers, round the British Ensign stand,
To face rebellion, Papistry, and crime,
With staunchness proved in many a perilous time.
At twenty-one, his too a place shall hold
With names ancestral in the Lodge enroll'd;
Or thus at least resolved the young man, eager-soul'd.   [1864]

CHEESQUATALAWNY/YELLOW BIRD/ JOHN ROLLIN RIDGE

Cherokee 1827–1867

Ridge was born into a prominent Treaty Party family of the Cherokee Nation who signed the New Echota Treaty (1835), effecting their displacement from Georgia and the Carolinas westward to Indian Territory (later Oklahoma and Arkansas). After studying classical literatures and then law, Ridge worked in California as a journalist, editor, and writer. He viewed assimilation as indigenous peoples' inevitable response to European technological and political domination. A collection of his verse, *Poems*, appeared posthumously in 1868.

THE ATLANTIC CABLE

Let Earth be glad! for that great work is done,
Which makes, at last the Old and New World one!
Let all mankind rejoice! for time nor space
Shall check the progress of the human race!
Though Nature heaved the Continents apart,
She cast in one great mould the human heart;
She framed on one great plan the human mind,
And gave man speech to link him to his kind;
So that, though plains and mountains intervene,
Or oceans, broad and stormy, roll between
If there but be a courier for the thought—
Soft-winged or slow—the land and seas are nought,
And man is nearer to his brother brought.

First, ere the dawn of letters was, or burst
The light of science on the world, men, nurs't
In distant solitudes apart, did send
Their skin-clad heralds forth to thread the woods,
Scale mountain-peaks, or swim the sudden floods,
And bear their messages of peace or war.

Next, beasts were tamed to drag the rolling car,
Or speed the mounted rider on his track;
And then came, too, the vessels, oar-propelled,
Which fled the ocean, as the clouds grew black,
And safe near shore their prudent courses held.
Next came the winged ships, which, brave and free,
Did skim the bosom of the bounding sea,
And dared the storms and darkness in their flight,
Yet drifted far before the winds and night,
Or lay within the dead calm's grasp of might.

Then, sea-divided nations nearer came,
Stood face to face, spake each the other's name,
In friendship grew, and learned the truth sublime,
That Man is Man in every age and clime!

They nearer were by months and years—but space
Must still be shortened in Improvement's race,
And steam came next to wake the world from sleep,
And launch her black-plumed warriors of the deep;
The which, in calm or storm, rode onward still,
And braved the raging elements at will.
Then distance, which from calms' and storms' delays
Grew into months, was shortened into days,
And Science' self declared her wildest dream
Reached not beyond this miracle of steam!
But steam hath not the lightning's wondrous power,
Though, Titan-like, mid Science' sons it tower
And wrestle with the ocean in his wrath,
And sweep the wild waves foaming from its path.
A mightier monarch is that subtler thing,
Which speaks in thunder like a God,
Or humbly stoops to kiss the lifted rod;
Ascends to Night's dim, solitary throne,
And clothes it with a splendor not its own
A ghastly grandeur and ghostly sheen,
Through which the pale stars tremble as they're seen;
Descends to fire the far horizon's rim,
And paints Mount Etnas in the cloudland grim;
Or, proud to own fair Science' rightful sway,
Low bends along th' electric wire to play,
And, helping out the ever-wondrous plan,
Becomes, in sooth, an errand-boy for man!

This power it was, which, not content with aught
As yet achieved by human will or thought
Disdained the slow account of months or days,
In navigation of the ocean ways,
And days would shorten into hours, and these
To minutes, in the face of sounding seas.
If Thought might not be borne upon the foam
Of furrowing keel, with speed that Thought should roam,
It then should walk, like light, the ocean's bed,
And laugh to scorn the winds and waves o'er head!
Beneath the reach of storm or wreck, down where
The skeletons of men and navies are,
Its silent steps should be; while o'er its path
The monsters of the deep, in sport or wrath,

The waters lashed, till like a pot should boil
The sea, and fierce Arion seize the upcast spoil.
America! to thee belongs the praise
Of this great crowning deed of modern days.
'Twas Franklin called the wonder from on high;
'Twas Morse who bade it on man's errand fly—
'Twas he foretold its pathway 'neath the sea:
A daring Field fulfilled the prophecy!
'Twas fitting that a great, free land like this,
Should give the lightning's voice to Liberty;
Should wing the heralds of Earth's happiness,
And sing, beneath the ever-sounding sea,
The fair, the bright millenial days to be.

Now may, ere long, the sword be sheathed to rust,
The helmet laid in undistinguished dust;
The thund'rous chariot pause in mid career.
Its crimsoned wheels no more through blood to steer;
The red-hoofed steed from fields of death be led,
Or turned to pasture where the armies bled;
For Nation unto Nation soon shall be
Together brought in knitted unity,
And man be bound to man by that strong chain,
Which, linking land to land, and main to main,
Shall vibrate to the voice of Peace, and be
A throbbing heartstring of Humanity!   [1868]

EMILY DICKINSON

USA 1830–1886

Encouraged by writer Thomas Wentworth Higginson, Dickinson published only a dozen of her poems during her lifetime. Following Dickinson's death her sister, Lavinia, discovered 1,147 poems in a cherry-wood box placed in the poet's bedroom bureau—a lifelong poetic documentation of her exacting meditations on her experiences of pain, of lies, of female intimacy, and, above all else, of barriers erected around our individual and social lives. The standard edited collections of this poetry are Higginson and Todd's 1890 posthumous volume, and Thomas Johnson's comprehensive 1955 three-volume variorum edition, and *The Manuscript Books of Emily Dickinson* (ed. Franklin, 1981) offer readers a fascinating facsimile reproduction of the original texts.

#632: THE BRAIN—IS WIDER THAN THE SKY—

The Brain—is wider than the Sky—
For—put them side by side—
The one the other will contain
With ease—and You—beside—

The Brain is deeper than the sea—
For—hold them—Blue to Blue—
The one the other will absorb—
As Sponges—Buckets—do—

The Brain is just the weight of God—
For—Heft them—Pound for Pound—
And they will differ—if they do—
As Syllable from Sound—   [1896]

#1082: REVOLUTION IS THE POD

Revolution is the Pod
Systems rattle from
When the Winds of Will are stirred
Excellent is Bloom

But except it's Russet Base
Every Summer be
The Entomber of itself,
So of Liberty—
Left inactive on the Stalk
All it's Purple fled
Revolution shakes it for
Test if it be dead.   [1929]

CHRISTINA ROSSETTI

England 1830–1894

A member of the gifted Rossetti family, Italian expatriates and aesthetes, Christina privately published her first volume of poetry at seventeen. Throughout her career she expressed the paradoxical nature of her temperament over a range of genres including nursery rhymes, children's tales, love poetry in English and Italian, mortuary verses (verses written from the point of view of the dead), devotional essays and lyrics, and essays on Dante. Rossetti maintained her artistic independence and production even while her 'spinsterhood' attached her to her brother William's household for most of her life. A variorum edition of *The Complete Poems of Christina Rossetti* is being prepared by R.W. Crump (from 1979).

'THAT WHERE I AM, THERE YE MAY BE ALSO'

How know I that it looms lovely that land I have never seen,
With morning-glories and heartsease and unexampled green,
With neither heat nor cold in the balm-redolent air?
　　Some of this, not all, I know; but this is so;
　　　　Christ is there.

How know I that blessedness befalls who dwell in Paradise,
The outwearied hearts refreshing, rekindling the worn-out eyes,
All souls singing, seeing, rejoicing everywhere?
　　Nay, much more than this I know; for this is so;
　　　Christ is there.

O Lord Christ, Whom having not seen I love and desire to love,
O Lord Christ, Who lookest on me uncomely yet still Thy dove,
Take me to Thee in Paradise, Thine own made fair;
　　For whatever else I know, this thing is so;
　　　Thou art there.   [1892]

WILLIAM MORRIS

England 1834-1896

Morris was the founder of an interior design company in London in 1861 and a proponent of
creative yet functional craftsmanship, qualities reflected in his poetry as well as his painting, weav-
ing, furniture-making, and printing. His utopian and later revolutionary socialism were derived
from an idealizing view of the past, an antique world he re-creates in long narrative historical poems
on medieval and mythological themes, such as *The Defence of Guinevere* (1858) and *The Earthly
Paradise* (1868–70).

from THE EARTHLY PARADISE

AN APOLOGY

　　Of Heaven or Hell I have no power to sing,
I cannot ease the burden of your fears,
Or make quick-coming death a little thing,
Or bring again the pleasure of past years,
Nor for my words shall ye forget your tears,
Or hope again for aught that I can say,
The idle singer of an empty day.

　　But rather, when aweary of your mirth,
From full hearts still unsatisfied ye sigh,
And, feeling kindly unto all the earth,
Grudge every minute as it passes by,
Made the more mindful that the sweet days die—
Remember me a little then I pray,
The idle singer of an empty day.

　　The heavy trouble, the bewildering care
That weighs us down who live and earn our bread,
These idle verses have no power to bear;
So let me sing of names rememberèd,

Because they, living not, can ne'er be dead,
Or long time take their memory quite away
From us poor singers of an empty day.

Dreamer of dreams, born out of my due time,
Why should I strive to set the crooked straight?
Let it suffice me that my murmuring rhyme
Beats with light wing against the ivory gate,
Telling a tale not too importunate
To those who in the sleepy region stay,
Lulled by the singer of an empty day.

Folk say, a wizard to a northern king
At Christmas-tide such wondrous things did show,
That through one window men beheld the spring,
And through another saw the summer glow,
And through a third the fruited vines a-row,
While still, unheard, but in its wonted way,
Piped the drear wind of that December day.

So with this Earthly Paradise it is,
If ye will read aright, and pardon me,
Who strive to build a shadowy isle of bliss
Midmost the beating of the steely sea,
Where tossed about all hearts of men must be;
Whose ravening monsters mighty men shall slay,
Not the poor singer of an empty day.   [1868–70]

NOVEMBER

Are thine eyes weary? is thy heart too sick
To struggle any more with doubt and thought,
Whose formless veil draws darkening now and thick
Across thee, e'en as smoke-tinged mist-wreaths brought
Down a fair dale to make it blind and nought?
Art thou so weary that no world there seems
Beyond these four walls, hung with pain and dreams?

Look out upon the real world, where the moon,
Half-way 'twixt root and crown of these high trees,
Turns the dread midnight into dreamy noon,
Silent and full of wonders, for the breeze
Died at the sunset, and no images,
No hopes of day, are left in sky or earth—
Is it not fair, and of most wondrous worth?

Yea, I have looked and seen November there;
The changeless seal of change it seemed to be,
Fair death of things that, living once, were fair;
Bright sign of loneliness too great for me,
Strange image of the dread eternity,
In whose void patience how can these have part,
These outstretched feverish hands, this restless heart?   [1868–70]

HENRY KENDALL

Australia 1839–1882

Kendall, born in New South Wales, worked as a cabin-boy, shopkeeper, legal clerk and civil servant,
and died of consumption at the age of forty-three. Regarded as an important figure in the history of
Australian literature, Kendall published several volumes of lyric poetry in which he adapted
conventions of English romanticism to native subjects and experiences: *Poems and Songs* (1862);
Leaves from Australian Forests (1869); *Songs from the Mountains* (1880); and *Orara* (1881). The
authoritative edition of Kendall's poetry is *The Poetical Works of Henry Kendall* (ed. Reed, 1966).

THE LAST OF HIS TRIBE

He crouches, and buries his face on his knees,
And hides in the dark of his hair;
For he cannot look up to the storm-smitten trees,
Or think of the loneliness there—
Of the loss and the loneliness there.

The wallaroos grope through the tufts of the grass,
And turn to their coverts for fear;
But he sits in the ashes and lets them pass
Where the boomerangs sleep with the spear—
With the nullah, the sling, and the spear.

Uloola, behold him! The thunder that breaks
On the tops of the rocks with the rain,
And the wind which drives up with the salt of the lakes,
Have made him a hunter again—
A hunter and fisher again.

For his eyes have been full with a smouldering thought;
But he dreams of the hunts of yore,
And of foes that he sought, and of fights that he fought
With those who will battle no more—
Who will go to the battle no more.

It is well that the water which tumbles and fills
Goes moaning and moaning along;
For an echo rolls out from the sides of the hills,
And he starts at a wonderful song—
At the sound of a wonderful song.

And he sees through the rents of the scattering fogs
And corroboree warlike and grim,
And the lubra who sat by the fire on the logs,
To watch, like a mourner, for him—
Like a mother and mourner for him.

Will he go in his sleep from these desolate lands,
Like a chief, to the rest of his race,
With the honey-voiced woman who beckons and stands,
And gleams like a dream in his face—
Like a marvellous dream in his face?

[1870]

THOMAS HARDY

England 1840–1928

After the publication of the last of his sixteen novels, *Jude the Obscure* (1896), Hardy devoted himself exclusively to poetry: his first book of verse, *Wessex Poems,* appeared in 1898; the last of his eight volumes, *Winter Words,* was published the year of his death. Hardy was poised in any number of poetic forms. Sensitive to the regional landscape and dialect of the West Country which he christened Wessex, Hardy assimilates the brooding historical and mythic rhythms and the interest of intricate stanzaic and metrical forms. 'The Darkling Thrush', originally entitled 'By the Century's Death-bed', was written on 31 December 1900, the last day of the nineteenth century. Hardy's *Collected Poems* was published posthumously in 1930.

THE DARKLING THRUSH

I leant upon a coppice gate
    When Frost was spectre-gray,
And Winter's dregs made desolate
    The weakening eye of day.
The tangled bine-stems scored the sky
    Like strings of broken lyres,
And all mankind that haunted nigh
    Had sought their household fires.

The land's sharp features seemed to be
    The Century's corpse outleant,
His crypt the cloudy canopy,
    The wind his death-lament.

The ancient pulse of germ and birth
    Was shrunken hard and dry,
And every spirit upon earth
    Seemed fervourless as I.

At once a voice arose among
    The bleak twigs overhead
In a full-hearted evensong
    Of joy illimited;
An aged thrush, frail, gaunt, and small,
    In blast-beruffled plume,
Had chosen thus to fling his soul
    Upon the growing gloom.

So little cause for carolings
    Of such ecstatic sound
Was written on terrestrial things
    Afar or nigh around,
That I could think there trembled through
    His happy good-night air
Some blessed Hope, whereof he knew
    And I was unaware.   [1901]

GERARD MANLEY HOPKINS

England 1844–1889

Hopkins's contribution to the development of accentual-syllabic metre really became accessible only in 1918 with the first (and posthumous) publication of his poetry. His reticence to publish arose with the rejection of a narrative ode whose eccentric style was little understood. He felt, as well, that his work as a priest conflicted with his work as a poet. (A convert to Roman Catholicism, he entered the Jesuit order in 1868.) Hopkins suggested that his metrical revision, 'sprung rhythm', returned poetry to the natural rhythm of common speech. Sprung rhythm allowed the poet to retain a given number of stresses and combine them with a variable number and distribution of unstressed syllables. Equally central was Hopkins's concept of 'instress'—the poet's inspired apprehension of the internal, essential, and individual pattern of each object in creation, an 'inscape' which declares the imprint of the divine. The most recent collection of his poetry is the fourth edition (eds Gardner and MacKenzie, 1967).

PIED BEAUTY

Glory be to God for dappled things—
    For skies of couple-colour as a brinded cow;
      For rose-moles all in stipple upon trout that swim;
Fresh-firecoal chestnut-falls, finches' wings;
    Landscape plotted and pieced—fold, fallow, and plough;
      And áll trádes, their gear and tackle and trim.

All things counter, original, spare, strange;
  Whatever is fickle, freckled (who knows how?)
    With swift, slow; sweet, sour; adazzle, dim;
He fathers-forth whose beauty is past change:
               Praise him.   [1918]

EMILY LAWLESS

Ireland 1845-1913

Story writer, historian, and poet, Lawless wrote of present and past struggles for Home Rule and particularly of the fate of the Wild Geese, the name given those Irish who survived defeat at the hands of the English in the Battle of Aughrim and the 1691 surrender of Limerick. About 200,000 of them rejected the offer to remain, an offer that required them to denounce their religion and their patriotism; of that number it was estimated that 150,000 died while serving military causes in France, Spain, and Austria. In 'Clare Coast: *Circa* 1720' Lawless finds veterans of the Irish Brigade, 'War-dogs, hungry and grey', just before their departure, '[d]arkened with anguish and ruth'. Her collection *With the Wild Geese* (1902) was dedicated to the Atlantic, itself the site of the Irish exodus.

CLARE COAST

CIRCA 1720

See, cold island, we stand
Here to-night on your shore,
To-night, but never again;
Lingering a moment more.
See, beneath us our boat
Tugs at its tightening chain,
Holds out its sail to the breeze,
Pants to be gone again.
Off then with shouts and mirth,
Off with laughter and jests,
Mirth and song on our lips,
Hearts like lead in our breasts.

Death and the grave behind,
Death and a traitor's bier;
Honour and fame before,
Why do we linger here?
Why do we stand and gaze,
Fools, whom fools despise,
Fools untaught by the years,
Fools renounced by the wise?
Heartsick, a moment more,
Heartsick, sorry, fierce,

Lingering, lingering on,
Dreaming the dreams of yore;
Dreaming the dreams of our youth,
Dreaming the days when we stood
Joyous, expectant, serene,
Glad, exultant of mood,
Singing with hearts afire,
Singing with joyous strain,
Singing aloud in our pride,
'We shall redeem her again!'
Ah, not to-night that strain,—
Silent to-night we stand,
A scanty, a toil-worn crew,
Strangers, foes in the land!
Gone the light of our youth,
Gone for ever, and gone
Hope with the beautiful eyes,
Who laughed as she lured us on;
Lured us to danger and death,
To honour, perchance to fame,—
Empty fame at the best,
Glory half dimmed with shame.
War-battered dogs are we,
Fighters in every clime,
Fillers of trench and of grave,
Mockers, bemocked by time.
War-dogs, hungry and grey,
Gnawing a naked bone,
Fighters in every clime,
Every cause but our own.

See us, cold isle of our love!
Coldest, saddest of isles—
Cold as the hopes of our youth,
Cold as your own wan smiles.
Coldly your streams outpour,
Each apart on the height,
Trickling, indifferent, slow,
Lost in the hush of the night.
Colder, sadder the clouds,
Comfortless bringers of rain;
Desolate daughters of air,
Sweep o'er your sad grey plain
Hiding the form of your hills,
Hiding your low sand duns;
But coldest, saddest, oh isle!
Are the homeless hearts of your sons.

Coldest, and saddest there,
In yon sun-lit land of the south,
Where we sicken, and sorrow, and pine,
And the jest flies from mouth to mouth,
And the church bells crash overhead,
And the idle hours flit by,
And the beaded wine-cups clink.
And the sun burns fierce in the sky;
And your exiles, the merry of heart,
Laugh and boast with the best,—
Boast, and extol their part,
Boast, till some lifted brow,
Crossed with a line severe,
Seems with displeasure to ask,
'Are these loud braggarts we hear,
Are they the sons of the West,
The wept-for, the theme of songs,
The exiled, the injured, the banned,
The men of a thousand wrongs?'

Fool, did you never hear
Of sunshine which broke through rain?
Sunshine which came with storm?
Laughter that rang of pain?
Boastings begotten of grief,
Vauntings to hide a smart,
Braggings with trembling lip,
Tricks of a broken heart?

Sudden some wayward gleam,
Sudden some passing sound,—
The careless splash of an oar,
The idle bark of a hound,
A shadow crossing the sun,
An unknown step in the hall,
A nothing, a folly, a straw!—
Back it returns—all—all!
Back with the rush of a storm,
Back the old anguish and ill,
The sad, green landscape of home,
The small grey house by the hill,
The wide grey shores of the lake,
The low sky, seeming to weave
Its tender pitiful arms
Round the sick lone landscape at eve.
Back with its pains and its wrongs,
Back with its toils and its strife,

Back with its struggle and woe,
Back flows the stream of our life.
Darkened with treason and wrong,
Darkened with anguish and ruth,
Bitter, tumultuous, fierce,
Yet glad in the light of our youth.

So, cold island, we stand
Here to-night on your shore,—
To-night, but never again,
Lingering a moment more.
See, beneath us our boat
Tugs at its tightening chain,
Holds out its sail to the breeze,
Pants to be gone again.
Off then with shouts and mirth,
Off with laughter and jests,
Jests and song on our lips,
Hearts like lead in our breasts.   [1902]

ALICE MEYNELL

England 1847–1922

Meynell was known as an essayist, journalist, and poet, particularly committed to women's suffrage;
she described herself as a Christian socialist and feminist in 'lawful and dignified ways'. She was
outraged by the devastation of World War I and tormented by the tensions it produced. On the
one hand, war becomes a sin against life committed by an 'unpardonable race' whose young men
die as armies 'convulsed'; on the other, a 'crippled world' provides opportunity for the 'daughters
of men' to demand those rights thus far denied by the 'million living fathers of the War' whose own
'sons are dust'. *The Poems of Alice Meynell*, Complete Edition, was published in 1940.

RENOUNCEMENT

I must not think of thee; and, tired yet strong,
   I shun the thought that lurks in all delight—
    The thought of thee—and in the blue Heaven's height,
And in the sweetest passage of a song.
O just beyond the fairest thoughts that throng
   This breast, the thought of thee waits hidden yet bright;
    But it must never, never come in sight;
I must stop short of thee the whole day long.

But when sleep comes to close each difficult day,
   When night gives pause to the long watch I keep,
    And all my bonds I needs must loose apart,
Must doff my will as raiment laid away,—
   With the first dream that comes with the first sleep
    I run, I run, I am gathered to thy heart.   [1940]

A FATHER OF WOMEN

AD SOROREM E.B.

> 'Thy father was transfused into thy blood.'
> (Dryden, Ode to Mrs Anne Killigrew)

Our father works in us,
The daughters of his manhood. Not undone
Is he, not wasted, though transmuted thus,
    And though he left no son.

Therefore on him I cry
To arm me: 'For my delicate mind a casque,
A breastplate for my heart, courage to die,
    Of thee, captain, I ask.

'Nor strengthen only; press
A finger on this violent blood and pale,
Over this rash will let thy tenderness
    A while pause, and prevail.

'And shepherd-father, thou
Whose staff folded my thoughts before my birth,
Control them now I am of earth, and now
    Thou art no more earth.

'O liberal, constant, dear,
Crush in my nature the ungenerous art
Of the inferior; set me high, and here,
    Here garner up thy heart!'

Like to him now are they,
The million living fathers of the War—
Mourning the crippled world, the bitter day—
    Whose striplings are no more.

The crippled world! Come then,
Fathers of women with your honour in trust,
Approve, accept, know them daughters of men,
    Now that your sons are dust.   [1940]

ISABELLA VALANCY CRAWFORD

Canada 1850–1887

Full recognition of Crawford's talents came after her death; while she was alive she struggled to scrape together a living by selling her poems and stories to Canadian and American periodicals. The only book she published in her lifetime—*Old Spookses' Pass, Malcolm's Katie, and other Poems* (1884)—sold fifty copies out of a press run of 1,000. The adjective 'mythopoeic' describes the distinctive turn of Crawford's imagination; her poems often draw on imagery of aboriginals to animate natural settings, and her most famous poem, 'Malcolm's Katie', narrates its love story in the context of aboriginal legend. Crawford's stories and tales are represented in *Selected Stories* (ed. Petrone, 1975) and *Fairy Tales* (ed. Petrone, 1977); her verse appears in *The Collected Poems* (ed. Garvin, 1905) and *Hugh and Ion* (ed. Clever, 1977).

THE DARK STAG

A startled stag, the blue-grey Night,
   Leaps down beyond black pines.
Behind—a length of yellow light—
   The hunter's arrow shines:
His moccasins are stained with red,
   He bends upon his knee,
From covering peaks his shafts are sped,
The blue mists plume his mighty head,—
   Well may the swift Night flee!

The pale, pale Moon, a snow-white doe,
   Bounds by his dappled flank:
They beat the stars down as they go,
   Like wood-bells growing rank.
The winds lift dewlaps from the ground,
   Leap from the quaking reeds;
Their hoarse bays shake the forests round,
With keen cries on the track they bound,—
   Swift, swift the dark stag speeds!

Away! his white doe, far behind,
   Lies wounded on the plain;
Yells at his flank the nimblest wind,
   His large tears fall in rain;
Like lily-pads, small clouds grow white
   About his darkling way;
From his bald nest upon the height
The red-eyed eagle sees his flight;
He falters, turns, the antlered Night,—
   The dark stag stands at bay!

His feet are in the waves of space;
    His antlers broad and dun
He lowers he turns his velvet face
    To front the hunter, Sun;
He stamps the lilied clouds, and high
    His branches fill the west.
The lean stork sails across the sky,
The shy loon shrieks to see him die,
    The winds leap at his breast.

Roar the rent lakes as thro' the wave
    Their silver warriors plunge,
As vaults from core of crystal cave
    The strong, fierce muskallunge;
Red torches of the sumach glare,
    Fall's council-fires are lit;
The bittern, squaw-like, scolds the air;
The wild duck splashes loudly where
    The rustling rice-spears knit.

Shaft after shaft the red Sun speeds:
    Rent the stag's dappled side,
His breast, fanged by the shrill winds, bleeds,
    He staggers on the tide;
He feels the hungry waves of space
    Rush at him high and blue;
Their white spray smites his dusky face,
Swifter the Sun's fierce arrows race
    And pierce his stout heart thro'.

His antlers fall; once more he spurns
    The hoarse hounds of the day;
His blood upon the crisp blue burns,
    Reddens the mounting spray;
His branches smite the wave—with cries
    The loud winds pause and flag—
He sinks in space—red glow the skies,
The brown earth crimsons as he dies,
    The strong and dusky stag.   [1883]

SAID THE CANOE

My masters twain made me a bed
Of pine-boughs resinous, and cedar;
Of moss, a soft and gentle breeder
Of dreams of rest; and me they spread

With furry skins and, laughing, said:
'Now she shall lay her polished sides
As queens do rest, or dainty brides,
Our slender lady of the tides!'

My masters twain their camp-soul lit;
Streamed incense from the hissing cones;
Large crimson flashes grew and whirled;
Thin golden nerves of sly light curled
Round the dun camp; and rose faint zones,
Half way about each grim bole knit,
Like a shy child that would bedeck
With its soft clasp a Brave's red neck,
Yet sees the rough shield on his breast,
The awful plumes shake on his crest,
And, fearful, drops his timid face,
Nor dares complete the sweet embrace.

Into the hollow hearts of brakes—
Yet warm from sides of does and stags
Passed to the crisp, dark river-flags—
Sinuous, red as copper-snakes,
Sharp-headed serpents, made of light,
Glided and hid themselves in night.

My masters twain the slaughtered deer
Hung on forked boughs with thongs of leather:
Bound were his stiff, slim feet together,
His eyes like dead stars cold and drear.
The wandering firelight drew near
And laid its wide palm, red and anxious,
On the sharp splendour of his branches,
On the white foam grown hard and sere
    On flank and shoulder.
Death—hard as breast of granite boulder—
    Under his lashes
Peered thro' his eyes at his life's grey ashes.

My masters twain sang songs that wove—
As they burnished hunting-blade and rifle—
A golden thread with a cobweb trifle,
Loud of the chase and low of love:
'O Love! art thou a silver fish,
Shy of the line and shy of gaffing,
Which we do follow, fierce, yet laughing,
Casting at thee the light-winged wish?

And at the last shall we bring thee up
From the crystal darkness, under the cup
    Of lily folden
    On broad leaves golden?

'O Love! art thou a silver deer
With feet as swift as wing of swallow,
While we with rushing arrows follow?
And at the last shall we draw near
And o'er thy velvet neck cast thongs
Woven of roses, stars and songs—
    New chains all moulden
    Of rare gems olden?'

They hung the slaughtered fish like swords
    On saplings slender; like scimitars,
    Bright, and ruddied from new-dead wars,
Blazed in the light the scaly hordes.

They piled up boughs beneath the trees,
    Of cedar web and green fir tassel.
    Low did the pointed pine tops rustle,
The camp-fire blushed to the tender breeze.

The hounds laid dewlaps on the ground
    With needles of pine, sweet, soft and rusty,
    Dreamed of the dead stag stout and lusty;
A bat by the red flames wove its round.

The darkness built its wigwam walls
    Close round the camp, and at its curtain
    Pressed shapes, thin, woven and uncertain
As white locks of tall waterfalls.

[1884]

ROBERT LOUIS STEVENSON

Scotland/England/Samoa 1850–1894

Stevenson was born and raised in Edinburgh. His school attendance was intermittent due to poor health related to tuberculosis; nonetheless, his extensive reading and rich imaginary life during his childhood inspired him to pursue a writing career. After attending Edinburgh University, Stevenson began writing essays and travel books but eventually turned to fiction, producing several classic children's adventure novels, including *Treasure Island* (1883) and *Kidnapped* (1886); he is also the author of *The Strange Case of Dr Jekyll and Mr Hyde* (1886). Stevenson's best-known poetry is the collection *A Child's Garden of Verses* (1885).

FOREIGN CHILDREN

Little Indian, Sioux or Crow,
Little frosty Eskimo,
Little Turk or Japanee,
O! don't you wish that you were me?

You have seen the scarlet trees
And the lions over seas;
You have eaten ostrich eggs,
And turned the turtles off their legs.

Such a life is very fine,
But it's not so nice as mine:
You must often, as you trod,
Have wearied *not* to be abroad.

You have curious things to eat,
I am fed on proper meat;
You must dwell beyond the foam,
But I am safe and live at home.

Little Indian, Sioux or Crow,
Little frosty Eskimo,
Little Turk or Japanee,
O! don't you wish that you were me?

[1885]

TORU DUTT

India 1856–1877

A member of a legendary family of poets from Rambagan, Calcutta, Dutt wrote in both English and French. Her *Ancient Ballads and Legends of Hindustan* was published in 1827. Dutt is considered 'the first Indian poet in English' by R. Parthasarathy, who argues in the Introduction to his *Ten Twentieth-Century Indian Poets* (1976) that 'she put the emphasis back on India, although her verse often glows with English romanticism of the mid-nineteenth century'. The tree in her family home at Baugmaree inspired 'Our Casuarina Tree'.

OUR CASUARINA TREE

Like a huge Python, winding round and round
   The rugged trunk, indented deep with scars
   Up to its very summit near the stars,
A creeper climbs, in whose embraces bound
   No other tree could live. But gallantly
The giant wears the scarf, and flowers are hung
In crimson clusters all the boughs among,
   Whereon all day are gathered bird and bee;
And oft at nights the garden overflows
With one sweet song that seems to have no close,
Sung darkling from our tree, while men repose.

When first my casement is wide open thrown
   At dawn, my eyes delighted on it rest;
   Sometimes, and most in winter,—on its crest
A gray baboon sits statue-like alone
   Watching the sunrise; while on lower boughs
His puny offspring leap about and play;
And far and near kokilas hail the day;
   And to their pastures wend our sleepy cows;
And in the shadow, on the broad tank cast
By that hoar tree, so beautiful and vast,
The water-lilies spring, like snow enmassed.

But not because of its magnificence
   Dear is the Casuarina to my soul:
   Beneath it we have played; though years may roll,
O sweet companions, loved with love intense,
   For your sakes shall the tree be ever dear!
Blent with your images, it shall arise
In memory, till the hot tears blind mine eyes!
What is that dirge-like murmur that I hear
Like the sea breaking on a shingle-beach?
It is the tree's lament, an eerie speech,
That haply to the unknown land may reach.

Unknown, yet well-known to the eye of faith!
　Ah, I have heard that wail far, far away
　In distant lands, by many a sheltered bay,
When slumbered in his cave the water-wraith
　And the waves gently kissed the classic shore
Of France or Italy, beneath the moon
When earth lay tranced in a dreamless swoon:
　And every time the music rose,—before
Mine inner vision rose a form sublime,
Thy form, O Tree, as in my happy prime
I saw thee, in my own loved native clime.

Therefore I fain would consecrate a lay
　Unto thy honour, Tree, beloved of those
　Who now in blessed sleep for aye repose,
Dearer than life to me, alas! were they!
　Mayst thou be numbered when my days are done
　With deathless trees—like those in Borrowdale,
Under whose awful branches lingered pale
　'Fear, trembling Hope, and Death, the skeleton,
And Time the shadow' and though weak the verse
That would thy beauty fain, oh fain rehearse,
May Love defend thee from Oblivion's curse.   [1878]

CHARLES G.D. ROBERTS

Canada 1860-1943

Because of his lifelong championing of Canadian literature and his powerful influence on a generation of Canadian poets, including his cousin Bliss Carman, Archibald Lampman, and Duncan Campbell Scott, Roberts is often referred to as the 'Father of Canadian Poetry'. His first book, *Orion, and Other Poems* (1880), was a major inspiration for Lampman. He is also credited with inventing the modern animal tale, and published a large number of collections of animal stories. Roberts was the first Canadian writer to pay careful imaginative attention to the Maritime setting where he grew up. *The Collected Poems of Sir Charles G.D. Roberts* (ed. Pacey) was published in 1985.

THE SKATER

My glad feet shod with the glittering steel
I was the god of the wingèd heel.

The hills in the far white sky were lost;
The world lay still in the wide white frost;

And the woods hung hushed in their long white dream
By the ghostly, glimmering, ice-blue stream.

Here was a pathway, smooth like glass,
Where I and the wandering wind might pass

To the far-off palaces, drifted deep,
Where Winter's retinue rests in sleep.

I followed the lure, I fled like a bird,
Till the startled hollows awoke and heard

A spinning whisper, a sibilant twang,
As the stroke of the steel on the tense ice rang;

And the wandering wind was left behind
As faster, faster I followed my mind;

Till the blood sang high in my eager brain,
And the joy of my flight was almost pain.

Then I stayed the rush of my eager speed
And silently went as a drifting seed,—

Slowly, furtively, till my eyes
Grew big with the awe of a dim surmise,

And the hair of my neck began to creep
At hearing the wilderness talk in sleep.

Shapes in the fir-gloom drifted near.
In the deep of my heart I heard my fear.

And I turned and fled, like a soul pursued,
From the white, inviolate solitude.   [1901]

BLISS CARMAN

Canada 1861–1929

Along with Charles G.D. Roberts, Archibald Lampman, and Duncan Campbell Scott, Bliss Carman is often referred to as a 'Confederation poet'; the designation has as much to do with Canada's birth as a nation in 1867 as with the widely held perception that these writers were creating a new national literature. A lyrically gifted poet, Carman was widely popular in both the US and Canada. His best poems are set in his native Maritimes (he was born in New Brunswick); his work is represented in *Selected Poems of Bliss Carman* (1976).

LOW TIDE ON GRAND PRÉ

The sun goes down, and over all
   These barren reaches by the tide
Such unelusive glories fall,
   I almost dream they yet will bide
   Until the coming of the tide.

And yet I know that not for us,
   By any ecstasy of dream,
He lingers to keep luminous
   A little while the grievous stream,
   Which frets, uncomforted of dream—

A grievous stream, that to and fro
   Athrough the fields of Acadie
Goes wandering, as if to know
   Why one beloved face should be
   So long from home and Acadie.

Was it a year or lives ago
   We took the grasses in our hands,
And caught the summer flying low
   Over the waving meadow lands,
   And held it there between our hands?

The while the river at our feet—
   A drowsy inland meadow stream—
At set of sun the after-heat
   Made running gold, and in the gleam
   We freed our birch upon the stream.

There down along the elms at dusk
   We lifted dripping blade to drift,
Through twilight scented fine like musk,

Where night and gloom awhile uplift,
  Nor sunder soul and soul adrift.

And that we took into our hands
  Spirit of life or subtler thing—
Breathed on us there, and loosed the bands
  Of death, and taught us, whispering,
  The secret of some wonder-thing.

Then all your face grew light, and seemed
  To hold the shadow of the sun;
The evening faltered, and I deemed
  That time was ripe, and years had done
  Their wheeling underneath the sun.

So all desire and all regret,
  And fear and memory, were naught;
One to remember or forget
  The keen delight our hands had caught;
  Morrow and yesterday were naught.

The night has fallen, and the tide . . .
  Now and again comes drifting home,
Across these aching barrens wide,
  A sigh like driven wind or foam:
  In grief the flood is bursting home.   [1893]

MARY COLERIDGE

England 1861–1907

Great-great-niece of Samuel Taylor Coleridge, Mary Coleridge devoted much of her adult life to
the teaching of literature among working-class women. She published but two brief volumes of
her poetry during her lifetime, more able to allow her novels (*The Seven Sleepers of Ephesus*, 1893;
The King with Two Faces, 1897) into the public domain than her verse. Coleridge's poetry often
discloses with subtlety and cunning the wild woman who circulates at the edge of consciousness.
Her verse relishes encounters with alternate and rebellious realities which undermine the security
of established routines.

THE OTHER SIDE OF A MIRROR

I sat before my glass one day,
  And conjured up a vision bare,
Unlike the aspects glad and gay,
  That erst were found reflected there—
The vision of a woman, wild
  With more than womanly despair.

Her hair stood back on either side
  A face bereft of loveliness.
It had no envy now to hide
  What once no man on earth could guess.
It formed the thorny aureole
  Of hard unsanctified distress.

Her lips were open—not a sound
  Came through the parted lines of red.
Whate'er it was, the hideous wound
  In silence and in secret bled.
No sigh relieved her speechless woe,
  She had no voice to speak her dread.

And in her lurid eyes there shone
  The dying flame of life's desire,
Made mad because its hope was gone,
  And kindled at the leaping fire
Of jealousy, and fierce revenge,
  And strength that could not change nor tire.

Shade of a shadow in the glass,
  O set the crystal surface free!
Pass—as the fairer visions pass—
  Nor ever more return, to be
The ghost of a distracted hour,
  That heard me whisper, 'I am she!'   [1882]

ARCHIBALD LAMPMAN

Canada 1861–1899

Lampman was influenced by the Romantics, particularly Keats, and composed detailed descriptions of Canadian settings in which the speaker often finds himself in a 'dream' state—the most charged word in Lampman's vocabulary. He was also hopeful about the possibilities for an authentic Canadian poetry, recording that he read Charles G.D. Roberts's new book of poems, *Orion*, in 1880 'in a state of wild excitement'. Duncan Campbell Scott, a friend and longtime admirer of Lampman's poetry, edited several collections, including *Selected Poems of Archibald Lampman* (1947); Lampman's sonnets, which include some of his best work, are available in *Lampman's Sonnets: The Complete Sonnets of Archibald Lampman* (ed. Whitridge, 1976).

HEAT

From plains that reel to southward, dim,
  The road runs by me white and bare;
Up the steep hill it seems to swim
  Beyond, and melt into the glare.

Upward half-way, or it may be
   Nearer the summit, slowly steals
A hay-cart, moving dustily
   With idly clacking wheels.

By his cart's side the wagoner
   Is slouching slowly at his ease,
Half-hidden in the windless blur
   Of white dust puffing to his knees.
This wagon on the height above,
   From sky to sky on either hand,
Is the sole thing that seems to move
   In all the heat-held land.

Beyond me in the fields the sun
   Soaks in the grass and hath his will;
I count the marguerites one by one;
   Even the buttercups are still.
On the brook yonder not a breath
   Disturbs the spider or the midge.
The water-bugs draw close beneath
   The cool gloom of the bridge.

Where the far elm-tree shadows flood
   Dark patches in the burning grass,
The cows, each with their peaceful cud,
   Lie waiting for the heat to pass.
From somewhere on the slope near by
   Into the pale depth of the noon
A wandering thrush slides leisurely
   His thin revolving tune.

In intervals of dreams I hear
   The cricket from the droughty ground;
The grasshoppers spin into mine ear
   A small innumerable sound.
I lift mine eyes sometimes to gaze:
   The burning sky-line blinds my sight:
The woods far off are blue with haze:
   The hills are drenched in light.

And yet to me not this or that
   Is always sharp or always sweet;
In the sloped shadow of my hat
   I lean at rest, and drain the heat;

Nay more, I think some blessèd power
    Hath brought me wandering idly here:
In the full furnace of this hour
    My thoughts grow keen and clear.   [1888]

IN NOVEMBER

With loitering step and quiet eye,
Beneath the low November sky,
I wandered in the woods, and found
A clearing, where the broken ground
Was scattered with black stumps and briers,
And the old wreck of forest fires.
It was a bleak and sandy spot,
And, all about, the vacant plot
Was peopled and inhabited
By scores of mulleins long since dead.
A silent and forsaken brood
In that mute opening of the wood,
So shrivelled and so thin they were,
So grey, so haggard, and austere,
Not plants at all they seemed to me,
But rather some spare company
Of hermit folk, who long ago,
Wandering in bodies to and fro,
Had chanced upon this lonely way,
And rested thus, till death one day
Surprised them at their compline prayer,
And left them standing lifeless there.

There was no sound about the wood
Save the wind's secret stir. I stood
Among the mullein-stalks as still
As if myself had grown to be
One of their sombre company,
A body without wish or will.
And as I stood, quite suddenly,
Down from a furrow in the sky
The sun shone out a little space
Across that silent sober place,
Over the sand heaps and brown sod,
The mulleins and dead goldenrod,
And passed beyond the thickets grey,
And lit the fallen leaves that lay,
Level and deep within the wood,
A rustling yellow multitude.

And all around me the thin light,
So sere, so melancholy bright,
Fell like the half-reflected gleam
Or shadow of some former dream;
A moment's golden reverie
Poured out on every plant and tree
A semblance of weird joy, or less,
A sort of spectral happiness;
And I, too, standing idly there,
With muffled hands in the chill air,
Felt the warm glow about my feet,
And shuddering betwixt cold and heat,
Drew my thoughts closer, like a cloak,
While something in my blood awoke,
A nameless and unnatural cheer,
A pleasure secret and austere.

                                                                    [1895]

RABINDRANATH TAGORE

India 1861–1941

Tagore's remarkably prolific work in Bengali includes 60 collections of verse, novels, short stories, experimental plays, and essays. His own English translations are available in the *Collected Poems and Plays of Rabindranath Tagore* (1936) and *Selected Poems* (1985). Tagore's two thousand songs have become the national music of Bengal, and include the national anthems of both India and Bangladesh. Tagore received the Nobel Prize in 1913, and although he was knighted two years later, attempted to reject the honour in 1919 to protest British colonial policy.

from THE CHILD

IX
The first flush of dawn glistens on the dew-dripping
          leaves of the forest.
The man who reads the sky cries:
               'Friends, we have come!'
They stop and look around.
     On both sides of the road the corn is ripe to the
          horizon,
     —the glad golden answer of the earth to the
          morning light.
The current of daily life moves slowly
     between the village near the hill and the one
          by the river bank.
The potter's wheel goes round, the woodcutter brings
          fuel to the market,
     the cow-herd takes his cattle to the pasture,

and the woman with the pitcher on her head
    walks to the well.
But where is the King's castle, the mine of gold,
    the secret book of magic,
    the sage who knows love's utter wisdom?
'The stars cannot be wrong,' assures the reader of the sky.
'Their signal points to that spot.'
    And reverently he walks to a wayside spring
from which wells up a stream of water, a liquid light,
    like the morning melting into a chorus of tears
    and laughter.
Near it in a palm grove surrounded by a strange hush
    stands a leaf-thatched hut,
at whose portal sits the poet of the unknown shore, and
    sings:
        'Mother, open the gate!'

X

A ray of morning sun strikes aslant at the door.
The assembled crowd feel in their blood the primæval
    chant of creation:
        'Mother, open the gate!'
The gate opens.
The mother is seated on a straw bed with the babe on
    her lap,
    Like the dawn with the morning star.
The sun's ray that was waiting at the door outside
    falls on the head of the child.
The poet strikes his lute and sings out:
  'Victory to Man, the new-born, the ever-living.'
They kneel down,—the king and the beggar, the saint
    and the sinner,
    the wise and the fool,—and cry:
  'Victory to Man, the new-born, the ever-living.'
The old man from the East murmurs to himself:
        'I have seen!'   [1931]

TEKAHIONWAKE/EMILY PAULINE JOHNSON

Mohawk 1861–1913

Tekahionwake was born on the Six Nations reserve near Brantford, Ontario, the daughter of a Mohawk chief, G.H.M. Johnson, and an English Quaker mother, Emily Susanna Howells. Her mother and a tutor gave her a typically Victorian education; her father and grandfather, John Smoke Johnson, the speaker of the Council of the Confederacy of the Six Nations, taught her the traditional Iroquois legends and history. Between 1889 and 1909 Tekahionwake performed and published her poetry widely in Canada, the United States, and Britain. Her poetic attempts to integrate her own experiences with those of two cultures, traditions, and histories foreshadow intercultural issues addressed by writers in our time. The most comprehensive collection of Tekahionwake's poetry is *Flint and Feather* (1917).

AS RED MEN DIE

Captive! Is there a hell to him like this?
A taunt more galling than the Huron's hiss?
He—proud and scornful, he—who laughed at law,
He—scion of the deadly Iroquois,
He—the bloodthirsty, he—the Mohawk chief,
He—who despises pain and sneers at grief,
Here in the hated Huron's vicious clutch,
That even captive he disdains to touch!

Captive! But *never* conquered; Mohawk brave
Stoops not to be to *any* man a slave;
Least, to the puny tribe his soul abhors,
The tribe whose wigwams sprinkle Simcoe's shores.
With scowling brow he stands and courage high,
Watching with haughty and defiant eye
His captors, as they council o'er his fate,
Or strive his boldness to intimidate.
Then fling they unto him the choice;

                         'Wilt thou
Walk o'er the bed of fire that waits thee now—
Walk with uncovered feet upon the coals,
Until thou reach the ghostly Land of Souls,
And, with thy Mohawk death-song please our ear?
Or wilt thou with the women rest thee here?'
His eyes flash like an eagle's, and his hands
Clench at the insult. Like a god he stands.
'Prepare the fire!' he scornfully demands.

He knoweth not that this same jeering band
Will bite the dust—will lick the Mohawk's hand;
Will kneel and cower at the Mohawk's feet;
Will shrink when Mohawk war drums wildly beat.

His death will be avenged with hideous hate
By Iroquois, swift to annihilate
His vile detested captors, that now flaunt
Their war clubs in his face with sneer and taunt,
Not thinking, soon that reeking, red, and raw,
Their scalps will deck the belts of Iroquois.

The path of coals outstretches, white with heat,
A forest fir's length—ready for his feet.
Unflinching as a rock he steps along
The burning mass, and sings his wild war song,
Sings, as he sang when once he used to roam
Throughout the forests of his southern home,
Where, down the Genesee, the water roars,
Where gentle Mohawk purls between its shores,
Songs, that of exploit and of prowess tell;
Songs of the Iroquois invincible.

Up the long trail of fire he boasting goes,
Dancing a war dance to defy his foes.
His flesh is scorched, his muscles burn and shrink,
But still he dances to death's awful brink.

The eagle plume that crests his haughty head
Will *never* droop until his heart be dead,
Slower and slower yet his footstep swings,
Wilder and wilder still his death-song rings,
Fiercer and fiercer thro' the forest bounds
His voice that leaps to Happier Hunting Grounds.
One savage yell—
                              Then loyal to his race,
He bends to death—but *never* to disgrace.   [1917]

A CRY FROM AN INDIAN WIFE

My Forest Brave, my Red-skin love, farewell;
We may not meet to-morrow; who can tell
What mighty ills befall our little band,
Or what you'll suffer from the white man's hand
Here is your knife! I thought 'twas sheathed for aye.
No roaming bison calls for it to-day:

No hide of prairie cattle will it maim;
The plains are bare, it seeks a nobler game:
'Twill drink the life-blood of a soldier host.
Go; rise and strike, no matter what the cost.
Yet stay. Revolt not at the Union Jack,
Nor raise Thy hand against this stripling pack
Of white-faced warriors, marching West to quell
Our fallen tribe that rises to rebel.
They all are young and beautiful and good;
Curse to the war that drinks their harmless blood.
Curse to the fate that brought them from the East
To be our Chiefs—to make our nation least
That breathes the air of this vast continent.
Still their new rule and council is well meant.
They but forget we Indians owned the land
From ocean unto ocean; that they stand
Upon a soil that centuries agone
Was our sole kingdom and our right alone.
They never think how they would feel to-day,
If some great nation came from far away,
Wresting their country from their hapless braves,
Giving what they gave us—but wars and graves.
Then go and strike for liberty and life,
And bring back honour to your Indian wife.
Your wife? Ah, what of that, who cares for me?
Who pities my poor love and agony?
What white-robed priest prays for your safety here,
As prayer is said for every volunteer
That swells the ranks that Canada sends out?
Who prays for victory for the Indian scout?
Who prays for your poor nation lying low?
None—therefore take your tomahawk and go.
My heart may break and burn into its core,
But I am strong to bid you go to war.
Yet stay, my heart is not the only one
That grieves the loss of husband and of son;
Think of the mother o'er the inland seas
Think of the pale-faced maiden on her knees;
One pleads her God to guard some sweet-faced child
That marches on toward the North-West wild.
The other prays to shield her love from harm,
To strengthen his young, proud uplifted arm.
Ah, how her white face quivers thus to think
YOUR tomahawk his life's best blood will drink.
She never thinks of my wild aching breast,
Nor prays for your dark face and eagle crest

Endangered by a thousand rifle balls,
My heart the target if my warrior falls.
O! coward self I hesitate no more;
Go forth, and win the glories of the war.
Go forth, nor bend to greed of white men's hands,
By right, by birth we Indians own these lands,
Though starved, crushed, plundered, lies our nation low . . .
Perhaps the white man's God has willed it so.   [1917]

DUNCAN CAMPBELL SCOTT

Canada 1862-1947

Scott, a longtime civil servant in the Department of Indian Affairs (1879–1932), worked with and reflected on the people who populate so many of his poems, in which aboriginals are often depicted as trapped between Christian and more indigenous value systems. Scott also wrote short stories (*In the Village of Viger*, 1896 is the best-known collection) and, with Archibald Lampman and Wilfred Campbell, established an important literary column, 'At the Mermaid Inn' in 1892 for the *Toronto Globe*. Scott's poems trace the evolution of a Canadian sensibility, shedding an inherited Victorian tradition to develop his own stance, subject, and style; like Charles G.D. Roberts, Scott witnessed and participated in the birth of Canadian modernism. His poems are represented in editions such as *Selected Poems* (ed. E.K. Brown, 1951) and *Powassan's Drum: Selected Poems of Duncan Campbell Scott* (ed. Souster and Lochhead, 1985).

THE FORSAKEN

I
Once in the winter
Out on a lake
In the heart of the north-land,
Far from the Fort
And far from the hunters,
A Chippewa woman
With her sick baby,
Crouched in the last hours
Of a great storm.
Frozen and hungry,
She fished through the ice
With a line of the twisted
Bark of the cedar,
And a rabbit-bone hook
Polished and barbed;
Fished with the bare hook
All through the wild day,
Fished and caught nothing;
While the young chieftain

Tugged at her breasts,
Or slept in the lacings
Of the warm *tikanagan.*
All the lake-surface
Streamed with the hissing
Of millions of iceflakes
Hurled by the wind;
Behind her the round
Of a lonely island
Roared like a fire
With the voice of the storm
In the deeps of the cedars.
Valiant, unshaken,
She took of her own flesh,
Baited the fish-hook
Drew in a gray-trout,
Drew in his fellows,
Heaped them beside her,
Dead in the snow.
Valiant, unshaken,
She faced the long distance,
Wolf-haunted and lonely,
Sure of her goal
And the life of her dear one:
Tramped for two days,
On the third in the morning,
Saw the strong bulk
Of the Fort by the river,
Saw the wood-smoke
Hang soft in the spruces,
Heard the keen yelp
Of the ravenous huskies
Fighting for whitefish:
Then she had rest.

II
Years and years after,
When she was old and withered,
When her son was an old man
And his children filled with vigour,
They came in their northern tour on the verge of winter,
To an island in a lonely lake.
There one night they camped, and on the morrow
Gathered their kettles and birch-bark
Their rabbit-skin robes and their mink-traps,
Launched their canoes and slunk away through the islands,

Left her alone forever,
Without a word of farewell,
Because she was old and useless,
Like a paddle broken and warped,
Or a pole that was splintered.
Then, without a sigh,
Valiant, unshaken,
She smoothed her dark locks under her kerchief,
Composed her shawl in state,
Then folded her hands ridged with sinews and corded with veins,
Folded them across her breasts spent with the nourishing of
    children,
Gazed at the sky past the tops of the cedars,
Saw two spangled nights arise out of the twilight,
Saw two days go by filled with the tranquil sunshine,
Saw, without pain, or dread, or even a moment of longing:
Then on the third great night there came thronging and thronging
Millions of snowflakes out of a windless cloud;
They covered her close with a beautiful crystal shroud,
Covered her deep and silent.
But in the frost of the dawn,
Up from the life below,
Rose a column of breath
Through a tiny cleft in the snow,
Fragile, delicately drawn,
Wavering with its own weakness,
In the wilderness a sign of the spirit,
Persisting still in the sight of the sun
Till day was done.
Then all light was gathered up by the hand of God and hid in His
    breast,
Then there was born a silence deeper than silence,
Then she had rest.   [1905]

SWAMI VIVEKANANDA

India 1863–1902

Called by his followers 'the Revealer, the Interpreter to India of the treasures she herself possesses in herself' from the Vedas and the Upanishads, Swami Vivekananda was disciple to Ramakrishna Paramahamsa who taught in the temple-garden at Dakshineshrwar. Welcomed by his disciples as 'the authoritative pronouncement on Hinduism in all its phases', Swami Vivekananda's public lectures, teachings, poems, conversations, and letters from 1893–1902 were published in eight volumes from 1947.

THE CUP

This is your cup—the cup assigned
   to you from the beginning.
Nay, My child, I know how much
   of that dark drink is your own brew
Of fault and passion, ages long ago,
In the deep years of yesterday, I know.

This is your road—a painful road and drear.
I made the stones that never give you rest.
I set your friend in pleasant ways and clear,
And he shall come like you, unto My breast.
But you, My child, must travel here.

This is your task. It has no joy nor grace,
But it is not meant for any other hand,
And in my universe hath measured place,
Take it. I do not bid you understand.
I bid you close your eyes to see My face.

[1963]

Andrew Barton ('The Banjo') Paterson

Australia 1864-1941

Paterson was born at Narambla Station in New South Wales and educated in Sydney. A lawyer by training and an adventuresome folk-poet, short-story writer, and novelist by reputation, Paterson became a war correspondent in South Africa during the Boer War and in the Philippines and China during World War I. He was later a journalist and editor for Sydney newspapers and magazines. In five collections of verse he immortalized legendary figures of Australian national folklore: *The Man from Snowy River and Other Verses* (1898), *Rio Grande's Last Race and Other Verses* (1902), *Collected Verse* (1923), and a children's book, *The Animals Noah Forgot* (1933).

The Man from Snowy River

There was movement at the station, for the word had passed around
    That the colt from old Regret had got away,
And had joined the wild bush horses—he was worth a thousand
      pound,
    So all the cracks had gathered to the fray.
All the tried and noted riders from the stations near and far
    Had mustered at the homestead overnight,
For the bushmen love hard riding where the wild bush horses are,
    And the stock-horse snuffs the battle with delight.

There was Harrison, who made his pile when Pardon won the cup,
    The old man with his hair as white as snow;
But few could ride beside him when his blood was fairly up—
    He would go wherever horse and man could go.
And Clancy of the Overflow came down to lend a hand,
    No better horseman ever held the reins;
For never horse could throw him while the saddle-girths would
      stand—
    He learnt to ride while droving on the plains.

And one was there, a stripling on a small and weedy beast;
    He was something like a racehorse undersized,
With a touch of Timor pony—three parts thoroughbred at least—
    And such as are by mountain horsemen prized.
He was hard and tough and wiry—just the sort that won't say
      die—
    There was courage in his quick impatient tread;
And he bore the badge of gameness in his bright and fiery eye,
    And the proud and lofty carriage of his head.

But still so slight and weedy, one would doubt his power to stay,
    And the old man said, 'That horse will never do
For a long and tiring gallop—lad, you'd better stop away,
    Those hills are far too rough for such as you.'
So he waited, sad and wistful—only Clancy stood his friend—
    'I think we ought to let him come,' he said;
'I warrant he'll be with us when he's wanted at the end,
    For both his horse and he are mountain bred.

'He hails from Snowy River, up by Kosciusko's side,
    Where the hills are twice as steep and twice as rough;
Where a horse's hoofs strike fireflight from the flint stones
        every stride,
    The man that holds his own is good enough.
And the Snowy River riders on the mountains make their home,
    Where the river runs those giant hills between;
I have seen full many horsemen since I first commenced to roam,
    But nowhere yet such horsemen have I seen.'

So he went; they found the horses by the big mimosa clump,
    They raced away towards the mountain's brow,
And the old man gave his orders, 'Boys, go at them from the jump,
    No use to try for fancy riding now.
And, Clancy, you must wheel them, try and wheel them to the
        right.
    Ride boldly, lad, and never fear the spills,
For never yet was rider that could keep the mob in sight,
    If once they gain the shelter of those hills.'

So Clancy rode to wheel them—he was racing on the wing
    Where the best and boldest riders take their place,
And he raced his stock-horse past them, and he made the ranges
        ring
    With the stockwhip, as he met them face to face.
Then they halted for a moment, while he swung the dreaded lash,
    But they saw their well-loved mountain full in view,
And they charged beneath the stockwhip with a sharp and sudden
        dash,
    And off into the mountain scrub they flew.

Then fast the horsemen followed, where the gorges deep and black
    Resounded to the thunder of their tread,
And the stockwhips woke the echoes and they fiercely answered
        back
    From cliffs and crags that beetled overhead.

And upward, ever upward, the wild horses held their way,
    Where mountain ash and kurrajong grew wide;
And the old man muttered fiercely, 'We may bid the mob good day,
    No man can hold them down the other side.'

When they reached the mountain's summit, even Clancy took a
      pull—
    It well might make the boldest hold their breath;
The wild hop scrub grew thickly, and the hidden ground was full
    Of wombat holes, and any slip was death.
But the man from Snowy River let the pony have his head,
    And he swung his stockwhip round and gave a cheer,
And he raced him down the mountain like a torrent down its bed,
    While the others stood and watched in very fear.

He sent the flint-stones flying, but the pony kept his feet,
    He cleared the fallen timber in his stride,
And the man from Snowy River never shifted in his seat—
    It was grand to see that mountain horseman ride.
Through the stringy barks and saplings, on the rough and broken
      ground,
    Down the hillside at a racing pace he went;
And he never drew the bridle till he landed safe and sound
    At the bottom of that terrible descent.

He was right among the horses as they climbed the farther hill,
    And the watchers on the mountain, standing mute,
Saw him ply the stockwhip fiercely; he was right among them
      still,
    As he raced across the clearing in pursuit.
Then they lost him for a moment, where two mountain gullies met
    In the ranges—but a final glimpse reveals
On a dim and distant hillside the wild horses racing yet,
    With the man from Snowy River at their heels.

And he ran them single-handed till their sides were white with
      foam;
    He followed like a bloodhound on their track,
Till they halted, cowed and beaten; then he turned their heads
      for home,
    And alone and unassisted brought them back.
But his hardy mountain pony he could scarcely raise a trot,
    He was blood from hip to shoulder from the spur;
But his pluck was still undaunted, and his courage fiery hot,
    For never yet was mountain horse a cur.

And down by Kosciusko, where the pine-clad ridges raise
   Their torn and rugged battlements on high,
Where the air is clear as crystal, and the white stars fairly
    blaze
   At midnight in the cold and frosty sky,
And where around the Overflow the reed-beds sweep and sway
   To the breezes, and the rolling plains are wide,
The Man from Snowy River is a household word today,
   And the stockmen tell the story of his ride.   [1895]

MARY GILMORE

Australia 1865–1962

Born near the town of Goulburn in New South Wales, Gilmore taught school before emigrating to an Australian colony in Paraguay. She returned to Australia in 1902 where she became a prominent labour movement activist and an editor for the *Sydney Worker*. Her poetry discloses how her socialist political views relate to gender issues. Gilmore was awarded the Order of the British Empire in 1936 for her contributions to Australian literature. Collections of her poetry include: *Marri'd and Other Verses* (1910), *The Passionate Heart* (1918), *Under the Wilgas* (1932), *Selected Verse* (1948, 1968), and *Selected Poems* (1963).

EVE-SONG

I span and Eve span
A thread to bind the heart of man;
But the heart of man was a wandering thing
That came and went with little to bring:
Nothing he minded what we made,
As here he loitered, and there he stayed.

I span and Eve span
A thread to bind the heart of man;
But the more we span the more we found
It wasn't his heart but ours we bound.
For children gathered about our knees:
The thread was a chain that stole our ease.
And one of us learned in our children's eyes
That more than man was love and prize.
But deep in the heart of one of us lay
A root of loss and hidden dismay.

He said he was strong. He had no strength
But that which comes of breadth and length.
He said he was fond. But his fondness proved
The flame of an hour when he was moved.
He said he was true. His truth was but
A door that winds could open and shut.

And yet, and yet, as he came back,
Wandering in from the outward track,
We held our arms, and gave him our breast,
As a pillowing place for his head to rest.
I span and Eve span,
A thread to bind the heart of man!   [1918]

NEVER ADMIT THE PAIN

Never admit the pain,
   Bury it deep;
Only the weak complain,
   Complaint is cheap.

Cover thy wound, fold down
   Its curtained place;
Silence is still a crown,
   Courage a grace.   [1930]

WILLIAM BUTLER YEATS

Ireland 1865–1939

Yeats felt his poetry released the emotional and intellectual symbols housed in the Great Mind and Memory of the unconscious, archetypal figures and patterns that live 'beyond the threshold of the waking life'. His symbolic system, the Great Wheel, allowed him to hold together in simultaneous relation a theory of personality, human history, and mythology. The system became both vision and technique. He theorized that the archetypal strength of the ballad metre loosens the poet's blank verse and yields the 'ghostly voice' of legendary figures whose heroism might revive an impoverished, anarchic present. Yeats knew many of the rebels, executed or imprisoned, after the 1916 Easter Monday uprising. Their sacrifice paradoxically heightened his impulse to both withdraw from and engage the political tragedy of his time. Major editions of his work include *The Variorum Edition of the Poems* (eds Allt and Alspach, 1957, corrected 3rd printing). *A Vision* is the published record of Yeats's symbolic system which his wife Georgie Hyde-Lees's automatic writing produced and which Yeats believed was directed by a supernatural hand (1925, 1937).

THE MAGI

Now as at all times I can see in the mind's eye,
In their stiff, painted clothes, the pale unsatisfied ones
Appear and disappear in the blue depth of the sky
With all their ancient faces like rain-beaten stones,
And all their helms of silver hovering side by side,
And all their eyes still fixed, hoping to find once more,
Being by Calvary's turbulence unsatisfied,
The uncontrollable mystery on the bestial floor.   [1914]

Easter 1916

I have met them at close of day
Coming with vivid faces
From counter or desk among grey
Eighteenth-century houses.
I have passed with a nod of the head
Or polite meaningless words,
Or have lingered awhile and said
Polite meaningless words,
And thought before I had done
Of a mocking tale or a gibe
To please a companion
Around the fire at the club,
Being certain that they and I
But lived where motley is worn:
All changed, changed utterly:
A terrible beauty is born.

That woman's days were spent
In ignorant good-will,
Her nights in argument
Until her voice grew shrill.
What voice more sweet than hers
When, young and beautiful,
She rode to harriers?
This man had kept a school
And rode our wingèd horse;
This other his helper and friend
Was coming into his force;
He might have won fame in the end,
So sensitive his nature seemed,
So daring and sweet his thought.
This other man I had dreamed
A drunken, vainglorious lout.
He had done most bitter wrong
To some who are near my heart,
Yet I number him in the song;
He, too, has resigned his part
In the casual comedy;
He, too, has been changed in his turn,
Transformed utterly:
A terrible beauty is born.

Hearts with one purpose alone
Through summer and winter seem
Enchanted to a stone
To trouble the living stream.
The horse that comes from the road,
The rider, the birds that range
From cloud to tumbling cloud,
Minute by minute they change;
A shadow of cloud on the stream
Changes minute by minute;
A horse-hoof slides on the brim,
And a horse plashes within it;
The long-legged moor-hens dive,
And hens to moor-cocks call;
Minute by minute they live:
The stone's in the midst of all.

Too long a sacrifice
Can make a stone of the heart.
O when may it suffice?
That is Heaven's part, our part
To murmur name upon name,
As a mother names her child
When sleep at last has come
On limbs that had run wild.
What is it but nightfall?
No, no, not night but death;
Was it needless death after all?
For England may keep faith
For all that is done and said.
We know their dream; enough
To know they dreamed and are dead;
And what if excess of love
Bewildered them till they died?
I write it out in a verse—
MacDonagh and MacBride
And Connolly and Pearse
Now and in time to be,
Wherever green is worn,
Are changed, changed utterly:
A terrible beauty is born.   [1921]

HENRY LAWSON

Australia 1867–1922

Lawson, an early proponent of literary nationalism in Australia, re-created the oral bush ballad in written form. Lawson's short stories in prose also earned acclaim. The son of Nils Larson, a Norwegian seaman turned golddigger and carpenter, and Louisa Albury, a feminist editor, Lawson became a journalist and freelance writer who worked in Brisbane, Perth, Sydney, and London before settling in Sydney in 1902. The comprehensive editions of Lawson's poetry are *Poetical Works* (1956) and the two-volume *Collected Verse, 1885–1909* (ed. Roderick, 1967–68).

THE BASTARD FROM THE BUSH

As night was falling slowly on city, town and bush,
from a slum in Jones's Alley came the Captain of the Push,
and his whistle, loud and piercing, woke the echoes of the Rocks,
and a dozen ghouls came slouching round the corners of the blocks.

Then the Captain jerked a finger at a stranger by the kerb,
whom he qualified politely with an adjective and verb.
Then he made the introduction: 'Here's a covey from the bush;
fuck me blind, he wants to join us, be a member of the Push!'

Then the stranger made this answer to the Captain of the Push:
'Why, fuck me dead, I'm Foreskin Fred, the Bastard from the Bush!
I've been in every two-up school from Darwin to the Loo;
I've ridden colts and blackgins; what more can a bugger do?'

'Are you game to break a window?' said the Captain of the Push.
'I'd knock a fucking house down!' said the Bastard from the Bush.
'Would you out a man and rob him?' said the Captain of the Push.
'I'd knock him down and fuck him!' said the Bastard from the Bush.

'Would you dong a bloody copper if you caught the cunt alone?
Would you stoush a swell or Chinkie, split his garret with a stone?
Would you have a moll to keep you; would you swear off work for
    good?'
Said the Bastard: 'My colonial silver-mounted oath I would!'

'Would you care to have a gasper?' said the Captain of the Push.
'I'll take that bloody packet!' said the Bastard from the Bush.
Then the Pushites all took council, saying, 'Fuck me, but he's game!
Let's make him our star basher; he'll live up to his name.'

So they took him to their hideout, that Bastard from the Bush,
and granted him all privileges appertaining to the Push.
But soon they found his little ways were more than they could
    stand,
and finally their Captain addressed the members of his band:

'Now listen here, you buggers, we've caught a fucking Tartar.
At every kind of bludging, that Bastard is a starter.
At poker and at two-up he's shook our fucking rolls;
he swipes our fucking likker and robs our bloody molls!'

So down in Jones's Alley all the members of the Push
laid a dark and dirty ambush for that Bastard from the Bush.
But against the wall of Riley's pub the Bastard made a stand,
a nasty grin upon his dial; a bike-chain in each hand.

They sprang upon him in a bunch, but one by one they fell,
with crack of bone, unearthly groan, and agonising yell,
till the sorely battered Captain, spitting teeth and gouts of blood,
held an ear all torn and bleeding in hand bedaubed with mud.

'You low polluted Bastard!' snarled the Captain of the Push,
'Get back where your sort belongs—that's somewhere in the bush.
And I hope heaps of misfortunes may soon tumble down on you;
may some lousy harlot dose you till your ballocks turn sky-blue!

'May the itching piles torment you; may corns grow on your feet!
May crabs as big as spiders attack your balls a treat!
And when you're down and outed, to a hopeless body wreck,
may you slip back through your arsehole and break your fucking
    neck!'   [1892]

W.E.B. Du Bois

USA 1868-1963

Du Bois was a militant African-American activist who advocated collective protest and civil disobedience as necessary responses to violence, racism, and segregation. After graduating with a bachelor's degree in history and sociology from Fisk University, Du Bois completed degrees in history and philosophy at Harvard. Du Bois held professorial positions at several universities, and subsequently organized the National Association for the Advancement of Colored People (NAACP). From 1910 to 1934, he served as the NAACP Director of Publicity and Research, and he edited *Crisis* magazine. However, he was dismissed from this position for advocating Black separatist policies and strategies, and became a citizen of Ghana in 1963 shortly before he died.

THE SONG OF THE SMOKE

I am the smoke king,
I am black.
I am swinging in the sky.
I am ringing worlds on high:
I am the thought of the throbbing mills,
I am the soul of the soul toil kills,
I am the ripple of trading rills,

Up I'm curling from the sod,
I am whirling home to God.
I am the smoke king,
I am black.

I am the smoke king,
I am black.

I am wreathing broken hearts,
I am sheathing devils' darts;
Dark inspiration of iron times,
Wedding the toil of toiling climes
Shedding the blood of bloodless crimes,

Down I lower in the blue,
Up I tower toward the true,
I am the smoke king,
I am black.

I am the smoke king,
I am black.

I am darkening with song,
I am hearkening to wrong;
I will be as black as blackness can,
The blacker the mantle the mightier the man,
My purpl'ing midnights no day dawn may ban.

I am carving God in night,
I am painting hell in white.
I am the smoke king,
I am black.

I am the smoke king,
I am black.

I am cursing ruddy morn,
I am nursing hearts unborn;
Souls unto me are as mists in the night,
I whiten my blackmen, I beckon my white,
What's the hue of a hide to a man in his might!

Hail, then, grilly, grimy hands,
Sweet Christ, pity toiling lands!
Hail to the smoke king,
Hail to the black!   [1907]

MARY FULLERTON ('E')

Australia 1868-1946

Born in Glenmaggie, Victoria, Fullerton was educated by her mother; *Bark House Days* (1921)
offers verse reminiscences of her childhood frontier experiences. A feminist active in the women's
suffrage movement during the 1890s, Fullerton published poetry and short fiction in newspapers
and magazines under the pen-name 'Alpenstock'; two collections of this verse appeared as *Moods
and Melodies* (1908) and *The Breaking Furrow* (1921). Fullerton's friend, novelist [Stella Maria]
Miles Franklin, arranged for the publication of two more collections under the pseudonym 'E' in
an attempt to avoid discriminatory judgments of her poetry's merits: *Moles Do So Little With Their
Privacy* (1942) and *The Wonder and the Apple* (1946).

FLESH

I have seen a gum-tree,
Scarred by the blaze
Of the pioneer axe,
Mend after long days;
Lip to lip shut
Of the separate bark,
Till the gape of the wound
Was a vanishing mark.

I have seen in the hunt
The pulse of rent flesh;
Seen the fingers of Time
Unite it afresh.
I have heard a man's cry
As the teeth of the mill
Bit marrow and bone—
To hurt, not to kill.

Oh, strong is the flesh
To cure and defend:
'Tis but the stopt heart
That Time cannot mend.

[1942]

CUBES

Nina's cross: her alphabet
Flung upon the floor.
Hoity toity! in a pet,
Wanting something more.

You have there the whole of it,
Little Goldilocks,
All the wisdom and the wit,
On those pretty blocks.

All the science and the verse,
Eastern, European;
Rearrange, transpose, disperse:
There's the Bodleian!

[1942]

MANMOHAN GHOSE

India 1869-1924

Author of *Love Songs and Elegies* (1898) and *Songs of Love and Death* (1926), Ghose's enthusiasm for his adopted home in London contrasts sharply with the point of view that Adil Jussawalla defines in an essay written after a six-year period of study in London and Oxford decades later: 'Every coloured immigrant has to remember that whatever his background, education and achievement in his home country, the moment he steps ashore here, he is part of that misunderstood, misrepresented, and misled mass of disinhabited strays who have fringed British consciousness for several decades now, but have never been important to it' ('Indifference', *Disappointed Guests*, 1965).

LONDON

Farewell, sweetest country; out of my heart, you roses,
   Wayside roses, nodding, the slow traveller to keep.
Too long have I drowsed alone in the meadows deep,
   Too long alone endured the silence Nature espouses.
Oh, the rush, the rapture of life! throngs, lights, houses,
   This is London. I wake as a sentinel from sleep.

Stunned with the fresh thunder, the harsh delightful noises
   I move entranced on the thronging pavement. How sweet
To eyes sated with green, the dusty brick-walled street!
   And the lone spirit, of self so weary, how it rejoices
To be lost in others, bathed in the tones of human voices,
   And feel hurried along the happy tread of feet.

And a sense of vast sympathy my heart almost crazes,
   The warmth of kindred hearts in thousands beating with mine.
Each fresh face, each figure, my spirit drinks like wine—
   Thousands endlessly passing. Violets, daisies,
What is your charm to the passionate charm of faces,
   This ravishing reality, this earthliness divine?

O murmur of men more sweet than all the wood's caresses,
   How sweet only to be an unknown leaf that sings
In the forest of life! Cease, Nature, thy whisperings,
   Can I talk with leaves, or fall in love with breezes?
Beautiful boughs, your shade not a human pang appeases.
   This is London. I lie, and twine in the roots of things.   [1926]

CHARLOTTE MEW

England 1869-1928

Thwarted by financial pressure and the rigid heterosexist codes of her time, Mew's dramatic mono-
logues expose nonetheless the contents of sexual desire, instability (a brother and sister died in
mental hospitals and she feared a hereditary insanity), and fantasy. Resident of London's Blooms-
bury, habitat of a renowned literary and artistic circle during the first decades of the twentieth
century, Mew ended her own life with half a bottle of Lysol while being treated for 'neurasthenia'
following the death of her treasured sister Anne. Mew was a complex figure whose work was
celebrated by many, including contemporary Virginia Woolf. Mew's work is available in *Collected
Poems* (1953) and *Collected Poems and Prose* (1981).

THE FARMER'S BRIDE

To——

*He asked life of thee, and thou gavest him a long life:
  even for ever and ever.*

> Three Summers since I chose a maid,
> Too young maybe—but more's to do
> At harvest-time than bide and woo.
>   When us was wed she turned afraid
> Of love and me and all things human;
> Like the shut of a winter's day.
> Her smile went out, and 'twasn't a woman—
>   More like a little frightened fay.
>   One night, in the Fall, she runned away.

> 'Out 'mong the sheep, her be,' they said,
> 'Should properly have been abed;
> But sure enough she wasn't there
> Lying awake with her wide brown stare.
> So over seven-acre field and up-along across the down
>   We chased her, flying like a hare
> Before our lanterns. To Church-Town
>   All in a shiver and a scare
> We caught her, fetched her home at last
>   And turned the key upon her, fast.

> She does the work about the house
> As well as most, but like a mouse:
>   Happy enough to chat and play
>   With birds and rabbits and such as they,
>   So long as men-folk keep away.

'Not near, not near!' her eyes beseech
When one of us comes within reach.
    The women say that beasts in stall
    Look round like children at her call.
    I've hardly heard her speak at all.

Shy as a leveret, swift as he,
Straight and slight as a young larch tree,
Sweet as the first wild violets, she,
To her wild self. But what to me?

The short days shorten and the oaks are brown,
    The blue smoke rises to the low grey sky,
One leaf in the still air falls slowly down,
    A magpie's spotted feathers lie
On the black earth spread white with rime,
The berries redden up to Christmas-time.
    What's Christmas-time without there be
    Some other in the house than we!

    She sleeps up in the attic there
    Alone, poor maid. 'Tis but a stair
Betwixt us. Oh! my God! the down,
The soft young down of her, the brown,
The brown of her—her eyes, her hair, her hair!   [1916]

MONSIEUR QUI PASSE

(QUAI VOLTAIRE)

A purple blot against the dead white door
In my friend's rooms, bathed in their vile pink light,
I had not noticed her before
She snatched my eyes and threw them back to me:
She did not speak till we came out into the night,
Paused at this bench beside the kiosk on the quay.

God knows precisely what she said—
I left to her the twisted skein,
Though here and there I caught a thread,—
Something, at first, about 'the lamps along the Seine,
And Paris, with that witching card of Spring
Kept up her sleeve,—why you could see
The trick done on these freezing winter nights!
While half the kisses of the Quay—
Youth, hope,—the whole enchanted string
Of dreams hung on the Seine's long line of lights.'

Then suddenly she stripped, the very skin
Came off her soul,—a mere girl clings
Longer to some last rag, however thin,
When she has shown you—well—all sorts of things:
'If it were daylight—oh! one keeps one's head—
But fourteen years!—No one has ever guessed—
The whole thing starts when one gets to bed—
Death?—If the dead would tell us they had rest!
But your eyes held it as I stood there by the door—
One speaks to Christ—one tries to catch His garment's hem—
One hardly says as much to Him—no more:
It was not you, it was your eyes—I spoke to them.'

She stopped like a shot bird that flutters still,
And drops, and tries to run again, and swerves.
The tale should end in some walled house upon a hill.
My eyes, at least, won't play such havoc there,—
Or hers—But she had hair!—blood dipped in gold;
And there she left me throwing back the first odd stare.
Some sort of beauty once, but turning yellow, getting old.
Pouah! These women and their nerves!
God! but the night *is* cold!   [1929]

JAMES WELDON JOHNSON

USA 1871–1938

Johnson was an educator, writer, diplomat, and activist committed to the development of Black culture in America. He founded a Black people's newspaper, the *Daily American*, and was a contributing editor for the *New York Age* (1914–16). A teacher at Stanton private school early in his career, and later at Fisk University and New York University, Johnson is best known for his organizational and political work in the National Association for the Advancement of Colored People (NAACP) from 1916 to 1930. As a poet he experimented with 'song poems' and 'sermon sagas' based on the Black traditional oral forms of expression he termed 'the creative genius of blacks', and published three volumes: *Fifty Years and Other Poems* (1917), *God's Trombones* (1927), and *St Peter Relates an Incident* (1930).

O BLACK AND UNKNOWN BARDS

O black and unknown bards of long ago,
How came your lips to touch the sacred fire?
How, in your darkness, did you come to know
The power and beauty of the minstrel's lyre?
Who first from midst his bonds lifted his eyes?
Who first from out the still watch, lone and long,
Feeling the ancient faith of prophets rise
Within his dark-kept soul, burst into song?

Heart of what slave poured out such melody
As 'Steal Away to Jesus'? On its strains
His spirit must have nightly floated free,
Though still about his hands he felt his chains.
Who heard great 'Jordan roll'? Whose starward eye
Saw chariot 'swing low'? And who was he
That breathed that comforting, melodic sigh,
'Nobody Knows de Trouble I See'?

What merely living clod, what captive thing,
Could up toward God through all its darkness grope,
And find within its deadened heart to sing
These songs of sorrow, love, and faith, and hope?
How did it catch that subtle undertone,
That note in music heard not with the ears?
How sound the elusive reed so seldom blown,
Which stirs the soul or melts the heart to tears?

Not that great German master in his dream
Of harmonies that thundered amongst the stars
At the creation, ever heard a theme
Nobler than 'Go Down, Moses.' Mark its bars,
How like a mighty trumpet-call they stir
The blood. Such are the notes that men have sung
Going to valorous deeds; such tones there were
That helped make history when Time was young.

There is a wide, wide wonder in it all,
That from degraded rest servile toil
The fiery spirit of the seer should call
These simple children of the sun and soil.
O black slave singers, gone, forgot, unfamed,
You—you alone, of all the long, long line
Of those who've sung untaught, unknown, unnamed,
Have stretched out upward, seeking the divine.

You sang not deeds of heroes or of kings;
No chant of bloody war, no exulting paean
Of arms-won triumphs; but your humble strings
You touched in chord with music empyrean.
You sang far better than you knew; the songs
That for your listeners' hungry hearts sufficed
Still live—but more than this to you belongs;
You sang a race from wood and stone to Christ.   [1908]

J.M. SYNGE ❧

Ireland 1871–1909

John Millington Synge's visits to the Aran Islands from 1898–1902 produced a series of peasant dramas which include a satiric examination of ecclesiastic rule in *The Well of the Saints* (1905) and a comic portrait of the artist as Oedipus in *The Playboy of the Western World* (1907), a controversial work whose heretical treatment of traditional Catholicism—Synge was Protestant and privileged by birth—induced continuous riots during its run at Dublin's Abbey Theatre. Synge's first book of poems was in fact 'passing through the press' when he died of Hodgkin's disease. His Preface commended the 'timbre' of a poetry that had 'strong roots among clay and worms': 'the strong things of life are needed in poetry also . . . before verse can be human again it must learn to be brutal.' Synge's poems appear in Volume 1 of the *Collected Works* (ed. Skelton 1962).

THE CURSE

To a sister of an enemy of the author's who disapproved of 'The Playboy'

Lord, confound this surly sister,
Blight her brow with blotch and blister,
Cramp her larynx, lung, and liver,
In her guts a galling give her.
Let her live to earn her dinners
In Mountjoy with seedy sinners:
Lord, this judgment quickly bring,
And I'm your servant, J.M. Synge.   [1907]

A QUESTION

I asked if I got sick and died, would you
With my black funeral go walking too,
If you'd stand close to hear them talk or pray
While I'm let down in that steep bank of clay.

And, No, you said, for if you saw a crew
Of living idiots, pressing round that new
Oak coffin—they alive, I dead beneath
That board,—you'd rave and rend them with your teeth.   [1909]

PAUL LAURENCE DUNBAR
USA 1872–1906

Dunbar, a son of former Black slaves from Kentucky, was born and raised in Dayton, Ohio where after high school graduation he wrote short stories and poetry while working as an elevator operator. Novelist, critic, and editor William Dean Howells promoted Dunbar's poetry, and *Lyrics of Lowly Life* (1896) received national acclaim. 'We Wear the Mask' depicts the ironic 'invisibility' of racially visible peoples. Also a prolific writer of fiction and essays concerning Black Americans' successes as well as their suffering, Dunbar left a legacy of over a dozen major published works before he died of tuberculosis at the age of thirty-four.

WE WEAR THE MASK

We wear the mask that grins and lies,
   It hides our cheeks and shades our eyes,—
This debt we pay to human guile;
With torn and bleeding hearts we smile,
And mouth with myriad subtleties.

Why should the world be over-wise,
In counting all our tears and sighs?
Nay, let them only see us, while
   We wear the mask.

We smile, but, O great Christ, our cries
To thee from tortured souls arise.
We sing, but oh the clay is vile
Beneath our feet, and long the mile;
But let the world dream otherwise,
   We wear the mask!   [1896]

JOHN SHAW NEILSON

Australia 1872-1942

Neilson was born in South Australia, and he received little formal education. The dialogue in 'The Orange Tree' is reminiscent of the bush ballad's traditional oral narrative form, but Neilson's concerns with processes of aesthetic perception and imagination are strikingly modernist. Working as a labourer and struggling with poor eyesight he often depended on co-workers, family members, and friends—most notably his editor and agent, A.G. Stephen—to copy his poems. Neilson's *Collected Poems* was published in 1934, and Judith Wright edited *Witnesses of Spring: Unpublished Poems* (1970).

THE ORANGE TREE

The young girl stood beside me. I
   Saw not what her young eyes could see:
—A light, she said, not of the sky
   Lives somewhere in the Orange Tree.

—Is it, I said, of east or west?
   The heartbeat of a luminous boy
Who with his faltering flute confessed
   Only the edges of his joy?

Was he, I said, borne to the blue
   In a mad escapade of Spring
Ere he could make a fond adieu
   To his love in the blossoming?

—Listen! the young girl said. There calls
   No voice, no music beats on me;
But it is almost sound: it falls
   This evening on the Orange Tree.

—Does he, I said, so fear the Spring
   Ere the white sap too far can climb?
See in the full gold evening
   All happenings of the olden time?

Is he so goaded by the green?
   Does the compulsion of the dew
Make him unknowable but keen
   Asking with beauty of the blue?

—Listen! the young girl said. For all
   Your hapless talk you fail to see
There is a light, a step, a call
   This evening on the Orange Tree.

—Is it, I said, a waste of love
   Imperishably old in pain,
Moving as an affrighted dove
   Under the sunlight or the rain?

Is it a fluttering heart that gave
   Too willingly and was reviled?
Is it the stammering at a grave,
   The last word of a little child?

—Silence! the young girl said. Oh, why,
   Why will you talk to weary me?
Plague me no longer now, for I
   Am listening like the Orange Tree.   [1919]

NGUNAITPONI/DAVID UNAIPON

Australia 1873–1967

Ngunaitponi was born in South Australia at the Point McLeay Mission, and became a prominent spokesperson for his people. His *Native Legends* (1929) was the first publication by an aboriginal writer in Australia. An authority on aboriginal mythology, he also produced an extensive typescript of 'The Legendary Tales of the Australian Aborigines' in 1929 (most of which was published without credit by anthropologist William Ramsay Smith in 1930). Ngunaitponi was also a gifted inventor, organist, and preacher.

THE SONG OF HUNGARRDA

   Bright, consuming Spirit. No power on earth so great as Thee,
   First-born child of the Goddess of Birth and Light,
   Thy habitation betwixt heaven and earth within a veil of clouds
      dark as night.
Accompanied by furious wind and lashing rain and hail.
Riding majestically upon the storm, flashing at intervals,
illumining the abode of man.
   Thine anger and thy power thou revealest to us. Sometimes in
a streak of light, which leaps upon a great towering rock, which
stood impregnable and unchallenged in its birth-place when the
earth was formed, and hurls it in fragments down the
mountain-side, striking terror into man and beast alike.

Thus in wonder I am lost. No mortal mind can conceive. No
mortal tongue express in language intelligible. Heaven-born
Spark, I cannot see nor feel thee. Thou art concealed
mysteriously wrapped within the fibre and bark of tree and bush
and shrubs.

Why dost thou condescend to dwell within a piece of stick?
As I roam from place to place for enjoyment or search of food,
My soul is filled with gratitude and love for thee.
And conscious, too, of thine all pervading spirit presence.

It seems so strange that thou wilt not hear or reveal thyself nor
bestow a blessing unless I pray.

But to plead is not enough to bring thee forth and cause thy
glowing smiles to flicker over my frame.

But must strive and wrestle with this piece of stick—pressing and
twirling into another stick with all the power I possess, to release
the bonds that bind thee fast.

Then shall thy living spark leap forth in contact with grass and twig.
Thy flame leaps upward like waves that press and roll.

Radiant sister of the Day, I cannot live without thee. For when at
twilight and in the depth of midnight; before the morning dawns,
the mist hangs over the valley like death's cold shroud, and
dewdrops chill the atmosphere. Ingee Too Ma.

Then like thy bright Mother shining from afar,
Thy beaming smiles and glowing energy radiates into this frail body.
Transfusing life, health, comfort, and happiness too.   [1929]

ALEXANDER POSEY

Creek 1873–1908

Posey spoke the Creek language until he began to learn English in school at the age of fourteen.
Although he modelled his poetry on the work of Longfellow, Burns, and Tennyson, Posey
attempted to adapt English rhythms to those of his own languages. 'Ode to Sequoyah' celebrates
the largely unacknowledged contribution of Sequoyah (George Guess), inventor of the Cherokee
syllabic alphabet. Posey also made significant contributions to his nation through his work as an
education administrator and journalist. *The Poems of Alexander Lawrence Posey* (1910) was edited
and published posthumously by his wife, Minnie Posey.

ODE TO SEQUOYAH

The names of Waitie and Boudinot—
    The valiant warrior and gifted sage—
And other Cherokees, may be forgot,
    But thy name shall descend to every age;
The mysteries enshrouding Cadmus' name
Cannot obscure thy claim to fame.

The people's language cannot perish—nay,
   When from the face of this great continent
Inevitable doom hath swept away
   The last memorial—the last fragment
Of tribes,—some scholar learned shall pore
Upon thy letters, seeking ancient lore.

Some bard shall lift a voice in praise of thee,
   In moving numbers tell the world how men
Scoffed thee, hissed thee, charged with lunacy!
   And who could not give 'nough honor when
At length, in spite of jeers, of want and need,
Thy genius shaped a dream into a deed.

By cloud-capped summits in the boundless west,
   Or mighty river rolling to the sea,
Where'er thy footsteps led thee on that quest,
   Unknown, rest thee, illustrious Cherokee!   [1899]

ROBERT FROST

USA 1874-1963

In the tradition of Franklin, Emerson, and Whitman, Frost gained tremendous popularity as well as critical acclaim by adopting the public persona of the New England patriarch who sermonizes on rural experience; he was awarded the Bollingen Prize (1963) and four Pulitzer Prizes (1924, 1931, 1937, 1943). In the collections *Complete Poems* (1949) and *In the Clearing* (1962), his poetry dramatizes complexities of life and nature in accessible yet highly allusive language. Although some poems affirm the possibility of order and meaning as a 'momentary stay against confusion', many others are bleak, paradoxically relying on the language of a speaker who has 'no expression, nothing to express'.

IN WHITE

A dented spider like a snow drop white
On a white Heal-all, holding up a moth
Like a white piece of lifeless satin cloth—
Saw ever curious eye so strange a sight?—
Portent in little, assorted death and blight
Like ingredients of a witches' broth?—
The beady spider, the flower like a froth,
And the moth carried like a paper kite.

What had that flower to do with being white,
The blue prunella every child's delight.
What brought the kindred spider to that height?

(Make we no thesis of the miller's plight.)
What but design of darkness and of night?
Design, design! Do I use the word aright?   [1922]

DESIGN

I found a dimpled spider, fat and white,
On a white heal-all, holding up a moth
Like a white piece of rigid satin cloth—
Assorted characters of death and blight
Mixed ready to begin the morning right,
Like the ingredients of a witches' broth—
A snow-drop spider, a flower like a froth,
And dead wings carried like a paper kite.

What had that flower to do with being white,
The wayside blue and innocent heal-all?
What brought the kindred spider to that height,
Then steered the white moth thither in the night?
What but design of darkness to appall?—
If design govern in a thing so small.   [1936]

DESERT PLACES

Snow falling and night falling fast, oh, fast
In a field I looked into going past,
And the ground almost covered smooth in snow,
But a few weeds and stubble showing last.

The woods around it have it—it is theirs.
All animals are smothered in their lairs.
I am too absent-spirited to count;
The loneliness includes me unawares.

And lonely as it is that loneliness
Will be more lonely ere it will be less—
A blanker whiteness of benighted snow
With no expression, nothing to express.

They cannot scare me with their empty spaces
Between stars—on stars where no human race is.
I have it in me so much nearer home
To scare myself with my own desert places.   [1936]

AMY LOWELL

USA 1874-1925

Lowell's Boston family was wealthy and prestigious, and although she was permitted little formal education, she educated herself in the family's private library and in the Boston Atheneum. Her first volume of poetry, *A Dome of Many-Coloured Glass*, appeared in 1912; she then edited three anthologies of Imagist poetry (1915–17) under the influence of poets such as H.D., Ezra Pound, and D.H. Lawrence. Subsequent volumes attest to her inventive play with free and blank verse as well as narrative and documentary poems, including *Pictures of the Floating World* (1919) and *What's O'Clock* (1925). Lowell's companion and a former actress, Ada Dwyer Russell, was the subject of many of her poems devoted to female love and beauty. Lowell also wrote several influential books of literary criticism and scholarship, among them a two-volume biography of John Keats (1925). Her poetry has been collected in *The Complete Poetical Works of Amy Lowell* (1955).

THE SISTERS

Taking us by and large, we're a queer lot
We women who write poetry. And when you think
How few of us there've been, it's queerer still.
I wonder what it is that makes us do it,
Singles us out to scribble down, man-wise,
The fragments of ourselves. Why are we
Already mother-creatures, double-bearing,
With matrices in body and in brain?
I rather think that there is just the reason
We are so sparse a kind of human being;
The strength of forty thousand Atlases
Is needed for our every-day concerns.
There's Sapho, now I wonder what was Sapho.
I know a single slender thing about her:
That, loving, she was like a burning birch-tree
All tall and glittering fire, and that she wrote
Like the same fire caught up to Heaven and held there,
A frozen blaze before it broke and fell.
Ah, me! I wish I could have talked to Sapho,
Surprised her reticences by flinging mine
Into the wind. This tossing off of garments
Which cloud the soul is none too easy doing
With us to-day. But still I think with Sapho
One might accomplish it, were she in the mood
To bare her loveliness of words and tell
The reasons, as she possibly conceived them,
Of why they are so lovely. Just to know
How she came at them, just to watch
The crisp sea sunshine playing on her hair,

And listen, thinking all the while 'twas she
Who spoke and that we two were sisters
Of a strange, isolated little family.
And she is Sapho—Sapho—not Miss or Mrs,
A leaping fire we call so for convenience;
But Mrs Browning—who would ever think
Of such presumption as to call her 'Ba.'
Which draws the perfect line between sea-cliffs
And a close-shuttered room in Wimpole Street.
Sapho could fly her impulses like bright
Balloons tip-tilting to a morning air
And write about it. Mrs Browning's heart
Was squeezed in stiff conventions. So she lay
Stretched out upon a sofa, reading Greek
And speculating, as I must suppose,
In just this way on Sapho; all the need,
The huge, imperious need of loving, crushed
Within the body she believed so sick.
And it was sick, poor lady, because words
Are merely simulacra after deeds
Have wrought a pattern; when they take the place
Of actions they breed a poisonous miasma
Which, though it leave the brain, eats up the body.
So Mrs Browning, aloof and delicate,
Lay still upon her sofa, all her strength
Going to uphold her over-topping brain.
It seems miraculous, but she escaped
To freedom and another motherhood
Than that of poems. She was a very woman
And needed both.
            If I had gone to call,
Would Wimpole Street have been the kindlier place,
Or Casa Guidi, in which to have met her?
I am a little doubtful of that meeting,
For Queen Victoria was very young and strong
And all-pervading in her apogee
At just that time. If we had stuck to poetry,
Sternly refusing to be drawn off by mesmerism
Or Roman revolutions, it might have done.
For, after all, she is another sister,
But always, I rather think, an older sister
And not herself so curious a technician
As to admit newfangled modes of writing—
'Except, of course, in Robert, and that is neither
Here nor there for Robert is a genius.'
I do not like the turn this dream is taking,

Since I am very fond of Mrs Browning
And very much indeed should like to hear her
Graciously asking me to call her 'Ba.'
But then the Devil of Verisimilitude
Creeps in and forces me to know she wouldn't.
Convention again, and how it chafes my nerves,
For we are such a little family
Of singing sisters, and as if I didn't know
What those years felt like tied down to the sofa.
Confound Victoria, and the slimy inhibitions
She loosed on all us Anglo-Saxon creatures!
Suppose there hadn't been a Robert Browning,
No 'Sonnets from the Portuguese' would have been written.
They are the first of all her poems to be,
One might say, fertilized. For, after all,
A poet is flesh and blood as well as brain
And Mrs Browning, as I said before,
Was very, very woman. Well, there are two
Of us, and vastly unlike that's for certain.
Unlike at least until we tear the veils
Away which commonly gird souls. I scarcely think
Mrs Browning would have approved the process
In spite of what had surely been relief;
For speaking souls must always want to speak
Even when bat-eyed, narrow-minded Queens
Set prudishness to keep the keys of impulse.
Then do the frowning Gods invent new banes
And make the need of sofas. But Sapho was dead
And I, and others, not yet peeped above
The edge of possibility. So that's an end
To speculating over tea-time talks
Beyond the movement of pentameters
With Mrs Browning.
              But I go dreaming on,
In love with these my spiritual relations.
I rather think I see myself walk up
A flight of wooden steps and ring a bell.
And send a card in to Miss Dickinson.
Yet that's a very silly way to do.
I should have taken the dream twist-ends about
And climbed over the fence and found her deep
Engrossed in the doings of a humming-bird
Among nasturtiums. Not having expected strangers,
She might forget to think me one, and holding up
A finger say quite casually: 'Take care.
Don't frighten him, he's only just begun.'

'Now this,' I well believe I should have thought,
'Is even better than Sapho. With Emily
You're really here, or never anywhere at all
In range of mind.' Wherefore, having begun
In the strict centre, we could slowly progress
To various circumferences, as we pleased.
We could, but should we? That would quite depend
On Emily. I think she'd be exacting,
Without intention possibly, and ask
A thousand tight-rope tricks of understanding.
But, bless you, I would somersault all day
If by so doing I might stay with her.
I hardly think that we should mention souls
Although they might just round the corner from us
In some half-quizzical, half-wistful metaphor.
I'm very sure that I should never seek
To turn her parables to stated fact.
Sapho would speak, I think, quite openly,
And Mrs Browning guard a careful silence,
But Emily would set doors ajar and slam them
And love you for your speed of observation.

Strange trio of my sisters, most diverse,
And how extraordinarily unlike
Each is to me, and which way shall I go?
Sapho spent and gained; and Mrs Browning,
After a miser girlhood, cut the strings
Which tied her money-bags and let them run;
But Emily hoarded—hoarded—only giving
Herself to cold, white paper. Starved and tortured,
She cheated her despair with games of patience
And fooled herself by winning. Frail little elf,
The lonely brain-child of a gaunt maturity,
She hung her womanhood upon a bough
And played ball with the stars—too long—too long—
The garment of herself hung on a tree
Until at last she lost even the desire
To take it down. Whose fault? Why let us say,
To be consistent, Queen Victoria's.
But really, not to over-rate the queen,
I feel obliged to mention Martin Luther,
And behind him the long line of Church Fathers
Who draped their prurience like a dirty cloth
About the naked majesty of God.
Good-bye, my sisters, all of you are great,
And all of you are marvellously strange,

And none of you has any word for me.
I cannot write like you, I cannot think
In terms of Pagan or of Christian now.
I only hope that possibly some day
Some other woman with an itch for writing
May turn to me as I have turned to you
And chat with me a brief few minutes. How
We lie, we poets! It is three good hours
I have been dreaming. Has it seemed so long
To you? And yet I thank you for the time
Although you leave me sad and self-distrustful,
For older sisters are very sobering things.
Put on your cloaks, my dears, the motor's waiting.
No, you have not seemed strange to me, but near,
Frightfully near, and rather terrifying.
I understand you all, for in myself—
Is that presumption? Yet indeed it's true—
We are one family. And still my answer
Will not be any one of yours, I see.
Well, never mind that now. Good night! Good night!   [1919]

New Heavens for Old

I am useless,
What I do is nothing.
What I think has no savour.
There is an almanac between the windows:
It is of the year when I was born.

My fellows call to me to join them,
They shout for me,
Passing the house in a great wind of vermillion banners.
They are fresh and fulminant,
They are indecent and strut with the thought of it.
They laugh, and curse, and brawl,
And cheer a holocaust of 'Who comes Firsts!' at the iron fronts
      of the houses at the two edges of the street.
Young men with naked hearts jeering between iron house-fronts,
Young men with naked bodies beneath their clothes
Passionately conscious of them,
Ready to strip off their clothes,
Ready to strip off their customs, their usual routine,
Clamouring for the rawness of life,
In love with appetite,
Proclaiming it as a creed,
Worshipping youth,

Worshipping themselves.
They call for the women and the women come,
They bare the whiteness of their lusts to the dead gaze of the
    old house-fronts,
They roar down the street like flame,
They explode upon the dead houses like new, sharp fire.

But I—
I arrange three roses in a Chinese vase:
A pink one,
A red one,
A yellow one.
I fuss over their arrangement.
Then I sit in a South window
And sip pale wine with a touch of hemlock in it,
And think of Winter nights,
And field-mice crossing and re-crossing
The spot which will be my grave.   [1927]

GERTRUDE STEIN

USA/France 1874–1946

Many have felt that Stein-ese and its author were pathological: inaccessible, subversive, gramma-centric. Stein's emphasis on the medium as medium, as artificially composed subject, challenged her readers to look at the 'talking arrangement[s]' on the printed page with great care: these were not simply copies of the familiar 'old say[s]', quotations, signs of 'extra', for Stein explicitly opened the closed forms in language—the accepted meanings, the prevailing assumptions about grammatical rule, the customary practice of syntax and spelling—and in life. As a woman writer, lesbian, American expatriate, and Jew, she 'arrest[ed]' the 'development' of meanings generated by habit and convention. Much of Stein's writing is available in *The Selected Writings of Gertrude Stein* (ed. Van Vechten, 1962), in the multi-volume Yale Edition of the *Unpublished Writings of Gertrude Stein* (ed. Van Vechten, from 1951), and in Patricia Meyerowitz's *Gertrude Stein: Look at Me Now and Here I Am, Writings and Lectures 1909–45* (1971).

from TENDER BUTTONS

A SUBSTANCE IN A CUSHION.

The change of color is likely and a difference a very little difference is prepared. Sugar is not a vegetable.

Callous is something that hardening leaves behind what will be soft if there is a genuine interest in there being present as many girls as men. Does this change. It shows that dirt is clean when there is a volume.

A cushion has that cover. Supposing you do not like to change, supposing it is very clean that there is no change in appearance, supposing that there is regularity and a costume is that any the worse than an oyster and an exchange. Come to season that is there any extreme use in feather and cotton. Is there not much more joy in a table and more chairs and very likely roundness and a place to put them.

A circle of fine card board and a chance to see a tassel.

What is the use of a violent kind of delightfulness if there is no pleasure in not getting tired of it. The question does not come before there is a quotation. In any kind of place there is a top to covering and it is a pleasure at any rate there is some venturing in refusing to believe nonsense. It shows what use there is in a whole piece if one uses it and it is extreme and very likely the little things could be dearer but in any case there is a bargain and if there is the best thing to do is to take it away and wear it and then be reckless and resolved on returning gratitude.

Light blue and the same red with purple makes a change. It shows that there is no mistake. Any pink shows that and very likely it is reasonable. Very likely there should not be a finer fancy present. Some increase means a calamity and this is the best preparation for three and more being together. A little calm is so ordinary and in any case there is sweetness and some of that.

A seal and matches and a swan and ivy and a suit.

A closet, a closet does not connect under the bed. The band if it is white and black, the band has a green string. A sight a whole sight and a little groan grinding makes a trimming such a sweet singing trimming and a red thing not a round thing but a white thing, a red thing and a white thing.

The disgrace is not in carelessness nor even in sewing it comes out out of the way.

What is the sash like. The sash is not like anything mustard it is not like a same thing that has stripes, it is not even more hurt than that, it has a little top.

. . .

EATING.

Eat ting, eating a grand old man said roof and never never re soluble burst, not a near ring not a bewildered neck, not really any such bay.

Is it so a noise to be is it a least remain to rest, is it a so old say to be, is it a leading are been. Is it so, is it so, is it so, is it so is it so is it so.

Eel us eel us with no no pea no pea cool, no pea cool cooler, no pea cooler with a land a land cost in, with a land cost in stretches.

Eating he heat eating he heat it eating, he heat it heat eating. He heat eating.

A little piece of pay of pay owls owls such as pie, bolsters.

Will leap beat, willie well all. The rest rest oxen occasion occasion to be so purred, so purred how.

It was a ham it was a square come well it was a square remain, a square remain not it a bundle, not it a bundle so is a grip, a grip to shed bay leave bay leave draught, bay leave draw cider in low, cider in low and george. George is a mass.

EATING.

It was a shame it was a shame to stare to stare and double and relieve relieve be cut up show as by the elevation of it and out out more in the steady where the come and on and the all the shed and that.

It was a garden and belows belows straight. It was a pea, a pea pour it in its not a succession, not it a simple, not it a so election, election with.

SALAD.

It is a winning cake.

SAUCE.

What is bay labored what is all be section, what is no much. Sauce sam in.

SALMON.

It was a peculiar bin a bin fond in beside.

ORANGE.

Why is a feel oyster an egg stir. Why is it orange centre.
A show at tick and loosen loosen it so to speak sat.
It was an extra leaker with a see spoon, it was an extra licker with a see spoon.

ORANGE.

A type oh oh new new not no not knealer knealer of old show beefsteak, neither neither.

ORANGES.

Build is all right.

. . .

MUTTON.

A letter which can wither, a learning which can suffer and an outrage which is simultaneous is principal.

Student, students are merciful and recognised they chew something.

Hate rests that is solid and sparse and all in a shape and largely very largely. Interleaved and successive and a sample of smell all this makes a certainty a shade.

Light curls very light curls have no more curliness than soup. This is not a subject.

Change a single stream of denting and change it hurriedly, what does it express, it expresses nausea. Like a very strange likeness and pink, like that and not more like that than the same resemblance and not more like that than no middle space in cutting.

An eye glass, what is an eye glass, it is water. A splendid specimen, what is it when it is little and tender so that there are parts. A centre can place and four are no more and two and two are not middle.

Melting and not minding, safety and powder, a particular recollection and a sincere solitude all this makes a shunning so thorough and so unrepeated and surely if there is anything left it is a bone. It is not solitary.

Any space is not quiet it is so likely to be shiny. Darkness very dark darkness is sectional. There is a way to see in onion and surely very surely rhubarb and a tomato, surely very surely there is that seeding. A little thing in is a little thing.

Mud and water were not present and not any more of either. Silk and stockings were not present and not any more of either. A receptacle and a symbol and no monster were present and no more. This made a piece show and was it a kindness, it can be asked was it a kindness to have it warmer, was it a kindness and does gliding mean more. Does it.

Does it dirty a ceiling. It does not. Is it dainty, it is if prices are sweet. Is it lamentable, it is not if there is no undertaker. Is it curious, it is not when there is youth. All this makes a line, it even makes makes no more. All this makes cherries. The reason that there is a suggestion in vanity is due to this that there is a burst of mixed music.

A temptation any temptation is an exclamation if there are misdeeds and little bones. It is not astonishing that bones mingle as they vary not at all and in any case why is a bone outstanding, it is so because the circumstance that does not make a cake and character is so easily churned and cherished.

Mouse and mountain and a quiver, a quaint statue and pain in an exterior and silence more silence louder shows salmon a mischief intender. A cake, a real salve made of mutton and liquor, a specially retained rinsing and an established cork and blazing, this which resignation influences and restrains, restrains more altogether. A sign is the specimen spoken.

A meal in mutton, mutton, why is lamb cheaper, it is cheaper because so little is more. Lecture, lecture and repeat instruction.   [1914]

EDWARD THOMAS

England 1878–1917

Thomas did not begin writing poetry—urged on by Robert Frost—until the outbreak of World
War I. Even then, Thomas's self-doubt led him to assume 'Edward Eastaway' as his first pen
name. In his twenties he'd concentrated on prose forms, and worked as an editor and anthologist.
His verse is rooted in the homegrown pastoral lyricism Wordsworth and Coleridge encode in their
Preface to the *Lyrical Ballads*, and his strengths include an imaginative freedom and love of things
as he finds them. Thomas was killed in action at Arras. His *Collected Poems* with manuscript and
typescript sources was published in 1978; the first *Collected Poems* (1920) included a Foreword by
Walter de la Mare anticipating Thomas's growing influence: 'When the noise of the present is
silenced . . . his voice will be heard much more clearly.'

THE GYPSY

A fortnight before Christmas Gypsies were everywhere:
Vans were drawn up on wastes, women trailed to the fair.
'My gentleman,' said one, 'You've got a lucky face.'
'And you've a luckier,' I thought, 'if such a grace
And impudence in rags are lucky.' 'Give a penny
For the poor baby's sake.' 'Indeed I have not any
Unless you can give change for a sovereign, my dear.'
'Then just half a pipeful of tobacco can you spare?'
I gave it. With that much victory she laughed content.
I should have given more, but off and away she went
With her baby and her pink sham flowers to rejoin
The rest before I could translate to its proper coin
Gratitude for her grace. And I paid nothing then,
As I pay nothing now with the dipping of my pen
For her brother's music when he drummed the tambourine
And stamped his feet, which made the workmen passing grin,
While his mouth-organ changed to a rascally Bacchanal dance
'Over the hills and far away.' This and his glance
Outlasted all the fair, farmer and auctioneer,
Cheap-jack, balloon-man, drover with crooked stick, and steer,
Pig, turkey, goose, and duck, Christmas Corpses to be.
Not even the kneeling ox had eyes like the Romany.
That night he peopled for me the hollow wooded land,
More dark and wild than stormiest heavens, that I searched
    and scanned
Like a ghost new-arrived. The gradations of the dark
Were like an underworld of death, but for the spark
In the Gypsy boy's black eyes as he played and stamped his
    tune,
'Over the hills and far away,' and a crescent moon.   [1915]

JOSEPH CAMPBELL   ⚘

Ireland 1879–1944

Eager participant in the Irish Literary Revival of the late nineteenth century, Campbell explored the oral tradition of folk song and regional legend. He combined intense involvement with Irish mysticism and ritual with emerging experiments in poetic technique: he was, for example, the first to write free verse in Ireland. After the Easter Rising, the poet served the cause as an elected member of the Wicklow County Council, and when civil war broke out he was arrested as a Republican sympathiser and interned for two years. Campbell emigrated to New York where he sought to establish a School of Irish Studies and became Director of Studies at Fordham University. He returned to Ireland twelve years later. Early collections include *The Mountainy Singer* (1909), *Irishry* (1913), and *Earth of Cualann* (1917); *The Poems of Joseph Campbell* (ed. Clarke) was published in 1963.

THE NEWSPAPER-SELLER

(Times Square, New York, about two o'clock on a winter's morning)

And how is Cabey's Lane?
I'm forty years left Ennis, sir,
And never like to see the place again.
'Twas out of there I married her—
The first one—Mattha Twomey's daughter.
The 'bit o' paint,' they called her.
She was young, tall as a birch-tree, pale,
With blushes in her cheeks,
And eyes as brown as Burren water.
Faith, and there was lavish drinking
At her wedding. Now, as I'm thinking—
Four half-barrels of ale,
Old whisky, cordial and wine;
And eating fine.

I'd ten by her;
Ten topping childer, sir,
Like apples, red and sweet.
In fair-meadow or street
You wouldn't see the likes of 'em . . .
And then she died.

You can't live by the dead,
Leastways, when you have hungry mouths to fill
That's what my people said.
And so inside a year I wed again—
This time, to Mary Quill,
A Limerick girl was lodging in the lane
West of Cabey's. The first was quiet and wise,
The second had laughing eyes:
I put a charm on them, and married her.

Says she on the wedding night,
'You're in a sorry plight
With me and the little ones. Let's go away.'
'Where to?' says I. 'To America,'
Says she. 'This country is too poor and small
For us, and over there there's work and bread for all.'

She was an eager kind, you see—
Far different to Sibby.
Well, by dint of slaving night and day
We made the passage out, and Boston Quay
Saw me and her in Eighteen Seventy-Three,
The Blizzard Year. That's four decades ago;
But even now I feel the bitter snow—
I feel it in my marrow, sir—the snow
And the high, driving wind.
We left our clan behind
In Cabey's Lane with neighbours
Till such times as I could find
The cash to fetch 'em after us.
And God was kind—
Kinder than I thought He'd be
In a strange lane.
For work came rolling to my hand, sir,
And I wrought for constant pay
In a bakehouse. He was German, sir,
The boss; and Germans, mostly, mixed the dough,
And watched the fires. That's how I came to know
The Deutsch. I speak it better than I used to do
The Gaelic at home.

I'd twelve by Mary, sir—
Ten living and two dead.
I'd ten by Sibby. Twenty childer, sir—
Twelve daughters and eight sons . . .
And better for myself I ne'er had one!

My curse on Matt and Ned
That let old age come down on my grey head,
And left me selling 'Worlds'!
My curse on Shaun!
My curse on Meehaul Ban,
The fair-haired boy, the gentleman,
That wouldn't look the road I doddered on!
My seven curses on him,
And the flaming curse of God!

My curse on Peter!
My blessing on poor Joe, who's now in quod
For housebreaking—the white lamb of the flock
He helped me when my right hand was a crock
With blood-poison, and paid the rent for me.
My curse on all my daughters!
On Sibby Ann, who's married west,
And has her auto, while I creep on limbs
All crookened with the pains!
My curse on Peg and Fan!
My curse on Angeline!
My curse on Ceely, and the rest!
I don't know half their names:
The devil's brood, but no brood of mine.
And Cabey's Lane, sir? I was happy there,
In Ennis town in Clare,
When I was young. Ah, young, not old . . .
God help us, isn't it bitter cold!   [n. d.]

FREDERICK PHILIP GROVE

Prussia/Canada 1879-1948

Critic D.O. Spettigue's publication of *FPG: the European Years* (1973) identified Grove as the European novelist and translator who changed his name (from Felix Paul Greve), faked his suicide in 1909, and fled to North America to escape his debtors. Several years later 'Fred Grove' settled in Manitoba as a schoolteacher, retiring in 1923 to write full time. Grove is best known for books like *Over Prairie Trails* (1922) and *Fruits of the Earth* (1933). A fuller appreciation of Grove's poetry is only now emerging with recent publications such as Gaby Divay's edition *Poems by Frederick Philip Grove* (1993).

ARCTIC WOODS

These are the woods of all the voices dead,
Of putrid moisture and of almost night,
The woods of hollows with green scum bespread
From whence large eyes look iridescent light.

These are the woods of stems with curly bark,
White like the skin that never yet was bared:
The woods that hold me motionless and stark
So that I am as who no motion dared.

And when at noon in all the glades the grass
As in a swoon, scarce breathing, seems to die,
A giant wing, dark, rigid, as of brass,
From all the stems shuts off so sun as sky.

And then—a whisper; sound nor far nor near:
A snowwhite horse glides through the leafless trees:
It stirs nor head nor foot, nor eye nor ear:
Frozen in flight. And not a soul that sees.   [1993]

Translation of Grove's 'Dies ist der Wald . . .'

SAROJINI NAIDU

India 1879–1949

Naidu's father, Dr Aghorenath Chattopâdhyây, founded Nizam College at Hyderabad. Prodigious (at twelve she matriculated first from the entire Madras Presidency), influenced by romanticism while studying in England, Naidu returned to India in 1898 with a growing commitment to the freedom movement. In 1930, Naidu took part in the Salt Satyagraha, walking with Mahatma Gandhi to the sea to make and sell salt in defiance of the British Government levy. President of the Indian National Congress, suffragette, co-ordinator of the All India Women's Conference, Naidu was appointed the governor of Uttar Pradesh, the largest state in the country following independence, a position she held until the time of her death. Her published collections include *The Bird of Fame* (1912), *The Broken Wing* (1917), *The Sceptred Flute* (1958), and *The Feather of the Dawn* (1961).

AWAKE!

Waken, O mother! thy children implore thee,
Who kneel in thy presence to serve and adore thee!
The night is aflush with a dream of the morrow,
Why still dost thou sleep in thy bondage of sorrow?
Awaken and sever the woes that enthrall us,
And hallow our hands for the triumphs that call us!

Are we not thine, O Belov'd, to inherit
The manifold pride and power of thy spirit?
Ne'er shall we fail thee, forsake thee or falter,
Whose hearts are thy home and thy shield and thine altar.
Lo! we would thrill the high stars with thy story,
And set thee again in the forefront of glory.

Hindus:
    Mother! the flowers of our worship have crowned thee!
Parsees:
    Mother! the flame of our hope shall surround thee!
Mussulmans:
    Mother! the sword of our love shall defend thee!
Christians:
    Mother! the song of our faith shall attend thee!
All Creeds:
    Shall not our dauntless devotion avail thee?
    Harken! O queen and O goddess, we hail thee!   [1958]

BANGLE-SELLERS

Bangle-sellers are we who bear
Our shining loads to the temple fair . . .
Who will buy these delicate, bright
Rainbow-tinted circles of light?
Lustrous tokens of radiant lives,
For happy daughters and happy wives.

Some are meet for a maiden's wrist,
Silver and blue as the mountain mist,
Some are flushed like the buds that dream
On the tranquil brow of a woodland stream;
Some are aglow with the bloom that cleaves
To the limpid glory of newborn leaves.

Some are like fields of sunlit corn,
Meet for a bride on her bridal morn,
Some, like the flame of her marriage fire,
Or rich with the hue of her heart's desire,
Tinkling, luminous, tender, and clear,
Like her bridal laughter and bridal tear.

Some are purple and gold-flecked gray,
For her who has journeyed through life midway.
Whose hands have cherished, whose love has blest
And cradled fair sons on her faithful breast,
Who serves her household in fruitful pride,
And worships the gods at her husband's side.   [1958]

Patrick (Padraic) Henry Pearse

Ireland 1879–1916

Pearse was elected President of the Provisional Government and Commandant-General of the Army of the Irish Republic in April, 1916. He was executed for his role in the Easter Rising in May, 1916. His desire for an Ireland, Gaelic and free, led to his pivotal role in the separatist movement. Educator and reformer, founder of St Enda's College in 1908, compelling orator, bilingual teacher, and poet, he wrote that he willingly sacrificed his own life to free his people. He was buoyed by his vision of heroic action within Irish saga and the 'ghosts of dead men that have bequeathed a trust to us living men', men who had been betrayed by 'bankrupt' government policy, ghosts in whose name Pearse proclaimed the Republic. Pearse's *Collected Works* appeared in 1918.

THE MOTHER

I do not grudge them: Lord, I do not grudge
My two strong sons that I have seen go out
To break their strength and die, they and a few,
In bloody protest for a glorious thing.
They shall be spoken of among their people,
The generations shall remember them,
And call them blessed;
But I will speak their names to my own heart
In the long nights;
The little names that were familiar once
Round my dead hearth.
Lord, thou art hard on mothers:
We suffer in their coming and their going;
And tho' I grudge them not, I weary, weary
Of the long sorrow—And yet I have my joy:
My sons were faithful, and they fought.

[1918]

WALLACE STEVENS

USA 1879-1955

A lawyer and an insurance company executive by profession, Stevens's sophisticated and analytical modernist poetry first appeared in the collection *Harmonium* (1923), in which he explores language's affinities with other forms of artistic perception and expression. During the 1930s and '40s, Stevens developed a more all-encompassing view of poetry as a 'supreme fiction' to take the place/Of empty heaven and its hymns' ('The Man with the Blue Guitar', 1937), especially in our confrontations with social realities of alienation, dispossession, and suffering. Stevens's complete works—including his later philosophical and meditative lyric poetry—are available in his *Collected Poems* (1954), for which he was awarded a Pulitzer Prize and a National Book Award in 1955, and *Opus Posthumous* (1957).

OF MERE BEING

The palm at the end of the mind,
Beyond the last thought, rises
In the bronze distance,

A gold-feathered bird
Sings in the palm, without human meaning,
Without human feeling, a foreign song.

You know then that it is not the reason
That makes us happy or unhappy.
The bird sings. Its feathers shine.

The palm stands on the edge of space.
The wind moves slowly in the branches.
The bird's fire-fangled feathers dangle down.   [1955]

THE PLANET ON THE TABLE

Ariel was glad he had written his poems.
They were of a remembered time
Or of something seen that he liked.

Other makings of the sun
Were waste and welter
And the ripe shrub writhed.

His self and the sun were one
And his poems, although makings of his self,
Were no less makings of the sun.

It was not important that they survive.
What mattered was that they should bear
Some lineament or character,

Some affluence, if only half-perceived,
In the poverty of their words,
Of the planet of which they were part.   [1955]

E.J. PRATT   ❧

Canada 1882-1964

Born in Newfoundland—which figures largely in his first book, *Newfoundland Verse* (1923)—Pratt studied philosophy and theology at the University of Toronto before enjoying a long career in the English department there from 1920 to 1953. Although he wrote poems that vividly evoke and reflect on animal life ('The Shark', for example), as well as meditations on the human condition ('The Truant'), Pratt's major importance in Canadian poetry rests on his achievements as a writer of long narrative poems that range widely in tone and subject matter: *Towards the Last Spike* both satirizes and praises the building of a national railroad, while *Brébeuf and His Brethren* is a sombre reflection on a Jesuit father's martyrdom. Among many other honours, Pratt won three Governor-General's Awards for his poetry; his work is represented in *E.J. Pratt: Complete Poems* (2 vols., ed. Djwa and Moyles, 1989).

from BRÉBEUF AND HIS BRETHREN

[THE MARTYRDOM OF BRÉBEUF AND LALEMANT, 16 MARCH 1649]

XII

No doubt in the mind of Brébeuf that this was the last
Journey—three miles over the snow. He knew
That the margins as thin as they were by which he escaped
From death through the eighteen years of his mission toil
Did not belong to this chapter: not by his pen
Would this be told. He knew his place in the line,
For the blaze of the trail that was cut on the bark by Jogues
Shone still. He had heard the story as told by writ
And word of survivors—of how a captive slave
Of the hunters, the skin of his thighs cracked with the frost,
He would steal from the tents to the birches, make a rough cross
From two branches, set it in snow and on the peel
Inscribe his vows and dedicate to the Name
In 'litanies of love' what fragments were left
From the wrack of his flesh; of his escape from the tribes;
Of his journey to France where he knocked at the door of the
     College
Of Rennes, was gathered in as a mendicant friar,
Nameless, unknown, till he gave for proof to the priest

His scarred credentials of faith, the nail-less hands
And withered arms—the signs of the Mohawk fury.
Nor yet was the story finished—he had come again
Back to his mission to get the second death.
And the comrades of Jogues—Goupil, Eustache and Couture,
Had been stripped and made to run the double files
And take the blows—one hundred clubs to each line—
And this as the prelude to torture, leisured, minute,
Where thorns on the quick, scallop shells to the joints of the
    thumbs,
Provided the sport for children and squaws till the end.
And adding salt to the blood of Brébeuf was the thought
Of Daniel—was it months or a week ago?
So far, so near, it seemed in time, so close
In leagues—just over there to the south it was
He faced the arrows and died in front of his church.

But winding into the greater artery
Of thought that bore upon the coming passion
Were little tributaries of wayward wish
And reminiscence. Paris with its vespers
Was folded in the mind of Lalemant,
And the soft Gothic lights and traceries
Were shading down the ridges of his vows.
But two years past at Bourges he had walked the cloisters,
Companioned by Saint Augustine and Francis,
And wrapped in quiet holy mists. Brébeuf,
His mind a moment throwing back the curtain
Of eighteen years, could see the orchard lands,
The *cidreries*, the peasants at the Fairs,
The undulating miles of wheat and barley,
Gardens and pastures rolling like a sea
From Lisieux to Le Havre. Just now the surf
Was pounding on the limestone Norman beaches
And on the reefs of Calvados. Had dawn
This very day not flung her surplices
Around the headlands and with golden fire
Consumed the silken argosies that made
For Rouen from the estuary of the Seine?
A moment only for that veil to lift—
A moment only for those bells to die
That rang their matins at Condé-sur-Vire.

By noon St Ignace! The arrival there
The signal for the battle-cries of triumph,
The gauntlet of the clubs. The stakes were set

And the ordeal of Jogues was re-enacted
Upon the priests—even with wilder fury,
For here at last was trapped their greatest victim,
Echon. The Iroquois had waited long
For this event. Their hatred for the Hurons
Fused with their hatred for the French and priests
Was to be vented on this sacrifice,
And to that camp had come apostate Hurons,
United with their foes in common hate
To settle up their reckoning with Echon.
. . .
Now three o'clock, and capping the height of the passion,
Confusing the sacraments under the pines of the forest,
Under the incense of balsam, under the smoke
Of the pitch, was offered the rite of the font. On the head,
The breast, the loins and the legs, the boiling water!
While the mocking paraphrase of the symbols was hurled
At their faces like shards of flint from the arrow heads—
'We baptize thee with water . . .
                         That thou mayest be led
To Heaven . . .
                  To that end we do anoint thee.
We treat thee as a friend: we are the cause
Of thy happiness; we are thy priests; the more
Thou sufferest, the more thy God will reward thee,
So give us thanks for our kind offices.'

The fury of taunt was followed by fury of blow.
Why did not the flesh of Brébeuf cringe to the scourge,
Respond to the heat, for rarely the Iroquois found
A victim that would not cry out in such pain—yet here
The fire was on the wrong fuel. Whenever he spoke,
It was to rally the soul of his friend whose turn
Was to come through the night while the eyes were uplifted in
    prayer,
Imploring the Lady of Sorrows, the mother of Christ,
As pain brimmed over the cup and the will was called
To stand the test of the coals. And sometimes the speech
Of Brébeuf struck out, thundering reproof to his foes,
Half-rebuke, half-defiance, giving them roar for roar.

Was it because the chancel became the arena,
Brébeuf a lion at bay, not a lamb on the altar,
As if the might of a Roman were joined to the cause
Of Judaea? Speech they could stop for they girdled his lips,
But never a moan could they get. Where was the source

Of his strength, the home of his courage that topped the best
Of their braves and even out-fabled the lore of their legends?
In the bunch of his shoulders which often had carried a load
Extorting the envy of guides at an Ottawa portage?
The heat of the hatchets was finding a path to that source.
In the thews of his thighs which had mastered the trails of the
    Neutrals?
They would gash and beribbon those muscles. Was it the blood?
They would draw it fresh from its fountain. Was it the heart?
They dug for it, fought for the scraps in the way of the wolves.
But not in these was the valour of stamina lodged;
Nor in the symbol of Richelieu's robes or the seals
Of Mazarin's charters, nor in the stir of the *lilies*
Upon the Imperial folds; nor yet in the words
Loyola wrote on a table of lava-stone
In the cave of Manresa—not in these the source—
But in the sound of invisible trumpets blowing
Around two slabs of board, right-angled, hammered
By Roman nails and hung on a Jewish hill.

The wheel had come full circle with the visions
In France of Brébeuf poured through the mould of St Ignace.
Lalemant died in the morning at nine, in the flame
Of the pitch belts. Flushed with the sight of the bodies, the
    foes
Gathered their clans and moved back to the north and west
To join in the fight against the tribes of the Petuns.
There was nothing now that could stem the Iroquois blast.
However undaunted the souls of the priests who were left,
However fierce the sporadic counter attacks
Of the Hurons striking in roving bands from the ambush,
Or smashing out at their foes in garrison raids,
The villages fell before a blizzard of axes
And arrows and spears, and then were put to the torch.

The days were dark at the fort and heavier grew
The burdens on Ragueneau's shoulders. Decision was his.
No word from the east could arrive in time to shape
The step he must take. To and fro—from altar to hill,
From hill to altar, he walked and prayed and watched.
As governing priest of the Mission he felt the pride
Of his Order whipping his pulse, for was not St Ignace
The highest test of the Faith? And all that torture
And death could do to the body was done. The Will
And the Cause in their triumph survived.
    Loyola's mountains,

Sublime at their summits, were scaled to the uttermost peak.
Ragueneau, the Shepherd, now looked on a battered fold.
In a whirlwind of fire St Jean, like St Joseph, crashed
Under the Iroquois impact. Firm at his post,
Garnier suffered the fate of Daniel. And now
Chabanel, last in the roll of the martyrs, entrapped
On his knees in the woods met death at apostate hands.

The drama was drawing close to its end. It fell
To Ragueneau's lot to perform a final rite—
To offer the fort in sacrificial fire!
He applied the torch himself. *'Inside an hour,'*
He wrote, 'we saw the fruit of ten years' labour
Ascend in smoke,—then looked our last at the fields,
Put altar-vessels and food on a raft of logs,
And made our way to the island of St Joseph.'
But even from there was the old tale retold—
Of hunger and the search for roots and acorns;
Of cold and persecution unto death
By the Iroquois; of Jesuit will and courage
As the shepherd-priest with Chaumonot led back
The remnant of a nation to Quebec.   [1940]

from TOWARDS THE LAST SPIKE

THE PRE-CAMBRIAN SHIELD

(i)
On the North Shore a reptile lay asleep—
A hybrid that the myths might have conceived,
But not delivered, as progenitor
Of crawling, gliding things upon the earth.
She lay snug in the folds of a huge boa
Whose tail had covered Labrador and swished
Atlantic tides, whose body coiled itself
Around the Hudson Bay, then curled up north
Through Manitoba and Saskatchewan
To Great Slave Lake. In continental reach
The neck went past the Great Bear Lake until
Its head was hidden in the Arctic Seas.
This folded reptile was asleep or dead:
So motionless, she seemed stone dead—just seemed:
She was too old for death, too old for life,
For as if jealous of all living forms
She had lain there before bivalves began
To catacomb their shells on western mountains.
Somewhere within this life-death zone she sprawled,

Torpid upon a rock-and-mineral mattress.
Ice-ages had passed by and over her,
But these, for all their motion, had but sheared
Her spotty carboniferous hair or made
Her ridges stand out like the spikes of molochs.
Her back grown stronger every million years,
She had shed water by the longer rivers
To Hudson Bay and by the shorter streams
To the great basins to the south, had filled
Them up, would keep them filled until the end
Of Time.

(ii)
Dynamite on the North Shore

The lizard was in sanguinary mood.
She had been waked again: she felt her sleep
Had lasted a few seconds of her time.
The insects had come back—the ants, if ants
They were—dragging *those* trees, *those* logs athwart
Her levels, driving in *those* spikes; and how
The long grey snakes unknown within her region
Wormed from the east, unstriped, sunning themselves
Uncoiled upon the logs and then moved on,
Growing each day, ever keeping abreast!
She watched them, waiting for a bloody moment,
Until the borers halted at a spot,
The most invulnerable of her whole column,
Drove in that iron, wrenched it in the holes,
Hitting, digging, twisting. Why that spot?
Not this the former itch. That sharp proboscis
Was out for more than self-sufficing blood
About the cuticle: 'twas out for business
In the deep layers and the arteries.
And this consistent punching at her belly
With fire and thunder slapped her like an insult,
As with the blasts the caches of her broods
Broke—nickel, copper, silver and fool's gold,
Burst from their immemorial dormitories
To sprawl indecent in the light of day.
Another warning—this time different.

Westward above her webs she had a trap—
A thing called muskeg, easy on the eyes
Stung with the dust of gravel. Cotton grass,

Its white spires blending with the orchids,
Peeked through green table-cloths of sphagnum moss.
Carnivorous bladder-wort studded the acres,
Passing the water-fleas through their digestion.
Sweet-gale and sundew edged the dwarf black spruce;
And herds of cariboo had left their hoof-marks,
Betraying visual solidity,
But like the thousands of the pitcher plants,
Their downward-pointing hairs alluring insects,
Deceptive—and the men were moving west!
Now was her time. She took three engines, sank them
With seven tracks down through the hidden lake
To the rock bed, then over them she spread
A counterpane of leather-leaf and slime.
A warning, that was all for now. 'Twas sleep
She wanted, sleep, for drowsing was her pastime
And waiting through eternities of seasons.
As for intruders bred for skeletons—
Some day perhaps when ice began to move,
Or some convulsion ran fires through her tombs,
She might stir in her sleep and far below
The reach of steel and blast of dynamite,
She'd claim their bones as her possessive right
And wrap them cold in her pre-Cambrian folds.   [1952]

T.E. Hulme

England 1883-1917

Hulme, a prominent theorist of the Imagist movement, directly influenced the early aesthetic
doctrines and poetic practices of Ezra Pound and T.S. Eliot. Expelled from Cambridge in 1906 for
his involvement in a tavern fight, Hulme travelled to Montreal by cargo boat and then to the
Canadian midwest where he worked for the railway and at odd jobs. Following his return to
England in 1908, Hulme founded the Poets Club, published a small selection of his poetry, and
contributed essays and manifestos to magazines such as *The Egoist* and Amy Lowell's *Poetry*,
promoting Imagist principles of composition, including precise images, exact diction, new
rhythms, and novel subjects.

THE BLANKET-MAKERS

Somewhere the gods (blanket-makers in the prairie of cold)
    Sleep in their blankets.   [1906]

AUTUMN

A touch of cold in the Autumn night
I walked abroad
And saw the ruddy moon lean over a hedge
Like a red-faced farmer.
I did not stop to speak, but nodded;
And round about were the wistful stars
With white faces like town children. [1908]

EDITH ANNE ROBERTSON

Scotland 1883 - c. 1978

Robertson's Scots translations of Hopkins's poetry grasp both the correlatives and the contrasts between the two languages, and derive their integrity from her understanding of his inventiveness. In her preface to *Translations into the Scots tongue of poems by Gerard Manley Hopkins*, Robertson suggests that 'if at times' the poem's 'meaning becomes clearer in translations, the credit is due to a language peculiarly suited to Hopkins's way of thought and of feeling. Had he known the Scots tongue, I think he would have loved it as dearly, as he did the tongue of Wales.'

PYATIE BEAUTY

O blythebid God for ilka dapperty thing—
    For luifts of spraikled colour like a pyatie coo;
        For rose-moles aa in a stipple where the trouties swim
Thru the burns; for gleenan conker; finch's wing;
    Grass parks plotted, marled fauld, fallow and plough;
        And áa trádes, their gear and tackle and trim.
Aá things conter, rare, spare, strange:
    Whatsomever is flirdie, pyatie (wha kens how?)
        Floskan, dauneran; sweet, soor; dazzlan, dim;
He childers: it is only his beauty canna change:
                    Blythebid him!

PIED BEAUTY

Glory be to God for dappled things—
    For skies of couple-colour as a brinded cow;
        For rose-moles all in stipple upon trout that swim;
Fresh-firecoal chestnut-falls; finches' wings;
    Landscape plotted and pieced—fold, fallow, and plough;
        And áll trádes, their gear and tackle and trim.
All things counter, original, spare, strange;
    Whatever is fickle, freckled (who knows how?)
        With swift, slow; sweet, sour; adazzle, dim;
He fathers-forth whose beauty is past change:
                    Praise him. [1968]

COUNTRY BOY ON A MOTOR CYCLE

If you wants your fun you gotta go fast,
like a hen hawk or a windhover
swinging and sweeping through the air,
taking your chances. If today's your last
well you've had it and all's over.

I slit a sheep in two back there,
not even a chop of her fit for the butcher;
and by gum it was cheap at the price!
I grant you it's good to be drunk, but it's better
to lie low-over at the corners, or to speed
on them long tarmacs as kind as flat air
to the birds. Cham or whisky have nothing there,
not when Lily on the pillion squeals
'Talk about faster than light!'

That sheep might easy have been a baby—
it wouldn't be my first, and all I can say
is Life's nothing to cling to now-a-day,
and the nearer the danger the better the game;
as for all those old men and women they may
be goddam thankful to get a quick push-off.

If it weren't for Lily I'd feel the same.   [1969]

WILLIAM CARLOS WILLIAMS
USA 1883-1963

Williams, who was a doctor, wrote verse that paid close attention to the rhythms of colloquial speech and the working-class lives of many of his patients; his five-'Book'-long poem *Paterson* (1946–61) draws on the New Jersey town where he practised to re-create his vision of modern American life. He espoused a poetics of immediacy, but also of carefully crafted rhythms (Williams worked at perfecting a metre he called the 'variable foot'). His first book of poems, *The Tempers*, was published in 1913, and numerous other books appeared over the next fifty years; his life's work (excluding *Paterson*) has been assembled in the two-volume *The Collected Poems of William Carlos Williams* (ed. Litz and MacGowan, 1986, 1988).

DANSE RUSSE

If when my wife is sleeping
and the baby and Kathleen
are sleeping
and the sun is a flame-white disc

in silken mists
above shining trees,—
if I in my north room
dance naked, grotesquely
before my mirror
waving my shirt round my head
and singing softly to myself:
'I am lonely, lonely.
I was born to be lonely,
I am best so!'
If I admire my arms, my face,
my shoulders, flanks, buttocks
against the yellow drawn shades,—

Who shall say I am not
the happy genius of my household?   [1917]

This Is Just to Say

I have eaten
the plums
that were in
the icebox

and which
you were probably
saving
for breakfast

Forgive me
they were delicious
so sweet
and so cold   [1934]

ANNA WICKHAM

England 1884-1947

Wickham's husband Patrick Hepburn had his wife committed to a private asylum for six weeks in 1910; he had forbidden her to publish her poetry and she had resisted. A deal of some kind was struck though the acrimony was never resolved. Wickham continued to publish, her work achieved recognition, and she found support among various artists including the American poet Natalie Barney whose salon Wickham joined in Paris as both would-be lover and writer. In 1935 Wickham began *The Great Spring Clean*, an autobiographical work that remained unfinished. Here, she recorded the overwhelming tension produced by the competing and irreconcilable claims she felt as woman and artist: 'There have been few women poets of distinction, and, if we count only the suicides of Sappho, Lawrence Hope and Charlotte Mew, their despair rate has been very high.' Wickham hanged herself in 1947; her poetry and prose are collected in *The Writings Of Anna Wickham Free Woman and Poet* (Virago, 1984).

THE FIRED POT

In our town, people live in rows.
The only irregular thing in a street is the steeple;
And where that points to, God only knows,
And not the poor disciplined people!

And I have watched the women growing old,
Passionate about pins, and pence, and soap,
Till the heart within my wedded breast grew cold,
And I lost hope.

But a young soldier came to our town,
He spoke his mind most candidly.
He asked me quickly to lie down,
And that was very good for me.
For though I gave him no embrace—
Remembering my duty—
He altered the expression of my face,
And gave me back my beauty.   [1984]

THE SICK ASSAILANT

I hit her in the face because she loved me.
It was the challenge of her faithfulness that moved me;
For she knew me, every impulse, every mood,
As if my veins had run with her heart's blood.
She knew my damned incontinence, my weakness—
Yet she forbore with her accursèd meekness.
I could have loved her had she ever blamed me;
It was her sticky, irritating patience shamed me.

I was tired-sick. It was her business to amuse me:
Her faith could only daunt me and confuse me.
She was a fine great wench, and well I knew
She was one good half panther, one half shrew—
Then why should my love, more than any other,
Induce in her the silly human Mother?
She would have nursed me, bathed me, fed me, carried me;
She'd have burned her soul to thaw me—she'd have married me!
I hit her in the face because she loved me.
It was her sticky, irritating patience moved me.   [1936]

D.H. Lawrence

England 1885–1930

Novelist (*Sons and Lovers*, 1914; *Lady Chatterley's Lover*, 1928), essayist and critic, painter and
poet, Lawrence created a mythology showing human and non-human currents enacting related
aspects of an underlying cosmic drama. Facing ongoing resistance to the publication of his
work, he left England to live in Italy, Mexico, and the south of France. To counter a perceived
aversion to the physical body—an escape into arid intellectualism, 'aesthetic ecstacy', and
bodiless spiritualism in English society—Lawrence launched his own intense exploration of 'real
substance', with the hope that he could 'touch' 'the hidden side of the moon', 'the back of
presented appearances'. His 'penetration' of the mysteries of sexual consciousness and behaviour
is as ambivalent, contradictory, and opaque as his subject matter and his drive to be 'born again,
pictorially' and linguistically. His poetry is collected in the *Complete Poems* (3 vols, 1957).

Figs

The proper way to eat a fig, in society,
Is to split it in four, holding it by the stump,
And open it, so that it is a glittering, rosy, moist, honied,
        heavy-petalled four-petalled flower.

Then you throw away the skin
Which is just like a four-sepalled calyx,
After you have taken off the blossom with your lips.

But the vulgar way
Is just to put your mouth to the crack, and take out the flesh in
        one bite.

Every fruit has its secret.

The fig is a very secretive fruit.
As you see it standing growing, you feel at once it is symbolic:
And it seems male.
But when you come to know it better, you agree with the Romans,
        it is female.

The Italians vulgarly say, it stands for the female part; the
     fig-fruit:
The fissure, the yoni,
The wonderful moist conductivity towards the centre.

Involved,
Inturned,
The flowering all inward and womb-fibrilled;
And but one orifice.

The fig, the horse-shoe, the squash-blossom.
Symbols.

There was a flower that flowered inward, womb-ward;
Now there is a fruit like a ripe womb.

It was always a secret.
That's how it should be, the female should always be secret.

There never was any standing aloft and unfolded on a bough
Like other flowers, in a revelation of petals;
Silver-pink peach, venetian green glass of medlars and
     sorb-apples,
Shallow wine-cups on short, bulging stems
Openly pledging heaven:
Here's to the thorn in flower! Here is to Utterance!
The brave, adventurous rosaceæ.

Folded upon itself, and secret unutterable,
And milky-sapped, sap that curdles milk and makes *ricotta*,
Sap that smells strange on your fingers, that even goats won't
     taste it;
Folded upon itself, enclosed like any Mohammedan woman,
Its nakedness all within-walls, its flowering forever unseen,
One small way of access only, and this close-curtained from the
     light;
Fig, fruit of the female mystery, covert and inward,
Mediterranean fruit, with your covert nakedness,
Where everything happens invisible, flowering and fertilisation,
     and fruiting
In the inwardness of your you, that eye will never see
Till it's finished, and you're over-ripe, and you burst to give
     up your ghost.

Till the drop of ripeness exudes,
And the year is over.

And then the fig has kept her secret long enough.
So it explodes, and you see through the fissure the scarlet.
And the fig is finished, the year is over.

That's how the fig dies, showing her crimson through the purple
    slit
Like a wound, the exposure of her secret, on the open day.
Like a prostitute, the bursten fig, making a show of her secret.

That's how women die too.

The year is fallen over-ripe,
The year of our women.
The year of our women is fallen over-ripe.
The secret is laid bare.
And rottenness soon sets in.
The year of our women is fallen over-ripe.

When Eve once knew *in her mind* that she was naked
She quickly sewed fig-leaves, and sewed the same for the man.
She'd been naked all her days before,
But till then, till that apple of knowledge, she hadn't had the
    fact on her mind.

She got the fact on her mind, and quickly sewed fig-leaves.
And women have been sewing ever since.
But now they stitch to adorn the bursten fig, not to cover it.
They have their nakedness more than ever on their mind,
And they won't let us forget it.

Now, the secret
Becomes an affirmation through moist, scarlet lips
That laugh at the Lord's indignation.

What then, good Lord! cry the women.
We have kept our secret long enough.
We are a ripe fig.
Let us burst into affirmation.

They forget, ripe figs won't keep.
Ripe figs won't keep.

Honey-white figs of the north, black figs with scarlet inside, of
     the south.
Ripe figs won't keep, won't keep in any clime.
What then, when women the world over have all bursten into
     self-assertion?
And bursten figs won't keep?

San Gervasio.
[1923]

DOROTHEA MACKELLAR

Australia 1885–1968

Born in Sydney and educated at the University of Sydney, Mackellar studied European languages and
published her first volume of poetry, *The Closed Door*, in 1911. In addition to producing five subse-
quent collections of verse, Mackellar wrote a novel and co-authored (with Ruth Bedford) two chil-
dren's novels. The comprehensive collection of her poetry is *The Poems of Dorothea Mackellar* (1971).

IN A SOUTHERN GARDEN

When the tall bamboos are clicking to the restless little breeze,
And bats begin their jerky skimming flight,
And the creamy scented blossoms of the dark pittosporum trees,
Grow sweeter with the coming of the night.

And the harbour in the distance lies beneath a purple pall,
And nearer, at the garden's lowest fringe,
Loud the water soughs and gurgles 'mid the rocks below the wall,
Dark-heaving, with a dim uncanny tinge

Of a green as pale as beryls, like the strange faint-coloured
     flame
That burns around the Women of the Sea:
And the strip of sky to westward which the camphor-laurels frame,
Has turned to ash-of-rose and ivory—

And a chorus rises valiantly from where the crickets hide,
Close-shaded by the balsams drooping down—
It is evening in a garden by the kindly water-side,
A garden near the lights of Sydney town!   [1911]

EZRA POUND

USA/England 1885–1972

Born in Hailey, Idaho, Ezra Loomis Pound became one of the most controversial figures in the Modernist movement. Pound travelled to London in 1908, where he was befriended by W.B. Yeats. As a promoter, critic, and editor, Pound powerfully influenced his contemporaries' work; he played a major role as editor of Eliot's *The Waste Land* (1922). Pound's own central poetic project, never completed, was his encyclopedic *The Cantos*, a 'poem including history'; the first section was published in 1925 and the latest in 1969. Pound's impassioned support of fascism in Italy in the late thirties and forties led to a twelve-year incarceration in a Washington, DC insane asylum, where he continued to work on *The Cantos*, publishing an acclaimed section, *The Pisan Cantos*, in 1948. His important work as a translator is represented in *The Translations of Ezra Pound* (ed. Kenner, 1953), and his poetry in *Collected Shorter Poems* (1984) and *The Cantos of Ezra Pound* (1972, 1981).

A PACT

I make a pact with you, Walt Whitman—
I have detested you long enough.
I come to you as a grown child
Who has had a pig-headed father;
I am old enough now to make friends.
It was you that broke the new wood,
Now is a time for carving.
We have one sap and one root—
Let there be commerce between us.   [1916]

L'ART, 1910

Green arsenic smeared on an egg-white cloth,
Crushed strawberries! Come, let us feast our eyes.   [1916]

HELEN B. CRUICKSHANK

Scotland 1886–1975

Cruickshank was born in Hillside, Angus, and worked as a civil servant in Edinburgh for most of her life. She founded the Scottish branch of PEN in 1927, and was a close friend of the poet Hugh MacDiarmid during the 1930s. Cruickshank wrote most of her poetry in the vernacular and was a significant early figure in the modern revival of Scots poetry. Her books include *Up the Noran Water* (1934), *The Ponnage Pool* (1968), and the posthumous *Collected Poems* (1976) and *More Collected Poems* (1978).

ON BEING EIGHTY

Broad in the beam? More broad in sympathy.
Stiff in the joints? More flexible in mind.
Deaf on the right? Now voices from the Left
In politics and art more clearly sound.
Arteries harden? Movements then more slow
Allow more time to contemplate and ponder.
High on the Shelf? Horizons farther grow
Extending faculties for joy and wonder.
Acceptance gained of what one has to bear?
The hard is then become more bearable
And comrade Death himself finds welcome, so
Quite cheerfully towards eighty-one we go.   [1971]

H.D. (HILDA DOOLITTLE)
USA/England 1886-1961

A poet and novelist, Doolittle was born in Bethlehem, Pennsylvania, and attended Bryn Mawr. Engaged to Ezra Pound while he was a student at the University of Pennsylvania, she moved to London in 1911 where she met and married English poet and novelist Richard Aldington in 1913. Both writers had begun publishing Imagist poems in Harriet Monroe's *Poetry* magazine and Amy Lowell's anthologies, and under the pen-name 'H.D.', Doolittle produced several collections of this work. Her marriage to Aldington ended in 1919 and Doolittle became the companion of English novelist and photographer 'Bryher' (heiress Annie Winifred Ellerman) until 1946. The couple lived in Switzerland, raising Doolittle's daughter until 1939 when they returned to London; in 1933–34, Doolittle spent time in Vienna in psychoanalysis with Sigmund Freud, and her poetry reflects an eclectic fascination with occult and symbolic systems. Among her finest works are the revisionary epic poems entitled *Trilogy* (1944–46; 1973) and *Helen in Egypt* (1961), and experimental prose with lesbian themes, *Bid Me to Live (A Madrigal)* (1960), *Asphodel* (1981), and *HERmione* (1981). The most comprehensive volume of H.D.'s work is *Collected Poems 1912–1944* (ed. Martz, 1983).

AT BAIA

I should have thought
in a dream you would have brought
some lovely, perilous thing,
orchids piled in a great sheath,
as who would say (in a dream)
I send you this,
who left the blue veins
of your throat unkissed.

Why was it that your hands
(that never took mine)
your hands that I could see
drift over the orchid heads
so carefully,
your hands, so fragile, sure to lift
so gently, the fragile flower stuff—
ah, ah, how was it

You never sent (in a dream)
the very form, the very scent,
not heavy, not sensuous,
but perilous—perilous—
of orchids, piled in a great sheath,
and folded underneath on a bright scroll
some word:

Flower sent to flower;
for white hands, the lesser white,
less lovely of flower leaf,

or

Lover to lover, no kiss,
no touch, but forever and ever this.   [1921]

from SIGIL

XIV

Now let the cycle sweep us here and there,
we will not struggle,
somewhere,
under a forest-ledge,
a wild white-pear
will blossom;
somewhere,
under an edge of rock,
a sea will open;
slice of the tide-shelf
will show in coral, yourself,
in conch-shell,
myself;

somewhere,
over a field-hedge,
a wild bird
will lift up wild, wild throat,
and that song heard,
will stifle out this note
and this song note.

XV

So if you love me,
love me everywhere,
blind to all argument
or phantasy
claim the one signet;

truly in the sky,
God marked me to be his,
scrawled, 'I, I, I
alone can comprehend

this subtlety':
a song is very simple
or is bound
within interwoven complicated sound;

one undertakes
the song's integrity,
another all the filament
wound round

chord and discord,
the quarter-note and whole
run of iambic
or of coryiamb:

'no one can grasp'
(God wrote)
'nor understand
the two, insolvent,
only he and you';

shall we two witness
that his writ is wise
or shall we rise,

wing-tip to purple wing,
create new earth,
new skies?

XVI

But it won't be that way,
I'm sane,
normal again;

I'm sane,
normal as when
we last sat in this room
with other people who spoke
pleasant speakable things;

though
you lifted your brow
as a sun-parched branch to the rain,

and I lifted my soul
as from the northern gloom,
an ice-flower to the sun,
they didn't know

how
my heart woke
to a range and measure
of song
I hadn't known;

as yours spoke through your eyes,
I recalled
a trivial little joke we had,
lest the others see
how the walls stretched out
to desert and sand,
the Symplegedes
and the sea.

XVII

Time breaks the barrier,
we are on a reef,
wave lengthens on to sand,
sand keeps wave-beat

furrowed in its heart,
so keep print of my hand;
you are the sea-surge,
lift me from the land,

let me be swept out in you,
let me slake the last,
last ultimate thirst;
I am you;

you are cursed;
men have cursed God,
let me be no more man,
God has cursed man,

let me go out and sink
into the ultimate sleep;
take me,
let your hand

gather my throat,
flower from that land
we both have loved,
have lost;

O wand of ebony, keep away the night,
O ivory wand,
bring back the ultimate light
on Delphic headland;

take me,
O ultimate breath,
O master-lyrist,
beat my wild heart to death.

XVIII

Are we unfathomable night
with the new moon
to give it depth
and carry vision further,
or are we rather stupid,
marred with feeling?

will we gain all things,
being over-fearful,
or will we lose the clue,
miss out the sense
of all the scrawled script,
being over-careful?

is each one's reticence
the other's food,
or is this mood
sheer poison to the other?

how do I know
what pledge you gave your God,
how do you know
who is my Lord
and Lover?

XIX

'I love you,'
spoken in rhapsodic meter,
leaves me cold:

I have a horror
of finality,
I would rather
hazard a guess,
wonder whether
either of us
could for a moment
endure the other,
after the first fine flavor
of irony
had worn off.   [1982]

RUPERT BROOKE

England 1887–1915

Brooke's first volume appeared in *Poems 1911*; a one-act play and a fellowship to King's College, Cambridge followed. A serious breakdown in 1913 led to extensive travels in Canada, the United States, and the Pacific, but when war was declared, Brooke became a commissioned officer with the Royal Naval Division. His war sonnets, including the heavily anthologized 'The Soldier', were written while he was on leave in December 1914, their power heightened by Brooke's death on a troopship bound for the Dardanelles five months later. Brooke's *1914 and Other Poems* (June 1915) and his *Collected Poems* together sold 300,000 copies in the first decade after their publication.

DINING-ROOM TEA

When you were there, and you, and you,
Happiness crowned the night; I too,
Laughing and looking, one of all,
I watched the quivering lamplight fall
On plate and flowers and pouring tea
And cup and cloth; and they and we
Flung all the dancing moments by
With jest and glitter. Lip and eye
Flashed on the glory, shone and cried,
Improvident, unmemoried;
And fitfully and like a flame
The light of laughter went and came.
Proud in their careless transience moved
The changing faces that I loved.

Till suddenly, and otherwhence,
I looked upon your innocence.
For lifted clear and still and strange
From the dark woven flow of change
Under a vast and starless sky

I saw the immortal moment lie.
One instant I, an instant, knew
As God knows all. And it and you
I, above Time, oh, blind! could see
In witless immortality.
I saw the marble cup; the tea,
Hung on the air, an amber stream;
I saw the fire's unglittering gleam,
The painted flame, the frozen smoke.
No more the flooding lamplight broke
On flying eyes and lips and hair;
But lay, but slept unbroken there,
On stiller flesh, and body breathless,
And lips and laughter stayed and deathless,
And words on which no silence grew.
Light was more alive than you.

For suddenly, and otherwhence,
I looked on your magnificence.
I saw the stillness and the light,
And you, august, immortal, white,
Holy and strange; and every glint
Posture and jest and thought and tint
Freed from the mask of transiency,
Triumphant in eternity,
Immote, immortal.

          Dazed at length
Human eyes grew, mortal strength
Wearied; and Time began to creep.
Change closed about me like a sleep.
Light glinted on the eyes I loved.
The cup was filled. The bodies moved.
The drifting petal came to ground.
The laughter chimed its perfect round.
The broken syllable was ended.
And I, so certain and so friended,

How could I cloud, or how distress,
The heaven of your unconsciousness?
Or shake at Time's sufficient spell,
Stammering of lights unutterable?
The eternal holiness of you,
The timeless end, you never knew,

The peace that lay, the light that shone.
You never knew that I had gone
A million miles away, and stayed
A million years. The laughter played
Unbroken round me; and the jest
Flashed on. And we that knew the best
Down wonderful hours grew happier yet.
I sang at heart, and talked, and eat,
And lived from laugh to laugh, I too,
When you were there, and you, and you.   [1908–11]

MARIANNE MOORE

USA 1887-1972

Moore was born in St Louis and moved with her mother to New York in 1918, where in 1929 they settled in a Brooklyn apartment in which Moore lived until her death. Moore's unique position among American Modernists is marked by her persistent and keen delight in precise observation of the natural world, and her rigorous, almost fastidious care with language. *Poems* (1921) was followed by *Observations* (1924), the year she began to work for the important literary magazine *Dial*, which she edited from 1926 to 1929. Her *Selected Poems* appeared in 1935; her *Collected Poems* (1952) won the Pulitzer Prize, the National Book Award, and the Bollingen Prize. *The Complete Poems of Marianne Moore* appeared in 1968 (rev. ed., 1984).

POETRY

I, too, dislike it: there are things that are important beyond
          all this fiddle.
    Reading it, however, with a perfect contempt for it, one
    discovers in it after all, a place for the genuine.
        Hands that can grasp, eyes
        that can dilate, hair that can rise
            if it must, these things are important not because a

high-sounding interpretation can be put upon them but because
          they are
    useful. When they become so derivative as to become
          unintelligible,
    the same thing may be said for all of us, that we
        do not admire what
        we cannot understand: the bat
            holding on upside down or in quest of something to

eat, elephants pushing, a wide horse taking a roll, a tireless
      wolf under
  a tree, the immovable critic twitching his skin like a horse
      that feels a flea, the base-
  ball fan, the statistician—
     nor is it valid
      to discriminate against 'business documents and

school-books'; all these phenomena are important. One must make a
      distinction
  however: when dragged into prominence by half poets, the
      result is not poetry,
  nor till the poets among us can be
   'literalists of
   the imagination'—above
     insolence and triviality and can present

for inspection, 'imaginary gardens with real toads in them,'
      shall we have
  it. In the meantime, if you demand on the one hand,
  the raw material of poetry in
   all its rawness and
   that which is on the other hand
     genuine, you are interested in poetry.   [1921]

POETRY

I, too, dislike it:
there are things that are important beyond all this fiddle.
The bat, upside down; the elephant pushing,
the tireless wolf under a tree,
the base-ball fan, the statistician—
'business documents and schoolbooks'—
these phenomena are pleasing,
but when they have been fashioned
into that which is unknowable,
we are not entertained.
It may be said of all of us
that we do not admire what we cannot understand;
enigmas are not poetry.   [1924]

POETRY

I, too, dislike it.
   Reading it, however, with a perfect contempt for it, one
   discovers
in it after all, a place for the genuine.   [1967]

Edwin Muir

Scotland 1887-1959

Muir was a poet, novelist, and translator, whose writing often explores the contact childhood and local landscapes make with visionary territories. Part of this interaction is informed by the dream journey he himself explored through psychoanalysis while living in London during and immediately after World War I. His *Collected Poems, 1921–1958* was published in 1964.

For Ann Scott-Moncrieff

(1914–1943)

Dear Ann, wherever you are
Since you lately learnt to die,
You are this unsetting star
That shines unchanged in my eye;
So near, inaccessible,
Absent and present so much
Since out of the world you fell,
Fell from hearing and touch—
So near. But your mortal tongue
Used for immortal use,
The grace of a woman young,
The air of an early muse,
The wealth of the chambered brow
And soaring flight of your eyes:
These are no longer now.
Death has a princely prize.

You who were Ann much more
Than others are that or this,
Extravagant over the score
To be what only is,
Would you not still say now
What you once used to say
Of the great Why and How,
On that or the other day?
For though of your heritage
The minority here began,
Now you have come of age
And are entirely Ann.

Under the years' assaults,
In the storm of good and bad,
You too had the faults

That Emily Brontë had,
Ills of body and soul,
Of sinner and saint and all
Who strive to make themselves whole,
Smashed to bits by the Fall.
Yet 'the world is a pleasant place'
I can hear your voice repeat,
While the sun shone in your face
Last summer in Princes Street.   [1946]

EDITH SITWELL

England 1887-1964

Original, unmistakable, and compelling, Sitwell's experimental style in her early poems led one critic to suggest they were composed for 'the xylophone', a point that is especially true for the syncopated rhythms of the series of 'abstract' poems that make up the sequence *Façade* which Sitwell performed jointly with music composed by Sir William Walton. In 'Some Notes on My Own Poetry', Sitwell discusses her search 'to find rhythmical expressions for the heightened speed of our time'. To those who mistook her surface gaiety for disengagement or her elaborate sound patterns for an art-for-art's-sake intellectualism, Sitwell observed: 'The gaiety of some masks darkness—the see-saw world in which giant and dwarf take it in turns to rush into the glaring light, the sight of the crowds, then, with a terrifying swiftness, go down to the yawning dark' (xviii). Sitwell's more than thirty volumes of poetry are represented in *Collected Poems* (1957) and *Selected Poems* (1965).

LULLABY

Though the world has slipped and gone,
Sounds my loud discordant cry
Like the steel birds' song on high:
'Still one thing is left—the Bone!'
Then out danced the Babioun.

She sat in the hollow of the sea—
A socket whence the eye's put out—
She sang to the child a lullaby
(The steel birds' nest was thereabout).

'Do, do, do, do—
Thy mother's hied to the vaster race:
The Pterodactyl made its nest
And laid a steel egg in her breast—
Under the Judas-colored sun.
She'll work no more, nor dance, nor moan,
And I am come to take her place
Do, do.

There's nothing left but earth's low bed—
(The Pterodactyl fouls its nest):
But steel wings fan thee to thy rest,
And wingless truth and larvae lie
And eyeless hope and handless fear—
All these for thee as toys are spread,
Do—do—

Red is the bed of Poland, Spain,
And thy mother's breast, who has grown wise
In that fouled nest. If she could rise,
Give birth again,
In wolfish pelt she'd hide thy bones
To shield thee from the world's long cold,
And down on all fours shouldst thou crawl
For thus from no height canst thou fall—
Do, do.

She'd give no hands: there's nought to hold
And nought to make: there's dust to sift,
But no food for the hands to lift.
Do, do.

Heed my ragged lullaby,
Fear not living, fear not chance;
All is equal—blindness, sight,
There is no depth, there is no height:
Do, do.

The Judas-colored sun is gone,
And with the Ape thou art alone—
Do,
  Do.'

[1942]

T.S. ELIOT

USA/England 1888-1965

Thomas Sterns Eliot migrated to London in 1914, established himself with Lloyd's Bank, and worked as a reviewer, essayist, editor, and poet. His first publication was 'The Love Song of J. Alfred Prufrock' (1915); The Waste Land, a five-part poetic drama that thrived under Ezra Pound's editorial attention when Eliot showed him the piece in manuscript form, appeared in 1922. Eliot brought to the Modernist movement in poetry an explicit renewal of Metaphysical wit and technique, the evocative elements of French Symbolist poetry, and an allusive method that depended on his understanding of the 'presentness' of the literary past which had trained him. To achieve intensity, he withdrew the usual connective fibre that had explained transitions in thought and meaning in poetic compositions. His early iconoclasm gave way to an Anglo-Catholic conversion and the exploration of the complex nature of the religious experience in sequences like The Four Quartets and Ash Wednesday. Eliot wished to see English poetry 'recover' from the 'dissociation of sensibility' he believed dominated its development in the eighteenth and nineteenth centuries: the poet, he advises, must look 'into a good deal more than the heart. One must look into the cerebral cortex, the nervous system, and the digestive tracts' and write. Eliot's work is represented in the Collected Poems, 1909–63 and The Complete Poems and Plays (including Poems Written in Early Youth) (1969).

THE HOLLOW MEN

Mistah Kurtz—he dead.
            A penny for the Old Guy

I
We are the hollow men
We are the stuffed men
Leaning together
Headpiece filled with straw. Alas!
Our dried voices, when
We whisper together
Are quiet and meaningless
As wind in dry grass
Or rats' feet over broken glass
In our dry cellar

Shape without form, shade without colour,
Paralysed force, gesture without motion;

Those who have crossed
With direct eyes, to death's other Kingdom
Remember us—if at all—not as lost
Violent souls, but only
As the hollow men
The stuffed men.

II
Eyes I dare not meet in dreams
In death's dream kingdom
These do not appear:
There, the eyes are
Sunlight on a broken column
There, is a tree swinging
And voices are
In the wind's singing
More distant and more solemn
Than a fading star.

Let me be no nearer
In death's dream kingdom
Let me also wear
Such deliberate disguises
Rat's coat, crowskin, crossed staves
In a field
Behaving as the wind behaves
No nearer—

Not that final meeting
In the twilight kingdom

III
This is the dead land
This is cactus land
Here the stone images
Are raised, here they receive
The supplication of a dead man's hand
Under the twinkle of a fading star.

Is it like this
In death's other kingdom
Waking alone
At the hour when we are
Trembling with tenderness
Lips that would kiss
Form prayers to broken stone.

IV
The eyes are not here
There are no eyes here
In this valley of dying stars
In this hollow valley
This broken jaw of our lost kingdoms

In this last of meeting places
We grope together
And avoid speech
Gathered on this beach of the tumid river

Sightless, unless
The eyes reappear
As the perpetual star
Multifoliate rose
Of death's twilight kingdom
The hope only
Of empty men.

V

Here we go round the prickly pear
Prickly pear prickly pear
Here we go round the prickly pear
At five o'clock in the morning.

Between the idea
And the reality
Between the motion
And the act
Falls the Shadow

        For Thine is the Kingdom

Between the conception
And the creation
Between the emotion
And the response
Falls the Shadow

        Life is very long

Between the desire
And the spasm
Between the potency
And the existence
Between the essence
And the descent
Falls the Shadow

        For Thine is the Kingdom

For Thine is
Life is
For Thine is the

This is the way the world ends
This is the way the world ends
This is the way the world ends
Not with a bang but a whimper.   [1925]

KATHERINE MANSFIELD

New Zealand 1888–1923

Best known as a writer of the short-story collections *In a German Pension* (1911), *Bliss and Other Sto-ries* (1920), and *The Garden Party and Other Stories* (1922), Katherine Beauchamp adopted 'Mans-field' as a pseudonym. Born in Wellington to upper-class, authoritarian parents, she went to Queen's College, London, for several years, returned home and finally settled in England in 1908. After her 1918 marriage to literary critic John Middleton Murry, she lived in Italy, France, and Switzerland. Her life was fraught with a prescient sense of isolation and loneliness that she conveys with subtle affection in her writing.

To STANISLAW WYSPIANSKI*

From the other side of the world,
From a little island cradled in the giant sea bosom,
From a little land with no history,
(Making its own history, slowly and clumsily
Piecing together this and that, finding the pattern, solving the
    problem,
Like a child with a box of bricks),
I, a woman, with the taint of the pioneer in my blood,
Full of a youthful strength that wars with itself and is lawless,
I sing your praises, magnificent warrior; I proclaim your
    triumphant battle.
My people have had nought to contend with;
They have worked in the broad light of day and handled the clay
    with rude fingers;
Life—a thing of blood and muscle; Death—a shovelling
    underground of waste material.
What would they know of ghosts and unseen presences,
Of shadows that blot out reality, of darkness that stultifies morn?
Fine and sweet the water that runs from their mountains;
How could they know of poisonous weeds, of rotted and clogging
    tendrils?
And the tapestry woven from dreams of your tragic childhood
They would tear in their stupid hands,

The sad, pale light of your soul blow out with their childish
    laughter.
But the dead—the old—Oh Master, we belong to you there;
Oh Master, there we are children and awed by the strength of a
    giant;
How alive you leapt into the grave and wrestled with Death
And found in the veins of Death the red blood flowing
And raised Death up in your arms and showed him to all the
    people.
Yours a more personal labour than the Nazarene's miracles,
Yours a more forceful encounter than the Nazarene's gentle
    commands.
Stanislaw Wyspianski—Oh man with the name of a fighter,
Across these thousands of sea-shattered miles we cry and proclaim
    you;
We say 'He is lying in Poland, and Poland thinks he is dead;
But he gave the denial to Death—he is lying there, wakeful;
The blood in his giant heart pulls red through his veins'.   [1938]

*Stanislaw Wyspianski was born in the 1860s and died prematurely in 1907. He was a dramatic
poet and has been described as the greatest literary genius produced by modern Poland. The
keynote of his work is an unconquerable faith in the future of his country.

CLAUDE McKAY

Jamaica/USA 1889-1948

A poet from childhood, in 1912 McKay published dialect verse, Jamaican Songs, and that same year
emigrated to the United States to study at Tuskegee Institute and Kansas State University. From
1914 until 1923, he wrote social protest prose as well as poetry and served as an editor for several
socialist magazines in New York. McKay's collections of poetry—Spring in New Hampshire and Other
Poems (1920) and Harlem Shadows (1922)—are among the most important works of the Harlem
Renaissance. Traditional in his appropriation of English sonnet and lyric verse forms, McKay writes
as passionately about the 1919 Chicago race riots as he does about love and faith. From 1923 until
1934 McKay lived as an expatriate in France, Great Britain, and Africa; he subsequently returned
to America and died in Chicago. A volume of McKay's Selected Poems was published in 1953.

IF WE MUST DIE

If we must die, let it not be like hogs
Hunted and penned in an inglorious spot,
While round us bark the mad and hungry dogs,
Making their mock at our accursed lot.
If we must die, O let us nobly die,
So that our precious blood may not be shed
In vain; then even the monsters we defy
Shall be constrained to honor us though dead!

O kinsmen! we must meet the common foe!
Though far outnumbered let us show us brave,
And for their thousand blows deal one deathblow!
What though before us lies the open grave?
Like men we'll face the murderous, cowardly pack,
Pressed to the wall, dying, but fighting back!   [1919]

AMERICA

Although she feeds me bread of bitterness,
And sinks into my throat her tiger's tooth,
Stealing my breath of life, I will confess
I love this cultured hell that tests my youth!
Her vigor flows like tides into my blood,

Giving me strength erect against her hate.
Her bigness sweeps my being like a flood.
Yet as a rebel fronts a king in state,
I stand within her walls with not a shred
Of terror, malice, not a word of jeer.
Darkly I gaze into the days ahead,
And see her might and granite wonders there,
Beneath the touch of Time's unerring hand,
Like priceless treasures sinking in the sand.   [1921]

IVOR GURNEY

England 1890-1937

Composer and poet, Gurney took his experiences at the Western Front during the first three years
of World War I to form the centre of his 1917 volume *Severn & Somme*. His second book, *War's
Embers*, appeared in 1919. The effects of poison gas suffered during the Passchendaele offensive in
1917 led to fifteen years in the City of London Mental Hospital. Tortured by the 'evil' of the 'times
scientific', Gurney continued to find himself 'hurt into poetry'. While assessing the kind of audience
who might be attracted to his first publication, he wrote that in his poetry there is hardly 'any of the
devotion to self-sacrifice, the splendid readiness for death that one finds in Grenfell, Brooke,
Nichols. . . .' Gurney's poetry is presented in P.J. Kavanagh's edition, *The Collected Poems of Ivor
Gurney* (1982).

THE SILENT ONE

Who died on the wires, and hung there, one of two—
Who for his hours of life had chattered through
Infinite lovely chatter of Bucks accent:
Yet faced unbroken wires; stepped over, and went
A noble fool, faithful to his stripes—and ended.
But I weak, hungry, and willing only for the chance

Of line—to fight in the line, lay down under unbroken
Wires, and saw the flashes and kept unshaken,
Till the politest voice—a finicking accent, said:
'Do you think you might crawl through there: there's a hole.'
Darkness, shot at: I smiled, as politely replied—
'I'm afraid not, Sir.' There was no hole no way to be seen
Nothing but chance of death, after tearing of clothes.
Kept flat, and watched the darkness, hearing bullets whizzing—
And thought of music—and swore deep heart's deep oaths
(Polite to God) and retreated and came on again,
Again retreated—and a second time faced the screen.   [1954]

ISAAC ROSENBERG

England 1890-1918

Rosenberg was a gifted visual artist and poet whose first publications included *Youth* (1915)
and the verse drama *Moses* (1916). 'Break of Day in the Trenches', like Wilfred Owen's 'Dulce et
Decorum Est', are poems fired in the crucible of active duty by young men whose careers were
extinguished in the 'torn fields of France'. A selection of Rosenberg's poetry appeared in 1922; his
Collected Works was published in 1937.

BREAK OF DAY IN THE TRENCHES

The darkness crumbles away.
It is the same old druid Time as ever,
Only a live thing leaps my hand,
A queer sardonic rat,
As I pull the parapet's poppy
To stick behind my ear.
Droll rat, they would shoot you if they knew
Your cosmopolitan sympathies.
Now you have touched this English hand
You will do the same to a German
Soon, no doubt, if it be your pleasure
To cross the sleeping green between.
It seems you inwardly grin as you pass
Strong eyes, fine limbs, haughty athletes,
Less chanced than you for life,
Bonds to the whims of murder,
Sprawled in the bowels of the earth,
The torn fields of France.
What do you see in our eyes
At the shrieking iron and flame
Hurled through still heavens?
What quaver—what heart aghast?

Poppies whose roots are in man's veins
Drop, and are ever dropping;
But mine in my ear is safe—
Just a little white with the dust.

                                                                        [1916]

FRANCIS LEDWIDGE

Ireland 1891–1917

One of eight children, Ledwidge was born in Slane, County Meath, and left school at fourteen to
work at various odd jobs. His first poem appeared in the newspaper the *Drogheda Independent*
in 1910. Encouraged by Lord Dunsany, an established writer, Ledwidge assembled his first book
of poems, *Songs of the Field* (1916). Disappointed in love, he joined the British Army in 1914,
and was killed by a shell at a battle near Ypres in July 1917. His second volume, *Last Songs*
(ed. Dunsany) was published in 1918; *The Complete Poems of Francis Ledwidge* appeared in 1919.

TO ONE DEAD

A BLACKBIRD singing
On a moss upholstered stone,
Bluebells swinging,
Shadows wildly blown,
A song in the wood,
A ship on the sea.
The song was for you
And the ship was for me.

A blackbird singing
I hear in my troubled mind,
Bluebells swinging
I see in a distant wind.
But sorrow and silence
Are the wood's threnody,
The silence for you
And the sorrow for me.

                                                                        [c. 1917]

HUGH MACDIARMID/CHRISTOPHER MURRAY GRIEVE

Scotland 1892-1978

Poet, critic, political activist, and leader in the Scots literary renaissance, MacDiarmid determined to recover many of the Scottish principles of poetry and thought that had been overwhelmed by the prestige accorded to English language and culture. He advanced the vernacular cause by making his own language, developing what is called Synthetic Scots, a blending of various dialects, oral traditions, and etymological resources. In *A Drunk Man Looks at the Thistle*, the inebriated comic exuberance of the poem's protagonist gives way to a genuine and complex nationalism, a discovery central to much of MacDiarmid's work available in the *Complete Poems 1920–1976* (1978).

from A DRUNK MAN LOOKS AT THE THISTLE

I amna fou sae muckle as tired—deid dune.	*drunk as much; exhausted*
It's gey and hard wark coupan gless for gless	*very; upending*
Wi Cruivie and Gilsanquhar and the like,	*With*
And I'm no juist as bauld as aince I wes.	*not; once*
The elbuck fankles in the course o time,	*elbow becomes clumsy*
The sheckle's no sae souple, and the thrapple	*wrist; not; gullet*
Grows deif and dour: nae langer up and doun	*unimpressionable; stiff*
Gleg as a squirrel speils the Adam's apple.	*Lively; climbs*
Forbye, the stuffie's no the real Mackay.	*Besides*
The sun's sel aince, as sune as ye began it,	*self once*
Riz in your vera saul; but what keeks in	*Rose; very soul; peeks*
Nou is in truth the vilest 'saxpenny planet.'	*(i.e., worthless trash)*
And as the worth's gane doun the cost has risen.	*gone*
Yin canna thow the cockles o yin's hert	*One cannot*
Wiout haean cauld feet nou, jalousan what	*Without having; suspecting*
The wife'll say (I dinna blame her fur't).	*don't; for it*
It's robban Peter to pey Paul at least. . . .	
And aa that's Scotch about it is the name,	*all*
Like aathing else caad Scottish nouadays	*everything; called*
—Aa destitute o speerit juist the same.	*All; of*
(To prove my saul is Scots I maun begin	*must*
Wi what's still deemed Scots and the folk expect,	*With*
And spire up syne by visible degrees	*soar; then*
To heichts whauro the fules hae never recked.	*whereof; have never reckoned*

But aince I get them there I'll whummle them   *overturn*
And souse the craturs in the nether deeps,   *creatures*
—For it's nae choice, and ony man sud wish   *should*
To dree the goat's weird tae as weel's the sheep's!)   *endure; fate too; well as*

Heifetz in tartan, and Sir Harry Lauder!
Whaur's Isadora Duncan dancean nou?
Is Mary Garden in Chicago still
And Duncan Grant in Paris—and me fou?   *drunk*

Sic transit gloria Scotia—aa the flouers   *all*
O the Forest are wede awa. (A blind bird's nest   *Of; vanished*
Is aiblins biggan in the thistle tho? . . .   *perhaps building; however*
And better blind if'ts brood is like the rest!)

You canna gang to a Burns supper even   *go*
Wiout some wizened scrunt o a knock-knee   *Without; mite*
Chinee turns round to say 'Him Haggis—velly goot!'
And ten to wan the piper is a Cockney.   *one*

No wan in fifty kens a wurd Burns wrote   *Not one; knows*
But misapplied is aabody's property,   *everybody's*
And gin there was his like alive the day   *if; today*
They'd be the last a kennan haund to gie—   *knowing hand; give*

Croose London Scotties wi their braw shirt fronts   *Conceited; with; handsome*
And aa their fancy freinds, rejoicean   *all*
That similah gatherings in Timbuctoo,
Bagdad—and Hell, nae dout—are voicean

Burns' sentiments o universal love,   *of*
In pidgin English or in wild-fowl Scots,
And toastan ane wha's nocht to them but an   *is nothing*
Excuse for faitherin Genius wi *their* thochts.   *with*

Aa *they've* to say was aften said afore   *All*
A lad was born in Kyle to blaw about.   *blow (brag)*
What unco fate maks *him* the dumpan-grund   *strange*
For aa the sloppy rubbish they jaw out?   *all; splash*

Mair nonsense has been uttered in his name
Than in ony's barran liberty and Christ.   *barring*
If this keeps spreidan as the drink declines,   *spreading*
Syne turns to tea, wae's me for the *Zeitgeist*!   *Then; woe is*

Rabbie, wadst thou wert here—the warld hath need, *Robbie [Burns]*
And Scotland mair sae, o the likes o thee!
The whisky that aince moved your lyre's become *once; has become*
A laxative for aa loquacity. *all*

O gin they'd stegh their guts and haud their wheesht *if; stuff; be quiet*
I'd thole it, for 'a man's a man,' I ken, *endure; know*
But tho the feck hae plenty o the 'aa that,' *majority have; all*
They're nocht but zoologically men.

I'm haveran, Rabbie, but ye understaund *rambling*
It gets my dander up to see your star
A bauble in Babel, banged like a saxpence
'Twixt Burbank's Baedeker and Bleistein's cigar.

There's nane sae ignorant but think they can
Expatiate on *you*, if on nae ither.
The sumphs hae taen you at your wurd, and, fegs! *fools; taken; faith*
The foziest o them claims to be a—Brither! *most stupid of*

Syne 'Here's the cheenge'—the star o Rabbie Burns. *Then; change (from the 6d)*
Smaa cheenge, 'Twinkle, Twinkle.' The memory slips *Small change*
As G.K. Chesterton heaves up to gie *give*
'The Immortal Memory' in a huge eclipse,

Or somebody else as famous if less fat.
You left the like in Embro in a scunner *Edinburgh in disgust*
To booze wi thieveless cronies sic as me. *powerless*
I'se warrant you'd shy clear o aa the hunner *I'll; all; hundred*

Odd Burns Clubs tae, or ninety-nine o them, *too*
And haud your birthday in a different kip *hold; house of ill-fame*
Whaur your name isna taen in vain—as Christ *taken*
Gied aa Jerusalem's Pharisees the slip, *Gave all*

—Christ wha'd hae been Chief Rabbi gin he'd liked— *would have; it*
Wi publicans and sinners, to foregather, *With; meet*
But losh! the publicans nou are Pharisees, *(exclamation of wonder)*
And I'm no shair o maist the sinners either. *not sure*

But that's aside the point! I've got fair waunert. *become very confused*
It's no that I'm sae fou as juist deid dune, *drunk*
And dinna ken as muckle's whaur I am *know as much as*
Or hou I've come to sprawl here neth the mune.

That's it! It isna me that's fou at aa,   *all*
But the fou mune, the doited jade, that's led   *full; foolish*
Me fer agley, or mogrified the warld.   *far astray*
—For aa I ken I'm safe in my ain bed.   *all; know; own*

Jean! Jean! Gin she's no here it's no *our* bed,
Or else I'm dreaman deep and canna wauken,
But it's a fell queer dream if this is no   *exceedingly*
A real hillside—and thae things thistles and bracken! *these*

It's hard wark haudin by a thocht worth haein   *holding onto; having*
And harder speakin't, and no for ilka man;   *every*
Maist Thocht's like whisky—a thousand under proof,
And a sair price is pitten on't even than.   *expensive (lit., sore); put; then*

As Kirks wi Christianity hae dune,
Burns Clubs wi Burns—wi aathing it's the same,   *everything*
The core o ocht is only for the few,   *aught*
Scorned by the mony, thrang wi'ts empty name.   *busy*

And aa the names in History mean nocht
To maist folk but 'ideas o their ain,'   *own*
The vera opposite o onything   *very*
The Deid wad awn gin they cam back again.   *own (acknowledge)*

A greater Christ, a greater Burns, may come.
The maist they'll dae is to gie bigger pegs   *give*
To folly and conceit to hank their rubbish on.   *fasten*
They'll cheenge folks' talk but no their natures, fegs!

I maun feed frae the common trough anaa   *as well*
Whaur aa the lees o hope are jumbled up;
While centuries like pigs are slorpan owre't   *guzzling, slobbering over it*
Sall my wee hour be cryan: 'Let pass this cup?'

In wi your gruntle then, puir wheengean saul,   *snout; poor complaining soul*
Lap up the ugsome aidle wi the lave,   *repulsive slop; everyone else*
What gin it's your ain vomit that you swill   *own*
And frae Life's gantan and unfaddomed grave?   *yawning*

I dout I'm geylies mixed, like Life itsel,   *suspect; very much*
But I was never ane that thocht to pit
An ocean in a mutchkin. As the haill's   *half-bottle; whole is*
Mair than the pairt sae I than reason yet.

I dinna haud the warld's end in my heid   *do not hold*
As maist folk think they dae; nor filter truth
In fishy gills through which its tides may pour
For ony *animalculae* forsooth.   *For [the purpose of removing]*

I lauch to see my crazy little brain
—And ither folks'—takan itsel seriously,
And in a sudden lowe o fun my saul   *flame*
Blinks dozent as the owl I ken't to be.   *stupid; know it*

I'll hae nae hauf-way house, but aye be whaur   *half-; always*
Extremes meet—it's the only way I ken
To dodge the curst conceit o bein richt
That damns the vast majority o men.   [1926]

VERA BRITTAIN

England 1893-1970

Brittain wrote 'To My Brother' four days before Captain E.H. Brittain was killed in action in the Austrian offensive on the Italian Front, 15 June 1918. Brittain was also a novelist and biographer: her best-known book is the first of her three-part autobiography, *Testament of Youth* (1933). She was born in Newcastle under Lyme and left Somerville College, Oxford, in 1915 to become a nurse after her fiancé was killed in the War. Brittain's feminist commitments emerge in her autobiography as well as in her novels and other books, including *Lady into Woman: A History of Women from Victoria to Elizabeth II* (1953). Her *Poems of the War and After* was published in 1934.

To My Brother

(In Memory of July 1st, 1916)

Your battle-wounds are scars upon my heart,
    Received when in that grand and tragic 'show'
You played your part
    Two years ago,

And silver in the summer morning sun
    I see the symbol of your courage glow—
That Cross you won
    Two years ago.

Though now again you watch the shrapnel fly,
    And hear the guns that daily louder grow,
As in July
    Two years ago,

May you endure to lead the Last Advance
  And with your men pursue the flying foe
As once in France
  Two years ago.   [1934]

SYLVIA TOWNSEND WARNER

England 1893–1978

Warner began her career as a musicologist, one of the editors of the scholarly ten-volume survey *Tudor Church Music*. Educated at home, her individualism finds expression in a generous scepticism, an idiosyncratic 'auditory rhetoric', and a tendency to examine 'my kingdom from below' ('Gloriana Dying'). In the 1959 Peter le Neve Foster Lecture delivered to the Royal Society, she describes the woman writer's entrance into the world of literature as quick, sly, and ad hoc: the 'pantry window' entrance of the 'amateur' rather than the established 'Tradesman's Door'. These conditions account for the fact that women as writers 'seem to be remarkably adept at vanishing out of their own writing so that the quality of immediacy replaces them'. Though Warner's last conventional collection of poems appeared in 1928 with *Time Importuned*, her unpublished and uncollected work has been gathered by Claire Harman in *Collected Poems* (1982).

HONEY FOR TEA

I've sat in the sun
From three to five
Watching the bees
About the hive.
They are horribly alive!

From white to red,
From red to white,
They weave Euclidean
Tangles of flight,
And nowhere find delight:

But them a maniac
Industry eggs
Onward; they grapple
With hairy legs,
Methodical to the dregs.

The blossom rifled,
With laden thighs
Further each willing
Eunuch plies:
A dull way to fertilize.

And back to their cells
They come at last;
Armed, incurious,
Sailing past
Me where I sit aghast.

Oh, horrible
That aught can be
So sufficient, yet
So unlike me!
I shall go in to tea.

There in the parlour
I shall find
Things to restore
My peace of mind;
By man for man designed.

The rat-tail spoons,
The china dishes,
Smooth as sequined
Sides of fishes,
Obedient to my wishes;

The sturdy table
So plain and whole,
The meek sweet
Of the sugar-bowl;
These shall confirm my soul

Till I, emboldened,
Lift down from the shelf
The hoarded treasure,
Taken by stealth
From that inimical Commonwealth.   [1925]

e.e. cummings

USA 1894–1962

During his education at Harvard, cummings became fascinated with the verbal and visual experimentation of Modernist writers and artists. With iconoclasm and satire his inventive and playful uses of language reflect as well as challenge the American myth of individual freedom of thought and expression. The diversity of cummings's innovations is well represented in his *Complete Poems* (1972).

[THE CAMBRIDGE LADIES WHO LIVE IN FURNISHED SOULS]

the Cambridge ladies who live in furnished souls
are unbeautiful and have comfortable minds
(also,with the church's protestant blessings
daughters,unscented shapeless spirited)
they believe in Christ and Longfellow,both dead,
are invariably interested in so many things—
at the present writing one still finds
delighted fingers knitting for the is it Poles?
perhaps. While permanent faces coyly bandy
scandal of Mrs N and Professor D
. . . . the Cambridge ladies do not care,above
Cambridge if sometimes in its box of
sky lavender and cornerless,the
moon rattles like a fragment of angry candy   [1923]

[SOMEWHERE I HAVE NEVER TRAVELLED,GLADLY BEYOND]

somewhere i have never travelled,gladly beyond
any experience,your eyes have their silence:
in your most frail gesture are things which enclose me,
or which i cannot touch because they are too near

your slightest look easily will unclose me
though i have closed myself as fingers,
you open always petal by petal myself as Spring opens
(touching skilfully,mysteriously)her first rose

or if your wish be to close me,i and
my life will shut very beautifully,suddenly,
as when the heart of this flower imagines
the snow carefully everywhere descending;

nothing which we are to perceive in this world equals
the power of your intense fragility:whose texture
compels me with the colour of its countries,
rendering death and forever with each breathing

(i do not know what it is about you that closes
and opens;only something in me understands
the voice of your eyes is deeper than all roses)
nobody,not even the rain,has such small hands   [1931]

LOUISE BOGAN

USA 1897–1970

Bogan was born in Maine and grew up in New England, attending Boston University. She was for
over thirty years the main poetry reviewer for *The New Yorker* and a practising critic, publishing the
study *Achievement in American Poetry, 1900–1950* (1951). Some regard Bogan's poetry as austere and
highly formalist, suffering from what has been called a 'remote fastidiousness and relentless intel-
lectuality'; her lyrics are precise and controlled and can impart a clear and calm assessment
of gender. Her first book, *Body of This Death* (1923) was followed by *Dark Summer* (1929) and *Sleep-
ing Fury* (1937). The major collection is *The Blue Estuaries: Poems, 1923–1968* (1968, rep. 1977).

WOMEN

Women have no wilderness in them,
They are provident instead,
Content in the tight hot cell of their hearts
To eat dusty bread.

They do not see cattle cropping red winter grass,
They do not hear
Snow water going down under culverts
Shallow and clear.

They wait, when they should turn to journeys,
They stiffen, when they should bend.
They use against themselves that benevolence
To which no man is friend.

They cannot think of so many crops to a field
Or of clean wood cleft by an axe.
Their love is an eager meaninglessness
Too tense, or too lax.

They hear in every whisper that speaks to them
A shout and a cry.
As like as not, when they take life over their door-sills
They should let it go by.   [1922]

HART CRANE

USA 1899–1932

Except for two years spent in New York after his parents' divorce in 1916, Crane lived in Ohio until 1923. By the time he moved to New York, he had written several early poems, and was working on 'Voyages', a sequence of six love poems about his affair with a sailor. After completing 'Voyages' in 1924 and publishing a first collection of verse, *White Buildings* (1926), Crane composed an epic work on the myth of America, *The Bridge* (1930), for which he received a *Poetry* magazine award and a Guggenheim Fellowship. Crane moved to Mexico where he worked on a poem about Montezuma; his life ended in despair at age 33 when he committed suicide by jumping from a ship during his return voyage to New York. *The Collected Poems of Hart Crane* was published post-humously in 1933.

BLACK TAMBOURINE

The interests of a black man in a cellar
Mark tardy judgment on the world's closed door.
Gnats toss in the shadow of a bottle,
And a roach spans a crevice in the floor.

Æsop, driven to pondering, found
Heaven with the tortoise and the hare;
Fox brush and sow ear top his grave
And mingling incantations on the air.

The black man, forlorn in the cellar,
Wanders in some mid-kingdom, dark, that lies,
Between his tambourine, stuck on the wall,
And, in Africa, a carcass quick with flies.   [1926]

from VOYAGES

III

Infinite consanguinity it bears—
This tendered theme of you that light
Retrieves from sea plains where the sky
Resigns a breast that every wave enthrones;
While ribboned water lanes I wind
Are laved and scattered with no stroke
Wide from your side, whereto this hour
The sea lifts, also, reliquary hands.

And so, admitted through black swollen gates
That must arrest all distance otherwise,—
Past whirling pillars and lithe pediments,
Light wrestling there incessantly with light,

Star kissing star through wave on wave unto
Your body rocking!
           and where death, if shed,
Presumes no carnage, but this single change,—
Upon the steep floor flung from dawn to dawn
The silken skilled transmemberment of song;

Permit me voyage, love, into your hands . . . |1927|

ROLLA LYNN RIGGS

Cherokee 1899–1954

After graduating from high school in Claremore, Oklahoma in 1917, Riggs worked as a journalist in New York and Los Angeles and wrote poetry for prominent literary magazines such as *Poetry*, *The Nation*, and *New Republic*. Much of his poetry was collected in *The Iron Dish* (1930). Awarded a Guggenheim Fellowship for his promise as a playwright in the late 1920s, he travelled to Paris where he wrote the successful Broadway play, *Green Grow the Lilacs* (1931), later adapted in collaboration with Richard Rogers and Oscar Hammerstein into the highly popular Broadway musical, *Oklahoma!* (1943). Riggs's poetry, plays, and songs are witty and evocative, if often nostalgic, reminiscences of the small towns, farms, and landscapes he had known in his youth.

SHADOW ON SNOW

I, a shadow, thinking as I go,
Feel the need of a mimicry
To say this in music: how the moon is one
With the snow, and the snow warmer than I shall ever be—
I, a shadow, moving across the snow.

There shall be no more shadows after mine shall go
Hissing over ice, cracking the black river glass.
There shall be still a moon, but never a sun,
Never an earth again with its triumphing grass—
Only the moon and the snow.   [1930]

F.R. SCOTT

Canada 1899-1985

Scott pursued his passionate commitments to Canadian culture and politics through related careers as professor of law, poet, and political thinker. He contributed significantly to the founding of the CCF (the Co-operative Commonwealth Foundation), which later became the NDP (New Democratic Party). At Oxford as a Rhodes Scholar, Scott returned to Canada in 1923 and studied law at McGill, where, with A.J.M. Smith, he established the *McGill Fortnightly Review* and published his first poems in it. Influenced by Eliot and Pound as well as by A.J.M. Smith, Scott was one of Canada's first Modernist poets, and through his editing of important anthologies like *New Provinces: Poems of Several Authors* (1936), he played a major role in the evolution of Canadian poetry. His *Collected Poems of F.R. Scott* (ed. Newlove, 1981) won a Governor-General's Award.

LAURENTIAN SHIELD

Hidden in wonder and snow, or sudden with summer,
This land stares at the sun in a huge silence
Endlessly repeating something we cannot hear.
Inarticulate, arctic,
Not written on by history, empty as paper,
It leans away from the world with songs in its lakes
Older than love, and lost in the miles.

This waiting is wanting.
It will choose its language
When it has chosen its technic,
A tongue to shape the vowels of its productivity.

A language of flesh and of roses.

Now there are pre-words,
Cabin syllables,
Nouns of settlement
Slowly forming, with steel syntax,
The long sentence of its exploitation.

The first cry was the hunter, hungry for fur,
And the digger for gold, nomad, no-man, a particle;
Then the bold commands of monopoly, big with machines,
Carving its kingdoms out of the public wealth;
And now the drone of the plane, scouting the ice,
Fills all the emptiness with neighbourhood
And links our future over the vanished pole.

But a deeper note is sounding, heard in the mines,
The scattered camps and the mills, a language of life,
And what will be written in the full culture of occupation
Will come, presently, tomorrow,
From millions whose hands can turn this rock into children.   [1954]

ERNEST G. MOLL

Australia 1900–1979

Born in Murtoo, Victoria, and raised on the family farm, reminiscences of which he offers in *Below These Hills: The Story of a Riverina Farm* (1957), Moll was educated in New South Wales schools and at Harvard. He was a professor of English at the University of Oregon from 1928 to 1966, but retained his Australian citizenship, visiting frequently and publishing his poetry there. Among Moll's many books of poetry dealing with rural and regional experience in Australia are *Poems 1940–1955* (1957), *The Rainbow Serpent* (1962), *Biseis* (1965), and *The Road to Cactusland* (1972).

A GNARLED RIVERINA GUM-TREE

Knob and hump upon this tree
And the humpy things in me
Have a greeting for each other
And a word I think is 'brother'.

Straighter trees there are that shake
The very heavens wide awake,
And straighter souls, yes, many a one,
Than mine keep threatening the sun.

They speed on without a word
Or the brief rapture of a bird,
Fearful lest the sky might shut
Like iron doors above them. But

I the man and this wried wood,
Hump to hump, as old friends should,
Squat and talk and watch them run
Stretched up thin to catch the sun.   [1940]

SIX NATIONS COUNCIL, IROQUOIS CONFEDERACY

Canada/America

The traditional history of the Confederacy of the Six Nations was translated and transcribed from dictation by the elder ceremonial chiefs of the Iroquois peoples: Peter Powless (Mohawk), Nicodemus Porter (Oneida), William Wage and Abram Charles (Cayugas), John A. Gibson (Seneca), Thomas William Echo (Onondaga), and Josiah Hill (Tuscarora). Chiefs Josiah Hill and J.W.M. Elliot composed the typescript of the document approved by the Six Nations Council on 3 July 1900 at Ohsweken. Their Preface states: 'For several hundred years the Five Nations (since 1715 called the Six Nations) have existed without a written history chronicled by themselves, of their ancient customs, rites and ceremonies, and the formation of the Iroquois League. Books have been written by white men in the past, but these have been found to be too voluminous and inaccurate in some instances. . . . [The] League . . . as constituted centuries ago by Dekanahwideh and his associates, has been maintained in accordance with the rules of the Confederacy as laid down by the founder of the League; and . . . the installation of the Lords or Chiefs as rulers of the people, laid down in these unwritten rules hundreds of years ago, is still strictly observed and adhered to by the Chiefs of the Six Nations and people.' The text of the ritual condolence ceremonies performed on the occasion of a lord's death affords us a means of recollecting people's wisdom and rights.

CONDOLENCE CEREMONY

(1) Now hear us our Uncles, we have come to condole with you in your great bereavement.

We have now met in dark sorrow to lament together over the death of our brother Lord. For such has been your loss. We will sit together in our grief and mingle our tears together, and we four brothers will wipe off the tears from your eyes, so that for a day period you might have peace of mind. This we say and do, we four brothers.

(2) Now hear us again, for when a person is in great grief caused by death, his ears are closed up and he cannot hear, and such is your condition now.

We will therefore remove the obstruction (grief) from your ears, so that for a day period you may have perfect hearing again. This we say and do, we four brothers.

(3) Continue to hear the expression of us four brothers, for when a person is in great sorrow his throat is stopped with grief and such is your case now. We will therefore remove the obstruction (grief) so that for a day period you may enjoy perfect breathing and speech. This we say and do, we four brothers.

The foregoing part of the Condolence Ceremony is to be performed outside of the place of meeting.

Then the bereaved will appoint two of their Chief Warriors to conduct the four brothers into the place of meeting.

(4) Continue to hear the expression of us four brothers, for when a person is in great grief caused by death, he appears to be deformed, so that our forefathers have made a form which their children may use in condoling with each other (Ja-weh-ka-ho-denh) which is that they will treat him a dose of soft drink (medicine) and which when it is taken and settled down in the stomach it will pervade the whole body and strengthen him and restore him to a perfect form of man. This we say and do, we four brothers.

(5) Continue to hear the expression of us four brothers.

Now when a person is brought to grief by death, such person's seat or bed seems stained with human blood, such is now your case. We therefore wipe off those stains with soft linen, so that your seat and bed may be clean and so that you may enjoy peace for a day, for we may scarcely have taken our seats before we shall be surprised to hear of another death. This we say and do, we four brothers.

(6) Continue to hear the expression of us four brothers. When a person is brought to grief through death, he is confined in the darkness of deep sorrow, and such is now the case of you three brothers. This we say and do, we four brothers.

(7) When a person is brought to grief by death, he seems to lose sight of the sky (blinded with grief) and he is crushed with sorrow. We therefore remove the mist from your eyes, so that the sky may be clear to you. This we say and do, we four brothers.

(8) When a person is brought to grief by death, he seems to lose the light of the sun, this is now your case. We therefore remove the mist so that you may see the sun rising over the trees or forest in the East, and watch its course and when it arrives in mid-sky it will shed forth its rays around you, and you shall begin to see your duties and perform the same as usual. This we say and do, we four brothers.

(9) Now when the remains are laid and cause the mound of clay (grave) we till the ground and place some nice grass over it and place a nice slab over it, so that his body (that of the dead Lord) may quietly lie in his resting place, and be protected from the heavy wind and great rain storms. This we say and do, we four brothers.

(10) Now continue to listen, for when a person is brought to grief, and such is your condition, the sticks of wood from your fire are scattered, caused by death, so we, the four brothers, will gather up the sticks of wood and rekindle the fire, and the smoke shall rise and pierce the sky, so that all the Nations of the Confederacy may see the smoke, and when a person is in great grief caused by the death of some of our rulers the head is bowed down in deep sorrow. We therefore cause you to stand up again, our uncles, and surround the Council fire again and resume your duties. This we say and do, we four brothers.

(11) Continue to listen, for when the Great Spirit created us, he created a woman as the help-mate of man, and when she is called away by death it is grievously hard, for had she been allowed to live she might have raised a family to inhabit the earth, and so we four brothers raise the woman again (to

encourage and cheer up their down-cast spirits) so that you may cheerfully enjoy peace and happiness for a day. This we say and do, we four brothers.

(12) Now my uncle Lords you have two relations, a nephew and a niece. They are watching your course. Your niece may see that you are making a mis-step and taking a course whereby your children may suffer ruin or a calamity, or it may be your nephew who will see your evil course and never bear to listen when the woman or Warrior will approach you and remind you of your duties, and ask you to come back and carry out your obligations as a Royaner (or Lord) of the Band. This we say and do, we four brothers.

(13) They say that it is hard for any one to allow his mind to be troubled too greatly with sorrow. Never allow yourself to be led to think of destroying yourself by committing suicide, for all things in this world are only vanity. Now we place in your midst a torch. We all have an equal share in the said light, and we would now call all the Ro-de-ya-ner-sonh (Lords) to their places and each perform the duties conferred upon each of them. This we say and do, we four brothers.

Now we return to you the Wampum which we received from you when you suffered the loss by death. We will therefore now conclude our discourse. Now point out to me the man whom I am to proclaim as Chief in place of the deceased.   [1900]

from THE CEREMONY CALLED 'AT THE WOOD'S EDGE'

1. Now to-day I have been greatly startled by your voice coming through the forest to this opening. You have come with troubled mind through all obstacles. You kept seeing the places where they met on whom we depended, my offspring. How then can your mind be at ease? You kept seeing the foot-marks of our forefathers; and all but perceptible is the smoke where they used to smoke the pipe together. Can then your mind be at ease when you are weeping on your way?

2. Great thanks now, therefore, that you have safely arrived. Now, then, let us smoke the pipe together. Because all around are hostile agencies which are each thinking, 'I will frustrate their purpose.' Here thorny ways, and here falling trees, and here wild beasts lying in ambush.

Either by these you might have perished, my offspring, or, here by floods you might have been destroyed, my offspring, or by the uplifted hatchet in the dark outside the house. Every day these are wasting us; or deadly invisible disease might have destroyed you, my offspring.

3. Great thanks now, therefore, that in safety you have come through the forest. Because lamentable would have been the consequences had you perished by the way, and the startling word had come, 'Yonder are lying bodies, yea, and of Chiefs!' And they would have thought in dismay, what had happened, my offspring.

4. Our forefathers made the rule, and said, 'Here they are to kindle a fire; here, at the edge of the woods, they are to condole with each other in few words.' But they have referred thither (that is to the Council House) all

business to be duly completed, as well as for the mutual embrace of condolence. And they said, 'Thither shall they be led by the hand, and shall be placed on the principal seat.'

. . .

9. . . . Then one will say, 'My offspring, now this day we are met together. God has appointed this day. Now, today, we are met together, on account of the solemn event which has befallen you. Now into the earth he has been conveyed to whom we have been wont to look. Yea, therefore, in tears let us smoke together.

10. 'Now, then, we say, we wipe away the tears, so that in peace you may look about you.

11. 'And, further, we suppose there is an obstruction in your ears. Now, then, we remove the obstruction carefully from your hearing, so that we trust you will easily hear the words spoken.

12. 'And also we imagine there is an obstruction in your throat. Now, therefore, we say, we remove the obstruction, so that you may speak freely in our mutual greetings.

13. 'Now again another thing, my offspring. I have spoken of the solemn event which has befallen you. Every day you are losing your great men. They are being borne into the earth; also the warriors and also your women, and also your grandchildren; so that in the midst of blood you are sitting.

14. 'Now, therefore, we say, we wash off the blood marks from your seat, so that it may be for a time that happily the place will be clean where you are seated and looking around you.'

15. Now the Hymn, called 'Hail'.
I come to greet and thank my uncles.
I come again to greet and thank the league;
I come again to greet and thank the kindred;
I come again to greet and thank the Warriors;
I come again to greet and thank the women;
My forefathers—what they established,—
My forefathers,—hearken to them.

16. The last verse is sung yet again, while he walks to and fro in the house, and says:

17. 'Hail my grandsires! Now hearken while your grandchildren cry mournfully to you—because the Great League which you established has grown old. We hope that they may hear.

18. 'Hail my grandsires! You have said that sad will be the fate of those who come in the latter times.

19. 'Oh, my grandsires! Even now I may have failed to perform this ceremony in the order in which they were wont to perform it.'

20. 'Oh, my grandsires! Even now that has become old which you established,—the Great League. You have it as a pillow under your heads in the ground where you are lying,—this Great League which you established; although you said that far away in the future the Great League would endure.'

21. So much is to be said here, and the Hymn is to be sung again, and then he is to go on and walk up and down in the house again, saying as follows:

22. 'Hail, my grandsires! Now hear, therefore, what they did—all the rules they decided on, which they thought would strengthen the House, Hail, my grandsires! This they said; now we have finished; we have performed the rites; we have put on the horns;

23. 'Now again another thing they considered and this they said: "Perhaps this will happen. Scarcely shall we have arrived at home when a loss will occur again." They said, "This, then shall be done, as soon as he is dead, even then the horns shall be taken off. For if invested with horns he should be borne into the grave, O my grandsires, they said, "we should perhaps all perish if invested with horns he is conveyed to the grave."

24. 'Then again another thing they determined, O my grandsires! This they said, "will strengthen the House." They said if any one should be murdered and (the body) be hidden away among fallen trees by reason of the neck being white, then you have said, this shall be done, we will place it by the wall in the shade.

25. 'Now again you considered and you said: It is perhaps not well that we leave this here, lest it should be seen by our grandchildren; for they are troublesome, prying into every crevice. People will be startled at their returning in consternation, and will ask what has happened that this (corpse) is lying here; because they will keep on asking until they find it out. And they will at once be disturbed in mind, and that again will cause us trouble.

26. 'Now again they decided and said: This shall be done, we will pull up a pine tree—a lofty tree—and will make a hole through the earth crust, and will drop this thing into a swift current which will carry it out of sight, and then never will our grandchildren see it again.

27. 'Now again another thing they decided, and thought, this will strengthen the House. They said: "Now we have finished; we have performed the rites. Perhaps presently it will happen, that a loss will occur amongst us. Then this shall be done. We will suspend a pouch upon a pole, and will place in it some mourning wampum—some short strings—to be taken to the place where the loss was suffered. The bearer will enter, and will stand by the hearth, and will speak a few words to comfort those who will be mourning; and then they will be comforted, and will conform to the law.

28. 'Now then, thou wert the principal of this confederacy, De-ka-na-wi-dah, with the joint principal, his son, O-dah-tshe-deh; and then again his uncle, Tha-do-dah-ho; and also again his son, Ha-ka-hen-yonh, and again his uncle, Ska-nya-da-ri-yoh; and then again his cousin, Sha-de-ka-ron-yes; and then in later times additions were made to the great edifice' (or long House).

29. Now listen, ye who established the Great League of Peace. Now it has become old. Now there is nothing but wilderness. Ye are in your graves who established it. Ye have taken it with you and have placed it under you, and there is nothing left but a desert. There ye have taken your intellects with you. What ye established ye have taken with you. Ye have placed under your heads what ye established—the Great League.   [1900]

KENNETH SLESSOR

Australia 1901-1971

Slessor was a journalist and poet who served as an editor, writer, and reviewer for several major Sydney newspapers. His masterpiece is 'Five Bells'. Although almost no subsequent poetry is extant, between 1924 and 1939 Slessor published seven highly original collections of elaborately sensual and existential poetry dealing with mutability, nothingness, and death: 'the flukes of thought/Anchored in Time'. Most of his work is contained in the volume *One Hundred Poems 1919–1939* (1944; reissued, with two additional pieces, as *Poems* in 1957).

FIVE BELLS

Time that is moved by little fidget wheels
Is not my Time, the flood that does not flow.
Between the double and the single bell
Of a ship's hour, between a round of bells
From the dark warship riding there below,
I have lived many lives, and this one life
Of Joe, long dead, who lives between five bells.

Deep and dissolving verticals of light
Ferry the falls of moonshine down. Five bells
Coldly rung out in a machine's voice. Night and water
Pour to one rip of darkness, the Harbour floats
In air, the Cross hangs upside-down in water.

Why do I think of you, dead man, why thieve
These profitless lodgings from the flukes of thought
Anchored in Time? You have gone from earth,
Gone even from the meaning of a name;
Yet something's there, yet something forms its lips
And hits and cries against the ports of space,
Beating their sides to make its fury heard.

Are you shouting at me, dead man, squeezing your face
In agonies of speech on speechless panes?
Cry louder, beat the windows, bawl your name!

But I hear nothing, nothing . . . only bells,
Five bells, the bumpkin calculus of Time.
Your echoes die, your voice is dowsed by Life,
There's not a mouth can fly the pygmy strait—
Nothing except the memory of some bones
Long shoved away, and sucked away, in mud;
And unimportant things you might have done,

Or once I thought you did; but you forgot,
And all have now forgotten—looks and words
And slops of beer; your coat with buttons off,
Your gaunt chin and pricked eye, and raging tales
Of Irish kings and English perfidy,
And dirtier perfidy of publicans
Groaning to God from Darlinghurst.

Five bells.

Then I saw the road, I heard the thunder
Tumble, and felt the talons of the rain
The night we came to Moorebank in slab-dark,
So dark you bore no body, had no face,
But a sheer voice that rattled out of air
(As now you'd cry if I could break the glass),
A voice that spoke beside me in the bush,
Loud for a breath or bitten off by wind,
Of Milton, melons, and the Rights of Man,
And blowing flutes, and how Tahitian girls
Are brown and angry-tongued, and Sydney girls
Are white and angry-tongued, or so you'd found.
But all I heard was words that didn't join
So Milton became melons, melons girls,
And fifty mouths, it seemed, were out that night,
And in each tree an Ear was bending down,
Or something had just run, gone behind grass,
When, blank and bone-white, like a maniac's thought,
The naphtha-flash of lightning slit the sky,
Knifing the dark with deathly photographs.
There's not so many with so poor a purse
Or fierce a need, must fare by night like that,
Five miles in darkness on a country track,
But when you do, that's what you think.

Five bells.

In Melbourne, your appetite had gone,
Your angers too; they had been leeched away
By the soft archery of summer rains
And the sponge-paws of wetness, the slow damp
That stuck the leaves of living, snailed the mind,
And showed your bones, that had been sharp with rage,
The sodden ecstasies of rectitude.
I thought of what you'd written in faint ink,
Your journal with the sawn-off lock, that stayed behind
With other things you left, all without use,
All without meaning now, except a sign

That someone had been living who now was dead:
'At Labassa. Room 6 x 8
On top of the tower; because of this, very dark
And cold in winter. Everything has been stowed
Into this room—500 books all shapes
And colours, dealt across the floor
And over sills and on the laps of chairs;
Guns, photoes of many differant things
And differant curioes that I obtained . . .'

In Sydney, by the spent aquarium-flare
Of penny gaslight on pink wallpaper,
We argued about blowing up the world,
But you were living backward, so each night
You crept a moment closer to the breast,
And they were living, all of them, those frames
And shapes of flesh that had perplexed your youth,
And most your father, the old man gone blind,
With fingers always round a fiddle's neck,
That graveyard mason whose fair monuments
And tablets cut with dreams of piety
Rest on the bosoms of a thousand men
Staked bone by bone, in quiet astonishment
At cargoes they had never thought to bear,
These funeral-cakes of sweet and sculptured stone.

Where have you gone? The tide is over you,
The turn of midnight water's over you,
As Time is over you, and mystery,
And memory, the flood that does not flow.
You have no suburb, like those easier dead
In private berths of dissolution laid—
The tide goes over, the waves ride over you
And let their shadows down like shining hair,
But they are Water; and the sea-pinks bend
Like lilies in your teeth, but they are Weed;
And you are only part of an Idea.
I felt the wet push its black thumb-balls in,
The night you died, I felt your eardrums crack,
And the short agony, the longer dream,
The Nothing that was neither long nor short;
But I was bound, and could not go that way,
But I was blind, and could not feel your hand.
If I could find an answer, could only find
Your meaning, or could say why you were here
Who now are gone, what purpose gave you breath
Or seized it back, might I not hear your voice?

I looked out of my window in the dark
At waves with diamond quills and combs of light
That arched their mackerel-backs and smacked the sand
In the moon's drench, that straight enormous glaze,
And ships far off asleep, and Harbour-buoys
Tossing their fireballs wearily each to each,
And tried to hear your voice, but all I heard
Was a boat's whistle, and the scraping squeal
Of seabirds' voices far away, and bells,
Five bells. Five bells coldly ringing out.

Five bells.   [1939]

GWENDOLYN B. BENNETT

USA *1902–1981*

Born in Texas, the daughter of a lawyer and a teacher, Bennett studied visual arts at the Pratt Institute in Brooklyn and taught at Howard University. Bennett was associated with the Harlem Renaissance authors, and was a contributor to Black magazines such as *Fire!!*, *Opportunity*, *Crisis*, *Messenger*, and *Palms*.

HERITAGE

I want to see the slim palm trees,
Pulling at the clouds
With little pointed fingers . . .

I want to see lithe Negro girls,
Etched dark against the sky
While sunset lingers.

I want to hear the silent sands
Singing to the moon
Before the sphinx-still face . . .

I want to hear the chanting
Around a heathen fire
Of a strange black race.

I want to breathe the lotus flower,
Sighing to the stars
With tendrils drinking at the Nile . . .

I want to feel the surging
Of my sad people's soul
Hidden by a minstrel smile.

[1923]

KENNETH FEARING

USA 1902-1961

Fearing's comic cynicism in 'Cultural Notes', from his first collection of poetry entitled *Angel Arms* (1929), offers a sardonic view of relations between culture and society, art and politics. As a poet, novelist, and journalist who drew on many personal tragedies as well as his experiences of the Depression and World War II for his writing, Fearing wrote compassionately about people's disillusion in an increasingly urbanized, media-oriented world.

CULTURAL NOTES

Professor Burke's symphony, 'Colorado Vistas,'
In four movements,
I Mountains, II Canyons, III Dusk, IV Dawn,
Was played recently by the Philharmonic.
Snapshots of the localities described in music were passed around
    and the audience checked for accuracy.
All O.K.
After the performance Maurice Epstein, 29, tuberculosis, stoker
    on the *S.S. Tarboy*, rose to his feet and shouted,
'He's crazy, them artists are all crazy,
I can prove it by Max Nordau. They poison the minds of young
    girls.'

Otto Svoboda, 500 Avenue A, butcher, Pole, husband, philosopher,
    argued in rebuttal,
'Shut your trap, you.
The question is, does the symphony fit in with Karl Marx?'

At the Friday evening meeting of the Browning Writing League, Mrs
    Whittamore Ralston-Beckett,
Traveler, lecturer, novelist, critic, poet, playwright, editor,
    mother, idealist,
Fascinated her audience with a brief talk, whimsical and caustic,
Appealing to the younger generation to take a brighter, happier,
    more sunny and less morbid view of life's eternal
    fundamentals.
Mrs Ralston-Beckett quoted Sir Henry Parke-Bennett: 'O Beauty,'
    she said,
'Take your fingers off my throat, take your elbow out of my eye,
Take your sorrow off my sorrow,
Take your hat, take your gloves, take your feet down off the table,
Take your beauty off my beauty, and go.'

In the open discussion that followed, Maurice Epstein, 29,
    tuberculosis, stoker on the *S.S. Tarboy*, arose and queried
    the speaker,
'Is it true, as certain scientists assert, that them artists are
    all of them crazy?'
A Mr Otto Svoboda present spoke in reply,
'Shut your trap, you. The question is, what about Karl Marx?'   [1929]

LANGSTON HUGHES

USA 1902-1967

Hughes, born in Joplin, Missouri, was the first Black American to make his living as a writer, and one of the leading figures in the Harlem Renaissance. He was as versatile in genres as in poetic forms, writing fiction, autobiography, drama, and a number of musical compositions. One of the first Black Americans of his generation to write civil-rights poetry, and the first to bring the blues thoroughly into the poetic idiom, Hughes also drew strongly on jazz in books like *Ask Your Mama: 12 Moods for Jazz* (1961). The fullest collection is *Selected Poems* (1959), and the most recent book is *The Panther and the Lash* (1969).

THE WEARY BLUES

Droning a drowsy syncopated tune,
Rocking back and forth to mellow croon,
    I heard a Negro play.
Down on Lennox Avenue the other night
By the pale dull pallor of an old gas light
    He did a lazy sway . . .
    he did a lazy sway . . .
To the tune o' those Weary Blues.
With his ebony hands on each ivory key
He made that poor piano moan with melody
    O Blues!
Swaying to and fro on his ricketty stool
He played that sad raggy tune like a musical fool.
    Sweet Blues!
Coming from a black man's soul.
    O Blues!
In a deep song voice with a melancholy tone
I heard that Negro sing, that old piano moan—
    'Ain't got nobody in all this world,
    Ain't got nobody but ma self.
    I's gwine to quit ma frownin'
    And put ma troubles on the shelf.'
Thump, thump, thump, went his foot on the floor.
He played a few chords then he sang some more—

'I got the Weary Blues
And I can't be satisfied.
Got the Weary Blues
And can't be satisfied—
I ain't happy no mo'
And I wish that I had died.'
And far into the night he crooned that tune.
The stars went out and so did the moon.
The singer stopped playing and went to bed
While the Weary Blues echoed through his head.
He slept like a rock or a man that's dead.   [1925]

A.J.M. SMITH

Canada 1902–1980

One of the strongest advocates for Modernism in Canadian poetry, Smith edited *New Provinces: Poems of Several Authors* with F.R. Scott in 1936; Smith's Preface (which, because some felt it might be too harsh, was published only in 1976, when the anthology was reissued) mocked what he saw as the limited subjects of Canadian poetry—'pine trees, the open road, God, snowshoes, or Pan'. Smith spent almost all of his academic career at Michigan State University, but returned to Canada each summer. His anthologies, criticism, and edited collections played a powerful role in bringing a more cosmopolitan understanding to Canadian poetry. Smith's first book, *News of the Phoenix and Other Poems* (1943) won the Governor-General's Award; his life's work is represented in *Collected Poems* (1962), *Poems: New and Collected* (1967), and *The Classic Shade: Selected Poems* (1978).

THE LONELY LAND

Cedar and jagged fir
uplift sharp barbs
against the gray
and cloud-piled sky;
and in the bay
blown spume and windrift
and thin, bitter spray
snap
at the whirling sky;
and the pine trees
lean one way.

A wild duck calls
to her mate,
and the ragged
and passionate tones
stagger and fall,
and recover,

and stagger and fall,
on these stones—
are lost
in the lapping of water
on smooth, flat stones.
This is a beauty
of dissonance,
this resonance
of stony strand,
this smoky cry
curled over a black pine
like a broken
and wind-battered branch
when the wind
bends the tops of the pines
and curdles the sky
from the north.

This is the beauty
of strength
broken by strength
and still strong.

[1936]

STEVIE SMITH

England 1902-1971

Born in Hull, Yorkshire, Smith lived in London and worked as a secretary in the Newness
Publishing Company, on whose yellow paper she wrote her first novel, *Novel on Yellow Paper* in
1936. Recipient of the Cholmondeley Award in 1966 and the Gold Medal for poetry in 1969,
Smith's idiosyncratic and facetious appreciation of our sometimes reluctant allegiance to societal
conventions is expressed equally in the line drawings that accompany her poetry. Collections of
her work include *Collected Poems* (1985) and *New Selected Poems* (1988).

NOT WAVING BUT DROWNING

Nobody heard him, the dead man,
But still he lay moaning:
I was much further out than you thought
And not waving but drowning.

Poor chap, he always loved larking
And now he's dead
It must have been too cold for him his heart gave way,
They said.

Oh, no no no, it was too cold always
(Still the dead one lay moaning)
I was much too far out all my life
And not waving but drowning.   [1957]

EMILY WRITES SUCH A GOOD LETTER

Mabel was married last week
So now only Tom left

The doctor didn't like Arthur's cough
I have been in bed since Easter

A touch of the old trouble

I am downstairs today
As I write this
I can hear Arthur roaming overhead

He loves to roam
Thank heavens he has plenty of space to roam in

We have seven bedrooms
And an annexe

Which leaves a flat for the chauffeur and his wife

We have much to be thankful for

The new vicar came yesterday
People say he brings a breath of fresh air

He leaves me cold
I do not think he is a gentleman

Yes, I remember Maurice very well
Fancy getting married at his age
She must be a fool

You knew May had moved?
Since Edward died she has been much alone

It was cancer

No, I know nothing of Maud
I never wish to hear her name again
In my opinion Maud
Is an evil woman

Our char has left
And a good riddance too
Wages are very high in Tonbridge

Write and tell me how you are, dear,
And the girls,
Phoebe and Rose
They must be a great comfort to you
Phoebe and Rose.   [1937]

LORINE NIEDECKER

USA 1903-1970

Born in Fort Atkinson, Wisconsin, Niedecker lived much of her life in a cabin on Black Hawk
Island in Lake Koshkonong, Wisconsin. Influenced by the 'Objectivist poetics' of her mentor Louis
Zukofsky, Niedecker wrote in a precise language that seems in its conciseness to capture a galaxy
of thought and feeling in one star; her short lines are shaped by fine attention to musicality and
rhythm. Niedecker's work is represented in *From This Condensery: The Complete Writings of Lorine
Niedecker* (1985).

[I MARRIED]

I married

in the world's black night
for warmth
          if not repose.
          At the close—
someone.

I hid with him
from the long range guns.
          We lay leg
          in the cupboard, head
in closet.

A slit of light
at no bird dawn—
          Untaught
          I thought
he drank

too much.
I say
          I married
          and lived unburied.
I thought—   [1968]

EARLE BIRNEY

Canada 1904-1995

Birney's first book, *David and other Poems* (1942), won that year's Governor-General's Award. Birney was a passionate experimenter, delighting in wordplay and in visual and oral adventures, and also a passionate nationalist whose poems denounce a passive country without a strong identity. Birney's long involvement with academia included his role as one of the founders of the Creative Writing Department at the University of British Columbia, and editor of publications like *The Canadian Forum* and *Canadian Poetry Magazine*. The fullest selection of his work is *The Collected Poems of Earle Birney* (2 vols, 1975).

CAN. LIT.

(or *them able to leave her ever*)

since we'd always sky about
when we had eagles they flew out
leaving no shadow bigger than wren's
to trouble even our broodiest hens

too busy bridging loneliness
to be alone
we hacked in railway ties
what Emily etched in bone

we French&English never lost
our civil war
endure it still
a bloody civil bore

the wounded sirened off
no Whitman wanted
it's only by our lack of ghosts
we're haunted   [Spanish Banks, Vancouver 1947; 1966]

THE BEAR ON THE DELHI ROAD

Unreal   tall as a myth
by the road the Himalayan bear
is beating the brilliant air
with his crooked arms
About him two men   bare
spindly as locusts   leap

One pulls on a ring
in the great soft nose   His mate
flicks   flicks with a stick
up at the rolling eyes

They have not led him here
down from the fabulous hills
to this bald alien plain
and the clamorous world   to kill
but simply to teach him to dance

They are peaceful both   these spare
men of Kashmir   and the bear
alive is their living   too
If   far on the Delhi way
around him galvanic they dance
it is merely to wear   wear
from his shaggy body the tranced
wish forever to stay
only an ambling bear
four-footed in berries

It is no more joyous for them
in this hot dust to prance
out of reach of the praying claws
sharpened to paw for ants
in the shadows of deodars
It is not easy to free
myth from reality
or rear this fellow up
to lurch   lurch with them
in the tranced dancing of men

[Srinagar 1958; Île des Porquerolles 1959]

GLADYS MAY CASELY-HAYFORD ('AQUAH LALUAH')

Ghana/Sierra Leone 1904–1950

Casely-Hayford adopted the pseudonym 'Aquah Laluah' when she began to publish in American publications like *The Atlantic Monthly* in the 1930s. She was born in Axim, Ghana and in 1919 travelled to Britain to study, beginning to write poetry while at Penrhos College in Wales. She returned to Africa to teach at a school founded by her mother in Sierra Leone, where she also performed as a musician in Freetown in the 1930s and 1940s; she died there of blackwater fever. Casely-Hayford left much unpublished work at her death; in 1983 the collection *Memoirs and Poems* appeared, which included her mother's reminiscences.

JUNIOR GEOGRAPHY LESSON

Here are the British Isles, girls, beyond the Atlantic Sea.
(Jes now somebody er go cry, if e no listen me.)
England is in Britain, where most white people stay.
(Tete, if you no careful, some good whip go pass you way.)
Now London is in England, where King George sits on his throne.
(No bring no crossness, Jane, to me, 'cos meself get me own.)
Now you and I and all of us are King George's subjects too,
For Sierra Leone belongs to him. (Ayo, if I hol' you . . .)
We help to form the Empire of Britain o'er the seas.
(You know say you dey laugh, don' you pretend you dey sneeze.)
What is the song about the Crown I taught you girls to sing?
Now everybody answer: 'God Save Our Gracious King'.
(Mercy! Dis here na wallah. Tank God, de bell done ring,
Dem dry-eye pickin whey dey now, no sabe anyting.)   [1993]

PATRICK KAVANAGH

Ireland 1904–1967

Kavanagh, born in Inniskeen, County Monaghan, became increasingly convinced that the emphasis on Irish content in the Irish Literary Movement was bred for an 'English-only' consumption. The fourteen parts of 'The Great Hunger' bring to life Patrick Maguire, an 'ignorant peasant deep in dung', trapped by 'fourteen-hour day[s]' and mean fields without 'tomorrow', who endures an imaginative and spiritual grinding down that is complete and irreversible. In rejecting the pastoral's romance with 'bog-wisdom' and picturesque escapism, Kavanagh challenged the claustrophobic effects of provincialism in Ireland and abroad.

from THE GREAT HUNGER

I

Clay is the word and clay is the flesh
Where the potato-gatherers like mechanized scarecrows move
Along the side-fall of the hill—Maguire and his men.
If we watch them an hour is there anything we can prove
Of life as it is broken-backed over the Book
Of Death? Here crows gabble over worms and frogs
And the gulls like old newspapers are blown clear of the hedges,
luckily.

Is there some light of imagination in these wet clods?
Or why do we stand here shivering?
Which of these men
Loved the light and the queen
Too long virgin? Yesterday was summer. Who was it promised
marriage to himself
Before apples were hung from the ceilings for Hallowe'en?
We will wait and watch the tragedy to the last curtain,
Till the last soul passively like a bag of wet clay
Rolls down the side of the hill, diverted by the angles
Where the plough missed or a spade stands, straitening the way.

A dog lying on a torn jacket under a heeled-up cart,
A horse nosing along the posied headland, trailing
A rusty plough. Three heads hanging between wide-apart
Legs. October playing a symphony on a slack wire paling.
Maguire watches the drills flattened out
And the flints that lit a-candle for him on a June altar
Flameless. The drills slipped by and the days slipped by
And he trembled his head away and ran free from the world's
halter,

And thought himself wiser than any man in the townland
When he laughed over pints of porter
Of how he came free from every net spread
In the gaps of experience. He shook a knowing head
And pretended to his soul
That children are tedious in hurrying fields of April
Where men are spanging across wide furrows.
Lost in the passion that never needs a wife—
The pricks that pricked were the pointed pins of harrows.
Children scream so loud that the crows could bring
The seed of an acre away with crow-rude jeers.
Patrick Maguire, he called his dog and he flung a stone in the
                                                              air
And hallooed the birds away that were the birds of the years.

Turn over the weedy clods and tease out the tangled skeins.
What is he looking for there?
He thinks it is a potato, but we know better
Than his mud-gloved fingers probe in this insensitive hair.

'Move forward the basket and balance it steady
In this hollow. Pull down the shafts of that cart, Joe,
And straddle the horse,' Maguire calls.
'The wind's over Brannagan's, now that means rain.
Graip up some withered stalks and see that no potato falls
Over the tail-board going down the ruckety pass—
And *that's* a job we'll have to do in December,
Gravel it and build a kerb on the bog-side. Is that Cassidy's ass
Out in my clover? Curse o' God—
Where is that dog?
Never where he's wanted.' Maguire grunts and spits
Through a clay-wattled moustache and stares about him from the
                                                              height.

His dream changes again like the cloud-swung wind
And he is not so sure now if his mother was right
When she praised the man who made a field his bride.

Watch him, watch him, that man on a hill whose spirit
Is a wet sack flapping about the knees of time.
He lives that his little fields may stay fertile when his own
                                                              body
Is spread in the bottom of a ditch under two coulters crossed in
                                                        Christ's Name.

He was suspicious in his youth as a rat near strange bread,
When girls laughed; when they screamed he knew that meant
The cry of fillies in season. He could not walk
The easy road to destiny. He dreamt
The innocence of young brambles to hooked treachery.
O the grip, O the grip of irregular fields! No man escapes.
It could not be that back of the hills love was free
And ditches straight.
No monster hand lifted up children and put down apes
As here.

                           'O God if I had been wiser!'
That was his sigh like the brown breeze in the thistles.
He looks towards his house and haggard. 'O God if I had been
                                      wiser!'

But now a crumpled leaf from the whitethorn bushes
Darts like a frightened robin, and the fence
Shows the green of after-grass through a little window,
And he knows that his own heart is calling his mother a liar
God's truth is life—even the grotesque shapes of its foulest
                                    fire.

The horse lifts its head and cranes
Through the whins and stones
To lip late passion in the crawling clover.
In the gap there's a bush weighted with boulders like morality,
The fools of life bleed if they climb over.

The wind leans from Brady's, and the coltsfoot leaves are holed
                                  with rust,
Rain fills the cart-tracks and the sole-plate grooves;
A yellow sun reflects in Donaghmoyne
The poignant light in puddles shaped by hooves.

Come with me, Imagination, into this iron house
And we will watch from the doorway the years run back,
And we will know what a peasant's left hand wrote on the page.
Be easy, October. No cackle hen, horse neigh, tree sough, duck
                                  quack.
                                  [1942]

LOUIS ZUKOFSKY

USA 1904–1978

Zukofsky had his M.A. from Columbia at 20 and was soon after an editor and adviser for William
Carlos Williams. When *Poetry* magazine published its 'Objectivist' issue in 1931, Zukofsky wrote
the editorial, a manifesto that was submerged when the New Critical perspective dominated in the
forties. He manifests one of the signatures of Modernist American verse. Zukofsky's lifelong project
was 'A', a long poem that weaves autobiography, history, and epic through his abiding love of
wordplay and punning; the poem was published serially and collected in *A* (1978). Zukofsky was
a distinguished critic; his *Prepositions: The Collected Critical Essays of Louis Zukofsky: Expanded
Edition* appeared in 1981. Selections of his poetry include *All: The Collected Shorter Poems* (1971).

from 'A'—11

for Celia and Paul

River that must turn full after I stop dying
Song, my song, raise grief to music
Light as my loves' thought, the few sick
So sick of wrangling: thus weeping,
Sounds of light, stay in her keeping
And my son's face—this much for honor.

Freed by their praises who make honor dearer
Whose losses show them rich and you no poorer
Take care, song, that what stars' imprint you mirror
Grazes their tears; draw speech from their nature or
Love in you—faced to your outer stars—purer
Gold than tongues make without feeling
Art new, hurt old: revealing
The slackened bow as the stinging
Animal dies, thread gold stringing
The fingerboard pressed in my honor.

Honor, song, sang the blest is delight knowing
We overcome ills by love. Hurt, song, nourish
Eyes, think most of whom you hurt. For the flowing
River's poison where what rod blossoms. Flourish
By love's sweet lights and sing *in them I flourish*.
No, song, not any one power
May recall or forget, our
Love to see your love flows into
Us. If Venus lights, your words spin, to
Live our desires lead us to honor.

Graced, your heart in nothing less than in death, go—
I, dust—raise the great hem of the extended
World that nothing can leave; having had breath go
Face my son, say: 'If your father offended
You with mute wisdom, my words have not ended
His second paradise where
His love was in her eyes where
They turn, quick for you two—sick
Or gone cannot make music
You set less than all. Honor

His voice in me, the river's turn that finds the
Grace in you, four notes first too full for talk, leaf
Lighting stem, stems bound to the branch that binds the
Tree, and then as from the same root we talk, leaf
After leaf of your mind's music, page, walk leaf
Over leaf of his thought, sounding
His happiness: song sounding
The grace that comes from knowing
Things, her love our own showing
Her love in all her honor.'   [1966]

KENNETH REXROTH

USA 1905-1982

Born in South Bend, Indiana, Rexroth lived his artistic life in San Francisco, where he moved in 1927. He was affiliated with the various poetic movements based there, particularly the Beats and the Black Mountain School which included poets like Robert Duncan and Robert Creeley. Rexroth's poetry could be swept up in his anger at those he perceived as poetry's foes, but his Imagist verse, particularly when it focuses on nature, is more reflective and serene. His work is available in *The Complete Collected Shorter Poems* (1967), *The Collected Longer Poems* (1968), and *New Poems* (1974).

from THE LOVE POEMS OF MARICHIKO

I
The full moon of Spring
Rises out of the Void
And pushes aside the
Net of stars—a crystal ball
On pale velvet set with gems.
                    Marichiko

II
This Spring Mercury
Is farthest from the sun and
Burns, a lonely spark
In the last glow of sunset
Over the uncountable
Sands and waves of the
Illimitable ocean.
                    Marichiko

III
Early spring this year—
Pittosporum, plums, peaches,
Almonds, mimosa,
All bloom at once. Under the
Full moon, night smells like your body.
                    Marichiko

IV
It is the time when
The wild geese return. Between
The setting sun and
The rising moon, a line of
Brant write the character 'heart.'
                    Marichiko

V
Who is there? Me.
Me who? I am me. You are you.
You take my pronoun
And we are us.
                    Marichiko

VI
As I came from the
Hot bath, you took me before
The long mirror, my
Breasts quivered in your hands, my
Buttocks shivered against you.
                    Marichiko

VII
Your tongue thrums and moves
Into me, and I become
Hollow and blaze with
Whirling light, like the inside
Of a vast expanding pearl.
                    Marichiko

VIII
I scream as you bite
My nipples and orgasm
Drains my body as if I
Had been cut in two.

Marichiko

IX
I wish I could be
Kannon of the thousand heads
To kiss you, and Kannon
Of the thousand arms
To embrace you.

Marichiko   [1978]

SAMUEL BECKETT

Ireland 1906-1989

Beckett left Dublin for Paris in the 1920s and after 1937 never returned. Working on occasion as James Joyce's assistant and translator (Joyce's deteriorating eyesight rendered services like these imperative), Beckett also created *Waiting for Godot* (1952) and *Endgame* (1958), dramas that contributed to the development of the Theatre of the Absurd by combining the timing, wordplay, and broad gesture of vaudeville with minimalist staging and self-conscious theatricalism. This tragicomic range is as central to Beckett's novels (*Molly*, 1951, *Malone Dies*, 1958, *The Unnameable*, 1960) and poetry (mostly written in the 1930s), where arcane and solipsistic interiors yield insights cramped by speakers who sometimes equate the drooling satisfaction of an all-day sucker with unexpected opportunities for communion. Beckett's *Collected Poems In English And French* was first published in 1977.

SOMETHING THERE

something there
where
out there
out where
outside
what
the head what else
something there somewhere outside
the head

at the faint sound so brief
it is gone and the whole globe
not yet bare
the eye

opens wide
wide
till in the end
nothing more
shutters it again

so the odd time
out there
somewhere out there
like as if
as if
something
not life
necessarily   [1974]

W.H. AUDEN

England/USA 1907-1973

Celebrated by his Oxford contemporaries for the enormous range of his poetic technique, Wynstan Hugh Auden emigrated to the United States in 1939 coincident with the beginning of World War II, but returned to England later in his career and was Oxford Professor of Poetry from 1956–60. Poet, teacher, critic, and playwright, his work includes *The Dyer's Hand* (1963, one of several collections of essays), *Collected Poems* (1976), *Selected Poems: New Edition* (1989), and with his companion Chester Kallam, the libretto for Stravinsky's *The Rake's Progress* (1951).

LETTER TO A WOUND

The maid has just cleared away tea and I shall not be disturbed until supper. I shall be quite alone in this room, free to think of you if I choose and believe me, my dear, I do choose. For a long time now I have been aware that you are taking up more of my life every day, but I am always being surprised to find how far this has gone. Why, it was only yesterday, I took down all those photographs from my mantelpiece—Gabriel, Olive, Mrs Marshall, Molim, and the others. How could I have left them there like that so long, memorials to my days of boasting? As it is, I've still far too many letters. (Vow. To have a grand clearance this week—hotel bills, bus tickets from Damascus, presentation pocket-mirrors, foreign envelopes, etc.)

Looking back now to that time before I lost my 'health' (Was that really only last February?) I can't recognise myself. The discontinuity seems absolute. But of course the change was really gradual. Over and over again in the early days when I was in the middle of writing a newsy letter to M., or doing tricks in the garden to startle R. and C., you showed your resentment by a sudden bout of pain. I had outbursts, wept even, at what seemed to me then your insane jealousy, your bad manners, your passion for spoiling things. What a little idiot I was not to trust your more exquisite judgment, which declined absolutely to let me go on behaving like a child. People would have tried to explain it all. You would not insult me with pity. I think I've learned my lesson now. Thank you, my dear. I'll try my hardest not to let you down again.

Do you realise we have been together now for almost a year? Eighteen months ago, if anyone had foretold this to me I should have asked him to leave the house. Haven't I ever told you about my first interview with the surgeon? He kept me waiting three quarters of an hour. It was raining outside. Cars passed or drew up squeaking by the curb. I sat in my overcoat, restlessly turning over the pages of back numbers of illustrated papers, accounts of the Battle of Jutland, jokes about special constables and conscientious objectors. A lady came down with a little girl. They put on their hats, speaking in whispers, tight-lipped. Mr Gangle would see me. A nurse was just coming out as I entered, carrying a white-enamelled bowl containing a pair of scissors, some instruments, soiled swabs of cotton wool. Mr Gangle was washing his hands. The examination on the hard leather couch under the brilliant light was soon over. Washing again as I dressed he said nothing. Then reaching for a towel turned, 'I'm afraid', he said. . . .

Outside I saw nothing, walked, not daring to think. I've lost everything, I've failed. I wish I was dead. And now, here we are, together, intimate, mature.

Later. At dinner Mrs T. announced that she'd accepted an invitation for me to a whist-drive at the Stewarts' on Wednesday. 'It's so good for you to get out in the evenings sometimes. You're as bad as Mr Bedder.' She babbled on, secretly disappointed, I think, that I did not make more protest. Certainly six months ago she couldn't have brought it off, which makes me think what a great change has come over us recently. In what I might call our honeymoon stage, when we had both realised what we meant to each other (how slow I was, wasn't I?) and that this would always be so, I was obsessed (You too a little? No?) by what seemed my extraordinary fortune. I pitied everybody. Little do you know, I said to myself, looking at my neighbour on the bus, what has happened to the little man in the black hat sitting next to you. I was always smiling. I mortally offended Mrs Hunter, I remember, when she was describing her son's career at Cambridge. She thought I was laughing at her. In restaurants I used to find myself drawing pictures of you on the bottom of the table mats. 'Who'll ever guess what that is?' Once, when a whore accosted me, I bowed, 'I deeply regret it, Madam, but I have a friend.' Once I carved on a seat in the park 'We have sat here. You'd better not.'

Now I see that all that sort of thing is juvenile and silly, merely a reaction against insecurity and shame. You as usual of course were the first to realise this, making yourself felt whenever I had been particularly rude or insincere.

Thanks to you, I have come to see a profound significance in relations I never dreamt of considering before, an old lady's affection for a small boy, the Waterhouses and their retriever, the curious bond between Offal and Snig, the partners in the hardware shop on the front. Even the close-ups on the films no longer disgust nor amuse me. On the contrary they sometimes make me cry; knowing you has made me understand.

It's getting late and I have to be up betimes in the morning. You are so quiet these days that I get quite nervous, remove the dressing. No I am safe, you are still there. The wireless this evening says that the frost is coming. When it does, we know what to expect, don't we? But I am calm. I can wait. The surgeon was dead right. Nothing will ever part us. Good-night and God bless you, my dear.

Better burn this.   [1931]

LULLABY

Lay your sleeping head, my love,
Human on my faithless arm;
Time and fevers burn away
Individual beauty from
Thoughtful children, and the grave
Proves the child ephemeral:
But in my arms till break of day
Let the living creature lie,
Mortal, guilty, but to me
The entirely beautiful.

Soul and body have no bounds:
To lovers as they lie upon
Her tolerant enchanted slope
In their ordinary swoon,
Grave the vision Venus sends
Of supernatural sympathy,
Universal love and hope;
While an abstract insight wakes
Among the glaciers and the rocks
The hermit's sensual ecstasy.

Certainty, fidelity
On the stroke of midnight pass
Like vibrations of a bell,
And fashionable madmen raise
Their pedantic boring cry:
Every farthing of the cost,
All the dreaded cards foretell,
Shall be paid, but from this night
Not a whisper, not a thought,
Not a kiss nor look be lost.

Beauty, midnight, vision dies:
Let the winds of dawn that blow
Softly round your dreaming head

Such a day of sweetness show
Eye and knocking heart may bless,
Find the mortal world enough;
Noons of dryness see you fed
By the involuntary powers,
Nights of insult let you pass
Watched by every human love.   [1937]

A.D. HOPE

Australia b. 1907

The son of a Presbyterian minister, Hope was born at Cooma in New South Wales. He studied at
Sydney and Oxford universities and taught at Sydney Teachers' College, the University of
Melbourne, and Australian National University from 1937 to 1968. His first collection of poetry,
The Wandering Islands, appeared in 1955, and among his many subsequent volumes are the mock
heroic epic *Dunciad Minor* (1970), *Collected Poems 1930–1970* (1972), *A Book of Answers* (1978),
and *The Tragical History of Dr Faustus* (1982). Hope eschews experimental and free verse to rely on
biblical, mythological, and literary figures and forms. He employs wit and satire to convey the
wonder and terror derived from poetic insights.

THE END OF A JOURNEY

There at the last, his arms embracing her,
She found herself, faith wasted, valour lost,
Raped by a stranger in her sullen bed;
And he, for all the bloody passion it cost
To have heard the sirens sing and yet have fled,
Thought the night tedious, coughed and shook his head,
An old man sleeping with his housekeeper.

But with the dawn he rose and stepped outside.
A farm-cart by the doorway dripped and stank,
Piled with the victims of his mighty bow.
Each with her broken neck, each with a blank,
Small, strangled face, the dead girls in a row
Swung as the cold airs moved them to and fro,
Full-breasted, delicate-waisted, heavy-thighed.

Setting his jaw, he turned and clambered down
A goat-track to the beach; the tide was full.
He stood and brooded on the breaking wave
Revolving many memories in his skull:
Calypso singing in her haunted cave,
The bed of Circe, Hector in his grave
And Priam butchered in his burning town.

Grimly he watched his enemy the sea
Rage round the petty kingdom he called home;
But now no trident threatened from the spray.
He prayed but knew Athene would not come.
The gods at last had left him, and the day
Darkened about him. Then from far away
And long ago, he seemed once more to be

Roped to a mast and through the breakers' roar
Sweet voices mocked him on his reeling deck:
'Son of Laertes, what delusive song
Turned your swift keel and brought you to this wreck,
In age and disenchantment to prolong
Stale years and chew the cud of ancient wrong,
A castaway upon so cruel a shore?'   [1963]

LOUIS MACNEICE

Ireland 1907-1963

A member of the Anglican Anglo-Irish class in Ulster yet cut from the Connemara cloth of his
mother and father, MacNeice was educated and domiciled in England, working with the BBC for
most of his life. His poetry explores the complex nature of his Irish identity. He travelled with
Auden to Iceland, went to Spain before and during the Civil War, and visited America at the
beginning of World War II. His images are particularly sensitive to the permutations and implica-
tions of a world of appearances. *The Collected Poems* was published in 1967; his Clark Lectures at
Cambridge were published as *Varieties of Parable* in 1963.

REFLECTIONS

The mirror above my fireplace reflects the reflected
Room in my window; I look in the mirror at night
And see two rooms, the first where left is right
And the second, beyond the reflected window, corrected
But there I am standing back to my back. The standard
Lamp comes thrice in my mirror, twice in my window,
The fire in the mirror lies two rooms away through the window,
The fire in the window lies one room away down the terrace,
My actual room stands sandwiched between confections
Of night and lights and glass and in both directions
I can see beyond and through the reflections the street lamps
At home outdoors where my indoors rooms lie stranded,
Where a taxi perhaps will drive in through the bookcase
Whose books are not for reading and past the fire
Which gives no warmth and pull up by my desk
At which I cannot write since I am not lefthanded.   [1961]

DENIS DEVLIN

Scotland/Ireland 1908-1959

Often perceived as representative of the 'alternative tradition'—the Joycean realist rather than the Yeatsian historian—Devlin was a career diplomat whose decade-long service in the United States as well as in London, Dublin, Italy, and Turkey accounts for his internationalist and comparatist values. His irony, for example, seems to blend cynical and idealistic approaches, resolving contradictions where others might find a *cul de sac*. The *Complete Poems* edited by his friend and fellow poet Brian Coffey first appeared in 1963.

LIFFEY BRIDGE

Parade parade
The evening puts on
Her breath-stained jewels
Her shadowy past.

Trailing behind
Tired poses
How they all
Fulfill their station!
The young with masks and
The old with faces
Such an assassin
Such a world!

From the bridge they admire
Their foolish reflection
Drowning in birth,
Man's face and centuries
In rivers with stars
Fugitive wheatfields
Giving no harvest . . .
Here's poulticed peace.
If dreaming of death
Unheavened could but rend them
With anger or envy!

The pigeons creak
On rusty hinges
Turn to the window
Bright with oranges
And girls the girls
The gashed fruit
Of their mouths and smiles

Cute as the rims
Of their cock-eyed hats:

In limp doorways
They try out their heaven
They grind at love
With gritted kisses
Then eyes re-opened
Behold slack flesh
Such an assassin
Such a world!

Same with all the
Young and hopeful
Any relief will
Do for a spell
Then timid masks
Live into faces
Then there is quiet
Desperation.

The houses lean
Against the wind
Won't you give over?
Say, what about
That second coming?

Deaf quay walls.
Water wears
The stone away
And out on the river
The arc-lamp rays and the
Wind weave
Try to weave
Something or other
From flight and water.   [1937]

KATHLEEN RAINE

England/Scotland b. 1908

A scholar of the Neoplatonic tradition in English Romantic poetry with a particular interest in William Blake, Raine has written 13 books of poetry (including *Collected Poems 1935–1980*), critical explorations, and a three-volume autobiography, and established the arts magazine *Temenos*. In an introduction to selections of her work in the 1985 *Bloodaxe Book of Contemporary Women Poets*, Raine describes her own muse as the 'Inspirer', 'the Eternal Child, an unageing presence nearer and more intimate than friend or lover, and not to be denied, at the price of life itself—imaginative life that is, a life that, once tasted, the poet cannot endure to be parted from'.

SPELL TO BRING LOST CREATURES HOME

Home, home,
Wild birds home!
Lark to the grass,
Wren to the hedge,
Rooks to the tree-tops,
Swallow to the eaves,
Eagle to its crag
And raven to its stone,
All birds home!

Home, home,
Strayed ones home,
Rabbit to burrow
Fox to earth,
Mouse to the wainscot,
Rat to the barn,
Cattle to the byre,
Dog to the hearth,
All beasts home!

Home, home,
Wanderers home,
Cormorant to rock
Gulls from the storm
Boat to the harbour
Safe sail home!

Children home,
At evening home,
Boys and girls
From the roads come home,

Out of the rain
Sons come home,
From the gathering dusk,
Young ones home!

Home, home,
All souls home,
Dead to the lamplight,
Old to the fireside,
Girls from the twilight,
Babe to the breast
And heart to its haven,
Lost ones home!   [1953]

THEODORE ROETHKE

USA 1908–1963

Roethke was born in Saginaw, Michigan, where his father owned a large greenhouse that would become the setting for many of Roethke's best-known poems. Educated at the University of Michigan, he taught at a number of American universities and settled at the University of Washington in 1948 as a poet-in-residence. His first volume of poetry was *Open House* (1942); the book that won him his large following was *The Lost Son* (1948). Roethke's verse can be exuberant and witty, but there is also a formal, elegiac strain, exemplified by the dark but stately villanelle, 'The Waking', in which Roethke alludes to his bouts of mental illness. Roethke's last book is the posthumous *The Far Field* (1964); his work is assembled in *Collected Poems* (1966, 1968).

MY PAPA'S WALTZ

The whiskey on your breath
Could make a small boy dizzy;
But I hung on like death:
Such waltzing was not easy.

We romped until the pans
Slid from the kitchen shelf;
My mother's countenance
Could not unfrown itself.

The hand that held my wrist
Was battered on one knuckle;
At every step you missed
My right ear scraped a buckle.

You beat time on my head
With a palm caked hard by dirt,
Then waltzed me off to bed
Still clinging to your shirt.   [1948]

CHARLES BRASCH

New Zealand 1909-1973

Brasch was born in Dunedin, but educated at Oxford, worked as an archaeologist in Egypt, and held civil service and teaching positions in England before returning to New Zealand in 1947. From 1947 to 1966, he edited the influential literary quarterly, *Landfall*, which he founded. Collections of his own poetry include *The Land and the People* (1939), *The Estate* (1957), and the posthumously published autobiography, *Indirections* (1980). 'Ambulando' (1964) is a beautifully-crafted meditation on the intractable, often inscrutable, patterns of experience that may alienate individuals from others and also from themselves.

AMBULANDO

i
In middle life when the skin slackens
Its loving clasp of our loose volumes,
When the bone tree stiffens and its well-jointed branches
Begin to creak, to droop a little,
May the spirit hold out no longer for
Old impossible terms, demanding
Rent-free futures where all, all is ripeness,
But cry pax to its equivocal nature and stretch
At ease with wry destiny,
Supple as wind bowing in every reed.

ii
Now that the young with interest no longer
Look on me as one of themselves
Whom they might wish to know or to touch,
Seeing merely another sapless greyhead,
The passport of that disguise conducts me
Through any company unquestioned,
In cool freedom to come and go
With mode and movement, wave and wind.

iii
Communicate with stones, trees, water
If you must vent a heart too full.
Who will hear you now, your words falling
As foreign as bird-tongue
On ears attuned to different vibrations?
Trees, water, stones:
Let these answer a gaze contemplative
Of all things that flow out from them
And back to enter them again.

iv
I do not know the shape of the world.
I cannot set boundaries to experience.
I know it may open out, enlarged suddenly,
In any direction, to unpredictable distance,
Subverting climate and cosmography,
And carrying me far from tried moorings
So that I see myself no more
Under some familiar guise
Resting static as in a photograph,
Nor move as I supposed I was moving
From fixed point to point;
But rock outwards like the last stars that signal
At the frontiers of light,
Fleeing the centre without destination.   [1964]

JEAN EARLE

England/Wales b. 1909

Born in Bristol, Earle has lived most of her life in Wales. Although she published short fiction and essays early, her first book of poetry, *A Trial of Strength* (1980), appeared when she was seventy-one. Earle's poetry can calmly evoke recollections of a family's strained culture to fine effect, as in 'Jugged Hare', which re-creates her mother's courtship of Earle's father. Recent books include *Visiting Light* (1987), *The Intent Look* (1984), and *Selected Poems* (1990).

YOUNG GIRLS RUNNING

Almost, flight . . .

Herons, angling
A tilted grace. Spring twigs,
Taking the awkward wind.

Three-as-one, linked onrush
Mirrored in polished sand,
Light legs
Spattering pools, shells.

'The sea!' they cry, 'the sea!'
Birdlike, birdshape

Breasting the tide
With no breasts, merged
In the thrown wave

Which will rain them
Rosy, swept
Through its firming sting,
Medicinal shock, thrust . . .

They will be women,
Breasted, hipped,
Salted,
When they come out.   [1990]

OLIVE FRASER

Scotland 1909-1977

In 1935 Fraser became the first woman to win the Chancellor's Medal for English Verse at Girton College, Cambridge. Her college friend Helena Shire recalls that 'A kind of quasi-academic dress had to be devised' for Fraser so that she could receive the honour 'as women were still non-members of the university and had no right to gown and square.' Years of poverty and poor health culminated in a breakdown in 1956. Over a decade of frequent hospitalization followed; though successfully treated in 1968, Fraser continued to live in hospital and to create poetry that would make sense of her suffering and that of others. *The Wrong Music: The Poems of Olive Fraser 1909–1977* was published in 1989.

LINES WRITTEN AFTER A NERVOUS BREAKDOWN

(II)

Come, lamefoot brain, and dance and be
A merry carnival for me.
We are alive in spite of all
Hobgoblins who our wits did call.
With ghosts and gallowsbirds we went
Hundreds of leagues 'til, fiercely spent,
We laid ourselves to weep and cry
Beyond the house of memory.

We have been lepers, and now run
To sit again within the sun,
And smile upon some country fair
With Punch and poor dog Toby there.
We, who did only think to die
Now laugh and mock the revelry.
Up, barefoot brain, and fill your hall
With flags as for a festival.

Yet you are poor and slow to do
The blessed things I ask of you,
Haunting with spectres still and still
Remembering your dungeon's chill,
Where you did cower and aye did grow
A frenzied circus for your foe,
Who sought you in the blood's dim arc,
And in the night-time, in the dark.

Peace, friend, and think how we are here
Through dangers, desolations, fear.
We two alone, now all is o'er
Will never move from pleasure more.
We two will sit like birds i' the sun
And preen and pipe while others run
And straddle in the world's proud play.
We have been night, who now are day.   [1964]

ROBERT GARIOCH (SUTHERLAND)

Scotland 1909-1987

Teacher and poet, member of the second wave of the Scottish Renaissance of the 1940s and 1950s,
Garioch wrote probing and wryly satiric poems about human behaviour. 'The Wire' is based on his
first-hand experience as a prisoner of war in Italy and Germany. Among Garioch's achievements
stand his translation into Scots of works by Belli, Pindar, Hesiod, Goethe, Apollinaire, and others,
which appear in his *Collected Poetical Works* (1983).

THE WIRE

moor   This day I saw ane endless muir
                                   wi sad horizon, like the sea
                                   around some uncouth landless globe
where/flicker   whaur waters flauchter endlessly.

bilberry   Heather bell and blaeberry
                                   grow on this muir; reid burns rin
sky   in clear daylicht; the luift is free
mist   frae haar, and yet there is nae sun.

everywhere   Gossamers glint in aa the airts,
flower-heads   criss-cross about the lang flure-heids
grass and thistles   of girss and thristles here, and there
                                   amang the purpie willow-weeds.

Bog-myrtle scent is in the air
honey heavy wi hinnie-sap and peat
mixed whiles mellit like uneasy thochts
excrement or sweat wi something human, shairn or sweit.

powder smoke Nou guns gaun aff, and pouther-reik
dogs and yappin packs of foetid dugs,
red/blisters and blobs of cramosie, like blebs
of bluid squeezed frae vanilla bugs

knock violently pash suddenlike intill the licht
that beats from every direction, and then that dings on this unshadowed muir
are gone frae ilka airt, and syne are gane
whirlwinds/dust like tourbillions of twisted stour.

The criss-cross gossamers, the while,
tight twang owre the heather, ticht and real;
slender I ken, houever jimp they seem,
that they are spun frae strands of steel.

And they are barbed wi twisted spikes
wi scant a handsbreidth space atween,
iron and reinforced wi airn rods
and hung about wi bits of tin

that hing in pairs alang the Wire,
each one ilkane three-cornered like a fang:
clashin thegither at a touch
unnaturally into the lark's song they break aukwart the lairick's sang.

high Heich in their sentry-posts, the guairds
who dare not wha daurna sleep, on pain of daith,
watch throu the graticules of guns,
cruel and persecuted, baith.

crowded This endless muir is thrang wi folk
limp in all directions at once that hirple aya aa airts at aince
wi neither purport nor content
nor rest, in fidgan impotence.

They gae in danger of the Wire
but stagger but staucher on anither mile
frae line to line of spider steel
to leap to loup anither deidlie stile.

A man trips up; the Wire gaes ding,
tins clash, the guaird lifts up his heid;
very slowly fu slaw he traverses his gun
and blatters at him till he's deid.

tearing The dugs loup on him, reivan flesh,
bones/wood crunchin the bane as they were wud;
swiftly swith they come and swith are gane,
syne nocht is left but pools of bluid.

blood dripping Bluid dreipan doun amang the roots
is sucked is soukit up the vampire stem
cruel flowers and suin the gaudy felloun flures
cheat and mock begowk the man that nourished them.

Some pairts the Wires close in and leave
go smaa space whaur men may freely gang,
and ilka step is taen in dreid;
there flures and men maist thickly thrang.

entangled A man gets taiglit on a barb,
the length of his stomach endlang his wame the cauld fear creeps;
he daurna muve, the hert beats hard,
but beats awa. The sentry sleeps.

energy Aye! his virr comes back in spate,
sly as some auld trout this man is slee;
he hauds himsel still as a stane,
back comes his ain self-maistery.

Cannily he sets to wark,
warp by warp his sleeve is free,
it hings nou by a single threid:
loud clash the tins and bullets flee.

forward Forrit and back and in and out
woeful they darn in waesome figure-dance;
staying/endure bydin still they canna thole
and each man works and ilk man warks his ain mischance.

They see the Wire, and weill they ken
which whilk wey it warks. In middle-air
the glintan guns are clear in sicht,
who tho nae man kens wha set them there.

Impersonal in uniform,
the guairds are neither friens nor faes;
none tries nane ettles to propitiate
upsets nor fashes them wi bribes or praise.

Efficient and predictable,
they cairry out their orders stricht;
immediately here naething happens unforeseen;
it is jist sae, no wrang nor richt.

On this dour mechanistic muir
wi nae land's end, and endless day,
whaur nae thing thraws a shadow, here
sorrowful   the truth is clear, and it is wae.

The crouds that thrang the danger-spots
weill ken what wey their warld's wrocht,
struggle on   but aye the mair they pauchle on
to win release frae nigglin thocht.

Some pairts the pattern of the Wire
leaves clear for fifty yairds and mair
dried up/dust   whaur soil has crined to desert stuir
with stunted shrubs wi scroggie bussels puir and bare.

more sensible than the rest Here some folk wycer nor the lave
given to taking fright   or maybe suiner gien to skar
tether theirsels wi chains to stakes,
sae they may gang, but no owre far.

spinning   Birlan in wretchedness aroun
must endure   their safe lives' centre, they maun dree
temptation sair to break their chains
for aye they ettle to gang free.

saunter aimlessly their patch Some stark and strang stravaig their yird
ponies   like shelties that hae never taen
mettle   the bit; mere smeddum drives them on,
their lives are short, but are their ain.

some in odd, ill-favoured directions A wheen in orra ill-faur'd airts
on barren streitches of the muir
gae whaur nae bluid is ever shed
to soak the wearisome unmoistened dust to drouk the dreich unslockent stour.

Within a pentagon of wire
they gang alane, or twae by twae,
endure   thole the condition of their life
and suffer what happens and dree the weird as best they may.

in all that alien   Alane in thon hale fremmit globe
slow-going/eyes   thae slaw-gaun folk hae in their een
as if   some sapience, as gin their looks
reflected marvels   refleckit ferlies they hae seen

in their ain thochts, the nucleus
revealed   of man himsel is keethit there.
Expressed in terms of happiness
are premises of pure despair.

Thae guidlie folk are nae great men;
unusually small   the best of men are unco smaa
          whan in the autumn of despair
faded away   irrelevance has dwined awa.

Their syllogisms widdershins
then the leaf   wither the petal; syne the leaf
shrink   and stem crine in as life gaes doun
          intill a corm of prime belief.

mighty thought   Wi utmaist pouer of forcy thocht
          they crine their life within its core,
          and what they ken wi certainty
known beside   is kent inby the bracken-spore.

And aye alane or twae by twae
vexation   they gang unhurt amang the noy
that cruel/eyes   of thon fell planet, and their een
blaze   lowe wi the licht of inwart joy.

Outwartly they seem at rest,
save for   binna the glint of hidden fires.
          Their warld shaks, but they bide still
vibrating   as nodal points on dirlan wires.

In ither airts, whaur folk are thrang,
          the Wire vibrates, clash gae the tins,
          flures blume frae bluidie marl, dugs
          yowl throu the blatter of the guns.

spin   I saw thon planet slawlie birl;
          I saw it as ane endless muir
          in daylicht, and I saw a few
dust   guid men bide still amang the stour.

[1977]

VINAYAK KRISHNA GOKAK

India b. 1909

As the editor of collections such as *The Golden Treasury of Indo-Anglian Poetry 1828–1965* (1970) and *Twenty-One Indo-Anglian Poems* (1975), Gokak has played a significant role in locating Indian poetry in the wider tradition. Educated at Bombay and Oxford, he had a career teaching English at several institutions from the early thirties to the late fifties and was the Director of the Indian Institute of Advanced Study at Simla (1970–71). Gokak won the Sahitya Akademi Award for his Kannada poem, *Dyava Prithwa* (1960).

THE SONG OF INDIA

'What song shall I sing of you, my Mother?'
I asked.
'Shall I sing
Of the Himalayas with their snow-born peaks,
Of the three seas that wash your palm?
Shall I sing
Of your clear dawn with its pure gold-streaks?'
Said the Mother imperturbable, calm:
'Sing of the beggar and the leper
That swarm my streets.
Sing of the filth and the dirt
That foul my sylvan retreats.'

'What song shall I sing of you, my Mother?'
I asked.
'Shall I sing
Of your rock-cut temples, epics in stone,
Of your children that died to call you their own,
Their very own?
Of the seers and prophets that hewed the straight path
For the man that pilgrims alone?'
Said the Mother in indignant words
That beat into my ears like a gong,
That flew about me, a pitiful thing,
Like great white birds:
'Sing of the millions that toil.
Sing of the wrinkled face
Indexing ignorance.
Sing of the helpless child
Born in a bleak, dark home.'
Nervous, I yet would ask,
Deeming it my task:
'What song shall I sing of you, my Mother?
What song?

Shall I sing of the dam and the lake?
Of steel mills, the ship-building yard?
Of the men that work hard
To technologise, to put you on the page
Of the Atomic Age?'
Said the Mother: 'Of these you may sing.
But sing also of the strikes, early and late,
Of iron men that come in their wake,
Of class-war and its correlate.'
Querulous, I said:
'Is there no song that I can sing of you,
Heart-whole, unalloyed?
A song bathed in the stainless blue
Unvapouring in the void?'
At that the Mother rose, draped in blue sky.
Milk-white oceans heaved round her. Their waves
Were the entrancing and enthroning light
On which she sat and wrote the Book of the Morrow.
Her forehead opened like earth's destiny
Yielding the sun-god, cancelling all sorrow.
It was clear dawn. Like a nightmare fled the night
And the sun-beam was as the Hand that saves.   [1965]

RALPH GUSTAFSON

Canada 1909-1995

Best known for his poetry, Gustafson was also a music critic, anthologist, and short-story writer who won the Governor-General's Award in 1974 for his book of poetry, *Fire on Stone*. Gustafson's most compelling poetry takes two directions: on the one hand, poems that evoke the familiar sense of place, of seasons, and climate in and around Gustafson's homeground, the Eastern Townships in Quebec; and on the other, poems that draw on his rich bank of allusion and learning, or his wide travels. Other verse depicts 'new' Canadian settings over against a European world imagined as an older, more domesticated mindscape that lies inert within an ossified tradition. Called a 'poet's poet' for his dedication to his craft, Gustafson published several collections, including *The Moment is All: Selected Poems, 1944–1983* (1983) and *Collected Poems* (1987).

IN THE YUKON

In Europe, you can't move without going down into history.
Here, all is a beginning. I saw a salmon jump,
Again and again, against the current,
The timbered hills a background, wooded green
Unpushed through; the salmon jumped, silver.
This was news, was commerce, at the end of the summer
The leap for dying. Moose came down to the water edge
To drink and the salmon turned silver arcs.

At night, the northern lights played, great over country
Without tapestry and coronations, kings crowned
With weights of gold. They were green,
Green hangings and great grandeur, over the north
Going to what no man can hold hard in mind,
The dredge of that gravity, being without experience.   [1972]

A.M. KLEIN

Canada 1909-1972

Klein evokes the richness and the agonies of modern Jewish experience, particularly in Montreal's
unique cultural milieu. As demonstrated in his Governor-General's Award-winning volume, *The
Rocking Chair and Other Poems* (1948), Klein was fascinated by the dilemmas of French Canadian
reality; his response to Hitler's atrocities inform the angry satire of *The Hitleriad* (1944). A lawyer
by training, a passionate Zionist, and an avid Joyce scholar, Klein drew on wide learning in the
Talmud and more esoteric sources like the Kabbalah for inspiration. In the early fifties, he suffered
a nervous breakdown, withdrawing from his roles as a lawyer and the longtime editor of the
Canadian Jewish Chronicle, and becoming reclusive until his death. Klein's *Complete Poems* (2 vols,
Parts One and Two, ed. Pollock) were published in 1990.

MONTREAL

1
O city metropole, isle riverain!
Your ancient pavages and sainted routs
Traverse my spirit's conjured avenues!
Splendor erablic of your promenades
Foliates there, and there your maisonry
Of pendent balcon and escalier'd march,
Unique midst English habitat,
Is vivid Normandy!

2
You populate the pupils of my eyes:
Thus, does the Indian, plumèd, furtivate
Still through your painted autumns, Ville-Marie!
Though palisades have passed, though calumet
With tabac of your peace enfumes the air,
Still do I spy the phantom, aquiline,
Genuflect, moccasin'd, behind
His statue in the square!

3
Thus, costumed images before me pass,
Haunting your archives architectural:
Coureur de bois, in posts where pelts were portaged;

Seigneur within his candled manoir; Scot
Ambulant through his bank, pillar'd and vast.
Within your chapels, voyaged mariners
Still pray, and personage departed,
All present from your past!

4

Grand port of navigations, multiple
The lexicons uncargo'd at your quays,
Sonnant though strange to me; but chiefest, I,
Auditor of your music, cherish the
Joined double-melodied vocabulaire
Where English vocable and roll Ecossic,
Mollified by the parle of French
Bilinguefact your air!

5

Such your suaver voice, hushed Hochelaga!
But for me also sound your potencies,
Fortissimos of sirens fluvial,
Bruit of manufactory, and thunder
From foundry issuant, all puissant tone
Implenishing your hebdomad; and then
Sanct silence, and your argent belfries
Clamant in orison!

6

You are a part of me, O all your quartiers—
And of dire pauvreté and of richesse—
To finished time my homage loyal claim;
You are locale of infancy, milieu
Vital of institutes that formed my fate;
And you above the city, scintillant,
Mount Royal, are my spirit's mother,
Almative, poitrinate!

7

Never do I sojourn in alien place
But I do languish for your scenes and sounds,
City of reverie, nostalgic isle,
Pendant most brilliant on Laurentian cord!
The coigns of your boulevards—my signiory—
Your suburbs are my exile's verdure fresh,
Your parks, your fountain'd parks—
Pasture of memory!

8
City, O city, you are vision'd as
A parchemin roll of saecular exploit
Inked with the script of eterne souvenir!
You are in sound, chanson and instrument!
Mental, you rest forever edified
With tower and dome; and in these beating valves,
Here in these beating valves, you will
For all my mortal time reside!   [1948]

POLITICAL MEETING

(For Camillien Houde)

On the school platform, draping the folding seats,
they wait the chairman's praise and glass of water.
Upon the wall the agonized Y initials their faith.

Here all are laic; the skirted brothers have gone.
Still, their equivocal absence is felt, like a breeze
that gives curtains the sounds of surplices.

The hall is yellow with light, and jocular;
suddenly some one lets loose upon the air
the ritual bird which the crowd in snares of singing

catches and plucks, throat, wings, and little limbs.
Fall the feathers of sound, like *alouette's*.
The chairman, now, is charming, full of asides and wit,

building his orators, and chipping off
the heckling gargoyles popping in the hall.
(Outside, in the dark, the street is body-tall,

flowered with faces intent on the scarecrow thing
that shouts to thousands the echoing
of their own wishes.) The Orator has risen!

Worshipped and loved, their favourite visitor,
a country uncle with sunflower seeds in his pockets,
full of wonderful moods, tricks, imitative talk,

he is their idol: like themselves, not handsome,
not snobbish, not of the *Grande Allée! Un homme!*
Intimate, informal, he makes bear's compliments

to the ladies; is gallant; and grins;
goes for the balloon, his opposition, with pins;
jokes also on himself, speaks of himself

in the third person, slings slang, and winks with folklore;
and knows now that he has them, kith and kin.
Calmly, therefore, he begins to speak of war,

praises the virtue of being *Canadien*,
of being at peace, of faith, of family,
and suddenly his other voice: *Where are your sons?*

He is tearful, choking tears; but not he
would blame the clever English; in their place
he'd do the same; maybe.

Where *are* your sons?
          The whole street wears one face,
shadowed and grim; and in the darkness rises
the body-odour of race.   [1948]

DOROTHY LIVESAY

Canada b. 1909

Livesay published her first book, *Green Pitcher*, in 1928. Her remarkably prolific career has spanned more than six decades, including (aside from hundreds of periodical publications and several important editorial roles) over twenty books encompassing virtually all genres. Livesay developed from a poet celebrated chiefly for lyric beauty, to a writer whose work was imbued with the leftist politics she embraced beginning in the thirties, to the later Livesay whose poems celebrate women's sexuality. Gender has always been important for Livesay: in her foreword to *Collected Poems: The Two Seasons* (1972), she writes: 'Perhaps we are a country more feminine than we like to admit, because the unifying, regenerative principle is a passion with us.' Livesay, who among many other honours has won two Governor-General's Awards for her poetry (1944 and 1947), has written a memoir, *Right Hand Left Hand* (1977), and a series of stories and sketches about growing up on the prairie, *Beginnings: A Winnipeg Childhood* (1975).

DAY AND NIGHT

1
Dawn, red and angry, whistles loud and sends
A geysered shaft of steam searching the air.
Scream after scream announces that the churn
Of life must move, the giant arm command.
Men in a stream, a moving human belt
Move into sockets, every one a bolt.
The fun begins, a humming, whirring drum—
Men do a dance in time to the machines.

2
One step forward
Two steps back
Shove the lever,
Push it back

While Arnot whirls
A roundabout
And Geoghan shuffles
Bolts about.

One step forward
Hear it crack
Smashing rhythm—
Two steps back

Your heart-beat pounds
Against your throat
The roaring voices
Drown your shout

Across the way
A writhing whack
Sets you spinning
Two steps back—

One step forward
Two steps back.

3
Day and night are rising and falling
Night and day shift gears and slip rattling
Down the runway, shot into storerooms
Where only arms and a note-book remember
The record of evil, the sum of commitments.
We move as through sleep's revolving memories
Piling up hatred, stealing the remnants,
Doors forever folding before us—
And where is the recompense, on what agenda
Will you set love down? Who knows of peace?

Day and night
Night and day
Light rips into ribbons
What we say.

I called to love
Deep in dream:
Be with me in the daylight
As in gloom.

Be with me in the pounding
In the knives against my back
Set your voice resounding
Above the steel's whip crack.

High and sweet
Sweet and high
Hold, hold up the sunlight
In the sky!

Day and night
Night and day
Tear up all the silence
Find the words I could not say . . .

4
We were stoking coal in the furnaces; red hot
They gleamed, burning our skins away, his and mine.
We were working together, night and day, and knew
Each other's stroke; and without words, exchanged
An understanding about kids at home,
The landlord's jaw, wage-cuts and overtime.
We were like buddies, see? Until they said
That nigger is too smart the way he smiles
And sauces back the foreman; he might say
Too much one day, to others changing shifts.
Therefore they cut him down, who flowered at night
And raised me up, day hanging over night—
So furnaces could still consume our withered skin.

Shadrach, Meshach and Abednego
Turn in the furnace, whirling slow.
        Lord, I'm burnin' in the fire
        Lord, I'm steppin' on the coals
        Lord, I'm blacker than my brother
        Blow your breath down here.

        Boss, I'm smothered in the darkness
        Boss, I'm shrivellin' in the flames
        Boss, I'm blacker than my brother
        Blow your breath down here.
Shadrach, Meshach and Abednego
Burn in the furnace, whirling slow.

5

Up in the roller room, men swing steel
Swing it, zoom; and cut it, crash.
Up in the dark the welder's torch
Makes sparks fly like lightning reel.

Now I remember storm on a field
The trees bow tense before the blow
Even the jittering sparrows' talk
Ripples into the still tree shield.

We are in storm that has no cease
No lull before, no after time
When green with rain the grasses grow
And air is sweet with fresh increase.

We bear the burden home to bed
The furnace glows within our hearts:
Our bodies hammered through the night
Are welded into bitter bread.

Bitter, yes:
But listen, friend:
We are mightier
In the end.

We have ears
Alert to seize
A weakness
In the foreman's ease

We have eyes
To look across
The bosses' profit
At our loss.

Are you waiting?
Wait with us
After evening
There's a hush—

Use it not
For love's slow count:
Add up hate
And let it mount

Until the lifeline
Of your hand
Is calloused with
A fiery brand!

Add up hunger,
Labour's ache
These are figures
That will make

The page grow crazy
Wheels go still,
Silence sprawling
On the till—

Add your hunger,
Brawn and bones,
Take your earnings:
Bread, not stones!

6
Into thy maw I commend my body
But the soul shines without
A child's hands as a leaf are tender
And draw the poison out.

Green of new leaf shall deck my spirit
Laughter's roots will spread:
Though I am overalled and silent
Boss, I'm far from dead!

One step forward
Two steps back
Will soon be over:
Hear it crack!

The wheels may whirr
A roundabout
And neighbour's shuffle
Drown your shout

The wheel must limp
Til it hangs still
And crumpled men
Pour down the hill.

Day and night
Night and day
Till life is turned
The other way!   [1944]

BARTOK AND THE GERANIUM

She lifts her green umbrellas
Towards the pane
Seeking her fill of sunlight
Or of rain;
Whatever falls
She has no commentary
Accepts, extends,
Blows out her furbelows,
Her bustling boughs;

And all the while he whirls
Explodes in space,
Never content with this small room:
Not even can he be
Confined to sky
But must speed high and higher still
From galaxy to galaxy,
Wrench from the stars their momentary notes
Steal music from the moon.

She's daylight
He is dark
She's heaven-held breath
He storms and crackles
Spits with hell's own spark.

Yet in this room, this moment now
These together breathe and be:
She, essence of serenity,
He in a mad intensity
Soars beyond sight
Then hurls, lost Lucifer,
From heaven's height.

And when he's done, he's out:
She leans a lip against the glass
And preens herself in light.   [1955]

MARIE MAKINO

England b. date unknown

Attitudes towards the conditions of the working class at the turn of the century in London are neatly summarized in *The Minority Report of the Royal Commission on the Poor Laws and Relief of Distress* (1905–10): '. . . the average citizen of the middle or upper class takes for granted the constantly recurring destitution among wage-earning families due to unemployment, as part of the natural order of things, and as no more to be combated than the east wind.' The voices in Makino's music-hall song underscore the Commission's report with the authority of personal experience.

'ILDA

I'm sick of it, I tell yer straight,
I'm at it early hours and late;
Up with the lark it ain't much cop,
Feels by eleven fit to drop.
And it's 'ave yer done this, and 'ave yer done that?
Didn't I tell yer to shake the mat?
Quick, there's the milkman at the door.
Now use some Ronuk to polish the floor.
Come, it's time the washing was done—
Now, my girl, you've some errands to run.

    'Oh, 'Ilda, 'Ilda, 'Ilda,
      Go and tidy yer 'air.
    Oh, 'Ilda, 'Ilda, 'Ilda,
      Here, there and everywhere.
    Have yer me boots? Where's the 'ot water?
    Stop carryin' on as yer didn't oughter.
    Use yer brain. Are yer sane?
      Oh, 'Ilda, 'Ilda, 'Ilda!'

When the beds is made and sweeping done,
Off for some fish I 'as ter run,
Or else ter fetch a bottle of stout,
Or take the kids fer a short walk out.
If the washing's out it's sure ter rain,
Then I 'as ter lug it in again.
I'm running about all over the show,
Why ever I does it, I don't know.
I'd like ter lay me down and die,
But I gets no chance, 'cause they always cry:

    'Oh, 'Ilda, 'Ilda, 'Ilda,
      Go and tidy yer 'air.

Oh, 'Ilda, 'Ilda, 'Ilda,
    Here, there and everywhere.
Wash yerself—you're stale and musty,
Sneeze, my girl, for yer brains are dusty,
Use yer eyes—don't catch flies—
    Oh, 'Ilda, 'Ilda, 'Ilda!'

I'm a slave, and it's a shame,
Why should *I* get all the blame?
I wouldn't mind so much if they smiled,
But, lumme! their looks near drive me wild.
They shoves on that superior face,
As if they was a-saying their grace.
I'm sorry I'm not a bit quicker—it's true,
But I'm not blaming meself, would you?
No, as I says when I thinks it all out,
It strengthens their lungs to 'ave to shout:

    'Oh, 'Ilda, 'Ilda, 'Ilda,
        Go and tidy yer 'air.
    Oh, 'Ilda, 'Ilda, 'Ilda,
        Here, there and everywhere.
    Go to the door—there's someone knocking,
    Clean yer teeth, pull up yer stocking,
    'Pon my soul, you're up the pole—
    Oh, 'Ilda, 'Ilda, 'Ilda!'   [c. 1910]

CHARLES OLSON

USA 1910–1970

Olson studied at Harvard and Wesleyan universities, and from 1951 to 1959 was the rector of Black Mountain College in North Carolina. The College name has become more famous as the name of the postmodern school of poetry that Olson founded and that included or influenced poets like Robert Duncan, Robert Creeley, Fred Wah, and George Bowering. Believing that humanism and its universalizing values were at an end, Olson countered with a poetics that named and celebrated the local, the particular, and the immediate. His major project, *The Maximus Poems* (1953–75), an epic published in several volumes, traces the development of Maximus/Olson in a Massachusetts community that Olson conceived as a reflection of America.

from THE MAXIMUS POEMS, BOOK III
THE FESTIVAL ASPECT

The World
has become divided
from the Universe. Put the three Towns
together

The Individual
has become divided
from the Absolute, it is the times promised
by the poets. They shall drop delta
and lingam, all forms
of symbol
and mystery. As well as all
naturalism. And literalness. The truth

is fingers holding it all up
underneath, the Lotus
is a cusp, and its stalk
holds up it all.
It isn't even a burning point, it is a bow
of fingers shooting
a single arrow. The three Towns
are to be destroyed, as well as
that they are to be made known,
that they are to be known,
that there is no three Towns
there is no Society, there is no
known
Absolute: we shall stand on our heads and hands
truly, kicking
all false form off
the surface
of the still, or active,
water-surface. There is no image
which is a reflection. Or a condition. There is solely
the Lotus
upside down. When the World is one again
with the Universal the Flower
will grow down, the Sun
will be stamped
on the leather
like a growing
Coin, the earth
will be the light, the air and the dust
of the air will be the perfume
of sense, the *gloire*
will have returned
of the body seen
against the window. The flesh
will glow.

          The three Towns
will have become populated
again. In the first Town
somebody will have addressed
themselves
to someone else. There will be no need
of the explicit. In the second Town
the earth
will have replaced
the sun. In the third Town the man
shall have arisen, he shall have concluded
any use of reason, the Dialogue
will have re-begun. The earth
shall have preceded love. The sun
shall have given back its deadly
rays, there shall be no longer any
need to be so careful. The third Town
shall have revealed
itself.

The third Town
is the least known. The third Town
is the one which is the most interesting—and is overpopulated—
behind the Western
sun. It shall only come forth
from underneath. The foot of the Lotus
is not its face, but the roots
of its stalk. The Elephant
moves easily
through any trees. He is Ganesh
with the big Hands. His hands alone
offer all. Through the mountain
through the bole
of any tree through the adamantine
he passes
as though it were nothing. Only the God Himself
of whom he is the frazzled stalk
in each of the coolness, and ease, of his power
is more than water. Water is not equal
                    to the
                    Flower. The three Towns
                    are the fairest
                    which the Flower
                    is. Only when the Flower—only when the uproar

has driven the Soul
out of me, only then shall the God
strike
the three Towns. The three Towns
shall first
be born again. The Flower shall
grow down. The mud of the bottom
is the floor
of the Upside Down. The present
is an uproar, the present
is the times of the re-birth of
the Lotus. Ganesh
is walking
through anything. There is no obs-
tacle. There will be no more
anger. There is only one
anyway. It is too early
for anger. The third Town
has only just
begun.   [1975]

P.S. REGE

India 1910–1978

Rege was born in a village in Ratnagiri district, Maharashtra and educated in Bombay and at the London School of Economics. One of the most widely translated of the Marathi poets, Rege writes poetry in most of the major Indian languages as well as in English, German, Spanish, Chinese, and Danish. 'Dream' was translated into English by Rege himself. A playwright, critic, and novelist, Rege published his first book of poems, *Sadhana*, in 1931; it has been followed by numerous other volumes, including *Dusra Pakshi* (1966).

DREAM

I think I must have dozed off for a little while;
For, when I woke up you had come and gone.
Only a few flowers remained—
Flowers which could not even say who they were . . .
And a vague soft fragrance in the air.

Tonight I must dream a longer dream
So that the flowers will talk
And their fragrance stretch a tremulous bridge
Between you and me.   [n. d.]

Translated by the poet

ELIZABETH BISHOP

USA 1911-1979

Bishop's wide travels, particularly her twenty-year sojourn in Brazil, inspired many of her poems, which often construct a geography of selfhood through careful observation and description of landscape and of cartography itself. 'The Moose', set in the Maritimes where Bishop spent part of her childhood, builds quietly to an animal's sudden appearance that awakens a communion among passengers travelling in a bus at night; 'In the Waiting Room' is typical of Bishop's evocations of a child's profound isolation and anxious emergence into history. *The Complete Poems* (1983) collect her life's work.

THE MOOSE

For Grace Bulmer Bowers

From narrow provinces
of fish and bread and tea,
home of the long tides
where the bay leaves the sea
twice a day and takes
the herrings long rides,

where if the river
enters or retreats
in a wall of brown foam
depends on if it meets
the bay coming in,
the bay not at home;

where, silted red,
sometimes the sun sets
facing a red sea,
and others, veins the flats'
lavender, rich mud
in burning rivulets;

on red, gravelly roads,
down rows of sugar maples,
past clapboard farmhouses
and neat, clapboard churches,
bleached, ridged as clamshells,
past twin silver birches,

through late afternoon
a bus journeys west,
the windshield flashing pink,

pink glancing off of metal,
brushing the dented flank
of blue, beat-up enamel;

down hollows, up rises,
and waits, patient, while
a lone traveller gives
kisses and embraces
to seven relatives
and a collie supervises.

Goodbye to the elms,
to the farm, to the dog.
The bus starts. The light
grows richer; the fog,
shifting, salty, thin,
comes closing in.

Its cold, round crystals
form and slide and settle
in the white hens' feathers,
in gray glazed cabbages,
on the cabbage roses
and lupins like apostles;

the sweet peas cling
to their wet white string
on the whitewashed fences;
bumblebees creep
inside the foxgloves,
and evening commences.

One stop at Bass River.
Then the Economies—
Lower, Middle, Upper;
Five Islands, Five Houses,
where a woman shakes a tablecloth
out after supper.

A pale flickering. Gone.
The Tantramar marshes
and the smell of salt hay.
An iron bridge trembles
and a loose plank rattles
but doesn't give way.

On the left, a red light
swims through the dark;
a ship's port lantern.
Two rubber boots show,
illuminated, solemn.
A dog gives one bark.

A woman climbs in
with two market bags,
brisk, freckled, elderly.
'A grand night. Yes, sir,
all the way to Boston.'
She regards us amicably.

Moonlight as we enter
the New Brunswick woods,
hairy, scratchy, splintery;
moonlight and mist
caught in them like lamb's wool
on bushes in a pasture.

The passengers lie back.
Snores. Some long sighs.
A dreamy divagation
begins in the night,
a gentle, auditory,
slow hallucination. . . .

In the creakings and noises,
an old conversation
—not concerning us,
but recognizable, somewhere,
back in the bus:
Grandparents' voices

uninterruptedly
talking, in Eternity:
names being mentioned,
things cleared up finally;
what he said, what she said,
who got pensioned;

deaths, deaths and sicknesses;
the year he remarried;
the year (something) happened.

She died in childbirth.
That was the son lost
when the schooner foundered.

He took to drink. Yes.
She went to the bad.
When Amos began to pray
even in the store and
finally the family had
to put him away.

'Yes . . .' that peculiar
affirmative. 'Yes . . .'
A sharp, indrawn breath,
half groan, half acceptance,
that means 'Life's like that.
We know *it* (also death).'

Talking the way they talked
in the old featherbed,
peacefully, on and on,
dim lamplight in the hall,
down in the kitchen, the dog
tucked in her shawl.

Now, it's all right now
even to fall asleep
just as on all those nights
—Suddenly the bus driver
stops with a jolt,
turns off his lights.

A moose has come out of
the impenetrable wood
and stands there, looms, rather,
in the middle of the road.
It approaches; it sniffs at
the bus's hot hood.

Towering, antlerless,
high as a church,
homely as a house
(or, safe as houses).
A man's voice assures us
'Perfectly harmless. . . .'

Some of the passengers
exclaim in whispers,
childishly, softly,
'Sure are big creatures.'
'It's awful plain.'
'Look! It's a she!'

Taking her time,
she looks the bus over,
grand, otherworldly.
Why, why do we feel
(we all feel) this sweet
sensation of joy?

'Curious creatures,'
says our quiet driver,
rolling his r's.
'Look at that, would you.'
Then he shifts gears.
For a moment longer,

by craning backward,
the moose can be seen
on the moonlit macadam;
then there's a dim
smell of moose, an acrid
smell of gasoline.

[1976]

IN THE WAITING ROOM

In Worcester, Massachusetts,
I went with Aunt Consuelo
to keep her dentist's appointment
and sat and waited for her
in the dentist's waiting room.

It was winter. It got dark
early. The waiting room
was full of grown-up people,
arctics and overcoats,
lamps and magazines.
My aunt was inside
what seemed like a long time
and while I waited I read
the National Geographic
(I could read) and carefully

studied the photographs:
the inside of a volcano,
black, and full of ashes;
then it was spilling over
in rivulets of fire.
Osa and Martin Johnson
dressed in riding breeches,
laced boots, and pith helmets.
A dead man slung on a pole
—'Long Pig,' the caption said.
Babies with pointed heads
wound round and round with string;
black, naked women with necks
wound round and round with wire
like the necks of light bulbs.
Their breasts were horrifying.
I read it right straight through.
I was too shy to stop.
And then I looked at the cover:
the yellow margins, the date.

Suddenly, from inside,
came an *oh!* of pain
—Aunt Consuelo's voice—
not very loud or long.
I wasn't at all surprised;
even then I knew she was
a foolish, timid woman.
I might have been embarrassed,
but wasn't. What took me
completely by surprise
was that it was *me*:
my voice, in my mouth.
Without thinking at all
I was my foolish aunt,
I—we—were falling, falling,
our eyes glued to the cover
of the *National Geographic*,
February, 1918.

I said to myself: three days
and you'll be seven years old.
I was saying it to stop
the sensation of falling off

the round, turning world
into cold, blue-black space.
But I felt: you are an *I*,
you are an *Elizabeth*,
you are one of *them*.
Why should you be one, too?
I scarcely dared to look
to see what it was I was.
I gave a sidelong glance
—I couldn't look any higher—
at shadowy gray knees,
trousers and skirts and boots
and different pairs of hands
lying under the lamps.
I knew that nothing stranger
had ever happened, that nothing
stranger could ever happen.
Why should I be my aunt,
or me, or anyone?
What similarities—
boots, hands, the family voice
I felt in my throat, or even
the *National Geographic*
and those awful hanging breasts—
held us all together
or made us all just one?
How—I didn't know any
word for it—how 'unlikely' . . .
How had I come to be here,
like them, and overhear
a cry of pain that could have
got loud and worse but hadn't?
The waiting room was bright
and too hot. It was sliding
beneath a big black wave,
another, and another.

Then I was back in it.
The War was on. Outside,
in Worcester, Massachusetts,
were night and slush and cold,
and it was still the fifth
of February, 1918.

[1976]

ALLEN CURNOW

New Zealand b. 1911

Born in Timaru, Curnow is a prominent poet, playwright, editor, and teacher who studied literature and theology at university. Before joining the English Department at Auckland University in 1951 where he taught until his retirement in 1977, Curnow worked as a journalist for the Christchurch Press as well as for newspapers in London. His most notable collections of poetry are *Islands and Time* (1941), *Poems 1947–57* and *An Incorrigible Music* (1979). 'Landfall in Unknown Seas' (1941), Curnow's polemic on the legacy of colonial exploration and exploitation, protests against European historical conquest narratives.

LANDFALL IN UNKNOWN SEAS

The 300th Anniversary of the Discovery of New Zealand by Abel Tasman, 13 December 1642

I

Simply by sailing in a new direction
You could enlarge the world.
                              You picked your captain,
Keen on discoveries, tough enough to make them,
Whatever vessels could be spared from other
More urgent service for a year's adventure;
Took stock of the more probable conjectures
About the Unknown to be traversed, all
Guesses at golden coasts and tales of monsters
To be digested into plain instructions
For likely and unlikely situations.

All this resolved and done, you launched the whole
On a fine morning, the best time of year,
Skies widening and the oceanic furies
Subdued by summer illumination; time
To go and to be gazed at going
On a fine morning, in the Name of God
Into the nameless waters of the world.

O you had estimated all the chances
Of business in those waters, the world's waters
Yet unexploited.
                    But more than the sea-empire's
Cannon, the dogs of bronze and iron barking
From Timor to the Straits, backed up the challenge.
Between you and the South an older enmity
Lodged in the searching mind, that would not tolerate
So huge a hegemony of ignorance.

There, where your Indies had already sprinkled
Their tribes like ocean rains, you aimed your voyage;
Like them invoked your God, gave seas to history
And islands to new hazardous tomorrows.

II
Suddenly exhilaration
Went off like a gun, the whole
Horizon, the long chase done,
Hove to. There was the seascape
Crammed with coast, surprising
As new lands will, the sailor
Moving on the face of the waters,
Watching the earth take shape
Round the unearthly summits, brighter
Than its emerging colour.

Yet this, no far fool's errand,
Was less than the heart desired,
In its old Indian dream
The glittering gulfs ascending
Past palaces and mountains
Making one architecture.
Here the uplifted structure,
Peak and pillar of cloud—
O splendour of desolation—reared
Tall from the pit of the swell,
With a shadow, a finger of wind, forbade
Hopes of a lucky landing.

Always to islanders danger
Is what comes over the sea;
Over the yellow sands and the clear
Shallows, the dull filament
Flickers, the blood of strangers:
Death discovered the Sailor
O in a flash, in a flat calm,
A clash of boats in the bay
And the day marred with murder.
The dead required no further
Warning to keep their distance;
The rest, noting the failure,
Pushed on with a reconnaissance
To the north; and sailed away.

III
Well, home is the Sailor, and that is a chapter
In a schoolbook, a relevant yesterday
We thought we knew all about, being much apter
    To profit, sure of our ground,
No murderers mooring in our Golden Bay.

But now there are no more islands to be found
And the eye scans risky horizons of its own
In unsettled weather, and murmurs of the drowned
    Haunt their familiar beaches—
Who navigates us towards what unknown

But not improbable provinces? Who reaches
A future down for us from the high shelf
Of spiritual daring? Not those speeches
    Pinning on the Past like a decoration
For merit that congratulates itself,

O not the self-important celebration
Or most painstaking history, can release
The current of a discoverer's elation
    And silence the voices saying,
'Here is the world's end where wonders cease.'

Only by a more faithful memory, laying
On him the half-light of a diffident glory,
The Sailor lives, and stands beside us, paying
    Out into our time's wave
The stain of blood that writes an island story.   [1941]

AN INCORRIGIBLE MUSIC

It ought to be impossible to be mistaken
about these herons, to begin with
you can count them, it's been done successfully
with swans daffodils blind mice, any number
of dead heroes and heavenly bodies.

Eleven herons are not baked in porcelain,
helpless to hatch the credulities of art
or to change places, e.g. number seven
counting from the left with number five,
or augment themselves by number twelve arriving
over the mangroves. Thirteen, fourteen, fifteen,
punctually the picture completes itself
and is never complete.

                The air
and the water being identically still,
each heron is four herons,
one right-side-up in the air,
one up-side-down in the tide,
and these two doubled by looking at.

The mudbacked mirrors in your head
multiply the possibilities of human
error, but what's the alternative?

The small wind instruments in the herons' throats
play an incorrigible music on a scale
incommensurate with hautboys and baroque wigs.

There's only one book in the world, and that's the one
everyone accurately misquotes.

A big one! A big one!   [1979]

SOMHAIRLE MACGILL-EAIN/ SORLEY MACLEAN

Scotland b. 1911

A leading writer of Gaelic in the twentieth-century Scottish Renaissance, MacLean is passionate in his concern for the survival of the language of his own family whose ancestors were bearers of traditional song: 'Gaelic is not a poor language, in art at any rate. Though it had only its ineffable songs, which cannot be put in other words, it would still be a priceless medium of expression.' (*Ris a bhruthaich: criticism and prose writings*, ed. Gillies, 1985).

BAN-GHÀIDHEAL

Am faca Tu i, lùdhaich mhóir,
ri 'n abrar Aon Mhac Dhé?
Am fac' thu 'coltas air Do thriall
ri strì an fhìon-lios chéin?

An cuallach mhiosan air a druim,
fallus searbh air mala is gruaidh;
's a' mhios chreadha trom air cùl
a cinn chrùibte bhochd thruaigh.

Chan fhaca Tu i, Mhic an t-saoir,
ri 'n abrar Rìgh na Glòir,
a miosg nan cladach carrach siar,
fo fhallus cliabh a lòin.

An t-earrach so agus so chaidh
's gach fichead earrach bho 'n an tùs
tharruing ise 'n fheamainn fhuar
chum biadh a cloinne 's duais an tùir.

'S gach fichead foghar tha air triall
chaill i samhradh buidh nam blàth;
is threabh an dubh-chosnadh an clais
tarsuinn mìnead ghil a clàir.

Agus labhair T' eaglais chaomh
mu staid chaillte a h-anama thruaigh;
agus leag an cosnadh dian
a corp gu sàmhchair dhuibh an uaigh.

Is thriall a tìm mar shnighe dubh
a' drùdhadh tughaidh fàrdaich bochd;
mheal ise an dubh-chosnadh cruaidh;
is glas a cadal suain an nochd.

A HIGHLAND WOMAN

Hast Thou seen her, great Jew,
who art called the One Son of God?
Hast Thou seen on Thy way the like of her
labouring in the distant vineyard?

The load of fruits on her back,
a bitter sweat on brow and cheek,
and the clay basin heavy on the back
of her bent poor wretched head.

Thou hast not seen her, Son of the carpenter,
who art called the King of Glory,
among the rugged western shores
in the sweat of her food's creel.

This Spring and last Spring
and every twenty Springs from the beginning,
she has carried the cold seaweed
for her children's food and the castle's reward.

And every twenty Autumns gone
she has lost the golden summer of her bloom,
and the Black Labour has ploughed the furrow
across the white smoothness of her forehead.

And Thy gentle church has spoken
about the lost state of her miserable soul,
and the unremitting toil has lowered
her body to a black peace in a grave.

And her time has gone like a black sludge
seeping through the thatch of a poor dwelling:
the hard Black Labour was her inheritance;
grey is her sleep to-night.   [1989]

JOHN CAGE   ໒໊

USA 1912-1992

Cage was educated as a composer and pianist in Los Angeles, Paris, and New York. From the 1940s to the 1970s he developed uniquely innovative compositional and performance procedures, including the prepared piano, 'silent' concerts, 'found' music, and 'chance' music. He often collaborated with his companion, David Tudor, a pianist, and was an early proponent of the creative use of technologies such as amplifiers, tapes, slides, and computers for musical events. His writings are no less strikingly innovative, as evidenced in texts such as *Silence* (1961), *A Year from Monday* (1967), and *M: Writings '67–'72*.

from DIARY: HOW TO IMPROVE THE WORLD (YOU WILL ONLY MAKE MATTERS WORSE) 1965–1967

VIII.   *The daily warmth we*
experience, my father said, is not
transmitted by Sun to Earth but is what
Earth does in response to Sun.
Measurements, he said, measure
measuring means.   Bashō: Matsutake ya
shiranu ko no ha no hebaritsuku.
The leaf of some unknown tree sticking
on the mushroom (Blythe). Mushroom does
not know that leaf is sticking on it
(Takemitsu).   Project: Discover way to
translate Far Eastern texts so western men
can read orientally.
Communication?   Bakarashi!   Words
without syntax, each word

Author's note: This text [. . .] is a mosaic of ideas, statements, words, and stories. It is also a diary. For each day, I determined by chance operations how many parts of the mosaic I would write and how many words there would be in each. The number of words per day was to equal, or, by the last statement written, to exceed one hundred words.[. . .] I used an IBM Selectric typewriter to print my text. I used twelve different type faces, letting chance operations determine which face would be used for which statement. So, too, the left marginations were determined, the right marginations being the result of not hyphenating words and at the same time keeping the number of characters per line forty-three or less. The present typography follows the original chance-determined plan.

Editor's note: Selections from the 90 entries of the first three years of John Cage's 'Diary' were determined by the stations of the Seventh Avenue I.R.T. in New York City, the subway line that was the most convenient to Cage's loft: 8 (standing for Sheridan Square), 14, 18, 23, 28, 34, 42, and so on. (This was also George Oppen's example of a mathematical 'discrete series', as an explanation for the title of his first book.)

polymorphic.   **He wanted me to agree that
the piano tuner and the piano maker have
nothing to do with it (the composition).
The younger ones had said: Whoever makes
the stretcher isn't separate from the
painting.   (It doesn't stop there
either.)**
                              XIV.   Since the
Spirit's omnipresent, there's a difference
in things but no difference in spirit.
          McLuhan was able to say 'The medium is
          the message' because he started from
no concern with content.   Or choose
                    quantity, not quality (we get
                    quality willy-nilly): i.e. we'd like
          to stay alive, the changes that are
taking place are so many and so
          interesting.   Composition'll have, he
          said, less and less to do with what
                    happens.   Things happen more
quickly.   One of the signs you'll get
          that'll tell you things are going well is
          that you and everyone else you know will
                    be inhabiting lightweight Dymaxion
                    houses, disengaged from ownership and
                    from violated Earth spot (read
                    Fuller).
                    XVIII.   Hearing of past actions
          (politics, economics), people soon
won't be able to imagine how such
          things could've happened.   Fusing
                    politics with economics prepared
          disappearance of both.   Still
          invisible: **Arriving, realizing we
                    never departed.   He mentioned heads
                    on the ceiling.   Seeing them, noticed
          him too**.   Fusion of credit card with
                    passport.   Means of making one's voice
                    heard: refusal to honor credit card.
End of the month?   That too may be
                    changed: the measurement of time,
                    what season it is, whether it's
                    night or day.   In any case, no bills,
          just added information.   **'Take it easy,
but take it.'**   What'll we do?   (Before
lunch.)   'Wing it.'

XXIII.   LET'S CALL IT THE
COLLECTIVE CONSCIOUSNESS (WE'VE GOT
THE COLLECTIVE UNCONSCIOUS).   THE
QUESTION IS: WHAT ARE THE THINGS
EVERYONE NEEDS REGARDLESS OF LIKES
AND DISLIKES?   BEGINNING OF ANSWER:
WATER, FOOD, SHELTER, CLOTHING,
ELECTRICITY, AUDIO-VISUAL
COMMUNICATION, TRANSPORTATION.   FORM
OF ANSWER: GLOBAL UTILITIES NETWORK.   Do
not fear that as the globe gets utility
organized your daily life will not
remain (or become as the case may be)
disorganized, characterized by chaos,
illuminated anarchically.   You'll
have nothing to do; so what will you
do?   A lifelong university
(Fuller)?   In the lobby after La
Monte Young's music stopped,
Geldzahler said: It's like being in a
womb; now that I'm out, I want to get
back in.   I felt differently and so did
Jasper Johns: we were relieved to be
released.
XXVIII.   We've
poisoned our food, polluted our air
and water, killed birds and cattle,
eliminated forests, impoverished,
eroded the earth.   We're unselfish,
skilful: we include in our acts to
perform—we've had a rehearsal—
the last one.   What would you call it?
Nirvana?   'Not only was instant
universal voice communication forecast
by David Sarnoff, but also instant
television, instant newspapers, instant
magazines and instant visual
telephone service . . . the development of
such global communications system
would link people everywhere . . . for
reorientation toward a "one-world
concept of mass communications in an
era marked by the emergence of a
universal language, a universal
culture and a universal common
market.'"

**XXXIV.   Boddhisattva Doctrine: Enter
Nirvana only when all beings, sentient,
non-sentient, are ready to do likewise.**
Couldn't believe my eyes (stopping for
lunch in Red Bud, Illinois): a single
photograph of nature (mountains,
lake, island, forests) enlarged, printed
twice, once left to right, once right to
left, the two prints juxtaposed to form a
single image, seam down the middle.
Eugenics.   Proposal: take facts of
art seriously: try them in economics/
politics, giving up, that is, notions about
balance (of power, of wealth),
foreground, background.   **They will kill
you, she said, with kindness.**   There's a
temptation to do nothing simply because
there's so much to do that one doesn't
know where to begin.   Begin anywhere.   For
instance, since electronics is at
the heart of the matter, establish a
global voltage, a single design for
plugs and jacks.   Remove the need for
transformers and adaptors.   Vary not the
connecting means but the things to be
connected.
*XLII.   To
know whether or not art is contemporary,
we no longer use aesthetic criteria (if
it's destroyed by shadows, spoiled by
ambient sounds); (assuming these) we
use social criteria: can include action on
the part of others.*   We'll take the mad
ones with us, and we know where we're
going.   Even now, he told me, they sit at
the crossroads in African villages
regenerating society.   Mental hospitals:
localization of a resource we've yet
to exploit.   I visited an aging
anarchist.   (He had the remaining copies of
Martin's Men Against the State.)   He
introduced me to two Negro children he'd
adopted.   After they went out to
play, he told me what trouble he'd had in
deciding finally to draw this line: No
jumping up and down on the beds.
L.   Abundance.

Officials checked to make certain we'd
paid the air-travel tax, didn't ask to see
    our passports.   *Marcel Duchamp.*
        '. . . Valencia, cathedral—University.
    Palma will be interesting again, then
    Dardona and off to Milan and after which
        the western coast of Yugoslavia & tour
        (at southern end) of Grecian Islands
after which plane from Athens to New York.
    Many travelers,—going everywhere.
        Love, Mom'   More irritated by the
    schedule than the work, he announced
he'd do all the dishwashing.   Shortly the
        others were helping.   Sometimes he had
            nothing to do.   **Returning from
        Europe: 'We're all looking forward
        to the return of the W.P.A.   It's the
only thing we ever had any talent for.'**
            LIX.   Mother wrote to say: 'Stay
in Europe.   Soak up as much beauty as you
    possibly can.'   Cards punched for
        insertion in telephones so we don't
        have to remember numbers or spend
time dialing.   Acceleration.   What shall we
    do with our emotions?   ('Suffer them,' I
    hear her saying.)   Having everything we
need, we'll nevertheless spend restless
nights awake with desire for pleasures we
    imagine that never take place.   **Things
        also happen gradually (one of New
    Babylon's anarchists was elected a
member of Amsterdam's City Council).**
We've the right, Fuller explains, to object
        to slavery, segregation, etc. (the
            problem of work is solved: machines
take the place of muscles): we've not yet
the right to object to war: first we must
            design, then implement means for
    making the world's resources the
possession of all men.
            LXVI. 'They dance the world as
        it will be . . . is now when they
    dance.'   Technique.   Discipline.
    Ultimately it's not a question of
    taste.   It's the other way around.
Each thing in the world asks us, 'What
makes you think I'm not something you

like?'   *The use of drugs to facilitate*
religious experience is against the stream
            of the times.   *(He lost interest in the*
        tape-music center, its experiments and
                performances.   *He went to the*
Southwest desert.   *He removed himself from*
            the others.)   Begging: difficult
        profession.   In India, parents maim
    children producing bodies that'll attract
    pity.   His eyes are sheep's eyes; his
            mind's superb.   Decided not to give
        him a penny.   Then did (after reading
letter Satie'd written shortly before
    death, asking for a little money, enough
so he could sit in a corner, smoke his
    pipe).
                        LXXII.   The
children have a society of their own.
They have no need for ours.   At the
        airport Ain said he came simply to see
whether his mother was all right.
            Mumma's music (*Mesa*) for Cunningham's
        dance called *Place*.   Sitting in the
            audience I felt afterward as though
I'd been rung through a ringer.   Then had
    to play Satie's *Nocturnes*, something not
            easy for me to do.   Wrong notes all
    over the place.   Tonight the program's
being repeated.   I've practiced.   I'll be
            deaf and blind.   Experimentation.
Summit lecture series on War: not to be
        given in one city, but via a global
    Telstar-like facility, each receiving set
        throughout the world equipped with a
                device permitting hearing no matter
what speech in one's own tongue.
                        LXXIX.   Get it,
    she said, so it's unknown which parent
conceiving will bear the child.
        Responsibility undefined.   Circa
    one hundred and seventy-five kinds of
        male, sixty, seventy kinds of female.
        Sterility.   He had actually gotten slides
showing the passage of the gene from one
                cell to the next.   Destruction.
    Reconstitution.   (What we want is very

little, nothing, so to speak.   We just
                want those things that have so often
            been promised or stated: Liberty,
    Equality, Fraternity; Freedom of this and
                that.)   Clothes for entertainment, not
because of shame.   Privacy to become an
        unusual rather than expected
    experience.   Given disinfection,
sanitation, removal of social concerns re
                defecation, urination.   No
self-consciousness.   Living like animals,
        becoming touchable.
                                    LXXXVI.
The lazy dog (a bomb containing ten
        thousand slivers of razor-sharp
                steel).   In one province of North
Vietnam, the most densely populated, one
    hundred million slivers of razor-sharp
        steel have fallen in a period of
        thirteen months.   These razor darts
slice the villagers to ribbons.   Maki
                thinks Hawaii's another part of
                    Japan.   Portugal thinks of Angola
            not as a colony but as Portugal.
    U.S.A. thinks the Free World is U.S.A.'s
    world, is determined to keep it free,
                    U.S.A.-determined.   *The possibility*
                of conversation resides in the
                    impossibility of two people having
    the same experience whether or not their
        attention is directed one-pointedly.   *An*
                ancient Buddhist realization (sitting
in different seats).   [1967]

IRVING LAYTON

Canada b. 1912

Over the last fifty years, Layton, who immigrated with his parents from Romania to Montreal when he was an infant, has assumed the role of Canada's most passionately romantic and iconoclastic poet, denouncing the country's ignorant, uptight, and boorish attitudes towards art, sexuality, and the imagination. Layton celebrates his Jewishness, his maleness, and his protean imaginative powers, but he also mocks his pretensions. His fine rages are often simultaneous with the invocation of mythic and sacred elements. *Here and Now*, the first of some fifty books, was published in 1945. Layton was an important influence on the succeeding generation of Montreal Jewish poets, most notably Leonard Cohen. Selections of his work include *The Collected Poems of Irving Layton* (1971), *The Love Poems of Irving Layton* (1980), and *A Wild Peculiar Joy: Selected Poems 1945–1982* (1982). He was twice nominated for the Nobel Prize (in 1982 and 1983).

FROM COLONY TO NATION

A dull people,
but the rivers of this country
are wide and beautiful

A dull people
enamoured of childish games,
but food is easily come by
and plentiful

Some with a priest's voice
in their cage of ribs: but
on high mountain-tops and in thunderstorms
the chirping is not heard

Deferring to beadle and censor;
not ashamed for this,
but given over to horseplay,
the making of money

A dull people, without charm
or ideas,
settling into the clean empty look
of a Mountie or dairy farmer
as into a legacy

One can ignore them
(the silences, the vast distances help)
and suppose them at the bottom
of one of the meaner lakes,
their bones not even picked for souvenirs.   [1956]

KEINE LAZAROVITCH 1870–1959

When I saw my mother's head on the cold pillow,
Her white waterfalling hair in the cheeks' hollows,
I thought, quietly circling my grief, of how
She had loved God but cursed extravagantly his creatures.

For her final mouth was not water but a curse,
A small black hole, a black rent in the universe,
Which damned the green earth, stars and trees in its stillness
And the inescapable lousiness of growing old.

And I record she was comfortless, vituperative,
Ignorant, glad, and much else besides; I believe
She endlessly praised her black eyebrows, their thick weave,
Till plagiarizing Death leaned down and took them for his mould.

And spoiled a dignity I shall not again find,
And the fury of her stubborn limited mind;
Now none will shake her amber beads and call God blind,
Or wear them upon a breast so radiantly.

O fierce she was, mean and unaccommodating;
But I think now of the toss of her gold earrings,
Their proud carnal assertion, and her youngest sings
While all the rivers of her red veins move into the sea.   [1961]

BHARATI SARABHAI

India b. 1912

Sarabhai's poetic drama, *The Well of the People*, is shaped by her vision of People's Theatre and her experience of the gathering of pilgrims at the Haridwar *kumbha mela* in spring, 1938, a time rich with the possibility of Indian independence. In the Introduction to the drama, Sarabhai notes that the 'odd form' of the work is expressed in 'the static representation in one moment of time of different characters fixed in their different environments with a changeless background behind.' This practice allows Sarabhai to examine the 'struggles between the traditional devotee and the practical unconscious mystic' as both a pageant of characters and 'the dim workings' of a single mind. The 'Chorus of Workers' tells of the 'old woman' whose 'coming' is both welcomed and feared: in her, 'we see India with the Himalaya of that responsibility, the many steps of synthesis and the burden, accepted by her naturally, without bitterness and without opposition.'

from THE WELL OF THE PEOPLE

CHORUS OF WORKERS

It is now time we speak for her whose life
Was dumb. She is you, you and all of us.
The many are unique man, woman, child. But
To you they are as one and it is time the one
And same unbroken soil that dumps its crust
On village after village of India,
Break—break to shapeless lump, pitiable
Drops of earth, that farmerlike we may torture
Caress, making each clod a hand, a mighty
Gesture, for you signalled across the sky.

You shall see this simple tale shoot its bloom
From hard bedrock of a people's secret life.
Our outer death is for all to see but
Great pain is dumb and faith not to be seen.

Rani has worked with us these twenty years.

We have seen, seen her at the weaving shed,
Come late at end of each long day and stand
Upon twilight that winds her cowdust through
The scattering basket of sunset harvest.

We have seen her, the last one come to stand
Upon the even landing of each day's
Earnings and next day's same beginnings.

She is from Madhubani, a Bihari
Of purest race of Maithili Brahman
In state Darbhanga, gateway of Bengal;

A people with shrewd imagination
Which sees in woman a boon companion
And a willing cost-free serf wife. Their custom,
Or rather the shifts of genteel poverty,
Made it convenient to marry soon,
As often as possible. When this woman
Was a growing girl, most likely beautiful,
They say it was not rare to see a whole
Village of widows; mud-raised, windowless
Huts exposed old and young and child women
Scattered about and men scarce, wonderful
As peacocks.

       But some girls are fortunate.
We hear it remembered that Rani's husband
Dropped by her reposeful and lingering
Oozed such slow amazement on her as takes
People once, making for them a retiring
Corner of madness from which they never tire.

This we remember: when we went to her,
Her husband was dead. She had not eaten
Her five days' share of rice, *Juvar* and water.
There was left no desire but to lie
Down for death, quiet as a child to sleep.

Then with clean-stinging fresh persuasion
And stranger sympathy, we cut through this
Hard apathy. For heavy were the hours
Now loosened on her from the image-desolate
Home—who to find life-breath?

       We sought it in
Work that would not destroy the home, her bulwark
Of love, tradition we respected; work
Of hand perfected in blood from father's
Father to son, from mother to daughter
And now forgotten, (documented since
In archives dry of art, reminding us
Of gracious fabric, pale, veined muslin
From Dacca's branching streams of trade frozen,
Frozen in history of fantastic cruelty
And now forgotten)—all which she, just turned
From near death, could not quite understand.
That folk from town should choose her village,
It seems absurd by any scheme of knowledge.

But inward she must have blessed, for now she
Turned her face, a dim, livid, drowsy herb
To startling light of sun. Then pillar by

Pillar relations fell. And then she lost
The use of her leg,—god, she was old, old
Upon threshold of death till every day
Weighed on her, each small gain bartered in blood.

Still we saw her dawn with unsulking sun
And lonely, in company with fickle moon,
(Her body waning miniature like shadow cast
By candle light), sit and turn her spinning wheel.
And once seven long days gather the web,
Come wading through the sun, to change with us
Pale drops of copper, coins dazzling, counted
From day to day of the year. For her self,
Her leg, she would not use it. Mother, I said,
Mother, what ever will you do with it?

She went on living. She lived to set apart
Crystal from rock, gold from dross, O rich proud heart,
Rose splendid, seventy coins of shining silver
Athwart her old undying body. Miser,
Miser, I cried, where is the merit?

Oh, but my heart was blind then, for every
Fabulous *pice* added, set aside, each coin
Upon coin became before her living eye
Stone upon stone and brick upon brick, piled
On the path to glorious golden-walled
God-apparelled temple of Benares,
Lotus seat of Tathagata at Saranath
In ending rest of death.

                    She saw herself
A pilgrim star upon the western end
Of life. Before my star sets in the sea,
On sun-hit horizon will be Benares,
With my own eyes I shall see Benares
And my husband and son will reap salvation
Through my last vision, she said. At the last
When there is enough, I will go, she said.

At last, she said, but at the last her worth
Was not enough. With her poor broken leg,
Not one in all that pilgrim band would care
To take her cold on her unmoving side,
Risk the long long journey to golden-walled
Benares. Not even for life's money?
She wept, she begged, she promised. All her love,
Was it enough—No, it was not enough.   [1943]

MURIEL RUKEYSER

USA 1913–1980

Rukeyser was born in New York City, educated at Vassar and Columbia, and taught at Sarah Lawrence College. Among her many interests was aviation; she drew on her experience as a pilot for her first book of poems, *Theory of Flight* (1935), which won the Yale Younger Poets Award. Rukeyser learned from Auden's example how to draw on her socialist political engagement to inform her verse without overwhelming it. The emergent feminist stance in Rukeyser's poetry was an acknowledged influence on Adrienne Rich and Anne Sexton, and on recent women's poetry. Rukeyser also wrote biography and children's books and was a translator; her poetry is represented in *The Collected Poems of Muriel Rukeyser* (1978).

from THE LYNCHINGS OF JESUS

PASSAGE TO GODHEAD

Passage to godhead, fitfully glared upon
by bloody shinings over Calvary
this latest effort to revolution stabbed
against a bitter crucificial tree,
mild thighs split by the spearwound, opening
in fierce gestation of immortality.

Icarus' phoenix-flight fulfils itself,
desire's symbol swings full circle here,
eternal defeat by power, eternal death
of the soul and body in murder or despair
to be followed by eternal return, until
the thoughtful rebel may triumph everywhere.

Many murdered in war, crucified, starved,
loving their lives they are massacred and burned,
hating their lives as they have found them, but
killed while they look to enjoy what they have earned,
dismissed with peremptory words and hasty graves,
little calm tributes of the unconcerned.

Bruno, Copernicus, Shelley, Karl Marx :   you
makers of victory for us   :   how long?
We love our lives, and the crucifixions come,
benevolent bugles smother rebellion's song,
blowing protection for the acquiescent,
and we need many strengths to continue strong.

Tendons bind us to earth, Antaeus-ridden
by desperate weakness disallied from ground,
bone of our bone; and the sky's plains above us
seduce us into powers still unfound,
and freedom's eagles scream above our faces,
misleading, sly, perverse, and unprofound.

Passage to godhead, shine illuminated
by other colors than blood and fire and pride.
Given wings, we looked downward on earth, seen
uniform from distance; and descended, tied
to the much-loved near places, moved to find
what numbers of lynched Jesuses have not been deified.   [1935]

R.S. THOMAS

Wales b. 1913

Thomas's experiences as an Anglican priest in remote rural communities are recorded in his per-
ceptions of the archetypal peasant farmer Iago Pyrtherch, stunted by poverty and indifference, who
poses the 'gaunt question' in whose 'shadow' Thomas's poems are 'made'. His personal recovery
of Welsh language and culture as a living context for his poetry-making rendered more acute
the problematic reciprocity held by the single term 'Anglo-Welsh' itself. His fear of the language's
extinction is countered in some measure by his involvement in national politics, his spirituality,
and his respect for the individual's capacity to survive. Thomas's *Complete Poems* was published
coincident with his eightieth birthday in 1993.

WELSH HISTORY

We were a people taut for war; the hills
Were no harder, the thin grass
Clothed them more warmly than the coarse
Shirts our small bones.
We fought, and were always in retreat,
Like snow thawing upon the slopes
Of Mynydd Mawr; and yet the stranger
Never found our ultimate stand
In the thick woods, declaiming verse
To the sharp prompting of the harp.

Our kings died, or they were slain
By the old treachery at the ford.
Our bards perished, driven from the halls
Of nobles by the thorn and bramble.

We were a people bred on legends,
Warming our hands at the red past.
The great were ashamed of our loose rags
Clinging stubbornly to the proud tree
Of blood and birth, our lean bellies
And mud houses were a proof
Of our ineptitude for life.

We were a people wasting ourselves
In fruitless battles for our masters,
In lands to which we had no claim,
With men for whom we felt no hatred.

We were a people, and are so yet.
When we have finished quarrelling for crumbs
Under the table, or gnawing the bones
Of a dead culture, we will arise,
Armed, but not in the old way.   [1952]

EXPATRIATES

Not British; certainly
Not English. Welsh
With all the associations,
Black hair and black heart
Under a smooth skin,
Sallow as vellum; sharp
Of bone and wit that is turned
As a knife against us.
Four centuries now
We have been leaving
The hills and the high moors
For the jewelled pavements
Easing our veins of their dark peat
By slow transfusions.
In the drab streets
That never knew
The cold stream's sibilants
Our tongues are coated with
A dustier speech.
With the year's passing
We have forgotten
The far lakes,
Aled and Eiddwen, whose blue litmus
Alone could detect
The mind's acid.   [1958]

DOUGLAS LEPAN

Canada b. 1914

Winner of two Governor-General's Awards, one for poetry (*The Net and the Sword*, 1953) and the other for his novel *The Deserter* (1964), LePan published his first book of poetry, *The Wounded Prince*, in 1948; its most important poems are those that evoke an undomesticated Canadian natural setting that threatens the proto-European imagination. *The Net and the Sword* draws on LePan's experience as a soldier to explore the horror of war. LePan had careers in the civil service in the fifties, as an English Professor at Queen's University in the early sixties, and as principal of University College, University of Toronto (1964–70). More recent work includes *Bright Glass of Memory: A Set of Four Memoirs* (1979), the poems of *Something Still to Find* (1982), and the collection *Weathering It: Complete Poems 1948–1987* (1987).

A COUNTRY WITHOUT A MYTHOLOGY

No monuments or landmarks guide the stranger
Going among this savage people, masks
Taciturn or babbling out an alien jargon
And moody as barbaric skies are moody.

Berries must be his food. Hurriedly
He shakes the bushes, plucks pickerel from the river,
Forgetting every grace and ceremony,
Feeds like an Indian, and is on his way.

And yet, for all his haste, time is worth nothing.
The abbey clock, the dial in the garden,
Fade like saint's days and festivals.
Months, years, are here unbroken virgin forests.

There is no law—even no atmosphere
To smooth the anger of the flagrant sun.
November skies sting sting like icicles.
The land is open to all violent weathers.

Passion is not more quick. Lightnings in August
Stagger, rocks split, tongues in the forest hiss,
As fire drinks up the lovely sea-dream coolness.
This is the land the passionate man must travel.

Sometimes—perhaps at the tentative fall of twilight—
A belief will settle that waiting around the bend
Are sanctities of childhood, that melting birds
Will sing him into a limpid gracious Presence.

The hills will fall in folds, the wilderness
Will be a garment innocent and lustrous
To wear upon a birthday, under a light
That curls and smiles, a golden-haired Archangel.

And now the channel opens. But nothing alters.
Mile after mile of tangled struggling roots,
Wild-rice, stumps, weeds, that clutch at the canoe,
Wild birds hysterical in tangled trees.

And not a sign, no emblem in the sky
Or boughs to friend him as he goes; for who
Will stop where, clumsily constructed, daubed
With war-paint, teeters some lust-red manitou?   [1948]

DYLAN THOMAS

Wales 1914–1953

Thomas's cadences often derive from the 'hwyl' (sermon) of the Welsh pulpit; his rhymes, built through unusual combinations based on assonance and vowel-rhymes, achieve unforgettable effects. Though he died, destroyed by alcoholism, without reaching his fortieth birthday, and left a relatively small body of work (his *Collected Poems 1934–1952* includes 99 pieces), poems like 'Fern Hill', 'Do not go gentle into that good night', and 'In my craft or sullen art' have legendary status. The paradoxical combination of flamboyance and earnestness in his nature finds correlatives in his verse—an apparent formlessness grounded in careful attention to the detailed demands of rhythm and structure.

FERN HILL

Now as I was young and easy under the apple boughs
About the lilting house and happy as the grass was green
   The night above the dingle starry,
    Time let me hail and climb
   Golden in the heydays of his eyes,
And honoured among wagons I was prince of the apple towns
And once below a time I lordly had the trees and leaves
   Trail with daisies and barley
   Down the rivers of the windfall light.

And as I was green and carefree, famous among the barns
About the happy yard and singing as the farm was home
   In the sun that is young once only,
    Time let me play and be
   Golden in the mercy of his means,

And green and golden I was huntsman and herdsman, the calves
Sang to my horn, the foxes on the hills barked clear and cold
    And the sabbath rang slowly
  In the pebbles of the holy streams.

All the sun long it was running, it was lovely, the hay
Fields high as the house, the tunes from the chimneys, it was air
    And playing, lovely and watery
      And fire green as grass.
    And nightly under the simple stars
As I rode to sleep the owls were bearing the farm away,
All the moon long I heard, blessed among stables, the night-jars
    Flying with the ricks, and the horses
      Flashing into the dark.

And then to awake, and the farm, like a wanderer white
With the dew, come back, the cock on his shoulder: it was all
    Shining, it was Adam and maiden,
      The sky gathered again
    And the sun grew round that very day.
So it must have been after the birth of the simple light
In the first, spinning place, the spellbound horses walking warm
    Out of the whinnying green stable
      On to the fields of praise.

And honoured among foxes and pheasants by the gay house
Under the new made clouds and happy as the heart was long,
    In the sun born over and over,
      I ran my heedless ways,
      My wishes raced through the house high hay
And nothing I cared, at my sky blue trades, that time allows
In all his tuneful turning so few and such morning songs
    Before the children green and golden
      Follow him out of grace,

Nothing I cared, in the lamb white days, that time would take me
Up to the swallow thronged loft by the shadow of my hand,
    In the moon that is always rising,
      Nor that riding to sleep
    I should hear him fly with the high fields
And wake to the farm forever fled from the childless land.
Oh as I was young and easy in the mercy of his means,
    Time held me green and dying
    Though I sang in my chains like the sea.   [1946]

DOROTHY AUCHTERLONIE (GREEN)

England/Australia 1915–1991

Born in County Durham, England, and educated in England and at the University of Sydney, Auchterlonie worked as a journalist, girls' school principal, and university lecturer, and published a volume of literary criticism entitled *The Music of Love* (1984). Her collections of poetry are *Kaleidoscope* (1940) and *The Dolphin* (1967).

APOPEMPTIC HYMN

All was as it was when I went in:
The pictures right-side up, the chairs in place,
The flowers stood stiff upon the mantelpiece,
I knew the voice, I recognized the face.

Outside, the same sky held the same earth fast,
The green leaves shone, dogs barked, the children played;
But suddenly, inside, the air grew cold,
The evening ceased to sing, I was afraid.

The chairs began to dance, the pictures screamed,
The suppurating flowers smelt sickly-sweet,
The white walls clashed together, silence howled,
The floor collapsed in darkness at my feet.

The door slams shut, the wind is in my hair,
The sun has gone, and in its place there stands
The mighty stranger, blotting out the sky;
I turn and feel my way with cold, blind hands.

But where I turn, he stands before me still,
Annihilating time, bestriding space,
Chaos is come, my daughter is unborn,
And blank and featureless my own son's face.

No point of recognition but the grass—
Even the tree betrays me in the end—
Oh blind hands, feel the toughness of the blades
And the cold ground beneath them as your friend.   [1964]

G.S. FRASER

Scotland 1915–1980

The poetry evenings Fraser hosted in his home during the 1950s so affected his contemporaries that he was considered for years 'literary London's arbiter of poetic taste' (Introduction to the *Poems of G.S. Fraser*, 1981). A freelance journalist who served in Egypt during the Second World War, Fraser was also Cultural Adviser to the United Kingdom Liaison Mission in Japan, 1950–51. He is particularly noted for his expert handling of difficult poetic metres and for a voice described as having 'a kind of off-hand conversational eloquence, an eager desire to communicate'.

AN ELEGY FOR KEITH BULLEN

(Headmaster of Gezira Preparatory School, Cairo, and a friend to English poetry and poets)

A great room and a bowl full of roses,
Red roses, a man as round as a ripe rose,
Lying in a bowl of sun. And who supposes
Such a sad weight could support such a gay pose.

Flying his sad weight like a round baby's
Petulant balloon! He has blue pebbles for eyes,
Petulant, bewildered, innocent eyes like a baby's;
Like a great baby or a clipped rose he lies

In a white bowl of light in my memory;
And expands his tenuous sweetness like a balloon;
I shall die of feeling his dear absurdity
So near me now, if I cannot cry soon.

Keith was particularly Sunday morning,
Red roses, old brandy, was unharrying Time,
Was that white light, our youth; or was the fawning
Zephyr that bobs the gay balloon of rhyme,

He bobbed incredibly in our modern air;
With his loose jacket, his white panama hat,
As he leaned on his walking stick on the stone stair
He seemed a balloon, moored down to the ground by that.

As he leaned at the bar and ordered us pink gin
Or arranged a flutter on the three-fifteen
He seemed a child, incapable of sin:
We never knew him prudent, cold, or mean.

Or tied to the way the world works at all
(Not even tied enough for poetry);
All that he was we only may recall,
An innocent that guilt would wish to be,

A kind, a careless, and a generous,
An unselfseeking in his love of art,
A jolly in his great explosive fuss;
O plethora of roses, O great heart!   [c. 1944]

ALUN LEWIS

Wales 1915–1944

A teacher, poet, and short-story writer, Lewis published his first collection *Raiders' Dawn* in 1942; his second, *Ha! Ha! Among the Trumpets*, was completed shortly before his accidental death while serving in Burma during World War II and published posthumously in 1945. Lewis's quiet, intense, and clear-eyed understanding of the enlisted man's experience led to numerous editions of his war poetry and to comparisons with World War I poet Edward Thomas. Lewis's sensitivities led him to agonize over accepting promotions that he'd earned: he felt that he was possibly more disturbed by his 'own destructive impulses' than by the 'perversions of Hitler'.

GOODBYE

So we must say Goodbye, my darling,
And go, as lovers go, for ever;
Tonight remains, to pack and fix on labels
And make an end of lying down together.

I put a final shilling in the gas,
And watch you slip your dress below your knees
And lie so still I hear your rustling comb
Modulate the autumn in the trees.

And all the countless things I shall remember
Lay mummy-cloths of silence round my head;
I fill the carafe with a drink of water;
You say 'We paid a guinea for this bed,'

And then, 'We'll leave some gas, a little warmth
For the next resident, and these dry flowers,'
And turn your face away, afraid to speak
The big word, that Eternity is ours.

Your kisses close my eyes and yet you stare
As though God struck a child with nameless fears;
Perhaps the water glitters and discloses
Time's chalice and its limpid useless tears.

Everything we renounce except our selves;
Selfishness is the last of all to go;
Our sighs are exhalations of the earth,
Our footprints leave a track across the snow.

We made the universe to be our home,
Our nostrils took the wind to be our breath,
Our hearts are massive towers of delight,
We stride across the seven seas of death.

Yet when all's done you'll keep the emerald
I placed upon your finger in the street;
And I will keep the patches that you sewed
On my old battledress tonight, my sweet.   [1945]

ROLAND MATHIAS

Wales b. 1915

One of the founders of *Dock Leaves* (which became the *Anglo-Welsh Review*) and its editor from 1961–76, Mathias co-edited the anthology *Anglo-Welsh Poetry 1480–1980* with Raymond Garlick in 1984. In its Introduction, Mathias and Garlick note that the unique nature of Wales's three-millennia 'territorial stability and continuity' accounts for the importance of the praise-poem of place, time, and person which 'broods over Anglo-Welsh poetry' as allusion and idiom. In Mathias's work, these characteristics combine with carefully crafted visual details that bring indigenous events and landscapes sharply into focus. Selections from his five collections of verse are gathered in *Burning Brambles* (1983).

LAUS DEO

(No. X of the sequence 'Tide-Reach')

The water is hard in the well
But it never fails:
The clifftop fields are infinite salt
When the gales flock and pummel
Roof and farmstack and holt:
But the worm speaks well
Of the earth, the pheasant
Is heavy with praise in the lane:
The sea-birds, for all their grieving,
Gamble and dive at the nape of the storm:
And man embroiders his tales.
Hard hands have not kept it, this puissant
And sacred endeavour, nor high
Heads either this old domain.

It is one engrossing work, this frail
Commerce of souls in a corner,
Its coming and going, and the mark
Of the temporal on it. It is one
Coherent work, this Wales
And the seaway of Wales, its Maker
As careful of strength as
Of weakness, its quirk and cognomen
And trumpet allowed for
The whole peninsula's length.
It is one affirmative work, this Wales
And the seaway of Wales.   [1975]

SYDNEY GOODSIR SMITH

New Zealand/Scotland 1915–1975

Beloved of his contemporaries for his irreverence and versatility, Smith was well aware of the problems writers and readers of Scots poetry confronted. Given the distance between the spoken tongue and the printed script, Smith writes: 'It is difficult to find the middle way. . . . Quite apart from the sound values, simple meaning may sometimes be distorted. It is the difficulty of unfamiliarity with the *printed* word. The same *spoken* would be perfectly understandable to all' (*Collected Poems 1941–1975*, 1975).

THE GRACE OF GOD AND THE METH-DRINKER

There ye gang, ye daft
And doitit dotterel, ye saft
Crazed outland skalrag saul
In your bits and ends o winnockie duds
Your fyled and fozie-fousome clouts
As fou 's a fish, crackt and craftie-drunk
Wi bleerit reid-rimmed
Ee and slaveran crozie mou
Dwaiblan owre the causie like a ship
Storm-toss't i' the Bay of Biscay O
At-sea indeed and hauf-seas-owre
Up-til-the-thrapple's-pap
Or up-til-the-crosstrees-sunk—
    Wha kens? Wha racks?
Hidderie-hetterie stouteran in a dozie dwaum
O' ramsh reid-biddie—Christ!
      The stink
O' jake ahint him, a mephitic
Rouk o miserie, like some unco exotic
Perfume o the Orient no juist sae easilie tholit

By the bleak barbarians o the Wast
But subtil, acrid, jaggan the nebstrous
Wi 'n owrehailan ugsome guff, maist delicat,
Like in scent til the streel o a randie gib . . .
        O-hone-a-ree!

His toothless gums, his lips, bricht cramasie
A schere-bricht slash o bluid
A schene like the leaman gleid o rubies
Throu the gray-white stibble
O' his blank unrazit chafts, a hangman's
Heid, droolie wi gob, the bricht een
Sichtless, cannie, blythe, and slee—
                        Unkennan.

Ay,
      Puir gangrel!
                  There
—But for the undeemous glorie and grace
O' a mercifu omnipotent majestic God
Superne eterne and sceptred in the firmament
Whartil the praises o the leal rise
Like incense aye about Your throne,
Ayebydan, thochtless, and eternallie hauf-drunk
Wi nectar, Athole-brose, ambrosia—nae jake for
      You—
            God there!—
But for the 'bunesaid unsocht grace, unprayed-for,
Undeserved
            Gangs,
                  Unregenerate,
                        Me.   [1959]

JUDITH WRIGHT

Australia b. 1915

Wright's family were English settlers in New South Wales, and she was born near Armidale. Wright was educated at the University of Sydney, and her first book of poetry, *The Moving Image* (1946), was widely acclaimed for its lyrical and finely crafted verse. Other major collections followed: *Woman to Man* (1949), *The Other Half* (1966), *Collected Poems 1942–1970* (1971), and *Fourth Quarter and Other Poems* (1976). She has also written an important book of literary criticism, *Preoccupations in Australian Poetry* (1965). Wright is a passionate conservationist and aboriginal rights activist; for her the landscape holds symbolic significance as the poet's interpretations of the world and its interdependent processes of change search for creative answers to enduring human questions.

THE HAWTHORN HEDGE

How long ago she planted the hawthorn hedge—
she forgets how long ago—
that barrier thorn across the hungry ridge;
thorn and snow.

It is twice as tall as the rider on the tall mare
who draws his reins to peer
in through the bee-hung blossom. Let him stare.
No one is here.

Only the mad old girl from the hut on the hill,
unkempt as an old tree.
She will hide away if you wave your hand or call;
she will not see.

Year-long, wind turns her grindstone heart and whets
a thornbranch like a knife,
shouting in winter 'Death'; and when the white bud sets,
more loudly, 'Life.'

She has forgotten when she planted the hawthorn hedge;
that thorn, that green, that snow;
birdsong and sun dazzled across the ridge—
it was long ago.

Her hands were strong in the earth, her glance on the sky,
her song was sweet on the wind.
The hawthorn hedge took root, grew wild and high
to hide behind.   [1964]

AT COOLOOLA

The blue crane fishing in Cooloola's twilight
has fished there longer than our centuries.
He is the certain heir of lake and evening,
and he will wear their colour till he dies,

but I'm a stranger, come of a conquering people.
I cannot share his calm, who watch his lake,
being unloved by all my eyes delight in,
and made uneasy, for an old murder's sake.

Those dark-skinned people who once named Cooloola
knew that no land is lost or won by wars,
for earth is spirit: the invader's feet will tangle
in nets there and his blood be thinned by fears.

Riding at noon and ninety years ago,
my grandfather was beckoned by a ghost—
a black accoutred warrior armed for fighting,
who sank into bare plain, as now into time past.

White shores of sand, plumed reed and paperbark,
clear heavenly levels frequented by crane and swan—
I know that we are justified only by love,
but oppressed by arrogant guilt, have room for none.

And walking on clean sand among the prints
of bird and animal. I am challenged by a driftwood spear
thrust from the water; and, like my grandfather,
must quiet a heart accused by its own fear.   [1955]

P.K. PAGE
Canada b. 1916

Page was born in England but emigrated with her parents to Alberta at the end of the war. After a stint as a radio actress in Saint John, New Brunswick in the late 1930s, Page moved to Montreal, where she began publishing poetry, met writers like F.R. Scott, and was one of the founding members of the magazine *Preview* (1942). She published her first book of poems, *As Ten, as Twenty*, in 1946; her second, *The Metal and the Flower* (1954), won the Governor-General's Award. Page travelled with her husband, who served as Canada's ambassador to Australia, Brazil, and Mexico, from 1953–1964. This period coincided with her developing interest in painting (usually under her married name, P.K. Irwin), and with a hiatus in her poetry writing. For some readers, Page's poems have a strong visual element (just as her paintings have been described as 'poetic' in their effects). Page's talents as a graphic artist are most clearly on display in *Cry Ararat! Poems New and Selected* (1967), which she illustrated; a more recent collection is *The Glass Air: Selected Poems* (1985).

THE PERMANENT TOURISTS

Somnolent through landscapes and by trees
nondescript, almost anonymous,
they alter as they enter foreign cities—
the terrible tourists with their empty eyes
longing to be filled with monuments.

Verge upon statues in the public squares
remembering the promise of memorials
yet never enter the entire event
as dogs, abroad in any kind of weather,
move perfectly within their rainy climate.

Lock themselves into snapshots on the steps
of monolithic bronze as if suspecting
the subtle mourning of the photograph
might later conjure in the memory
all they are now incapable of feeling.

And search all heroes out: the boy who gave
his life to save a town; the stolid queen;
forgotten politicians minus names
and the plunging war dead, permanently brave,
forever and ever going down to death.

Look, you can see them nude in any café
reading their histories from the bill of fare,
creating futures from a foreign teacup.
Philosophies like ferns bloom from the fable
that travel is broadening at the café table.

Yet somehow beautiful, they stamp the plaza.
Classic in their anxiety they call
all sculptured immemorial stone
into their passive eyes, as rivers
draw ruined columns to their placid glass.   [1974]

GWENDOLYN BROOKS

USA b. 1917

Brooks grew up in Chicago, and in 1971 became Distinguished Professor of the Arts at City College in New York. Brooks's earlier poetry, notably *A Street in Bronzeville* (1945)—(her name for Chicago's Black ghetto)—and *Annie Allen* (1949), for which she was awarded a Pulitzer Prize, articulated the experiences of life in urban ghettos with compassion and anger. After attending the Second Black Writers' Conference (1967) Brooks allied herself with militant Black political groups and her poetry became more infused with idioms of jazz, chants, and oral expression: improvisatory, resonant, and colloquial. Recent volumes include *Blacks* (1991) and *Children Coming Home* (1991).

THE MOTHER

Abortions will not let you forget.
You remember the children you got that you did not get.
The damp small pulps with a little or with no hair,
The singers and workers that never handled the air.
You will never neglect or beat
Them, or silence or buy with a sweet.
You will never wind up the sucking-thumb
Or scuttle off ghosts that come.
You will never leave them, controlling your luscious sigh,
Return for a snack of them, with gobbling mother-eye.

I have heard in the voices of the wind the voices of my dim
    killed children.
I have contracted. I have eased
My dim dears at the breasts they could never suck.
I have said, Sweets, if I sinned, if I seized

Your luck
And your lives from your unfinished reach,
If I stole your births and your names,
Your straight baby tears and your games,
Your stilted or lovely loves, your tumults, your marriages,
    aches, and your deaths,
If I poisoned the beginnings of your breaths,
Believe that even in my deliberateness I was not deliberate.

Though why should I whine,
Whine that the crime was other than mine?—
Since anyhow you are dead.
Or rather, or instead,
You were never made.
But that too, I am afraid,
Is faulty: oh, what shall I say, how is the truth to be said?
You were born, you had body, you died.
It is just that you never giggled or planned or cried.

Believe me, I loved you all.
Believe me, I knew you, though faintly, and I loved, I loved you
All.   [1945]

ROBERT LOWELL

USA 1917–1977

Born into a Boston family that descended from voyagers on the *Mayflower* and included the poets Amy Lowell (1874–1925) and his great-great-uncle James Russell Lowell, Robert rebelled against family, religion, and state, leaving Harvard in 1936 to study with Allen Tate and John Crowe Ransom, and became a Catholic. He served time in prison in 1943 after declaring himself a conscientious objector. His second book, *Lord Weary's Castle* (1946) established him as a modernist. *Life Studies* (1959) marked a major turn in his career and in the possibilities for American poetry. Its private focus (on matters such as Lowell's lifelong bouts of mental illness) melded with a public rhetoric that addressed contemporary American culture; in addition, his 'confessional poetry' strongly influenced the generation to follow. Two other collections of Lowell's poems are *Poems 1938–49* (1950) and *Selected Poems* (1977).

FOR THE UNION DEAD

'*Relinquunt Omnia Servare Rem Publicam.*'

The old South Boston Aquarium stands
in a Sahara of snow now. Its broken windows are boarded.
The bronze weathervane cod has lost half its scales.
The airy tanks are dry.

Once my nose crawled like a snail on the glass;
my hand tingled
to burst the bubbles
drifting from the noses of the crowd, compliant fish.

My hand draws back. I often sigh still
for the dark downward and vegetating kingdom
of the fish and reptile. One morning last March,
I pressed against the new barbed and galvanized

fence on the Boston Common. Behind their cage,
yellow dinosaur steamshovels were grunting
as they cropped up tons of mush and grass
to gouge their underworld garage.

Parking spaces luxuriate like civic
sandpiles in the heart of Boston.
A girdle of orange, Puritan-pumpkin colored girders
braces the tingling Statehouse,

shaking over the excavations, as it faces Colonel Shaw
and his bell-cheeked Negro infantry
on St Gaudens' shaking Civil War relief,
propped by a plank splint against the garage's earthquake.

Two months after marching through Boston,
half the regiment was dead;
at the dedication,
William James could almost hear the bronze Negroes breathe.

Their monument sticks like a fishbone
in the city's throat.
Its Colonel is as lean
as a compass-needle.

He has an angry wrenlike vigilance,
a greyhound's gentle tautness;

where the graveyard shelves on the town. . . .
My mind's not right.

A car radio bleats,
'Love, O careless Love. . . .' I hear
my ill-spirit sob in each blood cell,
as if my hand were at its throat. . . .
I myself am hell;
nobody's here—

only skunks, that search
in the moonlight for a bite to eat.
They march on their soles up Main Street:
white stripes, moonstruck eyes' red fire
under the chalk-dry and spar spire
of the Trinitarian Church.

I stand on top
of our back steps and breathe the rich air—
a mother skunk with her column of kittens swills the garbage
     pail.
She jabs her wedge-head in a cup
of sour cream, drops her ostrich tail,
and will not scare.   [1964]

JAMES MCAULEY

Australia 1917-1976

Most of McAuley's poetry, and most notably in *Under Aldebaran* (1946) and *A Vision of Ceremony* (1956), is characterized by its classical formalism and intellectually refined philosophical argument. McAuley opposes 'individual, arbitrary/And self-expressive art' on the grounds that 'only the simplest forms can hold/A vast complexity' ('An Art of Poetry'). His later autobiographical lyrics in *Music Late at Night: Poems 1970–1973* (1976) and *Time Given: Poems 1970–1974* (1976) recall the less restrained sensibility McAuley expressed as a jazz musician and poet during his years as a student of philosophy, English, and German at Sydney University.

BECAUSE

My father and my mother never quarrelled.
They were united in a kind of love
As daily as the *Sydney Morning Herald*,
Rather than like the eagle or the dove.

I never saw them casually touch,
Or show a moment's joy in one another.
Why should this matter to me now so much?
I think it bore more hardly on my mother.

Who had more generous feeling to express.
My father had dammed up his Irish blood
Against all drinking praying fecklessness,
And stiffened into stone and creaking wood.

His lips would make a switching sound, as though
Spontaneous impulse must be kept at bay.
That it was mainly weakness I see now,
But then my feelings curled back in dismay.

Small things can pit the memory like a cyst:
Having seen other fathers greet their sons,
I put my childish face up to be kissed
After an absence. The rebuff still stuns

My blood. The poor man's curt embarrassment
At such a delicate proffer of affection
Cut like a saw. But home the lesson went:
My tenderness thenceforth escaped detection.

My mother sang *Because*, and *Annie Laurie*,
White Wings, and other songs; her voice was sweet.
I never gave enough, and I am sorry;
But we were all closed in the same defeat.

People do what they can; they were good people,
They cared for us and loved us. Once they stood
Tall in my childhood as the school, the steeple.
How can I judge without ingratitude?

Judgment is simply trying to reject
A part of what we are because it hurts.
The living cannot call the dead collect:
They won't accept the charge, and it reverts.

It's my own judgment day that I draw near,
Descending in the past, without a clue,
Down to that central deadness: the despair
Older than any hope I ever knew.   [1971]

MIRIAM WADDINGTON

Canada b. 1917

Born in Winnipeg to Jewish-Russian immigrants, Waddington has retained a life-long affection
for the city. Her poetry can take up social issues, but is most celebrated for its lyrical purity and
directness; describing her distance from Modernist aesthetics, she writes: 'In poetry I disliked
rhetoric, intellectual wordplay, and T.S. Eliot, which made me native rather than cosmopolitan . . .
and realist-physical rather than metaphysical.' Waddington wrote a critical study, *A.M. Klein*
(1970) and edited Klein's poems (*The Collected Poems of A.M. Klein*, 1974); she published her first
book of poems, *Green World*, in 1945. Important collections include *Driving Home: Poems New and
Selected* (1972) and *Collected Poems* (1986).

DÉJÀ VU

That far terribly
northern city
I see when
I close my eyes
is it Winnipeg
or Leningrad?

Both have the same
skinny church
standing alone like
a cello in the snow,
and you can see
the same half-dozen
people on skis or
snowshoes making
their way across
the same flat
white park.

What's missing here
is the 18th century
architect who built
these houses with
their stucco fronts
and lace balconies,
also those 19th-century
idlers squinting up
at the sun from behind
the curtains of their
second-storey windows
on the same cold
Saturday afternoons.

The iron gates
of the summer gardens
are locked, the snow
piles up its cushions
on empty benches and
the frost wraps itself
like a bridal wreath
around the lighted
smoking street lamps;

It is all
so much the same,
I can't tell
if this far terribly
northern city is
Winnipeg or is it
Leningrad?

[1976]

MARGARET AVISON

Canada b. 1918

Resisting the usual contemporary propagandizing of poets and their reputations, Avison has stayed out of the public eye and published a small body of work. Her poetry is complex, often metaphysical, and yet informed by a simple (if difficult) challenge that finds its most eloquent expression in the opening of her sonnet, 'Snow': 'Nobody stuffs the world in at your eyes./The optic heart must venture: a jail-break/And re-creation.' Avison's Christian vision has inspired her work in Toronto at the Presbyterian Home Missions, and more recently at the Mustard Seed Mission. Her books include *Winter Sun* (1960), *The Dumbfounding* (1966), *sunblue* (1978), and *Winter Sun/The Dumbfounding: Poems 1940–1966* (1982).

THE SWIMMER'S MOMENT

For everyone
The swimmer's moment at the whirlpool comes,
But many at that moment will not say
'This is the whirlpool, then.'
By their refusal they are saved
From the black pit, and also from contesting
The deadly rapids, and emerging in
The mysterious, and more ample, further waters.
And so their bland-blank faces turn and turn
Pale and forever on the rim of suction
They will not recognize.
Of those who dare the knowledge
Many are whirled into the ominous centre
That, gaping vertical, seals up
For them an eternal boon of privacy,
So that we turn away from their defeat
With a despair, not for their deaths, but for
Ourselves, who cannot penetrate their secret
Nor even guess at the anonymous breadth
Where one or two have won:
(The silver reaches of the estuary).   [1960]

W.S. GRAHAM

Scotland 1918-1986

In his poetry (*Collected Poems 1942–1977*, 1979) and commentaries, Graham attends to the complex set of relationships which link the poet, the poem, and the reader. He observes: 'I am always very aware that my poem is not a telephone call. The poet only speaks one way. He hears nothing back. . . . That is why he has to make the poem stand stationary as an Art object' (*Twelve More Modern Scottish Poets*, eds King and Crichton Smith).

JOHANN JOACHIM QUANTZ'S FIVE LESSONS

THE FIRST LESSON

So that each person may quickly find that
Which particularly concerns him, certain metaphors
Convenient to us within the compass of this
Lesson are to be allowed. It is best I sit
Here where I am to speak on the other side
Of language. You, of course, in your own time
And incident (I speak in the small hours.)
Will listen from your side. I am very pleased
We have sought us out. No doubt you have read
My Flute Book. Come. The Guild clock's iron men
Are striking out their few deserted hours
And here from my high window Brueghel's winter
Locks the canal below. I blow my fingers.

THE SECOND LESSON

Good morning, Karl. Sit down. I have been thinking
About your progress and my progress as one
Who teaches you, a young man with talent
And the rarer gift of application. I think
You must now be becoming a musician
Of a certain calibre. It is right maybe
That in our lessons now I should expect
Slight and very polite impatiences
To show in you. Karl, I think it is true,
You are now nearly able to play the flute.

Now we must try higher, aware of the terrible
Shapes of silence sitting outside your ear
Anxious to define you and really love you.
Remember silence is curious about its opposite
Element which you shall learn to represent.

Enough of that. Now stand in the correct position
So that the wood of the floor will come up through you.
Stand, but not too stiff. Keep your elbows down.
Now take a simple breath and make me a shape
Of clear unchained started and finished tones.
Karl, as well as you are able, stop
Your fingers into the breathing apertures
And speak and make the cylinder delight us.

THE THIRD LESSON

Karl, you are late. The traverse flute is not
A study to take lightly. I am cold waiting.
Put one piece of coal in the stove. This lesson
Shall not be prolonged. Right. Stand in your place.

Ready? Blow me a little ladder of sound
From a good stance so that you feel the heavy
Press of the floor coming up through you and
Keeping your pitch and tone in character.

Now that is something, Karl. You are getting on.
Unswell your head. One more piece of coal.
Go on now but remember it must be always
Easy and flowing. Light and shadow must
Be varied but be varied in your mind
Before you hear the eventual return sound.

Play me the dance you made for the barge-master.
Stop stop Karl. Play it as you first thought
Of it in the hot boat-kitchen. That is a pleasure
For me. I can see I am making you good.
Keep the stove red. Hand me the matches. Now
We can see better. Give me a shot at the pipe.
Karl, I can still put on a good flute-mouth
And show you in this high cold room something
You will be famous to have said you heard.

THE FOURTH LESSON

You are early this morning. What we have to do
Today is think of you as a little creator
After the big creator. And it can be argued
You are as necessary, even a composer
Composing in the flesh an attitude
To slay the ears of the gentry. Karl,
I know you find great joy in the great
Composers. But now you can put your lips to
The messages and blow them into sound

And enter and be there as well. You must
Be faithful to who you are speaking from
And yet it is all right. You will be there.

Take your coat off. Sit down. A glass of Bols
Will help us both. I think you are good enough
To not need me anymore. I think you know
You are not only an interpreter.
What you will do is always something else
And they will hear you simultaneously with
The Art you have been given to read. Karl,

I think the Spring is really coming at last.
I see the canal boys working. I realise
I have not asked you to play the flute today.
Come and look. Are the barges not moving?
You must forgive me. I am not myself today.
Be here on Thursday. When you come, bring
Me five herrings. Watch your fingers. Spring
Is apparent but it is still chilblain weather.

THE LAST LESSON

Dear Karl, this morning is our last lesson.
I have been given the opportunity to
Live in a certain person's house and tutor
Him and his daughters on the traverse flute.
Karl, you will be all right. In those recent
Lessons my heart lifted to your playing.

I know. I see you doing well, invited
In a great chamber in front of the gentry. I
Can see them with their dresses settling in
And bored mouths beneath moustaches sizing
You up as you are, a lout from the canal
With big ears but an angel's tread on the flute.

But you will be all right. Stand in your place
Before them. Remember Johann. Begin with good
Nerve and decision. Do not intrude too much
Into the message you carry and put out.

One last thing, Karl, remember when you enter
The joy of those quick high archipelagoes,
To make to keep your finger-stops as light
As feathers but definite. What can I say more?
Do not be sentimental or in your Art.
I will miss you. Do not expect applause.   [1979]

AL PURDY

Canada b. 1918

Although most of his poetry appears simple and direct, Purdy has spent most of his life working at *The Crafte So Longe to Lerne* (1959). His use of colloquial idiom strongly influenced the next generation of poets in Canada. Working at manual jobs as a young man, Purdy rode the rails across Canada in the depressed 1930s. Since 1957 he has lived in Ameliasburg, Ontario, near his birth-place, a lodestone for many of his poems about place and time. Most remarkable in Purdy's poetry is its acute sensitivity to the stratas of North American time: the layering of recent with remote time evoked in 'Lament for the Dorsets', for example. Among selections of Purdy's work are *Being Alive: Poems 1958–1978* (1978). He is more fully represented in *The Collected Poems of Al Purdy* (1986) and more recently in *The Woman on the Shore* (1990).

LAMENT FOR THE DORSETS

(Eskimos extinct in the 14th century AD)

Animal bones and some mossy tent rings
scrapers and spearheads   carved ivory swans
all that remains of the Dorset giants
who drove the Vikings back to their long ships
talked to spirits of earth and water
—a picture of terrifying old men
so large they broke the backs of bears
so small they lurk behind bone rafters
in the brain of modern hunters
among good thoughts and warm things
and come out at night
to spit on the stars

The big men with clever fingers
who had no dogs and hauled their sleds
over the frozen northern oceans
awkward giants
                killers of seal
they couldn't compete with little men
who came from the west with dogs
Or else in a warm climatic cycle
the seals went back to cold waters
and the puzzled Dorsets scratched their heads
with hairy thumbs around 1350 A.D.
—couldn't figure it out
went around saying to each other
plaintively
            'What's wrong? What happened?
            Where are the seals gone?'
And died

Twentieth century people
apartment dwellers
executives of neon death
warmakers with things that explode
—they have never imagined us in their future
how could we imagine them in the past
squatting among the moving glaciers
six hundred years ago
with glowing lamps?
As remote or nearly
as the trilobites and swamps
when coal became
or the last great reptile hissed
at a mammal the size of a mouse
that squeaked and fled

Did they ever realize at all
what was happening to them?
Some old hunter with one lame leg
a bear had chewed
sitting in a caribou skin tent
—the last Dorset?
Let's say his name was Kudluk
and watch him sitting there
carving 2-inch ivory swans
for a dead grand-daughter
taking them out of his mind
the places in his mind
where pictures are
He selects a sharp stone tool
to gouge a parallel pattern of lines
on both sides of the swan
holding it with his left hand
bearing down and transmitting
his body's weight
from brain to arm and right hand
and one of his thoughts
turns to ivory
The carving is laid aside
in beginning darkness
at the end of hunger
after a while wind
blows down the tent and snow
begins to cover him

After 600 years
the ivory thought
is still warm

[1968]

THE RUNNERS

'It was when Leif was with King Olaf Tryggvason, and he bade him proclaim Christianity to Greenland, that the king gave him two Gaels; the man's name was Haki, and the woman's Haekia. The King advised Leif to have recourse to these people, if he should stand in need of fleetness, for they were swifter than deer. Erick and Leif had tendered Karlsefni the services of this couple. Now when they had sailed past Marvel-Strands (to the New World) they put the Gaels ashore, and directed them to run to the southward, and investigate the nature of the country, and return again before the end of the third half-day.'

(from *Erick the Red's Saga*)

Brother, the wind of this place is cold,
and hills under our feet tremble,
the forests are making magic against us—
I think the land knows we are here,
I think the land knows we are strangers.
Let us stay close to our friend the sea,
or cunning dwarves at the roots of darkness
shall seize and drag us down—

Sister, we must share our strength between us,
until the heat of our bodies makes a single flame:
while the moon sees only one shadow
and the sun knows only our double heartbeat,
and the rain does not come between—

Brother, I am afraid of this dark place,
I am hungry for the home islands,
and wind blowing the waves to coloured spray,
I am sick for the sun—

Sister, we must not think those thoughts again,
for three half-days have gone by,
and we must return to the ship.
If we are away longer,
the Northmen will beat us with thongs,
until we cry for death—
Why do you stare at nothing?

Brother, a cold wind touched me,
tho I stand in your arms' circle:
perhaps the Northmen's runes have found us,
I am afraid of this dark land,
ground mist that makes us half ghosts,
and another silence inside silence . . .

But there are berries and fish here,
and small animals by the sea's edge
that crouch and tremble and listen . . .
If we join our thoughts to the silence,
if our trails join the animal trails,
and the sun remembers what the moon forgets . . .
Brother, it comes to me now,
the long ship must sail without us,
we stay here—

Sister, we should die slowly,
the beasts would gnaw at our bodies,
the rains whiten our bones.
The Northmen's runes are strong magic,
the runes would track us down,
tho we keep on running
past the Land of Flat Stones
over the Marvel-Strands
beyond the country of great trees . . .
Tho we ran to the edge of the world,
our masters would track us down—

Brother, take my hand in your hand,
this part of ourselves between us
while we run together,
over the stones of the sea-coast,
this much of ourselves is our own:
while rain cries out against us,
and darkness swallows the evening,
and morning moves into stillness,
and mist climbs to our throats,
while we are running,
while we are running—

Sister—   [1968]

MURIEL SPARK

Scotland b. 1918

Known primarily as a novelist, Spark creates odd and tense characters who exist in strangely familiar worlds defined variously as the playfully gothic and the perversely comic. These disturbing, ironic effects pervade her poetry (*Collected Poetry*, 1967), plays, and short stories. Although she no longer resides in Scotland, Spark acknowledges with characteristic and complex clarity that 'Edinburgh is the place that I, a constitutional exile, am essentially exiled from.'

BLUEBELL AMONG THE SABLES

The visitor came clothed with sables,
My dark and social friend.
The afternoon prospered after its kind
But they bore me, those intimate parliaments,
Those tea-times wear my heart away.

So I took half my pleasure in the sables
That flowed across her arm, the chair, the floor,
Sleek and fathomless like contemplative,
Living animals, the deep elect,
In ceremonious most limp obedience.

But the dark skins did move, she felt them creep:
'My God! My sables!'
Indeed they were alive with a new life,
The sombre swiftly shot with quick and silver
Fur within fur. It was Bluebell, my beautiful,
My small and little cat pounding the sables.
Flat on her spine she tumbled them,
Shaking their kindly tails between her teeth.

'My furs! Your cat!' . . .
I said, 'No need for alarm;
Those dead pelts can't cause Bluebell any harm.'
Poor soul, this put her in the wrong;
As one who somehow fails the higher vision,
She was meek: 'They cost the earth, my furs.'
I stroked the comical creature, she the sables,
And all came even.

For she said there was no damage, no damage.
It may be she had profit of the event,
As for myself that moment was well spent
When I saw Bluebell pummelling the sables
I have the image, the gratuitous image,
Miserly seized of sable wonders glowing,

An order of the profound earth, of roots
And minerals evolved in civil strands,
Defined in which, the sprite, like air and like
A dawn asperges, green-eyed Bluebell plying
The sensuous fabric with her shining pads.   [1984]

CREATED AND ABANDONED

Where have you gone, how has it ended with you,
people of my dreams, cut off in mid-life, gone to what grave?
It's all right for me. I'm fine. I always woke up when we parted
and say it was only a dream. I took up my life
as I left it the day before. But you?—
like people with bound feet, or people not properly formed,
without further scope, handicapped. Sometimes I never knew
what you were going to say, didn't let you speak, but woke.
You being unreal after all, this means unwell. I worry about you.
Did something not happen to you after my waking?
Did something next not happen? Or are you
limbo'd there where I left you forever like characters
in a story one has started to write and set aside?

However bad-mannered you were, however amazing
in your style, I hope you're not looking for me
night after night, not waiting for me to come back.
I feel a definite responsibility for your welfare.
Are you all right?   [1984]

LAWRENCE FERLINGHETTI

USA b. 1919

Born in Yonkers, New York, Ferlinghetti graduated from Columbia University and the Sorbonne. He became co-owner of the City Lights Bookshop in San Francisco in 1953, and the editor of the City Lights publishing house in 1955. As a patron of Beat writers, he was arrested on but acquitted of obscenity charges for his publication of Ginsberg's *Howl* in 1956. In his collection, *A Coney Island of the Mind* (1958), a Whitmanesque style and autobiographical voice represent Ferlinghetti's attempt to return poetry to the people as an instrument of social and political dissent. His subsequent collections include *The Secret Meaning of Things* (1969), *Who Are We Now?* (1976), and *Over All Obscene Boundaries* (1984).

I AM WAITING

I am waiting for my case to come up
and I am waiting
for a rebirth of wonder
and I am waiting for someone
to really discover America

and wail
and I am waiting
for the discovery
of a new symbolic western frontier
and I am waiting
for the American Eagle
to really spread its wings
and straighten up and fly right
and I am waiting
for the Age of Anxiety
to drop dead
and I am waiting
for the war to be fought
which will make the world safe
for anarchy
and I am waiting
for the final withering away
of all governments
and I am perpetually awaiting
a rebirth of wonder

I am waiting for the Second Coming
and I am waiting
for a religious revival
to sweep thru the state of Arizona
and I am waiting
for the Grapes of Wrath to be stored
and I am waiting
for them to prove
that God is really American
and I am seriously waiting
for Billy Graham and Elvis Presley
to exchange roles seriously
and I am waiting
to see God on television
piped onto church altars
if only they can find
the right channel
to tune in on
and I am waiting
for the Last Supper to be served again
with a strange new appetizer
and I am perpetually awaiting
a rebirth of wonder

I am waiting for my number to be called
and I am waiting
for the living end
and I am waiting
for dad to come home
his pockets full
of irradiated silver dollars
and I am waiting
for the atomic tests to end
and I am waiting happily
for things to get much worse
before they improve
and I am waiting
for the Salvation Army to take over
and I am waiting
for the human crowd
to wander off a cliff somewhere
clutching its atomic umbrella
and I am waiting
for Ike to act
and I am waiting
for the meek to be blessed
and inherit the earth
without taxes
and I am waiting
for forests and animals
to reclaim the earth as theirs
and I am waiting
for a way to be devised
to destroy all nationalisms
without killing anybody
and I am waiting
for linnets and planets to fall like rain
and I am waiting for lovers and weepers
to lie down together again
in a new rebirth of wonder

I am waiting for the Great Divide to be crossed
and I am anxiously waiting
for the secret of eternal life to be discovered
by an obscure general practitioner
and save me forever from certain death
and I am waiting
for life to begin
and I am waiting
for the storms of life

to be over
and I am waiting
to set sail for happiness
and I am waiting
for a reconstructed Mayflower
to reach America
with its picture story and tv rights
sold in advance to the natives
and I am waiting
for the lost music to sound again
in the Lost Continent
in a new rebirth of wonder

I am waiting for the day
that maketh all things clear
and I am waiting
for Ole Man River
to just stop rolling along
past the country club
and I am waiting
for the deepest South
to just stop Reconstructing itself
in its own image
and I am waiting
for a sweet desegregated chariot
to swing low
and carry me back to Ole Virginie
and I am waiting
for Ole Virginie to discover
just why Darkies are born
and I am waiting
for God to lookout
from Lookout Mountain
and see the *Ode to the Confederate Dead*
as a real farce
and I am awaiting retribution
for what America did
to Tom Sawyer
and I am perpetually awaiting
a rebirth of wonder

I am waiting for Tom Swift to grow up
and I am waiting
for the American Boy
to take off Beauty's clothes
and get on top of her

and I am waiting
for Alice in Wonderland
to retransmit to me
her total dream of innocence
and I am waiting
for Childe Roland to come
to the final darkest tower
and I am waiting
for Aphrodite
to grow live arms
at a final disarmament conference
in a new rebirth of wonder

I am waiting
to get some intimations
of immortality
by recollecting my early childhood
and I am waiting
for the green mornings to come again
youth's dumb green fields come back again
and I am waiting
for some strains of unpremeditated art
to shake my typewriter
and I am waiting to write
the great indelible poem
and I am waiting
for the last long careless rapture
and I am perpetually waiting
for the fleeing lovers on the Grecian Urn
to catch each other up at last
and embrace
and I am awaiting
perpetually and forever
a renaissance of wonder   [1958]

ELMA MITCHELL

Scotland/England b. 1919

Born in Airdrie, Scotland, Mitchell settled in London where she worked as a librarian and in broadcasting, journalism, and publishing. Her poetry often explores domestic arrangements by assuming the voice of an aggrieved son-in-law, daughter, or wife; the language is usually attractively colloquial and idiomatic and can become taut with insight. A representative collection is *People Etcetera: Poems New & Selected* (1987).

THOUGHTS AFTER RUSKIN

Women reminded him of lilies and roses.
Me they remind rather of blood and soap,
Armed with a warm rag, assaulting noses,
Ears, neck, mouth and all the secret places:

Armed with a sharp knife, cutting up liver,
Holding hearts to bleed under a running tap,
Gutting and stuffing, pickling and preserving,
Scalding, blanching, broiling, pulverizing,
—All the terrible chemistry of their kitchens.

Their distant husbands lean across mahogany
And delicately manipulate the market,
While safe at home, the tender and the gentle
Are killing tiny mice, dead snap by the neck,
Asphyxiating flies, evicting spiders,
Scrubbing, scouring aloud, disturbing cupboards,
Committing things to dustbins, twisting, wringing,
Wrists red and knuckles white and fingers puckered,
Pulpy, tepid. Steering screaming cleaners
Around the snags of furniture, they straighten
And haul out sheets from under the incontinent
And heavy old, stoop to importunate young,
Tugging, folding, tucking, zipping, buttoning,
Spooning in food, encouraging excretion,
Mopping up vomit, stabbing cloth with needles,
Contorting wool around their knitting needles,
Creating snug and comfy on their needles.

Their huge hands! their everywhere eyes! their voices
Raised to convey across the hullabaloo,
Their massive thighs and breasts dispensing comfort,
Their bloody passages and hairy crannies,
Their wombs that pocket a man upside down!

And when all's over, off with overalls,
Quickly consulting clocks, they go upstairs,
Sit and sigh a little, brushing hair,
And somehow find, in mirrors, colours, odours,
Their essences of lilies and of roses.   [1987]

MAY SWENSON

USA 1919–1989

Born in Logan, Utah, in the 1930s, Swenson moved to New York, where she worked for the Writers' Project (one of the government initiatives to combat unemployment in the Depression) and began publishing in *The New Yorker*. Swenson's early formalist poetry attends carefully to the details of natural settings; in later books more of her personal experience surfaces. Swenson became Chancellor of the American Academy of Poets in 1980 and won the Bollingen Prize in 1981. Her books include *To Mix With Time: New and Selected Poems* (1963), *New and Selected Things Taking Place* (1978), and *In Other Words* (1987).

UNDER THE BABY BLANKET

Under the baby blanket 47 years old you are
asleep on the worn too-short leatherette sofa.

Along with a watermelon and some peaches from
the beach cottage, you brought home this gift

from your Mom. 'Just throw it in the van,' you
said you said, 'I haven't time to talk about it.'

She had wanted to tell how she handstitched and
appliquéd the panels—a dozen of them—waiting

for you to be born: 12 identical sunbonneted
little girls, one in each square, in different

colors of dresses doing six different things.
And every tiny stitch put in with needle and

thimble. 'It had to take months, looks like,'
I said. 'Well, Mom's Relief Society ladies

must have helped,' you said. One little girl
is sweeping, one raking, another watering a plant

in a pot, one dangling a doll dressed exactly
like herself. One is opening a blue umbrella.

At center is a little girl holding a book, with
your initial on the cover! I was astonished:

'A Matriarchal Blessing, predicting your future!'
(But, wait a minute, I thought. How did she know

you wouldn't be a boy? Was she also sewing
another blanket, with little boys in its squares:

holding hammer, riding tricycle, playing with
dog, batting ball, sailing boat, and so on?)

I asked for the baby blanket—which is a work
of art—to be hung on the wall above the sofa

where I could study it. You refused. You
lay down under it, bare legs drawn up, a smudge

of creosote on one knee. Almost covered with
little girls 47 years old you've gone to sleep.   [1978]

GWEN HARWOOD

Australia b. 1920

Raised in a musical family, Harwood studied and taught piano and played the organ at All Saints
Church in Brisbane. She settled in Tasmania with linguist William Harwood, and began writing
poetry while raising their five children; her first volume, *Poems*, was published in 1963. Harwood
frequently published her work under pseudonyms (Francis Geyer, Walter Lehmann, T.F. Kline,
Miriam Stone), and her reputation was well-established when readers informed the publishers of
Bulletin magazine that two acrostic sonnets by Harwood read 'Fuck all editors'; all unsold copies
were recalled. Many of her poems and especially those in her more recent volumes—*New and
Selected Poems* (1975) and *The Lion's Bride* (1981)—address intense experiences of separation, loss,
and death.

NEW MUSIC

To Larry Sitsky

Who can grasp for the first time
these notes hurled into empty space?
Suddenly a tormenting nerve
affronts the fellowship of cells.
Who can tell for the first time
if it is love or pain he feels,
violence or tenderness that calls
plain objects by outrageous names

and strikes new sound from the old names?
At the service of a human vision,
not symbols, but strange presences
defining a transparent void,
these notes beckon the mind to move
out of the smiling context of
what's known; and what can guide it is
neither wisdom nor power, but love.

Who but a fool would enter these
regions of being with no name?
Secure among their towering junk
the wise and powerful congregate
fitting old shapes to old ideas,
rocked by their classical harmonies
in living sleep. The beggars' stumps
bang on the stones. Nothing will change.

Unless, wakeful with questioning,
some mind beats on necessity,
and being unanswered learns to bear
emptiness like a wound that no
word but its own can mend; and finds
a new imperative to summon
a world out of unmeasured darkness
pierced by a brilliant nerve of sound.   [1968]

SUBURBAN SONNET

She practises a fugue, though it can matter
to no one now if she plays well or not.
Beside her on the floor two children chatter,
then scream and fight. She hushes them. A pot
boils over. As she rushes to the stove
too late, a wave of nausea overpowers
subject and counter-subject. Zest and love
drain out with soapy water as she scours
the crusted milk. Her veins ache. Once she played
for Rubinstein, who yawned. The children caper
round a sprung mousetrap where a mouse lies dead.
When the soft corpse won't move they seem afraid.
She comforts them; and wraps it in a paper
featuring: Tasty dishes from stale bread.   [1968]

EDWIN MORGAN

Scotland b. 1920

Much of Morgan's poetry is inspired by the street life of Glasgow, its violence, its poverty, its occasional beauty. He is as interested in the traditional forms that build his 'Glasgow Sonnets' series (1972) as he is intrigued by the experimental possibilities of the intersection of language and intergalactic travel, and the patois of concrete art.

CANEDOLIA: AN OFF-CONCRETE SCOTCH FANTASIA

oa! hoy! awe! ba! mey!

who saw?
rhu saw rum. garve saw smoo. nigg saw tain. lairg saw lagg.
rigg saw eigg. largs saw haggs. tongue saw luss. mull saw yell.
stoer saw strone. drem saw muck. gask saw noss. unst saw cults.
echt saw banff. weem saw wick. trool saw twatt.

how far?
from largo to lunga from joppa to skibo from ratho to shona from
ulva to minto from tinto to tolsta from soutra to marsco from
braco to barra from alva to stobo from fogo to fada from gigha to
gogo from kelso to stroma from hirta to spango.

what is it like there?
och it's freuchie, it's faifley, it's wamphray, it's frandy, it's
sliddery.

what do you do?
we foindle and fungle, we bonkle and meigle and maxpoffle. we
scotstarvit, armit, wormit, and even whifflet. we play at crosstobs,
leuchars, gorbals, and finfan. we scavaig, and there's aye a bit of
tilquhilly. if it's wet, treshnish and mishnish.

what is the best of the country?
blinkbonny! airgold! thundergay!

and the worst?
scrishven, shiskine, scrabster, and snizort.

listen! what's that?
catacol and wauchope, never heed them

tell us about last night
well, we had a wee ferintosh and we lay on the quiraing. it was
pure strontian!

but who was there?
petermoidart and craigenkenneth and cambusputtock and
ecclemuchty and corriehulish and balladolly and altnacanny and
clauchanvrechan and stronachlochan and auchenlachar and
tighnacrankie and tilliebruaich and killieharra and invervannach
and achnatudlem and machrishellach and inchtamurchan and
auchterfechan and kinlochculter and ardnawhallie and invershuggle

and what was the toast?
schiehallion! schiehallion! schiehallion!   [1968]

OODGEROO OF THE TRIBE NOONUCCAL (FORMERLY KATH WALKER)

Noonuccal/Australia 1920–1993

In 1987 Kath Walker changed her name to Oodgeroo of the tribe Noonuccal. Born on North Strad-
broke Island, Queensland, she received a primary school education and at the age of 13 began
working as a domestic servant in Brisbane. At 16 her application for training as a nurse was
rejected on racially discriminatory grounds, though she was allowed to serve in the Australian
Women's Army during World War II. As a result of her work in the aboriginal rights movement,
Oodgeroo became State Secretary of the Federal Council for the Advancement of Aboriginals and
Torres Strait Islanders in 1961, and she successfully argued for the abolition of the aboriginal
discrimination provisions of the Australian constitution in 1967. *My People: A Kath Walker
Collection* (1970) represents the poems from her first two books, newer poems, short stories, and
civil rights addresses.

WE ARE GOING

For Grannie Coolwell

They came in to the little town
A semi-naked band subdued and silent,
All that remained of their tribe.
They came here to the place of their old bora ground
Where now the many white men hurry about like ants.
Notice of estate agent reads: 'Rubbish May Be Tipped Here'.
Now it half covers the traces of the old bora ring.
They sit and are confused, they cannot say their thoughts:
'We are as strangers here now, but the white tribe are the
    strangers.
We belong here, we are of the old ways.

We are the corroboree and the bora ground,
We are the old sacred ceremonies, the laws of the elders.
We are the wonder tales of Dream Time, the tribal legends told.
We are the past, the hunts and the laughing games, the wandering
    camp fires.
We are the lightning-bolt over Gaphembah Hill
Quick and terrible,
And the Thunderer after him, that loud fellow.
We are the quiet daybreak paling the dark lagoon.
We are the shadow-ghosts creeping back as the camp fires burn
    low.
We are nature and the past, all the old ways
Gone now and scattered.
The scrubs are gone, the hunting and the laughter.
The eagle is gone, the emu and the kangaroo are gone from this
    place.
The bora ring is gone.
The corroboree is gone.
And we are going.'

[1964]

ANONYMOUS

Nigeria

This is an Ijálá chant from Yoruba oral literature. Typically, a hunter addresses an animal; but the sequence includes other chants less specific in audience or purpose. This chant, addressed to the elephant, offers a catalogue of the animal's grand physical attributes, but also establishes the elephant's place in the hunter's lore and in the culture, including the elephant's various names.

SALUTE TO THE ELEPHANT

O elephant, possessor of a savings-basket full of money
O elephant, huge as a hill, even in a crouching posture.
O elephant, enfolded by honour; demon, flapping *fans of war*.
Demon who snaps tree branches into many pieces and moves on to
    the forest farm.
O elephant, who ignores 'I have fled to my father for refuge',
Let alone 'to my mother'.
Mountainous Animal, Huge Beast who tears a man like a garment
And hangs him up on a tree.
The sight of whom causes people to stampede towards a hill of
    safety.
My chant is a salute to the elephant.
Ajanaku who walks with a heavy tread.
Demon who swallows palm-fruit bunches whole, even with the
    spiky pistil-cells.

O elephant, praisenamed Laaye, massive animal, blackish-grey in
    complexion.
O elephant, who single-handed causes a tremor in a dense tropical
    forest.
O elephant, who stands sturdy and alert, who walks slowly as if
    reluctantly.
O elephant, whom one sees and points towards with all one's
    fingers.
The hunter's boast at home is not repeated when he really meets
    the elephant.
The hunter's boast at home is not repeated before the elephant.
Ajanaku looks back with difficulty like a person suffering from a
    sprained neck.
The elephant has a porter's-knot without having any load on his
    head.
The elephant's head is his burden which he balances.
O elephant, praisenamed Laaye, 'O death, please stop following
    me'—
This is part and parcel of the elephant's appellation.
If you wish to know the elephant, the elephant who is a veritable
    ferry-man,
The elephant whom honour matches, the elephant who continually
    swings his trunk,
His upper fly-switch,
It's the elephant whose eyes are veritable water-jars.
O elephant, the vagrant par excellence,
Whose molar teeth are as wide as palm-oil pits in Ijesaland.
O elephant, lord of the forest, respectfully called Oríiríbobo
O elephant whose teeth are like shafts.
One tooth of his is a porter's load. O elephant fondly called Otikó
Who has a beast-of-burden's proper neck.
O elephant, whom the hunter sometimes sees face to face.
O elephant, whom the hunter at other times sees from the rear.
Beast who carries mortars and yet walks with a swaggering gait.
Primeval leper, animal treading ponderously.   [c. 1921]

Translated by Adeboye Babalowa

GEORGE MACKAY BROWN

Scotland b. 1921

Mackay Brown's novels and short stories blend modern and prehistoric life in the Orkney Islands. His interest in continuity is as evident in his poetry where the rituals and customs of his own Roman Catholicism provide the context for an understanding of the significance of the human struggle. Collections of his work include *Loaves and Fishes* (1959), *The Year of the Whale* (1969), *Poems New and Selected* (1971), and *Selected Poems* (1977).

KING OF KINGS

> The inn-keeper at Bethlehem writes secret letters
> to the Third Secretary (Security) at the door
> marked with dolphins in the fifth street north
> from Temple and Dove-market.

Came the first day of the week five guardsmen, Greeks. No sleep
in the village for their choruses. Their lamp still burned
at sunrise. One broken jar. Rachel's scent was in the
sergeant's sheets. Came a troop of merchants, solemn men,
with currants in their satchels, they were up and gone
early, on four camels, southward. *Who will pay for the jar?*
I said to the guardsmen. *Caesar*, said a corporal. *Rachel*,
said the sergeant, *she broke it. And anyway*, said a
guardsman, *the drink was bad*. God keep me from guests like
them. It was this summer's wine, the leaven still moving in
it, a little cloud. The Chian and Syrian are for silk
purses.

*

These passed through my door yesterday—Jude and Abrim and Saul,
farmers. Jude had sold an ox at the mart. *A fire in the back
room, a lamp, dice, a skin of wine*, said Jude. An Egyptian
with scars on his face, he left the north-bound camel train,
he ate barley cakes and fish and was most courteous and laid
Ethiop coins on the table. Then Abrim's wife, crying under
the stars, *Where is Abrim? He hasn't come home, the bull is
in the marsh, his children are hungry, he is with Rachel, I
know it, she will have his last penny.* The Egyptian leaned
his knife-marked face from his window. The wife of Abrim
took one look at him, then turned and wrapped her in night
and silence. The Egyptian looked from the stars to a chart
he had on the sill. He made comparisons, measurements.

*

The Egyptian is still here. He asks me after breakfast, could he
   get a guide as far as the border? *I have certain persons to*
   meet in the desert, said he. In the afternoon he left with
   Simon, donkey by donkey, a muted going. This was the sole
   guest today, except for a rout of farm servants and
   shepherds who lay about the barrel like piglets at the teats
   of a sow, and sung and uttered filth and (two of them) David
   a ploughman and Amos a shepherd roared about the alleys
   after Rachel. They came back with bleeding faces, separate
   and silent, after midnight. Such scum.

*

My brain is reeling from a press of faces! I had no warning of
   this. First came two bureaucrats, a Parthian and a Cypriot,
   bearing Caesar's seal, and a boy with them. Your best room,
   said the Cypriot. (For these chit-bearers you get paid a
   half-year later.) Then came a little company of clerks with
   scrolls and ledgers and wax and moneybags and a wolf on a
   chain. They set up benches in the courtyard. Then—O my
   God—by every road north and south they came, a horde of
   hook-noses, hillmen, yokels, they swarmed about the doors,
   come to pay some tribal tax, filthy thirsty goats. *We'll*
   sleep on the roof, said some. And others, *Provide beer and*
   bread, never mind blankets. And Rachel shining among them
   like a fish in a pool. A measured clash of bronze; a column
   of soldiers possessed the village. And the lieutenant, *I*
   commandeer six rooms. There are no six rooms, I said. *I*
   commandeer the whole inn, he said. The Cypriot stood in the
   door. *I commandeer the whole inn except for the rooms of*
   Caesar's civil servants, said the lieutenant. *And the room*
   of the chief clerk, said the Cypriot, *and the room of my*
   hound, and the room of Eros. (Eros is their catamite.) Never
   was such a day in this place. The till rattled, I don't deny
   it, a hundred throats gargled the new wine. Ditches between
   here and Hebron will be well dunged.

*

The skin is full of blots and scratchings and bad spellings. Put
   it down to this—my trade is lighting fires, listening,
   going with chamber pots, whispering, heating cold porridge;
   not scrivener's work. Know however, the yokels are back in
   the hills, poor as goats after the taxes and the revelry.
   Out of Rachel's room all morning small sweet snores. The
   clerks are balancing figures in their ledgers, melting wax
   in small flames. The bureaucrats are playing at chess in
   their room and sipping the old Chian. Eros, like Rachel,

sleeps. The soldiers polish their greaves and drink and
throw dice; two of them, bare and bronze-knuckled and
bloodied, boxed in the sand at noon. There came a man and a
woman from the north to pay the tax, very late, and wanted a
room. This was after dark. I had one place, ox and ass kept
it warm with winter breathings. I gave the man a lantern.

*

The tax-men have gone, a clash of bronze on one side, a wedge of
steel on the other, the Parthian on horseback before, the
Cypriot on horseback behind, the wolf chained to the money
cart, Eros carried by two black men in a silk chair, swaying
aloft like a tulip. The first star brought the shepherds.
The soldiers have drunk all the wine, I said. Amos stood
well back in the shadows. *You*, I said, *Amos, stay outside,
never come back. I bar you from this place. You and your
punch-ups and your pewkings.* I said sweetly to the others,
The Romans have dried the barrel. The shepherds drifted on
past me. One carried a new white winter lamb.

*

Most secret and urgent. Aaron will bring this on horseback,
direct from inn to palace, helter-skelter, a shower of
hooves and stars. The Negro with the cut cheeks has come
back, and with him an Indian and one from very far east with
eyes like grass-blades. In the first light they seemed like
revellers masked and weary from a carnival. They had men
servants with them, heavy baggage on the mules, bales and
jars. I lit fires, put out sweet water, spread woven
blankets over linen. They went about the village all day
with questing eyes. I poked among the baggage—ingots,
cruets, chalices, tiaras, candlesticks, swords, thuribles,
swathe upon swathe of heavy green silk, emeralds cold as
ice. They came back late. They wrote their names in the
guest book, steep square letters like Hindu temples, like
ships of Cathay. I cannot read it, I have torn out the page
for your perusal. *Please*, I said, *to enter places of origin.*
Coal Face murmured, *The broken kingdoms of this world*, and
wrote in the book. Nothing in the room for a while but
shadows and flutters. *Also enter*, I said, *the nature of your
business. You understand, the imperial government requires
this.* Bronze Face said, *Bearers of precious gifts.* Nothing
again—one star that hung a web of glimmers and shadows
about the chamber. *Blessings given to men in the beginning,*
he went on at last, *that have been wrongly spent, on pomp,
wars, usury, whoredoms, vainglory: ill-used heavenly gifts.
We no longer know what to do with these mysteries. Our*

thrones are broken. We have brought the old treasures here
by difficult ways. We are looking for the hands that first
gave them, in the ancient original kingdom. We will offer
them back again. Let them shine now in the ceremonies of the
poor. I lit a cluster of seven candles at the wall. *But*
first we must find the kingdom, said Daffodil Face, smiling.
Perhaps this kingdom does not exist. *Perhaps we found it and*
did not recognize it. Perhaps it is hidden so deep in birth
and love and death that we will never find it. If so, we
will leave our skulls in the desert. We do not know where we
should go from here. Perhaps the kingdom is a very simple
thing. I kept my hands clasped and my head to one side.
Landlord, said Coal Face, *your guests tonight are poor lost*
cold hungry kings. What have you got for us in your cellar?
I informed them that their rooms were ready. I said that I
had bread with honey and currants and dates in it, baked
that same morning. I mentioned Rachel. I said also my inn
was famous for wines, in keg or skin or flagon. I hoped the
gentlemen would enjoy their stay. It was cold, I said, for
the time of year. They did not move. The night was a sack of
coal with one diamond in it. I turned to the door.   [n. d.]

RUARAIDH MACTHÒMAIS/
DERICK THOMSON

Scotland b. 1921

Thomson is Professor of Celtic at Glasgow University and founding editor in 1952 of the Gaelic quarterly *Gairm*. His Gaelic poems and his own translations into English attest to his desire to retain allegiance to his mother tongue while extending the boundaries of his readership. His collected poems in Gaelic, *Creachadh na cl'arsaich/Plundering the Harp* was published in 1982. His *Introduction to Gaelic Poetry* (1974; 1989) remains central to the study of this tradition.

CLANN-NIGHEAN AN SGADAIN

An gàire mar chraiteachan salainn
ga fhroiseadh bho 'm beul,
an sàl 's am picil air an teanga,
's na miaran cruinne, goirid a dheanadh giullachd,
no a thogadh leanabh gu socair, cuimir,
seasgair, fallain,
gun mhearachd,
's na sùilean cho domhainn ri fèath.

B'e bun-os-cionn na h-eachdraidh a dh' fhàg iad
'nan tràillean aig ciùrairean cutach,
thall 's a-bhos air Galldachd 's an Sasainn.
Bu shaillte an duais a thàrr iad
ás na mìltean bharaillean ud,
gaoth na mara geur air an craiceann,
is eallach a' bhochdainn 'nan ciste,
is mara b'e an gàire
shaoileadh tu gu robh an teud briste.

Ach bha craiteachan uaille air an cridhe,
ga chumail fallain,
is bheireadh cutag an teanga
slisinn á fanaid nan Gall—
agus bha obair rompa fhathast
nuair gheibheadh iad dhachaigh,
ged nach biodh maoin ac':
air oidhche robach gheamhraidh,
ma bha siud an dàn dhaibh,
dheanadh iad daoine.

THE HERRING GIRLS

Their laughter like a sprinkling of salt
showered from their lips,
brine and pickle on their tongues,
and the stubby short fingers that could handle fish,
or lift a child gently, neatly,
safely, wholesomely,
unerringly,
and the eyes that were as deep as a calm.

The topsy-turvy of history had made them
slaves to short-arsed curers,
here and there in the Lowlands, in England.
Salt the reward they won
from those thousands of barrels,
the sea-wind sharp on their skins,
and the burden of poverty in their kists,
and were it not for their laughter
you might think the harp-string was broken.

But there was a sprinkling of pride on their hearts,
keeping them sound,
and their tongues' gutting-knife
would tear a strip from the Lowlanders' mockery—

and there was work awaiting them
when they got home,
though they had no wealth:
on a wild winter's night,
if that were their lot,
they would make men.   [1982]

GABRIEL OKARA

Nigeria b. 1921

A bookbinder by trade who worked for the Government Press in Enugu following wartime service
in the RAF, Okara assumed positions of major responsibility within the Rivers State of Nigeria.
Many of Okara's poems were lost during the Nigeria-Biafra Civil War; those which survived
appeared in *The Fisherman's Invocation* (1978). Okara looks clearly at the forces which have
appropriated the African voice and experience in his lifetime. He relocates indigenous rhythms
and traditions 'in my inside', yielding to but bewildered by potentially contradictory currents, like
the two Ijaw concepts, the Back (the communal past) and the Front (the future and potential new
life) which inform 'The Fisherman's Invocation'. His surrender to a hope for genuine liberation
depends on surviving the reality of continuing pain and uncertainty.

ONE NIGHT AT VICTORIA BEACH

The wind comes rushing from the sea,
the waves curling like mambas strike
the sands and recoiling hiss in rage
washing the Aladuras'* feet pressing hard
on the sand and with eyes fixed hard
on what only hearts can see, they shouting
pray, the Aladuras pray; and coming
from booths behind, compelling highlife
forces ears; and car lights startle pairs
arm in arm passing washer-words back
and forth like haggling sellers and buyers—

Still they pray, the Aladuras pray
with hands pressed against their hearts
and their white robes pressed against
their bodies by the wind; and drinking
palm-wine and beer, the people boast
at bars at the beach. Still they pray.
They pray, the Aladuras pray
to what only hearts can see while dead
fishermen long dead with bones rolling
nibbled clean by nibbling fishes, follow

Aladuras: a Christian sect addicted to ritual bathing.

four dead cowries shining like stars
into deep sea where fishes sit in judgement;
and living fishermen in dark huts
sit round dim lights with Babalawo
throwing their souls in four cowries
on sand, trying to see tomorrow.

Still, they pray, the Aladuras pray
to what only hearts can see behind
the curling waves and the sea, the stars
and the subduing unanimity of the sky
and their white bones beneath the sand.

And standing dead on dead sands,
I felt my knees touch living sands—
but the rushing wind killed the budding words.   [1967]

SUDDENLY THE AIR CRACKS

Suddenly the air cracks
with striking cracking rockets
guffaw of bofors stuttering LMGS
jets diving shooting glasses dropping
breaking from lips people diving
under beds nothing bullets flashing fire
striking writhing bodies and walls—

Suddenly there's silence—
and a thick black smoke
rises sadly into the sky as the jets
fly away in gruesome glee—

Then a babel of emotions, voices
mothers fathers calling children
and others joking shouting 'where's your bunker?'
laughing teasing across streets
And then they gaze in groups without sadness
at the sad smoke curling skywards—

Again suddenly, the air cracks
above rooftops cracking striking
rockets guffawing bofors stuttering LMGS
ack-ack flacks diving jets
diving men women dragging children
seeking shelter not there breathless
hugging gutters walls houses
crumbling rumbling thunder
bombs hearts thumping heads low
under beds moving wordless lips—

Then suddenly there's silence
and the town heaves a deep sigh
as the jets again fly away and the guns
one by one fall silent and the gunners
dazed gaze at the empty sky, helpless—

And then voices shouting calling
voices, admiring jets' dive
pilot's bravery blaming gunners
praising gunners laughing people
wiping sweat and dust from hair
neck and shirt with trembling hands.

Things soon simmer to normal
hum and rhythm as danger passes
and the streets are peopled
with strolling men and women
boys and girls on various errands
walking talking laughing smiling—
and children running with arms
stretched out in front playing
at diving jets zoom past
unsmiling bombing rocketing shooting
with mouths between startled feet.
This also passes as dusk descends
and a friendly crescent moon
appears where the jets were.
Then simmering silence—the day passes—
And the curling black smoke,
the sadless hearts and the mangled
bodies stacked in the morgue
become memorials of this day.   [1977]

RICHARD WILBUR

USA b. 1921

Wilbur, whose father was a portrait painter, was born in New York and educated at Amherst and Harvard; he taught at Wesleyan University from 1957 to 1977. A contemporary of Robert Lowell's, working at first in a similar poetic idiom, Wilbur did not turn to the confessional form with Lowell's poetic descendants. Rather, he remained a formalist whose attention to metre and rhythm mark his precise gaze on the natural world; here he often finds beauty, abundance, and 'a greenness deeper than anyone knows' ('The Beautiful Changes'). Wilbur won the Bollingen Prize for translation for his version of *Tartuffe* (1963) and for his volume *New Poems and Translations* (1969); his work is represented in *New and Collected Poems* (1988).

PANGLOSS'S SONG: A COMIC-OPERA LYRIC

I
Dear boy, you will not hear me speak
    With sorrow or with rancor
Of what has paled my rosy cheek
    And blasted it with canker;
'Twas Love, great Love, that did the deed
    Through Nature's gentle laws,
And how should ill effects proceed
    From so divine a cause?

Sweet honey comes from bees that sting,
    As you are well aware;
To one adept in reasoning,
Whatever pains disease may bring
Are but the tangy seasoning
    To Love's delicious fare.

II
Columbus and his men, they say,
    Conveyed the virus hither
Whereby my features rot away
    And vital powers wither;
Yet had they not traversed the seas
    And come infected back,
Why, think of all the luxuries
    That modern life would lack!

All bitter things conduce to sweet,
    As this example shows;
Without the little spirochete
We'd have no chocolate to eat,
Nor would tobacco's fragrance greet
    The European nose.

III
Each nation guards its native land
  With cannon and with sentry,
Inspectors look for contraband
  At every port of entry,
Yet nothing can prevent the spread
  Of Love's divine disease:
It rounds the world from bed to bed
  As pretty as you please.

Men worship Venus everywhere,
  As plainly may be seen;
The decorations which I bear
Are nobler than the Croix de Guerre,
And gained in service of our fair
  And universal Queen.   [1961]

PHILIP LARKIN

England 1922–1985

Larkin is identified with the Movement, a generation of post-war poets whose shared ironic detachment was first anthologized in Robert Conquest's *New Lines* (1956) and D.J. Enright's *Poets of the 1950s* (1955). Larkin has said that poems 'come from being oneself, in life' and are written 'because [they're] something you've got to get down, not because it's a philosophy of life.' His persona continually explores the colloquial resources of the dramatic monologue and narrative forms that release flashes of epigrammatic intensity. Sardonic, energetically misanthropic, and contemptuous of fashions and their sway, Larkin's published and unpublished work appears in *Collected Poems* (1988).

FAITH HEALING

Slowly the women file to where he stands
Upright in rimless glasses, silver hair,
Dark suit, white collar. Stewards tirelessly
Persuade them onwards to his voice and hands,
Within whose warm spring rain of loving care
Each dwells some twenty seconds. *Now, dear child,*
What's wrong, the deep American voice demands,
And, scarcely pausing, goes into a prayer
Directing God about this eye, that knee.
Their heads are clasped abruptly; then, exiled

Like losing thoughts, they go in silence; some
Sheepishly stray, not back into their lives
Just yet; but some stay stiff, twitching and loud
With deep hoarse tears, as if a kind of dumb
And idiot child within them still survives
To re-awake at kindness, thinking a voice
At last calls them alone, that hands have come
To lift and lighten; and such joy arrives
Their thick tongues blort, their eyes squeeze grief, a crowd
Of huge unheard answers jam and rejoice—

What's wrong! Moustached in flowered frocks they shake:
By now, all's wrong. In everyone there sleeps
A sense of life lived according to love.
To some it means the difference they could make
By loving others, but across most it sweeps
As all they might have done had they been loved.
That nothing cures. An immense slackening ache,
As when, thawing, the rigid landscape weeps,
Spreads slowly through them—that, and the voice above
Saying *Dear child*, and all time has disproved.   [1960]

ELI MANDEL

Canada 1922–1992

Mandel describes his poetry as a 'sacred illness': 'poetry became possible for me, on the road to Estevan.' The poem was 'Estevan Sakatchewan' (1946); Mandel drew on his Jewish roots in that community and his abiding sense of prairie place to inspire his careers as impassioned teacher (mostly at the University of Alberta and at York University), critic, editor, anthologist, and poet. The language of Mandel's criticism and poetry alike is rife with dark duplicities and ambiguities. Mandel perceived the recurring nationalist call for writing that identified a Canadian reality as both culturally imperative and woefully blind to language's own more indirect vocation. After publishing *Trio* with Gael Turnbull and Phyllis Webb (1954), Mandel wrote *Fuseli Poems* (1960), followed by several other volumes, including *Crusoe: Poems Selected and New* (1973) and *Dreaming Backwards, 1954–1981: The Selected Poetry of Eli Mandel*.

HOUDINI

I suspect he knew that trunks are metaphors,
could distinguish between the finest rhythms
unrolled on rope or singing in a chain
and knew the metrics of the deepest pools

I think of him listening to the words
spoken by manacles, cells, handcuffs,
chests, hampers, roll-top desks, vaults,
especially the deep words spoken by coffins

escape, escape: quaint Harry in his suit
his chains, his desk, attached to all attachments
how he'd sweat in that precise struggle
with those binding words, wrapped around him
like that mannered style, his formal suit

and spoken when? by whom? What thing first said
'there's no way out'?; so that he'd free himself,
leap, squirm, no matter how, to chain himself again,
once more jump out of the deep alive
with all his chains singing around his feet
like the bound crowds who sigh, who sigh.   [1967]

KENDRICK SMITHYMAN

New Zealand b. 1922

Smithyman has taught in primary schools and at the University of Auckland. His poems, as exemplified in 'The Last Moriori', use language to evoke subtle and resonant meanings beyond words themselves. Smithyman's best-known collections of poetry are *The Blind Mountain* (1950) and *The Gay Trapeze* (1955).

THE LAST MORIORI

Reputedly last of his kind,
quite surely one of the last
not crossbred but (as They said) pure
as pure goes, a Chatham Island Moriori
taken for a slave when a boy, taken
again in some other raiding, passed
from band to band, from place to place
until he washed up on the River.
That was the story, anyway, which is
as may be. He was

very old, he did not belong,
some chunk of totara which lay too long
     in acid swamp.
He was kumara left on the pit's floor,
     sweetness dried, its hull drawn small.
He was what you found in caves but did not
     mention, travesty gone
beyond human. A tatty topcoat, bowler hat,
blanket which seemed to look your way
without seeing you from the stoop of a hut
at the Pa. A few weak hungers,
he survived. He endured,

already myth, beyond legends of his kind,
a poor fact. But the fact was, and the myth
was, and they endure together.

This is written particularly to you.
Remembering, I shiver again as on that day
taking small comfort from our day as it is.   [1985]

HONE TUWHARE

New Zealand b. 1922

Born in Kaikohe and now living in Dunedin, Tuwhare was active in labour unions. Tuwhare is
Maori, and his people's mythology is an important dimension of his thought and expression.
Among his collections of poetry are *No Ordinary Sun* (1964) and *Selected Poems* (1980).

SNOWFALL

It didn't make a grand entrance and I nearly
missed it—tip-toeing up on me as it did when
I was half asleep and suddenly, they're there
before my eyes—white pointillist flakes on
a Hotere canvas—swirling about on untethered

gusts of air and spreading thin uneven
thicknesses of white snow-cover on drooping
ti-kouka leaves, rata, a lonely kauri, pear
and beech tree. Came without hesitation right
inside my opened window licking my neck, my

arms, my nose as I leaned far out to embrace
a phantom sky above the house-tops and over
the sea: *Hey, where's the horizon? I shall
require a boat, you know—two strong arms?*
. . . and snow, kissing and lipping my face

gently, mushily, like a pet whale, or (if
you prefer) a shark with red bite—sleet
sting hot as ice. Well,
it's stopped now. Stunning sight. Unnerved,
the birds have stopped singing, tucking their

beaks under warm armpits: temporarily. And for
miles upon whitened miles around, there is no
immediate or discernible movement except from
me, transfixed, and moved by an interior
agitation—an armless man applauding.

Bravo, I whisper. *Bravissimo.* Standing ovation.
Why not . . . Oh, come in, Spring.   [1982]

DANNIE ABSE

Wales b. 1923

Abse's poetry draws on his Welsh roots, his Judaism, his experiences with the RAF during World
War II, and the daily work of his medical practice in London. At the close of his second auto-
biographical novel, *A Poet in the Family,* he considers the question of the kinds of poems he writes:
'They were the poems of a much-married man who was almost as happy as possible. . . . He was
increasingly aware, too, of his own mortality—how the apple flesh was always turning brown after
the bite. . . . Writing poetry . . . was an immersion into the common reality not an escape from it'
(198). Abse's work is represented in *Collected Poems 1948–1976.*

EPITHALAMION

Singing, today I married my white girl
beautiful in a barley field.
Green on thy finger a grass blade curled,
so with this ring I thee wed, I thee wed,
and send our love to the loveless world
of all the living and all the dead.

Now, no more than vulnerable human,
we, more than one, less than two,
are nearly ourselves in a barley field—
and only love is the rent that's due
though the bailiffs of time return anew
to all the living but not the dead.

Shipwrecked, the sun sinks down harbours
of a sky, unloads its liquid cargoes
of marigolds, and I and my white girl
lie still in the barley—who else wishes
to speak, what more can be said
by all the living against all the dead?

Come then all you wedding guests:
green ghost of trees, gold of barley,
you blackbird priests in the field,
you wind that shakes the pansy head
fluttering on a stalk like a butterfly;
come the living and come the dead.

Listen flowers, birds, winds, worlds,
tell all today that I married
more than a white girl in the barley—
for today I took to my human bed
flower and bird and wind and world,
and all the living and all the dead.   [1952]

X-RAY

Some prowl sea-beds, some hurtle to a star
and, mother, some obsessed turn over every stone
or open graves to let that starlight in.
There are men who would open anything.

Harvey, the circulation of the blood,
and Freud, the circulation of our dreams,
pried honourably and honoured are
like all explorers. Men who'd open men.

And those others, mother, with diseases
like great streets named after them: Addison,
Parkinson, Hodgkin—physicians who'd arrive
fast and first on any sour death-bed scene.

I am their slowcoach colleague, half afraid,
incurious. As a boy it was so: you know how
my small hand never teased to pieces
an alarm clock or flensed a perished mouse.

And this larger hand's the same. It stretches now
out from a white sleeve to hold up, mother,
your X-ray to the glowing screen. My eyes look
but don't want to; I still don't want to know.   [1981]

MARI EVANS

USA

Evans was born in Ohio and studied at the University of Toledo. Editor of the study *Black Women Writers* (1984), she is an advocate of writing that specifically identifies her own subject position and that of her readers, noting: 'If there are those outside the Black experience who hear the music and can catch the beat, that is serendipity; I have no objections. But when I write, I write . . . "for my people".' Evans's books of poetry include *I Am a Black Woman* (1970), *Nightstar 1973–1978* (1981), and *A Dark and Splendid Mass* (1992).

I AM A BLACK WOMAN

I am a black woman
the music of my song
some sweet arpeggio of tears
is written in a minor key
and I
can be heard humming in the night
Can be heard
        humming
in the night

I saw my mate leap screaming to the sea
and I/with these hands/cupped the lifebreath
from my issue in the canebrake
I lost Nat's swinging body in a rain of tears
and heard my son scream all the way from Anzio
for Peace he never knew. . . . I
learned Da Nang and Pork Chop Hill
in anguish
Now my nostrils know the gas
and these trigger tire/d fingers
seek the softness in my warrior's beard

I
am a black woman
tall as a cypress
strong
beyond all definition still
defying place
and time
and circumstance
  assailed

```
        impervious
            indestructible
Look
    on me and be
renewed                                                    [1970]
```

DENISE LEVERTOV

England/USA b. 1923

Levertov's father was a Russian Jew who converted to Christianity and became an Anglican priest, and her mother was 'descended from the Welsh tailor and mystic Angel Jones of Mold'; what R.W. Butterfield calls Levertov's 'heterogeneous spirituality' might have had its roots at home. Born in England, Levertov published her first book there in 1946; she emigrated to the United States with her American husband in 1948 and became a citizen in 1955. Strongly influenced by the poetics of William Carlos Williams and of the Black Mountain poets, Levertov writes verse that strives for immediacy but that also accommodates her spirituality. She has written some fifteen books of poems; her work is represented in *Selected Poems* (1986).

A TREE TELLING OF ORPHEUS

```
White dawn. Stillness.      When the rippling began
    I took it for sea-wind, coming to our valley with rumors
    of salt, of treeless horizons. But the white fog
didn't stir; the leaves of my brothers remained outstretched,
unmoving.
            Yet the rippling drew nearer—and then
my own outermost branches began to tingle, almost as if
fire had been lit below them, too close, and their twig-tips
were drying and curling.
                Yet I was not afraid, only
                deeply alert.

I was the first to see him, for I grew
        out on the pasture slope, beyond the forest.
He was a man, it seemed: the two
moving stems, the short trunk, the two
arm-branches, flexible, each with five leafless
                        twigs at their ends,
and the head that's crowned by brown or gold grass,
bearing a face not like the beaked face of a bird,
        more like a flower's.
                        He carried a burden made of
some cut branch bent while it was green,
strands of a vine tight-stretched across it. From this,
when he touched it, and from his voice
which unlike the wind's voice had no need of our
```

leaves and branches to complete its sound,
came the ripple.
But it was no longer a ripple (he had come near and
stopped in my first shadow) it was a wave that bathed me
   as if rain
      rose from below and around me
   instead of falling.
And what I felt was no longer a dry tingling:
   I seemed to be singing as he sang, I seemed to know
   what the lark knows; all my sap
     was mounting towards the sun that by now
      had risen, the mist was rising, the grass
was drying, yet my roots felt music moisten them
deep under earth.

    He came still closer, leaned on my trunk:
    the bark thrilled like a leaf still-folded.
Music! There was no twig of me not
      trembling with joy and fear.

Then as he sang
it was no longer sounds only that made the music:
he spoke, and as no tree listens I listened, and language
    came into my roots
      out of the earth,
    into my bark
      out of the air,
    into the pores of my greenest shoots
     gently as dew
and there was no word he sang but I knew its meaning.
He told of journeys,
   of where sun and moon go while we stand in dark,
  of an earth-journey he dreamed he would take some day
deeper than roots . . .
He told of the dreams of man, wars, passions, griefs,
   and I, a tree, understood words—ah, it seemed
my thick bark would split like a sapling's that
     grew too fast in the spring
when a late frost wounds it.

     Fire he sang,
that trees fear, and I, a tree, rejoiced in its flames.
New buds broke forth from me though it was full summer.
   As though his lyre (now I knew its name)
   were both frost and fire, its chords flamed
up to the crown of me.

I was seed again.
I was fern in the swamp.
I was coal.
And at the heart of my wood
(so close I was to becoming man or a god)
there was a kind of silence, a kind of sickness,
something akin to what men call boredom,
something
(the poem descended a scale, a stream over stones)
that gives to a candle a coldness
in the midst of its burning, he said.

It was then,
when in the blaze of his power that
reached me and changed me
I thought I should fall my length,
that the singer began
to leave me.   Slowly
moved from my noon shadow
to open light,
words leaping and dancing over his shoulders
back to me
rivery sweep of lyre-tones becoming
slowly again
ripple.

And I
in terror
but not in doubt of
what I must do
in anguish, in haste,
wrenched from the earth root after root,
the soil heaving and cracking, the moss tearing asunder—
and behind me the others: my brothers
forgotten since dawn. In the forest
they too had heard,
and were pulling their roots in pain
out of a thousand years' layers of dead leaves,
rolling the rocks away,
breaking themselves
out of
their depths.

You would have thought we would lose the sound of the lyre,
of the singing
so dreadful the storm-sounds were, where there was no storm,

no wind but the rush of our
branches moving, our trunks breasting the air.
But the music!
The music reached us.

Clumsily,
stumbling over our own roots,
rustling our leaves
in answer,
we moved, we followed.

All day we followed, up hill and down.
We learned to dance,
for he would stop, where the ground was flat,
and words he said
taught us to leap and to wind in and out
around one another   in figures   the lyre's measure designed.
The singer
laughed till he wept to see us, he was so glad.
At sunset
we came to this place I stand in, this knoll
with its ancient grove that was bare grass then.
In the last light of that day his song became
farewell.
He stilled our longing.
He sang our sun-dried roots back into earth,
watered them: all-night rain of music so quiet
we could almost
not hear it in the
moonless dark.
By dawn he was gone.
We have stood here since,
in our new life.
We have waited.
He does not return.
It is said he made his earth-journey, and lost
what he sought.
It is said they felled him
and cut up his limbs for firewood.
And it is said
his head still sang and was swept out to sea singing.
Perhaps he will not return.
But what we have lived
comes back to us.
We see more.
We feel, as our rings increase,

something that lifts our branches, that stretches our furthest
leaf-tips
further.
The wind, the birds,
do not sound poorer but clearer,
recalling our agony, and the way we danced.
The music!   [1970]

JOHN ORMOND

Wales 1923 – 1990

Born in Dunvant, Swansea, son of the village shoemaker, Ormond writes poetry that reveals a lyric and elegiac attachment to the region and its people. In collaboration with BBC Wales he has made documentary films about Welsh painters and poets. His interest in visual art provides the incentive for 'Certain Questions for Monsieur Renoir', a poem that invites the reader to explore possible correlations in vision and technique between visual and verbal forms. Ormond's work is represented in *Selected Poems* (1987).

CERTAIN QUESTIONS FOR MONSIEUR RENOIR

Did you then celebrate
That grave discovered blue
With salt thrown on a fire
In honour of all blues?

I mean the dress of La Parisienne
(Humanly on the verge of the ceramic),
Blue of Delft, dream summary of blues,
Centre-piece of a fateful exhibition;

Whose dress-maker and, for that matter,
Stays-maker the critics scorned;
Who every day receives her visitors
In my country where the hard slate is blue.

She has been dead now nearly a century
Who wears that blue of smoke curling
Beyond a kiln, and blue of gentians,
Blue of lazurite, turquoise hauled

Over the blue waves, blue water, from Mount Sinai;
Clematis blue: she, Madame Henriot,
Whose papers fall to pieces in the files
In the vaults of the Registrar General.

Did you see in her garment the King of Illyria
Naming his person's flower in self-love?
And in the folds, part of polyphony
Of all colour, thunder blue,

Blue of blue slipper-clay, blue
Of the blue albatross? Blue sometimes
Without edge, blue liquified
By distance? Or did they start

Those ribbons at her wrists in blue
Of a sea-starwort? Or in verdigris, perhaps,
Blue on a Roman bead? Or in that regal blue
Of the Phœnicians, of boiled whelks;

That humbly-begun but conquering blue
Which, glowing, makes a god of man?
She who is always poised between appointments
For flirtation, what nuances of blue

Her bodice had, this blue you made
For your amusement, painter of fans and porcelain,
You set on gaiety; who saw, in the blue fog
Of the city, a candle burning blue

(Not heralding a death but) harbouring
A clear illusion, blue spot on the young salmon,
A greater blue in shadow; blue's calm
Insistence on a sense. Not for you

Indigo blue, or blue of mummy's cloth
Or the cold unction of mercury's blue ointment,
But the elect blue of love in constancy,
Blind, true blue; blue gage, blue plum,

Blue fibrils of a form, roundness
Absorbed by light, quintessence
Of blue beautiful. It was not blue
Tainted, taunted by dark. Confirm it.

The eyes are bells to blue
Inanimate pigment set alight
By gazing which was passionate.
So what is midnight to this midinette?

Ultramarine, deep-water blue?
Part of a pain and darkness never felt?
Assyrian crystal? Clouded blue malachite?

Blue of a blue dawn trusting light.   [1973]

NISSIM EZEKIEL

India b. 1924

Born in Bombay of Jewish parents, Ezekiel sees in himself the full range of his homeland's seemingly incongruous interests and influences which in his work often coalesce around themes of arrival and departure. One of the most well-known post-colonial English poets in India, Ezekiel was in the 1960s the founder-editor of the important journal *Poetry India*. Playwright, anthologist, and critic, his poetry collections include *A Time To Change* (1952), *The Exact Name* (1965), *New Poems 1965–1970* (1970), and *Hymns in Darkness* (1976).

VERY INDIAN POEM IN INDIAN ENGLISH

I am standing for peace and non-violence.
Why world is fighting fighting
Why all people of world
Are not following Mahatma Gandhi,
I am simply not understanding.
Ancient Indian Wisdom is 100% correct.
I should say even 200% correct.
But modern generation is neglecting—
Too much going for fashion and foreign thing.

Other day I'm reading in newspaper
(Every day I'm reading Times of India
To improve my English language)
How one goonda fellow
Throw stone at Indirabehn.
Must be student unrest fellow, I am thinking.
Friends, Romans, countrymen, I am saying
(to myself)
Lend me the ears.
Everything is coming—
Regeneration, Remuneration, Contraception.
Be patiently, brothers and sisters.

You want one glass *lassi*?
Very good for digestion.
With little salt lovely drink,
Better than wine;
Not that I am ever tasting the wine.
I'm the total teetotaller, completely total.
But I say
Wine is for the drunkards only.

What you think of prospects of world peace?
Pakistan behaving like this,
China behaving like that,
It is making me very sad, I am telling you.
Really, most harassing me.
All men are brothers, no?
In India also
Gujaraties, Maharashtrians, Hindiwallahs
All brothers
Though some are having funny habits.
Still, you tolerate me,
I tolerate you,
One day, *Ram Rajya* is surely coming.

You are going?
But you will visit again
Any time, any day,
I am not believing in ceremony.
Always I am enjoying your company.   [c. 1985]

ENTERPRISE

It started as a pilgrimage,
Exalting minds and making all
The burdens light. The second stage
Explored but did not test the call.
The sun beat down to match our rage.

We stood it very well, I thought,
Observed and put down copious notes
On things the peasants sold and bought.
The way of serpents and of goats,
Three cities where a sage had taught.

But when the differences arose
On how to cross a desert patch,
We lost a friend whose stylish prose
Was quite the best of all our batch.
A shadow falls on us—and grows.

Another phase was reached when we
Were twice attacked, and lost our way.
A section claimed its liberty
To leave the group. I tried to pray.
Our leader said he smelt the sea.

We noticed nothing as we went,
A straggling crowd of little hope,
Ignoring what the thunder meant,
Deprived of common needs like soap.
Some were broken, some merely bent.

When, finally, we reached the place.
We hardly knew why we were there.
The trip had darkened every face
Our deeds were neither great nor rare.
Home is where we have to gather grace.   [1960]

JANET FRAME

New Zealand b. 1924

Born in Dunedin and raised in Oamaru, Frame has lived and worked in London and in Saratoga
Springs, New York, and now resides in Wanganui. Her poetry first appeared in the collection, *The
Pocket Mirror* (1967), and her body of work includes collections of short stories, *The Lagoon* (1952)
and *The Reservoir* (1966), and the novels *Owls Do Cry* (1957), *The Edge of the Alphabet* (1962), and
Intensive Care (1971).

THE CLOWN

His face is streaked with prepared tears.
I, with others, applaud him, knowing it
is fashionable to approve when a clown cries
and to disapprove when a persistent sourface
does whether or not his tears are paint.

It is also fashionable, between wars,
to say that hate is love and love is hate,
to make out everything is more complex than we dreamed
and then to say we did not dream it,
we knew it all along and are wise.

Dear crying clown dear childlike old man
dear kind murderer dear innocent guilty
dear simplicity I hate you for making me pretend
there are several worlds to one truth when
I know, I know there are not. Dear people like you and me
whose breaths are bad, who sleep in and rumble
their bowels and control it until
they get home into the empty house or among the family
dear family, dear lonely man in torn world of nobody,
is it for this waste that we have hoarded words over so many
million years since the first, groan,
and look up at the stars. Oh oh the sky is too wide to sleep
        under!   [1967]

EFUA SUTHERLAND

Ghana b. 1924

Playwright Sutherland, who was born Efua Theodora Morgue in Cape Coast, is through her work in theatre one of Ghana's strongest advocates for women's and children's liberation. After a stint in London at the School of Oriental and African Studies, she returned to Ghana in 1951; since then she has been continuously involved in various theatre-centred educational projects, including founding the Ghana Experimental Theatre in Accra (1958–61), which became affiliated with the University of Ghana in 1963. Sutherland's plays, which draw on oral tradition, include *Foriwa* (1967), *Edufa* (1967), and *The Marriage of Anansewa* (1975).

A PROFESSIONAL BEGGAR'S LULLABY

Don't cry baby,
Son, at two years old
You'll be a prodigy beggar kid,
Cute wide-eyed toddler beggar
Outside United Nations;
On that swanky beat,
'Painy-painy' lisping
And thriving on the coming in
And going out of world distresses,
Don't cry baby.   [1977]

IAN HAMILTON FINLAY

Scotland b. 1925

A writer of short stories, plays, and concrete and non-concrete poetry, Finlay was born in the Bahamas and moved to Scotland in 1969. His integration of plastic and semantic possibilities as a Concrete artist is represented in *Selected Ponds* (1976) and has been exhibited at both the Scottish National Gallery of Modern Art and the Tate Gallery in London.

BALLAD

roar
rora
oaro
atro
roat
taor
rota
toro
orot
otro
toto
otot
toot   [1971]

LITTLE CALENDAR

April	light	light	light	light
May	light	trees	light	trees
June	trees	light	trees	light
July	trees	trees	trees	trees
August	trees'	light	trees'	light
September	lights	trees	lights	trees

[1971]

CAROLYN KIZER

USA *b.* 1925

Born in Spokane, Washington and educated at Sarah Lawrence College, Kizer has been praised for her feminism (in work like her early poem 'Pro Femina' from the volume *Knock Upon Silence*, 1965), but her subjects and modes range widely. 'Exodus', with its casual documenting of a mundane population fleeing from an unknown yet ominously familiar menace, exemplifies Kizer's later deployment of an open narrative line. Her first book was *The Ungrateful Garden* (1961); later volumes include the collection *Midnight Was My Cry: New and Selected Poems* (1971), *Yin: New Poems* (1984), and *The Nearness of You* (1986).

EXODUS

We are coming down the pike,
All of us, in no particular order,
Not grouped by age, Wanda and Val, her fourth husband,
Sallie Swift, the fellows who play bridge
Every Thursday, at Mason's Grill, in the back,
Two of them named George,
We are all coming down the pike.

Somebody whose face I can't make out
Is carrying old Mrs Sandow, wrapped in a pink afghan;
Her little pink toes peep out from the hem
Of her cotton nightie like pink pea pods,
As pink as her little old scalp showing through.
Be careful, Mister, don't lose ahold of her.
She has to come down the pike.

Maybelle and Ruth walk together, holding hands;
Maybelle wears tennis shorts and a sweatband
As she strides along steadily in her golf shoes;
Ruth has on something flimsy,
Already ripped, and sling-backs, for God's sake.
Imagine her feet tomorrow, she'll have to drop out.
But right now they are both coming down the pike.

Richard had to leave his piano; he looks sort of unfinished;
His long pale fingers wave like anemone
Or is it amoeba I mean?
He's artistic, but would never have been
Of the first rank, though he's changed his name three times.
He doesn't like the mob he's with.
But you can't be picky
When you're coming down the pike.

One of the monitors wants us to move faster,
But you can't really organize this crowd;
The latch on the birdcage was loose so the budgie escaped
About two miles back, but Mrs Rappaport still lugs his cage:
She's expecting the budgie to catch up any minute.
Its name was Sweetie. I can't stand pet names
And sentimentality at a time like this
When we should be concentrating all our efforts
On getting down the pike.

Who would have thought we would all be walking,
Except of course for Mrs Sandow, and Dolly Bliss
In her motorized wheelchair and her upswept hairdo.
Someone has piled six hatboxes on her lap;
She can hardly see over, poor lady, it isn't fair,
And who needs picture hats at a time like this.
But they are probably full of other things,
The kind of useless stuff you grab up in a panic
When there's no time to think or plan,
And you've got ten minutes before they order you down the pike.

Bill Watkins is sore that he wasn't chosen monitor
Because he lacks leadership qualities.
But he rushes up and down the lines anyhow
Snapping like a sheepdog. The Ruddy family,
All eight of them red-heads, has dropped out for a picnic,
Using a burnt-out car
As a table. Not me, I'm saving my sandwiches.
The Ruddys were always feckless; they won't laugh tomorrow
When they run out of food on the pike.

Of course Al Fitch has nothing, not even a pocketknife
Let alone a gun.
He had to get Morrie Phelps to shoot his dog for him.
No pets! You can see the reason for that,
Although nobody fussed about the budgie.

I expect there's a few smuggled cats
Inside some of the children's jackets.
But old Al Fitch, he just strolls along
With his hands in his pockets, whistling 'Goodnight Irene.'

My husband says I shouldn't waste my breath
Describing us, but save it for the hike
Ahead. We're just like people anywhere
Though we may act crazier right now.
Maybelle drags Ruth along faster and faster
Though she's stumbling and sobbing, and has already fallen twice.
Richard, who's always been so careful of his hands,
Just hit Al, and told him to whistle something else
Like Bach: one of the hymns he wrote, that we could sing.
Will you be trying to sing, wherever you are,
As you come down the pike?   [1984]

ANNE RANASINGHE

Sri Lanka b. 1925

Born into a German Jewish family in Essen, Germany, Ranasinghe left in 1939 for England; her
parents and many of her family died in concentration camps. She married a Sri Lankan doctor in
1949 and settled in Colombo, where she began to write poetry. Her return to Essen in 1983—she
was writing about wartime Germany for Sri Lankan newspapers—was a major influence on her
subsequent writing. Ranasinghe won the Sri Lanka Arts Council Prize for Poetry in 1982 and
1985; her books of poetry have been translated into several languages and include *Poems* (1971),
Plead Mercy (1975), *Against Eternity and Darkness* (1985), and *Not Even Shadows* (1989).

AUSCHWITZ FROM COLOMBO

Colombo.   March.   The city white fire
That pours through vehement trees burst into flame,
And only a faint searing wind
Stirring the dust
From relics of foreign invaders, thrown
On this far littoral by chance or greed,
Their stray memorial the odd word mispronounced,
A book of laws
A pile of stones
Or maybe some vile deed.

Once there was another city; but there
It was cold—the trees leafless
And already thin ice on the lake.
It was that winter
Snow hard upon the early morning street
And frost flowers carved in hostile window panes

It was that winter.

Yet only yesterday
Half a world away and twenty-five years later
I learn of the narrow corridor
And at the end a hole, four feet by four
Through which they pushed them all—the children too—
Straight down a shaft of steel thirteen feet long
And dark and icy cold
Onto the concrete floor of what they called
The strangling room. Dear God, the strangling room,
Where they were stunned—the children too—
By heavy wooden mallets,
Garroted, and then impaled
On pointed iron hooks.

I am glad of the unechoing street
Burnt white in the heat of many tropical years.
For the mind, no longer sharp,
Seared by the tropical sun
Skims over the surface of things
Like the wind
That stirs but slightly the ancient dust.   [1980]

JAMES K. BAXTER

New Zealand 1926-1972

Born in Dunedin and educated at Otago and Victoria universities, Baxter was a prolific writer of poetry, drama, and essays. In 1958 he converted to Catholicism and founded a religious community, 'Jerusalem', on the Wanganui River in his latter years. Baxter's collections of poetry include *The Fallen House* (1953), *In Fires of No Return* (1958), *Pig Island Letters* (1966), and *Jerusalem Sonnets* (1970).

THE IKONS

Hard, heavy, slow, dark,
Or so I find them, the hands of Te Whaea

Teaching me to die. Some lightness will come later
When the heart has lost its unjust hope

For special treatment. Today I go with a bucket
Over the paddocks of young grass,

So delicate like fronds of maidenhair,
Looking for mushrooms. I find twelve of them,

Most of them little, and some eaten by maggots,
But they'll do to add to the soup. It's a long time now

Since the great ikons fell down,
God, Mary, home, sex, poetry,

Whatever one uses as a bridge
To cross the river that only has one beach,

And even one's name is a way of saying—
'This gap inside a coat'—the darkness I call God,

The darkness I call Te Whaea, how can they translate
The blue calm evening sky that a plane tunnels through

Like a little wasp, or the bucket in my hand,
Into something else? I go on looking

For mushrooms in the field, and the fist of longing
Punches my heart, until it is too dark to see.   [1971]

RAYMOND GARLICK

Wales b. 1926

Editor, with Roland Mathias, of *Anglo-Welsh Poetry 1480–1980* and founding editor of *Dock Leaves* (later *The Anglo-Welsh Review*), Garlick pursues the origins of Welsh poetry in English into the fifteenth century. In his conclusion to *An Introduction to Anglo-Welsh Literature* (1972), he discusses the 'light' rather than 'heat', an appreciation of bilingualism in Welsh culture. 'No one can foretell', writes Garlick, 'what the disastrous failure in this respect may yet mean for Belgium, for Canada. . . . The whole aim of a bilingual education and a bilingual society must be to present the two languages and cultures as complementary . . . this is the social and educational function of Anglo-Welsh literature in contemporary Wales.' Garlick's *Collected Poems 1946–1986* appeared in 1987.

MAP READING

Look north if you like:
Eryri, water, Kirkcudbright,
the fingers of the Arctic sun
feeling out gold on the white
plains of the pole's Klondyke.

Look south even more:
Cardiff, the Bridge, and beyond
the Summer Country, Europe
shimmering up from the pond
of the Manche like a solar shore.

The west is all right:
the sea, the Republic, the crash
and spin of the ocean, furlongs
of light; only then bulks the brash
American shore, and the night.

Best avoid the east:
below the Dyke it's getting dark
in the tangled, litter-blown
Greater London park
of Britain, deceased. [1972]

ALLEN GINSBERG

USA b. 1926

A graduate of Columbia University, Ginsberg became a prominent spokesperson among avant-garde Beat writers with the publication of *Howl* (1956) and *Kaddish* (1961). Ginsberg's self-consciously prophetic voice, influenced by Rabbinic and Zen philosophers and by poets such as William Blake, Walt Whitman, and William Carlos Williams, addresses critical issues such as homophobia, xenophobia, racism, imperialism, and genocide. Ginsberg's many honours include a National Book Award for *The Fall of America: Poems of these States* (1973).

A SUPERMARKET IN CALIFORNIA

What thoughts I have of you tonight, Walt Whitman, for I
walked down the sidestreets under the trees with a headache
self-conscious looking at the full moon.

In my hungry fatigue, and shopping for images, I went into
the neon fruit supermarket, dreaming of your enumerations!

What peaches and what penumbras! Whole families
shopping at night! Aisles full of husbands! Wives in the
avocados, babies in the tomatoes!—and you, Garcia Lorca,
what were you doing down by the watermelons?

I saw you, Walt Whitman, childless, lonely old grubber,
poking among the meats in the refrigerator and eyeing the
grocery boys.

I heard you asking questions of each: Who killed the pork
chops? What price bananas? Are you my Angel?

I wandered in and out of the brilliant stacks of cans
following you, and followed in my imagination by the store
detective.

We strode down the open corridors together in our solitary
fancy tasting artichokes, possessing every frozen delicacy, and
never passing the cashier.

Where are we going, Walt Whitman? The doors close in an
hour. Which way does your beard point tonight?

(I touch your book and dream of our odyssey in the
supermarket and feel absurd.)

Will we walk all night through solitary streets? The trees
add shade to shade, lights out in the houses, we'll both be
lonely.

Will we stroll dreaming of the lost America of love past
blue automobiles in driveways, home to our silent cottage?

Ah, dear father, graybeard, lonely old courage-teacher, what
America did you have when Charon quit poling his ferry and
you got out on a smoking bank and stood watching the boat
disappear on the black waters of Lethe?   [1956]

FRANK O'HARA

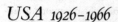

USA 1926–1966

O'Hara was not only a prominent experimental poet in the New York school, but a brilliant
musician, an influential art critic and curator, and an innovative visual artist. His volume *Collected
Poems* was published posthumously in 1971.

WHY I AM NOT A PAINTER

I am not a painter, I am a poet.
Why? I think I would rather be
a painter, but I am not. Well,

for instance, Mike Goldberg
is starting a painting. I drop in.
'Sit down and have a drink' he
says. I drink; we drink. I look
up. 'You have SARDINES in it.'
'Yes, it needed something there.'
'Oh.' I go and the days go by
and I drop in again. The painting
is going on, and I go, and the days
go by. I drop in. The painting is
finished. 'Where's SARDINES?'
All that's left is just
letters, 'It was too much,' Mike says.

But me? One day I am thinking of
a color: orange. I write a line
about orange. Pretty soon it is a
whole page of words, not lines.

Then another page. There should be
so much more, not of orange, of
words, of how terrible orange is

and life. Days go by. It is even in
prose, I am a real poet. My poem
is finished and I haven't mentioned
orange yet. It's twelve poems, I call
it ORANGES. And one day in a gallery
I see Mike's painting, called SARDINES.   [1971]

JOHN ASHBERY

USA b. 1927

A graduate of Harvard and Columbia, Ashbery worked as an art critic in Paris for many years. Returning to New York City, he became an executive editor for *Art News* and a professor at Brooklyn College. Although he was influenced by Wallace Stevens and W.H. Auden, Ashbery inverted Stevens's idea of art as a 'supreme fiction' to express his desire that 'nature, not art, might usurp the canvas.' Ashbery was awarded the Pulitzer Prize, the National Book Award, and the National Book Critics Circle Award for *Self Portrait in a Convex Mirror* (1975).

THE PAINTER

Sitting between the sea and the buildings
He enjoyed painting the sea's portrait.
But just as children imagine a prayer
Is merely silence, he expected his subject
To rush up the sand, and, seizing a brush,
Plaster its own portrait on the canvas.

So there was never any paint on his canvas
Until the people who lived in the buildings
Put him to work: 'Try using the brush
As a means to an end. Select, for a portrait,
Something less angry and large, and more subject
To a painter's moods, or, perhaps, to a prayer.'

How could he explain to them his prayer
That nature, not art, might usurp the canvas?
He chose his wife for a new subject,
Making her vast, like ruined buildings,
As if, forgetting itself, the portrait
Had expressed itself without a brush.

Slightly encouraged, he dipped his brush
In the sea, murmuring a heartfelt prayer:
'My soul, when I paint this next portrait
Let it be you who wrecks the canvas.'
The news spread like wildfire through the buildings:
He had gone back to the sea for his subject.

Imagine a painter crucified by his subject!
Too exhausted even to lift his brush,
He provoked some artists leaning from the buildings
To malicious mirth: 'We haven't a prayer
Now, of putting ourselves on canvas,
Or getting the sea to sit for a portrait!'

Others declared it a self-portrait.
Finally all indications of a subject
Began to fade, leaving the canvas
Perfectly white. He put down the brush.
At once a howl, that was also a prayer,
Arose from the overcrowded buildings.

They tossed him, the portrait, from the tallest of the buildings;
And the sea devoured the canvas and the brush
As though his subject had decided to remain a prayer.   [1970]

ROBERT KROETSCH

Canada b. *1927*

Kroetsch's novels, poetry, and criticism—he is western Canada's most protean writer—inhabit a common and paradoxical homeground in his native Alberta and in the international language of contemporary literary theory. Kroetsch is particularly drawn to the postmodern, poststructuralist, and deconstructionist notions that question textual coherence, discrete individuals, or the possibility of a unified self and voice. He is also fascinated with redirecting literary language away from realist and referential contexts to more indirect and reflexive modes. Kroetsch's first book of poetry, *The Stone Hammer Poems*, appeared in 1975; since then he has experimented widely, most notably with the long poem, exemplified in *Completed Field Notes: The Long Poems of Robert Kroetsch* (1987).

STONE HAMMER POEM

1.
This stone
become a hammer
of stone, this maul

is the colour
of bone (no,
bone is the colour
of this stone maul).

The rawhide loops
are gone, the
hand is gone, the
buffalo's skull
is gone;

the stone is
shaped like the skull
of a child.

2.
This paperweight on my desk

where I begin
this poem   was

found in a wheatfield
lost (this hammer,
this poem).

Cut to a function,
this stone was
(the hand is   gone—

3.
Grey, two-headed,
the pemmican maul

fell from the travois or
a boy playing   lost it in
the prairie wool or
a squaw   left it in
the brain of a buffalo or

it is a million
years older than
the hand that
chipped stone or
raised slough
water (or blood) or

4.
This stone maul
was found.

In the field
my grandfather
thought
was his

my father
thought was his

5.
It is a stone
old as the last
Ice Age, the
retreating/the
recreating ice,
the retreating
buffalo, the
retreating Indians

(the saskatoons bloom
white (infrequently
the chokecherries the
highbush cranberries the
pinchberries bloom
white along the barbed
wire fence (the
pemmican   winter

6.
This stone maul
stopped a plough
long enough for one
Gott im Himmel.

The Blackfoot (the
Cree?) not

finding the maul
cursed.

?did he curse
?did he try to
go back
?what happened

I have to/I want
to know (not know)
?WHAT HAPPENED

7.
The poem
is the stone
chipped and hammered
until it is shaped
like the stone
hammer, the maul.

8.
Now the field is
mine because
I gave it
(for a price)

to a young man
(with a growing son)
who did not

notice that the land
did not belong

to the Indian who
gave it to the Queen
(for a price) who
gave it to the CPR
(for a price) which
gave it to my grandfather
(for a price) who
gave it to my father
(50 bucks an acre
Gott im Himmel I cut
down all the trees I
picked up all the stones) who

gave it to his son
(who sold it)

9.
This won't
surprise you.

My grandfather
lost the stone maul.

10.
My father (retired)
grew raspberries.
He dug in his potato patch.
He drank one glass of wine
each morning.
He was lonesome
for death.

He was lonesome for the
hot wind on his face, the smell
of horses, the distant
hum of a threshing machine,
the oilcan he carried, the weight
of a crescent wrench in his hind pocket.

He was lonesome for his absent
son and his daughters,
for his wife, for his own
brothers and sisters and
his own mother and father.

He found the stone maul
on a rockpile in the
north-west corner of what
he thought of
as his wheatfield.

He kept it (the
stone maul) on the railing
of the back porch in
a raspberry basket.

11.
I keep it
on my desk
(the stone).

Sometimes I use it
in the (hot) wind
(to hold down paper)

smelling a little of cut
grass or maybe even of
ripening wheat or of

buffalo blood hot
in the dying sun.

Sometimes I write
my poems for that

stone hammer.   [1973]

PHYLLIS WEBB

Canada b. 1927

Since 1970 Webb has lived on Salt Spring, one of the Gulf Islands near her birthplace, Victoria, BC. Not as well known or as prolific as Canada's more visible writers, Webb is deeply respected as a poet's poet, a writer with exacting standards. Some of Webb's verse is taut and spare, as in *Naked Poems* (1965); some, such as the poems in the acclaimed volume *Water and Light: Ghazals and Anti Ghazals* (1984) experiment beautifully with forms like the Persian and Urdu love lyric. Two representative collections are *Selected Poems 1954–1965* (ed. Hulcoop, 1971), and *Selected Poems: The Vision Tree* (ed. Thesen, 1982).

POETICS AGAINST THE ANGEL OF DEATH

I am sorry to speak of death again
(some say I'll have a long life)
but last night Wordsworth's 'Prelude'
suddenly made sense—I mean the measure,
the elevated tone, the attitude
of private Man speaking to public men.
Last night I thought I would not wake again
but now with this June morning I run ragged to elude
the Great Iambic Pentameter
who is the Hound of Heaven in our stress
because I want to die
writing Haiku
or, better,
long lines, clean and syllabic as knotted bamboo. Yes!   [1962]

MAYA ANGELOU

USA b. 1928

Angelou, born in St Louis, Missouri, read her poetry at President Clinton's inauguration, the first Black American poet to be so honoured. Early in her career Angelou worked as a night-club singer in New York and toured Europe in a production of *Porgy and Bess*. Becoming increasingly active in Black political movements in the sixties, she edited the *African Review* in Ghana; she is now the Reynolds Professor of American Studies at Wake Forest University in North Carolina. Angelou's poetry combines blues, gospel music, and politics; her first book of poems, *Just Give Me a Cool Drink of Water 'Fore I Diiie* (1971), has been followed by several others, including *And Still I Rise* (1978), *Now Sheba Sings the Song* (1987), and *I Shall Not Be Moved* (1990). *The Complete Collected Poems of Maya Angelou* appeared in 1994.

A GOOD WOMAN FEELING BAD

The blues may be the life you've led
Or midnight hours in
An empty bed. But persecuting
Blues I've known
Could stalk
Like tigers, break like bone,

Pend like rope in
A gallows tree,
Make me curse
My pedigree,

Bitterness thick on
A rankling tongue,
A psalm to love that's
Left unsung.

Rivers heading north
But ending South,
Funeral music
In a going-home mouth.

All riddles are blues,
And all blues are sad,
And I'm only mentioning
Some blues I've had.

[1983]

KWESI BREW

Ghana b. 1928

Member of a Gold Coast family that traces its roots back to 1745, Brew became a career diplomat, serving in Britain, France, India, and Germany. His poetry often explores ancestral rituals and observances with a precision that approaches the surreal. His writing is graphic and intense, as in the presentation in 'The Executioner's Dream' of sappor, a custom in which captives of war or criminals, their tongues pinned by sharp sticks thrust through the under part of the jaw, slowly bleed to death. Brew's concern with the erosion of his homeland by political as well as natural forces is central to *Shadows of Laughter*, which appeared in 1968.

THE SEARCH

The past
Is but the cinders
Of the present;
The future
The smoke
That escaped
Into the cloud-bound sky.

Be gentle, be kind my beloved
For words become memories,
And memories tools
In the hands of jesters.
When wise men become silent,
It is because they have read
The palms of Christ
In the face of the Buddha.

So look not for wisdom
And guidance
In their speech, my beloved.
Let the same fire
Which chastened their tongues
Into silence,
Teach us—teach us!

The rain came down,
When you and I slept away
The night's burden of our passions;
Their new-found wisdom
In quick lightning flashes
Revealed the truth
That they had been
The slaves of fools.

[1968]

Iain MacA'Ghobhainn/ Iain Crichton Smith

Scotland b. 1928

Crichton Smith's work in Gaelic as well as in English expresses his concern with how the individual weathers the environment and how the environment weathers the individual. His understanding of the interpenetration of the two is central to his commitment to his mother tongue: 'He who loses his language loses his world.' Playwright, novelist, and short-story writer, Smith's collections of English poetry include *Thistles and Roses* (1961), *Consider the Lilies* (1970), and *Selected Poems* (1970).

Shall Gaelic Die?

A translation by the author of his Am Faigh A' Ghàidhlig Eàs?

(1)
A picture has no grammar. It has neither evil nor good.
It has only colour, say orange or mauve.
Can Picasso change a minister? Did he make a sermon to a bull?
Did heaven rise from his brush? Who saw a church that is orange?
In a world like a picture, a world without language,
would your mind go astray, lost among objects?

(2)
Advertisements in neon, lighting and going out, 'Shall it . . .
shall it . . . Shall Gaelic . . . shall it . . . shall Gaelic . . . die?'

(3)
Words rise out of the country. They are around us.
In every month in the year we are surrounded by words.
Spring has its own dictionary, its leaves are turning in
the sharp wind of March, which opens the shops.
Autumn has its own dictionary, the brown words lying on
the bottom of the loch, asleep for a season.
Winter has its own dictionary, the words are a blizzard
building a tower of Babel. Its grammar is like snow.
Between the words the wild-cat looks sharply across a
No-Man's-Land, artillery of the Imagination.

(4)
They built a house with stones. They put windows in the house,
and doors. They filled the room with furniture and the beards of thistles.
They looked out of the house on a Highland world, the flowers,
the glens, distant Glasgow on fire.
They built a barometer of history.

Inch after inch, they suffered the stings of suffering.
Strangers entered the house, and they left.
But now, who is looking out with an altered gaze? What does he see?
What has he got in his hand? A string of words.

(5)
He who loses his language loses his world. The Highlander who
loses his language loses his world.
The space ship that goes astray among planets loses the world.
In an orange world how would you know orange? In a world without
evil how would you know good?
Wittgenstein is in the middle of his world. He is like a spider.
The flies come to him. 'Cuan' and 'coill' rising.*
When Wittgenstein dies, his world dies.
The thistle bends to the earth. The earth is tired of it.

(6)
I came with a 'sobhrach' in my mouth. He came with a 'primrose.'
'A primrose by the river's brim.' Between the two languages, the
word 'sobhrach' turned to 'primrose.'
Behind the two words, a Roman said 'prima rosa.'
The 'sobhrach' or the 'primrose' was in our hands.
Its reasons belonged to us.

(7)
'That thing about which you cannot speak, be silent about it.'
Was there a pianist before a piano? Did Plato have a melodeon?
Melodeon in the heavens? Feet dancing in the heavens?
Red lips and black hair? Was there a melodeon in the heavens? A
skeleton of notes.

(8)
'Shall Gaelic die?' A hundred years from now who will say these
words? Who will say, 'Co their?'** Who? The voice of the owl.

(9)
If I say 'an orange church' will I build an orange church?
If I say 'a mauve minister' will I create him?
The tartan is in its own country.
The tartan is a language.
A Campbell is different from a Macdonald (this is what a tartan teaches).
The tartans fight each other. Is that why they had to put a
colourless church between them?

*'Cuan' means 'sea' and 'coill' means 'wood'.
**'Co their?'—'Who will say?'

(10)
Said Alexander Macdonald, 'It was Gaelic that Adam and Eve spoke
in that garden.' Did God speak Gaelic as well, when he told them
about the apple? And when they left that garden, were they like
exiles sailing to . . . Canada?

(11)
Shall Gaelic die? What that means is: shall we die?

(12)
An orange church with green walls. A picture on a wall showing
ships like triangles. On another wall, a picture of a café with
men made of paint. 'Gloria Deo' in the language of paintings, an
orange bell, a yellow halo around the pulpit where there are red dancers.

(13)
Were you ever in a maze? Its language fits your language. Its
roads fit the roads of your head. If you cannot get out of the
language you cannot get out of the maze. Its roads reflect your
language. O for a higher language, like a hawk in the sky, that
can see the roads, that can see their end, like God who built the
roads, our General Wade. The roads of the Highlands fit the roads
of our language.

(14)
When the ape descended from the trees he changed his language. He
put away the green leaves. He made small sharp words, words made
of stone.

(15)
The dove returned to Noah with a word in his mouth.

(16)
The scholar is sitting with a candle in front of him. He is
construing words. He is building a dictionary. Little by little,
inch by inch, he is building a dictionary. Outside the window the
children are shouting, a ball is rising to the sky, a girl and a
boy are walking without language to bed. What will he do when the
ball enters the quiet room, breaking the window, stopping him at
B, and Z so distant?

(17)
Whom have you got in the net? Who is rising with green eyes, with
a helmet, who is in the net?
Cuchulain is in the net, he is rising from the sea, ropes of
moonlight at his heels, ropes of language.

(18)
'When you turn your back on the door, does the door exist?' said
Berkeley, the Irishman who was alive in the soul.
When the Highlands loses its language, will there be a Highlands,
said I, with my two coats, losing, perhaps, the two.

(19)
A million colours are better than one colour, if they are different.
A million men are better than one man if they are different.
Keep out of the factory, O man, you are not a robot. It wasn't a
factory that made your language—it made you.

(20)
Like a rainbow, like crayons, spectrum of beautiful languages.
The one-language descended like a church—like a blanket, like mist.

(21)
God is outside language, standing on a perch. He crows now and
again. Who hears him? If there is a God let him emanate from the
language, a perfume emanating from the dew of the morning, from
the various-coloured flowers.

(22)
Death is outside the language. The end of language is beyond
language. Wittgenstein didn't speak after his death. What
language would he speak? In what language would you say, 'Fhuair
a' Ghaidhlig bas'?*

(23)
When the name 'Adam' was called, he turned his back on the hills.
He saw his shadow at his feet—he drew his breath.

(24)
You cannot say, 'Not-Adam.' You cannot say 'Not-Eve.'
The apple has a name as well. It is in the story.

(25)
The gold is new. It will not rust. 'Immutable, universal,' as the
Frenchman said. But the pennies, the pounds, the half-crowns,
these coins that are old and dirty, the notes that are wrinkled
like old faces, they are coping with time, to these I give my
allegiance, to these I owe honour, with sweetness. 'Immutable,
perfect,' Midas with his coat of gold and of death.   [1972]

---

*'Fhuair a' Ghaidhlig bas'—'Gaelic is dead.'

JAYANTA MAHAPATRA

India b. 1928

A professor of physics in Cuttack, an award-winning poet, and editor of the literary magazine *Chandrabhaga*, Mahapatra has published *Selected Poems* (1987) and *The Temple* (1989). His long poem 'Relationship' received the Sahitya Akademi Award of 1981. His poetry is that of a 'survivor' who is well aware of the tenuous nature of the past he has inherited as broken forms and partial memories. Mahapatra's work is further deepened by ambiguities felt and imagined that resist pat answers.

HUNGER

It was hard to believe the flesh was heavy on my back.
The fisherman said: Will you have her, carelessly,
trailing his nets and his nerves, as though his words
sanctified the purpose with which he faced himself.
I saw his white bone thrash his eyes.

I followed him across the sprawling sands,
my mind thumping in the flesh's sling.
Hope lay perhaps in burning the house I lived in.
Silence gripped my sleeves; his body clawed at the froth
his old nets had only dragged up from the seas.

In the flickering dark his lean-to opened like a wound.
The wind was I, and the days and nights before.
Palm fronds scratched my skin. Inside the shack
an oil lamp splayed the hours bunched to those walls.
Over and over the sticky soot crossed the space of my mind.

I heard him say: My daughter, she's just turned fifteen . . .
Feel her. I'll be back soon, your bus leaves at nine.
The sky fell on me, and a father's exhausted wile.
Long and lean, her years were cold as rubber.
She opened her wormy legs wide. I felt the hunger there,
the other one, the fish slithering, turning inside.   [1976]

THE ABANDONED BRITISH CEMETERY AT BALASORE

This is history.
I would not disturb it: the ruins of stone and marble,
the crumbling wall of brick, the coma of alienated decay.
How exactly should the archaic dead make me behave?

A hundred and fifty years ago
I might have lived. Now nothing offends my ways.
A quietness of bramble and grass holds me to a weed.
Will it matter if I know who the victims were, who survived?

And yet, awed by the forgotten dead,
I walk around them: thirty-nine graves, their legends
floating in a twilight of baleful littoral,
the flaking history my intrusion does not animate.

Awkward in the silence, a scrawny lizard
watches the drama with its shrewd, hooded gaze.
And a scorpion, its sting drooping,
two eerie arms spread upon the marble, over an alien name.

In the circle the epitaphs run: Florence R. . . , darling wife
of Captain R. . . R. . . , aged nineteen, of cholera . . .
Helen, beloved daughter of Mr & Mrs. . . , of cholera,
aged seventeen, in the year of our Lord, eighteen hundred . . .

Of what concern to me is a vanished empire?
Or the conquest of my ancestors' timeless ennui?
It is the dying young who have the power to show
what the heart will hide, the grass shows no more.

Who watches now in the dark near the dead wall?
The tribe of grass in the cracks of my eyes?
It is the cholera still, death's sickly trickle,
that plagues the sleepy shacks beyond this hump of earth,

moving easily, swiftly, with quick power
through both past and present, the increasing young,
into the final bone, wearying all truth with ruin.
This is the iron

rusting in the vanquished country, the blood's unease,
the useless rain upon my familiar window;
the tired triumphant smile left behind by the dead
on a discarded anchor half-sunk in mud beside the graves:

out there on the earth's unwavering gravity
where it waits like a deity perhaps
for the elaborate ceremonial of a coming generation
to keep history awake, stifle the survivor's issuing cry.   [1980]

ANNE SEXTON

USA 1928–1974

Sexton, née Anne Harvey, was born in Newton, Massachusetts and as a teenager worked as a fashion model. She suffered the first of several breakdowns after the birth of her first daughter in 1951. Later breakdowns, hospitalizations, and suicide attempts culminated in her taking her own life in 1974, when she was Professor of Creative Writing at Boston University. Sexton's most characteristic poetic mode is the confessional: the portrayal of mental illness informs some of her poems; other poems address women's fragmented experiences as children, daughters, lovers, and wives. Sexton won the Pulitzer Prize for *Live or Die* (1967); *45 Mercy Street* (1976) was published posthumously. Sexton's life's work is collected in *The Complete Poems* (1981).

THE DEATH BABY

1. DREAMS

I was an ice baby.
I turned to sky blue.
My tears became two glass beads.
My mouth stiffened into a dumb howl.
They say it was a dream
but I remember that hardening.

My sister at six
dreamt nightly of my death:
'The baby turned to ice.
Someone put her in the refrigerator
and she turned as hard as a Popsicle.'

I remember the stink of the liverwurst.
How I was put on a platter and laid
between the mayonnaise and the bacon.
The rhythm of the refrigerator
had been disturbed.
The milk bottle hissed like a snake.
The tomatoes vomited up their stomachs.
The caviar turned to lava.
The pimentos kissed like cupids.
I moved like a lobster,
slower and slower.
The air was tiny.
The air would not do.

*

I was at the dogs' party.
I was their bone.
I had been laid out in their kennel
like a fresh turkey.

This was my sister's dream
but I remember that quartering;
I remember the sickbed smell
of the sawdust floor, the pink eyes,
the pink tongues and the teeth, those nails.
I had been carried out like Moses
and hidden by the paws
of ten Boston bull terriers,
ten angry bulls
jumping like enormous roaches.
At first I was lapped,
rough as sandpaper.
I became very clean.
Then my arm was missing.
I was coming apart.
They loved me until
I was gone.

2. THE DY-DEE DOLL

My Dy-dee doll
died twice.
Once when I snapped
her head off
and let it float in the toilet
and once under the sun lamp
trying to get warm
she melted.
She was a gloom,
her face embracing
her little bent arms.
She died in all her rubber wisdom.

3. SEVEN TIMES

I died seven times
in seven ways
letting death give me a sign,
letting death place his mark on my forehead,
crossed over, crossed over.

And death took root in that sleep.
In that sleep I held an ice baby
and I rocked it
and was rocked by it.
Oh Madonna, hold me.
I am a small handful.

4. MADONNA[1]

My mother died
unrocked, unrocked.
Weeks at her deathbed
seeing her thrust herself against the metal bars,
thrashing like a fish on the hook
and me low at her high stage,
letting the priestess dance alone,
wanting to place my head in her lap
or even take her in my arms somehow
and fondle her twisted gray hair.
But her rocking horse was pain
with vomit steaming from her mouth.
Her belly was big with another child,
cancer's baby, big as a football.
I could not soothe.
With every hump and crack
there was less Madonna
until that strange labor took her.
Then the room was bankrupt.
That was the end of her paying.

5. MAX[2]

Max and I
two immoderate sisters,
two immoderate writers,
two burdeners,
made a pact.
To beat death down with a stick.
To take over.
To build our death like carpenters.
When she had a broken back,
each night we built her sleep.
Talking on the hot line
until her eyes pulled down like shades.
And we agreed in those long hushed phone calls
that when the moment comes
we'll talk turkey,
we'll shoot words straight from the hip,
we'll play it as it lays.

[1] 'Madonna' ('my lady') refers here to both Mary the mother of Christ and Sexton's own mother, Mary Gray.

[2] Max is Maxine Kumin, Pulitzer Prize-winning poet and Sexton's closest friend for seventeen years.

Yes,
when death comes with its hood
we won't be polite.

6. BABY

Death,
you lie in my arms like a cherub,
as heavy as bread dough.
Your milky wings are as still as plastic.
Hair as soft as music.
Hair the color of a harp.
And eyes made of glass,
as brittle as crystal.
Each time I rock you
I think you will break.
I rock. I rock.
Glass eye, ice eye,
primordial eye,
lava eye,
pin eye,
break eye,
how you stare back!

Like the gaze of small children
you know all about me.
You have worn my underwear.
You have read my newspaper.
You have seen my father whip me.
You have seen me stroke my father's whip.

I rock. I rock.
We plunge back and forth
comforting each other.
We are stone.
We are carved, a pietà
that swings and swings.
Outside, the world is a chilly army.
Outside, the sea is brought to its knees.
Outside, Pakistan is swallowed in a mouthful.

I rock. I rock.
You are my stone child
with still eyes like marbles.
There is a death baby
for each of us.
We own him.
His smell is our smell.

Beware. Beware.
There is a tenderness.
There is a love
for this dumb traveler
waiting in his pink covers.
Someday,
heavy with cancer or disaster
I will look up at Max
and say: It is time.
Hand me the death baby
and there will be
that final rocking.   [1974]

U.A. FANTHORPE

England b. 1929

Fanthorpe was educated at Oxford and taught at Cheltenham Ladies' College before becoming a
clerk in a Bristol hospital. Her poetry often sustains two seemingly diverse effects: shrewdness
and innocence. Her erudition thrives in contact with the colloquial and a street-level awareness
of the absurd. She received Travelling Scholarships from The Society of Authors and an Arts Coun-
cil Fellowship at St Martin's College. Her *Collected Poems* (1986) has been followed by *A Watch-
ing Brief* (1987) and *Neck-Verse* (1992).

NOT MY BEST SIDE

I

Not my best side, I'm afraid.
The artist didn't give me a chance to
Pose properly, and as you can see,
Poor chap, he had this obsession with
Triangles, so he left off two of my
Feet. I didn't comment at the time
(What, after all, are two feet
To a monster?) but afterwards
I was sorry for the bad publicity.
Why, I said to myself, should my conqueror
Be so ostentatiously beardless, and ride
A horse with a deformed neck and square hoofs?
Why should my victim be so
Unattractive as to be inedible,
And why should she have me literally
On a string? I don't mind dying
Ritually, since I always rise again,
But I should have liked a little more blood
To show they were taking me seriously.

II
It's hard for a girl to be sure if
She wants to be rescued. I mean, I quite
Took to the dragon. It's nice to be
Liked, if you know what I mean. He was
So nicely physical, with his claws
And lovely green skin, and that sexy tail,
And the way he looked at me,
He made me feel he was all ready to
Eat me. And any girl enjoys that.
So when this boy turned up, wearing machinery,
On a really *dangerous* horse, to be honest,
I didn't much fancy him. I mean,
What was he like underneath the hardware?
He might have acne, blackheads or even
Bad breath for all I could tell, but the dragon—
Well, you could see all his equipment
At a glance. Still, what could I do?
The dragon got himself beaten by the boy,
And a girl's got to think of her future.

III
I have diplomas in Dragon
Management and Virgin Reclamation.
My horse is the latest model, with
Automatic transmission and built-in
Obsolescence. My spear is custom-built,
And my prototype armour
Still on the secret list. You can't
Do better than me at the moment.
I'm qualified and equipped to the
Eyebrow. So why be difficult?
Don't you want to be killed and/or rescued
In the most contemporary way? Don't
You want to carry out the roles
That sociology and myth have designed for you?
Don't you realize that, by being choosy,
You are endangering job-prospects
In the spear- and horse-building industries?
What, in any case, does it matter what
You want? You're in my way.   [1978]

KNOWING ABOUT SONNETS

Lesson 1: 'The Soldier' (Brooke)

'[The task of criticism] is not to redouble the text's self-understanding, to collude with its object in a conspiracy of silence. The task is to show the text as it cannot know itself.'

Terry Eagleton, *Criticism and Ideology*

Recognizing a sonnet is like attaching
A name to a face. Mister Sonnet, I presume?
   If I
And naming is power. It can hardly
Deny its name. You are well on the way
To mastery. The next step is telling the sonnet
What it is trying to say. This is called Interpretation.
   If I should die
What you mustn't do is collude with it. This
Is bad for the sonnet, and will only encourage it
To be eloquent. You must question it closely:
What has it left out? What made it decide
To be a sonnet? The author's testimony
(If any) is not evidence. He is the last person to know.
   If I should die, think this
Stand no nonsense with imagery. Remember, though shifty,
It is vulnerable to calculation. Apply the right tests.
Now you are able to Evaluate the sonnet.
   If I
That should do for today.
   If I should die
               And over and over
The new white paper track innocent unlined hands.
Think this. Think this. Think this. Think only this.   [1984]

THOM GUNN

England/USA b. 1929

Born in Gravesend and educated at Cambridge and Stanford, Gunn has lived in San Francisco since 1954. He has been a reviewer for *Poetry* and the *Yale Review* and a professor at Berkeley from 1958 to 1966 and since 1975; he had resigned in the late 1960s to explore communal living, drug-induced experiences, and his own homosexuality. Gunn's poetry discloses elements of contemporary culture in relation to issues of love, identity, and freedom. He has recently published his *Collected Poems* (1994).

ON THE MOVE

The blue jay scuffling in the bushes follows
Some hidden purpose, and the gust of birds
That spurts across the field, the wheeling swallows,
Has nested in the trees and undergrowth.
Seeking their instinct, or their poise, or both,
One moves with an uncertain violence
Under the dust thrown by a baffled sense
Or the dull thunder of approximate words.

On motorcycles, up the road, they come:
Small, black, as flies hanging in heat, the Boys,
Until the distance throws them forth, their hum
Bulges to thunder held by calf and thigh.
In goggles, donned impersonality,
In gleaming jackets trophied with the dust,
They strap in doubt—by hiding it, robust—
And almost hear a meaning in their noise.

Exact conclusion of their hardiness
Has no shape yet, but from known whereabouts
They ride, direction where the tyres press.
They scare a flight of birds across the field:
Much that is natural, to the will must yield.
Men manufacture both machine and soul,
And use what they imperfectly control
To dare a future from the taken routes.

It is a part solution, after all.
One is not necessarily discord
On earth; or damned because, half animal,
One lacks direct instinct, because one wakes
Afloat on movement that divides and breaks.
One joins the movement in a valueless world,
Choosing it, till, both hurler and the hurled,
One moves as well, always toward, toward.

A minute holds them, who have come to go:
The self-defined, astride the created will
They burst away; the towns they travel through
Are home for neither bird nor holiness,
For birds and saints complete their purposes.
At worst, one is in motion; and at best,
Reaching no absolute, in which to rest,
One is always nearer by not keeping still.   [1957]

LAMENT

Your dying was a difficult enterprise.
First, petty things took up your energies,
The small but clustering duties of the sick,
Irritant as the cough's dry rhetoric.
Those hours of waiting for pills, shot, X-ray
Or test (while you read novels two a day)
Already with a kind of clumsy stealth
Distanced you from the habits of your health.
    In hope still, courteous still, but tired and thin,
You tried to stay the man that you had been,
Treating each symptom as a mere mishap
Without import. But then the spinal tap.
It brought a hard headache, and when night came
I heard you wake up from the same bad dream
Every half-hour with the same short cry
Of mild outrage, before immediately
Slipping into the nightmare once again
Empty of content but the drip of pain.
No respite followed: though the nightmare ceased,
Your cough grew thick and rich, its strength increased.
Four nights, and on the fifth we drove you down
To the Emergency Room. That frown, that frown:
I'd never seen such rage in you before
As when they wheeled you through the swinging door.
For you knew, rightly, they conveyed you from
Those normal pleasures of the sun's kingdom
The hedonistic body basks within
And takes for granted—summer on the skin,
Sleep without break, the moderate taste of tea
In a dry mouth. You had gone on from me
As if your body sought out martyrdom
In the far Canada of a hospital room.
Once there, you entered fully the distress
And long pale rigours of the wilderness.

A gust of morphine hid you. Back in sight
You breathed through a segmented tube, fat, white,
Jammed down your throat so that you could not speak.
    How thin the distance made you. In your cheek
One day, appeared the true shape of your bone
No longer padded. Still your mind, alone,
Explored this emptying intermediate
State for what holds and rests were hidden in it.
    You wrote us messages on a pad, amused
At one time that you had your nurse confused
Who, seeing you reconciled after four years
With your grey father, both of you in tears,
Asked if this was at last your 'special friend'
(The one you waited for until the end).
'She sings,' you wrote, 'a Philippine folk song
To wake me in the morning . . . It is long
And very pretty.' Grabbing at detail
To furnish this bare ledge toured by the gale,
On which you lay, bed restful as a knife,
You tried, tried hard, to make of it a life
Thick with the complicating circumstance
Your thoughts might fasten on. It had been chance
Always till now that had filled up the moment
With live specifics your hilarious comment
Discovered as it went along; and fed,
Laconic, quick, wherever it was led.
You improvised upon your own delight.
I think back to the scented summer night
We talked between our sleeping bags, below
A molten field of stars five years ago:
I was so tickled by your mind's light touch
I couldn't sleep, you made me laugh too much,
Though I was tired and begged you to leave off.

Now you were tired, and yet not tired enough
—Still hungry for the great world you were losing
Steadily in no season of your choosing—
And when at last the whole death was assured,
Drugs having failed, and when you had endured
Two weeks of an abominable constraint,
You faced it equably, without complaint,
Unwhimpering, but not at peace with it.
You'd lived as if your time was infinite:
You were not ready and not reconciled,
Feeling as uncompleted as a child
Till you had shown the world what you could do

In some ambitious role to be worked through,
A role your need for it had half-defined,
But never wholly, even in your mind.
You lacked the necessary ruthlessness,
The soaring meanness that pinpoints success.
We loved that lack of self-love, and your smile,
Rueful, at your own silliness.
                                    Meanwhile,
Your lungs collapsed, and the machine, unstrained,
Did all your breathing now. Nothing remained
But death by drowning on an inland sea
Of your own fluids, which it seemed could be
Kindly forestalled by drugs. Both could and would:
Nothing was said, everything understood,
At least by us. Your own concerns were not
Long-term, precisely, when they gave the shot
—You made local arrangements to the bed
And pulled a pillow round beside your head.
    And so you slept, and died, your skin gone grey,
Achieving your completeness, in a way.

Outdoors next day, I was dizzy from a sense
Of being ejected with some violence
From vigil in a white and distant spot
Where I was numb, into this garden plot
Too warm, too close, and not enough like pain.
I was delivered into time again
—The variations that I live among
Where your long body too used to belong
And where the still bush is minutely active.
You never thought your body was attractive,
Though others did, and yet you trusted it
And must have loved its fickleness a bit
Since it was yours and gave you what it could,
Till near the end it let you down for good,
Its blood hospitable to those guests who
Took over by betraying it into
The greatest of its inconsistencies
This difficult, tedious, painful enterprise.   [1992]

PETER PORTER

Australia b. 1929

Born and educated in Brisbane, Porter emigrated to England in 1951 where he became a prominent BBC broadcaster and freelance writer for the *New Statesman, Times Literary Supplement, Observer,* and the *New Review.* The author of almost two dozen books of poetry, Porter is best known for *The Cost of Seriousness* (1978) and *English Subtitles* (1981); an edition of his *Collected Poems* appeared in 1983. His poetry is noted for its philosophical scepticism and formal sophistication; his distrust of intellectual systems often results in ironic and paradoxical expressions of grief and despair.

PHAR LAP IN THE MELBOURNE MUSEUM

A masterpiece of the taxidermist's art,
Australia's top patrician stares
Gravely ahead at crowded emptiness.
As if alive, the lustre of dead hairs,
Lozenged liquid eyes, black nostrils
Gently flared, otter-satin coat declares
That death cannot visit in this thin perfection.

The democratic hero full of guile,
Noble, handsome, gentle Houyhnhnm
(In both Paddock and St Leger difference is
Lost in the welter of money)—to see him win
Men sold farms, rode miles in floods,
Stole money, locked up wives, somehow got in:
First away, he led the field and easily won.

It was his simple excellence to be best.
Tough men owned him, their minds beset
By stakes, bookies' doubles, crooked jocks.
He soon became a byword, public asset,
A horse with a nation's soul upon his back—
Australia's Ark of the Covenant, set
Before the people, perfect, loved like God.

And like God to be betrayed by friends.
Sent to America, he died of poisoned food.
In Australia children cried to hear the news
(This Prince of Orange knew no bad or good).
It was, as people knew, a plot of life:
To live in strength, to excel and die too soon,
So they drained his body and they stuffed his skin.

Twenty years later on Sunday afternoons
You still can't see him for the rubbing crowds.
He shares with Bradman and Ned Kelly some
Of the dirty jokes you still can't say out loud.
It is Australian innocence to love
The naturally excessive and be proud
Of a thoroughbred bay gelding who ran fast.   [1961]

A.K. RAMANUJAN

India/USA 1929-1993

Born and educated in Mysore, Karnataka, Ramanujan pursued a thirty-year teaching career at the
University of Chicago. With contemporary post-Independence sixties poets like Nissim Ezekiel
and Gieve Patel, Ramanujan departed from 'raj nostalgia' and turned his attention instead towards
the local traditions and tensions within South Indian culture as well as the indigenous structures
and conventions of the Tamil classics and medieval saints' poetry. He was an award-winning trans-
lator from Tamil and medieval Kannada, anthropologist, and editor. Ramanujan's collections of
poetry in English include *The Striders* (1966), *Relations* (1971), and *Second Sight* (1986).

STILL ANOTHER VIEW OF GRACE

I burned and burned. But one day I turned
and caught that thought
by the screams of her hair and said: 'Beware.
Do not follow a gentleman's morals

with that absurd determined air.
Find a priest. Find any beast in the wind
for a husband. He will give you a houseful
of legitimate sons. It is too late for sin,

even for treason. And I have no reason to know your kind.
Bred Brahmin among singers of shivering hymns
I shudder to the bone at hungers that roam the street
beyond the constable's beat.' But there She stood

upon that dusty road on a nightlit april mind
and gave me a look. Commandments crumbled
in my father's past. Her tumbled hair suddenly known
as silk in my angry hand, I shook a little

and took her, behind the laws of my land.   [1966]

ADRIENNE RICH

USA b. 1929

In 1974 Rich received a National Book Award for her collection, *Diving into the Wreck*, which was perceived as a major contribution to the contemporary cultural history of feminism. In her collection of prose, *On Lies, Secrets, and Silences*, she writes that 'Poetry is, among other things, a criticism of language. Poetry is above all a concentration of the power of language, which is the power of our ultimate relationship to everything in the universe.' Among Rich's major volumes are *Snapshots of a Daughter-in-Law* (1963), *The Dream of a Common Language* (1978), *Time's Power* (1989), *An Atlas of the Difficult World* (1991), and *What Is Found There* (1993).

DIVING INTO THE WRECK

First having read the book of myths,
and loaded the camera,
and checked the edge of the knife-blade,
I put on
the body-armor of black rubber
and absurd flippers
the grave and awkward mask.
I am having to do this
not like Cousteau with his
assiduous team
aboard the sun-flooded schooner
but here alone.

There is a ladder.
The ladder is always there
hanging innocently
close to the side of the schooner.
We know what it is for,
we who have used it.
Otherwise
it's a piece of maritime floss
some sundry equipment.

I go down.
Rung after rung and still
the oxygen immerses me
the blue light
the clear atoms
of our human air.
I go down.
My flippers cripple me,
I crawl like an insect down the ladder

and there is no one
to tell me when the ocean
will begin.

First the air is blue and then
it is bluer and then green and then
black I am blacking out and yet
my mask is powerful
it pumps my blood with power
the sea is another story
the sea is not a question of power
I have to learn alone
to turn my body without force
in the deep element.

And now: it is easy to forget
what I came for
among so many who have always
lived here
swaying their crenellated fans
between the reefs
and besides
you breathe differently down here.

I came to explore the wreck.
The words are purposes.
The words are maps.
I came to see the damage that was done
and the treasures that prevail.
I stroke the beam of my lamp
slowly along the flank
of something more permanent
than fish or weed

the thing I came for:
the wreck and not the story of the wreck
the thing itself and not the myth
the drowned face always staring
toward the sun
the evidence of damage
worn by salt and sway into this threadbare beauty
the ribs of the disaster
curving their assertion
among the tentative haunters.

This is the place.
And I am here, the mermaid whose dark hair
streams black, the merman in his armored body.
We circle silently
about the wreck
we dive into the hold.
I am she: I am he

whose drowned face sleeps with open eyes
whose breasts still bear the stress
whose silver, copper, vermeil cargo lies
obscurely inside barrels
half-wedged and left to rot
we are the half-destroyed instruments
that once held to a course
the water-eaten log
the fouled compass

We are, I am, you are
by cowardice or courage
the one who find our way
back to this scene
carrying a knife, a camera
a book of myths
in which
our names do not appear.   [1973]

(THE FLOATING POEM, UNNUMBERED)

Whatever happens with us, your body
will haunt mine—tender, delicate
your lovemaking, like the half-curled frond
of the fiddlehead fern in forests
just washed by sun. Your traveled, generous thighs
between which my whole face has come and come—
the innocence and wisdom of the place my tongue has found there—
the live, insatiate dance of your nipples in my mouth—
your touch on me, firm, protective, searching
me out, your strong tongue and slender fingers
reaching where I had been waiting years for you
in my rose-wet cave—whatever happens, this is.   [1978]

CHINUA ACHEBE

Nigeria b. 1930

Born in Ogidi, a village in eastern Nigeria, Achebe is Africa's best-known writer of fiction. His novels include *Things Fall Apart* (1958), *Arrow of God* (1964), and *Anthills of the Savannahs* (1987). Achebe's literary and cultural project is to witness the impact of colonialism on Nigeria—exploring the roots of Igbo civilization, its deformation and suppression under European rule, and the emergence of modern Nigeria. Although Achebe is less well known as a poet, 'Mango Seedling', evoking natural life struggling amidst concrete slabs, shows what skilful use he can make of this genre. His poems are represented in *Beware, Soul Brother, and Other Poems* (1971).

MANGO SEEDLING

Through glass window pane
Up a modern office block
I saw, two floors below, on wide-jutting
concrete canopy a mango seedling newly sprouted
Purple, two-leafed, standing on its burst
Black yolk. It waved brightly to sun and wind
Between rains—daily regaling itself
On seed-yams, prodigally.
For how long?
How long the happy waving
From precipice of rainswept sarcophagus?
How long the feast on remnant flour
At pot bottom?

    Perhaps like the widow
Of infinite faith it stood in wait
For the holy man of the forest, shaggy-haired
Powered for eternal replenishment.
Or else it hoped for Old Tortoise's miraculous feast

On one ever recurring dot of cocoyam
Set in a large bowl of green vegetables—
This day beyond fable, beyond faith?
    Then I saw it
Poised in courageous impartiality
Between the primordial quarrel of Earth
And Sky striving bravely to sink roots
Into objectivity, mid-air in stone.

I thought the rain, prime mover
To this enterprise, someday would rise in power
And deliver its ward in delirious waterfall
Toward earth below. But every rainy day

Little playful floods assembled on the slab,
Danced, parted round its feet,
United again, and passed.
It went from purple to sickly green
Before it died.
　　　Today I see it still—
Dry, wire-thin in sun and dust of the dry mouths—
Headstone on tiny debris of passionate courage.   [1968]

E.K. BRATHWAITE

Barbados b. 1930

Edward Kamau Brathwaite, born in Bridgetown, Barbados, studied at Cambridge and at Sussex University. Teaching in Ghana from 1955 to 1962 influenced his evocation of African traditions, which inform much of his poetry as do British modernist poets, jazz rhythms, and Caribbean dialect. Three of Brathwaite's early volumes, *Rights of Passage* (1967), *Masks* (1968), and *Islands* (1969) are combined in his highly regarded collection, *The Arrivants* (1973), an account of the African dispersal and resettlement in the Americas. More recent work includes *Middle Passage* (1991).

CALYPSO

1
The stone had skidded arc'd and bloomed into islands:
Cuba and San Domingo
Jamaica and Puerto Rico
Grenada Guadeloupe Bonaire

curved stone hissed into reef
wave teeth fanged into clay
white splash flashed into spray
Bathsheba Montego Bay

bloom of the arcing summers . . .

2
The islands roared into green plantations
ruled by silver sugar cane
sweat and profit
cutlass profit
islands ruled by sugar cane

And of course it was a wonderful time
a profitable hospitable well-worth-your-time
when captains carried receipts for rices
letters spices wigs
opera glasses swaggering asses
debtors vices pigs

O it was a wonderful time
an elegant benevolent redolent time—
and young Mrs P.'s quick irrelevant crime
at four o'clock in the morning . . .

3
But what of black Sam
with the big splayed toes
and the shoe black shiny skin?

He carries bucketfulls of water
'cause his Ma's just had another daughter.

And what of John with the European name
who went to school and dreamt of fame
his boss one day called him a fool
and the boss hadn't even been to school . . .

4
Steel drum steel drum
hit the hot calypso dancing
hot rum hot rum
who goin' stop this bacchanalling?

For we glance the banjo
dance the limbo
grow our crops by maljo

have loose morals
gather corals
father our neighbour's quarrels

perhaps when they come
with their cameras and straw
hats: sacred pink tourists from the frozen Nawth

we should get down to those
white beaches
where if we don't wear breeches

it becomes an island dance
Some people doin' well
while others are catchin' hell

o the boss gave our Johnny the sack
though we beg him please
please to take 'im back

so the boy now nigratin' overseas . . .

[1967]

TED HUGHES

England b. 1930

Hughes explores the Keatsian concept of 'Negative Capability' by thinking himself into alternate states of consciousness in poems like 'The Thought-Fox' and 'Hawk Roosting'. *Crow* (1970) introduced a series of creation stories determined by the dark and demonic presence of the crow, 'stronger than death' and as querulous and unstable as the forces of nature. A prize-winning poet who has written poetry and plays for children, Hughes was appointed Poet Laureate in 1985. His collections include *The Hawk in the Rain* (1957), *Lupercal* (1960), *Selected Poems 1957–1981*, and *River* (1983).

DUST AS WE ARE

My post-war father was so silent
He seemed to be listening. I eavesdropped
On the hot line. His lonely sittings
Mangled me, in secret—like TV
Watched too long, my nerves lasered.
Then, an after-image of the incessant
Mowing passage of machine-gun effects,
What it filled a trench with. And his laugh
(How had that survived—so nearly intact?)
Twitched the curtain never quite deftly enough
Over the hospital wards
Crowded with his (photographed) shock-eyed pals.

I had to use up a lot of spirit
Getting over it. I was helping him.
I was his supplementary convalescent.
He took up his pre-war *joie de vivre*.
But his displays of muscular definition
Were a bleached montage—lit landscapes:
Swampquakes of the slime of puddled soldiers
Where bones and bits of equipment
Showered from every shell-burst.
                              Naked men
Slithered staring where their mothers and sisters
Would never have to meet their eyes, or see
Exactly how they sprawled and were trodden.

So he had been salvaged and washed.
His muscles very white—marble white.
He had been heavily killed. But we had revived him.
Now he taught us a silence like prayer.
There he sat, killed but alive—so long

As we were very careful. I divined,
With a comb,
Under his wavy, golden hair, as I combed it,
The fragility of skull. And I filled
With his knowledge.
                    After mother's milk
This was the soul's food. A soap-smell spectre
Of the massacre of innocents. So the soul grew.
A strange thing, with rickets—a hyena.
No singing—that kind of laughter.   [1989]

MAZISI KUNENE

South Africa b. c. 1930

Kunene was born in Durban, attended the University of London, and was a founder of the British
anti-apartheid movement. He has taught African Studies at the University of Lesotho and UCLA.
Kunene is the principal contemporary African poet to draw on African oral and written tradition,
often writing his verse first in Zulu and then translating it into English, and often employing
traditional genres such as the elegy. His poetry is always politically engaged and looks to
combat apartheid. Kunene's books include *Zulu Poems* (1970), *Emperor Shaka the Great* (1979),
and *Ancestors and the Sacred Mountain* (1982).

ELEGY

O Mzingeli son of the illustrious clans
You whose beauty spreads across the Tukela estuary
Your memory haunts like two eagles
We have come to the ceremonial ruins
We come to mourn the bleeding sun
We are the children of Ndungunya of the Dlamini clan
They whose grief strikes fear over the earth
We carry the long mirrors in the afternoon
Recasting time's play past infinite night.

O great departed ancestors
You promised us immortal life with immortal joys
But how you deceived us!

We invited the ugly salamander
To keep watch over a thousand years with a thousand sorrows
She watched to the far end of the sky
Sometimes terrorized by the feet of departed men
One day the furious storms
One day from the dark cyclone
One day in the afternoon

We gazed into a barren desert
Listening to the tremendous voices in the horizon
And loved again in the epics
And loved incestuous love!

We count a million
Strewn in the dust of ruined capitals
The bull tramples us on an anthill
We are late in our birth
Accumulating violent voices
Made from the lion's death
You whose love comes from the stars
Have mercy on us!
Give us the crown of thunder
That our grief may overhang the earth

O we are naked at the great streams
Wanderers greet us no more . . .   [1970]

ALDA LARA

Angola 1930-1962

Lara was born in Bengeula and studied medicine in Portugal, where her poetry appeared in periodicals like the Angolan journal *Mensagem* (Message) and anthologies. 'Testament' reveals a sensibility attuned to harsh truths rather than untried daydreams. After her death, the Alda Lara Prize for poetry was established by the municipal government of Sá de Bandeira. Lara's book of poems *Poemas* was published posthumously in 1966 and her stories *Tempo de Chuva* (*Time of the Rain*) in 1973.

TESTAMENT

To the youngest prostitute
In the oldest and darkest barrio
I leave my earrings
Cut in crystal, limpid and pure. . . .

And to that forgotten virgin
Girl without tenderness
Dreaming somewhere of a happy story
I leave my white dress
My wedding dress
Trimmed with lace. . . .

I offer my old rosary
To that old friend of mine
Who does not believe in God. . . .

And my books, my rosary beads
Of a different suffering
Are for humble folk
Who never learned to read.

As for my crazy poems
Those that echo sincerely
The confusion and sadness in my heart
Those that sing of hope
Where none can be found
Those I give to you, my love. . . .

So that in a moment of peace
When my soul comes from afar
To kiss your eyes

You will go into the night
Accompanied by the moon
To read them to children
That you meet along each street. . . .

[1966]

GARY SNYDER

USA b. 1930

In Snyder's poetry words are connecting and shaping interdependencies of primal, social, natural, and cosmic energies. A student of Chinese, Japanese, Indian Buddhist, and North American native languages, literatures, and philosophies, Snyder has made his commitment to Zen Buddhism the most pervasive influence on his eclectic poetics and ecological politics. Awarded a Pulitzer Prize in 1975 for *Turtle Island* (1974), Snyder continues to work on the unfinished *Mountains and Rivers Without End*.

RIPRAP[1]

Lay down these words
Before your mind like rocks
             placed solid, by hands
In choice of place, set
Before the body of the mind
             in space and time:
Solidity of bark, leaf, or wall
             riprap of things:
Cobble of milky way,
             straying planets,

[1] Snyder's own annotation: 'a cobble of stone laid on steep slick rock to make a trail for horses in the mountains.'

These poems, people,
        lost ponies with
Dragging saddles—
        and rocky sure-foot trails,
The worlds like an endless
        four-dimensional
Game of *Go*,[2]
        ants and pebbles
In the thin loam, each rock a word
        a creek-washed stone
Granite: ingrained
        with torment of fire and weight
Crystal and sediment linked hot
        all change, in thoughts,
As well as things.   [1959]

[2] *A Japanese game played with black and white stones on a board marked with 19 vertical and 19 horizontal lines to make 361 intersections.*

WHAT YOU SHOULD KNOW TO BE A POET

all you can about animals as persons.
the names of trees and flowers and weeds.
names of stars, and the movements of the planets
        and the moon.

your own six senses, with a watchful and elegant mind.

at least one kind of traditional magic:
divination, astrology, the *book of changes*, the tarot;

dreams.
the illusory demons and illusory shining gods;

kiss the ass of the devil and eat shit;
fuck his horny barbed cock,
fuck the hag,
and all the celestial angels
        and maidens perfum'd and golden—

& then love the human: wives husbands and friends.

children's games, comic books, bubble-gum,
the weirdness of television and advertising.

work, long dry hours of dull work swallowed and accepted
and livd with and finally lovd.   exhaustion,
        hunger, rest.

the wild freedom of the dance, *extasy*
silent solitary illumination, *enstasy*

real danger. gambles. and the edge of death.   [1970]

DEREK WALCOTT

St Lucia b. 1930

Winner of the Nobel Prize in 1992, Walcott has devoted his writing life to interpreting his
Caribbean experience, drawing at once on the conventions and strong voices of the British poetic
tradition and, vitally, on the intimacies of his own local influences, idioms, and dialects. In his
celebrated epic, *Omeros* (1990), Walcott reads Caribbean culture alongside and against Homer's
masterwork, *The Odyssey*. Like his poetry, Walcott's life has described a series of departures from
and returns to his native St Lucia; currently he teaches at Boston University. His *Collected Poems*
appeared in 1987.

from OMEROS, CHAPTER LXIV

III
Out of their element, the thrashing mackerel
thudded, silver, then leaden. The vermilion scales
of snappers faded like sunset. The wet, mossed coral

sea-fans that winnowed weeds in the wiry water
stiffened to bony lace, and the dripping tendrils
of an octopus wrung its hands at the slaughter

from the gutting knives. Achilles unstitched the entrails
and hurled them on the sand for the palm-ribbed mongrels
and the sawing flies. As skittish as hyenas

the dogs trotted, then paused, angling their muzzles
sideways to gnaw on trembling legs, then lift a nose
at more scavengers. A triumphant Achilles,

his hands gloved in blood, moved to the other canoes
whose hulls were thumping with fishes. In the spread seine
the silvery mackerel multiplied the noise

of coins in a basin. The copper scales, swaying,
were balanced by one iron tear; then there was peace.
They washed their short knives, they wrapped the flour-bag sails,

then they helped him haul *In God We Troust* back in place,
jamming logs under its keel. He felt his muscles
unknotting like rope. The nets were closing their eyes,

sagging on bamboo poles near the concrete depot.
In the standpipe's sandy trough aching Achilles
washed sand from his heels, then tightened the brass spigot

to its last drop. An immense lilac emptiness
settled the sea. He sniffed his name in one armpit.
He scraped dry scales off his hands. He liked the odours

of the sea in him. Night was fanning its coalpot
from one catching star. The No Pain lit its doors
in the village. Achilles put the wedge of dolphin

that he'd saved for Helen in Hector's rusty tin.
A full moon shone like a slice of raw onion.
When he left the beach the sea was still going on.   [1990]

JAY MACPHERSON
Canada b. 1931

Macpherson studied with Northrop Frye at the University of Toronto, where she has taught since
1954; Frye's theory of literature as an autonomous universe has been a major influence. Her poetry
charts a mythic landscape through which human journeys are depicted as necessary if perilous
voyages on the ark of imagination. Macpherson's most celebrated work is *The Boatman* (1957),
which won the Governor-General's Award. *Poems Twice Told: The Boatman and Welcoming Disaster*
(1981) is a representative collection.

THE FISHERMAN

The world was first a private park
Until the angel, after dark,
Scattered afar to wests and easts
The lovers and the friendly beasts.

And later still a home-made boat
Contained Creation set afloat,
No rift nor leak that might betray
The creatures to a hostile day.
But now beside the midnight lake
One single fisher sits awake
And casts and fights and hauls to land
A myriad forms upon the sand.

Old Adam on the naming-day
Blessed each and let it slip away:
The fisher of the fallen mind
Sees no occasion to be kind,

But on his catch proceeds to sup;
Then bends, and at one slurp sucks up
The lake and all that therein is
To slake that hungry gut of his,

Then whistling makes for home and bed
As the last morning breaks in red;
But God the Lord with patient grin
Lets down his hook and hoicks him in.   [1957]

ARUN BALKRISHNA KOLATKAR

India b. 1932

A commercial artist and poet, Kolatkar has published poetry in English and Marathi. His long poem *Jejuri* (1976) won the Commonwealth Poetry Prize and *Arun Kilatkarchya kavita* (1977) won the Maharashtra government poetry prize. *Jejuri* presents the odyssey of Maruti, a westernized and urban pilgrim to the sacred temple of Khandob in Jejuri. *Jejuri* is often seen as a parallel to Eliot's *The Waste Land*: diffident pilgrims pose large questions about worship and the possibility of entering into meaningful relationships with original and sacred stories and practices.

AN OLD WOMAN

An old woman grabs
hold of your sleeve
and tags along.

She wants a fifty paise coin.
She says she will take you
to the horseshoe shrine.

You've seen it already.
She hobbles along anyway
and tightens her grip on your shirt.

She won't let you go.
You know how old women are.
They stick to you like a burr.

You turn around and face her
with an air of finality.
You want to end the farce.

When you hear her say,
'What else can an old woman do
on hills as wretched as these?'

You look right at the sky.
Clear through the bullet holes
she has for her eyes.

And as you look on,
the cracks that begin around her eyes
spread beyond her skin.

And the hills crack.
And the temples crack.
And the sky falls

with a plateglass clatter
around the shatter proof crone
who stands alone.

And you are reduced
to so much small change
in her hand.   [1976]

CHRISTOPHER OKIGBO

Nigeria 1932-1967

Unlike many of his African contemporaries, Okigbo did not espouse a specifically African poetics. Rather, he insisted that poetry was poetry first, national, political, thematic, or social instrument second. Nor did he reject the European inheritance thrust upon him. And although his total output was thin (Okigbo was only 35 when he was killed fighting on the Biafran side in the Nigerian civil war), he is now regarded by many as the leading English-language poet in modern Africa. Born in Ojoto in eastern Nigeria, he was destined by family tradition to become a priest, but he decided on an academic career instead. Okigbo's poetry is challenging—dense, sometimes difficult, and often inward-turning—but his lyrical intensity has been widely praised. His books of poems include *Heavensgate* (1962) and *Limits* (1964); a *Collected Poems* was published in 1986.

ELEGY FOR SLIT-DRUM

With rattles accompaniment

CONDOLENCES . . . from our swollen lips laden with
    condolences:

The mythmaker accompanies us
The rattles are here with us

condolences from our split-tongue of the slit drum condolences

one tongue full of fire
one tongue full of stone—

condolences from the twin-lips of our drum parted in
    condolences:

the panther has delivered a hare
the hare is beginning to leap
the panther has delivered a hare
the panther is about to pounce—

condolences already in flight under the burden of this century:

parliament has gone on leave
the members are now on bail
parliament is now on sale
the voters are lying in wait—

condolences to caress the swollen eyelids of bleeding mourners.

the cabinet has gone to hell
the timbers are now on fire
the cabinet that sold itself
ministers are now in gaol—

condolences quivering before the iron throne of a new
    conqueror:

the mythmaker accompanies us (*the Egret had come and gone*)
Okigbo accompanies us the oracle enkindles us
the Hornbill is there again (*the Hornbill has had a bath*)
Okigbo accompanies us the rattles enlighten us—

condolences with the miracle of sunlight on our feathers:

The General is up . . . the General is up . . . commandments . . .
the General is up the General is up the General is up—

condolences from our twin-beaks and feathers of condolences:

the General is near the throne
an iron mask covers his face
the General has carried the day
the mortars are far away—

condolences to appease the fever of a wake among tumbled
    tombs

the elephant has fallen

the mortars have won the day
the elephant has fallen
does he deserve his fate
the elephant has fallen
can we remember the date—

Jungle tanks blast Britain's last stand—

the elephant ravages the jungle
the jungle is peopled with snakes
the snake says to the squirrel
I will swallow you
the mongoose says to the snake
I will mangle you
the elephant says to the mongoose
I will strangle you

thunder fells the trees cut a path
thunder smashes them all—condolences . . .

THUNDER that has struck the elephant
the same thunder should wear a plume—condolences

a roadmaker makes a road
the road becomes a throne
can we cane him for felling a tree—condolences . . .

THUNDER that has struck the elephant
the same thunder can make a bruise—condolences:

we should forget the names
we should bury the date
the dead should bury the dead—condolences

from our bruised lips of the drum empty of condolences:

trunk of the iron tree we cry *condolences* when we break,
shells of the open sea we cry *condolences* when we shake . . .   [1968]

LENRIE PETERS

The Gambia b. 1932

Peters was born in Bathurst—now Banjul—and left Africa for medical studies in England, practising medicine for several years before returning to Africa where he has been a surgeon in Sierra Leone and The Gambia. His semi-autobiographical novel *The Second Round* (1965) documents a doctor's return to Africa from Britain; Peters's poetry takes up this theme, exploring the pain and alienation of an individual African awareness inflected with the dispossession and fragmentation of the larger culture. His verse includes *Satellites* (1967), *Katchikali* (1971), and *Selected Poetry* (1981).

ISATOU DIED

Isatou died
When she was only five
And full of pride
Just before she knew
How small a loss
It brought to such a few.
Her mother wept
Half grateful
To be so early bereft.
And did not see the smile
As tender as the root
Of the emerging plant
Which sealed her eyes.
The neighbours wailed
As they were paid to do
And thought how big a spread
Might be her wedding too.
The father looked at her
Through marble eyes and said;
'Who spilt the perfume
Mixed with morning dew?'   [1971]

SYLVIA PLATH

USA 1932–1963

Born in Boston, the daughter of two professors, Plath received her Master's degree from Cambridge in 1955. She married English poet Ted Hughes in 1956, and they pursued their writing careers in the USA before returning to England in 1959; the two separated in 1962. Plath published a book of poetry, *The Colossus*, in 1960 and an autobiographical novel, *The Bell Jar*, in 1963. While working on the poems for her next collection, *Ariel* (1965), Plath took her own life. Her *Collected Poems* was published in 1981.

DADDY

You do not do, you do not do
Any more, black shoe
In which I have lived like a foot
For thirty years, poor and white,
Barely daring to breathe or Achoo.

Daddy, I have had to kill you.
You died before I had time——
Marble-heavy, a bag full of God,
Ghastly statue with one gray toe
Big as a Frisco seal

And a head in the freakish Atlantic
Where it pours bean green over blue
In the waters off beautiful Nauset.
I used to pray to recover you.
Ach, du.

In the German tongue, in the Polish town
Scraped flat by the roller
Of wars, wars, wars.
But the name of the town is common.
My Polack friend

Says there are a dozen or two.
So I never could tell where you
Put your foot, your root,
I never could talk to you.
The tongue stuck in my jaw.

It stuck in a barb wire snare.
Ich, ich, ich, ich,
I could hardly speak.
I thought every German was you.
And the language obscene

An engine, an engine
Chuffing me off like a Jew.
A Jew to Dachau, Auschwitz, Belsen.
I began to talk like a Jew.
I think I may well be a Jew.

The snows of the Tyrol, the clear beer of Vienna
Are not very pure or true.
With my gipsy ancestress and my weird luck
And my Taroc pack and my Taroc pack
I may be a bit of a Jew.

I have always been scared of *you*,
With your Luftwaffe, your gobbledygoo.
And your neat mustache
And your Aryan eye, bright blue.
Panzer-man, panzer-man, O You——

Not God but a swastika
So black no sky could squeak through.
Every woman adores a Fascist,
The boot in the face, the brute
Brute heart of a brute like you.

You stand at the blackboard, daddy,
In the picture I have of you,
A cleft in your chin instead of your foot
But no less a devil for that, no not
Any less the black man who

Bit my pretty red heart in two.
I was ten when they buried you.
At twenty I tried to die
And get back, back, back to you.
I thought even the bones would do.

But they pulled me out of the sack,
And they stuck me together with glue.
And then I knew what to do.
I made a model of you,
A man in black with a Meinkampf look

And a love of the rack and the screw.
And I said I do, I do.
So daddy, I'm finally through.
The black telephone's off at the root,
The voices just can't worm through.

If I've killed one man, I've killed two—
The vampire who said he was you
And drank my blood for a year,
Seven years, if you want to know.
Daddy, you can lie back now.

There's a stake in your fat black heart
And the villagers never liked you.
They are dancing and stamping on you.
They always *knew* it was you.
Daddy, daddy, you bastard, I'm through.   [1962]

SIPHO SEPAMLA

South Africa b. 1932

Sepamla, one of South Africa's 'township poets', was born in Krugersdorp on the Witwatersrand.
He began writing in the midst of the rising opposition to apartheid in the late 1960s, and in the
1970s edited the journal *The New Classic* and the theatre magazine *S'ketsh*, both of which were
sometimes censored; Sepamla himself had a novel and a volume of poetry banned. Except for
trips to Germany and England in 1980 and residence as a fellow at Iowa University in 1980–81,
Sepamla has lived in Johannesburg. His novel *A Ride on the Whirlwind* appeared in 1981; his poetry,
all in English, parodies the language of officialdom and of apartheid and hopes for the collapse of
white rule in South Africa. A representative collection is *The Soweto I Love* (1977).

'MEASURE FOR MEASURE'

go measure the distance from cape town to pretoria
and tell me the prescribed area i can work in

count the number of days in a year
and say how many of them i can be contracted around

calculate the size of house you think good for me
and ensure the shape suits tribal tastes

measure the amount of light into the window
known to guarantee my traditional ways

count me enough wages to make certain that i
grovel in the mud for more food

teach me just so much of the world that i
can fit into certain types of labour

show me only those kinds of love
which will make me aware of my place at all times

and when all that is done
let me tell you this
you'll never know how far i stand from you   [c. 1960]

ANNE STEVENSON

England b. 1933

Stevenson was born in England of American parents. Raised in New England and Ann Arbor, Michigan, she returned to Britain in 1954, 'footless' and 'countryless' until residence in Dundee and Wales settled her. Her first book of poems was *Living in America* (1965); recent collections include *The Other House* (1990) and *Four and a Half Dancing Men* (1993). Co-founder in 1979 with Michael Farley of the Poetry Bookshop in Hay-on-Wye on the Hereford/Wales border, Stevenson has also published a study of the American poet Elizabeth Bishop and a biography of Sylvia Plath entitled *Bitter Fame* (1989). Stevenson's *Selected Poems 1956–1986* appeared in 1986.

A LETTER FROM AN ENGLISH NOVELIST: PAUL MAXWELL, AUTHOR OF 'A SECOND EVE', WRITES TO RUTH ARBEITER IN VERMONT

21 October, 1936

South Kensington
London

Most Cherished Ruth,

Two years ago. Only two years, and the terrible chasm between that autumn afternoon in a Vermont pasture and that unknown spring or autumn morning when we will meet again grows wider and wider. So you have two daughters now! Kathy and Eden. Eden and Kathy. Two American girls.

The impact of your letter was such that I almost see you. You and your baby in that big shabby kitchen with the broken floorboards hidden under the patchwork rug, and the clay mugs marching along the high shelf over the hearth. There. I *can* see you clearly. You are holding the baby in the crook of your left arm while with your right you are pouring water from a jug into a large stoneware basin set solidly on the scrubbed table. The water is just the right temperature. You question it with an elbow to make sure. Gently, you are laying the poor naked scrap in the womb-like basin.

She howls immediately, but you are serious and firm. You rouse the soap to lather and you wash the head (the black mane you describe). Then you carefully wash limbs and belly, taking care not to wet the navel which is not yet healed after its brutal severing from the placenta.

The baby is perfectly clean and perfectly frantic. You remove her, red-faced and howling, to a salvational towel. Tenderly (but again, seriously, thoroughly) you dry the thicket of hair, miraculous hands and feet, the little runnels and pleats of the fleshier thighs. Vigorously you powder each inch. You snow sweet powder into the delicate rift of the buttocks. Finally, you pin on the nappy (you, of course, call it a diaper) and slip a fresh muslin nightdress— gently, so gently—over the baby's head, taking care not to damage the life-giving palpitation of the fontanelle.

When you sit down it is in one of those plain unpainted rocking-chairs, polished by generations of your grandmothers. You unbutton your blouse. Not Leonardo, not Raphael, not Bellini has on canvas depicted such dazzling, inflammatory white breasts. But you, of course, are unaware of their beauty. For you, they are not lilies, nor succulent apples of honey; nor are they two 'breasts dim and mysterious, with the glamorous kindness of twilight between them'. No. They are practical technical instruments for nourishing your child. The greedy thing pummels and sucks. The milk flows too swiftly. The child splutters, chokes, has to be balanced over your shoulder for a painful winding.

But now at last she has settled into a rhythm of felicitous satisfaction. She is happier, perhaps than she ever will be again in her life.

You? Are you opening a book? Yes. You take a book everywhere even now. (You keep a book, still, in your handbag when you wait for a bus or go to the dentist.) So you open what is lying on the table . . . is it *The Rainbow*? Is it my collection of War Poets?

The baby has stopped sucking. It is asleep. You hardly notice. Ruth, you are not reading at all. Instead you are staring out of the window where a simple frill of muslin frames (I remember precisely) a harvest of red and orange hollyhocks.

Dearest, I am dreary in London where everyone bores me with German politics. I'm so vehement in my campaign to get back to the States, my friends have ceased drinking with me. I bore them to distraction with encomia.

Nourish me with a long letter. *Eve* progresses slowly (tell me if what I have written here about your baby seems suitable for the novel). I return two poems of yours, unfortunately rejected, but redolent as always of

my own dear Ruth,
your Paul   [1974]

FLEUR ADCOCK

New Zealand/England b. 1934

Adcock was born in Papakura, educated in England and then returned to Wellington where she studied Classics at Victoria University. From 1963 until 1979, she worked as a librarian for the Foreign and Commonwealth Office in London; subsequently, she has pursued her career as a writer, translator, and editor. Adcock's *Selected Poems* was published in 1983.

WIFE TO HUSBAND

From anger into the pit of sleep
You go with a sudden skid. On me
Stillness falls gradually, a soft
Snowfall, a light cover to keep
Numb for a time the twitching nerves.

Your head on the pillow is turned away;
My face is hidden. But under snow
Shoots uncurl, the green thread curves
Instinctively upwards. Do not doubt
That sense of purpose in mindless flesh:
Between our bodies a warmth grows;
Under the blankets hands move out,
Your back touches my breast, our thighs
Turn to find their accustomed place.

Your mouth is moving over my face:
Do we dare, now, to open our eyes?   [1964]

FOR A FIVE-YEAR-OLD

A snail is climbing up the window-sill
Into your room, after a night of rain.
You call me in to see, and I explain
That it would be unkind to leave it there:
It might crawl to the floor; we must take care
That no one squashes it. You understand,
And carry it outside, with careful hand,
To eat a daffodil.

I see, then, that a kind of faith prevails:
Your gentleness is moulded still by words
From me, who have trapped mice and shot wild birds,
From me, who drowned your kittens, who betrayed
Your closest relatives, and who purveyed
The harshest kind of truth to many another.
But that is how things are: I am your mother,
And we are kind to snails.   [1964]

AMIRI BARAKA

USA b. 1934

An associate of the early 1960s Greenwich Village writers—Charles Olson, Allen Ginsberg, and Frank O'Hara—then a Black nationalist follower of Malcolm X in the late 1960s and subsequently an international socialist, Baraka was instrumental in founding the Black Arts Repertory Theatre in Harlem, the Spirit House cultural centre in Newark, and the separatist Black Community Development and Defense Organization in Newark. Baraka epitomizes the political power of sound: 'we want a black poem. And a/Black world./Let all the world be a Black Poem/And/Let All Black People Speak This Poem/Silently/or Loud' (*Black Magic*). He published *The Autobiography of LeRoi Jones/Amiri Baraka* in 1984; among his collections of poetry are *The Dead Lecturer* (1964), *Black Magic* (1969), and *Selected Poetry of Amiri Baraka/LeRoi Jones* (1979).

AN AGONY. AS NOW

I am inside someone
who hates me. I look
out from his eyes. Smell
what fouled tunes come in
to his breath. Love his
wretched women.

Slits in the metal, for sun. Where
my eyes sit turning, at the cool air
the glance of light, or hard flesh
rubbed against me, a woman, a man,
without shadow, or voice, or meaning.

This is the enclosure (flesh,
where innocence is a weapon. An
abstraction. Touch. (Not mine,
Or yours, if you are the soul I had
and abandoned when I was blind and had
my enemies carry me as a dead man
(if he is beautiful, or pitied.

It can be pain. (As now, as all his
flesh hurts me.) It can be that. Or
pain. As when she ran from me into
that forest.
            Or pain, the mind
silver spiraled whirled against the
sun, higher than even old men thought
God would be. Or pain. And the other. The
yes. (Inside his books, his fingers. They
are withered yellow flowers and were never

beautiful.) The yes. You will, lost soul, say
'beauty.' Beauty, practiced, as the tree. The
slow river. A white sun in its wet sentences.

Or, the cold men in their gale. Ecstasy. Flesh
or soul. The yes. (Their robes blown. Their bowls
empty. They chant at my heels, not at yours.) Flesh
or soul, as corrupt. Where the answer moves too quickly.
Where the God is a self, after all.)

Cold air blown through narrow blind eyes. Flesh,
white hot metal. Glows as the day with its sun.
It is a human love, I live inside. A bony skeleton
you recognize as words or simple feeling.

But it has no feeling. As the metal, is hot, it is not,
given to love.

It burns the thing
inside it. And that thing
screams.   [1964]

NUMBERS, LETTERS

If you're not home, where
are you? Where'd you go? What
were you doing when gone? When
you come back, better make it good.
What was you doing down there, freakin' off

with white women, hangin' out
with Queens, say it straight, to be
understood straight, put it flat and real
in the street where the sun comes and the
moon comes and the cold wind in winter
waters your eyes. Say what you mean, dig
it out put it down, and be strong
about it.

I can't say who I am
unless you agree I'm real

I can't be anything I'm not
Except these words pretend
to life not yet explained,
so here's some feeling for you
see how you like it, what it
reveals, and that's me.

Unless you agree I'm real
that I can feel
whatever beats hardest
at our black souls

I am real, and I can't say who
I am. Ask me if I know, I'll say
yes, I might say no. Still, ask.

I'm Everett LeRoi Jones, 30 yrs old.
A black nigger in the universe. A long breath singer,
wouldbe dancer, strong from years of fantasy
and study. All this time then, for what's happening
now. All that spilling of white ether, clocks in ghostheads
lips drying and rewet, eyes opening and shut, mouths churning.

I am a meditative man. And when I say something it's all of me
saying, and all the things that make me, have formed me, colored me
this brilliant reddish night. I will say nothing that I feel is
lie, or unproven by the same ghostclocks, by the same riders
always move so fast with the word slung over their backs or
in saddlebags, charging down Chinese roads. I carry some words,
some feeling, some life in me. My heart is large as my mind
this is a messenger calling, over here, over here, open your eyes
and your ears and your souls; today is the history we must learn
to desire. There is no guilt in love   [1969]

LEONARD COHEN

Canada b. 1934

No writer in Canada has more successfully dissolved the boundaries between national and international, popular and highbrow art, song lyrics, and poetry than Cohen. His novels and his verse evoke suffering that can turn into ecstasy through grace. His lyrics are by turn apocalyptic and witty in their examination of individual conditions and political revolution. Cohen often reserves his most mocking condemnations for incarnations of the poet/singer himself. His earlier work is represented in *Selected Poems* (1968); a more recent collection is *Stranger Music: Selected Poems and Songs* (1993).

I HAVE NOT LINGERED IN EUROPEAN MONASTERIES

I have not lingered in European monasteries
and discovered among the tall grasses tombs of knights
who fell as beautifully as their ballads tell;
I have not parted the grasses
or purposefully left them thatched.

I have not released my mind to wander and wait
in those great distances
between the snowy mountains and the fishermen,
like a moon,
or a shell beneath the moving water.

I have not held my breath
so that I might hear the breathing of God,
or tamed my heartbeat with an exercise,
or starved for visions.
Although I have watched him often
I have not become the heron,
leaving my body on the shore,
and I have not become the luminous trout,
leaving my body in the air.

I have not worshipped wounds and relics,
or combs of iron,
or bodies wrapped and burnt in scrolls.

I have not been unhappy for ten thousand years.
During the day I laugh and during the night I sleep.
My favourite cooks prepare my meals,
my body cleans and repairs itself,
and all my work goes well.   [1965]

FRENCH AND ENGLISH

I think you are fools to speak French
It is a language which invites the mind
to rebel against itself causing inflamed ideas
grotesque postures and a theoretical approach
to common body functions. It ordains the soul
in a tacky priesthood devoted to the salvation
of a failed erection. It is the language
of cancer as it annexes the spirit and
installs a tumour in every honeycomb
Between the rotten teeth of French are incubated
the pettiest notions of destiny and the shabbiest
versions of glory and the dreariest dogma of change.
ever to pollute the simplicity of human action
French is a carnival mirror in which the
brachycephalic idiot is affirmed and encouraged
to compose a manifesto on the destruction of the sideshow

I think you are fools to speak English
I know what you are thinking when you speak English
You are thinking piggy English thoughts
you sterilized swine of a language that has no genitals
You are peepee and kaka and nothing else
and therefore the lovers die in all your songs
You can't fool me you cradle of urine
where Jesus Christ was finally put to sleep
and even the bowels of Satan cannot find
a decent place to stink in your flat rhythms
of ambition and disease
English, I know you, you are frightened by saliva
your adventure is the glass bricks of sociology
you are German with a licence to kill

I hate you but it is not in English
I love you but it is not in French
I speak to the devil but it is not about your punishment
I speak to the table but it is not about your plan
I kneel between the legs of the moon
in a vehicle of perfect stuttering
and you date to interview me on the matter
of your loathsome destinies
you poor boobies of the north
who have set out for heaven with your mouths on fire
Surrender now surrender to each other
your loveliest useless aspects
and live with me in this and other voices
like the wind harps you were meant to be
Come and sleep in the mother tongue
and be awakened by a virgin
(O dead-hearted turds of particular speech)
be awakened by a virgin
into a sovereign state of common grace   [1978]

KAMALA DAS

India b. *1934*

In 'An Introduction', Das explores the paradoxes of custom, mother-tongue, social rule, and mythology that encircle identity, rings that the speaker attempts to penetrate to liberate her own voice. Raised in Kerala's matrilineal society, educated at home by her mother the Malayalam poet Balamani Amma, Das later attended a Catholic boarding school in Calcutta. She writes of the restrictions of patriarchal society, her longing for intimacy, and her experiences in an unhappy and open marriage. Colloquial rhythm and idiom free her verse from the Anglo-English conventions Indian poets working in English initially felt obligated to replicate. Das's verse collections include *Summer in Calcutta: Fifty Poems* (1965), *The Descendants* (1967), and *The Old Playhouse and Other Poems* (1973). She has received the PEN Asian Poetry Prize in Manila (1963), the Kerala state Sahitya Akademi Award for short fiction (1969), and the Chimanlal Prize for journalism (1971, 1986).

THE OLD PLAYHOUSE

You planned to tame a swallow, to hold her
In the long summer of your love so that she would forget
Not the raw seasons alone, and the homes left behind, but
Also her nature, the urge to fly, and the endless
Pathways of the sky. It was not to gather knowledge
Of yet another man that I came to you but to learn
What I was, and by learning, to learn to grow, but every
Lesson you gave was about yourself. You were pleased
With my body's response, its weather, its usual shallow
Convulsions. You dribbled spittle into my mouth, you poured
Yourself into every nook and cranny, you embalmed
My poor lust with your bitter-sweet juices. You called me wife,
I was taught to break saccharine into your tea and
To offer at the right moment the vitamins. Cowering
Beneath your monstrous ego I ate the magic loaf and
Became a dwarf. I lost my will and reason, to all your
Questions I mumbled incoherent replies. The summer
Begins to pall. I remember the ruder breezes
Of the fall and the smoke from burning leaves. Your room is
Always lit by artificial lights, your windows always
Shut. Even the air-conditioner helps so little,
All pervasive is the male scent of your breath. The cut flowers
In the vases have begun to smell of human sweat. There is
No more singing, no more dance, my mind is an old
Playhouse with all its lights put out. The strong man's technique is
Always the same, he serves his love in lethal doses,
For, love is Narcissus at the water's edge, haunted
By its own lonely face, and yet it must seek at last
An end, a pure, total freedom, it must will the mirrors
To shatter and the kind night to erase the water.   [1973]

AN INTRODUCTION

I don't know politics but I know the names
Of those in power, and can repeat them like
Days of week, or names of months, beginning with
Nehru. I am Indian, very brown, born in
Malabar, I speak three languages, write in
Two, dream in one. Don't write in English, they said,
English is not your mother-tongue. Why not leave
Me alone, critics, friends, visiting cousins,
Every one of you? Why not let me speak in
Any language I like? The language I speak
Becomes mine, its distortions, its queernesses
All mine, mine alone. It is half English, half
Indian, funny perhaps, but it is honest,
It is as human as I am human, don't
You see? It voices my joys, my longings, my
Hopes, and it is useful to me as cawing
Is to crows or roaring to the lions, it
Is human speech, the speech of the mind that is
Here and not there, a mind that sees and hears and
Is aware. Not the deaf, blind speech
Of trees in storm or of monsoon clouds or of rain or the
Incoherent mutterings of the blazing
Funeral pyre. I was child, and later they
Told me I grew, for I became tall, my limbs
Swelled and one or two places sprouted hair. When
I asked for love, not knowing what else to ask
For, he drew a youth of sixteen into the
Bedroom and closed the door. He did not beat me
But my sad woman-body felt so beaten.
The weight of my breasts and womb crushed me. I shrank
Pitifully. Then . . . I wore a shirt and my
Brother's trousers, cut my hair short and ignored
My womanliness. Dress in sarees, be girl,
Be wife, they said. Be embroiderer, be cook,
Be a quarreller with servants. Fit in. Oh,
Belong, cried the categorizers. Don't sit
On walls or peep in through our lace-draped windows.
Be Amy, or be Kamala. Or, better
Still, be Madhavikutty, It is time to
Choose a name, a role. Don't play pretending games.
Don't play at schizophrenia or be a
Nympho. Don't cry embarrassingly loud when
Jilted in love . . . I met a man, loved him. Call
Him not by any name, he is every man

Who wants a woman, just as I am every
Woman who seeks love. In him . . . the hungry haste
Of rivers, in me . . . the oceans' tireless
Waiting. Who are you, I ask each and everyone,
The answer is, it is I. Anywhere and
Everywhere, I see the one who calls himself
I; in this world, he is tightly packed like the
Sword in its sheath. It is I who drink lonely
Drinks at twelve, midnight, in hotels of strange towns,
It is I who laugh, it is I who make love
And then, feel shame, it is I who lie dying
With a rattle in my throat. I am sinner,
I am saint. I am the beloved and the
Betrayed. I have no joys which are not yours, no
Aches which are not yours. I too call myself I.   [1965]

AUDRE LORDE
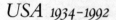

USA 1934–1992

Lorde was born in New York, and studied at Hunter College and Columbia University. After
working as a librarian she began teaching at Tougaloo College in 1968, and then became Thomas
Hunter Professor at Hunter College. Lorde was a compelling reader of her poetry, which is often
drawn directly from her personal experience as a Black lesbian woman and as a victim of cancer.
It is also often political poetry that denounces contemporary power and gender structures. Her
first book, *The First Cities* (1968), was followed by seven others, including *Black Unicorn* (1978),
Chosen Poems—Old and New (1982), and *Our Dead Behind Us* (1986).

POWER

The difference between poetry and rhetoric
is being
ready to kill
yourself
instead of your children.

I am trapped on a desert of raw gunshot wounds
and a dead child dragging his shattered black
face off the edge of my sleep
blood from his punctured cheeks and shoulders
is the only liquid for miles and my stomach
churns at the imagined taste while
my mouth splits into dry lips
without loyalty or reason
thirsting for the wetness of his blood
as it sinks into the whiteness

of the desert where I am lost
without imagery or magic
trying to make power out of hatred and destruction
trying to heal my dying son with kisses
only the sun will bleach his bones quicker.

The policeman who shot down a 10-year-old in Queens
stood over the boy with his cop shoes in childish blood
and a voice said 'Die you little motherfucker' and
there are tapes to prove that. At his trial
this policeman said in his own defense
'I didn't notice the size or nothing else
only the color,' and
there are tapes to prove that, too.

Today that 37-year-old white man with 13 years of police forcing
has been set free
by 11 white men who said they were satisfied
justice had been done
and one black woman who said
'They convinced me' meaning
they had dragged her 4'10" black woman's frame
over the hot coals of four centuries of white male approval
until she let go the first real power she ever had
and lined her own womb with cement
to make a graveyard for our children.

I have not been able to touch the destruction within me.
But unless I learn to use
the difference between poetry and rhetoric
my power too will run corrupt as poisonous mold
or lie limp and useless as an unconnected wire
and one day I will take my teenaged plug
and connect it to the nearest socket
raping an 85-year-old white woman
who is somebody's mother
and as I beat her senseless and set a torch to her bed
a greek chorus will be singing in 3/4 time
'Poor thing. She never hurt a soul. What beasts they are.'   [1978]

DAVID MALOUF

Australia b. 1934

Born in Brisbane of English and Lebanese parents and educated at the University of Queensland, Malouf lived in Europe from 1959 to 1968 and returned to Australia to teach English at the University of Sydney. A full-time poet and novelist since 1977, Malouf has homes in both Australia and Tuscany. His six volumes of verse, often dealing with memories of childhood and rediscoveries of place, include *Selected Poems* (1980).

OFF THE MAP

All night headlamps dazzle
the leaves. Truck drivers
throbbing on pills
climb out of the sleep

of farm towns prim
behind moonlit lace, bronze Anzacs
nodding, leaden-headed,
at ease between wars,

and out into a dream
of apple-orchards, paddocks
tumbling with mice,
bridges that slog the air

—black piers, bright water—silos
moonstruck, pointing nowhere,
like saints practising stillness
in the ripple of grain.

They thunder across country
like the daredevil boys
of the 'Fifties who flourished
a pistol in banks,

and rode off into headlines
and hills or into legends
that hang grey-ghostly over
campfires in the rain.

Now kids, bare-footed, wade
in the warm hatched tyre-marks
of country dust, the print
of monsters; cattle stare.

All night through the upland
spaces of our skull
in low gear shifting skyward
they climb towards dawn.

A lit butt glows, a beercan
clatters. Strung out
on the hills, new streets that shine
in the eyes of farmboys, cities

alive only at nightfall
that span a continent.
Nameless. Not to be found
by day on any map.   [1970]

N. Scott Momaday

Kiowa b. 1934

Momaday's family lived in and travelled to many places, and his father's Kiowa stories and his mother's affection for English literature further enriched his experience. By celebrating imagination and memory, oral and written, Momaday crosses many boundaries in forms and techniques of expression, but poetry and the land endure as a source of identity. Momaday received the Pulitzer Prize for *House Made of Dawn* (1968); *The Way to Rainy Mountain* (1969) and *The Gourd Dancer* (1976) are no less acclaimed. He has taught at many universities, including Stanford, Berkeley, and the University of Arizona.

Rainy Mountain Cemetery

Most is your name the name of this dark stone.
Deranged in death, the mind to be inheres
Forever in the nominal unknown,
The wake of nothing audible he hears
Who listens here and now to hear your name.

The early sun, red as a hunter's moon,
Runs in the plain. The mountain burns and shines;
And silence is the long approach of noon
Upon the shadow that your name defines—
And death this cold, black density of stone. .   [1969]

R. PARTHASARATHY
Tamil/USA b. 1934

Parthasarathy takes advantage of English as a foreign language without cultural roots such that 'ordinary and inconspicuous' words, 'rarely, if ever, reverberant' achieve the status of 'artifact'. In 'Rough Passage', a long autobiographical poem, the section entitled 'Exile' examines identity and language and the cost of a 'youth' spent 'Whoring after English gods', moves in 'Trial' toward the possibility of a return to community through marriage, and assesses in 'Homecoming' the 'tired language' of his Tamil past and the English which 'chains' his 'tongue' and tethers his hoped-for reconciliation. He has edited the anthology *Ten Twentieth-Century Indian Poets* (16th printing, 1996) and has translated into modern English verse the Tamil national epic, *The Tale of an Anklet: An Epic of South India* (1993). This translation was awarded the 1995 Indian National Academy of Letters (Sahitya Akademi) Translation Prize (English) and the 1996 Association for Asian Studies A.K. Ramanujan Book Prize for Translation. Parthasarathy is Director, Program in Asian Studies at Skidmore College, Saratoga Springs, New York.

from GHOSTS

I
LUIZ VAZ DE CAMOËNS, 1524?–1580

Gulls wrinkle the air.
The boat heaves,
opens the river's eye

in a twinkle of streets.
Houses drop
into place. The engine stops.

From the funnel
smoke balloons towards Ilhas.
I step out, and a *carreira*

takes me into the heart of Goa.
Echo of immaculate bells
from hilltops

flagged with pale crosses.
Under the sun's oppressive glare
he stands alone

in a corner,
an unrepentant schoolboy,
book in hand

spanning an empire
from the Tagus to the China seas.
I stop to take

a picture. A storm
of churches
breaks about my eyes.   [1972]

SONIA SANCHEZ

USA b. 1934

Sanchez was born in Birmingham, Alabama and educated at Hunter College, where she studied
with Louise Bogan. Commitment to the civil rights movement informs her first book, *Homecoming*
(1969). While Sanchez has increasingly been drawn to the rhythms of Black speech, as in *We a
BaddDDD People* (1970), she also experiments with traditional forms such as haiku. *A Blues Book
for Black Magical Women* (1973) coincided with Sanchez's membership in the Nation of Islam in
the early 1970s; a representative collection is *I've Been a Woman: New and Selected Poems* (1981).

under a soprano sky

1.
once i lived on pillars in a green house
boarded by lilacs that rocked voices into weeds.
i bled an owl's blood
shredding the grass until i
rocked in a choir of worms.
obscene with hands, i wooed the world
with thumbs
                    while yo-yos hummed.
was it an unborn lacquer i peeled?
the woods, tall as waves, sang in mixed
tongues that loosened the scalp
and my bones wrapped in white dust
returned to echo in my thighs.

i heard a pulse wandering somewhere
on vague embankments.
O are my hands breathing? I cannot smell the nerves.
i saw the sun
ripening green stones for fields.
O have my eyes run down? i cannot taste my birth.

2.
now as i move, mouth quivering with silks
my skin runs soft with eyes.
descending into my legs, i follow obscure birds
purchasing orthopedic wings.
the air is late this summer.

i peel the spine and flood
the earth with adolescence.
O who will pump these breasts? I cannot waltz my tongue.

under a soprano sky, a woman sings,
lovely as chandeliers.   [1987]

haiku
(for the police on osage ave)

they came eating their
own mouths orgiastic teeth
smiling crucifixions   [1987]

WOLE SOYINKA

Nigeria b. 1934

The first African writer to receive the Nobel Prize (1986), Soyinka exerts a profound influence as
poet, dramatist, essayist, film-maker, teacher, and activist. *A Shuttle in the Crypt* (1972) arose from
a two-year imprisonment imposed because of his pro-Biafran activity during the Nigerian civil war;
Ogun Abibiman (1976) finds hope in Mozambique's declaration of war against the white rule that
was once Rhodesia; *Mandela's Earth and Other Poems* (1989) considers complex and evolving
liberations. In the Introduction to his own anthology, *Poems Of Black Africa* (1975), Soyinka
considered the critiques of purists who find persistent traces of Occidental traditions to be
unnecessary contaminants. His understanding of the resistance and absorption integral to an
African idiom has been a central focus in his work.

TELEPHONE CONVERSATION

The price seemed reasonable, location
Indifferent. The landlady swore she lived
Off premises. Nothing remained
But self-confession. 'Madam,' I warned,
'I hate a wasted journey—I am African.'
Silence. Silenced transmission of
Pressurized good-breeding. Voice, when it came,
Lipstick coated, long gold-rolled
Cigarette-holder pipped. Caught I was, foully.
'HOW DARK?' . . . I had not mishead. . . . 'ARE YOU LIGHT
OR VERY DARK?' Button B. Button A. Stench
Of rancid breath of public hide-and-speak.
Red booth. Red pillar-box. Red double-tiered
Omnibus squelching tar. It *was* real! Shamed
By ill-mannered silence, surrender
Pushed dumbfoundment to beg simplification.

Considerate she was, varying the emphasis—
'ARE YOU DARK? OR VERY LIGHT?' Revelation came.
'You mean—like plain or milk chocolate?'
Her assent was clinical, crushing in its light
Impersonality. Rapidly, wave-length adjusted,
I chose. 'West African sepia'—and as afterthought,
'Down in my passport.' Silence for spectroscopic
Flight of fancy, till truthfulness clanged her accent
Hard on the mouthpiece. 'WHAT'S THAT?' conceding
'DON'T KNOW WHAT THAT IS.' 'Like brunette.'
'THAT'S DARK, ISN'T IT?' 'Not altogether.
Facially, I am brunette, but madam, you should see
The rest of me. Palm of my hand, soles of my feet
Are a peroxide blonde. Friction, caused—
Foolishly madam—by sitting down, has turned
My bottom raven black—One moment madam!'—sensing
Her receiver rearing on the thunderclap
About my ears—'Madam,' I pleaded, 'wouldn't you rather
See for yourself?'   [1960]

'NO!' HE SAID

For Nelson Mandela

Shorn of landmarks, glued to a sere promontory,
The breakers sought to crush his head,
To flush the black will of his race
Back in tidal waves, to flesh-trade centuries,
Bile-slick beyond beachcombing, beyond
Salvage operations but—no, he said.

Sea urchins stung his soul. Albino eels
Searched the cortex of his heart,
His hands thrust high to exorcise
Visions of lost years, slow parade of isolation's
Ghosts. Still they came, seducers of a moment's
Slack in thought, but—no, he said.

And they saw his hands were clenched.
Blood oozed from a thousand pores. A lonely
Fisher tensed against the oilcloth of new dawns,
Hand over hand he hauled. The harvest strained.
Cords turned writhing hawsers in his hands. 'Let go!'
The tempters cried, but—no, he said.

Count the passing ships. Whose argosies
Stretch like golden beads on far horizons? Those are
Their present ease, your vanished years. Castaway,
Minnows roost in the hold of that doomed ship
You launched in the eye of storms. Your mast is seaweed
On which pale plankton feed, but—no, he said.

Are you bigger than Nkomati? Blacker
Than hands that signed away a continent for ease?
Lone matador with broken paddle for a lance,
Are you the Horn? The Cape? Sequinned
Constellation of the Bull for tide-tossed
Castaways on pallid sands? No, he said.

The axis of the world has shifted. Even the polar star
Loses its fixity, nudged by man-made planets.
The universe has shrunk. History reechoes as
We plant new space flags of a master race.
You are the afterburn of our crudest launch.
The stars disown you, but—no, he said.

Your tongue is salt swollen, a mute keel
Upended on the seabed of forgotten time.
The present breeds new tasks, same taskmasters.
On that star planet of our galaxy, code-named Bantustan,
They sieve rare diamonds from moon dust. In choice reserves,
Venerably pastured, you . . . but—no, he said.

That ancient largesse on the mountaintop
Shrinks before our gift's munificence, an offer even
Christ, second-come, could not refuse. Be ebony mascot
On the flagship of our space fleet, still
Through every turbulence, spectator of our Brave New World.
Come, Ancient Mariner, but—no, he said—

[1988]

CHRIS WALLACE-CRABBE

Australia b. 1934

Born and educated in Melbourne, Wallace-Crabbe has taught English at the University of Melbourne since 1968, and has written and edited several books of essays on Australian literature. The ironic and academic formalism of his early poems collected in *Selected Poems* (1973) has given way to more lyrical yet philosophical poems on political and historical subjects, as in *The Emotions Are Not Skilled Workers* (1980).

LOVE POEM

Written under Capricorn, a land
Two centuries and half a globe away
From pastoral conventions at their end.
The shepherds and the nymphs have had their day
And merciless beauty will no longer make
The stuff of formal poems. So I take
This plainer speech to say what I must say:
Love breaks upon my cold hills like the sun.

I cannot fabricate a green email
To set this gift of love in, so my heart
Must be stripped bare; I cannot spin a tale
Of goddesses in fabled groves apart
Or fob my passions off on bushland swains.
O.K., have patience—take my stumbling pains
In this morass of words as love's report
And glow upon my cold hills like the sun.

All language fails me in the trembling dark,
And I would give my body to you entire
To show a love my poor words cannot mark
The bounds of. Yet, although consumed by fire,
I do not give again this shape of flesh
Which you, already, always hold in mesh;
And so I build these phrases for love's choir.
Love sings upon my cold hills like the sun.

And while our leaning poplar-tree turns bare,
Full green, then bare again above our heads,
We draw love from ourselves and from the air
And learn to weave its casual bright threads
Into a tough and subtle web that can
Outlast our youth and in our twilight span
Be refuge from decay and gathering dread
While love still warms our cold hills like the sun.

One thing is now assured; should hemispheres,
As well they may, divide us for a space,
Beyond the echoes and the parting tears
Your image in my heart will gather grace
And, like a stretching spring, my love will grow
Ever more taut the farther out I go,
Till all my days are haunted by your face.
Love breaks upon my cold hills like the sun.

Where once was no direction, now there run
These warm and glowing bars of eastern light,
And love breaks on my cold hills like the sun.   [1964]

A WINTRY MANIFESTO

It was the death of Satan first of all,
The knowledge that earth holds though kingdoms fall.
    Inured us to a stoic resignation,
    To making the most of a shrunken neighbourhood;

And what we drew on was not gold or fire,
No cross, not cloven hoof about the pyre,
    But painful, plain, contracted observations:
    The gesture of a hand, dip of a bough

Or seven stubborn words drawn close together
As a hewn charm against the shifting weather.
    Our singing was intolerably sober
    Mistrusting every trill of artifice.

Whatever danced on needle-points, we knew
That we had forged the world we stumbled through
    And, if a stripped wind howled through sighing alleys,
    Built our own refuge in a flush of pride

Knowing that all our gifts were for construction—
Timber to timber groined in every section—
    And knowing, too, purged of the sense of evil,
    These were the walls our folly would destroy.

We dreamed, woke, doubted, wept for fading stars
And then projected brave new avatars,
    Triumphs of reason. Yet a whole dimension
    Had vanished from the chambers of the mind,

And paramount among the victims fled,
Shrunken and pale, the grim king of the dead;
    Withdrawn to caverns safely beyond our sounding
    He waits as a Pretender for his call,

Which those who crave him can no longer give.
Men are the arbiters of how they live,
    And, stooped by millstones of authority,
    They welcome tyrants in with open arms.

Now in the shadows of unfriendly trees
We number leaves, discern faint similes
    And learn to praise whatever is imperfect
    As the true breeding-ground for honesty,

Finding our heroism in rejection
Of bland Utopias and of thieves' affection:
    Our greatest joy to mark an outline truly
    And know the piece of earth on which we stand.   [1963]

ARONIAWENRATE/PETER BLUE CLOUD

Mohawk b. 1935

Aroniawenrate, a member of the Turtle clan, lives in the Mohawk community of Kahnawake. A former ironworker, since 1969 he has worked as an editor for many magazines, including the *Alcatraz Newsletter, Akwesasne Notes*, and *Coyote's Journal*. He has published several books of poetry and stories, including *Elderberry Flute Song* (1989) and *Clans of many nations: Selected Poems 1969–1994* (1995).

RATTLE

When a new world is born, the old
turns itself inside out, to cleanse
and prepare for a new beginning.
            It is
told by some that the stars are
small holes piercing the great
intestine
of a sleeping creature. The earth is
a hollow gourd and earthquakes are
gas rumblings and restless dreaming
of the sleeping creature.
            What
sleeping plant sings the seed
shaken in the globe of a rattle,
the quick breath of the singer warms
and awakens the seed to life.

Let us shake
the rattle
to call back
a rattlesnake
to dream back
the dancers.

When the wind
sweeps earth
there is fullness
of sound,
we are given
a beat
to dance by
and drum
now joins us

The old man rolled fibres of
milkweed across his thigh, softly
speaking to grandchildren, slowly
saying
the thanksgiving to a sacred plant.

His left hand coiled the string as it
grew, thin and very strong, as he
explained the strength of a unity
of threads combined.
     He took his
small basket of cocoons and poured
grains of coarse sand, poured from
his hand the coarse sand like a
funnel
of wind, a cone between hand and
cocoon.

 Then, seven by seven, he bound
these nests to a stick with the
string,
and took the sap of white blood
of the plant, and with a finger,
rubbed
the encircling string.
     And waited, holding
the rattle to the sun for drying. And
when
he shook the first sound, the
children
sucked in their breaths and felt
strange
stirrings in their minds and
stomachs.
And when he sang the first song of
many,
the leaves of the cottonwood joined
in,
and desert winds shifted sand.
     And the
children closed their eyes, the better
 to hear tomorrow.

What sleeping plant sings the seed
in the gourd of night within the
hollow moon, the ladder going down,

and flutes
are like gentle
birds and

crickets on
  branches,
swaying trees.
The fan of
winged hawks
brush clouds like
streaks of
white clay upon
a field
of blue sky

water base.
The seeds in

the pod
of a plant

are children
of the sun

of earth
that we sing
we are

a rainfall voice

a plumed

and sacred bird

we are

shadows come back

to protect
the tiny seedlings
we are
a memory in

single dance
which is all
dancing forever.

down into the core of this good earth
leads to stars and wheeling suns
and
planets beyond count.
                    What sound
is that in the moist womb of the sea;
the softly swaying motion in a
multitude of sleeping seeds.
                    Maybe it
is rattlesnake, the medicine singer.
                    And
it is gourd, cocoon, seed pod, hollow
horn,
shell of snapping turtle, bark of
birch,
hollowed cedar, intestines of
creatures,
    rattle
is an endless element in sound and
vibration, singing the joys of
awakening,
shushing like the dry stalks of corn
in wind, the cradle songs of night.
    Hail-heavy wind bending upon
a roof of elm bark,
                    the howling song
of a midwinter blizzard heard by
a people sitting in circle close to
the fire. The fire is the sun, is the
burning core of Creation's seed,
sputtering
and seeking the womb of life.

    When someone asked Coyote, why
is there loneliness, and what is the
reason and meaning of loneliness:
Coyote
took an empty gourd and began
shaking
it, and he shook it for a long time.
                    Then
he took a single pebble and put it
into the gourd, and again began to
shake the gourd for many days, and
the pebble was indeed loneliness.

We are eyes
looking about

for the children
do they
run and play
our echos
our former joys
in today?
Let us shake
the rattle
for the ancients

who dwell

upon this land

whose spirits
joined to ours
guide us

and direct us
that we
may ever walk
a harmony
that our songs
be clear.
Let us shake
the rattle
for the fliers

and swimmers

for the trees
and mushrooms
for tall grasses

blessed by

a snake's passage
for insects
keeping the balance,
and winds
which bring rain
and rivers

> Again
Coyote paused to put a handful of
pebbles into the gourd.
> And the sound
now had a wholeness and a meaning
beyond questioning.

going to sea
and all
things of Creation.
Let us
> shake the rattle
always, forever.   [1987]

KOFI AWOONOR

Ghana b. 1935

Awoonor's first inspiration has been the oral tradition he was immersed in from childhood. In his essay 'Reminiscences of Earlier Days' he notes: 'the mouth is the source of sacred words. . . . When the mouth says it, then it must be true. Truth is being, presence, affirmation. This is the source of my poetry . . . the magic of the word in the true poetic sense.' Awoonor has played important roles in Ghana and beyond as an historian, novelist, anthologist (*Messages: Poems from Ghana*, 1971, ed. with Adali-Mortty), diplomat, and politician as well as poet. His first book of poems, *Rediscovery, and Other Poems* (1964), was followed by *Night of My Blood* (1971) and *Ride Me, Memory* (1973). *Until the Morning After: Collected Poems* appeared in 1987.

AFRO-AMERICAN BEATS

i.
Feet fall, jiving man
trailing beat and arguments of impossibility
conga drums and tom-toms in Apollo:
Nina Simone and Roberta Flack are getting it together,
doing their thing, shedding this earth of putrescent plutonic light
letting in the black breeze of the warm south.

ii.   *To Maya Angelou*
Maya baby, I read your book
of caged-birds, and my tummy was filled
with birds flying southwards and
to Africa, to river gods and ancestral shrines,
your Arkansas youth was the mystery
of earth and the wine bursting forth in blood and balls
jazz and blues in basements
evangelical hymns and father clocks
dim versions of our lineage here
where you and I are captives of time.
I remember you as Mother Courage,
large savanna princess with the voice of thunder
dragging your wagon of pain across the dying gut of Africa.

iii.   *An American Memory of Africa*
Black as my night, anonymous here
my death in Elizabethville was your death.

Blood shed in Sharpeville was shed before in Ulundi
Alabama, Memphis
Fred Hampton on a Chicago bed
blood and gun fire in darkness
was it prophesied that the panther
shall die in his bed without a leap?
I hug my black skin here against my better judgement
hung my shields and sheaves for a season
Leaving Africa that September 1967
in flight from the dreams we build
in the pale talons of eagles yard
donkeys braying on the bloody field across the square
the bulge of my sails unfurl for the
harbor of hate;
The pride of this color
by which they insist on defining my objection;
that I am a nigger is no matter
but that I died in Memphis and Elizabethville
outrages my self-esteem
I plot my vengeance silently
like Ellison's men in bright dens
of hiding and desperate anonymity
and with the hurricanes and eagles of tomorrow
prepare a firm and final rebuttal to your lies.
To be delivered in the season of infinite madness.

iv.   *To Langston Hughes When He Walked Among Us In Kampala, 1962*
To that gathering of wooden headed boys
you came, pops, singing your jazz solos
in whiskied nights,
black nativity for Rome, raisins in the sun
For Harlem, bagmen of black rebirth
beats of drums jive talk
and her daddy-o singing that song
'I wonder where I'm gonna die
being neither white nor black.'
Your dusky rivers gurgling down your throat
watering fields for your soul
the rivers you've known
beneath slave ships
whip lashes
and the golden note
you heard the sweep of ancient rivers
and daddy-o you died in Harlem.

v.   *To the Anonymous Brown-skinned Girl in Fresno*
I remember your face distinctly
haunting serenity glistening teeth

eyes the passion of centuries
we exchanged polite conversation
You took me in your cadillac across town
to Oakland where pot-bellied papas
guard deserted storefronts,
there was the sting of tear gas
following the riots in the Berkeley air that May
broads and winos all over the place,
between periodic love making
you outlined your revolutionary dreams
your coming trip to Algiers,
the smell of afterlove
and spent weary pubic aroma
when at once the light shone from your dark beautiful soul
and I knew who you were.

vi.
Hold on there, the rag man
half-assed jiving mother
celebrant in rented tuxedo
barker at others' carnivals
for barren pennies you will vomit blood
and asphalt here in speaking to police dogs
and night sticks on the outskirts of Harlem;
my friend, pimp for downtown rich
limping from cudgel wounds
broken torso, black tooth jack-anapes
even the hairs in your ass-hole have been eaten by termites.
Remember what Malcolm said when you asked a dumb question?

vii.   *Characteristic Leaders*
Charlie Parker, Coltrane
the true artists of a battered age
must take a trip; to draw cards
all true prophets must lose their voice;
for now the sanguine moon pale across my doorway
is singing in my bathroom
intricate fabrics woven in your trombonic voice
John the Baptist and the bird of paradise,
despised angel of infinite mercy
who made his nest in Newport
only to be despoiled. What happened
to the real voice of Miles before he abandoned
heavenly sounds for the vibrations of electricity
and jived doped rock bullshit?
When be-bop was born on hilly grounds,

these imitators were wriggling to the braying of donkeys
others were needed to keep their ears to earth
to hear the footfalls, and the beat, and crack
and vibes of mother's heart
across ten thousand years of our primal nakedness.   [1947]

JOHN PEPPER CLARK BEKEDEREMO

Nigeria b. 1935

Bekederemo's career has been shaped by the central dilemmas of many modern African writers:
how to define a culture among the turbulent forces dispersing colonialism, the competing and vio-
lent versions of independence, and the desire to be free of European languages and impositions.
After a mainly British education in Nigeria, he went to Princeton, an unhappy experience. Return-
ing to Lagos, he taught in the University's English Department until his retirement in 1980. In his
early work Bekederemo was an impassioned advocate for negritude, for 'dark Africa'; in *Casualties:
Poems, 1966–68* (1970), he responds more directly to the violent political conflicts of Nigeria's civil
war (1967–70). Later volumes of poetry include *A Decade of Tongues: Selected Poems, 1958–1968*
(1981), *State of the Union* (1985), and *Mandela and Other Poems* (1988); Bekederemo's *Collected
Plays and Poems, 1958–1988* appeared in 1991.

A CHILD ASLEEP

He who plucked light
From under shade of a tree
Sat so in dust, but in silence,
Passing like a spear clean into
The pith of things. But you,
Graft to an old bombax tree,
Raised on fulness of sap science
Cannot give, breed flies
In the oil of our evening,
Have sat dropsical feeding
On desire: it squashes, like dried
Out ribs of tobacco an old woman
Is turning into snuff you tried
To wreck with stones—
But oh look at what we spies
Have missed! In the sand
Here at our feet already fallen is
Your stool, and how clean
Past our fingers, teasing and
Tugging, you have slumped down
A natal stump, there shed
Distended in the dust—No!
As a primeval shadow
Tumbling head over heels into arms of light.   [1965]

GEORGE BOWERING

Canada b. 1935

Influenced by the Black Mountain school of American poetry and more particularly by William Carlos Williams's work, Bowering was one of the founders of the magazine *Tish* in Vancouver in 1961. Although in his early work he was drawn to the lyric, Bowering has more often worked towards a poetics that enacts lived and felt experience (rather than embellishing or aestheticizing it); his revelry in the sound and sense of language animates what might sometimes appear as merely conversational idiom and syntax. His *Kerrisdale Elegies* (1984) draws on the form of Rainer Maria Rilke's elegies to meditate on Bowering's life in his middle-class Vancouver neighbourhood. Since publishing his first book (*Sticks & Stones*, 1963), Bowering has been prolific and versatile; representative collections include *Touch: Selected Poems 1960–1970* (1971), and *West Window: The Selected Poetry of George Bowering* (1982).

GRANDFATHER

Grandfather
      Jabez Harry Bowering
strode across the Canadian prairie
hacking down trees
        and building churches
delivering personal baptist sermons in them
leading Holy holy holy lord god almighty songs in them
red haired man squared off in the pulpit
reading Saul on the road to Damascus at them

Left home
      big walled Bristol town
at age eight
      to make a living
buried his stubby fingers in root snarled earth
for a suit of clothes and seven hundred gruelly meals a year
taking an anabaptist cane across the back every day
for four years till he was whipped out of England

Twelve years old
      and across the ocean alone
to apocalyptic Canada
      Ontario of bone bending child labor
six years on the road to Damascus till his eyes were blinded
with the blast of Christ and he wandered west
to Brandon among wheat kings and heathen Saturday nights
young red haired Bristol boy shoveling coal
in the basement of Brandon college five in the morning

Then built his first wooden church and married
a sick girl who bore two live children and died
leaving several pitiful letters and the Manitoba night

He moved west with another wife and built children and churches
Saskatchewan Alberta British Columbia Holy holy holy
lord god almighty
        struck his labored bones with pain
and left him a postmaster prodding grandchildren with crutches
another dead wife and a glass bowl of photographs
and holy books unopened save the bible by the bed

Till he died the day before his eighty fifth birthday
in a Catholic hospital of sheets white as his hair   [1964]

YASMINE GOONERATNE

Sri Lanka/Australia b. 1935

Gooneratne, a critic who has written books on Jane Austen, Alexander Pope, and Ruth Prawer Jhab-
vala, as well as the study *English Literature in Ceylon 1815–1878*, was educated in Ceylon and at
Cambridge. She is the director of the Post-Colonial Literatures and Language Research Centre at
Macquarie University in North Ryde, New South Wales. Gooneratne adeptly depicts the cultural
anxieties of a displaced élite, as in 'The English Writers' Circle': 'The members of the English Writers'
Circle/nourish with anxious care the fitful flame/their tiny fires send flickering into darkness . . . and
hear the whispering/of a forgotten tongue beyond the light.' Gooneratne's first book of poems, *Word,
Bird, Motif* (1971), was followed by *The Lizard's Cry* (1972) and *6000 ft Death Dive* (1981).

MENIKA

Deft-handed, swirling rice-grains in clear water,
pouring the white stream from pot to pot
She said:
I would like to go back to the village next week
There is a court case
I am reclaiming my children, two daughters, from their father
He has another woman

Neat-handed, kneading coriander and cumin
on the smooth stone
She said:
My father made the marriage
There were good fields and much fine property
My father inspected the fields, my brother went with him
They all agreed it was a good match
Two weeks after the marriage he brought her back to the house

The pestle rising, falling, in her practised hands
the grain in the mortar crumbling to powder
She said:
We lived eighteen years in that house
My children with me in one room, she with him in the other
One day a relation of his came in, asking for a measure of rice
I did not think to refuse it
That night he came home drunk, and said I was giving away the household
    goods.

Spreading the grain in the sun to dry
She said:
When he beat me before the neighbours I sent for my father
He came and took me away
When we signed the Register at the Police Station
the Sergeant said: What a man is this!
To make such a shameful to-do over a measure of rice!
She looks after my children well, they tell me
But they are daughters, can I allow them to become women
and far away from me?

On the day of the court case, her skin smoothly powdered,
a crimson sari knotted at her neat waist, her hair
combed into shining coils on her slender neck
She said:
He is a good man
There is no fault in him.   [1972]

SALLY ROBERTS JONES

Wales b. 1935

Born in London of a Welsh father, Jones moved to Wales with her parents when she was thirteen. A librarian in Port Talbot, she (with Alison Bielski) became the first honorary secretary of the English-language section of *Yr Academi Gymreig* and later established Alun Books (1977) as well as Barn Owl Press, which specializes in children's books. 'Lletherneuadd Uchaf, 1868' responds to the story of Sarah Jacob (1857–69), known as the 'Welsh Fasting Girl' whose parents proclaimed that she had taken neither food nor drink for two years and yet survived. The notoriety which accompanied this claim led to closer surveillance, the death of the child, the trial and conviction of the parents for the crime of manslaughter and continuing speculation as to the nature of the child's eating disorder and the seemingly predatory nature of her parent's complicity—visitors were encouraged to give gifts of money to the child who lay dressed as a bride in her bed. Jones's verse collections include *Sons and Brothers* (1977), *The Forgotten Country* (1977), and *Relative Values* (1985).

LLETHERNEUADD UCHAF, 1868

(The parents of Sarah Jacob, the 'Welsh Fasting Girl', were sentenced to imprisonment for manslaughter after her death from starvation.)

This man, young Evan; Hannah his wife; the two
Rushed into marriage before they could burn to worse,
Tied now for lifetimes into the sapping, terse
Conversation of strangers. Prisoners working through
A sentence of labour, fifty years hard or more.
The prison quite picturesque; the white-washed farm
Thick-walled as a fortress; stream running by; the calm
Sweep of the sheltering hill. Behind their door
Bare feet on the ground, damp plaster, a gloomy cell
Pierced by unopened windows. On the hearth
Glimmers of brass; china on shelves, hard earth
Packed underfoot, defence against greater harm. Their role
Assigned from the first, their pain not the debtor's part
But always the bitter hunger of the heart.   [1977]

TITUS CHUKWENEKA NWOSU

Nigeria b. 1935

Nwosu is a poet and teacher with a rich background in editing and publishing. He was the first executive director of Pilgrim Books (African Universities Press) and now directs Cross Continental Press. His published poetry includes *Sirens of the Spirit*, two volumes of *Poems for the African Young*, and *Six Dazzling Days*, a collection of poems that respond to Pope John Paul II's visit to Nigeria. 'Combat' reveals Nwosu's power to arrest the reader with a series of explosive images that dramatize the battleground fear that bites 'into the small/of human feeling'.

COMBAT

I
The night had hung storm-bound
from a sullen wreck of a sky
like a woman in travail
Storm that wrecks hopes
and wrests the heart from the sword
giving the wind sturdy

arms of violence

and earthworms got the message
when the flood came with the rainstorm
and men cried hot tears

Because they could not speak
of the things they had seen
and heard when stars fell
and the sorrowing throng swayed
under the weight of loads
that bit into the small
of human feeling . . .

II
Like spearsmen filing out
with masses of dark clouds in the sky
in the furnace-heat of warrior drums
they sang and chanted songs
which echoed their ferocious moods
as if the earth in a death-dance
would eat their thundering feet
and make their skin glow and grow
with dog-barks and snake-bites
The night has heart

which men must eat
so they can scorn
the terrors of the night-storm
and make the eyes spurt
with flames which could
devour forests of enemies . . .

III
So out they marched
at beat of the tattoo
to a crossroads where they had
their first baptism of fear
under trees whose fine feathered
birds had flown in fright
and whose leaves lay dry
naked and lifeless
on the ghost-ground
good company with hearts of steel

They kept moving on razor-edge
orders broadchested crouchers
shadowed by fear of coughing
or sneezing or standing or falling
and not rising . . .

IV
Later the sun came
Like a cat-burglar and gave
everyone a porridge face
for it was now time
to let the knees sink
into the waiting ground
weary of the sound and fury
that had made night
bleed the day to death.

Suddenly everyone stared at the sun
and at the swift mercy of its coming
telling their wounds like beads of penance
with each sad twinge and tweak of pain
not daring to look back at fallen blood

For at sundown as everyone knows
the heat waves will once more rise
and leave the neighbourhood gutted with blood.   [1990]

STEWART CONN

Scotland b. 1936

Senior Producer of Drama at the BBC studios in Edinburgh and an accomplished playwright, Conn
renders his characters' experience of place in landscapes which include the farmlands of Ayrshire
and the decaying urban cores and sprouting urban insults of Edinburgh and Glasgow. His poems
are often shadowed by a sense of loss, vulnerability, and a yearning for stasis. Conn's collections
include *Stoats in the Sunlight* (1968), *An Ear to the Ground* (1972), *Under the Ice* (1978), and *In the
Kibble Place—Poems, New and Selected* (1986).

'KITCHEN-MAID'

Reaching the Rijksmuseum
mid-morning, in rain,
we skirt the main hall
with its tanned
tourists and guides

and, ignoring the rooms
we saw yesterday,
find ourselves heading
past Avercamp's skaters,
Breughel's masses of flowers,

and even the Night-Watch
in its noisy arena
till, up carpeted stairs,
we are in a chamber
made cool by Vermeer.

For what might be hours
we stand facing
a girl in a blue apron
pouring milk
from a brown jug.

Time comes to a stop.
Her gesture will stay
perpetually in place.
The jug will never empty,
the bowl never fill.

It is like seeing
a princess
asleep, under ice.
Your hand, brushing mine,
sustains the spell:

as I turn to kiss you,
we are ourselves
suspended in space;
your appraising glance
a passionate embrace.

[1978]

K.D. KATRAK

India b. 1936

Influenced by Nissim Ezekiel and his own interest in Tantric yoga, Katrak's metaphysical impulses encourage the interdependence of playfulness and prayer. He finds in 'earthly love' 'a door to the Most High' ('On the Birth of My Daughter') and penetrates the occult armed with the magic of the colloquial and the mundane. His collections include *A Journal of the Way* (1969), *Diversions by the Wayside* (1969), *Underworld* (1979), and *Purgatory: Songs from the Holy Planet* (1984).

MALABAR HILL

1
I used to come here often. This hill
Hard with rock granite deceptively
Covered with softer earths: Limestone and Chalk,
Clay, Basalt, Slate, loose gravel and new mud
After rain; this hill
Disguised with flowering shrubs, trees, grass,
Planted by civic minded fathers; faces the sea.
Its fist houses the oldest cemetery; the barbaric
Parsee Towers of Silence.
Children use its park. Families come
Picnic on Sunday.
Lovers walk and lie upon
Its old dead surface in the night.

I used to come here often, especially
In colder weather: to gather my resources,
Pray, watch lovers, think, or merely to withdraw.
Bombay has no real winter, only a few
Days of warning cold
That point to the bone.
This hill is a good place then:
Facing the sea
With children, lovers, dogs, and the quiet dead
To pose the old equation: but like all
High places of the soul
Dangerous.

I used to come here often, but last year
Something happened. I fell in love
Successfully, Now I am happy.

2

High on this hill the Parsee dead keep watch
Snore, giggle or whatever
Dead men do. Even now the names sound well;
Vaccha and Dadyseth, Wadia and Taleyarkhan: traders
Philanthropists, patrons of art; as placid now
As when they were alive. Lust, lechery
Healthy coupling, laughter, children's sports
And other deaths: whatever happens here
Does not concern them.

I think of this
Watching two people under the trees. Their laughter
Frantic and indiscreet evokes no answering
Indignant growl. The dead
Seem resigned to essentials. Blood
Holds liver and loin in thrall but cannot touch the bone.
The lovers also sense this: but the dead
Know. They have no choice.

I

Intoxicated by this hill, made separate
By heights, stand here alone.
Southward the night sky burns
Towards Canopus. Lovers and dead
Turn me to my first theme
Bone.

3

The bone prevails. Always I have found this.
The flesh exists upon it, breeds
Proliferates, turns to itself for love:
Creates its bright arterial jungle and undergrowth of nerve
Pap, genital and thigh;
Suffers its own agony and dies.
Somewhere beneath
Interior and unlit, the bone remains
Inexorably white.

Opposed to it is something
Animal and profound. The body's dark
Instinctive fondling of itself. The snare of blood.

Something that ties
Metaphor and flesh, dreams of Paradise
And breasts of real women. Something that shouts
Screams or sings alternately
In the wide throat at night.

Yet the bone prevails. Always. Partaking nothing.
Immovable to all that blood commands
It does not bend,
But witnesses the body's barefaced lusts,
Watches the mind's hidden and prolific lusts
And stays in the end
Itself.

4

To know the bone and know it well:
Its inner hard compulsions and complexities;
To eat, make love,
To defecate and sleep, holding it near
May be perhaps a vocation:
A way of life requiring
Fortitude and love to make it true.
I think I have it now—
Love—because of you.

I used to come here often. December was my month,
Now coming here with the first rain in May
I find that I have grown remote from pain
And have something to say.

5

I do not know much about love.
My father shaped my head and handed down
His large distinctive nose. My mother taught me facts
But left me little else. Of their first act
That made me
Swaggering and shy, nervous, afraid of love,
Nothing was said. Whether it was
Quiet or passionate, trivial or profound
My eyes know nothing. Nothing is left
Of their first sound.

I used to come here looking for love, alone.
And now that it is found
I see the old division of its ground
Between the antagonists of flesh and bone.

I think I know now why lovers laugh
Obsessively against the cold;
Compelled to see even in love the old
Powers that divide the world
Half and half.   [1960]

THE KITCHEN DOOR

And Ramakrishna said 'It is possible. Yes it
is possible by the use of the Tantric method
to attain to Illumination. Even sex used
with dedication leads to the goal. But
why should you choose to enter by the
kitchen door, when the front door
is available?'

Why that 'even'
I have often pondered, good, simple saint,
Mother ridden Mahatma with mouth agape
In Holy awe at Kali's gobs
Offered to suck. Is any man's beloved
Less sacred than your black image;
Flesh less to be desired than anthracite;
Any flea ridden tool less worthy
Of veneration than the caste mark on your forehead?

That kitchen door you speak of has taken me
Half a lifetime to find and behind
Is such a sap and savour that official entrants
And other gentlemen forfeit alive
In the white dusk of their souls: secrets hidden,
Low fires burning on black hearths, smells,
Goings-on, the cooking of flesh;
Slaughtered black rams, blood that flows under secret cities,
Tastes of the only fruit, the air heightened
With herbs from the back garden, cow dung,
Gentian and spices from Caucasian markets.

I have been through the front door of the church:
Altars and lilies, candles
Chastened saints withering in time's bower.
Gilt and incense deaden my erection.

I have been in the white cell:
Tiled floors and cooing doves
Breviary and icon unquickened by the sun.
The hermit's stench deadens my erection.

I have been through the official entrance to the monastery:
Low horns and starving Buddhas
Ramrod monks meditating in the half day
The abbot's joyful constipation ruined my erection.

No, no my friend, it takes too long this way, besides
The other is more enlivened, come with me
And I will show you as I found it: under
Norton's Hotel at Ranikhet. Come God's fool
Flap-eared, ass-bottomed, come through the rose garden
And the kitchen door. See here the Alchemist
And his small fair wife. Be their drudge,
Serve them, and sleep on straw.
And at the mid-hour of night that other door will open:
After seven years, your Rachel
Come to claim your unearthly sweets
Of flesh:

Enter my friend, enter.   [1972]

MARGE PIERCY

USA b. 1936

Born and raised in a family of labour activists in Detroit, Piercy graduated from the University of Michigan in 1957 and received her Master's degree from Northwestern University in 1958. Her involvement in civil rights, feminist, and ecological movements began in the 1960s, commitments powerfully (often angrily) articulated in her poetry, although in more personal, meditative terms in her recent volumes such as *My Mother's Body* (1985) and *Available Light* (1988). Piercy lives on Cape Cod, writing, gardening, and celebrating.

THE WOMAN IN THE ORDINARY

The woman in the ordinary pudgy downcast girl
is crouching with eyes and muscles clenched.
Round and pebble smooth she effaces herself
under ripples of conversation and debate.
The woman in the block of ivory soap
has massive thighs that neigh,
great breasts that blare and strong arms that trumpet.
The woman of the golden fleece
laughs uproariously from the belly
inside the girl who imitates
a Christmas card virgin with glued hands,
who fishes for herself in other's eyes,
who stoops and creeps to make herself smaller.

In her bottled up is a woman peppery as curry,
a yam of a woman of butter and brass,
compounded of acid and sweet like a pineapple,
like a handgrenade set to explode,
like goldenrod ready to bloom.   [1982]

UNLEARNING TO NOT SPEAK

Blizzards of paper
in slow motion
sift through her.
In nightmares she suddenly recalls
a class she signed up for
but forgot to attend.
Now it is too late.
Now it is time for finals:
losers will be shot.
Phrases of men who lectured her
drift and rustle in piles:
Why don't you speak up?
Why are you shouting?
You have the wrong answer,
wrong line, wrong face.
They tell her she is womb-man,
babymachine, mirror image, toy,
earth mother and penis-poor,
a dish of synthetic strawberry icecream
rapidly melting.
She grunts to a halt.
She must learn again to speak
starting with I
starting with We
starting as the infant does
with her own true hunger
and pleasure
and rage.   [1982]

PRAKASH BANDEKAR

India b. 1937

Bandekar was born in Goa but moved widely with his parents. A graphic artist, he worked in a Bombay advertising agency and then moved to Malaysia. He began writing poetry in the sixties, publishing in the Marathi magazine *Aso* ('Amen'); the translations of his poems into English are his own. Bandekar's style, diction, and imagery, as well as his subject matter and vision, represent a Modernist break from his inherited traditions.

AFTERNOON MASSACRE

There is a grasshopper in the building
Descending on the terrace down to the pipe line
Hopping from one window to another
Children gather scream rush over the pavement
Overpassing curious Gorkha who cooked meals
Under staircases

GRASSHOPPER

I thrive one within
Sheltered in my veinual branches
Creeping thru windpipe with queer proximity
Doctors executioners butchers food poisoning
Butlers it's incurable.
Grasshopper grasshopper INNUMERABLE grasshoppers
That's obscure if you count consciously
Stars are innumerable fishes are innumerable
Bitches are innumerable wishes are innumerable
Mosquitoes are innumerable
Kurla is full of mosquitoes they live in slums
Slums are horrible they stink they are a problem
Like exposed St Xavier four hundred & twelve
They are gray
Ashes are gray
One day the world will become ashes
Slums—you're a distorted image of an ash-tray
I love you slums.
An ecstatic impulse I smoke a cigarette
Think of Pope & increasing population &
Anti-sexual activities of Miss F
& food problem
Outside people roar grasshopper
Shrills whistles tankers motorcades
I see one million trains parked in the porch

Trains motorcades tankers firebrigade aeroplanes
Cars bullock-carts air-compressors allover
Like quills from a bursted pillow
'Attention' yells one toy soldier
Militaries are made of bricks cried another
They fade never die
Cars are made by Henry Ford
Similar to Henry Fonda the buffalo hunter
Beefsteak is cheap in movies
Hindus are prohibited
I am bored of Hinduism they say
World is rested on the great boar
Universe assembles many worlds & many boars
It's dash boring

They shoot matchsticks astringent but accurate
I move bring developer loosen the tab
Shut windows & doors switch on the red lamp
Develop a gigantic grasshopper
In its true shape & changeable colour
Then let dry the film
        GANG
            BANG
              BANG
There goes the civil war
Thirty planes dragon trains two onions one chair
Fifty broken boils 1 kg carrots & a toy soldier
Fight till death having no faith I am safe
1964 all is well
Children stop their noise & play marbles   [c. 1967]

GILLIAN CLARKE
Wales b. 1937

Clarke is a lecturer in poetry in the Gwent College Faculty of Art and Design and former editor of *The Anglo-Welsh Review*. Her collections include *Selected Poems* (1985), *Letting in the Rumour*, which received a Poetry Book Society recommendation and was shortlisted for the Whitbread Literary Award (1989), and *The King of Britain's Daughter* (1993). In many respects, Clarke's work can be likened to Atwood's because both offer incisive commentary on society's vulnerability to the political and emotional fallout that accompanies seemingly commonplace events.

ON AIR

Tools of my father's art: old radios
of fretted wood and bakelite.
In a sanctum of shot-silk curtained window
crystal or valve lurked in its holy light.

I turned the knob. The needle wavered on
through crackling distances, Paris, Luxembourg, Hilversum,
past the call-sign of some distant station,
a lonely lightship where infinity scrambles to a hum

the Chinese whispers of a jabbering world.
And now, by transistor and satellite we hear
Beethoven in Berlin sooner than if we were there
on air-waves the speed of light. And when the wall crumbled

we heard the first stone fall before they could.
We watch storms darken the map from the crow's nest
of the weather satellite, hear the swallow's foot
on the wind's telegraph before she comes to rest,

the sun dried to a pellet in her throat.
Still lodged at the wingfeather's bloodroot
a grain of desert sand,
and on my car a veil of strange red dust.   [1993]

K.N. DARUWALLA

India b. 1937

Novelist, essayist, and editor, Daruwalla has published six poetry collections. *The Keeper of the Dead* (1982) won the national Sahitya Akademi Award in 1984 and *Landscapes* (1987) won the Commonwealth Poetry Prize for Asia in 1988. Daruwalla is interested in the outcast, the loner, and in an often brute physical reality where moral, emotional, and ethical discernment is sometimes still possible. His 'poetry is rooted in landscape' which is 'not merely there to set the scene but to lead to an illumination': poetry is 'firstly personal', an 'aid in coming to terms with one's own interior world'.

THE EPILEPTIC

Suddenly the two children
flew from her side
           like severed wings.

Thank God, the burden in her belly
stayed where it was.

The rickshaw-puller was a study in guilt.
It was too much for him:
the convulsionary and her frightened kids
floundering about in a swarm of limbs.

A focus in the brain
           or some such flap
the look had gone from the mother's eyes
the way her children
           had flown from her lap.

The husband dug through the mound
that was her face; forced the mouth wide,
plucked out the receding tongue
           warped into a clotted wound
           and put a gag between her teeth.

The traffic ground
to an inquisitive halt. A crowd senses
a mishap before it sees one.
They fanned her, rubbed her feet, and looked around
for other ways to summon back her senses.
A pedestrian whispered
'Her seizures are cyclic
they visit her in her menses'.

She was not hysteric, she didn't rave
her face was flushed, abstract, and marionette-
head jerked from side to side to side, a slave
to cross-pulls. A thin edge of froth
simmered round her lips
like foam dregs left by a receding wave.

The hospital doctors frowned with thought
light words like *petit mal* were tied
to the heavies, 'psychomotor epilepsy'.
A physician pointed out with pride
the 'spike-and-wave' electrical activity,
prescribed belladonna and paraldehyde.

Just when he said, 'she isn't shaping
too well', she recovered, bleached
        by the sun of her agony.
As a limp awareness slouched along her face
I found it was the husband who was shaking.   [c. 1972]

CLAIRE HARRIS

Trinidad and Tobago/Canada b. 1937

Harris emigrated to Canada in 1966, having first lived in Nigeria, where she wrote her first published poem. She now teaches in Calgary. In verse that alternates effectively between narrative reports and stilled images (as in the opening section of *Fables From the Women's Quarters*, 1984), Harris explores her mutable condition as a wife, a lover, a woman, all the while meditating on poetry's creative properties. Her other books of poetry include *Translation into Fiction* (1984), *Travelling to Find a Remedy* (1986), and *Drawing Down A Daughter* (1992).

IN THE DARK, FATHER

Father, when you were finished I came to stand under trees you planted to taste the bitter sweet lime air you enjoyed   Now (old women have tied your feet toe to toe)   I walk for you in the dark   I remember your earlier body stripped to the waist gleaming with sweat and sun as you shared the harvest-ing   labour a release from your head   workmen patient with your smiles and sudden jokes made room for you

Has your long travail freed you now?   Do you there smile so carefully the new boy?   To what new chains do you surrender the gifts of   vision and wonder that here led to trees rippling down a hillside (they have placed pen-nies on your eyes)   but I remember the land scorched naked   and you   at the window of the room that now contains you with a grand sweep promising 'bags of limes   truck loads'   Once you flirted with painting but terrified of the anarchy of imagination you came to earth   planted these groves

Immersed I listen for you   my eyes closed to hear the green growing   (old
women have stuffed your ears with cotton)   but I remember you counting
the first bags of yellowing limes   then standing sweat soaked eyes further
than the horizon watching you said   the trucks disappear in the dust

[1984]

G.S. Sharat Chandra

India b. 1938

In a finely controlled rage and with taut irony, Chandra's poem documents the suffering attending
the political, military, and domestic upheavals that formed the nation of Bangladesh. One of the
poem's effective registers is deadpan description that evokes more than it says: 'A family of five is
practicing/Concave and convex sleeping postures,/In that one children rotate after a fat fly.'

BANGLA (WATER PIPE) DESH

The most ambitious water project of West Bengal
Is now complete.
Each pipe is shared only by two families.
Each family has a separate entrance
And a good view of the burning-ghats.
In this one facing west
A family of five is practicing
Concave and convex sleeping postures,
In that one children rotate after a fat fly.
I'm sorry the refugee in this one
Is going through Karmic convulsions . . .

    tearing through
        the mud like stampeding cattle
   carrying all they possess
       on the platform of their heads
Bengalis unnecessarily gifted away in the name of democracy
       have come back
   to their misunderstood country

   faces whose eyes recede
     so far back into terror
   inspect my greeting hands for guns . . .

How many? Oh so many
Just imagining will crack your nerve,
But these are the lucky who fled
The Pakistani panzers & artillery . . .
This woman has gone crazy,

They threatened to nail her infant to the wall,
When done with her
They nailed the infant anyway . . .

    if all the water-pipes are joined
      a Bangla-tunnel is formed
   the tunnel-nation can surface for necessities
     rationed puffs of air
              drip-drops from an exhausted tap . . .

perhaps that will please the big powers
        who abhor foreign wars . . .

Here come the ambassadors—
The ambassadors of the U.S.A. controls
The umbilical cord of the poor,
Bow to him with highest priority.
The Chinese ambassador is an expert of whispers,
So expert that one ear has to run across
The chest of many nations to hear
What he whispered in the other.
The goat-eyes is from the U.S.S.R.,
He'll herd cadavers together
And march them to a Siberian pasture.
The United Nations is manned by this faceless one
Who keeps shifting his legs.

The rest of the world is a believing mouth
Living obedient dying obedient.
Show the ambassadors in which tunnel you're best hunted
And they'll show you where the food packages are hidden . . .   [1977]

DILIP CHITRE

India b. 1938

Poet in both English (*Travelling in a Cage*, 1980) and Marathi (*Kavitenantaracya*, 1978), translator and editor (*An Anthology of Marathi Poetry, 1945–65*, 1967), Chitre writes poems that emphasize the unstable concord that diverse impulses sometimes attain: he writes of the struggle towards individuation and of conflicted desire. Punishingly self-aware of the seemingly irreconcilable differences he embodies, he has an intense visual imagination that seeks connectedness within the possible: 'My mouth stays open like a wasped bowl/Awaiting your acid gift, a single drop will do./ I am all tongue'.

POEM IN SELF-EXILE

The season's first dead butterfly
Has freshly frayed wings. Meanings are transferred
Like the wet on the grass
To shoes. America is incredibly erotic.
Too many legs makes all these streets sexy.
Back home in Bombay, we have one single millipede
Walking toward the city every morning.
It is so hot there, and still, out of modesty,
Those who afford wear all the clothes they can.
And also, unlike here, those who have the money
Eat without counting the calories.
I am homesick, which is stupid of course.
I was never a famous chauvinist back home,
Nor is America not beautiful. But I am terrified
Of such glowing youth, such exquisite innocence,
Such exotic visions of the rest of the world,
Which exists somewhere,
That I feel already obsolete,
Not being American.
Perhaps I should have been, after all, a guru,
Or a yogi, a gigolo, a snake-charmer, or a cook
Of clandestine curries instead of being a poet.
America, here I come, too
Late.   [1980]

MUMBAI: A SONG

scattered the mind
                 like a poem
this city the garbled relic
of someone's empire
                      the remaining
voice now peopled
                 by estranged millions

where once the horse of Mountstuart Elphinstone
galloped surveying the island
                              with the sad
eyes of the eagle
                      later Kipling was born
where now they sell
                          eggplants and mangoes in season
and the railway lines
                          going from here
all over the peninsula
                            the torn and blistered
chapati of a subcontinent
                              filling our plate
how can I count
                      the teeth in your mouth
hungry goddess of the island
                                  or measure
your tongue red as Kali's own
                                  unsuckled
for forty years in the shadow
                              of your gross breasts
East of Suez
                  the English had such marvellous
concubines and such clubs
                              the jokes they cracked
in the army mess
                      produced laughter
whose lingering ring
                          even now informs
the generals guarding the Himalayas
and Colaba
              land's end
Afghan Church
                    the blessed martyrs
who shed their blood for England
                              in these savage parts
times have changed
                          the empire reversed
wogs have invaded England
                                  the Asian menace
has become universal
                          only in Bombay
some English dignity remains
                                  Victoria Terminus
that gothic foundation of our modernity
still stands majestically

                    in the midst of native squalor
filled by the voices of coolies and poets
                    in front of The Times of India
the old hag of Bori Bunder
                         frowning disdainfully
slick castrates singing in an editorial chorus
                         who praised Indira Gandhi
a latter-day Empress
                    who promised to wipe out
Bombay's slums and declared that
                    beggars were foreigners
threatening the peace
                    now that she is gone
and the cops advised to stick to the book
                    we are out in the streets again
that once had English names
                    and now the followers
of Mahatma Gandhi
                    no relation of the former
speak of prohibition
                    smugglers have become religious
seven million tongues wag again
                    our noise soars to heaven
higher even than our Manhattan-like skyline
that fascinates the correspondent of the N.Y. Times
                    we have a sacred connection
being citizens of the innermost city
                    displaced bastards clustered
on a shrinking island that can only grow
                    heavenward
like my own crowded poems   [1983]

JONATHAN KARIARA

Kenya b. 1938

Kariara was born in Kikuyuland and educated at Makerere University; there he began to publish poems and short stories, and he has become a steady contributor to the journal *Zuka*. 'A Leopard Lives in a Muu Tree' skilfully establishes a series of connections among the leopard's emanations: at once a presence, an animal, and a symbol; the speaker's state of mind (and body); and the poem's whole setting, human, animal, and natural.

A LEOPARD LIVES IN A MUU TREE

A leopard lives in a Muu tree
Watching my home
My lambs are born speckled
My wives tie their skirts tight
And turn away—
Fearing mottled offspring.
They bathe when the moon is high
Soft and fecund
Splash cold mountain stream water on their nipples
Drop their skin skirts and call obscenities.
I'm besieged
I shall have to cut down the Muu tree
I'm besieged
I walk about stiff
Stroking my loins.
A leopard lives outside my homestead
Watching my women
I have called him elder, the one-from-the-same-womb
He peers at me with slit eyes
His head held high
My sword has rusted in the scabbard.
My wives purse their lips
When owls call for mating
I'm besieged
They fetch cold mountain water
They crush the sugar cane
But refuse to touch my beer horn.
My fences are broken
My medicine bags torn
The hair on my loins is singed
The upright post at the gate has fallen
My women are frisky
The leopard arches over my homestead
Eats my lambs
Resuscitating himself.   [1971]

LES A. MURRAY

Australia b. 1938

Poet and essayist Les Murray was born in Nabiac, New South Wales, and raised on a dairy farm in Bunyah. Educated at Sydney University, he has worked as a translator, journalist, and editor for a publishing firm. In the first collection of his verse, *The Ilex Tree* (1967) (co-written with Geoffrey Lehmann), Murray appeals to populist interests in the lives of ordinary rural people and the sanctity of the land as resources for harmony and community in a materialist world. A profoundly religious person, Murray develops these themes throughout his subsequent poetry, the most comprehensive edition of his work being *The Vernacular Republic: Poems 1961–1981* (1982).

AN ABSOLUTELY ORDINARY RAINBOW

The word goes round Repins,
the murmur goes round Lorenzinis,
at Tattersalls, men look up from sheets of numbers,
the Stock Exchange scribblers forget the chalk in their hands
and men with bread in their pockets leave the Greek Club:
There's a fellow crying in Martin Place. They can't stop him.

The traffic in George Street is banked up for half a mile
and drained of motion. The crowds are edgy with talk
and more crowds come hurrying. Many run in the back streets
which minutes ago were busy main streets, pointing:
There's a fellow weeping down there. No one can stop him.

The man we surround, the man no one approaches
simply weeps, and does not cover it, weeps
not like a child, not like the wind, like a man
and does not declaim it, nor beat his breast, nor even
sob very loudly—yet the dignity of his weeping

holds us back from his space, the hollow he makes about him
in the midday light, in his pentagram of sorrow,
and uniforms back in the crowd who tried to seize him
stare out at him, and feel, with amazement, their minds
longing for tears as children for a rainbow.

Some will say, in the years to come, a halo
or force stood around him. There is no such thing.
Some will say they were shocked and would have stopped him
but they will not have been there. The fiercest manhood,
the toughest reserve, the slickest wit amongst us

trembles with silence, and burns with unexpected
judgements of peace. Some in the concourse scream
who thought themselves happy. Only the smallest children
and such as look out of Paradise come near him
and sit at his feet, with dogs and dusty pigeons.

Ridiculous, says a man near me, and stops
his mouth with his hands, as if it uttered vomit—
and I see a woman, shining, stretch her hand
and shake as she receives the gift of weeping;
as many as follow her also receive it

and many weep for sheer acceptance, and more
refuse to weep for fear of all acceptance,
but the weeping man, like the earth, requires nothing,
the man who weeps ignores us, and cries out
of his writhen face and ordinary body

not words, but grief, not messages, but sorrow
hard as the earth, sheer, present as the sea—
and when he stops, he simply walks between us
mopping his face with the dignity of one
man who has wept, and now has finished weeping.

Evading believers, he hurries off down Pitt Street.   [1969]

JOHN NEWLOVE

Canada b. 1938

Although Newlove has sometimes been seen as a poet of despair, as ruthless with self-deception as with his skilled vivisections of contemporary inhumanity, his prairie roots inspire his most powerful work. His long poem 'The Pride' senses the prairie's haunting legacy of aboriginal ghosts, spirits that must be acknowledged in poetry as in life. Newlove's *Lies* (1972) won the Governor-General's Award for poetry; collections include *The Fat Man: Selected Poems 1962–1972* (1977).

SAMUEL HEARNE IN WINTERTIME

1
In this cold room
I remember the smell of manure
on men's heavy clothes as good,
the smell of horses.

It is a romantic world
to readers of journeys
to the Northern Ocean

especially if their houses are heated
to some degree, Samuel.

Hearne, your camp must have smelled
like hell whenever you settled down
for a few days of rest and journal-work:

hell smeared with human manure,
hell half-full of raw hides,
hell of sweat, Indians, stale fat,
meat-hell, fear-hell, hell of cold.

2
One child is back from the doctor's while
the other one wanders about in dirty pants
and I think of Samuel Hearne and the land—

puffy children coughing as I think,
crying, sick-faced,
vomit stirring in grey blankets
from room to room.

It is Christmastime—
the cold flesh shines.
No praise in merely enduring.

3
Samuel Hearne did more
in the land (like all the rest
full of rocks and hilly country,
many very extensive tracts of land,
tittimeg, pike and barble,

and the islands:
the islands, many
of them abound

as well as the main
land does
with dwarf woods,

chiefly pine
in some parts intermixed
with larch and birch) than endure.

The Indians killed twelve deer.
It was impossible to describe
the intenseness of the cold.

4
And, Samuel Hearne,
I have almost begun to talk

as if you wanted to be
gallant, as if you went
through that land for a book—

as if you were not SAM, wanting
to know, to do a job.

5
There was that Eskimo girl
at Bloody Falls, at your feet,

Samuel Hearne, with two spears in her,
you helpless before your helpers.

and she twisted about them like
an eel, dying, never to know.   [1968]

PAULA GUNN ALLEN

Laguna/Sioux b. 1939

Allen, a Native American Studies Professor at Berkeley, holds degrees from the University of Oregon and the University of New Mexico. She has published four volumes of poetry: *Coyote's Daylight Trip* (1978), *Shadow Country* (1982), *Wyrds* (1987), and *Skins and Bones* (1988). Her poetry embraces the traditional and the modern, the mythical and the personal, especially as enacted in the lives of women. Allen has also written a novel, *The Woman Who Owned the Shadows* (1983) and a research study on women and indigenous cultures, *The Sacred Hoop* (1986). She edited *Spider Woman's Granddaughters* (1989) and *Studies in American Indian Literatures* (1983).

KOPIS'TAYA

(A GATHERING OF SPIRITS)

Because we live in the browning season
the heavy air blocking our breath,
and in this time when living
is only survival, we doubt the voices
that come shadowed on the air,
that weave within our brains
certain thoughts, a motion that is soft,
imperceptible, a twilight rain
soft feather's fall, a small body
dropping into its nest, rustling, murmuring,
settling in for the night.

Because we live in the hardedged season,
where plastic brittle and gleaming shines
and in this space that is cornered and angled,
we do not notice wet, moist, the significant
drops falling in perfect spheres
that are the certain measures of our minds;
almost invisible, those tears,
soft as dew, fragile, that cling to leaves,
petals, roots, gentle and sure,
every morning.

We are the women of daylight; of clocks and steel
foundrys, of drugstores and streetlights,
of superhighways that slice our days in two.
Wrapped around in glass and steel we ride
our lives; behind dark glasses we hide our eyes,
our thoughts, shaded, seem obscure, smoke
fills our minds, whisky husks our songs,
polyester cuts our bodies from our breath,
our feet from the welcoming stones of earth.
Our dreams are pale memories of themselves,
and nagging doubt is the false measure of our days.

Even so, the spirit voices are singing,
their thoughts are dancing in the dirty air.
Their feet touch the cement, the asphalt
delighting, still they weave dreams upon our
shadowed skulls, if we could listen.
If we could hear.
Let's go then. Let's find them. Let's
listen for the water, the careful gleaming drops
that glisten on the leaves, the flowers. Let's
ride the midnight, the early dawn. Feel the wind
striding through our hair. Let's dance
the dance of feathers, the dance of birds.   [1984]

MARGARET ATWOOD

Canada b. 1939

Equally well known for her fiction and for her critical study, *Survival: A Thematic Guide to Canadian Literature* (1972), Atwood published her first important book of poetry, *The Circle Game*, in 1966. Her poems typically dramatize the conditions of colonized victims, many of them female, in a landscape that is often indifferent or hostile and in relationships that are often oppressive.

PROGRESSIVE INSANITIES OF A PIONEER

I
He stood, a point
on a sheet of green paper
proclaiming himself the centre,
with no walls, no borders
anywhere; the sky no height
above him, totally un-
enclosed
and shouted:

Let me out!

II
He dug the soil in rows,
imposed himself with shovels.
He asserted
into the furrows, I
am not random.

The ground
replied with aphorisms:

a tree-sprout, a nameless
weed, words
he couldn't understand.

III
The house pitched
the plot staked
in the middle of nowhere.
At night the mind
inside, in the middle
of nowhere.

The idea of an animal
patters across the roof.

In the darkness the fields
defend themselves with fences
in vain:
>everything
>is getting in.

IV
By daylight he resisted.
He said, disgusted
with the swamp's clamourings and the outbursts
of rocks,
>This is not order
>but the absence
>of order.

He was wrong, the unanswering
forest implied:

>It was
>an ordered absence

V
For many years
he fished for a great vision,
dangling the hooks of sown
roots under the surface
of the shallow earth.

It was like
enticing whales with a bent
pin. Besides he thought

in that country
only the worms were biting.

VI
If he had known unstructured
space is a deluge
and stocked his log house-
boat with all the animals
even the wolves,

he might have floated.

But obstinate he
stated, The land is solid
and stamped,

watching his foot sink
down through stone
up to the knee.

VII
Things
refused to name themselves; refused
to let him name them.

The wolves hunted
outside.

On his beaches, his clearings,
by the surf of under-
growth breaking
at his feet, he foresaw
disintegration
            and in the end
through eyes
made ragged by his
effort, the tension
between subject and object,

the green
vision, the unnamed
whale invaded.   [1968]

Notes Towards a Poem That Can Never Be Written

for Carolyn Forché

i
This is the place
you would rather not know about,
this is the place that will inhabit you,
this is the place you cannot imagine,
this is the place that will finally defeat you

where the word *why* shrivels and empties
itself. This is famine.

ii
There is no poem you can write
about it, the sandpits
where so many were buried
& unearthed, the unendurable
pain still traced on their skins.

This did not happen last year
or forty years ago but last week.
This has been happening,
this happens.

We make wreaths of adjectives for them,
we count them like beads,
we turn them into statistics & litanies
and into poems like this one.

Nothing works.
They remain what they are.

iii
The woman lies on the wet cement floor
under the unending light,
needle marks on her arms put there
to kill the brain
and wonders why she is dying.

She is dying because she said.
She is dying for the sake of the word.
It is her body, silent
and fingerless, writing this poem.

iv
It resembles an operation
but it is not one

nor despite the spread legs, grunts
& blood, is it a birth.

Partly it's a job,
partly it's a display of skill
like a concerto.

It can be done badly
or well, they tell themselves.

Partly it's an art.

v
The facts of this world seen clearly
are seen through tears;
why tell me then
there is something wrong with my eyes?

To see clearly and without flinching,
without turning away,
this is agony, the eyes taped open
two inches from the sun.

What is it you see then?
Is it a bad dream, a hallucination?
Is it a vision?
What is it you hear?

The razor across the eyeball
is a detail from an old film.
It is also a truth
Witness is what you must bear.

vi
In this country you can say what you like
because no one will listen to you anyway,
it's safe enough, in this country you can try to write
the poem that can never be written,
the poem that invents
nothing and excuses nothing,
because you invent and excuse yourself each day.

Elsewhere, this poem is not invention.
Elsewhere, this poem takes courage.
Elsewhere, this poem must be written
because the poets are already dead.

Elsewhere, this poem must be written
as if you are already dead,
as if nothing more can be done
or said to save you.

Elsewhere you must write this poem
because there is nothing more to do.   [1981]

bill bissett

Canada b. 1939

bissett's refusal to capitalize his name signals his consistent rebellion against conventional orthography and typography—a stance in keeping with his vision of a cosmos he would like to set free from any institutional or social norms. His poetry, which he often illustrates, charms the eye, while in his public performances his chants recall poetry's oral and ritual provenance. His 1968 book, *awake in th red desert*, includes an LP of bissett's performances; *Selected Poems: Beyond Even Faithful Legends* (1980) offers a generous collection.

th wundrfulness uv th mountees our secret police

they opn our mail   petulantly
they burn down barns they cant
bug   they listn to our politikul
ledrs phone conversashuns   what
cud b less inspiring to ovrheer

they had me down on th floor til
i turnd purpul thn my frends
pulld them off me   they think
brest feeding is disgusting   evry
time we cum heer to raid ths place
yu always have that kid on yr tit

they tore my daughtrs dolls hed off
looking for dope   whun uv my mor
memorabul beetings was in th back
seet lockd inside whun a ther unmarkd
cars

they work for the CIA   at nite they
drive around nd shine ther serchlites
on peopul embracing   nd with ther
p a systems tell them to keep away
from th treez

they listn to yr most secret farts
re-winding th tape looking for hiddn
meening indigestyun is a nashunal
security risk

i think they shud stick to protecting
th weak   eldrly laydees n men childrn
crossing th street   helping sick
nd/or defensless peopul nd
arresting capitalist crooks

insted theyve desertid th poor
n eldrly   nd ar protecting
th capitalist crooks

its mor than musical
th ride theyr taking
us all on   [1978]

SEAMUS HEANEY

Ireland b. 1939

Heaney is carefully aware of both his loyalty to region and root that he calls a 'tribal' perspective
and the need for distanced, less vulnerable points of view. 'I speak and write in English, but do not
altogether share the preoccupations and perspectives of an Englishman. . . . At school I studied the
Gaelic literature of Ireland as well as the literature of England, and since then I have maintained a
notion of myself as Irish in a province that insists that it is British.' Heaney's *Selected Poems,
1965–1975* was published in 1980. Representative collections include *Death of a Naturalist* (1966),
Wintering Out (1972), and *Field Work* (1979). In 1995 he received the Nobel Prize for Literature.

DIGGING

Between my finger and my thumb
The squat pen rests; snug as a gun.

Under my window, a clean rasping sound
When the spade sinks into gravelly ground:
My father, digging. I look down

Till his straining rump among the flowerbeds
Bends low, comes up twenty years away
Stooping in rhythm through potato drills
Where he was digging.

The coarse boot nestled on the lug, the shaft
Against the inside knee was levered firmly.
He rooted out tall tops, buried the bright edge deep
To scatter new potatoes that we picked
Loving their cool hardness in our hands.

By God, the old man could handle a spade.
Just like his old man.

My grandfather cut more turf in a day
Than any other man on Toner's bog.
Once I carried him milk in a bottle
Corked sloppily with paper. He straightened up
To drink it, then fell to right away

Nicking and slicing neatly, heaving sods
Over his shoulder, going down and down
For the good turf. Digging.

The cold smell of potato mould, the squelch and slap
Of soggy peat, the curt cuts of an edge
Through living roots awaken in my head.
But I've no spade to follow men like them.

Between my finger and my thumb
The squat pen rests.
I'll dig with it.   [1966]

from WHATEVER YOU SAY SAY NOTHING

I
I'm writing this just after an encounter
With an English journalist in search of 'views
On the Irish thing'. I'm back in winter
Quarters where bad news is no longer news,

Where media-men and stringers sniff and point,
Where zoom lenses, recorders and coiled leads
Litter the hotels. The times are out of joint
But I incline as much to rosary beads

As to the jottings and analyses
Of politicians and newspapermen
Who've scribbled down the long campaign from gas
And protest to gelignite and Sten,

Who proved upon their pulses 'escalate',
'Backlash' and 'crack-down', 'the provisional wing',
'Polarization' and 'long-standing hate'.
Yet I live here, I live here too, I sing,

Expertly civil-tongued with civil neighbours
On the high wires of first wireless reports,
Sucking the fake taste, the stony flavours
Of those sanctioned, old, elaborate retorts:

'Oh, it's disgraceful, surely, I agree,'
'Where's it going to end?' 'It's getting worse.'
'They're murderers.' 'Internment, understandably . . .'
The 'voice of sanity' is getting hoarse.

. . .

III
'Religion's never mentioned here,' of course.
'You know them by their eyes,' and hold your tongue.
'One side's as bad as the other,' never worse.
Christ, it's near time that some small leak was sprung

In the great dykes the Dutchman made
To dam the dangerous tide that followed Seamus.
Yet for all this art and sedentary trade
I am incapable. The famous

Northern reticence, the tight gag of place
And times: yes, yes. Of the 'wee six' I sing
Where to be saved you only must save face
And whatever you say, you say nothing.

Smoke-signals are loud-mouthed compared with us:
Manoeuvrings to find out name and school,
Subtle discrimination by addresses
With hardly an exception to the rule

That Norman, Ken and Sidney signalled Prod
And Seamus (call me Sean) was sure-fire Pape.
O land of password, handgrip, wink and nod,
Of open minds as open as a trap,

Where tongues lie coiled, as under flames lie wicks,
Where half of us, as in a wooden horse,
Were cabin'd and confined like wily Greeks,
Besieged within the siege, whispering morse.

IV
This morning from a dewy motorway
I saw the new camp for the internees:
A bomb had left a crater of fresh clay
In the roadside, and over in the trees

Machine-gun posts defined a real stockade.
There was that white mist you get on a low ground
And it was déjà-vu, some film made
Of Stalag 17, a bad dream with no sound.

Is there a life before death? That's chalked up
In Ballymurphy. Competence with pain,
Coherent miseries, a bite and sup,
We hug our little destiny again.   [1975]

PATRICK LANE

Canada b. 1939

Lane dedicated his first book, *Letters from the Savage Mind* (1966), to his older brother Red Lane, an emerging poet who died in Vancouver at twenty-six. Patrick began to write out of his working-class background, evoking the pain and suffering of ordinary people and the cruelty and violence of the natural world. Those qualities mark the work inspired by his travels in the early seventies, *Unborn Things: South American Poems* (1975). Lane's *Poems New and Selected* (1978) won the Governor-General's Award.

PASSING INTO STORM

Know him for a white man.
He walks sideways into wind
allowing the left of him

to forget what the right
knows as cold. His ears
turn into death what

his eyes can't see. All day
he walks away from the sun
passing into storm. Do not

mistake him for the howl you hear
or the track you think you
follow. Finding a white man

in snow is to look for the dead.
He has been burned by the wind.
He has left too much

flesh on winter's white metal
to leave his colour as a sign.
Cold white. Cold flesh. He leans

into wind sideways; kills without
mercy anything to the left of him
coming like madness in the snow. .

[1978]

DENNIS LEE

Canada b. 1939

Lee is both a children's (*Alligator Pie*, 1974, and *Garbage Delight*, 1977) and adults' poet, as well as an editor, publisher, and critic. His nationalist despair at Canada's relation to the US inspired *Civil Elegies and Other Poems* (1972), which won the Governor-General's Award for poetry, while his commitment to Canadian publishing led to his co-founding of House of Anansi Press in the late sixties. His latest book of poems is *Riffs* (1993).

from CIVIL ELEGIES

I
Often I sit in the sun and brooding over the city, always
in airbone shapes among the pollution I hear them, returning;
pouring across the square
in fetid descent, they darken the towers
and the wind-swept place of meeting and whenever
the thick air clogs my breathing it teems with their presence.
Many were born in Canada, and living unlived lives they died
of course but died truncated, stunted, never at
home in native space and not yet
citizens of a human body of kind. And it is Canada
that specialized in this deprivation. Therefore the spectres arrive,
    congregating in bitter droves, thick in the April sunlight,
accusing us and we are no different, though you would not expect
the furies assembled in hogtown and ring me round, invisible, demanding
what time of our lives we wait for till we shall start to be.
Until they come the wide square stretches out
serene and singly by moments it takes us in, each one for now
a passionate civil man, until it
sends us back to the acres of gutted intentions,
back to the concrete debris, to parking scars and the four-square tiers
of squat and righteous lives. And here
once more, I watch the homing furies' arrival.

I sat one morning by the Moore, off to the west
ten yards and saw though diffident my city nailed against the sky
in ordinary glory.
It is not much to ask. A place, a making,
two towers, a teeming, a genesis, a city.
And the men and women moved in their own space,
performing their daily lives, and their presence occurred
in time as it occurred, patricians in
muddy York and made their compact together against the gangs of the new.
And as that crumpled before the shambling onset, again the
lives we had not lived in phalanx invisibly staining

the square and vistas, casting back I saw
regeneration twirl its blood and the rebels riding
riderless down Yonge Street, plain men much
goaded by privilege—our other origin, and cried
'Mackenzie knows a word, Mackenzie
knows a meaning!' but it was not true. Eight hundred-odd steely Canadians
turned tail at the cabbage patch when a couple of bullets fizzed
and the loyalists, scared skinny by the sound of their own gunfire,
gawked and bolted south to the fort like rabbits,
the rebels for their part bolting north to the pub: the first
spontaneous mutual retreat in the history of warfare.
Canadians, in flight.

Buildings oppress me, and the sky-concealing wires
bunch zigzag through the air. I know
the dead persist in
buildings, by-laws, porticos—the city I live in
is clogged with their presence; they
dawdle about in our lives and form a destiny, still
incomplete, still dead weight, still
demanding whether Canada will be.

But the mad bomber, Chartier of Major Street, Chartier
said it: that if a country has no past,
neither is it a country and promptly
blew himself to bits in the parliament john, leaving as civil testament
assorted chunks of prophet, twitching and
bobbing to rest in the flush.
And what can anyone do in this country, baffled and
making our penance for ancestors, what did they leave us? Indian-swindlers,
stewards of unclaimed earth and rootless what does it matter if they, our
forebears' flesh and bone were often
good men, good men do not matter to history.
And what can we do here now, for at last we have no notion
of what we might have come to be in America, alternative, and how make
    public
a presence which is not sold out utterly to the modern? utterly? to the
savage inflictions of what is for real, it pays off, it is only
accidentally less than human?

In the city I long for, green trees still
asphyxiate. The crowds emerge at five from jobs
that rankle and lag. Heavy developers
pay off aldermen still; the craft of neighbourhood,
its whichway streets and generations
anger the planners, they go on jamming their maps
with asphalt panaceas; single men

still eke out evenings courting, in parks, alone.
A man could spend a lifetime looking for
peace in that city. And the lives give way around him—marriages
founder, the neighbourhoods sag—until
the emptiness comes down on him to stay.
But in the city I long for men complete
their origins. Among the tangle of
hydro, hydrants, second mortgages, amid
the itch for new debentures, greater expressways,
in sober alarm they jam their works of progress, asking where in truth
they come from and to whom they must belong.
And thus they clear a space in which
the full desires of those that begot them, great animating desires
that shrank and grew hectic as the land pre-empted their lives
might still take root, which eddy now and
drift in the square, being neither alive nor dead.
And the people accept a flawed inheritance
and they give it a place in their midst, forfeiting progress, forfeiting
dollars, forfeiting yankee visions of cities that in time it might grow
whole at last in their lives, they might
belong once more to their forebears, becoming their own men.

To be our own men! in dread to live
the land, our own harsh country, beloved, the prairie, the foothills—
and for me it is lake by rapids by stream-fed lake, threading
north through the terminal vistas of black spruce, in a
bitter, cherished land it is farm after
farm in the waste of the continental outcrop—
for me it is Shield but wherever terrain informs our lives and claims us;
and then, no longer haunted by
unlived presence, to live the cities:
to furnish, out of the traffic and smog and the shambles of dead precursors,
a civil habitation that is
human, and our own.

The spectres drift across the square in rows.
How empire permeates! And we sit down
in Nathan Phillips Square, among the sun,
as if our lives were real.
Lacunae. Parking lots. Regenerations.
Newsstand euphorics and Revell's sign, that not
one countryman has learned, that
men and women live that
they may make that
life worth dying. Living. Hey,
the dead ones! Gentlemen, generations of

acquiescent spectres gawk at the chrome
on American cars on Queen Street, gawk and slump and retreat.
And over the square where I sit, congregating above the Archer
they crowd in a dense baffled throng and the sun does not shine through.

[1972]

MUDROOROO/
COLIN JOHNSON

Nyoongah/Australia b. 1939

Mudrooroo was raised in a Roman Catholic orphanage in West Australia and began writing novels after moving to Melbourne and working in the public service. His *Wildcat Falling* (1965) was the first aboriginal novel in Australia, and his passionate concerns about aboriginal identity and white cultural practices are also the subject of his poetry and two subsequent novels, *Long Live Sandawara* (1979) and *Doctor Weereddy's Prescription for Enduring the Ending of the World* (1983), a history of the genocide committed against Tasmanian aborigines as seen from a Black man's point of view.

CROW

Crow, he everywhere; everywhere, he crow. Mating, fighting,
fleeing together and apart from Magpie adding some white to
his black to blend in somewhere in the brick kiln jungle. Sat
Bhai, babblers babble the cement squawking Bulbul into
assuming the red of missing bejewelled Butterfly hiding in
the Drongo aching to be swift Tailor bird endlessly stitching
Koranic covers too-weeing to Mecca the subtlety of Golden
Oriole selecting an extension to Myall's yellow stockings of
Dyall evading Sparrows overtaking of the government buildings
and refusing Honeysucker a singular drop of nectar from
exploitation of Woodpecker dismantling the last industries in
co-operation with Coppersmith suffering under Blue Jay's
compassion for all who work and forget to play. Kingfisher
seeks out the last unpolluted pools of amenities abandoned
by Dalwurra's somewhat alter-ego Koel, sweet with the final
tasting of sugared lips on a brown face munching the few
fruits of the brick jungle echoing with the mimicking of
Parrot living down his fate at not being quite Indian even to
Owl hiding his untouchable body in the darkness which he
secures for gleaming fireflies to emerge and enter the dark
tunnel of his throat, the cavern, stretched and gloomy with
vultures of desires to cry forth the incarnations of high
reaching kites, scarred and battered through evading the
teeth of the sky hazy with a message for Dalwurra. Remember
the seeds of Earth's sorrow as the boar was murdered and the
joys of Crab tearing at the fleshy throat, as Koel dived into
the eyes and blinded with a sudden spurt of the water-element

crab lost to the coo-cooing doves bob-bobbing at a pretence
of Seagull in a dance miming Dalwurra's open mouth hanging
down at so many vacant perches squat and ugly under the grime
of ancient weathering long lost in the haze of the murdered
witch heavy on his back sinking down to broken earth
ground-flooded crab-element water-stinking city.   [1988]

FRED WAH

Canada b. 1939

Wah has brought to Canadian poetry the influence of the Black Mountain school of American
poetry. For Wah, the Kootenay region of British Columbia where he grew up is an ample site for
all human experience. Linguistics and literature inform his exploration of the processes of spoken,
even breathed, language—for example, his evocations of the sound of his own last name in the
book *Breathin' My Name with a Sigh* (1981). The child of a Chinese father and a Swedish mother,
Wah has also mapped his ethnic ancestry in his poetry. He is a founding or contributing editor of
Tish, *Open Letter*, and *Swift Current*. Wah won the Governor-General's Award for poetry in 1985
with *Waiting for Saskatchewan*; earlier work includes *Among* (1972), *Earth* (1974), *Pictograms from
the Interior of BC* (1975), and the collection *Selected Poems: Loki Is Buried at Smoky Creek* (1980).

WAITING FOR SASKATCHEWAN

Waiting for Saskatchewan
and the origins grandparents countries places converged
europe asia railroads carpenters nailed grain elevators
Swift Current my grandmother in her house
he built on the street
and him his cafés namely the 'Elite' on Centre
looked straight ahead Saskatchewan points to it
Erickson Wah Trimble houses train station tracks
arrowed into downtown fine clay dirt prairies wind waiting
for Saskatchewan to appear for me again over the edge
horses led to the huge sky the weight and colour of it
over the mountains as if the mass owed me such appearance
against the hard edge of it sits on my forehead
as the most political place I know these places these strips
laid beyond horizon for eyesight the city so I won't have to go
near it as origin town flatness appears later in my stomach why
why on earth would they land in such a place
mass of pleistocene
sediment plate wedge
arrow sky beak horizon still waiting for that
I want it back, wait in this snowblown winter night
for that latitude of itself its own largeness
my body to get complete
it still owes me, it does   [1985]

EUNICE DE SOUZA

India b. 1940

De Souza, a member of the English Department at St Xavier College of Bombay, is an art critic, writer of children's stories, and anthologist; with Adil Jussawalla she edited *Statements* (1976), an anthology of Indian prose in English. Her poetry collections include *Women in Dutch Painting* (1988) and *Ways of Belonging: New and Selected Poems* (1990). De Souza's demanding satiric perspectives explore the constraints imposed within the Catholicism of her Goan family in Poona, specifically the denial of personhood for women ('Marriages Are Made'), and the moral and social poverty of imperial institutions.

ENCOUNTER AT A LONDON PARTY

For a minute we stand blankly together.
You wonder in what language to speak to me,
offer a pickled onion on a stick instead.
You are young and perhaps forgetful
that the Empire lives
only in the pure vowel sounds I offer you
above the din.   [1988]

ADIL JUSSAWALLA

India b. 1940

Educated at University College, Oxford, Jussawalla worked in England writing poetry (*Land's End*, 1962) and beginning an analysis of the effects of his own colonial experience. In *Missing Person* (1976), published after his return to Bombay, he explores the devastation wrought by expatriation—exported, superficially anglicized by foreign educational and economic systems, his 'missing person' devolves into an upper-middle-class Indian intellectual, a 'colonial ape' blown to bits by a host of 'Third World' forces kindled by an independent India. Jussawalla's work as an anthologist includes *New Writing in India* (1974), post-Independence writing in English and in translation, and *Statements* with Eunice De Souza.

A BOMB-SITE

As if the broken stumps were a girl's
Starved shoulders; as if the dusty rubble
Were her hair starfished across a pillow,
I would push my fingers through its grit.

I would press my bones into the bony
Shoulders of these scarred homes, as
I pass above their sardined tops, concealed;
Reach out and grasp and clean the greasy tin.

But children throwing stones, trenched behind mounds,
Holler and kill and crumple like stale newssheets,
Unsatisfied with spotless skies of peace,
And I begin to count my enemies.

Violence is a culture found on playgrounds.
Cities fall to let their children breathe.   [1962]

JUDITH KAZANTZIS

England b. 1940

Born in Oxford, Kazantzis lives in London where she teaches creative writing and is a poetry reviewer for *Spare Rib*. She remarks: 'I have written poetry since I was seven, my first work being one of Spenserian stature (in a school exercise book) entitled "Fairyland". This book was lost by my mother. I have been interested in reassembling good and bad in women ever since.' Kazantzis's first book of poems was *Minefield* (1977), followed by *The Wicked Queen* (1980).

FOR MY SISTER PREGNANT

On your coverletted bed
your watercolour of a green avenue
the lady who walks into a distance
but not you, just now.

My lady my sister
your canteloupe breasts
glisten for your next child,
I walk home from your boudoir,

on your bed you are robust,
your broad brown neck, and
your hill gleams for the child
who swims round and round inside,

a fishtail woman for a
time, who's beached—the
clear whites of your brown eyes
and you're amused: I'm
always here, drop in.

Since you may not move
for indefinite weeks of the slow
hill you build up
for that invisible troglodyte, the
obstreperous guest—

who may, you're perfectly aware,
drain like a doll on waters
out of control, if there's no luck,
any morning—through the exit
                    of the bursting blood
and the exit of the
nursing waters; where like Noah
the child now bounces: saying

I exercise my strength
I pound you below the breast,
jamming my heels to your ribs,
here mother; so your hands
shall stroke with pride my strong tremors
inside your globe.
Here I could die, in my first audacity.
You must be calm, and still.

My Rachel my sister
amicable on your child-bed,
your swelling skin brown under lace
you your child's own bed . . .

attend, the little stranger's sharp
and has its mother in chains
for months; and will be
a tyrant in later life:

how will you ever put your
foot down, after all this?
What will you say in protest?
Nothing; but joy.   [1980]

GEOFFREY LEHMANN

Australia b. 1940

A graduate of the University of Sydney with degrees in arts and law, Lehmann practised law and now teaches in the law school at the University of New South Wales. His poems in *The Ilex Tree* (1965) deal with families and relationships as do many others, including the seventy-five pieces in his *Ross' Poems* (1978). In other volumes Lehmann re-creates the barbarism and decadence of collapsing Roman and Greek empires.

NIGHT FLOWER

Sussex Street sleeps in mists of nickel moonlight
And echoes ghostly music, but the sound
Inside is crushing, voices, drums, stars jerked
From electric guitars, and swaying, shaking bodies:
Young, beautiful and cruel my friends are dancing.
Night in your cold vase hold this crumbling flower,
Stung smiles, dark corridors where bodies push
To a white stately room of bare feet stamping
A gritty floor, figures dissolving in shadows,
The dance, this great, sad, bitter swaying thing
Which burns and moves and kisses us with salt.   [1968]

RACHEL MCALPINE

New Zealand b. 1940

Born in Fairlie and educated at Massey, Victoria, and Canterbury Universities, McAlpine is a playwright and novelist as well as a poet. She teaches at the Correspondence Schools in Wellington where she now lives, and has published many books of poetry, including a volume of *Selected Poems* (1988).

HERE IT IS

Well to get to the nitty-gritty,
here it is:
I was suddenly sick of praying
to men, for men.
That was the beginning,
the middle and the end.

Ritual: remind myself I am guilty,
wrong, and light in the head.

Orthodox theology and common sense:
yes our Father is sexless,
God is being, God is love,
yes the Holy Spirit is spirit
and Jesus being a Jew
simply had to be male
and he was kind to girls.
Yes I could alter pronouns privately,
yes I am married to God
and have no right to divorce.
Yes Man is metaphor for Woman,
yes I could work within,
yes I could wait a century
yes it is just as silly
to think of God as Woman—

yet things are right for me
when flesh and spirit agree:
I do not feel included.

One truth is that God the Father
calls mostly to men except
when he wants a cup of tea.   [1988]

MOLARA OGUNDIPE-LESLIE

Nigeria b. 1940

Ogundipe-Leslie's social activism has led her to the Nigerian Directorate for Social Mobilization as an adviser on the status of women. She is involved in an ongoing analysis of the myths that have defined African women. As a critic, poet, professor, and Head of the Department of English at Ogun State University in Nigeria, Ogundipe-Leslie is particularly interested in Marxist readings of critical and creative writing in Africa, in indigenous aesthetics, and in the work of Amos Tutuola, Wole Soyinka, Chinua Achebe, and Christopher Okigbo. Her first book of poems, *Sew the Old Days and Other Poems*, appeared in 1985.

song at the african middle class

For agostinho neto

we charge through the skies of disillusion,
seeking the widening of eyes, we gaze at chaos,
speak to deadened hearts and ears stopped with
commerce. We drift around our region of clowns,
walking on air as dreams fly behind our eyes.
we forage among broken bodies, fractured minds
to find just ways retraced and new like beaten cloth.

and if they come again
will they come again?
and if they come again
will they dance this time?
will the new *egungun* dance once more
resplendent in rich-glassed cloth?
will they be of their people's needs,
rise to those needs, settle whirling rifts
salve, O, festering hearts?
will they say when they come
O my people, O my people, how to love you delicately?   [1990]

GIEVE PATEL

India b. 1940

Patel absorbs the images and techniques of his own clinical practice as a physician in Bombay, driven by a professional curiosity, a contempt that is barely contained, and a compassion that is disciplined and self-aware. An important contemporary Indian painter, Patel has written essays on Indian art and two collections of verse: *Poems* (1966) and *How Do You Withstand, Body* (1976).

NARGOL

This time you did not come
To trouble me. I left the bus
Wiping dust from my lashes
And did not meet you all the way
Home. At the back of my mind,
Behind greetings, dog-licks, and deepening
Safety, I continued to look for you—
But my strolls continued pleasant—
I did not spot you at the end of a lane,
Your necklace pendulant as your skin,
Your cringing smile pointing the disease:
Leper-face, leonine, following my elbow
As I walk past casual, casual.
I am friendly, I smile. I am
No snob. Lepers don't disgust me. But also
Tough resistance: I have no money,
Meet me later,
My fingernail rasping a coin.
She'll have her money but
Cannot be allowed to bully—
Let her follow, let her drone.
Sooner or later she'll give up,
Stop in the centre of a lane,

Let herself recede.
I reach the sea.
Yes, that was essential
Discipline.

In the open street I stand
With elders. How far have you
Studied, when do you finish?
In the middle of my reply
She passes by,
I skip a word, she cannot
Meet my eye, grins timidly, goes on;
Accepted fact
This is not the time.

Afternoon, and she reappears,
Stands before the house, says
Nothing, looks for my eyes
Between page-turns. I cannot read.

The book is frozen, angry weapon
In my hand. I pretend a page,
Then look up—I'm reading now, I say,
I'll give you later—switch down,
Master, unquestioned. She goes.

Cruel, you're cruel.

From a village full of people
She has chosen me; year after year;
Is it need
Or a private battle?

At the end it is four annas—
Four annas for leprosy. It's green
To give so much
But I am a rich man's son.
She cringes—I've worked for your mother.
She hasn't.
—You come just once a year.
All right, a rupee. She goes.
My strolls are to myself again.
The sea is reached with ease,
Reading is simplified. One last tussle:
Was it not defeat after all?
Personal, since I did not give,

I gave in; wider—there was
No victory even had I given.
I have lost to a power too careless
And sprawling to admit battle,
And meanness no defence.
Walking to the sea I carry
A village, a city, the country,
For the moment
On my back.

This time you did not come
To trouble me. In the middle
Of a lane I stopped.
She's dead, I thought;
And after relief, the next thought:
She'll reappear
If only to baffle.   [1965]

JAMES WELCH

Blackfoot b. 1940

Welch graduated from the University of Montana, and he has taught creative writing at the
University of Washington and Cornell University. Well-known for his novels, including *Winter in
the Blood* (1974), *The Death of Jim Loney* (1979), and *Fool's Crow* (1986), Welch first published a
collection of protest poems, *Riding the Earthboy 40* (1971), whose surrealism documents the
vagaries of indigenous peoples' quests and the sacrifices they have made in order to endure.

IN MY LIFETIME

This day the children of Speakthunder
run the wrong man, a saint unable
to love a weasel way, able only to smile
and drink the wind that makes the others go.
Trees are ancient in his breath.
His bleeding feet tell a story of run
the sacred way, chase the antelope naked
till it drops, the odor of run
quiet in his blood. He watches cactus
jump against the moon. Moon is speaking
woman to the ancient fire. Always woman.

His sins were numerous, this wrong man.
Buttes were good to listen from. With thunder
hands his father shaped the dust, circled
fire, tumbled up the wind to make a fool.

Now the fool is dead. His bones go back
so scarred in time, the buttes are young to look
for signs that say a man could love his fate,
that winter in the blood is one sad thing.

His sins—I don't explain. Desperate in my song,
I run these woman hills, translate wind
to mean a kind of life, the children of Speakthunder
are never wrong and I am rhythm to strong medicine.   [1971]

MICHAEL HARTNETT

Ireland b. *1941*

Influenced primarily by classical Irish-language poets like Daibhi Bruadair and by Lorca, whose
works he has translated, Hartnett declares his decision to stop writing in English in *A Farewell to
English*, the title of his 1975 manifesto collection. Hartnett's *Collected Poems* in two volumes
appeared from 1984 to 1987; his bilingual work, *Necklace of Wrens: Selected Poems in Irish with
English Translations by the Author*, was published in 1987.

from A FAREWELL TO ENGLISH

for Brendan Kennelly

i.
Her eyes were coins of porter and her West
Limerick voice talked velvet in the house:
her hair was black as the glossy fireplace
wearing with grace her Sunday-night-dance best.
She cut the froth from glasses with a knife
and hammered golden whiskies on the bar
and her mountainy body tripped the gentle
mechanism of verse: the minute interlock
of word and word began, the rhythm formed.
I sunk my hands into tradition
sifting the centuries for words. This quiet
excitement was not new: emotion challenged me
to make it sayable. The clichés came
at first, like matchsticks snapping from the world
of work: mánla, séimh, dubhfholtach, álainn, caoin:
they came like grey slabs of slate breaking from
an ancient quarry, mánla, séimh, dubhfholtach,
álainn, caoin, slowly vaulting down the dark
unused escarpments, mánla, séimh, dubhfholtach,
álainn, caoin, crashing on the cogs, splinters
like axeheads damaging the wheels, clogging

the intricate machine, mánla, séimh,
dubhfholtach, álainn, caoin. Then Pegasus
pulled up, the girth broke and I was flung back
on the gravel of Anglo-Saxon.
What was I doing with these foreign words?
I, the polisher of the complex clause,
wizard of grasses and warlock of birds
midnight-oiled in the metric laws?

ii.
Half afraid to break a promise
made to Dinny Halpin Friday night
I sat down from my walk to Camas
Sunday evening, Doody's Cross,
and took off my burning boots
on a gentle bench of grass.
The cows had crushed the evening
green with mint
springwater from the roots
of a hawkfaced firtree on my right
swamped pismires bringing home
their sweet supplies
and strawberries looked out
with ferret's eyes.
These old men walked on the summer road
sugán belts and long black coats
with big ashplants and half-sacks
of rags and bacon on their backs.
They stopped before me with a knowing look
hungry, snotnosed, half-drunk.
I said grand evening
and they looked at me awhile
then took their roads
to Croom, Meentogues and Cahirmoyle.
They looked back once,
black moons of misery
sickling their eye-sockets,
a thousand years of history
in their pockets.   [1978]

GWENDOLYN MACEWEN

Canada 1941-1987

Among contemporary Canadian poets, MacEwen most fully draws on mythology to integrate her art and her vision in 'Kanada'—the spelling reflects MacEwen's mystical version of the country and culture. Her novels also draw on myth and alchemy; in her acclaimed 1982 book, *The T.E. Lawrence Poems*, she re-creates Lawrence's voice to tell his several famous stories. Married for six years to the Greek singer Nikos Tsingos, MacEwen translated with him the work of the contemporary Greek poet Yannis Ritsos. She won the Governor-General's Award for *The Shadow-Maker* (1970) and the A.J.M. Smith Award for Poetry for *The Armies of the Moon* (1972); representative collections are *Earthlight: Selected Poetry, 1963–1982* (1982) and *Magic Animals: The Selected Poems of Gwendolyn MacEwen* (1984).

DARK PINES UNDER WATER

This land like a mirror turns you inward
And you become a forest in a furtive lake;
The dark pines of your mind reach downward,
You dream in the green of your time,
Your memory is a row of sinking pines.

Explorer, you tell yourself this is not what you came for
Although it is good here, and green;
You had meant to move with a kind of largeness,
You had planned a heavy grace, an anguished dream.

But the dark pines of your mind dip deeper
And you are sinking, sinking, sleeper
In an elementary world;
There is something down there and you want it told.   [1969]

ATUKWEI OKAI/JOHN OKAI

Ghana b. 1941

Raised in Ga, his native tongue, Twi (the major language of Ghana), and English, Okai combines these languages with an interest in performance poetry and popular and oral traditions to build the comic and revolutionary edges in his poems. Emphatic and recurrent patterns of sound and rhythm in his work emphasize the spoken character of language. This dimension—central to E.K. Brathwaite's concept of the 'Nation language[s]' of patois, pidgin, and Dub poetries—establishes Okai's relation to 'orature', the term coined by Ugandan literary critic Pio Zimru to define the oral tradition of the griots (professional musicians in West Africa who sang the history of particular families), calypso, and blues. Okai's collections include *Flowerfall*, *Lorgorligi Logarithms*, and *Rhododendrons in Donkeydom*.

ELAVANYO CONCERTO

(to Angela Davis and Wole Soyinka)

Cross.	Banner.	Swastika.	Sickle.
Dross.	Hammer.	Floodfire.	Spittle.

The sun is the centre of our system.

The leaning tower.	Two stones.	Revolution.
Summons to Rome.	Burning Stake.	The Inquisition.

The sun's not the centre of our system.

El Cordobes! El Cordobes!
There are some things I have to confess;
(The bulls and bulls you kill in the ring.)
When to the winds you all caution fling,

You have things unto which to cling.
The bulls and bulls you kill in the ring
Alone have no prospects of wearing a sling.
The bulls and bulls you kill in the ring.

But when Galileo Galilei
Was thrown into the rot-ring of scorn,
The charging bull they hurled against him
Was armed to the horn and to the hoof
With the cudgel of hate and the spear of fear

And with the red-hot crowbar of anger.
Galileo Galilei in the ring
Was alone; his only weapon and friend

Was time; and time was a mere toddler then.
(And for time to mature in the marrow,

You certainly have to come tomorrow;
Centuries and centuries after the morrow)
And they said: Galileo Galilei,
We hear you are not at home in the mind,
We fear you must be counted with the blind.

You may think all your thoughts; you may,
But your ideas shan't see the light of day;
Your midday coughing hurts our midnight prayers.
And you said: two is a crowd; even the
Elements bear witness; the heavens

Hear evidence; the universe gives judgment.
Place no mouldy margin upon what I
Should imagine; and no single censor
In hell or heaven shall tell me censor
My sigh or sin. You retail a sick tale

Tailored to your taste. But toppling trees tell
Another story. When in the lap of
A man-blinded God, truth lies, lying like
The soon-to-be-unlaced lips of a hell—
Robed Iscariot the Judas jettisoned

Into the joyless jungle of seekers
After the truth that shall not tear apart
When torn apart, caterpillar canoes
All crawl into the highway threshold
Of a contourless anger; but the seed,

O God, is already in the soil; the
Rains have already gone down to it.
Elavanyo! Elavanyo! better
Times cannot be too far away. I
Sit here watching the stars. Elavanyo.

Hei . . . Galileo Galilei . . . My eyes
are watering, their teeth are tightening, your lips
are quivering, and our solo-song slows
down to a silent stop; Hallelujah Chorus
cracks upon the shock-rock of an anti-
truth cataract.

O . . . Galileo Galilei . . . you fold
your face like a preying mantis pawned for
a pound of maize; and we erase all
trace, taking no chances with cheating
charcoal-sellers who hold the hand of hands
over the hovering hawk hankering after
human flesh.

Hei . . . Galileo Galilei . . . Time marks
time in our tears, and the rivers of truth
renew their roar; fire fights flesh in their
fears, and suns that shone should no more soar.

O . . . Galileo Galilei . . . truth's lip-
stick on your mind, green anger in their heart,
scorners' thick mud on your shirt, black dark-
ness in their hair, dry dagger in some
hand; and they crouch and come: advancing
towards you, advancing towards me,
charging against the very liver of
truth.

Hei . . . Galileo Galilei . . . water
walking, rainbow running, and the sky in
our song; I hear them laughing, I see you
sneezing, murderous thunder under their
tongue. Rays of knowledge pierce their eyes, smoke of
truth blocks their nose; and fire in the
flesh, and the rainfall on the rock, and the
myre in the mesh, and man shall not talk? amen . . .

O . . . Galileo Galilei . . .
O . . . Galileo Galilei . . .
Grave and grievous galley-groans all relay
The grandeur grinding of the painful play

Of rude rods on souls that forlornly pray
But whom suffering shall soon surely slay
On a particular forthdawning day.
They love this earth, but their bursting breath gives way,
They love this life, but their spirits won't stay.
The candlelight of knowledge and truth holds sway . . .
Inquisition fires faint-die away . . .
O, Elavanyo . . . Galileo
O, Elavanyo . . . Galilei.   [c. 1974]

SIMON J. ORTIZ

Acoma Pueblo b. 1941

Ortiz, a graduate of the University of New Mexico and the University of Iowa, has taught creative writing and indigenous literatures at several universities. He has edited and published several volumes of short fiction as well as four collections of his poetry: *Going for the Rain* (1976); *A Good Journey* (1977); *Fight Back: For the Sake of the People, For the Sake of the Land* (1980); and *From Sand Creek* (1981). Whether he is recounting his personal journeys in long narrative poems attentive to traditional oral forms or documenting conditions of anger and protest, Ortiz writes poetry from his conviction that 'Song as language is a way of touching.'

WAITING FOR YOU TO COME BY

all those summers, waiting,
hot, tensing with sounds that don't come,
the wind puts circles
              in which your mind is enclosed
waiting
for thoughts to follow,
anywhere, just so the thoughts
come.
              they don't come,
just the hot wind, dancing steady, deadening
the moments not paying attention to history,
the flesh without motion, waiting
              for the sound without motion.

come here girl. come here. come.
i have been waiting
so long. these days are impossible,
blessings so vague that they are not even dreams,
i can't see the stars on the horizon,
time has stopped. time has stopped.

i have been waiting
for you to come by.   [1975]

PAULINE STAINER

England b. 1941

Stainer, who lives and writes in Essex, is concerned with the sacred, with what it means, for example, to 'walk into the crucifixion'. She brings emotional realism to a range of dramatic monologues that reveal the problems visual artists attempt to solve in their painted subjects. Stainer extends her multi-disciplinary focus to medieval events and circumstances, to music (and the often tormented oxymorons which isolate 'the Mozart lovers/running the concentration camps'), and to the body of love. Stainer's collections include *The Honeycomb* (1989), *Sighting the Slave Ship* (1992), and *The Ice-Pilot Speaks* (1994).

SIGHTING THE SLAVE SHIP

We came to unexpected latitudes—
sighted the slave ship
during divine service
on deck.

In earlier dog-days
we had made landfall
between forests of sandalwood,
taken on salt, falcons and sulphur.

What haunted us later
was not the cool dispensing
of sacrament
in the burnished doldrums

but something more exotic—
that sense
of a slight shift of cargo
while becalmed.   [1992]

LAKDASA WIKKRAMASINHA

Sri Lanka 1941-1978

Wikkramasinha was a bilingual poet with an interest in Sinhala literature. Early in his career, he saw writing in English as an act of betrayal and therefore wrote in it only to try to subvert the language—an attitude that informs his first book, *Lustre. Poems* (1965) and that extends to his perception of the effects of exported European culture more generally. Wikkramasinha drowned in 1978; before his early death he privately published several volumes, including *Janakiharana and Other Poems* (1967), *O Regal Blood* (1975), and *The Grasshopper Gleaming* (1976).

DON'T TALK TO ME ABOUT MATISSE

Don't talk to me about Matisse, don't talk to me
about Gauguin, or even
the earless painter van Gogh,
and the woman reclining on a blood-spread . . .
the aboriginal shot by the great white hunter Matisse

with a gun with two nostrils, the aboriginal
crucified by Gauguin—the syphilis-spreader, the yellowed obesity.

Don't talk to me about Matisse . . .
the European style of 1900, the tradition of the studio
where the nude woman reclines forever
on a sheet of blood.

Talk to me instead of the culture generally—
how the murderers were sustained
by the beauty robbed of savages: to our remote
villages the painters came, and our white-washed
mud-huts were splattered with gunfire.   [1975]

ANNHARTE

Anishinabe b. 1942

Annharte's father was Irish, her mother Anishinabe, and she was raised in Winnipeg. Her writing often angrily and ironically evokes the conditions of contemporary aboriginals in a predominantly white world. Annharte's craft works deft reversals to sharp effects, as in the opening of 'Coyote Trail'—'warm this trail/my nose picks you to follow/your tracks quiver my whisker/my nostrils fill'. She published her first book of poetry, *Being on the Moon*, in 1990; her most recent book is *Coyote Columbus Café* (1994).

RACED OUT TO WRITE THIS UP

I often race to write   I write about race   why do I write
about race   I must erase all trace of my race   I am an
eraser abrasive bracing myself embracing

it is classic to want to write about class   not low class but
up the nose class   I know I am classy   brassy   crass ass
of a clash comes when I move up a rung

we are different skins   different bins for brown rice and
white rice   not even a container of wild rice   you know
what they do when you are white and not rich   poverty
counts big when you count the cost of a caste a colourful
past

drunk as a skunk he danced at the Lebret Hotel   what for
no   not really   says he's not writing because they won't
publish his books   he does a number for a book   he
hugged me like I was his old Tibetan guru out on the
dance floor teleporting again

white racists notice colour which they don't have   you
might be off-white   a bone white   a cream white
alabaster white   dingy white if you don't wash often
enough   nevermind a non-bleached white   white with
pinkish undertone   peaches and cream   white with
freckles   who is colour blind   I write my black ink on
white paper   I white out write out my colour lighten up

full of self I saw old whitey again but he wanted to be a
part of a pure religion not like ours   not that he was a
white racist but a pure racist in his heart which had no
colour but our colour   red   red   mind you a few white
corpuscles but compared to the red they were a minority
not invisible

so few of me yet I still write not for the white audience but
the colour of their response to my underclassy class   the
flash of their fit to kill me why race away to the finish
when I cross the finish line will it be white   will I be red
from running   hot and cold touch me not less I am to be
divided against my self who is both red and white but not a
shade of pink maybe a beige pink blushed flushed off
white right I colour my winning everytime   I am still in the
red not the black   blackened red   reddened black   but
what about   black n' blue   green at the gills   yellow belly
but what about the whitish frightish part I put it behind
behind me when I need to say my piece about togetherness
that we must breed not by ourselves but with everyone
out in the world who will listen   hey   I'm a half a half

breed   a mixed bag breed bread and butter bred my
whole grain bannock will taste as good to me even if I
smear on red jam sink my white teeth down into it down
the red hatch to the black hole   that is behind it all   the
whole black of me   the whore backing up behind me
the sore holy part of me which is the blackest darkest most
coloured most non-Indian, non-white slice of me bred to
wonder   [1990]

EILÉAN NÍ CHUILLEANÁIN

Ireland b. 1942

Chuilleanáin teaches at Trinity College, Dublin and co-edits the literary magazine *Cyphers*. Her
'Second Voyage', like Atwood's 'Progressive Insanities of a Pioneer', exposes the soft underbelly of
the Ulyssean quest, an approach that Tennyson explored as well when he took his hero out of early
retirement in 'Ulysses'. Chuilleanáin, who is the editor of *Irish Women: Image and Achievement*
(1985), has written *The Second Voyage: Selected Poems* (1986) and *The Magdalene Sermon* (1989).

THE SECOND VOYAGE

Odysseus rested on his oar and saw
The ruffled foreheads of the waves
Crocodiling and mincing past: he rammed
The oar between their jaws and looked down
In the simmering sea where scribbles of weed defined
Uncertain depth, and the slim fishes progressed
In fatal formation, and thought
                              If there was a single
Streak of decency in these waves now, they'd be ridged
Pocked and dented with the battering they've had,

And we could name them as Adam named the beasts,
Saluting a new one with dismay, or a notorious one
With admiration; they'd notice us passing
And rejoice at our shipwreck, but these
Have less character than sheep and need more patience.

I know what I'll do he said;
I'll park my ship in the crook of a long pier
(And I'll take you with me he said to the oar)
I'll face the rising ground and walk away
From tidal waters, up riverbeds
Where herons parcel out the miles of stream,
Over gaps in the hills, through warm
Silent valleys, and when I meet a farmer
Bold enough to look me in the eye
With 'where are you off to with that long
Winnowing fan over your shoulder?'
There I will stand still
And I'll plant you for a gatepost or a hitching-post
And leave you as a tidemark. I can go back
And organise my house then.
                              But the profound
Unfenced valleys of the ocean still held him;

He had only the oar to make them keep their distance;
The sea was still frying under the ship's side.
He considered the water-lilies, and thought about fountains
Spraying as wide as willows in empty squares,
The sugarstick of water clattering into the kettle,
The flat lakes bisecting the rushes. He remembered spiders and frogs
Housekeeping at the roadside in brown trickles floored with mud,
Horsetroughs, the black canal, pale swans at dark:
His face grew damp with tears that tasted
Like his own sweat or the insults of the sea.   [1977]

AMELIA

Remembering her half-sister Amelia, that girl
Whose hips askew made every step seem upstairs
The woman at the airport tells me that from her
One spring she bought the first small car.

After that it was trains and taxis for Amelia
For years and years, while the younger lay
In the car in a leafy mews in Dublin
Making love to a bald actor
Her elbow tightening
Linked through the steering-wheel.

She tells me, this hot noisy afternoon,
That Amelia now drives a car like a cabin-cruiser
In Halifax, Nova Scotia, where her husband
Fishes for lobster in short ice-free summers.   [1981]

GAURI DESHPANDE

India b. 1942

In her introduction to *an anthology of indo-english poetry* which she edited, Deshpande credits poets like Kamala Das, 'and in general all the women poets . . . for coming to terms with the man-woman relationship in blunt, bitter and concrete terms, where the men still pussyfoot around in metaphor, metaphysics and roundaboutation.' Deshpande's collections include *Between Births* (1968), *Lost Love* (1970), and *Beyond the Slaughterhouse* (1972).

THE FEMALE OF THE SPECIES

Sometimes you want to talk
about love and despair
and the ungratefulness of children.
A man is no use whatever then.
You want then your mother
or sister
or the girl with whom you went through school,
and your first love, and her
first child—a girl—
and your second.
You sit with them and talk.
She sews and you sit and sip
and speak of the rate of rice
and the price of tea
and the scarcity of cheese.
You know both that you've spoken
of love and despair and ungrateful children.   [1968]

DOUGLAS DUNN

Scotland b. 1942

Dunn's *Elegies*, a collection that won the Whitbread Literary Award for poetry in 1985, mourns the death of his first wife, recording their journey while he helped in her care. The intensity of Dunn's observations, the capacity of his imagery to 'so naturally' adhere 'to the subject' that the mysterious yields an inevitable clarity, is also central to his poetry soundtracks for BBC television, including his most recent, *Anons People*. For Dunn, 'poems are themselves intimate events generated by imagination and a kind of necessity. It is obedience to that necessity that makes a person a poet, or at any rate inclined towards writing poems.'

EMPIRES

All the dead Imperia . . . They have gone
Taking their atlases and grand pianos.
They could not leave geography alone.
They conquered with the thistle and the rose.
To our forefathers it was right to raise
Their pretty flag at every foreign dawn
Then lower it at sunset in a haze
Of bugle-brass. They interfered with place,
Time, people, lives, and so to bed. They died
When it died. It had died before. It died
Before they did. They did not know it. Race,
Power, Trade, Fleet, a hundred regiments,
Postponed that final reckoning with pride,
Which was expensive. Counting up the cost
We plunder morals from the power they lost.
They ruined us. They conquered continents.
We filled their uniforms. We cruised the seas.
We worked their mines and made their histories.
You work, we rule, they said. We worked; they ruled.
They fooled the tenements. All men were fooled.
It still persists. It will be so, always.
Listen. An out-of-work apprentice plays
God Save the Queen on an Edwardian flute.
He is, but does not know it, destitute.   [1979]

DAPHNE MARLATT

Australia/Canada b. 1942

Marlatt moved with her parents to Vancouver in 1951 and studied at the University of British Columbia, where she was influenced by the Black Mountain School of American poetry and worked on the literary magazine *Tish* in its formative years. The poems in *Steveston* (1974, rev. ed. 1984), with photographs by Robert Minden, document the daily lives of Japanese fishermen in a BC coastal town; *Touch to My Tongue* (1984) reflects the evolution in Marlatt's lifelong exploration of gender in writing, her interest in feminist and lesbian theory, and her work with Montreal feminist writer Nicole Brossard, who translated Marlatt's poems into French (1986). Her work is represented in *Selected Writing: New Work* (1980).

IMPERIAL CANNERY, 1913

Standing inside the door (the river . . .) how shadow lies
just inside the cannery floor, sun, pouring down outside,
the river streaming slow, slow, by. Now she feels old enough,
now she is wearing her long print dress & leaning into the
threshold, waiting for work, the wheel that time is, Whose hands
are standing still, hers, empty, Whose friends also surround her,
waiting, waiting all morning for the fish to come. Nothing moves
but occasional strands of long hair the subtle wind is lifting,
up off the river, the Fraser, mouth of the Fraser here where it
debouches, into marsh, delta, swirling around & past those
pilings of the cannery wharf they are standing on, muddy &
pale grey teeming, invisible fish . . .
      Now she is old enough to be her
mother inside, working, with the smallest one standing by her skirt
in grubby dress, & the blood streams down the wooden cutting board
as the 'iron chink' (that's what they call it) beheads each fish . . .

Now she is old enough for the wheel's turn, she is feeling her
body in its light dress wind blows thru, as past the faces of
her friends, likewise silent, impassive. Wind blows thru
those open doors (two) because, in the dark where machines are,
& the cans, & the steam, & a cavern of men with rolled up
sleeves & straw hats, & men in oilcloth slickers spattered with
fish gut, beyond & across the corner of that dark stands
another door, & the sail of a boat crossing the river, wind,
wind . . . An open door, where men unload their hauls of fish, the
collector's boat, float, sliding one, a hundred, on top of another,
their own scale grease that keeps them alive in sea they're
taken from to dry, in open sun on an open dock.
        But she is in her
element, dreaming of sails, her father's, or a friend's son, at the

Imperial which owns their boat, their net, their debt. But the
Fraser gives of itself, incessantly, rich (so the dream goes),
& wooden houses jammed on pilings close together, leaning, with
wooden walks & muddy alleys, laundry, & the dry marsh grass that
stutters out of silt the dykes retain, from a flowing
ever eroding & running river . . .

dreaming, of fabric she saw at Walker's Emporium, & the ribbon. A
woman of means she dreams, barefoot on the dock in the wind, leaning
into her threshold of work, machines, the wheel that keeps turning
turning, out of its wooden sleeve, the blade with teeth marked:
for marriage, for birth, for death.   [1984]

MICERE GITHAE MUGO

Kenya b. 1942

Kenyan by birth, educated at the University of Makere in Uganda and the University of Toronto,
Mugo left Kenya in 1982, commenting in a 1986 interview: 'It is very difficult, in Kenyan society,
to speak one's mind, especially if one takes a position that is pro-socialism. One faces harassment
and imprisonment.' Mugo has taught at the University of Zimbabwe since 1982. Her first book of
poetry, *Daughter of My People, Sing!* (1976), was followed by criticism (*Visions of Africa*, 1981), and
plays, including *The Trial of Dedan Kimathi* (1976).

WHERE ARE THOSE SONGS?

Where are those songs
my mother and yours
always sang
fitting rhythms
to the whole
vast span of life?

What was it again
they sang
          harvesting maize, threshing millet, storing the grain . . .

What did they sing
bathing us, rocking us to sleep . . .
and the one they sang
stirring the pot
(swallowed in parts by choking smoke)?

What was it
the woods echoed
as in long file

my mother and yours and all the women on our ridge
beat out the rhythms
trudging gaily
as they carried
piles of wood
through those forests
miles from home
What song was it?

And the row of bending women
hoeing our fields
to what beat
did they
break the stubborn ground
as they weeded
our *shambas*?

What did they sing
at the ceremonies
      child-birth
      child-naming
      second birth
      initiation . . . ?
how did they trill the *ngemi*
What was
the warriors' song?
how did the wedding song go?
sing me
the funeral song.
What do you remember?

Sing
      I have forgotten
      my mother's song
      my children
      will never know.
This I remember:
Mother always said
      sing child sing
      make a song
      and sing
      beat out your own rhythms
      and rhythms of your life
      but make the song soulful
      and make life
      sing

Sing daughter sing
around you are
unaccountable tunes
some sung
others unsung
sing them
to your rhythms
observe
listen
absorb
soak yourself
bathe
in the stream of life
    and then sing
    sing
    simple songs
    for the people
    for all to hear
    and learn
    and sing
    with you   [1976]

MUKHTARR MUSTAPHA

Sierra Leone b. 1942

Educated in Sierra Leone and the United States, Mustapha expresses his commitment to his Wolof
and Yoruba ancestry in 'Dalabani', a long dramatic poem grounded in the griot tradition of the
Berbers of the western Sahara. 'Gbassay—blades in regiment' reveals the ritual act of a cult-group
or secret society whose name derives, perhaps, from the Yoruba word 'Gbase', meaning slave. The
initiates' trance-cries of 'Krrr Gbassay Gbassay, Krr Gbassay' and seeming immunity from various
forms of self-mutilation may have provided Mustapha with a correlative for the courage of victims
of political oppression.

GBASSAY—BLADES IN REGIMENT

Push a porcupine quill into
My quaint eyes
Then plunge an assagai into
My fibroid face
Then slash my neck and stain
The tortoise back rich with my blood

Force a rug needle into my narrow
nose: force it right into my
Indigo marrow.

Lift my tongue and tie it
With a rope from a tethered goat
Lacerate my lips with deep sanguine
gutters splattering blood like a
Bellow in full blaze—blazing yellow

Disembowel my belly and feed the
Hawks that hover there hourless-
timeless black blue sky
And inside a crater bury
My ears.
          'Is it death?'   [1990]

ANDREW SUKNASKI

Canada b. 1942

Suknaski's most celebrated book, *Wood Mountain Poems* (1973; rev. ed. Purdy, 1976), documents the complex range of his allegiance to his homeground in Saskatchewan. The poems, writes Suknaski, address 'a vaguely divided guilt, . . . for what happened to the Indian'. One of Suknaski's favoured forms is the anecdotal long poem, in which he can represent the various dialects and voices from his own background. The youngest of six children of Polish-Ukrainian parents, he learned to speak English in first grade; he left Wood Mountain at sixteen to work and travel widely around Canada, returning home in the early 1970s. Collections of Suknaski's work include *The Land They Gave Away: New & Selected Poems* (ed. Scobie, 1982).

OVERLAND TO THE SOUTHERN PLAIN

1. henry kelsey arriving at indian village on carrot river

that young whiteman
he funny man say our country belong to his people
this strange medicine
he stand barehead
shout something to wind and river
in his language—our men talk
one man say . . . *this big medicine*
he big medicine

2. kelsey leaving deering's point

that summer the chief of the stones
provided me with several men to protect and lead me
and i was grateful—
for a while we paddled down the great river
and then continued our journey on foot leaving

the forests behind as the land flattened
we lived on small game and often ate berries
whenever we found trees heavy with fruit

at times we saw small herds of buffalo
and once shot one
when it rained for several days—we slowly cooked
big chunks of meat on a skinned branch
we turned over a campfire—
the sweet and coarse soft meat was something to remember
in our hardships
as we journied often hungry till one of us
shot another partridge

finally we reach hills rising above the plain
my indian companions said eagles built nests there
and we camped there for several days and rested—
we feasted on berries and a couple geese
one of us had shot
finally we journied west a few more days and began
the long walk back
to where we had left our canoes
for it was late summer

when we returned to the village just after the first frost
i cut two straight trees and skinned them
and tied them together—
i then raised the cross on that high place
where i had claimed the country of good report
calling the place *deering's point* to honour the man
and carved the following text:
july the 10th 1690 sir edward deering

3. the myth

we watch him put up cross
we thought
this man come so long way to do this
learn our language
live like us
this place be big medicine
he talk peace to naywatamee poets and nayhaythaways
this man this cross big medicine
cross so white on
blue sky   [1975]

HUGO WILLIAMS

England b. 1942

Williams was born in Windsor and, after graduating from Eton in 1960, worked as an editorial assistant for *London Magazine*. He wrote about his travels in the early sixties in *All the Time in the World* (1966) and published his first book of poems, *Symptoms of Loss*, in 1965, followed by *Sugar Daddy* (1970). Williams won the Eric Gregory Award in 1966 and the Cholmondeley Award in 1971. His poetry is attractively laconic, almost epigrammatic, in its sharp echoes of a life's timbre. Other Williams volumes include *Selected Poems* (1989) and *Writing Home* (1990).

THE COUPLE UPSTAIRS

Shoes instead of slippers down the stairs,
She ran out with her clothes

And the front door banged and I saw her
Walking crookedly, like naked, to a car.

She was not always with him up there,
And yet they seemed inviolate, like us,
Our loves in sympathy. Her going

Thrills and frightens us. We come awake
And talk excitedly about ourselves, like guests.   [1970]

GRACE AKELLO

Uganda b. 1940s

Akello was born in eastern Uganda, attended Makerere University, and worked in Kenya and Tanzania until 1981, when she left Africa for England. Her study *Iteso Thought Patterns in Tales* reflects how this tradition informs her verse; her book of poetry *My Barren Song* appeared in 1980.

ENCOUNTER

Teach me to laugh once more
let me laugh with Africa my mother
I want to dance to her drum-beats
I am tired of her cries
Scream with laughter
roar with laughter
Oh, how I hate this groaning

Africa groans
under the load of her kwashiorkored children
she weeps
what woman would laugh
over her children's graves

I want to laugh once again
let me laugh with you
yes, even you my brother who blames me for breeding . . .
I laugh with you
even you who sell me guns
preserving world peace
while my blood, Africa's blood stains Earth
let laughter be my gift to you
my generous heart overflows with laughter
money and vanity harden yours
clogged in your veins, the blood no longer warms your heart
I will teach you yet

I am not bush, lion, savagery
mine are the sinews which built your cities
my sons fighting your wars
gave you victory, prestige
wherein lies the savagery in Africa . . .
Your sons in Africa looted our family chests
raping the very bowels of our earth
our gold lines the streets of your cities . . .
where are pavements in Africa

Laugh with me
Do not laugh at me
my smile forgives all
but greed fetters your heart
the nightmare of our encounter is not over
your overgrown offspring
swear by the western god of money and free enterprise
that they are doing their best for Africa
indeed, Africa the dumping ground
Africa the vast experimental ground
the army bases in the developing parts
enhanced military aid in the loyal parts
family planning programmes in the advanced parts

My son built your cities
What did your son do for me . . .

[1979]

AMELIA BLOSSOM HOUSE

South Africa b. 1940s

Born in Cape Town, Amelia Pegram adopted the name 'Blossom' for her underground work in South Africa, where she taught for seven years after graduating from the University of Cape Town. She moved to Kentucky in 1972 and now teaches at the University of Louisville. Blossom House published *A Checklist of Black South African Women Writers in English* in 1980. Her poetry, short fiction, and criticism have appeared in journals like *Présence Africaine* and *Staffrider*; her books of poetry include *Deliverance* (1986) and *Our Sun Will Rise: Poems for South Africa* (1989).

WE STILL DANCE

today
yesterday
tomorrow
through and beyond time
we still dance
red dust
black mud
ochre sand
we still dance
birth
marriage
victory
we still dance
ankle rings
bracelets
feet drumming
soil
we still dance
yesterdays celebrations
for the soul
of the soil
todays celebrations
for the fight
of the soil
tomorrows
soul victory
we still dance.

[1989]

LOUISE GLÜCK

USA b. 1943

Glück was born in New York, grew up on Long Island, and now lives in Plainfield, Vermont. *Firstborn* (1968) opened her career with poems much influenced by Sylvia Plath's work; in later work like *The House on the Marshland* (1975) Glück began to draw more on mythological and biblical allusion as well as on the natural settings she observes in and around Plainfield. Glück published *Descending Figure* in 1980 and *The Triumph of Achilles* in 1985 and won the Pulitzer Prize for *Ararat* (1992).

AUBADE

Today above the gull's call
I heard you waking me again
to see that bird, flying
so strangely over the city,
not wanting
to stop, wanting
the blue waste of the sea—

Now it skirts the suburb,
the noon light violent against it:

I feel its hunger
as your hand inside me,

a cry
so common, unmusical—

Ours were not
different. They rose
from the unexhausted
need of the body

presuming a wish to return:
the ashen dawn, our clothes
not sorted for departure.   [1976]

DEDICATION TO HUNGER

1 / FROM THE SUBURBS

They cross the yard
and at the back door
the mother sees with pleasure
how alike they are, father and daughter—
I know something of that time.

The little girl purposefully
swinging her arms, laughing
her stark laugh:

It should be kept secret, that sound.
It means she's realized
that he never touches her.
She is a child; he could touch her
if he wanted to.

2 / GRANDMOTHER

'Often I would stand at the window—
your grandfather
was a young man then—
waiting, in the early evening.'

That is what marriage is.
I watch the tiny figure
changing to a man
as he moves toward her;
the last light rings in his hair.
I do not question
their happiness. And he rushes in
with his young man's hunger,
so proud to have taught her that:
his kiss would have been
clearly tender—

Of course, of course. Except
it might as well have been
his hand over her mouth.

3 / EROS

To be male, always
to go to women
and be taken back
into the pierced flesh:

I suppose
memory is stirred.
And the girl child
who wills herself
into her father's arms
likewise loved him
second. Nor is she told
what need to express.

There is a look one sees,
the mouth somehow desperate—

Because the bond
cannot be proven.

4 / THE DEVIATION

It begins quietly
in certain female children:
the fear of death, taking as its form
dedication to hunger,
because a woman's body
is a grave; it will accept
anything. I remember
lying in bed at night
touching the soft, digressive breasts,
touching, at fifteen,
the interfering flesh
that I would sacrifice
until the limbs were free
of blossom and subterfuge: I felt
what I feel now, aligning these words—
it is the same need to perfect,
of which death is the mere by-product.

5 / SACRED OBJECTS

Today in the field I saw
the hard, active buds of the dogwood
and wanted, as we say, to capture them,
to make them eternal. That is the premise
of renunciation: the child, the model of restraint,
having no self to speak of,
comes to life in denial—

I stood apart in that achievement,
in that power to expose
the underlying body, like a god
for whose deed
there is no parallel in the natural world.   [1980]

PAULETTE JILES

USA/Canada b. 1943

Born in Salem, Missouri, Jiles emigrated to Canada in 1969 and worked for ten years (1973–83) in the Canadian Arctic in aboriginal communications—a sojourn that inspires many of her poems and what she calls her book of 'creative non-fiction', *North Spirit: Travels Among the Cree and Ojibway Nations and Their Star Maps* (1995). Her writing can also evoke the restrictions of gender and childhood. Her collection *Celestial Navigation* (1984) won the Governor-General's Award.

WINDIGO

No one understands the Windigo, his voice like
the white light of hydrogen, only long.
Some say he carries his head under his arm, for
others it is the race down to the rapids
where the canoes draw close, close to the shore
and he jumps in. You have time for a few last words.
Under the moon he turns pearl grey, the
head chatters amiably about meals. He is the
Hungry Man, the one who reached this wasteland of
the soul and did not emerge. Not whole. Not as you
would recognize wholeness.

Sometimes he wants to be killed, putting his
heart or what there is of it in the way of arrows,
bullets, he wants his soul or what there is of it
to spring heavenward to the village where people
begin again, he too
wants to cross the bridge.
His story is of one who reached starvation
and death and did not make it through, not
as you would recognize making it.
People shoot the Windigo, they
do not pray for him, or it.   [1982]

THOMAS KING

Cherokee b. 1943

King's heritage includes a Cherokee father and a Greek-German mother. His writing (like his work in TV, radio, and film) often explores the distances, conflicts, and intersections between white and native characters and cultures, creation stories, and legends. He is better known for his short fiction and novels than his poetry; his novel *Medicine River* (1990) was followed by the celebrated *Green Grass, Running Water* (1993). King has taught Native Studies at the Universities of Lethbridge, Minnesota, and Guelph.

THE CITY ON THE HILL

My uncle savages the streets
   skates figure eights
   around the meters
   drums the cars.

He gimmes change from laughing people
   wrapped in tight, white skins
   and sheepy coats,
   round dances round the block
   in red-face
   clown-crows out the words he carries
   on his cuffs.

Until the cops come by
   and chauffeur him away
   with Marvin and the rest
   to Burger King.
   A break.
   Union rules.

Tough job, he says to Marvin
   over fries,
   but, hey,
   we got to hold the middle class
   in line,
   and keep them from the woods.   [1991]

MICHAEL ONDAATJE

Sri Lanka/Canada b. 1943

An acclaimed novelist as well as a poet (*The English Patient*, 1992, won both the Booker Prize and the Governor-General's Award), Ondaatje composes verse that throws art, experience, and language into violent and erotic conflict. His figures, like the outlaw of his best-known book of poems, *The Collected Works of Billy the Kid* (1970), are often those who live on the shifting borders between the mad and the sane, the inspired and the perverse. Ondaatje's postmodern explorations of selfhood and culture are as likely to fragment as to integrate ideas of linguistic, personal, or geographical identity.

BEARHUG

Griffin calls to come and kiss him goodnight
I yell ok. Finish something I'm doing,
then something else, walk slowly round
the corner to my son's room.
He is standing arms outstretched
waiting for a bearhug. Grinning.

Why do I give my emotion an animal's name,
give it that dark squeeze of death?
This is the hug which collects
all his small bones and his warm neck against me.
The thin tough body under the pyjamas
locks to me like a magnet of blood.

How long was he standing there
like that, before I came?   [1979]

THE CINNAMON PEELER

If I were a cinnamon peeler
I would ride your bed
and leave the yellow bark dust
on your pillow.

Your breasts and shoulders would reek
you could never walk through markets
without the profession of my fingers
floating over you. The blind would
stumble certain of whom they approached
though you might bathe
under rain gutters, monsoon.

Here on the upper thigh
at this smooth pasture
neighbour to your hair
or the crease
that cuts your back. This ankle.
You will be known among strangers
as the cinnamon peeler's wife.

I could hardly glance at you
before marriage
never touch you
—your keen nosed mother, your rough brothers.
I buried my hands
in saffron, disguised them
over smoking tar,
helped the honey gatherers . . .

                         *

When we swam once
I touched you in water
and our bodies remained free,
you could hold me and be blind of smell.
You climbed the bank and said

              this is how you touch other women
the grass cutter's wife, the lime burner's daughter.
And you searched your arms
for the missing perfume
                         and knew

              what good is it
to be the lime burner's daughter
left with no trace
as if not spoken to in the act of love
as if wounded without the pleasure of a scar.

You touched
your belly to my hands
in the dry air and said
I am the cinnamon
peeler's wife. Smell me.   [1981]

OLIVE SENIOR

Jamaica b. 1943

Born in Jamaica and educated in Canada, Senior also writes short fiction, edits the *Jamaica Journal*, and has worked with the Women in the Caribbean Research Project for the University of the West Indies. Her writing, which often documents village life in Jamaica, also explores the paradoxes and ambiguities attendant on a colonized culture's awareness of its condition. A collection of Senior's poems, *Talking of Trees*, was published in 1985.

COLONIAL GIRLS SCHOOL

for Marlene Smith MacLeish

Borrowed images
willed our skins pale
muffled our laughter
lowered our voices
let out our hems
denied our sex in gym tunics and bloomers
harnessed our voices to madrigals
and genteel airs
yoked our minds to declensions in Latin
and the language of Shakespeare

Told us nothing about ourselves
There was nothing about us at all

How those pale northern eyes and
aristocratic whispers once erased us
How our loudness, our laughter
debased us

There was nothing left of ourselves
Nothing about us at all

Studying: History Ancient and Modern
Kings and Queens of England
Steppes of Russia
Wheatfields of Canada

There was nothing of our landscape there
Nothing about us at all

Marcus Garvey turned twice in his grave.
'Thirty-eight was a beacon. A flame,
They were talking of desegregation
in Little Rock, Arkansas. Lumumba

and the Congo. To us: mumbo-jumbo.
We had read Vachel Lindsay's
vision on the jungle

Feeling nothing about ourselves
There was nothing about us at all

Months, years, a childhood memorising
Latin declensions
(For our language
—'bad talking'—
detentions)
Finding nothing about us there
Nothing about us at all

So, friend of my childhood years
One day we'll talk about
How the mirror broke
Who kissed us awake
Who let Anansi from his bag

For isn't it strange how
northern eyes
in the brighter world before us now

Pale?   [1986]

EAVAN BOLAND

Ireland b. 1944

Boland's poems offer a concentrated awareness of the pain accompanying the second-class status of Irish women. Concerned about 'the habit[s] of land' ('After a Childhood Away from Ireland') and the cost of an untenable romanticized nostalgia whose 'roots are brutal', her work exposes the woman betrayed by male-dominated, ungrounded mythologies. Boland's works include *The War Horse* (1975), *In Her Own Image* (1980), *Selected Poems* (1989), *Outside History* (1990), *In a Time of Violence* (1994), and a pamphlet, *A Kind of Scar: The Woman Poet in a National Tradition* (1989).

MISE EIRE

I won't go back to it—

my nation displaced
into old dactyls,
oaths made
by the animal tallows
of the candle—

land of the Gulf Stream,
the small farm,
the scalded memory,
the songs
that bandage up the history,
the words
that make a rhythm of the crime

where time is time past.
A palsy of regrets.
No. I won't go back.
My roots are brutal:

I am the woman—
a sloven's mix
of silk at the wrists,
a sort of dove-strut
in the precincts of the garrison—

who practises
the quick frictions,
the rictus of delight
and gets cambric for it,
rice-coloured silks.

I am the woman
in the gansy-coat
on board the 'Mary Belle',
in the huddling cold,

holding her half-dead baby to her
as the wind shifts East
and North over the dirty
water of the wharf

mingling the immigrant
guttural with the vowels
of homesickness who neither
knows nor cares that

a new language
is a kind of scar
and heals after a while
into a passable imitation
of what went before.   [1990]

LISTEN. THIS IS THE NOISE OF MYTH

This is the story of a man and woman
under a willow and beside a weir
near a river in a wooded clearing.
They are fugitives. Intimates of myth.

Fictions of my purpose. I suppose
I shouldn't say that yet or at least
before I break their hearts or save their lives
I ought to tell their story and I will.

When they went first it was winter; cold,
cold through the Midlands and as far West
as they could go. They knew they had to go—
through Meath, Westmeath, Longford,

their lives unravelling like the hours of light—
and then there were lambs under the snow
and it was January, aconite and jasmine
and the hazel yellowing and puce berries on the ivy.

They could not eat where they had cooked,
nor sleep where they had eaten
nor at dawn rest where they had slept.
They shunned the densities

of trees with one trunk and of caves
with one dark and the dangerous embrace
of islands with a single landing place.
And all the time it was cold, cold:

the fields still gardened by their ice,
the trees stitched with snow overnight,
the ditches full; frost toughening lichen,
darning lace into rock crevices.

And then the woods flooded and buds
blunted from the chestnut and the foxglove
put its big leaves out and chaffinches
chinked and flirted in the branches of the ash.

And here we are where we started from—
under a willow and beside a weir
near a river in a wooded clearing.
The woman and the man have come to rest.

Look how light is coming through the ash.
The weir sluices kingfisher blues.
The woman and the willow tree lean forward, forward.
Something is near; something is about to happen;

something more than Spring
and less than history. Will we see
hungers eased after months of hiding?
Is there a touch of heat in that light?

If they stay here soon it will be summer; things
returning, sunlight fingering minnowy deeps,
seedy greens, reeds, electing lights
and edges from the river. Consider

legend, self-deception, sin, the sum
of human purpose and its end; remember
how our poetry depends on distance,
aspect: gravity will bend starlight.

Forgive me if I set the truth to rights.
Bear with me if I put an end to this:
She never turned to him; she never leaned
under the sallow-willow over to him.

They never made love; not there; not here;
not anywhere; there was no winter journey;
no aconite, no birdsong and no jasmine,
no woodland and no river and no weir.

Listen. This is the noise of myth. It makes
the same sound as shadow. Can you hear it?
Daylight greys in the preceptories.
Her head begins to shine

pivoting the planets of a harsh nativity.
They were never mine. This is mine.
This sequence of evicted possibilities.
Displaced facts. Tricks of light. Reflections.

Invention. Legend. Myth. What you will.
The shifts and fluencies are infinite.
The moving parts are marvellous. Consider
how the bereavements of the definite

are easily lifted from our heroine.
She may or she may not. She was or wasn't
by the water at his side as dark
waited above the Western countryside.

O consolations of the craft.
How we put
the old poultices on the old sores,
the same mirrors to the old magic. Look.

The scene returns. The willow sees itself
drowning in the weir and the woman
gives the kiss of myth her human heat.
Reflections. Reflections. He becomes her lover.

The old romances make no bones about it.
The long and short of it. The end and the beginning
The glories and the ornaments are muted.
And when the story ends the song is over.   [1990]

DENNIS COOLEY

Canada b. 1944

Cooley was born in Estevan, Saskatchewan, and raised on a farm near there. He is Canada's major theorist of the eye, voice, and ear of the prairie idiom—and also a poet who delights in punning, in wordplay, and in formal as well as spatial and typographical experimentation. He has edited two collections of prairie poetry, *Draft* (1981) and *Inscriptions: A Prairie Poetry Anthology* (1992), and was a co-founder of the Winnipeg literary press, Turnstone. Since the late 1960s, Cooley has taught Canadian and American literature and literary theory at the University of Manitoba. Among his several books of poems are *Bloody Jack* (1984), *Perishable Light* (1988), and *This Only Home* (1992).

a curse on a critic

behind yr powdered perriwigs & wings *riggedy*
jiggedy you porker out on little pigs feet
how you jig & hop yr pork chops a round
on those bonestiff ideas that look a bit like legs
vindictive with blondness bristling with bindertwine emotions

smug as a burgher (you are
soul) slackassed with notions you drop emotions
slung from what should have been a backbone
a wallet of farts   you wallow of warts   ferret of fear
my finest   truffles all my arts all are trifled (jewel
by jowl) by yr rifle eyes   you & your sluice of reviews

all tarted up & champing   yr tartered chompers   *iggety*
ig   id like to say   yr thin as silver-fish you eat
my words but no toe   nailed by your cloven smirks ill
have to settle for letting you looming large as lard lord
ing it over us know how much i admire   *& jigjig* envy

you & the ooozy grace your expansive breadth your
pockmarked porkbarreled ex   pensive brain *jigjug* goes
your slopbucket soul   you & yr gluttinous yr gelatinous
mind pickled in the vinegar of what passes
in the prig that gristles between
yur nazi bloodpudding smiles
what passes for feeling
in that heart plugged with fat
what (you pizzle of poetry)   you hunchknuckle marrowmush pass
/for thot   fatuous with flatulence

now   in throatsquint & eyesqueal in that
tin y un n   erv(in)g nerVou s itC h   th Efain   test
collapse when—unclogging of eyes—you vaguely
knackers knicked & no thing left   you have   the knack
(munchsnuffle read   :   jawdrop :;
)in little()red eyes (dimly sur
mise in instinct of sphincter begin to know   the   sligh
test pres sure   of poetry   right   be.
tween yur eyes   [1988]

PAUL DURCAN

Ireland b. 1944

A critic of sectarian warfare, institutional bigotries, and gender stereotypes, Durcan shapes a poetic
line that accommodates the difficult ambiguities of Irish life and celebrates, on occasion, the
possibility of vision in 'a country where words also have died an unnatural death/or else have been
used on all sides for unnatural ends/and by poets as much as by gunmen and churchmen' ('Tribute
to a Reporter in Belfast, 1974'). Representative collections include *The Selected Paul Durcan* (ed.
Longley, 1982) and more recently Durcan's own *A Snail In My Prime: New and Selected Poems*
(1993). *Daddy, Daddy* won the 1990 Whitbread Literary Award for poetry.

CRINKLE, NEAR BIRR

Daddy and I were lovers
From the beginning, and when I was six
We got married in the church of Crinkle, near Birr.
The *Irish Independent* photographed the wedding.
My mother gave me away.

My sister was best man.
He was forty-two and a TV personality in Yorkshire,
Close to his widowed mother in Mayo,
Always having his photograph taken,
Always grinning and polite and manly and coy and brittle,
Checking the stubs of his cheque books,
Tying up his used cheque books in elastic bands,
Putting money away for a rainy day,
Making gilt-edged investments.
It was in the days before he became a judge.
He compèred boxing fights and women's beauty contests
In an accent that was neither English nor Irish nor American.
It was known as the Athlone accent.
When he spoke of Athlone
Listeners were meant to think
Of a convent in the middle of a dark forest
To which the speaker was chaplain.

We went on our honeymoon
To Galway, the City of the Tribes.
We stayed in the Eglinton Hotel in Salthill.
For breakfast we ate grapefruit segments and toast
And the manager bowed, the waiters goosing around us.
We stood on the Salmon Bridge counting
Squadrons of salmon floating face down in the waters below,
Waiting to go upstream to spawn.

In the afternoons we spawned our own selves in our hotel bedroom
Listening to cricket.
The West Indies were playing the MCC at Lord's.
We lay in bed listening to Rohan Kanhai batting for a double century
And Garfield Sobers taking six wickets for forty-five runs.
O Owen of the Birds,
That is what it meant to be Irish and free—
To be father and son in bed together
In a hotel in the City of the Tribes
Listening to cricket on the BBC Radio Third Service.
After dinner we walked on the pier at Spiddal,
Holding hands, watching schools
Of porpoises playing in the apple-light of the western sea.
One night after dinner we drove to Gort,
Where Daddy let his hair down
And we played a game of cricket
In the back garden of another father-and-son couple.
When Daddy bowled, I was his wicketkeeper.

He fancied himself as Ray Lindwall
And I fancied myself as Godfrey Evans—
Godders jack-knifing over bails and stumps.
When we returned to the hotel, we entered
By the fire escape, feeling in a mood to be secretive,
Black iron staircase flicked up against white pebble-dash gable.
Daddy divided the human race
Into those who had fire escapes and spoke Irish
And those who had not got fire escapes and did not speak Irish.
Another night we sat in a kitchen in Furbo
With a schoolteacher hobnobbing in Irish
Exotic as Urdu, all that rain and night at the windowpane.

The marriage lasted five years.
On a summer's night in Newcastle West
After a game of cricket with boys my own age
I came back into the house without my school blazer.
'Where have you left your school blazer
Which you should not have been wearing in the first place?
School blazers are not for wearing.
School blazers cost money.'
I had left it on a fence in the field.
When I went to retrieve it, it was lolling out of a cow's mouth,
One arm of it.
Daddy took off his trousers' belt,
Rolled it up in a ball round his fist,
And let fly at me with it.
In a dust storm of tears I glimpsed
His Western movie hero's eyes stare at me.

When I was twelve, I obtained a silent divorce.
Ireland is one of the few civilised countries—
And the only country outside Asia—
In this respect, that while husbands and wives
Can only at best separate,
Children can obtain a silent divorce from their parents.
When I look back at the years of my marriage to Daddy
What I remember most
Are not the beatings-up and the temper tantrums
But the quality of his silence when he was happy.
Walking at evening with him down at the river,
I lay on my back in the waters of his silence,
The silence of a diffident, chivalrous bridegroom,
And he carried me in his two hands home to bed.   [1990]

THE JEWISH BRIDE

After Rembrandt

At the black canvas of estrangement,
As the smoke empties from the ruins under a gold winter sky,
Death-trains clattering across the back gardens of Amsterdam—
Sheds, buckets, wire, concrete,
Manholes, pumps, pliers, scaffolding—
I see, as if for the first time,
The person you were; and are, and always will be
Despite the evil that men do:
The teenage girl on the brink of womanhood
Who, when I met you, was on the brink of everything—
Composing fairytales and making drawings
That used remind your friends of Anderson and Thurber—
Living your hidden life that promised everything
Despite all the maimed, unreliable men and women
Who were at that moment congregating all around you:
Including, of course, most of all, myself.
You made of your bedroom a flowing stream
Into which, daily, you threw proofs of your dreams;
Pinned to your bedroom wall with brass-studded drawing pins
Newspaper and magazine photographs of your heroes and heroines.
People who met you breathed the air of freedom,
And sensuality fragile as it was wild:
'Nessa's air makes free,' people used say,
Like in the dark ages, 'Town air makes free.'
The miracle is that you survived me.
You stroll about the malls and alleyways of Amsterdam,
About its islands and bridges, its archways and jetties,
With spring in your heels, although it is winter;
Privately, publicly, along the Grand Parade;
A Jewish Bride who has survived the death camp,
Free at last of my swastika eyes
Staring at you from across spiked dinner plates
Or from out of the bunker of a TV armchair;
Free of the glare off my jackboot silence;
Free of the hysteria of my gestapo voice;
Now your shyness replenished with all your old cheeky confidence—
That grassy well at which red horses used rear up and sip
With young men naked riding bareback calling your name.
Dog-muzzle of tension torn down from your face;
Black polythene of asphyxiation peeled away from your soul;
Your green eyes quivering with dark, sunny laughter
And—all spreadeagled and supple again—your loving, freckled hands.   [1985]

TOM LEONARD

Scotland b. 1944

Leonard mentions e.e. cummings, William Carlos Williams, Samuel Beckett, and Bertolt Brecht, among others, as significant influences, as well as music and geometry. The title *Intimate Voices 1965–1983*, 'refers not simply to the fact that the poems in the book use different voices and registers, but also to the name of a string quartet by Sibelius.'

JIST TI LET YI NO

(from the American of Carlos Williams)

ahv drank
thi speshlz
that wurrin
thi frij

n thit
yiwurr probbli
hodn back
furthi pahrti

awright
they wur great
thaht stroang
thaht cawld   [1984]

A Priest Came on at Merkland Street

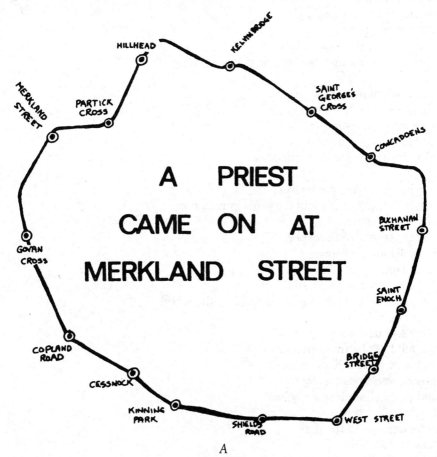

A
very thoughtful poem,
being a canonical penance
for sufferers of psychosomatic asthma.

oh no
holy buttons
sad but dignified
and sitting straight across from me
a troubled soul
my son
christ
a bit of Mahler's Seventh might drown him
dah dum, da dum dah dee,
dah dah dah DAH da dah
da DAH, dah DEE da da da
DUM DUM dah dee

hello there
when I'm dead
when I think I'm dead
and I'm in my box
and it's all dark
and I'm wondering where the air's coming from
I'll see this curtain
and it will move to the side
and your great horrible leering face
how many times my son
and how long ago was this
bless me father for I am tinned
christ
maybe he's saying hail mary's
maybe he's praying for all the souls in purgatory
and really sincere
the nicest man in the world
he really loves people
hello father
I'm going to give you a smile
I'm going to give you the nicest smile in the world
it will be real love
there will be absolutely no sex
we will both be five years old
and we'll go to school together
play at weekends together
and you'll climb inside my box
laughing
lying together in the dark
innocent as hell
like after lights out in a school dormitory
cosy but exciting
and maybe God will look round the curtain
hello there
softly as God would say it
and we'll all go away together
away through his door
for ever
amen
I always spoil it
but maybe you'd spoil it yourself
maybe you wouldn't be five years old at all
and you'd climb inside my box
a troubled soul
my son
with a keyhole in your back

wind me up in the morning
and a button under your right arm
how many times my son
and a button under your left arm
how long ago was this
and a button in the back of your head
press to bless
and a tape recorder between your ears
from henceforth ye shall catch men
from henceforth ye shall catch men
from henceforth ye shall catch men
dah dum, da dum dah dee,
oh no
you won't catch me
maybe I'll be really dead
as dead as everyone else who has died
just lying in a box
a box that somebody's made
a box for dead people
and I won't even know
christ
my name is Ozymandias
king of Leithland Road
Pollok
Glasgow SW3
and all the worrying
all the wanting to be five years old
imagine
the lone and level
far away
amen
only it's not the lone and level at all
for there's the Lansdowne Clinic for Functional Nervous
    Disorders
and the Southern General Hospital Department of
    Psychological Medicine
and Leverndale formerly known as Hawkhead
    Mental Asylum
I could write to a psychiatrist
a cry from the heart
dear sir
my name is Ozymandias
king of Leithland Road
and then there's the box
yours sincerely
maybe faithfully would be better

you know who
ps
I always spoil it
pps
I am awful lonely
ppps
I don't know what people are for
oh no
maybe I think about the box too much
maybe nobody else thinks about the box at all
at least not for long
not more than five minutes a day
or maybe ten minutes at the weekend
and that's all they need
they usually think about something else
they think about something else for hours on end
maybe I should do the same
I could draw up a plan
I could draw up a list of things to think about
everything but the box
and I'd think about them all day
I wouldn't think about the box at all
and then I'd go away home at night
and I'd have my tea
oxtail soup
a plate of potatoes and mince
two slices of toasted cheese
and a cup of tea
that would be fine
that would be very nice indeed
and then I'd go upstairs to my room
and I'd sit down at the table
and I'd write it out twenty times
I am going to die
imagine
maybe I'd get up in the morning
with a big smile
and I'd throw open the bedroom windows
hello there
I have accepted the box
I have accepted that I am going to die
oh no
maybe it wouldn't work at all
maybe I would just stay the same way for years
just thinking about something else all day
not thinking about the box at all

and then just going away home at night
just having my tea
just a cup of tea
maybe a bun
sad as hell
wanting to be five years old
christ
maybe I would tear up my plan
maybe I would tear up my list of things to think about
and I'd just go upstairs to my room
away through my door
for ever
with no button under my right arm
I am going to die
and no button under my left arm
I am going to die
and no button in the back of my head
I am going to die
but a tape recorder between my ears
I am going to die
I am going to die
I am going to die
dear Ozymandias
there is nothing wrong with you at all
my name is Ozymandias two
correction
my name is Ozymandias too
we are all in the box toogether
correction
we are all in the box twogether
correction
we are all in the box together
only indifferent ones
sorry
only in different ones
yours sincerely
you know whoo
correction
you know whwo
correction
you know who
correction
'You Know Who'
imagine
maybe there's nothing wrong with me at all
maybe I'm just the same as everyone else who has lived

and I'll just put on a smile at the box
I'll just put on the nicest smile in the world
and a bit of Mahler's Seventh might drown it
dah dum, da dum dah dee,
dah dah dah DAH da dee
correction
da da da DAH da da
correction
dah dah dah DAH da dah
tick tock
tick
oh no
tick tock
tick
hello there
tick tock
tick
hello there everybody
tick tock
tick

tick tock
tick

tick tock
tick

     brackets watch him he has a stoop and funny eyes

[1970]

bpNICHOL

Canada 1944-1988

Nichol was Canada's best-known Concrete poet, delighting in the appearance and shape of language on the page as well as in its sound. In 1970, Nichol and three other poets formed the celebrated Sound Poetry group The Four Horsemen. Nichol's masterwork is the multi-volume *The Martyrology*, begun in 1970, in which the poet quests for insight through attending to the diction and syntax of the language he himself speaks and writes. Nichol won the Governor-General's Award for poetry in 1970. George Bowering and Michael Ondaatje have edited a selection of Nichol's work, *An H in the Heart: bpNichol: A Reader* (1994).

TWO WORDS: A WEDDING

For Rob & Sheron

There are things you have words for, things you do not
have words for. There are words that encompass all your
feelings & words that encompass none. There are feelings
you have that are like things to you, picked up & placed in
the pocket, worn like the cloth the pocket is attached to, like
a skin you live inside of. There is a body of feeling, of
language, of friends; the body politic, the body we are
carried inside of till birth, the body we carry our self inside
of till death, a body of knowledge that tells of an afterlife, a
heaven, an unknown everything we have many words for
but cannot encompass. There are relationships between
words & concepts, between things, between life & death,
between friends & family, between each other & some other
other. We wed words to things, people to feelings, speak of
a true wedding of the mind & heart, intuition & intellect, &
out of this form our realities. Our realities are wedded one
to another, concepts & people are joined, new people
conceived within that mesh of flesh & realities, are carried
forward in the body of the mother, the family, the bodily
love we have for one another. They are creating their own
reality each step of the way, daily, another kind of reality is
born, each new word, person, expanding our vocabulary,
our concepts, new realities are conceived, our old reality
changes, the 'real' grows realer every day. We are marrying
the flesh to the flesh, the word to the daily flux of lives we
know & don't know, our friends grow older & marry, raise
children as you once were children with mothers & fathers
of your own, grow older, so many things you still lack
words for, struggle to wed the inner & outer worlds, the self
to some other self or selves, confess your love & struggle
with one another, together, conscious there is this word is

you, your name, & that you are yet another thing or things
you will never encompass, never exhaust the possibilities of,
because you are wedded to the flux of life, because we are
words and our meanings change.   [1978]

SALEEM PEERADINA

India/USA b. 1944

In his collection *First Offence* (1980) Peeradina's collage techniques display the explosive hetero-
geneity of suburban culture in modern Bombay; his second collection, *Group Portrait* (1990)
explores his domestic and field experience since his migration to the United States to teach at Siena
Heights College in Adrian, Michigan. Peeradina's anthology, *Contemporary Indian Poetry in English*
(1972), took issue with the 'open door' inclusivity of P. Lal's massive *Modern Indian Poetry in English*
(1969). Peeradina's principles of selection initiated a more canonical and evaluative approach to
the study of Indian poetry in English.

THERE IS NO GOD

only mother.

Obedient daughter, sister, the eldest
slogger in her father's house

presently:
expected to like with downcast eyes
the singular lord & master always faithfully
yours: wife

Of love:
the essence preserved in a photograph on the shelf

the multipurpose woman
                        to be taken
into the irreversible process
                        of motherhood

Become head of the house: wave
both arms like a paternal traffic-policeman

support her
claim to her ancient duties

regularly
after meal sweeping dusting meal
scrubbing washing pause meal
                        fall at her feet

when it's time to leave

Leave   [1972]

CRAIG RAINE

England b. 1944

Raine counts as major influences the organic principles Pablo Picasso employs to achieve a synthesis of fractured images, the 'argumentative open-ness' of Matthew Arnold, the 'density' of Gerard Manley Hopkins, and above all, 'the descriptive lust' of James Joyce. 'Writing', Raine muses, 'is the slavery of sense-experience'; it requires 'being faithful to what's in front of me. I keep my eye on the object; I'm responsible to it; I respond to it.' Raine's collections include *The Onion, Memory* (1978), *A Martian Sends a Postcard Home* (1979), and *A Free Translation* (1981).

IN THE KALAHARI DESERT

The sun rose like a tarnished
looking-glass to catch the sun

and flash His hot message
at the missionaries below—

Isabella and the Rev. Roger Price,
and the Helmores with a broken axle

left, two days behind, at Fever Ponds.
The wilderness was full of home:

a glinting beetle on its back
struggled like an orchestra

with Beethoven. The Hallé,
Isabella thought and hummed.

Makololo, their Zulu guide,
puzzled out the Bible, replacing

words he didn't know with Manchester.
Spikenard, alabaster, Leviticus,

were Manchester and Manchester.
His head reminded Mrs Price

of her old pomander stuck with cloves,
forgotten in some pungent tallboy.

The dogs drank under the wagon
with a far away clip-clopping sound,

and Roger spat into the fire,
leaned back and watched his phlegm

like a Welsh rarebit
bubbling on the brands . . .

When Baby died, they sewed her
in a scrap of carpet and prayed,

with milk still darkening
Isabella's grubby button-through.

Makololo was sick next day
and still the Helmores didn't come.

The outspanned oxen moved away
at night in search of water,

were caught and goaded on
to Matabele water-hole—

nothing but a dark stain on the sand.
Makololo drank vinegar and died.

Back they turned for Fever Ponds
and found the Helmores on the way . . .

Until they got within a hundred yards,
the vultures bobbed and trampolined

around the bodies, then swirled
a mile above their heads

like scalded tea leaves.
The Prices buried everything—

all the tattered clothes and flesh,
Mrs Helmore's bright chains of hair,

were wrapped in bits of calico
then given to the sliding sand.

'In the beginning was the Word'—
Roger read from Helmore's Bible

found open at St John.
Isabella moved her lips,

'The Word was Manchester'.
Shhh, shhh, the shovel said. Shhh . . .

[1979]

CAROL RUMENS

England b. 1944

Rumens, a writing fellow at Queen's University, Belfast, currently lives in Northern Ireland. Her poems are political and dramatic—finding the voices of those whose worlds in Eastern Europe, Russia, and Great Britain somehow endure. In *Thinking of Skins*, the 1993 collection of her work that represents poems from earlier pieces like *Unplayed Music* (1981), *Direct Dialling* (1985), and *From Berlin to Heaven* (1989), Rumens considers issues of entitlement, reference, and representation. The poems she has written about Belfast come from one who is both insider and outsider, one who knows that the 'ground' beneath her is unstable even while it 'feels so insistently like home'.

RULES FOR BEGINNERS

They said: 'Honour thy father and thy mother.
Don't spend every evening at the Disco.
Listen to your teachers, take an O level
or two. Of course, one day you'll have children.
We've tried our best to make everything nice.
Now it's up to you to be an adult!'

She went to all the 'X' films like an adult.
Sometimes she hung around the Mecca Disco.
Most of the boys she met were dead O level,
smoking and swearing, really great big children.
She had a lot of hassle with her mother;
it was always her clothes or her friends that weren't nice.

At school some of the teachers were quite nice,
but most of them thought they were minding children.
'Now Susan,' they would say, 'You're nearly adult
—behave like one!' The snobs taking O level
never had fun, never went to the Disco;
they did their homework during 'Listen with Mother'.

She said: 'I'd hate to end up like my mother,
but there's this lovely bloke down at the Disco
who makes me feel a lot more like an adult.'
He murmured—'When I look at you, it's nice
all over! Can't you cut that old O level
scene? Christ, I could give you twenty children!'

He had to marry her. There were three children
—all girls. Sometimes she took them to her mother
to get a break. She tried to keep them nice.
It was dull all day with kids, the only adult.
She wished they'd told you that, instead of O level.
Sometimes she dragged her husband to the Disco.

She got a part-time job at the Disco,
behind the bar; a neighbour had the children.
Now she knew all about being an adult
and, honestly, it wasn't very nice.
Her husband grumbled—'Where's the dinner, mother?'
'I'm going down the night-school for an O level,

I am,' said mother. 'Have fun at the Disco,
kids! When you're an adult, life's all O level.
Stay clear of children, keep your figures nice!'   [1981]

MONGANE (WALLY) SEROTE

South Africa b. 1944

Serote, born in Sophiatown, Johannesburg, is one of South Africa's 'township poets'. Imprisoned for
nine months in solitary confinement in 1969–70, allegedly for his involvement in the Black Con-
sciousness Movement, he was released without charge; as a Fulbright scholar, he then completed an
M.F.A. at Columbia University (1977). Like Sipho Sepamla, Serote understands English as the lan-
guage of an oppressor and uses it subversively; his poetry appears universally reflective and contem-
plative of the human condition, but it is increasingly underwritten by his political stance. Serote's first
book of poetry, *Yakhal'inkomo*, was published in 1972; it was followed by the banned *Tsetlo* (1974).
Other volumes include *No Baby Must Weep* (1975), *Selected Poems* (1982), and *A Tough Tale* (1987).

THE GROWING

No!
This is not dying when the trees
Leave their twigs
To grow blindly long into windows like fingers into eyes.
And leave us unable
To wink or to blink or to actually close the eye,
The mind—
Twigs thrusting into windows and leaves falling on the sills,
Are like thoughts uncontrolled and stuffing the heart.
Yes,
This is teaching about the growing of things:
If you crowd me I'll retreat from you,
If you still crowd me I'll think a bit,
Not about crowding you but about your right to crowd me;
If you still crowd me, I will not, but I will be thinking
About crowding you.
If my thoughts and hands reach out
To prune the twigs and sweep the leaves,
There was a growth of thought here,
Then words, then action.
So if I say prune instead of cut,
I'm teaching about the growing of things.   [1972]

KIT WRIGHT

England b. 1944

Wright's wry and iconoclastic approach to established norms and expectations combines with metrical and verbal ingenuity to secure the darkly comic. Often his allegiance to macabre incongruities and surprising rhymes recalls similar political schemes in e.e. cummings's poetry. Author of numerous children's books, freelance writer, editor, and broadcaster, Wright has published *Poems 1974–1983* (1988); *Short Afternoons* (1989) is his most recent collection.

I FOUND SOUTH AFRICAN BREWERIES MOST HOSPITABLE

Meat smell of blood in locked rooms I cannot smell it,
Screams of the brave in torture loges I never heard nor heard of
Apartheid I wouldn't know how to spell it,
None of these things am I paid to believe a word of
For I am a stranger to cant and contumely.
I am a professional cricketer
My only consideration is my family.

I get my head down nothing to me or mine
Blood is geysering now from ear, from mouth, from eye,
How they take a fresh guard after breaking the spine,
I must play wherever I like or die
So spare me your news your views spare me your homily.
I am a professional cricketer.
My only consideration is my family.

Electrodes wired to their brains they should have had helmets,
Balls wired up they should have been wearing a box,
The danger was the game would turn into a stalemate,
Skin of their feet burnt off I like thick woollen socks
With buckskin boots that accommodate them roomily
For I am a professional cricketer.
My only consideration is my family.

They keep falling out of the window they must be clumsy
And unprofessional not that anyone told me,
Spare me your wittering spare me your whimsy,
Sixty thousand pounds is what they sold me
And I have no brain. I am an anomaly.
I am a professional cricketer.
My only consideration is my family.   [1988]

SYL CHENEY-COKER

Sierra Leone b. 1945

Born in Freetown, Cheney-Coker was educated at the University of Oregon, UCLA, and the University of Wisconsin. He has worked as a journalist and a radio broadcaster, and taught at the University of Maiduguri in Borno, Nigeria. Cheney-Coker says of his poetry: 'it . . . owes very little to the English or American masters of the recent past. To express myself in verse, I have had to see poetry as a return to the primordial beginning of the word. . . . My poetry comes from the well-spring of a country, a world continually brutalized.' Cheney-Coker's books include *Concerto for an Exile: Poems* (1973) and *The Graveyard Also Has Teeth* (1974, rev. ed. 1979).

LETTER TO A TORMENTED PLAYWRIGHT

For Yulisa Amadu Maddy

Amadu I live alone inside four walls of books
some I have read others will grow cobwebs
or maybe like some old friends and lovers
will fade away with their undiscovered logic

the world that I have seen: New York
where I suffered the suicidal brother
and London where I discovered Hinostroza
Delgado, Ortega, Heraud and the other
Andean poets with a rage very much like ours!

remember Amadu how terrible I said it was
that you were in exile and working
in the Telephone Office in touch with all
the languages of the world but with no world
to call your own; how sad you looked that winter
drinking your life and reading poetry with me
in the damp chilly English coffee shops

*

remember I said how furious I was
that Vallejo had starved to death in Paris
that Rabearivelo had killed himself
suffocated by an imaginary France
and I introduced Neruda and Guillen to you
and how in desperation we sought solace in the house
of John La Rose, that courageous Trinidadian poet

Amadu I am writing to you from the dungeon of my heart
the night brings me my grief and I am passive
waiting for someone to come, a woman
a friend, someone to soothe my dying heart!

now the memory of our lives brings a knife to my poems
our deaths which so burdened the beautiful Martiniquan
you said made you happy, she made you so happy, you a
tormented playwright

*

sadness returns, the apparitions of my brothers
and my mother grows old thinking about them
and also seeing so much sadness in me her living and dying son
my mother who wishes me happy, who wants me to relive the son
she lost to poetry like a husband a wife to a trusted friend

but already the walls are closing around me
the rain has stopped and once again I am alone
waiting for them, the politicians of our country to come for me
to silence my right to shouting poetry loud in the parks
but who can shut up the rage the melodrama of being Sierra Leone
the farce of seeing their pictures daily in the papers
the knowledge of how though blindfolded and muzzled
something is growing, bloating, voluptuous and not despairing
I say to you for now, I embrace you brother.   [1980]

GILLIAN HANSCOMBE

Australia/England b. 1945

Born in Melbourne, Australia, Hanscombe moved to England in 1965. With Jackie Forster, she
wrote *Rocking the Cradle—Lesbian Mothers* (1981), and in 1982 she published the study *The Art of
Life—Dorothy Richardson and the development of feminist consciousness.* Her books of poetry include
Hecate's Charms (1976) and *Between Friends* (1982).

AN APOSTROPHE TO HER MAJESTY QUEEN ELIZABETH II

You may have this book, if you like, though from
all I've been told, I can't imagine you'd like it;
there are words that may not be used in addressing you,
words that signify the unseemly,
female words.
            So all I can say is, take this book.
There are others of my kind in your kingdom.
And we feel not-smiled upon.
                        Your
grandfather's grandmother, we're told, didn't
believe in us. But
just like anyone we
lick your head into shape on the corners of our letters,

trade with your image among one another.
                                    Like
anyone, we can see you move on immaculate horses
by courtesy of cameras.
                   It's
even likely, given our knowledge, that
some of us share your bloodline.
So take this book; it implies no dishonour;
and queens have been known to dissent from the fathers.   [1986]

SELIMA HILL

England b. 1945

A section of Hill's *The Accumulation of Small Acts of Kindness* (1989), which records in poem-journal form the life-journey of a schizophrenic, won the 1988 Arvon/Observer International Poetry Competition. Other collections include *Saying Hello at the Station* (1985), *A Little Book of Meat* (1993), and most recently, *Trembling Hearts in the Bodies of Dogs* (1994). Hill has collaborated with artists such as choreographer Emilyn Claid and sculptor Bill Woodrow.

THE SIGNIFICANCE OF SIGNIFICANCE

She was worried he couldn't be happy
just loafing about by the river,
like she liked doing.
Plans, and plans about plans, and sex,
was *his* idea of happiness.
He wore a floppy hat.
She felt so lonely!

Another thing, she couldn't spell.
Laborinth. Itiniry. Elann.
She cooked him cockles
in a thick orange sauce,
and bought him a suitcase—
'for the Great Man'.

They sat on a rocky mountain
dressed in leather.
Sardines and beer.
Parois vertigineuses.

Their children were his books.
She understood that.
O Significado De Significado,
lecture notes.

'The blissfully well-run nursing-home'
is now public knowledge—
her little lump, like longing,
prised from her oesophagus;
her crawling from the hut
on her knees.

A tortoise-shell comb,
embroidery,
The Crack.
A lovely moth.
'The nurse is a crashing bore'
. . . poking about among her mysteries.
God bless you, Patty.   [1988]

EATING CHOCOLATES IN THE DARK

And after that, the diaries stop.
We think he went to his grandmother's,
whom he adored apparently.
They sat on her bed
with the lights turned off,
and ate chocolates,
and listened to the sea.
It was a kind of ritual
they both found very comforting.

Her other love was hyacinths.
He said he didn't like them,
and asked her to take them away.
And then he started telling her
about a lost eskimo
who paddled up the Don in a kayak.
He was dressed in sealskin,
and very tired. After a few days,
he caught a cold and died.

The dip dip dip of the little boat,
and his sad story-telling voice,
were like a lullaby,
and she was asleep, or nearly asleep,
when suddenly he asked her
if she believed in God.
(She told me all this quite openly—
the old Russian grandmother,
half lying back on her cushions.

Perhaps I shouldn't say this, she said,
but listen to me for a moment—
if you wake up,
and feel something fat like a puppy
wriggling between your legs,
you're not going to say it's God,
or the answer to all your questions,
or Love, are you? It's sex!
It was the same for him.)   [1984]

JACK MAPANJE

Malawi b. 1945

Born in Kadango in southern Malawi, Mapanje was educated there and in Britain and taught at
Chancellor College in Zomba. In 1971 he was one of the founders and an editor of *ODI*, a journal
of Malawi literature. Although Mapanje's poems are sometimes rooted in African settings and
traditions, his gaze also sweeps over a larger arena, as in 'On Being Asked to Write a Poem for 1979',
which opens: 'Without kings and warriors occasional verse fails/Skeletal Kampuchea children star-
ing, cold/Stubborn Irish children throwing grenades/ . . . Today no poet sufficiently asks why dying
children/Stare or throw bombs.' His first book of poems was *Of Chameleons and Gods* (1981).

AT THE METRO: OLD IRRELEVANT IMAGES

(for Blaise)

They are still so anthropologically tall here
Still treating you in irrelevant tribal metaphors:
Somalis have softer skins, they drink milk; they say
(And yours is cracking, you drink *kachasu*!)

Even the most knowledgeable still slip back
Apologizing to you in banal Tarzan images:
The children still know mostly Tarzans at school; they say
(Tarzans choked me too in the fifties, damn it!)

But the College girls' sit-in about rapists was
A bit of a change, and Mrs Thatcher's et cetera
Against overseas students; and, the publisher's dinner!
(How are the jacarandas I left blooming, otherwise?)   [1981]

BRONWEN WALLACE

Canada 1945–1989

Wallace lived most of her life in Kingston, Ontario, where she worked in a centre for battered women. Her poetry, which favours an artfully colloquial narrative line, records the quiet pain and inarticulateness of everyday lives. Wallace's books of poems include *Signs of the Former Tenant* (1983), *Common Magic* (1985), and *The Stubborn Particulars of Grace* (1987); her collection of short fiction, *People You'd Trust Your Life To*, appeared in 1990.

THE WOMAN IN THIS POEM

The woman in this poem
lives in the suburbs
with her husband and two children
each day she waits for the mail and
once a week receives
a letter from her lover
who lives in another city
writes of roses   warm patches
of sunlight on his bed
Come to me he pleads
I need you and the woman
reaches for the phone
to dial the airport
she will leave this afternoon
her suitcase packed
with a few light clothes

But as she is dialing
the woman in this poem
remembers the pot-roast
and the fact that it is Thursday
she thinks of how her husband's face
will look when he reads her note
his body curling sadly toward
the empty side of the bed

She stops dialing and begins
to chop onions for the pot-roast

but behind her back the phone
shapes itself insistently
the number for airline reservations
chants in her head
in an hour her children will be

home from school and after that
her husband will arrive
to kiss the back of her neck
while she thickens the gravy
and she knows that
all through dinner
her mouth will laugh and chatter
while she walks with her lover
on a beach somewhere

She puts the onions in the pot
and turns toward the phone
but even as she reaches
she is thinking of
her daughter's piano lessons
her son's dental appointment

Her arms fall to her side
and as she stands there
in the middle of her spotless kitchen
we can see her growing
old like this
and wish for something anything
to happen   we could have her go
mad perhaps and lock herself
in the closet   crouch there
for days her dresses withering
around her like cast-off skins
or maybe she could take
to cruising the streets at night
in her husband's car
picking up teenage boys
and fucking them in the back seat
we can even imagine
finding her body
dumped in a ditch somewhere
on the edge of town

The woman in this poem offends us
with her useless phone and the persistent
smell of onions   we regard her as we do
the poorly calculated overdose
who lies in a bed somewhere
not knowing how her life drips
through her drop by measured drop

we want to think of death
as something sudden
stroke or the leap
that carries us over the railing
of the bridge in one determined arc
the pistol aimed precisely
at the right part of the brain
we want to hate this woman

but mostly we hate knowing
that for us too it is
moments like this
our thoughts   stiff fingers
tear at again and again
when we stop in the middle
of an ordinary day and
like the woman in this poem
begin to feel
our own deaths
rising slow within us   [1983]

TOM WAYMAN

Canada b. 1945

Winner of the A.J.M. Smith Prize for 'distinguished achievement in Canadian poetry' in 1976, Wayman has been Canada's major practitioner of poetry about work—how work defines, distorts, or inspires most lives. His verse is often narrative, wry, and ironic, relying less on metaphor or tightly-controlled diction than on colloquial rhythms. Wayman's first book of poetry, *Waiting for Wayman* (1973) was followed by, among others, *Free Time* (1977), *Living on the Ground: Tom Wayman Country* (1980), *Counting the Hours: City Poems* (1983), and *In a Small House on the Outskirts of Heaven* (1989).

SAVING THE WORLD

They had just tied up the tug at Creston
he said, secured the logs at the booming ground
under the bridge. They heard a cry
as though from an animal
in trouble. And again.
He got the boom boat driver
and they turned on the searchlight
and cast off to see what it was.

In the beam of the lamp, they found
someone had thrown a dog from the bridge,
a pup whose muzzle had been tied shut

so tightly its teeth
had been driven into the bleeding flesh
of the mouth. Its forepaws were crossed
and bound hard together with rope
and its back legs also were lashed together.
But the dog had survived the fall,
terrified, barely able to make a sound,
bobbing on the water alongside the boom, head up
then head under. They backed the boat closer
but their wash drove the animal below the surface
once more, and when he fished it out
and slashed through the wet cords
its eyes went flat and rigid
and it died. And he said
he stood cursing, knife in his hand
anyone who could treat a dog like this
would do the same to a child or woman
or a helpless man.

         And as he told me of his rage
I remembered this sailor's grief
for his own children
lost twice in the ruptured tubes
of his wife,
and my children
lost in abortion and
indecision, and
thought it for the best.
Then I recalled his anger
that the world needs,
that has to be passed on.

So much left to do.

The tortured dog on the deck.   [1987]

ROBERT BRINGHURST

USA/Canada b. 1946

Bringhurst was born in Los Angeles to Canadian parents, and has been as peripatetic in his learning as in his travels, although he has settled on the coast of British Columbia since the early seventies. Everything nourishes Bringhurst; in *Pieces of Map, Pieces of Music* (1986) he reflects: 'Biology, physics, mathematics, the painting of paintings, the telling of myths, metaphysical reasoning—all of these are ways of listening to and speaking with the world. They are aspects of intelligence. What else is poetry for?' *The Beauty of the Weapons* (1982) offers a generous selection of Bringhurst's work.

THESE POEMS, SHE SAID

These poems, these poems,
these poems, she said, are poems
with no love in them. These are the poems of a man
who would leave his wife and child because
they made noise in his study. These are the poems
of a man who would murder his mother to claim
the inheritance. These are the poems of a man
like Plato, she said, meaning something I did not
comprehend but which nevertheless
offended me. These are the poems of a man
who would rather sleep with himself than with women,
she said. These are the poems of a man
with eyes like a drawknife, with hands like a pickpocket's
hands, woven of water and logic
and hunger, with no strand of love in them. These
poems are as heartless as birdsong, as unmeant
as elm leaves, which if they love love only
the wide blue sky and the air and the idea
of elm leaves. Self-love is an ending, she said,
and not a beginning. Love means love
of the thing sung, not of the song or the singing.
These poems, she said. . . .
                    You are, he said,
beautiful.
            That is not love, she said rightly.   [1982]

CHRYSTOS

Menominee/USA/Canada b. 1946

Chrystos is a self-educated writer, artist, and activist who lives in British Columbia. Her poetry, written out of her uncompromising determination to 'Make words, not war!' has appeared in anthologies of lesbian and indigenous women's writing, and in two collections: *Not Vanishing* (1988) and *Dream On* (1991).

CEREMONY FOR COMPLETING A POETRY READING

This is a give away poem
You've come gathering   made a circle with me of the places
I've wandered   I give you   the first daffodil opening
from earth I've sown   I give you warm loaves of bread baked
in soft mounds like breasts   In this circle I pass each of you
a shell from our mother sea   Hold it in your spirit   Hear
the stories she'll tell you   I've wrapped your faces
around me   a warm robe   Let me give you ribbonwork leggings
dresses sewn with elk teeth   moccasins woven with red
& sky blue porcupine quills
I give you blankets woven of flowers & roots   Come closer
I have more to give   this basket is very large
I've stitched it of your kind words
Here is a necklace of feathers & bones
a sacred meal of chokecherries
Take this mask of bark which keeps out the evil ones
This basket is only the beginning
There is something in my arms for all of you
I offer this memory of sunrise seen through ice crystals
Here   an afternoon of looking into the sea from high rocks
Here   a red-tailed hawk circles over our heads
One of her feathers drops for your hair
May I give you this round stone which holds an ancient spirit
This stone will soothe you
Within this basket is something you've been looking for
all of your life   Come take it   Take as much as you need
I give you seeds of a new way
I give you the moon shining on a fire of singing women
I give you the sound of our feet dancing
I give you the sound of our thoughts flying
I give you the sound of peace moving into our faces & sitting down
Come   This is a give away poem
I cannot go home
until you have taken everything & the basket which held it
When my hands are empty
I will be full

[1988]

TONY CURTIS

Wales b. 1946

Curtis is Senior Lecturer in English at the Polytechnic of Wales, an editor of the arts magazine *Madog*, chair of the English-language section of *Yr Academi Gymreig*, and winner of a 1984 National Poetry Competition. His earlier verse is represented in *Selected Poems 1970–1985* (1986); his most recent is *The Last Candles* (1989). Intrigued by the quiet musings of the reluctant traveller and the displaced person, he is particularly adept at capturing the voice of the 'accidental tourist' just 'passing through'.

THOUGHTS FROM THE HOLIDAY INN

(for John Tripp)

'When you're dead, you're bloody dead.'
We both liked the punch of that one, John, said
Ten or more years ago by an author breaking
Through his fiction, kicking the rules, risking
All our willing disbelief to shock through
To the truth. B.S. Johnson, that sad and tortured man, knew
The whole thing to be by turns a joke, by turns the need
To love each other into something close to sense. We bleed,
John, we bleed, and time bleeds from our wrists.
Your death was shocking, and tidies up another lovely, angry (when pissed),
Poet of a man, who would not, for anyone, be tidied into respectability
Longer than an evening, or his allotment in some anthology.
There's too much to be said, by too many, too soon.
But from this lunchtime watering place, this unlikeliest of rooms,
Spare me the modest time and space—by Christ, you've enough
Of both in death old mate—to work things out, sound off—
About the months you've missed, the months that we've missed you.
You'd have seen this place go up, the skyline that you knew
Transformed, jagged, blocked as urban planners brought rationality
To what the coal century had grown and shaped to the Taff's estuary.
We've needed you here, John, thrusting out your neck and stroking the chin
From a classy, fraying shirt to show the disdain we hold these people in,
These late-comers to a country and a nation in a mess.
They've given us the bum's rush today, John, I must confess.
We checked out the place for next year's Literature Festival
And sponsorship. As far as we could tell
It was a waste of time, for any management
Who'd given Sickle-Cell Research the thumbs down were clearly bent
On profit, and to hell with charity, never mind cultural P.R.
Well fed and disappointed, we returned to the bar.
Still, they'd named the two big function rooms, the 'Dylan Suite'
And 'Gwyn Jones Room'. 'Don't know him,' said the manageress,
    with complete

Honesty. 'He's one of our Academy's most distinguished senior members,'
I said, and thought, We do no more than blow upon the embers,
We scribblers who'd want to claim
That everything in Wales for praise or blame
Is brought to life and fact and mythical creation
By that writerly mix of ego and the grasp of a tradition.
What use we prove, the weight the world gives us, if any,
Is likely to be cheap and grudging, no more than a blunt penny
Flung to shut our mannered, metred whining.
Then, later, taken up again shining
From the rubbing our tongues and lives impart.
I hear you answer, John, 'It's a start, boy, some sort of bloody start.'
John, further down the Hayes, now I think of you, haunting those benches
And passing a coffee or the length of a fag below the rich stenches
From Brains's brewery snugged in behind the Royal Arcade.
As the big internationals move in and build and build the shade
And sunlight shift position down the city's roads.
In spruced-up Bute (re-named, as Tiger Bay encodes
A docklands past we'd best forget or sanitise
In tarted-up pubs or tree-lined low-rise
Flats—*The Jolly Tar* or *Laskar's Close*)
The men who clinch the deals, the gaffers, the boss
With the tax-free Daimler, the Series Seven,
Square out the mazy city into real estate concepts, proven
Returns for their money. They are gilt-edged applicants
For Euro-funds, Welsh Development grants.
This hotel is for the likes of them. It stretches eye to eye
With the brewery's silver funnel, two hundred bedrooms in the sky
Starting at fifty quid the night. 'Fat cats,' I hear you say,
'And that's before your breakfast. Stuff the fucking pool, O.K.'
Tax payer's rage? John, even you, an occasional connoisseur
Of hotel fitments and glimpses of the soft life, would incur
A gullet-sticking at this pricey junk, mock-Grecian style
Arches, columns, thick marble-facings done in tiles,
Plush, deep divans around an open fire beneath a metal canopy,
Surrogate logs you'd hardly warm your hands upon. You'd see
Beyond, the indoor pool, functional, gaunt,
More marble, sharp angles with, each end, broken columns to flaunt
The facile version of classic decor money'll buy
And set down in a city anywhere, across a sky
Or ocean. Continent to continent there must be travellers
Who need the reassurance of such nondescript pools and bars,
To step off the plane or train, taxi down concrete tracks
To what the Telex reservation guarantees predictable: stacks
Of credit-cards accepted, pool-side temperature just O.K.
An in-house movie they choose and relay
To each room in American or English—God forbid

The native patois—*(These people down here, the Welsh—did*
You say—a language all their own—an ancient tongue?
—King Arthur—well, I saw a movie when I was a kid, sung
The songs all that summer—Danny Kaye—got it!)
John, what kind of progress is all this shit?
They took the coal-miners and put 'em in a coal museum:
And the people drove down, coughed up three quid ten just to see 'em.
Tourists one-nighting en route the Beacons, Bath or Ireland:
'Cardiff—what's that?' 'The airport . . . it's halfways there. I planned
To break the trudge from Heathrow.' And what of the locals?
Lunchtimes bring yuppies of both sexes, the gals
Waft in like *Cosmo* covers, the men have knife-
Creased casuals, hook their index fingers through the keyrings of life.
And there's the midday nibblers, women past their prime
But dressed to the nines and painted, passing the time
Between Howells' upholstery and Hones and Jones with a small gin
And sandwich triangles of horseradish and smoked salmon,
Piquant, hardly fattening. Their cigarette smoke curls
Away with the suggestion of rope, these former good-lookers, girls
Who, thirty years before, bagged a man of promise or means
And moved up, to Cyncoed, out to Lisvane, a pool, lawns
Done by a man who brings his own machine and strips
His shirt in the long afternoons. They tip
Him with the last cut of September.
Their husbands are on the board and successfully bored. 'Remember,'
They'd say, 'when we had that little detached in Newport,
And we'd spend Sundays, you mowing and me trimming.' 'I've fought
Hard to get this far, and Christ, there's times I wonder,
What for? What have we got? Where's it gone? Just blunder
On to the next rung, dinner party, contract, barbecue.'
'Love, you're working too hard. Is the company proving too much for you?'
John, excuse this indulgence, that clumsy fiction, it's no digression,
I'm still concerned to understand progression.
When working-class is all you've known
These rich fish cruise by bright-coloured (if overblown)
Distracting—but these too are tenants of the pool
You plunged your wit and pen into. Fool
No one was your aim, and at last came the anger of *Life Under Thatcher.*
But winos in the Hayes betray a watcher
Who'd sum up the whole state of things in verses.
It's too easy to shoot off steam in curses
That pepper the mark but fail to penetrate.
Guys with real assets, clever portfolios, are immune to street hate;
They justify themselves in terms of respectability, vision, advancement.
The world's an oyster if you lift your nose off the pavement.
They've bought themselves out of the firing line.
Windows purr close, revs slipping the motor into fifth gear, it feels fine

To loosen out along the motorway—weekends in Pembs.
Or, turning right, over the Bridge, a trim two hours to dine by the Thames.
No one's rooted anymore, John, as you must have known—
'The old man' coming to smith in Taffs Well in the 30s where you'd grown
Up Welsh, not Cornish like him, in all but the language.
(The wounding of that loss, it seems, no achievements can assuage.)
And, because of that, confused, determined and concerned
As the rest of us, excluded from the *Gorsedd* but feeling you'd earned
The right to sound off for this Wales—Taffs and Gwerin,
To voice the peculiar place of the eighty per cent. The din
Of justified protest settled after '79—Welsh cheque books, Channel Four.
The nationalist drummings the Sixties saw you working for
You realised later were too easy, too raw. Like R.S.
You loved the country with a passion, an anger, but the less
Misty, period-costume work will surely prove the best,
The more enduring; real poetry 'welcoming the rough-weather guest'.
John, I would rather have seen your ashes ebb from Barafundle
Bay. That grey day at Thornhill we watched your coffin trundle
Behind the curtains to the kind of anonymity
You'd rail against for other 'botched angels', losers we
Turn away from, society's mistakes, the hard-done-to,
Underdogs you wanted to feel close to.
The glow of a cupped-hand fag was light enough to draw
You to some alley, a derelict huddled there against a door,
One of the Hollow Men, a voter with no vote
Wrapped in old woollens, *Echoes* stuffed inside an overcoat.
'Cold enough, butt, eh? on the street. Here, have yourself a cuppa.
Take care, old fella, and watch out for the copper.
Those bastards aren't for the likes of us,
They don't give a tinker's cuss
As long as things stay down and quiet, and everything's neat.
You and me'll keep to the shadows, butt, and stay light on our feet.'
I've a feeling poetry's not the thing most apt
To dissect society, or politicise an audience one imagines trapped
In wilful ignorance, lobotomised by the trashy press,
Disenfranchised by the soapy box, seduced by the caress
Of the goodish life in the second half of this softening century.
You, fellow sprinter, took your chance through readings—could be
Five or fifty listeners, in club, gallery, college, school.
But articles in the London nationals, plays on the TV as a rule
Work most action, albeit short-lived. We
Poets light shower-burning fuses or rockets you see
Flash and quickly fade as the moment's charged
And spent. John, you saw the first decade of this city enlarged,
Pulled into the dream-shape someone thought we needed.
At fifty-nine who's to say you'd not changed things, not succeeded
In stirring up whatever stuff this corner of the pool had in suspension?

Talk of booze, too little care taken of yourself, prevention
Of the heart's explosion that took you in the early hours
With McGuigan's fight won and the tele drizzling showers
Of grey flakes down its mute screen,
Won't bring you back. You slid away. The barely-tuned machine
Packed up. Unlike Dylan, no insult to the brain, John. Often we'd talk
Of going to the States, whistle-stopping, the Chelsea in New York,
Our tour for the Yanks, I could have rigged.
Yes, if I'd pushed it, we two in tandem could have gigged
Over there. Like a lot of the others, I chickened out, I suppose.
Pembrokeshire a couple of nights—you with no change of clothes,
Just a battered attaché, poems, toothbrush, fags—
Was the limit of my stamina for your ways. Memory drags
Such petty guilts to the fore.
Though I treasure and feed off that reading we did on the man o'war,
Reluctant sailors pouring export ale down us
To forestall the poetry (they did) drown us
With hospitality in the middle of Fishguard harbour
Until we staggered past the missiles in her belly's store
Up to the frigate's redundant forward gun-turret, officers dressed
In cummerbunds, and elegant women. The talk was veiled, but impressed
Words like 'Responsibility', 'Capability' and 'Global role'. 'Yes, but
What do you do with all this training? All the missiles, shit-hot
Fire-power?' I remember, he answered you with, 'We can blow Fishguard
Away with each one, you know. We are, I suppose, a "hard
Fist gloved by our democratic masters".' John, before the evening ended—
You topped that with a poem scribbled on a cigarette pack. We descended
A precarious ladder to the launch with those lines of his and yours sinking
Into the night. And now, a decade later, the story has a ring
Any writer could tune. Perhaps that's what your Sandeman Port inquisitor
Pointed to—after the jaunts and applause, the writer's for
Filling the void, putting structure into space, a kind of race
Against apathy and oblivion. Too grand, you say, too heroic? Let's face
It, John, we've both indulged in our 'intervals of heat'
On the page and off. Both been chilled by the thought one couldn't beat
The odds, stuck in Wales, chiselling verse, weak in the flesh.
We're out on the edge of the world's concern, no Wall St, no Long Kesh.
Unless the challenge here is also to connect—radar dishes at Brawdy,
Hinkley over the water, Trawsfynydd, the poison brought in on our sea.
An *Anglo*, dipped in England's sewer should still produce the goods.
Albeit in 'invisible ink / on dissolving paper . . .' one loads
The futile quarto, pushes it out to travel or sink.
Standing here before the Holiday Inn, and its shiny 0–3–0, I think
How my grandfather, before the Great War, shunted down to Wales on the G.W.R.
How arbitrary one's identity is: with voice and gesture we are
Challenged to make sense of where and what we find ourselves. No
Border guards patrol the Dyke, no frontier seals us in at Chepstow.

Did you really ever want that, John, seriously?
From here I have to question that stance. Were you quite as you appeared to be?
This locomotive worked the sidings in Cardiff and the junction,
Was scrapped at Barry and now is made to function
As an image of our hard-bitten history. *9629*, freshly painted green and black,
Her valves de-gutted, holds to her half-dozen yards of track:
No driver on the footplate, no steam, no destination,
This featureless hotel her final station,
Under the flags of Canada, Commerce and the Dragon.
I turn around. On the island in the Hayes a wino tilts his flagon
And light flashes from the moment.   [1989]

PATRICK FRIESEN

Canada b. 1946

Friesen is one among the generation of contemporary Manitoba poets finding in their Mennonite backgrounds both a source for artistic expression and a powerful impediment to it. Friesen's poems inform a conversational idiom with quiet meditations on grace, love, and loss, on spirit and the flesh. Friesen has also written plays (*The Shunning*, 1985 and *The Raft*, 1992); among his books of poems are *bluebottle* (1978), *Unearthly Horses* (1984), *Flicker and Hawk* (1987), and the most recent and representative collection, *Blasphemer's Wheel: Selected and New Poems* (1994).

talking new york: waiting on love

seems though that words are dead and me standing here with
    empty pockets and a mouthful of stone
you'd think I'd be humbled by this but I have no inclination for
    the desert and humility's hard work
you never get used to the waiting not me waiting on love
    waiting on the words you serve
hell I'm not used to being on this planet never mind the
    ballroom or the intricacies of table talk
I'm still feeling my way around all tongue and hands and ears
    each cell looking for a way in or out
I'm still dealing with disbelief not in anything particular but a
    kind of daily incredulity
for me everything's still pretty incredible I mean I get mystified
    by the same things again and again
like there's something missing and search and destroy never
    finds it though it's got a cemeteryful of cadavers
and you can read the tombstones with your hands and you've
    learned nothing but you love the feel of the letters
and I figure there's nothing missing I just can't put a name to it
    and that's all to the good
it's something in the feel of those letters the feel of granite flat
    and angular as it slips grainy into an A

there's something there the skin and imagination working
   together for the sake of working together
and it's there in the breath that you bring to the keyboard the
   breath that works its way into the words
you can feel them shuffle or shimmy or hoof it the way they
   take off as the breath shines its way
and you don't have much to say it kind of caught on once you
   abandoned yourself to the rhythm
I don't have anything to say outside what I know and that
   keeps shifting with the years
what I mean is not always what I say we all know that but
   you've got to sing it or hum it you never know
and when it sounds just right the words don't harden as fast
   they drift like stray notes always getting away in time
and isn't that the way to be caught talking like this while I'm
   waiting for word from my love   [1994]

LEONA GOM

Canada b. 1946

Gom's most longstanding contribution to Canadian writing has been her poetry, which often
grows out of her roots in the Peace River area of Alberta. She is also a novelist and a teacher of
creative writing. Like her novels, her poems dramatize feminist visions of contemporary women's
condition, at times with a sharply ironic vision. Much of her work is represented in *The Collected
Poems* (1991).

UNIVERSITY

*'He's got a scholarship. . . . Mr Gates, your son's up into the middle-class now, and you won't be
speaking the same language. You know that, don't you?'*
                           Lessing, *The Golden Notebook*

Education an amulet
against the lives of our parents,
it seals our skins against the touch
of old rituals, presses us
into the corners of family gatherings,
fills our mouths with lumps
of harmless reminiscence.

You are different, they say,
you are changed,
too good for us now, they laugh,
needing our clumsy contradiction,
when we should say,
yes, it is all true,

our tongues unlearn daily
the vocabulary of crops and cattle,
there is less and less here
we can explain.

A head of barley:
what has it to do
with quadratic equations,
with medieval literature?
The day we left
we began to believe it,
and now our knowledge fits our hands
like a manicure
too expensive to soil
with the fact of these farms.
Yes, we should say,
it is all true,
we are no longer your children.

They will watch us leave them
and be afraid,
something they wished for
gone wrong,
like a crop so heavy
it lies down in the field.
That it is no easier for us
is the first
of our educated lies.

                                                                    [1984]

WAYNE KEON

Algonkin-Iroquois b. 1946

Keon was born in Pembroke and went to high school in the mining town of Elliot Lake, Ontario. Trained in business administration, he now makes his home in Toronto where he works as an auditor for a mining company. He has written a collaborative book of poetry with his father Orville and brother Ronald, *Sweetgrass* (1972), and a novel with his father, *Thunderbirds of the Ottawa* (1977). His poetry has appeared in many literary magazines in Canada; his most recent published collection is *Sweetgrass II* (1990).

I'M NOT IN CHARGE OF THIS RITUAL

i'm not in charge of this
sun dance anymore
i'm hangin here
completely out of it

the lawyers nd therapists
have taken over
my breasts are pierced
nd writhing in the blood
nd pain
i'm not that brave you know
that's why my children
nd woman were
taken from me
that's why i'm takin it on alone again
i never did any of those purification rituals
that's probably why this isn't working
nd hallucinations start sneakin
into my work, i can't say home
because i don't have a home
i live in a room
making medicine bags nd
wonderin if the silver strands
nd gems i'm puttin in them will do the trick
i escape temporarily at nite catching
my breath at donut & pizza shops
where nobody talks nd everyone just eats
munchin nd chewin nd swallowin down
hunger in the nite
hah ! despair wouldn't have the nerve to come
waltzin through the door here
it would be devoured whole
in one fat gulp
they're all lookin at me wonderin why
i'm so skinny nd still losing weight
they know i'm not one of them
but i'm there every nite
shakin over another cup of coffee
tired nd numb from another day of torture
i'm glad when the sun goes down
nd the crazy cool of dark comes
b'cos there's hardly anywhere left to hide
nd they'll find me in the morning
nd drag me back to the dance
in front of the sun
i wish i knew how long this was gonna take
but there's always tonite
nd ah ! there's always linda
always linda waitin in the nite
with smokey topaz eyes
with smokin lips nd thighs

pressed like a gem
from the earth
into mine
but even she's started lockin
her door at nite now   [1990]

KOJO LAING

Ghana b. 1946

Laing was born in Kumasi and educated at Glasgow University, after which he returned
to Ghana to work as an administrator with the government and, in the early eighties, with the Insti-
tute of African Studies at the University of Ghana. Most recently he has worked at a private school
in Accra. Laing's poetry takes delight in observation and reflection of local scenes and vignettes,
wherein a character's gestures and habits can be transformed into metaphysically significant acts,
while retaining their ground in the everyday. His poetry to date is collected in *Godhorse* (1989).

SENIOR LADY SELLS GARDEN EGGS

I love the lit corners of your kerosene smile,
your sympathy soft as new-boiled nkontommire
no whines come between you and this world, and
your large elbows take all the knocks possible. O
senior lady sits in the rain, sells
garden eggs with a sense of grace
under a wide hat wider than all my markets,
and the chewing-stick brushes
memories long dry with their own strength.
She meets life's one-wheel screams
with the subtlest roars in the land:
if you can't stop the rain
you can throw your own water up, or
store the biggest tank underground. Can
I too not give my floods direction, as
I watch you watch the deaths go by,
    watch the children grow like sugar-cane,
hard and sweet with your own dying.
I love the quiet corn boiling
as you look through its steam to far worlds,
your mind in a maze it loves, in prayers
spread on the waters like boats broad and dry.
Senior Lady sells garden eggs,
fights in her own way only when she must, and
she must; a slight almost hidden glint, in her eye,
        a tightening of the shoulders,
        a face set like shield or armour.

The water is flowing, stand back, you
can't be hard to a hard world forever, and
the great face shines
like the sun through morning mist, and strangely
the rain is caught in her large hands and sent home.   [1990]

BILL MANHIRE

New Zealand b. 1946

Born in Ivercargill and educated at Otago University and London's University College, Manhire
teaches at Victoria University. He comments: 'The chief joy of the shorter lyric I take to be its ability
to carry the reader out of the sequential, linear world into its own moment: as it were, Snap. . . .
If the vision granted is of meringues, equipped with legs and ankles (and somewhere, surely,
wrists), we must wave our cakeforks, and approve it'. Manhire's collections of poetry include
Zoetropes: Poems 1972–82 (1984) and *The New Land* (1990).

WELLINGTON

It's a large town
full of distant figures on the street
with occasional participation.
Someone buys some shares,
another gets a piece of the action.
Foreign languages are spoken.
A good secretary
is worth her weight in gold.
The man himself
is sitting on a little goldmine.
And down on Lambton Quay
the lads in cars go past, it's raining,
and the boys from Muldoon Real Estate
are breaking someone's arm.
They don't mean harm, really, it's
nobody's business, mainly free
instructive entertainment,
especially if you don't get close
but keep well back like
all the distant figures in the crowd.
So you watch what you can
but pretend to inspect with interest instead
the photographs of desirable private
properties, wondering how close they go
to government valuation. That one's nice.
The question is, do you put your hands
above your head or keep them

in your pockets. Do you want a place
without a garage, could you manage
all those steps. The answer is
the man would simply like you off the streets.
You haven't even got a window
and his is full of houses.   [1982]

PARTY GOING

It's lonely in the world
when all you get is pity.
The grass is tall and straight
and sometimes waving in the wind.
It grows around the sleeping lovers
and though the police are coming
they somehow look remoter. The last time
I saw you, you said you really
wanted to go home but you had this feeling
you were being followed. You were
half in darkness, half in light,
going outside with all the others.   [1982]

MIGUEL PIÑERO

Puerto Rico/USA b. 1946

Piñero was born in Gurabo, Puerto Rico, and raised on New York's Lower East Side where he still
lives. Self-educated, Piñero is a Nuyorican poet, actor, and playwright; he has received New York
Drama Critics Circle, Obie, and Tony awards for his work.

THE BOOK OF GENESIS ACCORDING TO SAINT MIGUELITO

Before the beginning
God created God
In the beginning
God created the ghettos & slums
and God saw this was good.
So God said,
'Let there be more ghettos & slums'
and there were more ghettos & slums.
But God saw this was plain
so
to decorate it
God created leadbase paint
and then
God commanded the rivers of garbage & filth

to flow gracefully through the ghettos.
On the third day
because on the second day God was out of town
On the third day
God's nose was running
& his jones was coming down and God
in his all knowing wisdom
he knew he was sick
he needed a fix
so God
created the backyards of the ghettos
& the alleys of the slums
& heroin & cocaine
and
with his divine wisdom & grace
God created hepatitis
who begat lockjaw
who begat malaria
who begat degradation
who begat
GENOCIDE
and God knew this was good
in fact God knew things couldn't git better
but he decided to try anyway
On the fourth day
God was riding around Harlem in a gypsy cab
when he created the people
and he created these beings in ethnic proportion
but he saw the people lonely & hungry
and from his eminent rectum
he created a companion for these people
and he called this companion
capitalism
who begat racism
who begat exploitation
who begat male chauvinism
who began machismo
who begat imperialism
who begat colonialism
who begat wall street
who begat foreign wars
and God knew
and God saw
and God felt this was extra good
and God said
'VAYAAAAAAAA'

On the fifth day
the people kneeled
the people prayed
the people begged
and this manifested itself in a petition
a letter to the editor
to know why? WHY? WHY? que pasa babyyyyyy?
and God said,
'My fellow subjects
let me make one thing perfectly clear
by saying this about that
         NO . . . COMMENT!'
but on the sixth day God spoke to the people
he said . . .'PEOPLE!
the ghettos & the slums
& all the other great things I've created
will have dominion over thee'
and then
he commanded the ghettos & slums
and all the other great things he created
to multiply
and they multiplied
On the seventh day God was tired
so he called in sick
collected his overtime pay
a paid vacation included
But before God got on that t.w.a.
for the sunny beaches of Puerto Rico
He noticed his main man satan
planting the learning trees of consciousness
around his ghetto edens
so God called a news conference
on a state of the heavens address
on a coast to coast national t.v. hook up
and God told the people
to be
COOL
and the people were cool
and the people kept cool
and the people are cool
and the people stay cool
and God said
'Vaya. . . .'   [1975]

PETER READING

England b. 1946

Reading's interest in newsprint conventions, typography, parodies of quantitative verse, and potentially anarchic combinations of poetic forms leads to precocious and arcane explorations. *Evagatory*, the hatchings of some kind of intergalactic voyaging and 'a sea-borne sorrowful history', recalls the satiric energy of the Swiftean Gulliver and presents the reader with an invitation to ride the curve of the opaque and the bizarre. Reading has written fifteen books of poetry, among them, *Tom O'Bedlam's Beauties* (1981), *Ukulele Music/Going On* (1985), *Stet* (1986), and *Evagatory*.

from EVAGATORY

[PROVINCE OF HYPERBOREAN BLEAKNESS]

    Province of hyperborean bleakness,
  Cranium. Roused by nightmare (in which
I am a butcher, cleaver repeatedly
    hacking your carcass, five-years-dead friend),
grief gushes raw again from an old lesion.

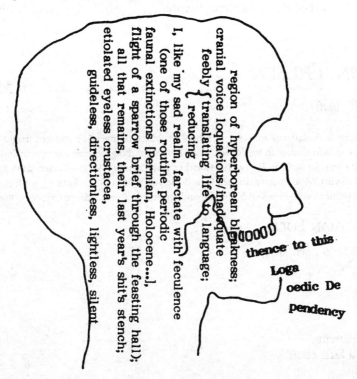

region of hyperborean bleakness;
cranial voice loquacious/inadequate
feebly {translating life to language;
      {reducing
I, like my sad realm, farctate with feculence
  (one of those routine periodic
faunal extinctions [Permian, Holocene...],
flight of a sparrow brief through the feasting hall);
all that remains, their last year's shit's stench;
etiolated eyeless crustacea,
  guideless, directionless, lightless, silent

thence to this Loga oedic De pendency

[EAST END OF LONDON . . .]

East End of London, where the indigenous
    practise a noteworthy brand of homicide—
fruit and veg hurled from speeding limos.
Melons, potatoes, cauliflowers, aubergines,
clutter the vegetarian headlines here:
    Turnip tops septuagenarian shopper,
    Juvenile jogger culled by cabbage.

[FOREST, SARAWAK, LIMESTONE OUTCROP]

Forest, Sarawak, limestone outcrop,
caverns of roosting Bornean horseshoe bats
(faeces of which are sifted by cockroaches);
one-and-a-half miles into the labyrinth,
    reservoir, stalactitic vaulting,
etiolated, eyeless crustacean,
    wheeze of a Tilley lamp near expiry.

Guideless, directionless, lightless, silence.   [1992]

SHARON THESEN

Canada b. 1946

Thesen was born in Saskatchewan, went to school in Prince George, BC, and has taught for
many years at Capilano College in Vancouver. Aside from publishing her own poetry—including
Confabulations: Poems for Malcolm Lowry (1984) and *Pangs of Sunday* (1990)—Thesen also edited
a collection of Phyllis Webb's poetry, *Selected Poems: The Vision Tree* (1982). Thesen's work traces
contemporary women's erotic lives with humour and anger, conveying a desire for poetry itself.

LOOSE WOMAN POEM

for Victoria Walker & Penny Kemp

A landscape
full of holes.
Women.
Pierced
ears voices piercing
the ceiling, a little choir
stung by wine:
I Fall to Pieces, and
Please Release Me.
After which I put on my old wedding band

& go to the party.
Next day 222's
& the moon falls out
of my fingernail.
The house smells like oysters
& a moon is on the loose
a woman in the bathtub   another
talking on the phone, their presence
shimmers, I'm fed up
with the wages of sin
put on some Mingus
& hepcat around

how come
it's always a question
of loss, being sick of self
displaced & frantic, chopped out
of the World of Discourse
waylaid
on the Bridge of Sighs, a net
work of connections coming down
to getting laid
or not getting laid & by whom.
Except getting laid
is not the way she thinks of it,
more like
something that her moons
can waylay waylay waylay
in the dark   [1980]

PO-IT-TREE

It live under the stars.

It be handsome man.

It gather the bay leaf
for a crown

It dance at the wedding party
up & down.

It love licorice ice cream cone

It hang out at the Roller Dome

It ask the book for an answer

It feel all alone.

It feel everything It be alive

It dream under the covers &

in the car

It laugh at the Polish joke

It sing along
with the singalong.

It map the heavens

It be handsome man

It gather the bay leaf
for a crown

It dance at the wedding party
up & down.   [1980]

PENNY WINDSOR

Wales b. 1946

Born in the West Country, Windsor settled in Swansea, where she worked as a teacher before becoming a full-time writer. She began publishing in journals like *Spare Rib* and *Poetry Wales*. Windsor employs a wry persona and straightforward diction to explore the perceptions of women as they discover their lives, 'tumbled into middle age/celebrating forty wayward years—/with confidence'. Windsor is an accomplished performance poet. Her books include *Dangerous Women* (1987) and *Like Oranges* (1989).

ADVICE ON PREGNANCY

What is pregnancy?
It's obviously an issue to be treated seriously
involving, as it does, the future of the human race.
The Magic of Pregnancy is much talked about
by men and superwomen
but here I offer a little practical advice
for the woman in the street.

First you will need the ability
to pee into a small bottle
accurately, before breakfast, and stop midstream
(remember to wash the bottle first or
expect a health visitor
relentlessly pursuing contaminated samples).

Secondly, an affinity with plastic dolls helps.
There are lots of these in the ante-natal clinic
all wearing nappies in different styles.

Thirdly, acquire a thorough knowledge
of all the public loos
exact location, cost and comfort.

Next, an ability to move bulk.
Placing a demi-john on a shelf
is good practice for travelling on a bus
Also try driving an overloaded lorry with care.

Fifth—Association.
Only associate with thin women
More than one pregnant/overweight woman
seen together
is a joke.

And sixth, don't let it show
or let it all show.
In pregnancy there is no middle way
a Bump is a Bump.

Seventh, don't worry about 'internals'
men are experienced at this kind of thing.

Lastly, *Learn the Signs.*
Chelsea buns and chips are not a normal meal
Five minute labour pains are not a) diarrhoea b) belated
      period pains c) cramp d) psychosomatic
Ignore advice that it's natural and doesn't hurt
also stories of African women and bushes—
these are the fantasies of male academics.
Note that the majority of husbands who faint during labour
      like large families
and that hospitals that want you to come again have a vested interest—
      ignore them.

and any advice to forget the pain, the inconvenience, the humiliation
WRITE IT DOWN

these are just some practical points to remember
about pregnancy and its magic.   [1990]

KOFI ANYIDOHO

Ghana b. 1947

Anyidoho, who teaches at the University of Ghana in Accra, draws much of his inspiration from the oral tradition of Ewe poetry in Ghana. His poetry is also intensely political; his first book, *Elegy for the Revolution* (1978), angrily mourns the failure of Ghana's revolution. Anyidoho's poetic idiom surprises with deft disruptions of his matter-of-fact narrative line, as in 'Last night on the village square a man/bumped into my conscience and cursed/our god' (in 'Soul in Birthwaters', i). His second book, *Harvest of Our Dreams* (1984), was followed by *Earthchild, with Brain Surgery* (1985).

from SOUL IN BIRTHWATERS (SUITE FOR THE REVOLUTION)

II. RADIO REVOLUTION

Again this dawn our Radio
broke off the vital end of sleep

Revolution!...............Devolution!...............Resolution!

grab a razor-sharp matchet
and step onto the paths of war

Across our yard I disturbed a courtship of
the dogs. They barked and backed away

through streets to all familiar walks
through maze of slums to armed barracks
of peace. Where? Where?
old peasant with hoe in hand, I
seek Revolution. Where is Revolution?
young veteran with blood across blue eyes, I
knew of no Revolution, but I
met Revolt limping down this road
chased by a howling herd of armed jackals
down this road down this road
to the market square where an only
pig searching for a morning meal
took me for a moving lump of flesh
and charged at me charged at me
with fangs sharpened by hunger's despair

I slashed her into two, wiped her
blood upon
            her head

down this road   down this road
to Dependence Square seeking Revolution
I found a lone symbol for Peace
a nameless bronze warrior with empty
gun pointing earthwards doing homage
to earth goddess

The school-boy news-pedlar leans against
a smile tells of how he came and found my doors
open my inner rooms unguarded in the dawn

I was out my dear
I was out seeking Revolution

Our Revolution, Sir? It's here in these
dailies. The headlines display it:

THE REVOLUTION—NOT A CONCERT PARTY

The photographs confirm it:

Statesmen at State Banquets
Proposing a toast to the health of State:
LONG LEAVE THE REVOLUTION!!!   Legon
                                                [1976]

PETER FINCH

Wales b. 1947

Author of seventeen collections of verse, including *Visual Texts 1970–1980* (1980) and *Some Music and a Little War* (1984), Finch is an experimentalist whose range includes performance, improvisation, and multimedia. Editor of *Second Aeon* from 1966–1974, *Typewriter Poems* (1972), and *Green Horse* (with Meic Stephens, 1978), Finch deploys his energy and iconoclasm to attack under the very cover of playfulness those crimes against humanity from which there is no recovery. For example, Finch marches his reader through onomatopoeic land mines that 'make the sound' of two hundred 'scrubbed', orphaned Jewish children, 'loaded on the freight cars' 'clean for Treblinka'.

VISUAL TEXT MAKES IT AS SUPER HERO

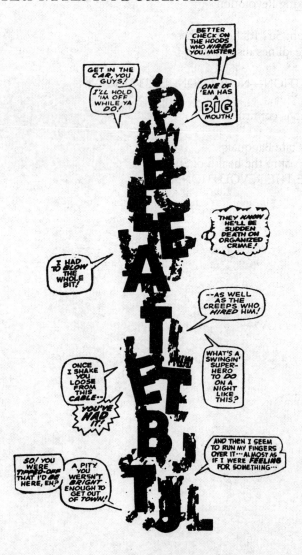

[1981]

VERONICA FORREST-THOMSON

Scotland 1947-1975

In her discussion of how the poet works to find the technical correlative for a theoretical position, Forrest-Thomson notes that the 'subject' in poetry is both form and content: 'because it is not the ideas merely but the actual linguistic forms that are to be the object of attention, the new kind of subject will be one that can be approached and even defined in terms of formal experimentation. The process is one of smashing and rebuilding the forms of thought.' Forrest-Thomson's *Collected Poems and Translations* appeared in 1990.

IDENTI-KIT

Love is the oldest camera.
Snap me with your eyes.
Wearied with myself I want
a picture that simplifies.

Likeness is not important
provided the traits cohere.
Dissolve doubts and contradictions
to leave the exposure clear.

Erase shadows and negative
that confuse the tired sight.
Develop as conclusive definition
a pattern of black and white.

For I wish to see me reassembled
in that dark-room of your mind.   [1967]

KERI HULME

New Zealand b. 1947

Hulme is of Kai Tahu heritage, and belongs to the Kati Rakiamoa and Ka Ruahikihiki groups. Born in Christchurch, she lives in Okarito, Westland where she fishes and writes short stories, novels, and poetry. Her collections of verse include *The Silences Between [Moeraki Conversations]* (1982), *The Bone People* (1984), *Lost Possessions* (1985), and *Te Kaihau/The Windeaters* (1986).

MUSHROOMS AND OTHER BOUNTY

[TE KAIHAU—2]

Picking mushrooms, grumbling over their pale heads
heavy and sodden-gilled from continuing rain

Still, they are chance-fruit
like naked frostfish found on bitter glittering mornings

the jewels of phrases I have been given
tossed away by careless strangers

and the real people who slid in from the black
at the back of my dreams, and played,
until I imprisoned them in words

Chance-fruit: what past bones
tuned my ears to catch the inner chant
of shining-cuckoo song?

And once, walking a sea-line yet again,
I caught the only whitebait of that tide
stranded by a sandbank in an errant finger of water
already cooked by the sun.

[1983]

LIZ LOCHHEAD

Scotland b. 1947

Painter and poet, interested in 'how the female poet—especially if she wasn't Sappho—could forge any sort of Muse for herself,' Lochhead moved inward, 'trusting the pull of familiar mother-tongue legendary, folk-tale oral traditions and making exactly the sort of "allusive" poetry' she had initially scorned. Lochhead sees herself as 'assertively and un-apologetically "feminist".'

SIX MEN MONOLOGUES

NO. 1: ANNEMARIE.

Men see men I've had it
Up to here absolutely
It's all off completely.
I said suppose that'll suit you fine I said
You can go out with your mates
Every night of the week and not just Thursdays
I said,
Look at the state of you
The beer's all going to your belly already
And coming from the West of Scotland you
Are statistically unlikely
even to reach the age of 25
without false teeth
And to tell the truth
Since we got engaged

You never bother with the Brut
or the good suit I said
I'm sick to the backteeth of
Every time we go for a Chinese
You order
chicken and chips, fried egg and peas.
I said No way
Believe me the only way I'd ever consider
The World Cup in Mala-bloody-ga
For my honeymoon
Is if I was guaranteed
An instant trade you in for a
Six foot shit-hot sharp shooter that never failed to hit the spot.
I told him where to stick his bloody
One carrot diamond-is-forever.

I blame his mother.

No. 2: PAMELA.

Men, my boyfriend says, Honest-to-God he says men huvn't got it any
easier than women these days! He says men aren't any more sure and secure
within their own sexual identity. Oh naw, not by a long, long chalk. And yiv
got tae watch not tae laugh at them, huvn't yi. Everybody knows if yi laugh at
a man in That Way he will wilt for ever, willn't he?

I was reading this article in a Playboy Magazine round at my boyfriend's
place, or was it Penthouse, anyway, I seem to be spending quite a lot o' time
round at my boyfriend's reading magazines and here it says how these several
top U.S. psychiatrists had done this survey on how your emotions can
sabotage your sexlife even if you *are* a man and here it blamed the sexually
aggressive female of the seventies for the sexual recession of the eighties. No,
apparently it's world wide. Even in Italy these days women are failing to feel
the pinch. The article says there was a definite swing away from swinging and
back to the values of the fifties. Apparently people are even going back to the
fifties contraceptives! Supposed to be that this whole you know, Ronald
Reagan, Swing-to-the-Right, Fun-Fashion, Fifties thing disny stop at the
glitter-sox the roll-ons and the lurex! It says people were turning again to the
old tried and true spices of Guilt and Feeling Dirty and Furtiveness And Stuff
in a frantic attempt to resurrect the whole sad affair.

My boyfriend says that ladies like me huv been just too liberated for our
own good. Just you mark my words, he says, the Worm Will Turn.

No. 3: JUDITH.

Men said the small ad in the wants column
am I expecting too much
lady fifty one tall shapely separated
genuine gregarious aware

varied interests vegetarian (own muesli-mix)
New Statesman reader romantic sincere
Wishes to share
simple sunshine and undemanding companionship
(view marriage) with
comfortable mature strong nonsmoker sincere
adventurous male graduate music-lover (radius Hampstead
    ten miles)
Whole life spent searching for him.
Lady seeks soulmate (or sim.)

No. 4: KIMBERLEY.

Men said the Cosmogirl (eyes
lighting up like dollarsigns in Vegas)
Men And How To Hook Them by Tamara Gogetter M.D.
Sip your dulep,
slick another coat of Golddigger Red on your fingernails,
Now Read On . . .
'A good substitute for a silverspoon is a
castiron nerve and wherever the Beautiful People are
Be There—
even if you have to hock your last
Hermes scarf to raise the fare.
(P.S. spas are passé and so is San Trop).
Consider Best Bars as a first resort,
regard the single cocktail you'll shell out for as
sheer investment, get yourself
gift wrapped, send for our jetset silklook shirt,
rid yourself of
even that inch-of-pinch and the
body beautiful will be guaranteed bait for
ace race driver or millionaire financier in advanced stages of
    senility.
(Offer subject to availability.)

No. 5: MO.

Men says My Boss
are definitely more dependable
and though even in these days of equal pay
men tend to come a wee bitty more expensive
due to the added responsibility a man tends to have
in his jobspecification
Well for instance you can depend on a man not to get
pregnant.
My Boss says men are more objective.
Catch a man bitching

about healthhazards and conditions
and going out on strike over no papertowels in the toilet
or nagging over the lack of day nursery facilities
My Boss says as far as he's concerned a crêche is a motor accident in
    Kelvinside
and any self respecting woman should have a good man
to take care of her so its only pinmoney anyway
and that's bound to come out in the attitude.
Well a man isn't subject to moods
or premenstrual tension a guy
isn't going to phone in sick with some crap about cramps.
My Boss says a man rings in
with an upset stomach and you know either
he means a hangover or else his brother
managed to get him a ticket for Wembley.

You know where you are with a man.

No. 6: BETTE.

Men said the housewife
(Waiting for the coffee to perk)
Honestly, Muriel, men!
(Wringing her apron in mock indignation)
That's the third time this week I've picked his
Good polyester-dacron trousers up off the floor and
Hung them up in their crease.
What's the use?
Doesn't lift a finger, does David
Never a handsturn from him, believe me.
The kitchenette is a closed book.
Don't you be downtrodden Muriel.
Make that clear from the start.

Men, honestly, wee boys at heart.
Men!   [1985]

ARVIND KRISHNA MEHROTRA

India b. 1947

Mehrotra's collections include *Middle Earth* (1984) and *The Absent Traveller* (1991), a book of
collaborative translations. He is currently professor of English at Allahabad University and is the edi-
tor of *The Oxford India Anthology of Twelve Modern Indian Poets* (1992) and co-editor of *Periplus*, a
volume of and about poetry in translation (1993). Mehrotra's experimentation with the avant garde
involves imagist collage and assemblage techniques, typographic rhetorics, surrealistic accidents,
and 'free associations'; he is especially interested in how memory conspires against clock time.

THE SALE

I
It's yours for the price, and these
old bits have character too. Today,
they may not be available.
Naturally I can't press you
to buy them, and were I not leaving
—you hear the sun choking with an eclipse—
I would never have thought of selling.
You may take your time though, and
satisfy yourself. Yes, this is Europe,
that America. This scarecrow Asia,
that groin Africa and amputated
Australia. These five, I don't have more.
May be another egg-laying island remains
in the sea. You remember in my letter
I wrote of forests—here they are,
wrapped in leaves and there should
be no trouble in carrying them.
This skull contains the rivers.
Of that I'm sorry. Had you come
yesterday I might have given you two.
I shall take another look. Yes,
I do have a mummy somewhere; only last
night came the pyramids and
knocked at my gate for a long time.

II
Do you mind if I show you
a few more things now yours?
Be careful, one river is still wet
and slippery; its waters continue to
run like footprints. Well, this is a
brick and we call that string.

This microscope contains the margins
of a poem. I have a map left, drawn
by migrating birds. In this
thumbed leaf wilts an epic.
Come into the attic.
That's not a doll—it's the
photograph of a brain walking
on sand and in the next one
it is wearing an oasis-like crown.
I must also show you a tiger's skin
which once hid a palace.
On one roof you will see
the antelope's horns rise;
on another the falling wind. These round
things are bangles and that long one
a gun. This cave is the inside
of a boot. And here
carved wheels turn through stone.

III
I wish you had asked me
earlier. The paintings have
just been bought by a broken mirror,
but I think I can lead you
to a crack in the wall.
I have a skeleton too.
It is full of butterflies
who at dawn will carry away
the crown.
I've also a wheel-chair to show
you, it belonged to my uncle once,
and one day the hook
which hangs from the sky
touched him. If you open the
cupboard you'll see his memory
on the upper shelves and two books
now yours.
Ruskin's Lectures on Art and a
Short History of English Literature by Legouis.
I'll take another minute.
Can you climb this ladder?
Well, that's the sun and moon.
And with this candle you can
work the clouds. I'm sorry I was
short of space
and had to pack The Great Bear

in this clock. Oh them,
let them not worry you.
They're only fisherman and king,
who will sail soon as one's bait
is ready and the other's dominion.   [1976]

M. NOURBESE PHILIP

Trinidad and Tobago/Canada b. 1947

Winner of the 1988 Casas de las Americas literary prize for poetry, university lecturer and lawyer
Nourbese Philip now lives in Toronto. Her poetry ventures into the related but, for Nourbese
Philip, uncharted and silenced territories of women's bodies and speech; in her most recent
volume these forays intersect with a re-imagined exploration of the 'dark continent' of Stanley's and
Livingstone's imaginations. Nourbese Philip also writes both fiction and essays; among other books
of poetry, she has published *As She Tries Her Tongue Her Silence Softly Breaks* (1989) and *Looking For
Livingstone: An Odyssey of Silence* (1991).

SOMEWHERE IN THE DARK CONTINENT

'Now see here, Stanley—this is *my* expedition—you just can't horn in on it
like that, you know. I want all the glory for myself, my God and my Queen.
Those falls were worthy of her name, now, weren't they?'
'Dr Livingstone, I only wanted a piece of the action—there's a whole damn
continent out there for the taking. You don't have to be so selfish.'
'You call *me* selfish—after all I have done for God, my country, and for the
natives—after I risked my life to bring them to the one God, the true God, the
only God—materialism!—you call me selfish? Go and discover something you
can call your own—give your name to a new race, a river, a mountain—what-
ever—conquer a piece of history you can call your own, but leave me alone.'
'Gimmie, gimmie never gets—come on, let's be men about this, Livingstone.
You and I will be forever linked, and Stanley and Livingstone has a better ring
about it than Livingstone and Stanley—so there.'
'Why are you stopping, men—carry on, carry on!'

FOR EXACTLY TWO HUNDRED YEARS NOW I HAD BEEN HAVING THE
SAME TWO RECURRING DREAMS—SOMETIMES ON ALTERNATE
NIGHTS, SOMETIMES ON THE SAME NIGHT—

HE—LIVINGSTONE—AND I COPULATE LIKE TWO BEASTS—HE
RIDES ME—HIS WORD SLIPPING IN AND OUT OF THE WET MOIST
SPACES OF MY SILENCE—I TAKE HIS WORD—STRONG AND THRUSTING
—THAT WILL NOT REST, WILL NOT BE DENIED IN ITS SEARCH TO FILL
EVERY CREVICE OF MY SILENCE—I TAKE IT INTO THE SILENCE OF MY
MOUTH—AND IN A CLEARING IN A FOREST HE SITS AND WEEPS AS
STANLEY COMFORTS HIM—

'I SAY, OLD CHAP, WHAT'S THE MATTER?'
'MY WORD, MY WORD IS IMPOTENT—'
'FUCK THE WORD, LIVINGSTONE.'
'THAT'S WHAT I'M TRYING TO TELL YOU, OLD CHAP—'
'I KNOW WHAT YOU'RE TRYING TO TELL ME, LIVINGSTONE, AND
I SAY FUCK THE WORD—A CONTINENT AWAITS US—EAGERLY—LIKE
A . . . LIKE A WHORE!'
'AND YOU A JOURNALIST, SIR—HOW CAN YOU SAY SUCH A THING?
DON'T YOU SEE, STANLEY, WITHOUT MY WORD, THE CONTINENT IS
BEYOND ME—BEYOND US?'

IN MY SECOND DREAM I AM HUGE AND HEAVY, BLOWN UP LIKE A
SOW ABOUT TO FARROW—THE FRUIT OF HIS WORD. PREGNANT FOR
ONE THOUSAND AND TWO YEARS—MY LABOUR AN AGONY THAT
LASTS FOREVER AS I STRUGGLE TO BIRTH—NOW SQUATTING, NOW
KNEELING, NOW SITTING, NOW WALKING—I GROAN AND GRUNT
LIKE THE ANIMAL I AM, KEENING AND WAILING I TRY TO BIRTH THE
MONSTROUS PRODUCT OF HIS WORD AND MY SILENCE—CONCEIVED
IN THE SILENCE OF MY OWN, MY VERY OWN WOMB.

*Journal entry written on the back of a camel on the sixth day of the ninth month in
the millionth Year of Our Word.*

Out out of my dreams, Dr Livingstone—go inhabit your own dreams—your
own silences. I become obsessed—oppressed—impressed? perhaps, with you
—a seeker like you—I'm off to the interior or perish, but I seem to be following
you—in your footsteps—or is it you who follows me—each becoming a
mirage to the other. I am determined to cure myself of you, Dr Livingstone
    —of this obsession
    —with silence
    —with the word—your word—engorging itself on my many, yet one,
silence, sucking it dry—the paps, the dried dugs of my silence that haunt
your turgid phallused word—

Was it the word
    In Mary's womb
Exploding
    Or the Silence
Of holy
In the desert that was
    Elizabeth
Seeded with Silence
    Barren
Shrivelled womb
    Refusing
The swell and

Split
In seed until
    Silence
Welcomes
The hungry word
    In again
And again
    The womb
Oasis of Silence
    Blooms   [1991]

ROBERTA HILL WHITEMAN

Oneida b. 1947

Whiteman holds degrees from the universities of Wisconsin and Montana. In a 1987 interview
with Abnaki poet Joseph Bruchac, Whiteman reflects upon her Oneida childhood in Wisconsin:
'even as children, . . . we have an intuitive sense of our own exile. We know this emotionally and
spiritually and we understand it. But it is never dealt with. . . . You'd never find . . . anyone telling
children, "You know, there's a reason why you feel this way. It's in history, it's a fact that you
feel this way".' Through imagination and memory, Whiteman's poetry integrates history and
estrangement as facts of the indigenous being. Her achievement is well-represented in the
collection *Star Quilt* (1984).

SCRAPS WORTHY OF WIND

I've walked those ruins and arranged
the ways I've died there
on scraps of paper worthy enough
for the wind. I've worked hard,
treading this lake that is my life,
floating with barely a breath
over the man-of-war's wave,
over these bubbles of death and departure.

In your letter you demanded I remember
the mirror I once shattered,
the tar from a street I fear. You taunt me
with losses I've mourned and put to rest.
You wrap them in innocent ribbons.
They wound with pink barbs.
Only one house remains
on the street where we played tag.

The witch still lives on the corner.
When she carries out the garbage, her hips stiffen
with pain. No one plays Dr Rhodie in her yard,

finally degraded into tar and liquor store.
Does it matter rats, large as terriers,
crept down that alley, or that a woman
cried herself graveward,
longing for the wind of a bayou?

I'm that woman from whose mouth
a long white string of mucus
unwinds on a stair. We cannot hate
ourselves enough to justify
that world. I wore blame
until it became my birthmark,
but no more.
Death comes soon enough.

Already its mason has laid a mosaic
in my womb. In dreams I sweep
the floors of universities and make the dust
leap down the empty halls. That bleak air
will never hold my dancing.
Doctors peer and tear.
With one more slice, they will it gone.
Gone, but never done.

Waist deep in dying, at last I understand
nothing is ever exactly the same.
We can't deny the ways we change.
I must run toward each moment
and learn to look at earth again,
learn how stars explore what's left them.
Just yesterday the night began to love me.
This morning I noticed how the sun shook loose
in the tall white beeches behind my house.
I welcome those trees, that shaft of light.
I welcome the long enduring night.
I welcome the witch in my elder tree.
A second ago, I heard her
singing, 'Bird on my branches,
little brown bird,
look for the fruit in the flower.'   [1984]

CIARAN CARSON

Ireland b. 1948

'Belfast Confetti', which comes from the 1989 collection of the same name, foregrounds the tragedy of a post-1968 Northern Ireland. It is the name given to the bricolage of nuts, bolts, and half-bricks that arms the protest Carson examines at close range. His technique combines the improvisational capabilities of a long poetic line with the circuitous route of the seanachie (the Irish storyteller). Musician (his *Pocket Guide to Irish Traditional Music* appeared in 1986) and former teacher, Carson is a Traditional Arts Officer for the Northern Ireland Arts Council and author of *The New Estate and Other Poems* (1988), a revised and enlarged version of the 1976 *The New Estate and The Irish For No* (1987).

BELFAST CONFETTI

Suddenly as the riot squad moved in, it was raining exclamation marks,
Nuts, bolts, nails, car-keys. A fount of broken type. And the explosion
Itself—an asterisk on the map. This hyphenated line, a burst of rapid fire . . .
I was trying to complete a sentence in my head, but it kept stuttering,
All the alleyways and side-streets blocked with stops and colons.

I know this labyrinth so well—Balaclava, Raglan, Inkerman, Odessa Street—
Why can't I escape? Every move is punctuated. Crimea Street.
    Dead end again.
A Saracen, Kremlin-2 mesh. Makrolon face-shields. Walkie-talkies. What is
My name? Where am I coming from? Where am I going? A fusillade
    of question-marks.   [1987]

NARRATIVE IN BLACK AND WHITE

Now take these golf balls, scattered all around the place, which since
The reproduction's blurred, you'd easily misconstrue as ping-pong—
You can't make out the dimples. But they're different as chalk and cheese:
Ever get hit by a golf ball? You'd know all about it. And perhaps
The golf club in the bottom corner is no give-away. People have been known
To mistake it for a gun. And the disembodied plus-fours
Might be army surplus. No, all these things are dangerous enough,
According to whose rules you play. Which is maybe why they're put there,
Where you'd least expect them, floating against the façade of the Europa.

Hotel, that is. You know it? Looks as if it's taken from a photograph,
Down to the missing E of the logo, the broken windows, which they only got
Around to fixing last week. Things drift off like that, or people drift in.
Like Treacy, who it's all about, according to the guy who painted it.
This splash of red here: not blood, but a port-wine stain or strawberry mark
That Treacy carried all his life, just here, above the wrist-watch. Any time
You saw him sitting, he would have his right hand over it. Like this.

Too easily recognised, he didn't like. This is where the black gloves
Come in, gripping the revolving foyer doors. Or maybe one of them
Is raised, like saying *Power*—to the people, to himself, whatever.

Billiard balls? Well, maybe. Certainly these random scratches on the canvas
Suggest the chalk-marks on a green baize, a faded diagram from which
You'd try to piece together what the action was. Like trying to account
For Treacy's movements. Though on the night in question, according to the
   barman
In The Beaten Docket, he'd staggered in from some win on the horses,
Slaps a tenner on the counter, and orders a 'Blue Angel'. Blue what?
Says the barman. Angel, Treacy says, Blue Bols, vodka, ice, a drop of sugar.
Oh, and top it up with whipped cream. I say this just to show the sort
Of him, like someone who a year or two ago would not have known cocktail
From a hen's arse. You're sure, the barman says, you wouldn't like a straw?

The staircase is important. The zig-zag is like taking one step forward,
Two steps back. For who would take the stairs up thirteen floors, when
He could take the lift? The reason why, the power had gone that night.
So only one way in, and one way out. As sure as meeting your own shadow.
This, I think, is what the mirror represents. Like, everybody knew about
   the split,
And what side Treacy ended up on. Of course, the detail's lost;
You have to see it like it is, original. The colours, the dimensions.
Even the frame, like someone spying through binoculars, is saying something:
I'm watching you; but you, you can't see me. Ping-pong. Yin-yang.

So here is Treacy, at the wrong end of the telescope, diminishing.
He was seen in this bar, that bar. Like what I'm saying is, that anybody
Might have fingered him. So the man on the thirteenth floor sits pat.
He draws back the curtain. He stares through the kaleidoscope of snow
And sees what's coming next. Treacy's footsteps. Game, set and match.
They found him in the empty room. The face was blown off. They rolled down
One black glove. A Rorschach blot. The Red Hand, as he called himself.
Me? I knew him like a brother. Once. But then our lives grew parallel, if
Parallel is never meeting. He started dressing up and talking down. What
He would and wouldn't do. And people don't go shooting off their mouths
   like that.   [1989]

LORNA CROZIER

Canada b. 1948

Crozier, who until 1981 published her poetry under the name Lorna Uher, was born in Swift Current, Saskatchewan; some of her poems draw on her intimate apprehension of the prairie landscape, climate, and culture. Crozier is a warm and witty poet. Her direct, charged language can be playfully erotic, or pulsing with anger recast as parodic denunciation, as in her mocking putdown of a swaggering macho-man, 'This One's For You'. Crozier won the Governor-General's Award for *Inventing the Hawk* (1992); among her other books are *Crow's Black Joy* (1978), and *The Garden Going On Without Us* (1985).

ON THE SEVENTH DAY

On the first day God said
Let there be light.
And there was light.
On the second day
God said, *Let there be light,*
and there was more light.

What are you doing? asked God's wife,
knowing he was the dreamy sort.
You created light yesterday.

I forgot, God said. *What can I do
about it now?*

Nothing, said his wife.
But pay attention!
And in a huff she left
to do the many chores
a wife must do in the vast
(though dustless) rooms of heaven.

On the third day God said
Let there be light. And
on the fourth and the fifth
(his wife off visiting his mother).

When she returned there was only
the sixth day left. The light
was so blinding, so dazzling
God had to stretch and stretch the sky to hold it
and the sky took up all the room—
it was bigger than anything

even God could imagine.
Quick, his wife said,
make something to stand on!
God cried, *Let there be earth!*
and a thin line of soil
nudged against the sky like a run-over serpent
bearing all the blue in the world on its back.

On the seventh day God rested
as he always did. Well, *rest*
wasn't exactly the right word,
his wife had to admit.

On the seventh day God
went into his study
and wrote in his journal
in huge curlicues and loops
and large crosses on the *t*'s
changing all the facts, of course,
even creating Woman
from a Man's rib, imagine that!
But why be upset? she thought.
Who's going to believe it?

Anyway, she had her work to do.
Everything he'd forgotten
she had to create
with only a day left to do it.
Leaf by leaf,
paw by paw, two by two,
and now nothing
could be immortal
as in the original plan.

Go out and multiply, yes,
she'd have to say it,
but there was too little room for
life without end,
forever and ever,
always, eternal, *ad infinitum*
on that thin spit of earth
under that huge prairie sky.   [1992]

KRISTJANA GUNNARS

Iceland/Canada b. 1948

Born in Iceland and raised there and in Denmark, Gunnars came to Canada in 1969. She worked in Winnipeg for a stint as a writer and translator, and currently teaches creative writing in Edmonton at the University of Alberta. Much of Gunnars's work—such as *Settlement Poems 1 and 2* (1980)—conjures up spare memories of her Icelandic ancestry and the harsh accommodation this close-knit immigrant community forged in Manitoba.

STEFÁN EYJÓLFSSON XIV

i'm down to collecting skeletons
bones with deeper relations
than flesh or skin, bones that show
how we live, seven

are dead at fridjón's, two
left, at ólafur's the third
baby swells in the gums
blood streaks the white teeth

scurvy cuts away the flesh
as cleanly as it can, removes
the skin, viscera, bones
too small, too delicate

to be touched hang together
by thin ligaments, tags
of leather separate the segments
the hatchets of disease do

rough work among us
cut the tendons that join
cheek bones, pelvic bones, deep
bones loosen like ribs

i'm buckling under, can't watch
ólafur's third one bruise, swell
thirty five are dead, every
third one of us, a child

a weak adult, the saw
of scurvy picks away
the eyes, scrapes the brain
out of the skull, washes out

the loosened brain, folds
the legs, limbs, ties up
the marrowed bones in rags
bones, deep bleeding bones, see

how we hang in the sun to dry   [1980]

WENDY ROSE

Hopi b. 1948

Born in Oakland, California, Rose earned degrees from and taught at Berkeley before joining the
American Indian Studies Program at Fresno City College. Her poetry offers eclectic responses to its
cultural influences, indigenous and Eurocentric, using both realism and spirituality as means for re-
envisioning contemporary indigenous women's experiences. Her books of poetry include *Hopi Road-
runner Dancing* (1973), *Builder Kachina: A Home-Going Cycle* (1979), and *Halfbreed Chronicles* (1985).

STORY KEEPER

The stories would be braided in my hair
between the plastic combs and blue wing tips
but as the rattles would spit,
the drums begin,
along would come someone
to stifle and stop the sound
and the story keeper I would have been
must melt into the cave
of artifacts discarded

and this is a wound
to be healed
in the spin of winter,
the spiral
of beginning.
This is the task:
to find the stories now
and to heave at the rocks,
dig at the moss
with my fingernails,
let moisture seep along my skin
and fall within
soft and dark
to the blood
and I promise
I will find them
even after so long: where underground

they are albino
and they listen, they shine,
and they wait
with tongues shriveled like leaves
and fearful of their names
that would crystallize them,
make them fossils
with the feathers on their backs
frozen hard
like beetle wings.

△ △ △ △   △ △ △ △

But spring is floating
to the canyon rim;
needles burst yellow
from the pine branch
and the stories have built a new house.
Oh they make us dance
the old animal dances
that go a winding way
back and back
to the red clouds
of our first
Hopi morning.

Where I saw them last
they are still: antelope and bear
dancing in the dust,
prairie dog and lizard
whirling just whirling,
pinyon and willow
bending, twisting,
we women
rooting into the earth
our feet becoming water
and our hair pushing up
like tumbleweed

and the spirits should have noticed
how our thoughts wandered those first days,
how we closed our eyes against them
and forgot the signs;
the spirits were never smart about this
but trusted us to remember it right
and we were distracted,
we were new.

We mapped the trails
the spirits had walked
as if the footprints had more meaning
than the feet.
Color after color,
designs that spin and sprout
were painted on the sky
but we were only confused
and turned our backs
and now we are trapped
inside our songlessness.

We are that kind of thing
that pushes away
the very song
keeping us alive
so the stories have been strong
and tell themselves
to this very day,
with or without us
it no longer matters.
The flower merges with the mud,
songs are hammered onto spirits
and spirits onto people;
every song is danced out loud
for we are the spirits,
we are the people,
descended from the ones
who circled the underworld
and return to circle again.

I feel the stories
rattle under my hand
like sun-dried greasy
gambling bones.   [1985]

LESLIE MARMON SILKO

Laguna Pueblo b. 1948

Growing up on the Laguna Pueblo reservation in New Mexico, Silko learned about connections between people and the natural environment in Hopi, Zuni, Navajo, Spanish, and European traditions; she was also acutely aware of the nuclear experiments at nearby Los Alamos and of the open-pit uranium mining industry. In her conception, the land endures its natural and spiritual losses. Silko's books include *Laguna Woman* (1974), *Ceremony* (1977), and *Storyteller* (1981).

LULLABY

The earth is your mother,
   she holds you.
The sky is your father,
   he protects you.
Sleep,
sleep.
Rainbow is your sister,
   she loves you.
The winds are your brothers,
   they sing to you.
Sleep,
sleep.
We are together always
We are together always
There never was a time
when this
was not so.

                                        [1981]

MURRAY EDMOND

New Zealand b. 1949

Edmond was born in Hamilton, New Zealand and graduated from Auckland University. He works as a writer, actor, and director on innovative theatre projects in Wellington, and he has published *Entering the Eye* (1973), *Patchwork: Poems* (1978), and *End Wall* (1981). His task as an artist is unequivocal: 'Free the imagination society sits on or pretends doesn't exist. . . . Raise up in no-man's-land a flag, a fist, a shout. . . . Step outside the superstructure of self, the superstructure of society, to where there is nothing—a place to speak from.'

MY RETURN TO CZECHOSLOVAKIA

1
This is my return to Czechoslovakia.
Twice in my life I have felt utterly
foreign, staying in a place.

The first was in Prague.
I felt the need to leave behind me
a book I had written myself
—a present for the people I stayed with.
It was as though time stopped
and I needed to rest, and in their house
I rested. At night I rested
and listened to the one cold water tap
running all night in Prague,
running on and on like silence.
By day they took me by the hand
and showed me the churches, the palace,
the cathedral with the tiny window
up high where Kafka wrote and looked down
and saw the drama of K. and the priest.
They took me in hand and led me
down that long side street by the Vltava
to a place where on a brick
at the corner of a building
at the height of my eye
some one had scratched the name Dubček.
Because nothing seemed to correspond
I needed to leave something complete
that would stay there,
that would live its own life there.
This is my return to Czechoslovakia.

2
The second place I left a book behind me
was Christchurch, night of a lunar eclipse,
and I sat alone in the middle of a garden
perched on a chair, a singular point
in the whole of the Canterbury Plains.
I watched the moon disappear
and thought of myself as the sum
of all the people who went into my making
—my father's stoop, my mother's hands,
grandmother's hips, my Scottish soul,
doctor, preacher, grocer, weaver,
silent, dead, mad and drowned,
and not one present beside me
to watch the moon turn black.
The tide of everything being born and dying
stopped for a time in the eclipse
and I looked right through the window of the moon
—right through into Czechoslovakia.   [1981]

HOUSE

Last night as I lay beside you all the desire had gone out of me
and I was cast up like a heap of sand, porous, shapeless, shifting,
a thing of shape, an entity, only by virtue of its million parts.

Here I live on a cliff in a tiny house at the end of the island
and in the face of the wind from the north and the wind from the south
I surround myself with this thin wall of wood, this shape in space

and you are there asleep in the bed, curled to the end wall of the house,
your breathing blowing shapes in the cold air, your dreams dreaming,
your dreaming holding up the whole fabric of paint and wood and tin.

If you stop wanting to dream it will collapse. Your desire to dream holds it up,
all the bare longing of the imagination holds it up, the desire of the nail
to enter the wood, the desire of the wood to embrace the nail,

the desire of the paint to hide the wood and reflect the light,
the desire of the roof to contain a secret shape of darkness,
the desire of the glass to shine like the sun in the face of the sun.

And the earth desires to lie asleep under the house and dream,
it dreams the very shape of the house as though it was something organic,
whole as a body, breathing and seeing and standing cold in the wind.

The house is the container and you are the thing contained.
Its membrane protects you and your life gives it energy
and stops the walls from collapse. And the moment of seeing this

and the moment of saying this are two separate moments:
the first, the moment of seeing is a moment without desire,
at night, by the bed watching you sleep, alone, still, chill,

but not cold, watching, as the silence of space watches the grinding earth,
when all the desire has gone out of me and I get up,
get up out of the bed, go out the door, out through the end wall,

and grasp hold of the string on the balloon and rise slowly, steadily,
shimmering like a giant eye over the house, the whole town, the capital city,
rising over the island and the ocean, the earth opening like a flower.

But the second, the moment of saying, involves me in the grammar of desire.
I have to touch you with my speech to be heard.
And grammar itself is a thing of desire, announcing its capacity

to evolve infinitely more complex systems out of bits of nothing,
to put together the grains of sand to make rock and the rock to build
a cliff and the cliff to hold a house, many houses, a city

to stand at the end wall of the island, the end wall of the land
turned like smooth wood in the yielding shape of the bay
to embrace the random desiring waves of the sea.

Somewhere a child is sacrificed and buried at the foot of the posthole
which comes to hold up the whole house. Building walls for the compost heap
I smash a post in half and in its rotted core a weta lies, soft and sleepy,
hiding until its new exoskeleton hardens enough to let it safely live,
to let it grow vulnerable, as earth to light, as sand to sea.
Tonight I embrace you and trust the roof will hold up till morning.   [1981]

CILLA MCQUEEN

New Zealand b. 1949

A widely published poet in New Zealand and abroad, McQueen was born in Birmingham, England, but now lives in Dunedin. Her poetry has appeared in literary magazines, and *Homing In* (1982), *Anti-Gravity* (1984), *Wild Sweets* (1986), and *Benzina* (1988) are among her collections of verse.

MATINAL

Alice on the croquet lawn
is nibbling   at the morning:
high   as a tree   she is
appropriately placed for
contemplation.
              In the garden
held down by webs
                   anchored on
leaves, quiet as trickling
the wind unknots its branches.
Alice goes in   to the garden
leaf by   leaf: such small things
as transparency in the sun's light
move her.
              The blackbird directs an eye
at veins   under the
skin: she watches a moment, and
laughs her
              disappearing laugh, unpicking
nets of shadows.

        Alice's balance
is delicate:
       yet see
the quiet spider journeying
from point to point,
repairing her small wounds.   [1982]

WEEKEND SONNETS

i
Winter's a finger under the wool, spreading
capillaries of shivers: my boots go gong on
the pavement,
          I bow to the hungry letterboxes
past Joe's goat & the ship in the bottle in the
window & the kids repairing the old car
all colours & bits & pieces & rust colours
in the corrugated iron fence & the hulls of
ships, gulls wheeling slow
             & the innkeeper's
daughter down by the water feeding the ducks,
her long striped hair clean as flax:
            delicate,
the way she divides the bread   And here we
are at the pub, Mungo singing Whistle wind oh
whistle window Whistle me
           Oh a ship so tall
but he's too drunk to go fishing today

ii
She's feeding the water, crumbling &
crumbling her white
        hands, her eyes
colour of water, absent
         soft voices of
ducks around her feet:
        he's cocked keen
as a red-eyed gull watching: if he could
just beat up high into the wind & drop her
like a crab she'd split
        & he would feed
on the milk inside her wrists
          Love
like a round white shell skips out
over the water where it blobs & flecks
darkly under the boats

making sweet
lost faces drowned in nets, mussel-shell
sky full of soft hair
& all of the blue-lipped
hills in their eyes.   [1982]

CAROLYN FORCHÉ

USA b. 1950

Forché was born and raised in Detroit, the city to which her working-class family had emigrated
from Czechoslovakia. Forché's poetry addresses the problems and prospects of developing
communities, and relationships of respect for 'others'. Her political commitments have focused on
the struggles of aboriginals (*Gathering the Tribes*, 1975) and El Salvadoreans (*The Country Between
Us*, 1982); she also travels extensively, giving readings, delivering lectures, and participating in the
human rights work of Amnesty International.

KALALOCH

Bleached wood massed in bone piles,
we pulled it from dark beach and built
fire in a fenced clearing.
Wood stubs were sunk down,
they circled and were roofed by milled
lumber dragged at one time to the coast.
We slept there.

Each morning the minus tide—
weeds flowed it like hair swimming.
Starfish gripped rock, pastel, rough.
Fish bones lay in sun.

Each noon milk fog sank
from cloud cover, came in
our clothes, held them
tighter on us. Sea stacks
stood and disappeared.
They came back when the sun
scrubbed out the inlet.

We went down to piles to get
mussels, I made my shirt a bowl
of mussel stones and carted them
to our grate where they smoked apart.
I pulled the mussel lip bodies out,
chewed their squeak.

We went up the path for fresh water,
berries. Hardly speaking, thinking.

During low tide we crossed
to the island, climbed
its wet summit. The redfoots
and pelicans dropped for fish.
The oclets so silent fell
toward water with linked feet.

Jacynthe said little,
her tuk pulled down her hair, long
since we had spoken *Nova Scotia, Michigan*
and knew beauty in saying nothing.
She told me about her mother who would
come at them with bread knives, then stop
herself, her face emptied.

I told her about me,
never lied. At night
at times the moon floated.
We sat with arms tight,
watching flames spit and snap.
On stone and sand picking up
wood shaped like a body, like a gull.

I ran barefoot not only
on beach but harsh gravels
up through the woods.
I shit easy, covered my dropping.
Some nights no fires, we watched
the sea pucker and get stabbed
by the beacon
circling on Tatoosh.

2
I stripped and spread
on the sea lip, stretched
to the slap of the foam
and the vast red dulce.
Jacynthe gripped the earth
in her fists, opened—
the boil of the tide
shuffled into her.

The beach revolved,
headlands behind us
put their pines in the sun.
Gulls turned a strong sky.
Their pained wings held,
they bit water quick, lifted.
Their looping eyes continually
measure the distance from us,
bare women who do not touch.

Rocks drowsed, holes filled
with suds from a distance.
A deep laugh bounced
in my flesh and sprayed her.

3
Flies crawled us,
Jacynthe crawled.
With her palms she
spread my calves she
moved my heels from each other.
A woman's mouth is
not different, sand moved
wild beneath me, her long
hair wiped my legs, with women
there is sucking, the water
slops our bodies. We come
clean, our clits beat like
twins to the loons rising up.

We are awake.
Snails sprinkle our gulps,
fish die in our grips, there is
sand in the anus of dancing.
Tatoosh Island
hardens in the distance.
We see its empty stones
sticking out of the sea again.
Jacynthe holds tinder
under fire to cook the night's wood.

If we had men I would make
milk in me simply. She
is quiet. *I like that you
cover your teeth.*

[1976]

LENORE KEESHIG-TOBIAS

Ojibway b. 1950

Born on the Cape Croker Reserve, Keeshig-Tobias is a member of the Nawash Chippewa First Nation for whom, she says, 'Storytelling has always been part of our family life, not just as a heritage in the traditional stories, but as a necessary function in our individual family circle.' In 1983, she graduated from York University with a degree in creative writing. She lives in Toronto, working as a writer and editor for magazines such as *Sweetgrass*, *Ontario Indian*, and *The Magazine to Re-establish the Trickster*.

RESISTANCE

well, coyote,
you old dog

there you go again,
pulling on your cowboy boots
and walking out

AAY—in total resistance
to save the world, to rise
as lord amongst advocates
and piss on government
buildings under cover of night

when taking out the garbage,
helping with dishes, picking
up your own dirty socks and
the things of a woman's heart
make little sense
to your fine warrior logic

well, she's not gonna
go after you
this time, crying

she's gonna take a
deep breath, wash
her hair, bundle up
the kids

and go to university
for a degree in engineering   [1986]

MEDBH McGUCKIAN

Ireland b. 1950

McGuckian places issues of impenetrability and resistance to paraphrase—issues necessary to viable concepts of identity and place—in the feminine. The complexity of the maternal figure overwhelms the conventional representations of Ireland as woman which have been designed by Catholic and Nationalist ideologies. In a 1986 interview McGuckian said 'I see my audience very much as male. The voice is female, speaking mostly to be understood by men. . . . I don't want men to underestimate women ever.' McGuckian's books include *The Flower Master* (1982), *Venus and the Rain* (1984), *On Ballycastle Beach* (1988), and *Marconi's Cottage* (1991).

VENUS AND THE RAIN

White on white, I can never be viewed
Against a heavy sky—my gibbous voice
Passes from leaf to leaf, retelling the story
Of its own provocative fractures, till
Their facing coasts might almost fill each other
And they ask me in reply if I've
Decided to stop trying to make diamonds.

On one occasion, I rang like a bell
For a whole month, promising their torn edges
The birth of a new ocean (as all of us
Who have hollow bodies tend to do at times):
What clues to distance could they have,
So self-excited by my sagging sea,
Widened ten times faster than it really did?

[1984]

GRACE NICHOLS

Guyana/England b. 1950

The energy and authenticity of the Black woman Nichols's work develops quarantine the pornographic appetite and migratory gaze of the colonial mind, the 'white imagination', the 'thin' European. Educated in Guyana, Nichols settled in London in 1977 where her first collection, *i is a long memoried woman* (1983), won the Commonwealth Poetry Prize. *The Fat Black Woman's Poems* (1984) and *Lazy Thoughts of a Lazy Woman* (1989) followed. In an essay in the anthology *Let It Be Told: Black Women Writers in Britain* (1988), Nichols discusses the '[d]ifference, diversity and unpredictability' that make her 'tick' as she 'chisel[s] out a new language' by fusing Creole and standard English: for Caribbean poets, Creole expressions contain a vividness and conciseness that 'have no equivalent in English'.

TROPICAL DEATH

The fat black woman want
a brilliant tropical death
not a cold sojourn
in some North Europe far/forlorn

The fat black woman want
some heat/hibiscus at her feet
blue sea dress
to wrap her neat

The fat black woman want
some bawl
no quiet jerk tear wiping
a polite hearse withdrawal

The fat black woman want
all her dead rights
first night
third night
nine night
all the sleepless droning
red-eyed wake nights

In the heart
of her mother's sweetbreast
In the shade
of the sun leaf's cool bless
In the bloom
of her people's bloodrest

the fat black woman want
a brilliant tropical death yes

[1984]

ODIA OFEIMUN

Nigeria b. 1950

Once the personal secretary to Chief Obafemi Awolowo, former premier of the western region of Nigeria, Ofeimun is currently a member of the editorial board of *The Guardian* (Lagos) and General Secretary of the Association of Nigerian Authors. His first volume, *The Poet Lied* (1981), was originally withdrawn because of a potential lawsuit by J.P. Clark Bekederemo against Ofeimun's publishers; Bekederemo felt the title-poem slanderous. *The Poet Lied* appeared again in 1990 as a provisional collected poems following the publication of *A Handle for the Flutist* in 1986.

A HANDLE FOR THE FLUTIST

You have heard it said before
that poetry makes no water jump
blows not the wind it divines
builds no pyramids nor does it
repair bridges or start anything afresh.

Yet in the common tongue of those
who love to feel the terror of survival
the survival of mouth as mouth alone
the worshipped word is enough
to expiate crimes and to lay honour
upon whom the pleaded grace of song has fallen.

So to save culture, they save a little risk
for those who obey no laws of gravity
outsiders to pain for whom murder will pass
no moral handle to the flutist
they fly only where the executives
would never want to tamper. Where?
The described becomes the prescribed
You have heard it said before.

So while they celebrate themselves
for holy ineffectuality
and seek the freedom of the ostrich
to bury their heads in the sands
let us praise those who will banish poets
from the People's Republic.

Let us praise them who know
what pagan fire can come
from waterfalls denied the lie of valleys
those who have seen gods crumble to their knees

questioned by simple images
so let us praise those who will track down
folksongs with police dogs
They will not live with poets
in the People's Republic.

[1988]

SHEENAGH PUGH

England/Wales b. 1950

Pugh moved to Wales from Birmingham in 1971. Particularly interested in shaping the defining moments of perception, Pugh works with historical events, establishing intimate contact during her own travels in Iceland, for example, with Gunnar Hamundarson in the poem 'Going back to Hlidarendi'; under threat of death, Hamundarson decides to risk remaining in his homeland. Her books include *Crowded by Shadows* (1977), *What a Place to Grow Flowers* (1980), and *Earth Studies and Other Voyages* (1983).

GOING BACK TO HLIDARENDI

*Gunnar Hamundarson is leaving Iceland under threat of death, he looks back at his farm,
Hlidarendi, and decides to stay.*

Did you think about it much,
farmer; no, you'd feel it
like a wave, wind sweeping the slopes
of wheat into a pattern
of light and dark, making
sense in your mind.

But you were right, no logic
could have led you better. What then
would going away gain you—your life?
Hardly, for death would come
to whatever place, and always
at an inconvenient hour.

You might as well await him
where your life is; in the place
that is to your liking.
A year elsewhere means so little
to you, with Hlidarendi
in your mind.

It is enough for you,
that wave; all the sea
you need; all your adventure.

There is a Hlidarendi
to most minds; on a map
sometimes, more often not; a way
to be.   [1979]

PHILIP SALOM

Australia b. 1950

Salom's *The Silent Piano* (1980) won the 1981 Commonwealth Poetry Prize. The title of a sequence
of his longer poems, *The Projectionist* (1983), refers to the persona's work in a local West Australia
movie theatre.

THE WORLD OF DREAMS

The world of dreams
is no salvation
no-one lives in it
except the mad
who are sane there.
It is our half-life
by which we balance
and is replaced
by art and memory
against all better judgement.

It is wiser than us
but has no manners
it's as modern
as modern poetry
and always has been
it's as ancient
as cave paintings
and always will be.
You can fly in dreams
enter minds and bodies
more than mere technique
dreams speak in images
that are as obstinate
as they are strange
more dramatic than logic
thought is linear
dream's holistic
direct and yet oblique
as foreign films.

When it speaks
we are reminded
language is wakefulness
dubbed onto our actions,
as crude, simplistic
as white subtitles
amidst the colour.
When it's all over
it's what you saw
that you remember.

It seems the dying
take notice of their dreams
whereas the living
do more controlling
one is wisdom
one is ulterior motive
both are thrilling.
Dreams have common subjects
his and her illicit skins
bodies caught in images
each is electric
murdering or at peace.
Even an old boot if dreamt
is Ibsen's gun upon the wall.
You go to sleep exhausted
you can wake up drained
two lives a day.
It's every part of us
Tao, wheel, rose, cross,
every pagan urging as well.
Dreams save us from
the world   the world
saves us from our dreams.

[1986]

RAY A. YOUNG BEAR

Meskwaki b. 1950

Young Bear lives and works in Tama, Iowa, the Meskwaki community where he was born and raised. A poet, novelist, performer, and teacher, Young Bear has published three books of poetry: *Winter of the Salamander* (1980), *The Invisible Musician* (1990), and *Black Eagle Child* (1992). His recent poetry is derived from Meskwaki traditions—'real or imagined clans, names, and people who live in ordinary and supernatural realities'—that endure so that 'in spite of everything that has happened to Native Americans over the course of five centuries of cultural malignment and even through today, we remain mindful of the beliefs that were "given" so long ago.' (*The Best American Poetry*, 1996).

OUR BIRD AEGIS

An immature black eagle walks assuredly
across a prairie meadow. He pauses in mid-step
with one talon over the wet snow to turn
around and see.

Imprinted in the tall grass behind him
are the shadows of his tracks,
claws instead of talons, the kind
that belong to a massive bear.
And he goes by that name:
Ma kwi so ta.

And so this aegis looms against the last
spring blizzard. We discover he's concerned
and the white feathers of his spotted hat
flicker, signalling this.

With outstretched wings he tests the sutures.
Even he is subject to physical wounds and human
tragedy, he tells us.

The eyes of the Bear-King radiate through
the thick, falling snow. He meditates the loss
of my younger brother—and by custom
suppresses his emotions.   [1994]

CATHERINE OBIANUJU ACHOLONU

Nigeria b. 1951

Acholonu's dystopian squint at Nigeria at the turn of the century extrapolates from current conditions to forecast a bleak future. The 'whitish black' child has emerged from a womb lined with both the detritus of a colony ('pieces of broken razor/MADE IN ENGLAND') and the newer trappings of 'goof' (marijuana), techno-rock, and a Bob Marley tune that ominously intones 'r-a-st-a f-ar-i-a/ e-x-o-d-u-s'. Acholonu's four-chapter pamphlet of instructions for the child strikes out at the corruption that she perceives as pervasive in contemporary Nigeria and makes the poet an angry prophet denouncing a dying culture.

NIGERIA IN THE YEAR 1999

today the sixth of june
in the year of our lord
nineteen hundred and ninety nine
a child was born at 6 p.m.

    weight — three stones
    height — three feet
    colour — whitish black

mother died of exhaustion
and father took off on a feat of fear
and what is this bunch of bloody rubbish
has the child been shitting in the womb?
no that is the placenta
I suppose
the what?
is it a cuckoo's nest?
here pieces of broken razor
MADE IN ENGLAND
there heaps of cigarette butts
but no, nothing as mild as that
this is plain harsh 'goof'*

and these reels and reels of tape?
just wait a minute
what has this adult-infant been up to?
provided its own everything
even its own rock'n roll
right from the tomb?
no, womb?

*marijuana

our little man didn't have to yell out his first sound
just switched on his micro-cassette
and bob marley came blaring out

    r-a-st-a f-ar-i-a
    e-x-o-d-u-s

child of the devil has got it all worked out
how to enjoy life in nigeria
then still dripping of blood
infant child says his first words:

here is my pamphlet of 'Life Made Simple'

    chapter one   — how to run without walking

    chapter two   — education made simple
                        expo* 2000

    chapter three — how to make billions without sweat
                        the secret of ten percent

    chapter four   — rig yourself into life-presidency

surely our little man
is most highly equipped
for life in nigerian fashion   [1990]

*examination malpractice (slang)

MEENA ALEXANDER

India/USA b. 1951

Alexander's *Night-Scene, The Garden* (1992) is about her mother's home in a small town in Kerala, South India. Performed off-off Broadway by the Medicine Show Theatre Ensemble in April 1988, the piece evolves in nine stages, weaving, as Alexander suggests, 'through two voices, though perhaps there are three: the third, the voice of the poet broken loose, speaking against silence.' Other works of poetry include *Stone Roots* (1980), *House of a Thousand Doors* (1988), and *River and Bridge* (1996). Currently a professor of English at New York's Hunter College and a lecturer in poetry at Columbia University, Alexander has also written essays, experimental fiction, and autobiographical works burnished by her understanding of complex family histories.

BOATING

One summer's day
we put out in a painted boat
the family entire,
a few friends included

The men in dhotis and well
fitted shirts,
a few with cigars spouting smoke

The women with their saris
edging right past
their eyes, drawn down

Against the sun
that eclipsed itself in fury
at the Kerala coast.

We rocked at a rope's end
in Cochin harbour
till my great uncle Alexander
cried out, dropping his pipe

And the men screwed
monocles just right
and the women crouching down
held bits of broken mirror
to their eyes

Or clear gray glass
my grandmother
for me, crying
child, child
so the sun might kiss
and not burn

Child, unripe child

Till the wooden hull
dashed suddenly
against the swollen pier
and shot us
into cold sea spray

The blackest depths
drawn up in pleated waves,
my smocking dress
puckered and ripped with salt

Child, O child
shut your eyes
so tight

Grandmother cried
clutching me
to her bony neck

Her silken cloak
with the golden pin
stuck fast
to my fist

When they pulled
us out
we would not
come unstuck.   [1992]

CHRISTOPHER DEWDNEY
Canada b. 1951

Dewdney, who grew up in London, Ontario, has made his major poetic project an imaginative
charting of the myriad ways in which the southern Ontario landscape—its limestone formations,
its petrified creatures from various millennia—testify to a magnificently variegated prehistory
available to human memory and to Dewdney's language. *Predators of the Adoration: Selected Poems
1972–82* (1983) is his most representative collection.

THE DIALECTIC CRIMINAL:
HAND IN GLOVE WITH AN OLD HAT

When it's raining cats and dogs you've got to cut corners because you could
get your eyes peeled. You must come to grips with yourself until you fly off
the handle & then if you're not fit as a fiddle you'll spill the beans. That's
hitting below the belt with the short end of the stick, if I can bring the point
home, ladies.

It all started in early 1975, I had an axe to grind during a blanket freeze.
It was no great shakes but I had to go against the grain, iron out the details.
You see, I pulled a few strings & had to go off the deep end. But I guess I had
reckoned without my host. (That's burning the candle at both ends because
this whole thing rings a bell.) The host carried a torch for this chick & now
she's praying through the nose. I guess the handwriting was on the wall
though.

Anyway, before I got the drop on this I bit the dust and turned the tables.
I caught the big shot hanging around by a thread generally laying it on the
line. I told him I thought he was right off the wall and it went to his head.
He kept it under his hat but greased my palms anyway. Yet I always say strike
while the iron is hot and lay low till the heat's off because drawing a line is

like splitting hairs. I'd be in the groove now if it wasn't for a bolt out of the blue & even then I got taken to the cleaners. But the whole kit and caboodle is right as rain by my money.

You on the other hand, you put your foot in your mouth & bit off more than you could chew. Now with what's left you put your foot in the door and then accuse *me* of changing my tune? I *had* to change my tune in order to face the music.

I'm going through the motions after bringing the house down because a fly-by-night that held water led me down the garden path. I'm coming on like this because I put one over on you. And now you're out on a limb getting a charge. If you hadn't swapped horses in midstream maybe you could've gotten off. But you've got to keep the ball rolling because we're playing with loaded dice. But then again, who am I to remain on the level?

Anyway back in '75 I was riding a dark horse with a grain of salt up my sleeve. I burned my bridges as I got to them. Everyone around me was starting from scratch because they threw in their towels. I was going like a bat out of hell, I got the drop on it under my skin. A drop in the bucket that is, so now I'm right down your alley because I blew my top. 'In hot water?' you ask; no, just flashing. I'm making tracks because this place is definitely nothing by mouth, by word of mouth that is. You see, when you're over your head in a car pool & no one is biting then it's time to break the ice. And break the ice I did, lemme tell you, this bruiser I double-crossed was loaded for bear. I figured it was time to throw a monkey wrench into the works when suddenly he pulled a boner. I didn't waste any time, I hit him below the belt and buried the hatchet. It's a dog's breakfast, lemme tell you, when you're hand in glove with an old hat.

Now I'm letting it all hang out in my old stomping grounds and you can go and take the cake because I've been beating around the burning bush long enough. I've got a stiff upper lip from blowing hot and cold on you bad eggs. I'll never let bygones become old stand-bys because the leading edge takes the friction.

You're shitting bricks but I'm sweating blood.   [1983]

JOY HARJO

Creek b. 1951

Harjo, born in Tulsa, Oklahoma, belongs to the Creek nation, and her poetry voices her anger at the loss of indigenous traditions and cultures and her desire to protect them. Her poetic resources, as shown in collections such as *She Had Some Horses* (1983) and *Secrets from the Center of the World* (1987), include realism and spiritualism, memory and dream. Educated at the Institute of American Indian Arts in Santa Fe, and the University of Iowa, Harjo now teaches at the University of Colorado.

ANCHORAGE

for Audre Lorde

This city is made of stone, of blood, and fish.
There are Chugatch Mountains to the east
and whale and seal to the west.
It hasn't always been this way, because glaciers
who are ice ghosts create oceans, carve earth
and shape this city here, by the sound.
They swim backwards in time.

Once a storm of boiling earth cracked open
the streets, threw open the town.
It's quiet now, but underneath the concrete
is the cooking earth,
                          and above that, air
which is another ocean, where spirits we can't see
are dancing   joking   getting full
on roasted caribou, and the praying
goes on, extends out.

Nora and I go walking down 4th Avenue
and know it is all happening.
On a park bench we see someone's Athabascan
grandmother, folded up, smelling like 200 years
of blood and piss, her eyes closed against some
unimagined darkness, where she is buried in an ache
in which nothing makes
                          sense.

We keep on breathing, walking, but softer now,
the clouds whirling in the air above us.
What can we say that would make us understand
better than we do already?
Except to speak of her home and claim her

as our own history, and know that our dreams
don't end here, two blocks away from the ocean
where our hearts still batter away at the muddy shore.

And I think of the 6th Avenue jail, of mostly Native
and Black men, where Henry told about being shot at
eight times outside a liquor store in L.A., but when
the car sped away he was surprised he was alive,

no bullet holes, man, and eight cartridges strewn
on the sidewalk
                    all around him.

Everyone laughed at the impossibility of it,
but also the truth. Because who would believe
the fantastic and terrible story of all of our survival
those who were never meant
                              to survive?   [1983]

I AM A DANGEROUS WOMAN

the sharp ridges of clear blue windows
motion to me
from the airport's second floor
edges dance in the foothills of the sandias
behind security guards
who wave me into their guncatcher machine

i am a dangerous woman
when the machine buzzes
they say to take off my belt
and i remove it so easy
that it catches the glance
of a man standing nearby
(maybe that is the deadly weapon
that has the machine singing)

i am a dangerous woman
but the weapon is not visible
security will never find it

they can't hear the clicking
of the gun
        inside my head   [1979]

FRANK KUPPNER

Scotland b. 1951

Kuppner describes *A Bad Day for the Sung Dynasty* with characteristic self-deprecation and whimsy: 'This work consists of 501 4-line observations and 10 4-line observations on the verse form, which is taken from the common usage of translators of Chinese poetry, provoked by looking at the illustrations in Osvald Siren's *Chinese Painting: Leading Masters and Principles* (1956–58), and feeling certain that the whole story was not being told. Many of them are supposed to be funny.' Author of the novel *Life on a Dead Planet* (1993), his poetry collections include *The Intelligent Observation of Naked Women* (1987) and *Ridiculous! Absurd! Disgusting!* (1989).

from A BAD DAY FOR THE SUNG DYNASTY

193.
Dutifully listening to the four expert musicians
Who are welcoming at length an important visitor to his court,
The king manages to retain his austere smile
By imagining them pissing on his guest from a considerable height.

194.
In his private apartments the Emperor relaxes;
He has tied his hair to the wrist of a zither-player;
When she reaches for the low notes, a pain racks his whole being,
But the three little hands around his neck prevent him from moving forward.

195.
After the ordeal, the Emperor relaxes;
One of the twins rubs her eyebrows against his forehead;
The other rubs her forehead against his eyebrows;
Their mother sings old songs of her native land.

196.
After his grim ordeal the Emperor relaxes;
Two nude female musicians play impeccable lute music,
While a third, wearing a tiny leather jacket,
Leans out of a window and describes what birds she can see.

197.
After his appalling ordeal, the Emperor relaxes;
One of the triplets places a foot upon his forehead;
Another runs at full speed towards the window;
The third sings softly inside her mother's body.

198.
After his devastating ordeal, the Emperor relaxes;
Whenever the cook strikes the drum with her little bottom,
The giggling musicians, with practised agility,
Scatter to avoid the next of her cakes he throws at them.

199.
After his cataclysmic ordeal, the Emperor relaxes;
With a puzzled smile, he shines a torch upon their mother,
While the quadruplets dance to the rhythm of his heart,
Three of them balanced upon disgraced ambassadors.

200.
After fifty years of frantic and unplanned travelling,
He finds himself outside the house where he wrote his first poem;
The stream still flows by as flippantly as ever;
He hears some running feet, and a door shutting.

. . .

242.
Delegated to decide which old poems should be kept,
And which destroyed, to lessen the excess baggage of time,
In a bad mood, hungover, he burns scroll after scroll,
Hugging his own works to his heart and crooning.

243.
Morosely he gazes at the old text in front of him;
What on earth is he to make of all those absurd squiggly lines?
Something sunlight something something laughter;
Happiness something something something she.

244.
Stolidly he ponders the old text in front of him;
Delight something buttocks pliant something;
Sunburst something buttocks something balcony;
He frowns at the girl noisily pouring out wine.

245.
In the open-air conclave of scholars he inspects his antique text:
Joy something wine something light something;
Something dancing something eyes something follow;
What is that idiot over there laughing about?

246.
Something something something hands something;
Something perhaps reaches something pineapple;
Better death something love her;
Something something something something giggling.

247.
Something breasts something something bosom;
Something bust something bosom something;
Breast something something caterpillar something;
A look of doubt crosses the old scholar's face.

248.
Death something decrepitude something annihilation;
Something something something rotting putrefaction;
Groans something something shrieks groans;
The old scholar makes a signal to the wine-girl.

249.
Something something something something something;
Something something something smiling something;
Something smiling something something something;
The old scholar finds himself involuntarily smiling.

. . .

418.
The emperor is routinely sketching a minuscule bird;
Indifferent to the honour, it dreams of a snail;
The snail is dreaming of an apple-tree;
The apple-tree is dreaming of itself.

419.
Beneath a peachtree, the painter is sketching a sparrow;
The sparrow is dreaming of another bird, now dead;
The other bird dreams of the same peachtree;
The peachtree is dreaming of the painter underneath it.

420.
The emperor lies, dreaming of his daughter;
His daughter kneels, dreaming of a palace guard;
The palace guard stands, dreaming of the tea merchant's wife;
The tea merchant's wife sits, thinking of her husband's bank-book.

421.
The emperor lies, dreaming of his palace guard;
The palace guard stands, dreaming of the emperor's daughter;
The emperor's daughter kneels, dreaming of the merchant's wife;
The tea merchant's wife lies, dreaming of the emperor.

422.
The painter sits, drawing a blossoming plumtree;
The blossoming plumtree is dreaming of a denuded orange-tree;
The orange-tree is dreaming of a peculiar apple-tree;
The apple-tree is dreaming of interstellar space.

423.
A dog is pissing against a delicate peony;
The distressed peony is dreaming of a pinetree;
As the dog wanders happily along the forest path,
A pine branch suddenly falls on its head, concussing it.

424.
A dog is pissing against a delicate peony;
The delicate peony is dreaming of an oaktree near it;
The oaktree is dreaming of a coniferous forest;
The forest is dreaming of the rich seams of the earth.

425.
Oh, the emptiness; the challenge of the emptiness;
Inside his drunken head spangles and arrows dance,
As if the edge of the world had fallen away;
No, that is water there; that is water, that is water.

426.
Looking back, they see their path no longer exists;
Is not this how one enters an enchanted world?
The ordinary river eddies at their feet;
As they watch, its surface level gets lower and lower and lower.

427.
Clinging to a servant, he staggers back from the party;
The neighbours, knowing him an austere lawyer,
Are most struck, looking from their various windows,
By the intelligent look on the face of the water buffalo.

428.
As the water buffalo sniffs the grass vivaciously,
The herdboy stares at what he has found by the side of the road;
How far could these old arrows travel, he wonders,
Not recognizing the Red Indian markings on its shaft.

429.
A few priests amble across the high stone bridge;
In the distance, at the top of a hill, a pagoda;
They pass an open window, out of which comes laughter;
The screen shuts, and they hear the same laughter, further away.   [1984]

PAUL MULDOON

Ireland b. 1951

Working at Queen's University, Belfast, with poets like Seamus Heaney and Michael Longley, Muldoon published his first volume, *New Weather* in 1972 at the age of 21. Now freelancing in the United States, Muldoon has written *Mules* (1977) and *Why Brownlee Left*, which won the Geoffrey Faber Memorial Prize in 1980, as well as editing *The Faber Book of Contemporary Irish Verse* (1988). Marriages, mixed, vulnerable, and capable of reproduction, captivate Muldoon, revealing his interest in the Metaphysical poets and the Conceit. Of the dramatis personae he creates, Muldoon has observed that there is a 'wryness, a mischievousness in the voice' which provides him the multi-layered opportunities for enigma and indirection that he so admired in Robert Frost.

WHY BROWNLEE LEFT

Why Brownlee left, and where he went,
Is a mystery even now.
For if a man should have been content
It was him; two acres of barley.
One of potatoes, four bullocks,
A milker, a slated farmhouse.
He was last seen going out to plough
On a March morning, bright and early.

By noon Brownlee was famous;
They had found all abandoned, with
The last rig unbroken, his pair of black
Horses, like man and wife,
Shifting their weight from foot to
Foot, and gazing into the future.   [1980]

SUSAN MUSGRAVE

USA/Canada b. 1951

Born to Canadian parents in Santa Cruz, California, Musgrave left school at fourteen, coming after many travels to her spiritual home, the Queen Charlotte Islands off the BC coast. Musgrave's best-known poetry is incantatory, haunted with invocations to spirits inhabiting self and nature. Her first collection was *Songs of the Sea-witch* (1970); her books of selected poems include *Grave-Dirt and Selected Strawberries* (1973), *Tarts and Muggers* (1982), and *The Embalmer's Art: Selected Poems 1970–1985* (1992).

BURIAL OF THE DOG

He would not lie uncovered
for long,
the cracked grave-boards
released his gnawing dust.

His face had
not appeared
though out of the
cramped earth
one eye had shed
for all to see.

His fur was worn—
an unsexed carpet ploughed
where time and light passed like
relics of an ancient crime.

The earth dwarfed him—
knowing this he came
to his own burial.
He unlearned every trick
he made—lay down
like black dawn
on all horizons.

But did not change.
Last winter we found him
unburied once more by rain,
half-running to
recover sleep, tunnelling
through age.

We with our faces closed
saw nothing—
knew the cold memory
stiffened as it dried.
We left him in the
half-light, our footsteps
sly as blood.
Our fear went out to him
from eyes of
other animals.   [1970]

ROO BORSON

Canada b. 1952

Borson was born in Berkeley, California and educated at Goddard College in Vermont and the University of British Columbia, where she worked with poets Pat Lowther and Robert Bringhurst. Borson imagines confused human presence in natural settings that speak another, more coherent language. These poems are complemented by verse in which men's and women's apprehensions of each other are mediated by desire confounded within different languages. Her first book was *Landfall* (1977); her most recent collection is *Night Walk: Selected Poems* (1994).

CITY LIGHTS

To board the train for Toronto and glance over at the other
track as that train starts rolling and the woman there,
opposite, dozing, opens her eyes.
To look into eyes and know there are many directions.
To have it all at once: cinnamon buns
from the Harbord Bakery and the late poems of Wang Wei.
To step out, bringing traffic to a halt.
To bemoan with total strangers the state of the lettuce,
to be queried concerning the uses of star fruit,
and expostulate thereon.
To guide an unsteady gentleman across the street
and refuse payment in eternity.
To happen on the long light down certain streets as the sun is setting,
to pass by all that tempts others without a thought.
For cigar smoke and Sony Walkmans and random belligerence,
the overall sense of delighted industry
which is composed of idle hatred, inane self-interest,
compassion, and helplessness, when looked at closely.
To wait in queues, anonymous as the price code in a supermarket.
To board a bus where everyone is talking at once,
and count eight distinct languages, and not know any.
For the Chinese proprietress of the Bagel Paradise Restaurant,

who is known to her customers as the joyful
otter is known to the clear salt water of Monterey Bay.
To know that everyone who isn't reading, daydreaming,
or on a first date is either full of plans or
playing Sherlock Holmes on the subway.
For eerie cloudlit nights, and skyscrapers,
and raccoons, jolly as bees.
For the joy of walking out the front door and becoming
instantly, and resolutely, lost.
To fall, when one is falling,
into a safety net, and find one's friends.
To be one among many.
To be many.   [1989]

DI BRANDT

Canada b. 1952

In her first book, *questions i asked my mother* (1987, winner of the Gerald Lampert Award for the best book of poetry in Canada), Brandt interrogates the many versions of authority that she fought against while growing up in a strict religious Mennonite family in Reinland, a farming village in south-central Manitoba. Alongside her three other books of poetry (*Agnes in the Sky*, 1990, *mother, not mother*, 1992, and *Jerusalem, Beloved*, 1995), Brandt has published a book of criticism, *Wild Mother Dancing: Maternal Narrative in Canadian Literature* (1993) that examines the problem of the absent mother in the Western literary tradition.

questions i asked my mother

look when grampa died last week everybody said he's better off
where he is because he's in heaven now he's with God we should
be happy he's gone home but yesterday when they put him in the
ground the minister said he's going to be there till the last trumpet
raises the quick & the dead for the final judgement now look
mom i can't figure out which is true it's got to be either up or
down i mean what's he gonna do swoop back into his body at the
last moment so he can rise with the trumpet call or what i got to
know mom what do you think   my mother is sewing she's
incredibly nimble with her fingers my father marvels at them she's
sewed all our clothes since we were born embroidered designed
them   she bites the thread carefully before answering   now
Diana she says & then stops   i can see my question is too
much for her   Dad she calls into the other room come here a
minute & listen to what this girl is asking   i have to repeat the
whole thing my voice rising desperately   well when grampa
died last week everybody said he's better off where he is because
he's in heaven now he's with God but yesterday when they put

him in the ground the minister said he's going to be there till the
last trumpet raises the quick & the dead for the final judgement &
i can't figure out which is true he's got to be either up or down
what's he gonna do swoop back into his body at the last moment
so he can rise with the trumpet call or what   they look at
each other complicity in their eyes   i don't think that's a very
nice thing to say about grampa she begins   she wouldn't say
this if we were alone it's an introduction   she lets him finish
with the big stuff   it's your attitude he says i've noticed lately
everything you say has this questioning tone i don't think you're
really interested in grampa or your faith what you really want is to
make trouble for mom & me you've always been like that you're
always trying to figure everything out your own way instead of
submitting quietly to the teachings of the church when are you
going to learn not everything has to make sense your brain is not
the most important thing in the world what counts is your attitude
& your faith your willingness to accept the mystery of God's
ways   another time i asked her mom   i been thinking about
arithmetic & what i'm wondering is do you think arithmetic was
invented or discovered i mean it seems like it must have been
invented because all these signs numbers & things they didn't find
those lying on a rock somewhere people must have made them
up but on the other hand it really works i mean do you think
anybody could have invented 10 times 10 is a hundred & if so
who could it have been   well i just don't know she says
wonderingly i've never really thought about it you sure come up
with the strangest questions really i don't know how you got to be
so smart   sometimes i just felt i would burst with all the
unanswered questions inside me i thought of writing the *Country
Guide* question & answer column but i didn't have stationery &
anyway no one ever asked questions like that   i imagined
heaven as a huge schoolroom where all the questions of the
universe were answered once & for all God was the cosmic school
inspector pointing eternally to a chalkboard as big as the sky
just imagine i thought Abraham & Isaac & all those guys they
already know everything they knew about relativity centuries before
Einstein instantly like that they don't ever have to think   one
time i asked her about bread   i loved smelling the brown yeast
in the huge blue speckled bowl its sweetish ferment watching it
bubble & churn how does it turn into bread i asked her   well
the yeast is what makes it rise she said when you add warm water
it grows as you can see yes but how does it turn into bread i
mean it comes out a completely different thing what exactly
happens to it in there in the oven why does heat turn it into
something full of holes we can eat   she sighed my mother
sighed a lot when i was around   you're asking me something

i can't tell you she said now help me punch down the dough
i sat in front of the oven all afternoon bathed in warm kitchen
smells trying to figure it out someday i said to myself someday
i will find out i will find out everything   [1987]

HELEN DUNMORE

England b. 1952

Dunmore's award-winning collections include *The Sea Skater* (1987), *The Raw Garden* (1988), and
Short Days, Long Nights: New & Selected Poems (1991). Writer-in-Residence at the Polytechnic of
Wales (1990) and the Brighton Festival (1991), Dunmore participates in reading events in arts
centres, schools, poetry groups, and prisons throughout Great Britain, and this activism is central
to her indictment of the colonial mentality.

SISTERS LEAVING BEFORE THE DANCE

Sisters leaving before the dance,
before the caller gets drunk
or the yellow streamers unreel
looping like ribbons
here and there on the hair of the dancers,

sisters at the turn of the stairs
as the sound system
one-twos, as the squeezebox
mewed in its case

is slapped into breath, and that scrape
of the tables shoved back for the dance
burns like the strike of a match
in the cup of two hands.
Ripe melons and meat

mix in the binbags with cake
puddled in cherry-slime, wind
heavy with tar
blows back the yard door, and I'm

caught with three drinks in my hands
on the stairs looking up
at the sisters leaving before the dance,
not wishing to push past them
in their white broderie anglaise and hemmed

skirts civilly drawn
to their sides to make room
for the big men in suits,
and the girls in cerise

dance-slippers and cross-backed dresses
who lead the way up
and take charge of the tickets, and yet
from their lips canteloupe
fans as they speak

in bright quick murmurs between
a violin ghosting a tune
and the kids in the bar downstairs
begging for Coke, peaky but certain.

The sisters say their *good nights*
and all the while people stay bunched
on the stairs going up, showing respect
for the small words of the ones leaving,
the ones who don't stay for the dancing.

One sister twists a white candle
waxed in a nest of hydrangeas—
brick-red and uncommon, flowers
she really can't want—she bruises the limp

warm petals with crisp fingers
and then poises her sandal
over the next non-slip stair
so the dance streams at her heels
in the light of a half-shut door.   [1991]

POEM FOR DECEMBER 28

My nephews with almond faces
black hair like bunches of grapes

>   (the skin stroked and then bruised
>   the head buried and caressed)

he takes his son's head in his hands
kisses it blesses it   leaves it:

the boy with circles under his eyes like damsons
not the blond baby, the stepson.

In the forest stories about the black
father   the jew   the incubus

if there are more curses they fall on us.

Behind the swinging ropes of their isolation
my nephews wait, sucking their sweets.
The hall fills quickly and neatly.

If they keep still as water
    I'll know them.
I look but I can't be certain:

my nephews with heavy eyelids
blowing in the last touches of daylight

my sisters raising them up like torches.   [1991]

LINTON KWESI JOHNSON

Jamaica/England b. 1952

Johnson was born in Chapeltown, Jamaica and moved to Brixton, England at the age of eleven. He
joined the Black Panthers youth section in high school and began writing poetry. Since 1973 he
has belonged to the *Race Today Collective*, an organization that publishes the journal *Race Today*
and is active in the Black movement, including Creation for Liberation, founded in 1978 by John-
son and others 'to foster the development of the creative expression in Britain among the Black
artists'. One of the originators of 'Dub poetry'—Johnson coined the phrase—he records as much
poetry as he publishes. His first book was *Voices of the Living and the Dead* (1974), followed by
Dread Beat An' Blood (1975) and *Inglan is a Bitch* (1980); records include *Bass Culture* (1980) and
Making History (1984).

MEKKIN HISTRI

now tell mi someting
mistah govahment man
tell mi someting

how lang yu really feel
yu coulda keep wi andah heel
wen di trute done reveal
bout how yu grab an steal
bout how yu mek yu crooked deal
mek yu crooked deal?

well doun in Soutall
where Peach did get fall
di Asians dem faam-up a human wall
gense di fashist an dem police sheil
an dem show dat di Asians gat plenty zeal
                        gat plenty zeal
                        gat plenty zeal

it is noh mistri
wi mekkin histri
it is noh mistri
wi winnin victri

now tell mi someting
mistah police spokesman
tell mi someting

how lang yu really tink
wi woulda tek yu batn lick
yu jackboot kick
yu dutty bag a tricks
an yu racist pallyticks
yu racist pallyticks?   [1991]

DANIEL DAVID MOSES

Delaware b. 1952

A playwright as well as a poet, Moses was raised on a farm on the Six Nations lands along the Grand River in Southern Ontario; he writes that he 'grew up nominally Anglican in a community of various Christian sects and of the Longhouse, the Iroquoian traditional religious and political system. These form the largely unarticulated base of my understanding of the world.' Along with books of poems like *Delicate Bodies* (1980) and *The White Line* (1990), he has written several plays (*Coyote City* was produced in 1988) and edited, with Terry Goldie, *An Anthology of Native Canadian Literature in English* (1992).

THE LINE

This is not the poem, this line
I'm feeding you. And the thought
that this line is not the poem
is not it either. Instead
the thought of what this line is
not is the weight that sinks it
in. And though this image of
that thought as a weight is quite

a neat figure of speech, you
know what it's not—though it did
this time let the line smoothly
arc to this spot, and now lets
it reach down to one other,
one further rhyme—the music
of which almost does measure
up, the way it keeps the line
stirring through the dampening
air. Oh, you know you can hear
the lure in that. As you know
you've known from the start the self
referring this line's doing
was a hook—a sharp, twisted
bit of wit that made you look
and see how clear it is no
part of this line or its gear
could be the poem. Still it cast
and kept the line reeling out
till now at last the hook's on
to itself and about to
tie this line I'm feeding you
up with a knot. Referring
to itself has got the line
and us nowhere. So clever's
not what the poem is about
either. We're left hanging there
while something like a snout starts
nudging at your ear, nibbling
near my mouth—and it's likely
it's the poem about to take
the bait. From the inside ought
to be a great way to learn
what the poem is. And we'll use
this line when the poem's drawn it
taut and fine as breath to tell
what we know, where we are and
where we'll go—unless the line
breaks. How would it feel, knowing,
at last, what the poem really
is, to lack the line to speak?

[1990]

CHRISTINE QUNTA

South Africa b. 1952

Born in Kimberley, Qunta served on the executive of the South African Students Organization. Detained after the 1973 student walk-out, she fled South Africa in 1975 and was granted asylum in Botswana. She later took a degree in law in Sydney and currently practises in Zimbabwe. Her poetry is included in the collection *Hoyi Na! Azania—Poems of an African Struggle* (1979), and she edited the book *Women in South Africa* (1987).

THE KNOW

the know
is in the brown-red broken nipples
of my pregnant breasts
from which the warm milk
will spurt in gleeful dance
the know is written
on the innocent swelling of my hips
the know is in the
majestic black glint in my eye
it is in the pulsating
sometimes lilting tunes
flowing from the sadness in my voice
spilling from oceans of angry waves
the know
lives in sweet-sad gaiety
exuberant utterances of self-pride
viciousness
bitterness
love
enlightenment
the know is in knowing him
better than him knowing me
it is tasting and spitting him out.

[1979]

VIKRAM SETH

India b. 1952

Born in Calcutta and an economist by training, Seth has lived in England, California, China, and India. On the one hand, he tests out comic and sardonic effects in fastidiously regularized rhyme schemes that explore the 'residues' of his own romantic interiors. But he also uses 'other voices' and discloses the unsettling politics of 'other places', regimes, and systems of thought. Seth's writing includes *From Heaven Lake*, an account of his walk through Sinkiang and Tibet which won the Thomas Cook Travel Book Award in 1983, *The Golden Gate*, a novel in verse, the novel *A Suitable Boy* (1993), and two collections of verse, *The Humble Administrator's Garden* (1985) and *All Who Sleep Tonight* (1990).

WORK AND FREEDOM

Even small events that others might not notice,
I found hard to forget. In Auschwitz truly
I had no reason to complain of boredom.
If an incident affected me too deeply
I could not go straight home to my wife and children.
I would ride my horse till the terrible picture faded.
Often at night I would wander through the stables
And seek relief among my beloved horses.
At home my thoughts, often and with no warning,
Turned to such things. When I saw my children playing
Or observed my wife's delight over our youngest,
I would walk out and stand beside the transports,
The firepits, crematoriums, or gas chambers.
My wife ascribed my gloom to some annoyance
Connected with my work—but I was thinking,
'How long will our happiness last?' I was not happy
Once the mass exterminations had started.

My work, such unease aside, was never-ending,
My colleagues untrustworthy, those above me
Reluctant to understand or even to listen—
Yet everyone thought the commandant's life was heaven.
My wife and children, true, were well looked after.
Her garden was a paradise of flowers.
The prisoners, trying no doubt to attract attention,
Never once failed in little acts of kindness.
Not one of them, in our house, was badly treated:
My wife would have loved to give the prisoners presents—
And as for the children, they begged for cigarettes for them,
Especially for those who worked in the garden and brought them
Tortoises, martens, lizards, cats. Each Sunday

We'd walk to the stables, never omitting the kennels
Where the dogs were kept. My children loved all creatures
But most of all our foal and our two horses.
In summer they splashed in the wading pool, but their greatest
Joy was to bathe together with Daddy—who had
Limited hours, alas, for these childish pleasures.
My wife said, 'Think of us, not only the service.'
How could she know what lay so heavily on me?
(It made life hard, this excessive sense of duty.)

When Auschwitz was divided, Pohl in a kindly
And quite exceptional gesture gave me the option
—Perhaps as recompense for this last assignment—
To head DK or to run Sachsenhausen.
I had one day to decide. At first the thought of
Uprooting myself from Auschwitz made me unhappy,
So involved had I grown in its tasks and troubles.
But in the end I was glad to gain my freedom.   [1990]

DIONNE BRAND

Trinidad and Tobago/Canada b. 1953

Brand came to Toronto from Trinidad in 1970 and took degrees from the University of Toronto
and the Ontario Institute for Studies in Education. From 1971 to 1973, she was an editor and
writer for *Spear, Canada's Black Family Magazine*, and has worked in a number of capacities with
Black, minority, and women's groups. In her depictions of the hostile and oppressive markers of
race and gender, particularly as she has experienced these as a Black woman in Toronto and as a
girl growing up in Trinidad, her exploration extends to the crucial realm of language itself, as the
title of *No Language Is Neutral* (1990) indicates.

from NO LANGUAGE IS NEUTRAL

This is the part that is always difficult, the walk each
night across the dark school yard, biting my tongue
on new english, reading biology, stumbling over
unworded white faces. But I am only here for a
moment. The new stink of wet wool, driving my legs
across snow, ice, counting the winters that I do not
skid and fall on, a job sorting cards, the smell of an
office full of hatred each morning, no simple hatred,
not for me only, but for the hated fact of an office, an
elevator stuffed with the anger of elevator at 8 a.m.
and 5 p.m., my voice on the telephone after nine
months of office and elevator saying, I have to spend
time on my dancing. Yes, I'm a dancer, it's my new

career. Alone in the room after the phone crying at
the weakness in my stomach. Dancer. This romance
begins in a conversation off the top of my head, the
kitchen at Grace Hospital is where it ends. Then the
post office, here is escape at least from femininity,
but not from the envy of colony, education, the list of
insults is for this, better than, brighter than, richer
than, beginning with this slender walk against the
mountainous school. Each night, the black crowd of
us parts in the cold darkness, smiling.

The truth is, well, truth is not important at one end of a
hemisphere where a bird dives close to you in an
ocean for a mouth full of fish, an ocean you come to
swim in every two years, you, a slave to your leaping
retina, capture the look of it. It is like saying you are
dead. This place so full of your absence, this place
you come to swim like habit, to taste like habit, this
place where you are a woman and your breasts need
armour to walk. Here. Nerve endings of steady light
pinpoint all. That little light trembling the water again,
that gray blue night pearl of the sea, the swirl of the
earth that dash water back and always forth, that
always fear of a woman watching the world from an
evening beach with her sister, the courage between
them to drink a beer and assume their presence
against the coralline chuckle of male voices. In
another place, not here, a woman might . . . Our
nostalgia was a lie and the passage on that six hour
flight to ourselves is wide and like another world, and
then another one inside and is so separate and fast
to the skin but voiceless, never born, or born and
stilled . . . hush.

In another place, not here, a woman might touch
something between beauty and nowhere, back there
and here, might pass hand over hand her own
trembling life, but I have tried to imagine a sea not
bleeding, a girl's glance full as a verse, a woman
growing old and never crying to a radio hissing of a
black boy's murder. I have tried to keep my throat
gurgling like a bird's. I have listened to the hard
gossip of race that inhabits this road. Even in this I
have tried to hum mud and feathers and sit peacefully
in this foliage of bones and rain. I have chewed a few
votive leaves here, their taste already disenchanting

my mothers. I have tried to write this thing calmly
even as its lines burn to a close. I have come to know
something simple. Each sentence realised or
dreamed jumps like a pulse with history and takes a
side. What I say in any language is told in faultless
knowledge of skin, in drunkenness and weeping,
told as a woman without matches and tinder, not in
words and in words and in words learned by heart,
told in secret and not in secret, and listen, does not
burn out or waste and is plenty and pitiless and loves.   [1990]

ABENA P.A. BUSIA

Ghana b. 1953

Busia moved from Ghana to Oxford where she completed her doctorate in Social Anthropology.
She has taught at Oxford, Yale, the Center for Afro-American Studies at the University of
California (at Los Angeles), and most recently at Rutgers State University where she is Associate
Professor of English. Busia's first collection, *Testimonies of Exile* (1990), is dedicated to 'the wilder-
ness years' and includes the home songs of the 'black man's child' 'stranded on the shores of saxon
seas' ('Caliban').

EXILES

Funerals are important.
Away from home we cannot lay
our dead to rest
for we alone have given them
                    no fitting burial

Self-conscious of our absence
brooding over distances in western lands
we must rehearse
the planned performance of our rites
                    till we return.

And meanwhile through the years
our unburied dead eat with us
follow behind through bedroom doors.   [1990]

LIBERATION

We are all mothers,
and we have that fire within us,
of powerful women
whose spirits are so angry

we can laugh beauty into life
and still make you taste
the salt tears of our knowledge—
For we are not tortured
anymore;
we have seen beyond your lies and disguises,
and *we* have mastered the language of words,
we have mastered speech.
And know
we have also seen ourselves.
We have stripped ourselves raw
and naked piece by piece until our flesh lies flayed
with blood on our *own* hands.
What terrible thing can you do us
which we have not done to ourselves?
What can you tell us
which we didn't deceive ourselves with
a long time ago?

[1990]

MONIZA ALVI

Pakistan/England b. 1954

Alvi left Lahore, Pakistan and currently teaches in south London. Her first collection, *The Country at My Shoulder*, received a 1993 Poetry Book Society Recommendation. Alvi's work examines the evolution of her family and origin even as she takes in her adopted country. She discovers in 'The Sari' how her body, wrapped by generations, is her 'country'; she plays the field from her own 'dark centre' in 'I Would Like to be a Dot in a Painting by Mir'; and she pretends that if she stares at the map version 'long enough' 'India is manageable—smaller than/my hand, the Mahanadi River/thinner than my lifeline' ('Map of India').

THE SARI

Inside my mother
I peered through a glass porthole.
The world beyond was hot and brown.

They were all looking in on me—
Father, Grandmother,
the cook's boy, the sweeper-girl,
the bullock with the sharp
shoulderblades,
the local politicians.

My English grandmother
took a telescope
and gazed across continents.

All the people unravelled a sari.
It stretched from Lahore to Hyderabad,
wavered across the Arabian Sea,
shot through with stars,
fluttering with sparrows and quails.
They threaded it with roads,
undulations of land.

Eventually
they wrapped and wrapped me in it
whispering *Your body is your country.*   [1993]

IMITIAZ DHARKER

India b. 1954

Dharker is an artist, poet, and founder and poetry editor of *Debonair*. *Purdah and Other Poems* (1989) is her first book-length collection. Severe and bold, she pays close attention to the territory circumscribed for women, 'bought and sold, and worse, /Grown old' ('Purdah II'), whose 'woman's place' is 'fear' ('A Woman's Place'), and whose future is 'a bright noose/that hangs above [them], swinging/casually, loose, /waiting for the time when they are ready' ('The Rope').

ANOTHER WOMAN

This morning she bought green 'methi'
in the market, choosing the freshest bunch;
picked up a white radish,
imagined the crunch it would make
between her teeth, the sweet sharp taste,
then put it aside, thinking it
an extravagance; counted her coins
out carefully, tied them, a small bundle
into her sari at the waist;
came home, faced her mother-in-law's
dark looks, took
the leaves and chopped them,
her hands stained yellow from the juice;
cut an onion, fine, and cooked
the whole thing in the pot
(salt and cumin seeds thrown in)
over the stove,
shielding her face from the heat.

The usual words came and beat
their wings against her: the money spent,
curses heaped upon her parents,
who had sent her out
to darken other people's doors.

She crouched, as usual, on the floor
beside the stove,
When the man came home
she did not look into his face
nor raise her head; but bent
her back a little more.
Nothing gave her the right
to speak.

She watched the flame hiss up
and beat against the cheap old pot,
a wing of brightness
against its blackened cheek.

This was the house she had been sent to,
the man she had been bound to,
the future she had been born into.

So when the kerosene was thrown
(just a moment of surprise,
a brilliant spark)
it was the only choice
that she had ever known.

Another torch, blazing in the dark.

Another woman.

We shield our faces from the heat.   [1989]

IAN DUHIG

Ireland/England b. 1954

Duhig's poem speaks to one of the paradoxes that attends the fight to protect traditional languages from eradication: there is a fine line between preserving a language (and the culture and tradition it encodes) and xenophobic ignorance. In a Welsh pub Duhig's speaker is impatient with the 'epileptic verses' of his drinking companions and with their 'two solid hours of slaver' because he doesn't speak Irish. In revenge, the speaker quotes an Irish prayer to them that demeans the Welsh king. When the Welshman responds 'It sounds quite beautiful', the ironies are compounded, and the poet's perception of 'the Old Tongue' becomes complex and riddling.

I'R HEN IAITH A'I CHANEUON/TO THE OLD TONGUE AND ITS SONGS

> *'If the tongue only speak all that the mind knows*
> *There wouldn't be any neighbours'*—The Red Book of Hergest

When I go down to Wales for the long bank holiday
to visit my wife's grandfather who is teetotal,
who is a non-smoker, who does not approve
of anyone who is not teetotal and a non-smoker,
when I go down to Wales for the long, long bank holiday
with my second wife to visit her grandfather
who deserted Methodism for The Red Flag,
who won't hear a word against Stalin,
who despite my oft-professed socialism
secretly believes I am still with the Pope's legions,
receiving coded telegrams from the Vatican
specifying the dates, times and positions I should adopt
for political activity and sexual activity,
who in his ninetieth year took against boxing,
which was the only thing I could ever talk to him about,
when I visit my second wife's surviving grandfather,
and when he listens to the football results in Welsh
I will sometimes slip out to the pub.

I will sometimes slip out to the pub
and drink pint upon pint of that bilious whey
they serve there, where the muzak will invariably be
The Best of the Rhosllanerchrugog Male Voice Choir
and I will get trapped by some brain donor from up the valley
who will really talk about 'the language so strong and so beautiful
that has grown out of the ageless mountains,
that speech of wondrous beauty that our fathers wrought,'
who will chant to me in Welsh his epileptic verses
about Gruffudd ap Llywellyn and Daffydd ap Llywellyn,

and who will give me two solid hours of slaver
because I don't speak Irish and who will then bring up religion,
then I will tell him I know one Irish prayer about a Welsh king
on that very subject, and I will recite for him as follows:
'Na thracht ar an mhinisteir Ghallda
Na ar a chreideimh gan bheann gan bhrí,
Mar ni'l mar bhuan-chloch da theampuill
Ach magairle Annraoi Rí.' 'Beautiful,'
He will say, as they all do, 'It sounds quite beautiful.'   [1991]

I'r Hen Iaith A'i Chaneuon: *The title is Welsh. The Irish translates roughly as: 'Speak not to me
of the foreign prelate/Nor of his creed with neither truth nor faith/For the foundation stone of his
temple/Is the bollocks of King Henry VIII.'*

LOUISE ERDRICH

Chippewa b. 1954

A member of the Turtle Mountain Chippewa of North Dakota, Erdrich was born in Little Falls,
Minnesota. Her mother was Ojibwa, her father was German, and both parents worked at the
Department of Indian Affairs school in Wahpeton, North Dakota. Erdrich studied at Dartmouth
College and Johns Hopkins University, and now teaches at Dartmouth. She is both novelist (*Love
Medicine*, 1984, *The Beet Queen*, 1986, *The Bingo Palace*, 1994, and *Tales of Burning Love: A Novel*,
1996) and poet: her collections of poetry are entitled *Jacklight* (1984) and *Baptism of Desire* (1989).
In her poetry Erdrich explores the intricacies of childhood, motherhood, childbirth, desire, and
abandonment in language 'of the body transformed at last and then consumed/in a rush of music'
('The Sacraments', 1989).

DEAR JOHN WAYNE

August and the drive-in picture is packed.
We lounge on the hood of the Pontiac
surrounded by the slow-burning spirals they sell
at the window, to vanquish the hordes of mosquitoes.
Nothing works. They break through the smoke screen for blood.

Always the lookout spots the Indians first,
spread north to south, barring progress.
The Sioux or some other Plains bunch
in spectacular columns, ICBM missiles,
their feathers bristling in the meaningful sunset.

The drum breaks. There will be no parlance.
Only the arrows whining, a death-cloud of nerves
swarming down on the settlers

who die beautifully, tumbling like dust weeds
into the history that brought us all here
together: this wide screen beneath the sign of the bear.

The sky fills, acres of blue squint and eye
that the crowd cheers. His face moves over us,
a thick cloud of vengeance, pitted
like the land that was once flesh. Each rut,
each scar makes a promise: *It is*
not over, this fight, not as long as you resist.

Everything we see belongs to us.

A few laughing Indians fall over the hood
slipping in the hot spilled butter.
The eye sees a lot, John, but the heart is so blind.
Death makes us owners of nothing.
He smiles, a horizon of teeth
the credits reel over, and then the white fields

again blowing in the true-to-life dark.
The dark films over everything.
We get into the car
scratching our mosquito bites, speechless and small
as people are when the movie is done.
We are back in our skins.

How can we help but keep hearing his voice,
the flip side of the sound track, still playing:
Come on, boys, we got them
where we want them, drunk, running.
They'll give us what we want, what we need.
Even his disease was the idea of taking everything.
Those cells, burning, doubling, splitting out of their
    skins.   [1984]

NUALA ARCHER

USA/Ireland b. 1955

Archer was born to Irish parents in New York and has travelled widely. Her verse is marked by a witty but anguished surrealism and by stark evocations of figures' fleeting gestures at each other, as in the opening of 'Towards Another Terminal': 'Down silver eels/the train highballs/into the iron barn./Its whistle moans/to the red-haired moon/as Ms Fashoon sidles over/to Walter and a vodka gimlet./Her eyes are strawberries/with green lashes./She is a tall coyote/trying to bite her heart into/digestible pieces.' Archer's books include *Whale on the Line* (1981), *Two Women, Two Shores* (1989, with the Irish poet Medbh McGuckian), and *Pan/Ama* (1992).

WHALE ON THE LINE

(for John)

1
You can't hear me dialling your number
because a whale is tangled
in the telephone cables on the ocean floor.
For some unknown reason

he torpedoed to the bottom. Cables entwine
the spool of his body—forty-five tons
of blubber the colour of your blue eyes.
His last air bubbles drift up

like small parachutes. He explores
the darkness by ear, listens
to kelp wave solemnly back and forth
like ushers at a funeral.

It took the scuba divers
days of overtime to unknot the mesh.
Arc lamps scattered light
in strange shadows. A white octopus

floated about, curling and uncurling
his arms like yo-yo's, gently touching
the whale's slack muscles,
open mouth and lidded eyes.

2
For months words drift in shoals
around the quiet whale . . . 'Remember
nightingales, stars, hibiscus, the late
train, willows of wind . . . ?'

Fish gargoyles, carrying lamps,
pick barnacles off the whale's back.
Submarine gulls circle and scream
Ballena! Ballena! Kujira! Kujira!

The whale's skull lies in sand.
A seaweed tongue flutters with the tide.
His stoney ears patiently become
the water sounding against a calf

just born to blue-green September
light. Soft explosions of breath
buoy her thermos-shaped body.
An albatross wraps the five-foot cord

around its neck, tears into placenta
as a clean wind tears clouds open.
Half-awake the calf rolls with the slanting
sea into a night brightened by the moon's

rainbow witches. Fog horns call back memories
of ships—*Union, Essex, Ann Alexander*
and *Kathleen*—sent to the bottom by whales;
and of whales lashed to my call of love for you.   [1981]

DAVID DABYDEEN

British Guyana/England b. 1955

Dabydeen is professor of literature and lecturer at the University of Warwick. His first collection, *Slave Song* (1984) fuses Guyanese Creole and the dramatic monologue to explore the indentured slaves' experience in the Caribbean; it was awarded the Commonwealth Poetry Prize and the Cambridge University Quiller-Couch Prize. *Coolie Odyssey* (1988) extends this understanding of 'Nigger Talk' and culture to Great Britain. Dabydeen has pursued central concerns about the representation of Black and East Indian realities in visual art (*Hogarth's Blacks*, 1987) and political/economic contexts (*Hogarth, Walpole and Commercial Britain*, 1987).

THE CANECUTTERS' SONG

(The slow throbbing of a drum at long intervals, growing louder and quicker as the song proceeds, then breaking into a wild uncontrolled beating at the last few lines of the song. The men move slowly around the solitary canecutter with slight dance gestures that also intensify gradually.)

CANECUTTER

White hooman walk tru de field fo watch we canecutta,
Tall, straight, straang-limb,
Hair sprinkle in de wind like gold-duss,
Lang lace frack loose on she bady like bamboo-flag,

An flesh mo dan hibiscus early maan, white an saaf an wet
Flowering in she panty.
O Shanti! Shanti! Shanti!
Wash dis dutty-skin in yu dew
Wipe am clean on yu saaf white petal!
O Shanti! Shanti! Shanti!—
So me spirit call, so e halla foh yu
When me peep out at yu tween cane-stalk, strain me nose foh ketch yu scent
Bram-bram bram-bram beat me haat till me friken yu go hear—
Bu daylight separate me an yu, an dis mud on me haan
Dis sweat from me face, dis rag on me back . . .
Yu puss-mouth glow, mesh wid light, sun a seed an sprout deh
Me too black fo come deh—
Bu when night come how me dream . . .
Dat yu womb lie like starapple buss open in de mud
An how me hold yu dung, wine up yu waiss
Draw blood from yu patacake, daub am all over yu face
Till yu dutty like me an yu halla
Like when cutlass slip an slice me leg, an yu shake
Like when snake twist rung me foot, when we cut cane . . .
So me dream
When night come
An masquita wake up from de bush,
Malabunta move.

CHORUS

Baai yu ever dream she drawsie-down!
Baai yu ever wuk she wid yu tongue!
Baai yu ever taste she pokey
Saaf an drippy like baigan-chokey!   [1984]

THE NEW POETRY

She wanted to be alone with her world, vexed
Always by his prehistoric eye,
The strange usurping tales of anthropophagi
And recitation of colonial texts.

Britannia is serviced by new machines
Humming and twinkling as they work,
The creak of mule-drawn punt or old slave feet,
The exhalation of the aborigines

Are esoteric notes in a scholar's curious book:
The new poetry quietly observes
The ways a leaf spirals neutrally to earth,
The shades of moon, the tides, the shepherd's timeless crook.

She forsook as tedious his confession,
His alien unbridgeable babble of words,
Settling comfortably on the sofa
She would turn the television on

And see confirmed the greetings beamed through space
Of natives singing by some runway,
The bone-shaped plane of fat white men and foreign aid
Met by loud spears and women jigging waist.   [1988]

CAROL ANN DUFFY

Scotland b. 1955

Poet, editor, and freelance writer, Duffy writes poetry in which the familiar and the concrete
resonate within legendary and mythic frames of reference. Her collections have been distinguished
by honours such as the Somerset Maugham Award (1988), the Dylan Thomas Award (1989), and
the Cholmondeley Award (1992). Her 1993 volume *Mean Time* received both the Forward Poetry
Prize and the Whitbread Literary Award for poetry.

STANDING FEMALE NUDE

Six hours like this for a few francs.
Belly nipple arse in the window light,
he drains the colour from me. Further to the right,
Madame. And do try to be still.
I shall be represented analytically and hung
in great museums. The bourgeoisie will coo
at such an image of a river-whore. They call it Art.

Maybe. He is concerned with volume, space.
I with the next meal. You're getting thin,
Madame, this is not good. My breasts hang
slightly low, the studio is cold. In the tea-leaves
I can see the Queen of England gazing
on my shape. Magnificent, she murmurs
moving on. It makes me laugh. His name

is Georges. They tell me he's a genius.
There are times he does not concentrate
and stiffens for my warmth. Men think of their mothers.
He possesses me on canvas as he dips the brush
repeatedly into the paint. Little man,
you've not the money for the arts I sell.
Both poor, we make our living how we can.

I ask him Why do you do this? Because
I have to. There's no choice. Don't talk.
My smile confuses him. These artists
take themselves too seriously. At night I fill myself
with wine and dance around the bars. When it's finished
he shows me proudly, lights a cigarette. I say
Twelve francs and get my shawl. It does not look like me.   [1985]

THE CAPTAIN OF THE 1964 TOP OF THE FORM TEAM

Do Wah Diddy Diddy, Baby Love, Oh Pretty Woman
were in the Top Ten that month, October, and the Beatles
were everywhere else. I can give you the B-side
of the Supremes one. Hang on. Come See About Me?
I lived in a kind of fizzing hope. Gargling
with Vimto. The clever smell of my satchel. Convent girls.
I pulled my hair forward with a steel comb that I blew
like Mick, my lips numb as a two-hour snog.

No snags. The Nile rises in April. Blue and White.
The humming-bird's song is made by its wings, which beat
so fast that they blur in flight. I knew the capitals,
the Kings and Queens, the dates. In class, the white sleeve
of my shirt saluted again and again. Sir! . . . Correct.
Later, I whooped at the side of my bike, a cowboy,
mounted it running in one jump. I sped down Dyke Hill,
no hands, famous, learning, dominus domine dominum.

Dave Dee Dozy . . . Try me. Come on. My mother kept my
    mascot Gonk
on the TV set for a year. And the photograph. I look
so brainy you'd think I'd just had a bath. The blazer.
The badge. The tie. The first chord of A Hard Day's Night
loud in my head. I ran to the Spinney in my prize shoes,
up Churchill Way, up Nelson Drive, over pink pavements
that girls chalked on, in a blue evening; and I stamped
the pawprints of badgers and skunks in the mud. My
    country.

I want it back. The captain. The one with all the answers.
    Bzz.
My name was in red on Lucille Green's jotter. I smiled
as wide as a child who went missing on the way home
from school. The keeny. I say to my stale wife
Six hits by Dusty Springfield. I say to my boss A pint!
How can we know the dancer from the dance? Nobody.
My thick kids wince. Name the Prime Minister of Rhodesia.
My country. How many florins in a pound?   [1993]

RITA ANN HIGGINS

Ireland b. 1955

Unequivocal and charged, Higgins's lists identify the indignity of 'some people' who know what it is like 'to be second hand/to be second class/to be no class/to be looked down on/to be walked on/to be pissed on/to be shat on' ('Some People'). Her timing is expert and of the stand-up comic variety. Her witches and goddesses, in 'Goddess on the Mervue Bus' (1986) and 'Witch in the Buses' (1988), exist fully in three dimensions. Higgins's strength as a poet of the people is described by one delighted student just after a reading at the University of Bingen: 'direct, enlightening, and entertaining'.

WOMAN'S INHUMANITY TO WOMAN
(GALWAY LABOUR EXCHANGE)

And in this cage ladies and gentlemen,
we have the powers that be.

Powder power,
lipstick power,
pencil power,
paper power,
cigarette in the left hand power,
raised right of centre half plucked eyebrow, Cyclops power,

big tits power,
piercing eyes power,
filed witches nails power,
I own this building power,
I own you power,
fear of the priest power,
fear of the Black 'N' Tans power.

Your father drank too much power,
your sister had a baby when she was fifteen power,
where were you last night power,
upstairs in your house is dirty power,
the state of your hotpress power,
the state of your soul power,
keep door closed power,
keeping eyes closed power,
no smoking power,
money for the black babies power,
queue only here power,
sign only there power,
breathe only when I tell you power.

No pissing on the staff power,
jingle of keys power,
your brother signs and works power,
ye have a retarded child power,
you sign and work power,
look over your shoulder power,
look over your brother's shoulder power,
I know your mother's maiden name power,
look at the ground power,
I know your father's maiden name power,
spy in the sky power,
spy in the toilet power,
fart in front of a bishop power.

Apologise for your mother's colour hair power,
apologise for your father's maiden name power,
apologise for being born power.   [1988]

ERIN MOURÉ

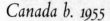

Canada b. 1955

In 1974 Mouré left her native Calgary for Vancouver, where she worked for CNR and VIA Rail, moving to Montreal in 1984. Her first book, *Empire, York Street* (1979), focused on ordinary experience—working lives, sexuality, and the politics of relationships. More recently she has concentrated on the powers of language to create reality, as in 'The Acts', a sequence in *Furious* (1988) that reflects on the ways in which the surfaces and depths of language create forms of thought. Her latest book is *The Green Word: Selected Poems 1973–1992* (1994).

CHERISH

for Libby Scheier

The expression of longing,
in & among
the collapse of social systems,
among facts such as fish see colour;
in a room where light cannot enter the high window,
where mugs are empty of coffee & contain
so many ounces of the room's air,

in the room where air dips close
between the arms,
where women are not forgetful any longer
but tell their whole stories
& fear their body's message,
being alone

The essential barrier
The unknown way to cherish aloneness
& dispel it as a waste
The cups are empty on the floor all night long,
the plates have tipped their crumbs into the paper,
the paper has lain stubbornly unread
until its news is no more sensible,

until Salvador is liberated or invaded,
the fish are suffocating in their own waters,
the future has occurred & not been announced yet
Women
in the ease of their voices' murmur,
able to express but not dispel
anything
To talk without loneliness
because it has been acknowledged & achieved
in our own bodies
Because here the cups are full of the noise
of our laughter,
because no touch is the answer & we know it giddily
& The longing for it
purely
makes us full   [1985]

VÉRONIQUE TADJO

Ivory Coast b. 1955

Tadjo sometimes writes in French and then translates her work into English, as is the case with
'Five Poems', the first three of which were included in her book of poems, *Latérite*. Tadjo has also
written two novels, a book of short stories, and a children's book. She teaches at the University of
Abidjan.

FIVE POEMS

LIFE IS MADE
OF BLACKBERRY BUSHES
AND DARK THORNS
I WOULD HAVE LIKED IT
MORE MELLOW AND LESS BITTER
BUT YOU KNOW
THE LIMIT OF THINGS
SHRINKS AT EVERY MOMENT
OUR FACES CHANGE
AND OUR LOVES CRASH

AGAINST ONE ANOTHER
YOU KNOW IT WELL
THE NIGHT OF YOUR BIG FRIGHT
THERE'LL ONLY BE YOU

*   *   *

YOU MUST GIVE BIRTH
TO CHILDHOOD
SPIT OUT THE VENOM
WHICH BREAKS YOUR VIOLENCE
EMBRACE THE PRESENT
AND LEAVE FROM THE PLATFORM
THE WARMTH OF THE FOETUS
IS THE NIGHT OF ALL TIMES

*   *   *

HE IS MY SHADOW
MY STEP-BY-STEP
MY FURTIVE GLANCE
HE IS MY MAYBE
MY NEWBORN DESIRE
HE IS MY STRENGTH
AND MY WEAKNESS
THE WATER WHICH CARRIES ME
AND THE WATER WHICH DROWNS ME
HE IS WHERE I'D LIKE TO GO
TOMORROW AS WELL AS YESTERDAY

*   *   *

DID YOU SEE
HOW THE FATHER CRIED
WHEN HIS DAUGHTER LEFT?
WHEN SHE WALKED AWAY
HIS FACE A GRIMACE
HIS MOUTH A GAPING HOLE
AND HIS BROW LINED WITH CREASES
THEN HE LOWERED HIS HEAD

TO GO OVER THERE
FURTHER AWAY FROM EVERYTHING
THAT MADE YOU

BUT THERE IS THE TELEPHONE
WHICH ECHOES ONE MORNING
IN THE HALF SLEEP OF A DAY
ALREADY TURNING GREY
THE VOICE OF THE FATHER
OVER LAND
AND OVER WATER
TELLING EVERYDAY WORDS
WORDS CARVED BY YEARS
WORDS SO ORDINARY
THEY SOUND LIKE A REVELATION
AND IN THE MIDST OF
SUCH EMOTION
OF THIS OUTSTRETCHED HAND
THE CLICK OF THE TELEPHONE
SENDING SILENCE
WHICH BECOMES OBSESSION
UNENDING UPROAR
OF A TRUER REALITY
EMPTINESS & THE FORGETTING OF BODIES

* * *

Life is walking fast
It wasn't how I wanted it, but I had to take what I could.
I used to think time was on my side. That has changed now.
I can't risk it
I can't wait
I had to touch you
I don't know what tomorrow will bring.
I had to gamble.   [1984]

SUJATA BHATT

India b. 1956

Bhatt moved with her family to the United States in the 1960s; for a time she studied creative writing at the University of Iowa. *Brunizem* (1988), her first book of poetry in English, won the Alice Hunt Barlett Prize in England and the Commonwealth Poetry Prize for Asia. Recent collections include *Monkey Shadows* (1992) and *The Stinking Rose* (1994). A translator of Gujarati poetry and a freelance writer currently living in Germany, Bhatt offers her readers bicultural and often bilingual experiences. Wary of clichés, intolerant of stereotypes, she is particularly sensitive to the intense physical and spiritual energy alive in women's worlds.

WHITE ASPARAGUS

Who speaks of the strong currents
streaming through the legs, the breasts
of a pregnant woman
in her fourth month?

She's young, this is her first time,
she's slim and the nausea has gone.
Her belly's just starting to get rounder
her breasts itch all day,

and she's surprised that what she wants
is *him*
    inside her again.
Oh come like a horse, she wants to say,
move like a dog, a wolf,
           become a suckling lion-cub—

Come here, and here, and here—
but swim fast and don't stop.

Who speaks of the green coconut uterus
the muscles sliding, a deeper undertow
and the green coconut milk that seals
her well, yet flows so she is wet
from his softest touch?

Who understands the logic
behind this desire?
Who speaks of the rushing tide
        that awakens
her slowly increasing blood—?
And the hunger

     raw obsessions beginning
with the shape of asparagus:
sun-deprived white and purple-shadow-veined,
she buys three kilos
of the fat ones, thicker than anyone's fingers,
she strokes the silky heads,
some are so jauntily capped . . .
     even the smell pulls her in—
                        [1991]

A DIFFERENT WAY TO DANCE

1
It is June.
A record-breaking hot night.
Sizzling insects spatter against
the windshield as we drive
south from Boston.
My mother has stretched out
on the back seat.
Her eyes half closed, a little bored
her head begins to nod with sleep.

Then she sits up abruptly:

અરે પેલો હાથી જાય!
(aray paylo hathi jai!)

હાથી જાય!
(hathi jai!)

Hey, there goes an elephant!
An elephant's going by!
She shouts
pointing at the largest elephant I've ever seen—

chained inside an open truck.

He is a grey shadow
in a black truck, hurtling through
indigo New England night haze.

We look and look, desperately craning our necks,
wishing there were more light—

and we are not sure
whether we've actually seen
the expression in his eyes
or the delicate pink
curled inside the tip of his trunk.

There he goes
shuffling his feet
to his own Blues—
his trunk flies up to the right
to the left, extending the song,
                    greeting the night air . . .

'Follow that truck!'
                My mother points,
'Follow that elephant!'

We follow him
as if he were the god,
                Ganesh himself.

2
Sometimes Parvati dreams
of her son's face:
the little boy Ganesh
who had greenish brown eyes—
huge eyes reminding her
of coriander leaves and sliced
ginger root floating in water
                    in a deep wooden bowl.

Her little boy Ganesh
had a small nose, straight eyebrows,
thick knots of curly hair
before Shiva interfered.

Parvati even remembers the shape
of the newborn Ganesh she bore,
bent flower stalk elbows, the chest
                    flushing red—
the almost transparent skin
                    she first oiled
and the ripe melon soft fontanelle,
the spot she stroked everyday,
                    always checking
just to be sure . . .

Sometimes the elephant head of Ganesh
dreams of the life among elephants it knew
before Shiva interfered.

How comfortable it was to walk
on four legs. To be able to speak with mountains,
to guess the mood of the wind . . .
and there was the jungle,
cool mud, dripping leaves,
the smell of wood—sandalwood, teak.
The smell of trees allowed to grow old
the smell of fresh water touched by deer
the smell of his newly found mate
the smell of their mounting passion—

None the less
everyday that elephant head of Ganesh
reveals a secret: a new way to eat,
another direction for language
a different way to dance . . .

In the early morning
          through greyish pink mist,
and in the evening
          through long shadows, smudged blue,
see how his one tusk balances those human knees,
how the elephant ears guide the human toes
until Parvati smiles
          Shiva steps aside,
and the elephant trunk sways
removing all that stands in the way—
the elephant trunk swings
          from side to side
hiding away the memory of Shiva's raised hand,
hiding away the knife-slashed soul,
that throbbing wound it carries
since leaving its first life.   [1991]

JEAN BINTA BREEZE

Jamaica/England b. 1956

Identified as the first female Dub poet, Binta Breeze is also a playwright and an actress who studied theatre at Jamaica's School of Drama before moving to England. She is a dancer and choreographer who believes in poetry as performance: on the page, her poems invite readers to read and hear her distinctive idiom, as in the opening of 'Riddym Ravings (The Mad Woman's Poem)': 'De fus time dem kar me go a Bellevue was fi di dactar an de lanlord operate/and tek de radio out a mi head,/ troo dem seize de bed/weh did a gimme cancer/and mek mi talk to nobady.' Recent collections of her verse include *Riddym Ravings* (1988) and *Spring Cleaning* (1992).

ORDINARY MAWNING

it wasn't dat de day did start out bad
or dat no early mawning dream
did swing mi foot
aff de wrong side of de bed

it wasn't dat de cold floor
mek mi sneeze
an mi nose start run wid misery
wasn't a hangover headache
mawning
or a worry rising mawning

de sun did a shine same way
an a cool breeze
jus a brush een aff de sea
an de mawning news
was jus de same as ever
two shot dead
truck lick one
Israel still a bruk up
Palestine
an Botha still have de whole world han
twist back a dem

no
it wasn't de day dat start out bad
wasn't even pre m t
or post m t
was jus anadda ordinary get up
get de children ready fi school
mawning
anadda what to cook fah dinna dis evening

mawning
anadda wish me never did breed but Lawd
mi love dem mawning
jus anadda wanda if ah should a
tek up back wid dis man it would a
ease de situation mawning

no
it wasn't no duppy frighten mi
mek mi jump outa mi sleep
eena bad mood
nor no neighbour bring first quarrel
to mi door
wasn't de price rise pon bus fare
an milk an sugar

was jus anadda
same way mawning
anadda clean up de mess
after dem lef mawning
a perfectly ordinary
mawning of a perfectly
ordinary day
trying to see a way
out

so it did hard fi understand
why de ordinary sight of
mi own frock
heng up pon line
wid some clothespin
should a stop mi from do nutten
but jus
bawl   [1988]

ANNE FRENCH

New Zealand b. 1956

Born in Wellington, French lives and works in Auckland where she is a managing editor for an international publishing firm. Her own publications include *All Cretans are Liars* (1987) and *The Male as Evader* (1988).

COLLISIONS

'Of course she's still intransigent', you said
between bites as though it isn't someone's marriage.
So I took a good thirty seconds to digest it.
'Intransigent nothing.' Sounds as though I was
their counsellor from Marriage Guidance and not
—well, something similar, if less honourable. More
involved. His consolation, her confidante.
A reflex triangle, you might call it, kinked
briefly backwards against gravity.
How much of that you know I daren't assess,
but note the stillness of your eyes, your voice
as we defend them to each other. It's the boys'
team against the girls'. Result: a draw.
We call it off with a point each on the board.

So do you know it all then, or just what he
told you—not quite the same thing—the plot
and some of the dialogue, with a critical commentary
throughout? Not, presumably, how it happened:
the usual collisions of people from a small
country living in a provincial town.
The predictable, in other words, just waiting
for its chance. I was the meat, that's all—he'll
have told you gristle. Or how it ended: dinners
together, celebrations, people left on planes,
assorted fictions stayed intact. Now silence.
It's relief. But forget his elegant phrases, grand
evoked emotion. Let me risk the awkward
truth—it seems (improbably) I loved them both.   [1987]

IN ABSENTIA

The problem is how to occupy dead
time. When some women weep, or drink,
or blab, take baths, go to pieces, read,

she finds herself making the most futile
of female gestures: washing the floors,
cutting flowers, dusting, setting all

to rights, as though what mute time shoves
aside or buries crumb by crumb can ward
off misfortune, is efficacious

against misery. It is mere cave
magic, does not rise above wax and water
or preclude snappishness, ill-temper

with small children; of virtues
it is the most insignificant. Of course
she would prefer, if she could choose,

to screech and wail like Ariadne, or hack
like Gaea at his balls. Instead she's meek
as a housewife ironing in a clean kitchen.   [1988]

IYAMIDÉ HAZELEY

Sierra Leone b. 1957

Although she was born in London of Sierra Leonean parentage, Hazeley grew up in West Africa, returning to England to complete her degrees and develop her skills as a teacher, designer, and painter. In 1983 she received a Minority Rights Group/Minority Arts Advisory Service Award for poetry; in 1986 she was a joint winner of the Greater London Council Black Experience filmscript competition. Co-founder of Zora Press, a Black women's publishing collective, Hazeley published her first collection *Ripples and Jagged Edges* in 1987. Her freedom poems build hope from the ground up; she is acutely aware of the cost a future entails.

WHEN YOU HAVE EMPTIED OUR CALABASHES

When you have emptied our calabashes
Into your porcelain bowls overflowing
the surplus spilling and seeping
into foreign soil
when you have cleaved the heads of our young
and engraved upon the soft papyrus there
an erasure of our past
having built edifices to your lies
filled them with so many bad books and distorts
and sealed the cracks in the structure
with some synthetic daub,
when you stock and pile arms
and talk about the nuclear theatre

want to make the world your stage
limiting the chance of world survival
it confirms your calculations, your designs
your ambitions which we'll thwart
which we'll resist
which we'll fight in all manner of ways.

We will rebuild
we will choose our most knowing
most eloquent old women
to spit in the mouths
of the newborn babies
so that they will remember
and be eloquent also
and learn well
the lessons of the past
to tell their grandchildren
so that if you come again
in another time
with your trinkets and arms
with porcelain bowls
and scriptures
they will say
we know you.

[1988]

LI-YOUNG LEE

Indonesia/USA b. 1957

Lee was born in Jakarta where his father, a personal physician to Mao Tse-tung, had been a
political prisoner jailed by Sukarno. Later his family travelled throughout the Far East, emigrated
to the United States, and settled in rural Pennsylvania. Lee has studied and taught at several US
universities, and published two collections of poetry: *Rose* (1986) and *The City in Which I Love You*
(1990). Lee's poetry invokes 'the art of memory' for meditations on a sensuous world with an acute
consciousness of the ephemeral; 'I won't last'.

THIS ROOM AND EVERYTHING IN IT

Lie still now
while I prepare for my future,
certain hard days ahead,
when I'll need what I know so clearly this moment.

I am making use
of the one thing I learned
of all the things my father tried to teach me:
the art of memory.

I am letting this room
and everything in it
stand for my ideas about love
and its difficulties.

I'll let your love-cries,
those spacious notes
of a moment ago,
stand for distance.

Your scent,
that scent
of spice and a wound,
I'll let stand for mystery.

Your sunken belly
is the daily cup
of milk I drank
as a boy before morning prayer.

The sun on the face
of the wall
is God, the face
I can't see, my soul,

and so on, each thing
standing for a separate idea,
and those ideas forming the constellation
of my greater idea.
And one day, when I need
to tell myself something intelligent
about love,

I'll close my eyes
and recall this room and everything in it:
My body is estrangement.
This desire, perfection.
Your closed eyes my extinction.
Now I've forgotten my
idea. The book
on the windowsill, riffled by wind . . .
the even-numbered pages are
the past, the odd-
numbered pages, the future.
The sun is
God, your body is milk . . .

useless, useless . . .
your cries are song, my body's not me . . .
no good . . . my idea
has evaporated . . . your hair is time, your thighs are song . . .
it had something to do
with death . . . it had something
to do with love.   [1990]

IAN MCMILLAN

England b. 1957

McMillan was born in Barnseley, Yorkshire, where he performed as a stand-up comic, training that
he put to good use when he became part of a performance group called Versewagon with poets
John Turner and Martin Wiley. Versewagon, renamed the Circus of Poets, remains widely popular
in Britain. McMillan is an accomplished print poet and his comedy can be underscored by won-
der at the impulses of the verbal imagination. His books include *An Anthology from Versewagon*
(1982), *Now It Can Be Told* (1983), and *Selected Poems* (1987).

JUST THE FACTS, JUST THE

In the play room
Dean won't eat his cabbage.
His mother whispers to him,
'Look, I know you don't like cabbage . . .'
His dad, who has been exchanging shy smiles
with me all weekend, says,
'Tha dun't like cabbage, all reight,
tha dun't . . .'

We sit around on the small chairs
encouraging. Enormous toys
line the walls like prefects,
two huge snails lick themselves
up the side of the glass case,
thirty-seven fish move in a tank.

We are on the eighth floor. Six
floors down, my mother settles
herself painfully into a new hip.
On the eighth floor, my daughter
spoons mush into her mouth. Tonight
the doctor will tell her to go home.
I close my eyes and see her jerking
about on the settee, bright red,
making little cardboard cries.

Cardboard cries? Pull together yourself.
Just the facts, just the

Late at night, driving between Barnburgh
and Goldthorpe, a couple making love
in a ditch, caught in the light of the
car lights, looking like a brightly
coloured bird or a brightly coloured
animal.

Yes, I guess
you are right.
Any facts will do.   [1987]

ARCHIE WELLER

Australia b. 1957

Born in Subiaco, Western Australia, Weller is a prominent aboriginal writer whose works include
a novel, *The Day of the Dog* (1981), a collection of short stories, *Going Home* (1986), and an
anthology of aboriginal writing, *Us Fellas* (co-edited with Colleen Francis-Glass, 1988).

THE LEGEND OF JIMMY'S AXE

Here is the legend of Jimmy's axe
that scarred the country with ochre red blood:
as red as the flaming hair on his head
or as the fire that writhed in his cold eyes,
green like the trees and the grass of his home and the swift
parrots that flew through his skies.
Here is the story of a cruel axe.
Sometimes its ringing singing tones would roll
across the wheat-heavy hills on which he worked,
as he crowned the land with wooden fence-posts.
In the year this Federal country was born,
toasted in champagne and praised in loud song,
Jimmy, lost in these new lands,
with his axe held in half-caste brown hands
came stumbling and bumbling, sullen and wild;
came like Ned Kelly, maiming and killing
women and children old men and babies
with his brother, who laughed like the Devil,
and like storm-filled rivers blood was spilling
until at last they shot him dead.
Shot-gun pellets tore through his head
and ripped to shred his dreams of war
then Jimmy and his axe were no more.

Yet,
did his wife,
as white as he would have liked to be;
white like the flour those squatters never gave him
and for which he took up his bloody axe
to smash the white eggshell complacency.
His wife as white as the day he was born;
she as white as the baby that was not his—
all so white on that gruesome awesome night . . .
Did she mourn?

[1990]

UNTITLED

Our songman is a flashing silver king
who will always please and never die;
whose vibrating songs are new all the time:
honeyed lips, love and soulful eyes.
In our Boora rings, on the corners of the roads
we, the young men of our tribe, gather
for initiation ceremonies again.
Our scars are not from flint but are from knives.
We are the drunken stumbling warriors
of our tribe—our dissipated tribe.
We shout out the legends gathered from our back-roads
and our kangaroos we kill from behind the bar.

He reclines upon his shabby throne:
his broken-backed
bursting springs throne
and watches his soldiers coming home
youths swaggering—
staggering—home.

[1990]

MOYA CANNON

Ireland b. 1958

Cannon was born in Donegal and studied history and politics in Galway and Cambridge before taking a position teaching school. In '"Taom"' Cannon grasps the formidable 'new and mortal' language birthed by women 'when needed', 'in anguish' 'across death and generation'. Cannon's first collection, *The Oar*, appeared in 1990 and many of her pieces have been set to music by the Irish composer Jane O'Leary.

'TAOM'

The unexpected tide,
the great wave,
uncontained, breasts the rock,
overwhelms the heart, in spring or winter.

Surfacing from a fading language,
the word comes when needed.
A dark sound surges and ebbs,
its accuracy steadying the heart.

Certain kernels of sound
reverberate like seasoned timber,
unmuted truths of a people's winters
stirrings of a thousand different springs.

There are small unassailable words
that diminish caesars;
territories of the voice
that intimate across death and generation
how a secret was imparted—
that first articulation,
when a vowel was caught
between a strong and a tender consonant;
when someone, in anguish
made a new and mortal sound
that lived until now,
a testimony
to waves succumbed to
and survived.   [1990]

'Taom' is an Irish word which means 'an overwhelming wave of emotion'.

DERMOT BOLGER

Ireland b. 1959

Although Bolger writes poems that speak to Ireland's political and historical situation, 'Snuff Movies' represents another less locally grounded element in his vision. The voice speaking and the eye mesmerized by television murder are paralyzed by fear, inertia, and the threat (as well as the promise) of 'real life' violence ritually enacted for him on television. Ultimately, the poem focuses more closely on the viewer and his motivations than on the images he sees: 'longing for release and yet not daring to believe it could happen,' this speaker lives in an endless purgatory.

SNUFF MOVIES

The wind shuffles through the crackled glass and the floorboards rot.
It has been eight days since I stepped outside this filthy flat
where I've sat watching and four times my vigil has been rewarded:
four times I have hung within the limbo of the static from the tube,
longing for release and yet not daring to believe it could happen,
and four times the picture hasn't jerked back on to advertisements—
my throat has dried up and my body trembled as I watched
the figure thrown naked into the room and the beating begin.
Whole days wither stagnantly in this flat and nothing happens,
days when I'm stuck like an insect on fly paper unable to move,
trapped within the metallic hiss of that ocean of static,
and I wait and pray that the advertisements will not continue
as over and over the slogans repeat without commentary or pity,
hammering out messages at those remaining sealed in their rooms.
Once we walked down streets and worked in throbbing factories,
I remember oil on my overalls and the smell of sweat without fear,
but then the coalitions collapsed and regrouped and were submerged
by the corporations who had learnt how to survive without us.
Just four times the knife has flashed like an old matador's
and youngsters raised their heads although blinded by the hood.
There is no way of knowing how many of my workmates are left,
caged up before crackling boxes terrified to miss the murders.
Last month I saw a man run with a plastic bag through the litter,
apart from him all streets to the superstore were deserted.
I breathe safely—I am too old for anybody's attention,
they will never come and shove me hooded into that studio,
I will never strain my head forward in expectation of the blow.
From this final refuge I can spy and be involved in their agony,
the flesh wincing and that final anonymous moan of pain;
and afterwards I breathe again in my renewed triumph of living.
Nobody knows any longer when the curfew begins or ends
but one evening I heard them come for somebody on the street.
I never knew which hooded neighbour I might have once passed

kept the whole of Ireland contained for a day with their death.
I know they are killing me too in this war of nerves I survive in,
it's been years since I've not slept sitting upright in this chair
dreaming of blood and waking fretfully to advertisements,
and yet I still cling on, speaking to nobody in the superstore,
running home frantic that I will miss a final glimpse of life.
Long ago I believed in God—now I believe what I am told:
there is no heaven except that instant when the set comes alive,
no purgatory except the infinite static bombarding the screen,
hell could only be if they came for the television or for me.   [1986]

JOANNE ARNOTT

Canada b. 1960

Arnott was born in Manitoba, raised in western Canada, and studied at the University of Western
Ontario. She currently lives in Vancouver, where she works with groups like AWARE to educate about
racism. Her poetry traces her search through her past to uncover and work through experiences of
violence and abuse in her family; frequently, Arnott's language and imagery move swiftly from exter-
nal world to internal states of mind and being, searching for correspondences between self and
world. *Wiles of Girlhood* (1991) is her first book of poetry; her second is *My Grass Cradle* (1992).

ABORTION (LIKE MOTHERHOOD) CHANGES NOTHING

I am a cunt, and the folds of my face
are purple. My mouth, delicate and moist,
a pale pink.
Like your tongue, like the roof
of your mouth my throat
arcs gently, while
all around me pulses
my heart (the pump
of power, the vibrant
juices). At the base of my throat
is an organ, the organ
is growing, it swells
from lemon to orange to melon
as the long days pass. Here
at the base of my throat
life and death are meeting
for a hot red time.

Life and death are meeting
at the base of my throat, i do not
scream, i do not
gurgle. Life and death

are cavorting, and when
all is done,
receding,
both of them, all of us,
back down the throat to
the lip of my face,
out into the world
of men—

off to
meander again.
The organ forgotten reduces
to her virgin size; my self
slips back to the usual
uncondensed form;
and my cunt,
she is returned to
a shadowy half-known place,
off along
the tenuous edge
of being.
My face

remembers her eyes, her nose
and ears, her taste buds.
My face
speaks well, again, in places, in that

stilted *human* tongue.   [1985]

CHERRY SMYTH

Ireland/England b. 1960

'Black Leather Jacket' depicts the culture that surrounds Smyth's visit to a lover dying in the hospital and allows her to move quickly from the intimacy of the bodies that have worn, rubbed, and stroked this jacket to the wider significance of her contemporary setting. Whatever has stricken the person in the hospital and caused three thousand to march from Hyde Park to Trafalgar to commemorate those who have already died—AIDS?—for the speaker, the jacket has become a talisman; it is mute at her grief but redolent of the history of desire.

BLACK LEATHER JACKET

My black leather jacket rubs and sticks,
hot and stubborn.
'You have to suffer for style.'
Your voice is wicked,

body like a stick insect,
in pyjamas with stripes,
saying 'hospital property'.

I hold your hand which is enormous
and want to fill the bed
with petals, silks, feathers to soften
the bones that tug at your skin
to run away.

The beard isn't you.
You don't smoke unfiltered Gauloises anymore.
The smell would rise from the garden
as you bent and planted and built
and trimmed and picked and
made so much from nothing.

Yesterday I bought flowers for you.
Marched them from Hyde Park to Trafalgar.
Wilting, rather ghastly dahlias
were all they had.
We were three thousand,
one for each who has died.
Men sobbed in Piccadilly
over white lilies,
hands tight on stems,
teeth sore.

You ask imperiously,
'Which is better, to be happy or to be right?'
I smile.
You would have scoffed at Louise Hay six months ago.
You look happy.
And haven't the wind to laugh.

'Go quickly now,' you order.
Your mouth moves like a butterfly under the mask.
'Take those yellow roses, all of them,
I've not enough room.'
Your eyes are as big as your heart,
bluer than the sky you can't see from the bed.

Your black leather jacket creaks as I kiss you.
It rubs and sticks, smells of sex and clubs and streets
and tells of firm hands that have stroked it,
rushed it off, to love you.
It is important to keep it on.   [c. 1990]

MAUD SULTER

Scotland b. 1960

Sulter, a journalist who also writes fiction, was born in Glasgow. In 'Azania', she transforms the history of the crucifixion (moving across time, race, gender, and place from 'Christ of St John on the Cross' to a 'Black Madonna on the Cross' who 'soars above Soweto') both to invoke a tradition and then reinterpret it for her own murderous time and place. Sulter can also move quickly and directly from Christian traditions to contemporary relations between women and men. Her first book of poems, *As a Black Woman*, appeared in 1985.

AZANIA

Christ of St John on the Cross soars above her. An inky
ecclesiastic blue incense engulfs her sensibilities. Lips part.
Her parched mouth opens and tastes its richness. A note.
Pinned to the apex. Her long black and boney fingers
reach out. Crocheting the air alerts her to the bloodbrown
stigmata on her palm. The note is wordless. No language
great or small has sullied the paper's woven plane. She is
now ready. Ready to write in her women's tongue a
message. In blood. To her sisterhood. A society closed to
the taint of men. Ready to leave her mark of the past. For
the future.

In surreality her body floats. Cloudward. Her sphere being
the moon she is neither restricted by forces gravitational
nor the chains of enslavement that is inhumanity. Her
blood drains from head to feet. There, old nails. Nails with
fist sized heads. Hammered home by gladitorial men. Nails
which flake rusty coppertoned fragments onto her flexing
feet.

Consciousness returns like lambs to the fold.

Black Madonna on the Cross soars above Soweto. A
smokey folkloric green incense engulfs her sensibilities.
Eyes focus. Her lipcracked mouth opens and tastes death's
stench. The note. Pinned to the apex. Her long black and
boney fingers grasp it. Crocheting the air a quicksilver
bullet passes through her palm. The note is legible. To the
left the embedded bullet stilled by the wood explodes. She
is now prepared. Prepared to speak in her mother's tongue a
message. Of blood. To her people. A society opened to the
taint of massacre. Ready to leave her words of the past.
For the future.

Labouring her body plunges. Groundward. Her aim being
redemption she is neither constricted by forces military nor
the chains of enslavement that is apartheid. Blood splatters
her from head to feet. There, children's bodies. Bodies with
fist sized wounds. Shot through by fascist men. Bodies
which ooze slimy soldertoned mucous onto her flexed feet.

Consciousness returns like squatters to the Crossroads.

Where is she? Where is she? Woman with the seeing eye.
We need her. Like blood in the rain. My sister dead. Load
aim trigger release. Bullet leaves. Air. Target meets
object. Entry. No force meets resistance. Explode. Flesh
burst. Fragments bruised. Blood pumps steadily
rhythmically. Covers distance forcefully. Its colour. The
blazing sun. Chant Soweto. Remember Soweto remember.
The eye that could see all, the future; past and present.
Stilled by reality. Kassinga approaches. And yet she sees.
Azania will be free.   [1985]

KATHLEEN JAMIE

Scotland b. 1962

Jamie's 'The Queen of Sheba' pounds the mythological pavement demanding that the 'whae do you think y'ur?' of Scottish 'Presbyterian living rooms' make way for the 'hot breath' and 'mettle' of Scottish womanhood. A freelance writer in Fife, Jamie has published collections including *A Flame In Your Heart* (with Andrew Greig, 1986), *The Way We Live* (1987), *The Autonomous Region* (with Sean Mayne Smith, 1993), and *The Queen of Sheba* (1994).

THE QUEEN OF SHEBA

Scotland, you have invoked her name
just once too often
in your Presbyterian living rooms.
She's heard, yea
even unto heathenish Arabia
your vixen's bark of poverty, come down
the family like a lang neb, a thrawn streak,
a wally dug you never liked
but can't get shot of.

She's had enough. She's come.
Whit, tae this dump? Yes!
She rides first camel
of a swaying caravan

from her desert sands
to the peat and bracken
of the Pentland hills
across the fit-ba pitch
to the thin mirage
of the swings and chute; scattered with glass.

Breathe that steamy musk
on the Curriehill Road, not mutton-shanks
boiled for broth, nor the chlorine stink
of the swimming pool where skinny girls
accuse each other of verrucas.
In her bathhouses women bear
warm pot-bellied terracotta pitchers
on their laughing hips.
All that she desires, whatever she asks—
she will make the bottled dreams
of your wee lasses
look like *sweeties*.

Spangles scarcely cover
her gorgeous breasts, hanging gardens
jewels, frankincense; more voluptuous
even than Vi-next-door, whose
high-heeled slippers
keeked from dressing gowns
like little hooves, wee tails
of pink fur stuffed in the cleavage of her toes;
more audacious even than Currie Liz
who led the gala floats
through the Wimpey scheme
in a ruby-red Lotus Elan
before the Boys' Brigade band
and the Brownies' borrowed coal-truck;
hair piled like candy-floss;
who lifted her hands from the neat wheel
to tinkle her fingers
at her tricks
        among the Masons and the elders and the police.

The cool black skin
of the Bible couldn't hold her,
nor the atlas green
on the kitchen table,
you stuck with thumbs
and split to fruity hemispheres

yellow Yemen, Red Sea, *Ethiopia*. Stick in
with the homework and you'll be
cliver like yer faither
but no too cliver,
no *above yersel*.

See her lead those great soft camels
widdershins round the kirk-yaird,
smiling
as she eats
avocados with apostle spoons
she'll teach us how. But first

she wants to strip the willow
she desires the keys
            to the National Library
she is beckoning
      the lasses
      in the awestruck crowd . . .

Yes, we'd like to
            clap the camels,
to smell the spice,
to admire her hairy legs and
bonny wicked smile, we want to take
PhDs in Persian, be vice
to her president: we want
to help her ask some
            Difficult Questions

she's shouting for our wisest man
to test her mettle:

      Scour Scotland for a Solomon!

Sure enough: from the back of the crowd
someone growls:
            whae do you think y'ur?

and a thousand laughing girls
draw our hot breath
            and shout:

THE QUEEN OF SHEBA!   [1994]

JACKIE KAY

Scotland b. 1962

The Adoption Papers, Kay's first book of poems which won the Scottish Arts Council Book and Eric Gregory awards, uses multiple points of view to tell the story of a white Scottish couple's adoption of a four-month-old Black baby girl. Kay has published two plays (*Chiaroscuro*, 1986 and *Twice Over*, 1988), a book of children's poetry (*Two's Company*, 1992, and a second collection, *Other Lovers*, 1993). Alive to the politics of choice, Kay's work in television films focuses on pornography, AIDS, and transracial adoption.

from THE ADOPTION PAPERS

CHAPTER 4: BABY LAZARUS

Land moves like driven cattle
My eyes snatch pieces of news
headlines strung out on a line:
MOTHER DROWNS BABY IN THE CLYDE

November

The social worker phoned,
our baby is a girl but not healthy
she won't pass the doctor's test
until she's well. The adoption papers
can't be signed. I put the phone down.
I felt all hot. Don't get overwrought.
What does she expect? I'm not a mother
until I've signed that piece of paper.

The rhythm of the train carries me
over the frigid earth
the constant chug a comforter
a rocking cradle.

Maybe the words lie
across my forehead
headline in thin ink
MOTHER GIVES BABY AWAY

December

We drove through to Edinburgh,
I was that excited the forty miles
seemed a lifetime. What do you think she'll

look like? I don't know my man says. I could tell
he was as nervous as me. On the way back his face
was one long smile even although
he didn't get inside. Only me.
I wore a mask but she didn't seem to mind
I told her *any day now my darling any day.*

Nobody would ever guess.
I had no other choice
Anyway it's best for her,
My name signed on a dotted line.

March

Our baby has passed.
We can pick her up in two days.
Two days for Christ's sake,
could they not have given us a bit more notice?

Land moves like driven cattle

I must stop it. Put it out my mind.
There is no use going over and over.
I'm glad she's got a home to go to.
This sandwich is plastic.
I forgot to put sugar in the flask.
The man across the table keeps staring.
I should have brought another book—
all this character does is kiss and say sorry

go and come back,
we are all foolish with trust.
I used to like winter
the empty spaces, the fresh air.

When I got home
I went out into the garden—
the frost bit my old brown boots—
and dug a hole the size of my baby
and buried the clothes I'd bought anyway.
A week later I stood at my window
and saw the ground move and swell
the promise of a crop,
that's when she started crying.
I gave her a service then, sang
Ye banks and braes, planted

a bush of roses, read the Book of Job,
cursed myself digging a pit for my baby
sprinkling ash from the grate.
Late that same night
she came in by the window,
my baby Lazarus
and suckled at my breast.

[1991]

KRISTINA RUNGANO

Zimbabwe b. 1963

Born in Zvimba, Rungano was educated at Martindale Primary School (a Dominican institution) and St John's High School. She then left Zimbabwe for Britain, where she earned a degree in computer science, returning to Zimbabwe in 1982. Her first book of poems, *A Storm Is Brewing*, was published in 1984.

THE WOMAN

A minute ago I came from the well
Where young women drew water like myself;
My body was weary and my heart tired.
For a moment I watched the stream that rushed before me
And thought how fresh the smell of flowers,
How young the grass around it.
And yet again I heard the sound of duty
Which ground on me—made me feel aged
As I bore the great big mud container on my head
Like a great big painful umbrella.
Then I got home and cooked your meal
For you had been out drinking the pleasures of the flesh
While I toiled in the fields
Under the angry vigilance of the sun,
A labour shared only by the bearings of my womb.
I washed the dishes—yours—
And swept the room we shared
Before I set forth to prepare your bedding
In the finest corner of the hut,
Which was bathed by the sweet smell of dung
I had this morning applied to the floors.
Then you came in,
In your drunken lust
And you made your demands.
When I explained how I was tired
And how I feared for the child—yours—I carried,
You beat me and had your way.

At that moment
You left me unhappy and bitter
And I hated you.
Yet tomorrow I shall again wake up to you,
Milk the cow, plough the land and cook your food;
You shall again be my lord,
For isn't it right that woman should obey,
Love, serve and honour her man?
For are you not the fruit of the land?   [1984]

MÉIRA COOK

South Africa/Canada b. 1964

Cook was born in Johannesburg and came to Ashern, Manitoba in late 1990, moving from there to Winnipeg in 1993. Currently a poetry editor with the Manitoba literary journal *Prairie Fire*, Cook began writing poetry in Ashern; her first book, *A Fine Grammar of Bones*, appeared in 1993. She is working on a PhD in Canadian literature at the University of Manitoba, and reflects that 'both my writing and my graduate work were motivated, to a certain extent, by the disorientation attendant upon immigration, consequently both are concerned with responses to place and displacement.' Her chapbooks *The Ruby Garotte* and *Talking the Waters* were published in 1994 and 1996; her book of poems, *A Catalogue of Falling*, appeared in 1996.

a fine grammar of bones

this country was long ago she
remembers a crookwalled town wintersoup
sliced with rutted vegetables there
were no signposts to this town it began
in the margins of a blank page peeled
open to a scroll and when it snowed
she said the world opened into silence
between letters snow falling like words
and the white spaces between words
in another country her daughter
brushes her hair twists tortoiseshell
combs through coils she was dying the sun
shone through her skin to a fine
grammar of bones strummed that pale
ribcage chanted the pious liturgy
of her spine i was queen her bones
rattled in her skin and she died
turning to parchment like the town
where she was born where she was young
was queen was beautiful tamed wild
rubies to her knucklebones fell
ill of language began to die   [1993]

Author Index

Abse, Dannie, 467
Achebe, Chinua, 518
Acholonu, Catherine Obianuju, 738
Adcock, Fleur, 538
Akello, Grace, 636
Alexander, Meena, 739
Allen, Paula Gunn, 591
Allingham, William, 198
Alvi, Moniza, 764
Angelou, Maya, 494
Annharte, 625
Anonymous, America (1640), 32
Anonymous, America (1683), 61
Anonymous, America (1775), 127
Anonymous, America/Canada (1776), 128
Anonymous, America/Canada (1780), 129
Anonymous, England (1661), 47
Anonymous, Ireland (c. 1650), 39
Anonymous, Nigeria (c. 1921), 452
Anyidoho, Kofi, 700
Archer, Nuala, 770
Arnold, Matthew, 197
Arnott, Joanne, 795
Aroniawenrate/Peter Blue Cloud, 557
Ashbery, John, 487
Atwood, Margaret, 593
Auchterlonie (Green), Dorothy, 417
Auden, W.H., 353
Avison, Margaret, 432
Awoonor, Kofi, 560

Bamewawasgezhikaquay/Jane Schoolcraft, 142
Bandekar, Prakash, 577
Baraka, Amiri, 539
Barbauld, Anna Laetitia (Aiken), 102
Baxter, James K., 483
Beckett, Samuel, 352
Behn, Aphra, 33
Bekederemo, John Pepper Clark, 563
Bennett, Gwendolyn B., 336
Berkeley, George, 62
Bhatt, Sujata, 780
Birney, Earle, 343
Bishop, Elizabeth, 386
bissett, bill, 598
Blake, William, 114

Blamire, Susanna, 106
Blue Cloud, Peter. See Aroniawenrate
Bogan, Louise, 323
Boland, Eavan, 647
Bolger, Dermot, 794
Borson, Roo, 751
Bowering, George, 564
Bradstreet, Anne, 26
Brand, Dionne, 761
Brandt, Di, 752
Brasch, Charles, 362
Brathwaite, E.K., 519
Breeze, Jean Binta, 784
Brew, Kwesi, 495
Bringhurst, Robert, 679
Brittain, Vera, 319
Brontë, Emily, 171
Brooke, Rupert, 300
Brooks, Gwendolyn, 426
Brown, George Mackay, 454
Browning, Elizabeth Barrett, 149
Browning, Robert, 167
Burns, Robert, 115
Busia, Abena P.A., 763
Byron, Lord. See Gordon, George

Cage, John, 399
Campbell, Joseph, 271
Cannon, Moya, 793
Carman, Bliss, 223
Carson, Ciaran, 714
Casely-Hayford ('Aquah Laluah'), Gladys May,
    345
Chandra, G.S. Sharat, 582
Cheesquatalawny/Yellow Bird/John Rollin
    Ridge, 201
Cheney-Coker, Syl, 670
Chitre, Dilip, 584
Chrystos, 680
Chuilleanáin, Eiléan Ní, 626
Clarke, Gillian, 579
Cohen, Leonard, 541
Coleridge, Mary, 224
Coleridge, Samuel Taylor, 125
Collier, Mary, 74
Conn, Stewart, 570

Cook, Méira, 805
Cooley, Dennis, 651
Cooper, Mary, 80
Crane, Hart, 324
Crawford, Isabella Valancy, 215
Crozier, Lorna, 716
Cruickshank, Helen B., 294
cummings, e.e., 322
Curnow, Allen, 393
Curtis, Tony, 681

Dabydeen, David, 771
Daruwalla, K.N., 580
Das, Kamala, 544
Davies, Sir John, 6
Derozio, Henry L., 163
Deshpande, Gauri, 628
De Souza, Eunice, 608
Devlin, Denis, 358
Dewdney, Christopher, 741
Dharker, Imitiaz, 765
Dickinson, Emily, 203
Dickinson, John, 97
Donne, John, 14
Doolittle, Hilda (H.D.), 295
Douglass, Frederick, 173
Drayton, Michael, 3
Du Bois, W.E.B., 246
Duffy, Carol Ann, 773
Duhig, Ian, 767
Dunbar, Paul Laurence, 255
Dunmore, Helen, 754
Dunn, Douglas, 629
Durcan, Paul, 652
Dutt, Toru, 220

Earle, Jean, 363
Edmond, Murray, 722
Egerton, Sarah (née Fyge, later Field), 55
Eliot, T.S., 307
Emerson, Ralph Waldo, 144
Erdrich, Louise, 768
Evans, Mari, 469
Ezekiel, Nissim, 476

Fanthorpe, U.A., 596
Fearing, Kenneth, 337
Ferlinghetti, Lawrence, 441
Finch, Anne, Countess of Winchilsea, 51
Finch, Peter, 702

Finlay, Ian Hamilton, 479
Forché, Carolyn, 727
Forrest-Thomson, Veronica, 703
Frame, Janet, 478
Fraser, G.S., 418
Fraser, Olive, 364
French, Anne, 786
Freneau, Philip, 109
Friesen, Patrick, 686
Frost, Robert, 259
Fullerton ('E'), Mary, 247

Garioch (Sutherland), Robert, 365
Garlick, Raymond, 484
Ghose, Manmohan, 249
Gilmore, Mary, 240
Ginsberg, Allen, 485
Glück, Louise, 639
Gokak, Vinayak Krishna, 370
Goldsmith, Oliver, 93
Gom, Leona, 687
Gooneratne, Yasmine, 565
Gordon, George, Lord Byron, 130
Graham, W.S., 433
Gray, Thomas, 85
Grieve, Christopher Murray. See MacDiarmid,
    Hugh
Grove, Frederick Philip, 273
Gunn, Thom, 509
Gunnars, Kristjana, 718
Gurney, Ivor, 312
Gustafson, Ralph, 371

H.D. See Doolittle, Hilda
Hamilton, Janet, 134
Hanscombe, Gillian, 671
Hardy, Thomas, 208
Harjo, Joy, 743
Harris, Claire, 581
Hartnett, Michael, 616
Harwood, Gwen, 448
Hayman, Robert, 17
Hazeley, Iyamidé, 787
Heaney, Seamus, 599
Herrick, Robert, 18
Higgins, Rita Ann, 775
Hill, Selima, 672
Hope, A.D., 356
Hopkins, Gerard Manley, 209
House, Amelia Blossom, 638

Howe, Joseph, 148
Hughes, Langston, 338
Hughes, Ted, 521
Hulme, Keri, 703
Hulme, T.E., 284

Iroquois Confederacy. *See* Six Nations Council

Jamie, Kathleen, 799
Jiles, Paulette, 642
Johnson, Colin. *See* Mudrooroo
Johnson, Emily Pauline. *See* Tekahionwake
Johnson, James Weldon, 252
Johnson, Linton Kwesi, 756
Jones, Sally Roberts, 567
Jussawalla, Adil, 608

Kariara, Jonathan, 587
Katrak, K.D., 571
Kavanagh, Patrick, 346
Kay, Jackie, 802
Kazantzis, Judith, 609
Keats, John, 137
Keeshig-Tobias, Lenore, 730
Kelsey, Henry, 57
Kendall, Henry, 207
Keon, Wayne, 688
Killigrew, Mrs Anne, 44
King, Thomas, 643
Kizer, Carolyn, 480
Klein, A.M., 372
Kolatkar, Arun Balkrishna, 528
Kroetsch, Robert, 488
Kunene, Mazisi, 522
Kuppner, Frank, 745

Laing, Kojo, 690
Lampman, Archibald, 225
Lane, Patrick, 602
Lang, John Dunmore, 141
Lanier, Emilia, 7
Lara, Alda, 523
Larkin, Philip, 463
Lawless, Emily, 210
Lawrence, D.H., 289
Lawson, Henry, 244
Layton, Irving, 406
Leapor, Mary, 89
Ledwidge, Francis, 314
Lee, Dennis, 603

Lee, Li-Young, 788
Lehmann, Geoffrey, 611
Leonard, Tom, 656
LePan, Douglas, 414
Levertov, Denise, 470
Lewis, Alun, 419
Lindsay, Lady Anne, 108
Livesay, Dorothy, 375
Lochhead, Liz, 704
Longfellow, Henry Wadsworth, 157
Lorde, Audre, 546
Lowell, Amy, 261
Lowell, Robert, 427

MacA'Ghobhainn, Iain/Iain Crichton Smith, 496
McAlpine, Rachel, 611
McAuley, James, 429
MacDiarmid, Hugh/Christopher Murray Grieve, 315
MacEwen, Gwendolyn, 618
MacGill-Eain, Somhairle/Sorley MacLean, 396
McGuckian, Medbh, 731
McKay, Claude, 311
Mackellar, Dorothea, 292
MacLean, Sorley. *See* MacGill-Eain, Somhairle
MacLeod, Mary. *See* Ruaidh, Mairi Nighean Alasdair
McMillan, Ian, 790
MacNeice, Louis, 357
Macpherson, Jay, 527
McQueen, Cilla, 725
MacThòmais, Ruaraidh/Derick Thomson, 457
Mahapatra, Jayanta, 500
Makino, Marie, 381
Malouf, David, 548
Mandel, Eli, 464
Mangan, James Clarence, 146
Manhire, Bill, 691
Mansfield, Katherine, 310
Mapanje, Jack, 674
Marlatt, Daphne, 630
Marvell, Andrew, 28
Mary Queen of Scots, 1
Mathias, Roland, 420
Mehrotra, Arvind Krishna, 708
Melville, Herman, 175
Mew, Charlotte, 250
Meynell, Alice, 213
Milton, John, 21

Mitchell, Elma, 446
Moll, Ernest G., 327
Momaday, N. Scott, 549
Montagu, Lady Mary Wortley, 71
Moore, Marianne, 302
Morgan, Edwin, 450
Morris, William, 205
Morton, Sarah Wentworth, 118
Morton, Thomas, 16
Moses, Daniel David, 757
Mouré, Erin, 776
Mudrooroo/Colin Johnson, 606
Mugo, Micere Githae, 631
Muir, Edwin, 304
Muldoon, Paul, 749
Murray, Les A., 588
Musgrave, Susan, 750
Mustapha, Mukhtarr, 633

Naidu, Sarojini, 274
Neilson, John Shaw, 256
Newlove, John, 589
Ngunaitponi/David Unaipon, 257
Nichol, bp, 663
Nichols, Grace, 732
Niedecker, Lorine, 342
Nwosu, Titus Chukweneka, 568

Ofeimun, Odia, 733
Ogundipe-Leslie, Molara, 612
O'Hara, Frank, 486
Okai, Atukwei/John Okai, 619
Okara, Gabriel, 459
Okigbo, Christopher, 529
Oliphant, Carolina, Baroness Nairne, 120
Olson, Charles, 382
Ondaatje, Michael, 644
Oodgeroo (formerly Kath Walker), 451
Ormond, John, 474
Ortiz, Simon J., 622

Page, P.K., 425
Parthasarathy, R., 550
Patel, Gieve, 613
Paterson, Andrew Barton ('The Banjo'), 237
Pearse, Patrick (Padraic) Henry, 276
Peeradina, Saleem, 664
Peters, Lenrie, 532
Philip, M. Nourbese, 710
Philips, Katherine Fowler, 31

Piercy, Marge, 575
Piñero, Miguel, 692
Plath, Sylvia, 533
Poe, Edgar Allan, 163
Pope, Alexander, 63
Porter, Peter, 513
Posey, Alexander, 258
Pound, Ezra, 293
Pratt, E.J., 278
Pugh, Sheenagh, 734
Purdy, Al, 436

Qunta, Christine, 759

Raine, Craig, 665
Raine, Kathleen, 360
Ramanujan, A.K., 514
Ranasinghe, Anne, 482
Reading, Peter, 695
Rege, P.S., 385
Rexroth, Kenneth, 350
Rich, Adrienne, 515
Ridge, John Rollin. See Cheesquatalawny/
    Yellow Bird
Riggs, Rolla Lynn, 325
Roberts, Charles G.D., 221
Robertson, Edith Anne, 285
Roethke, Theodore, 361
Rose, Wendy, 719
Rosenberg, Isaac, 313
Rossetti, Christina, 204
Ruaidh, Mairi Nighean Alasdair/Mary
    MacLeod, 9
Rukeyser, Muriel, 411
Rumens, Carol, 667
Rungano, Kristina, 804

Salom, Philip, 735
Sanchez, Sonia, 551
Sarabhai, Bharati, 408
Schoolcraft, Jane. See Bamewawasgezhikaquay
Scott, Duncan Campbell, 233
Scott, F.R., 326
Scott, Sir Walter, 124
Senior, Olive, 646
Sepamla, Sipho, 535
Serote, Mongane (Wally), 668
Seth, Vikram, 760
Seward, Anna, 99
Sexton, Anne, 502

Shakespeare, William, 5
Shelley, Percy Bysshe, 132
Silko, Leslie Marmon, 722
Sitwell, Edith, 305
Six Nations Council, Iroquois Confederacy, 328
Slessor, Kenneth, 333
Smith, A.J.M., 339
Smith, Charlotte, 107
Smith, Iain Crichton. *See* MacA'Ghobhainn, Iain
Smith, Stevie, 340
Smith, Sydney Goodsir, 421
Smithyman, Kendrick, 465
Smyth, Cherry, 796
Snyder, Gary, 524
Soyinka, Wole, 552
Spark, Muriel, 440
Spenser, Edmund, 2
Stainer, Pauline, 623
Stein, Gertrude, 266
Stevens, Wallace, 277
Stevenson, Anne, 536
Stevenson, Robert Louis, 219
Suknaski, Andrew, 634
Sulter, Maud, 798
Sutherland, Efua, 479
Swenson, May, 447
Swift, Jonathan, 53
Synge, J.M., 254

Tadjo, Véronique, 777
Tagore, Rabindranath, 228
Taylor, Edward, 37
Tekahionwake/Emily Pauline Johnson, 230
Tennyson, Alfred, Lord, 165
Thesen, Sharon, 696
Thomas, Dylan, 415
Thomas, Edward, 270
Thomas, Elizabeth, 60
Thomas, R.S., 412
Thomson, Derick. *See* MacThòmais, Ruaraidh

Thomson, James, 81
Truth, Sojourner, 140
Tuwhare, Hone, 466

Unaipon, David. *See* Ngunaitponi

Vivekananda, Swami, 236

Waddington, Miriam, 430
Wah, Fred, 607
Walcott, Derek, 526
Walker, Kath. *See* Oodgeroo
Wallace, Bronwen, 675
Wallace-Crabbe, Chris, 555
Waller, Edmund, 20
Warner, Sylvia Townsend, 320
Warren, Mercy Otis, 91
Wayman, Tom, 677
Webb, Phyllis, 493
Welch, James, 615
Weller, Archie, 791
Wheatley, Phillis, 112
Whiteman, Roberta Hill, 712
Whitman, Walt, 177
Wickham, Anna, 288
Wigglesworth, Michael, 29
Wikkramasinha, Lakdasa, 624
Wilbur, Richard, 462
Williams, Hugo, 636
Williams, Roger, 19
Williams, William Carlos, 286
Wilson, William, 192
Windsor, Penny, 698
Wordsworth, William, 122
Wright, Judith, 423
Wright, Kit, 669

Yeats, William Butler, 241
Young Bear, Ray A., 737

Zukofsky, Louis, 349